Challenges & Prospects
for Canadian Social Studies

Challenges & Prospects

for Canadian Social Studies

Edited by
Alan Sears and Ian Wright

Pacific Educational Press
Vancouver Canada

Published by Pacific Educational Press
Faculty of Education, University of British Columbia
6365 Biological Sciences Road
Vancouver, Canada V6T 1Z4
Telephone: 604-822-5385
Facsimile: 604-822-6603
email: pep@interchange.ubc.ca

The publisher would like to acknowledge the financial contribution made by Canadian Heritage in support of its publishing program.

Library and Archives Canada Cataloguing in Publication
    Challenges and prospects for Canadian social studies / Alan Sears
and Ian Wright, editors.

Includes index.
ISBN 978-1-895766-72-1

    1. Social sciences--Study and teaching--Canada. I. Wright, Ian,
1941- II. Sears, Alan, 1954-
LB1584.5.C3C453 2004   300'.71'071   C2004-903325-5

Edited by Barbara Kuhne
Endnotes edited by Robyn So
Cover design by Warren Clark

Printed and bound in Canada

 08 09 10   5 4 3 2

Acknowledgements
This book is obviously a collaborative effort and we gratefully acknowledge the scholarship and professionalism of the contributors who worked hard to meet deadlines and were patient with our questions and suggestions. We also deeply appreciate the dedicated work of the staff at Pacific Educational Press, particularly Catherine Edwards and Barbara Kuhne, who took our rough work and turned it into a polished publication. Our thanks to all.

Alan Sears, Fredericton, May 2004
Ian Wright, Vancouver, May 2004

This book is dedicated to Joe Kirman

Joe Kirman recently retired after many years in the Department of Elementary Education at the University of Alberta. Despite retirement, he still teaches there. Joe has always pushed the boundaries of social studies with his interest in technology, geography, and human rights. He is the author of *Elementary Social Studies: Creative Classroom Ideas*, now in its third edition. We are honouring him here especially for having rescued *Canadian Social Studies*, Canada's national social studies journal, which was in danger of disappearing. Joe took on the editorship and made it a viable electronic journal. You can find it at www.quasar.ualberta.ca/css. You can also find his Canadian Social Studies Super Site at www.ualberta.ca/~jkirman.

Thank you, Joe, for your significant contributions to social studies education.

Contents

Preface

Joseph M. Kirman

What challenges have there been for the Canadian social studies curriculum over the years? What are its prospects for the future? Curriculum change tends to follow societal change and since social studies deals with society in all its ramifications, as society has changed, so has what is taught in social studies. Much has changed in Canadian society; these changes pose significant challenges for social studies, including how to deal with a broadening sense of national identity; more open attitudes towards differing lifestyles; pressure to include a wider range of voices in curricula; and the explosion of information technology. I turn to these challenges first and will then address future prospects for social studies in Canada.

National Identity

A remarkable change has occurred since the late 1960s and early 1970s regarding national identity. At that time, "Who is a Canadian?" and "What is a Canadian?" were issues. That era was the start of a coming of age regarding a Canadian "self." It went as far as to generate hostility by some towards the British monarchy and an insistence on Canada's distinctiveness as a nation from the United States. My students at that time requested that I deal with how to teach about Canadianism. There was good reason for this. The uniqueness of Canadian culture was submerged by British and American social studies textbooks in use from elementary through post-sec-

ondary education, including for teacher education. And the influence of American media was pervasive. One letter by a parent to the *Edmonton Journal* decried a child's drawing of the stars and stripes as Canada's flag, and another parent complained that her child thought Richard Nixon was the prime minister of Canada.

In 1971 Alberta moved to address the lack of Canadian content by introducing a new social studies curriculum, Experiences in Decision Making. The curriculum committee had heard the complaints about the dominance of foreign material, and moved to eliminate foreign social studies textbooks. A call was issued for Canadian-produced materials. At about the same time, the federal government began regulating foreign media and implementing regulations mandating levels of Canadian content.

Today's students are more secure in their Canadian identity than were those of earlier decades. They no longer appear threatened by British or American influences. Perhaps some of the change came from Trudeau's in-your-face attitude in asserting Canadian interests and goals, as well as from the patriation of the Constitution of 1982. More recently, Jean Chretien's refusal, for better or for worse, to follow U.S. and British policy to invade Iraq without a broad international coalition reinforced this sense of Canada's distinctiveness.

Changing Attitudes towards Differing Lifestyles

There have been significant changes over the past thirty-five years in teaching about families in social studies. Traditionally curricula presented the stereotypical white, middle-class family with the breadwinner father and the homemaker mother. By the mid-1970s the push for gender equity mandated the elimination of stereotypical gender role models. Over time, single-parent families were included in the curriculum in recognition of social realities. By the 1990s, a fuller range of family structures was recognized in social studies curricula and teaching. These changes have not been without controversy and, as societal debates about same-sex marriages and the like continue, teaching about families will no doubt continue to raise challenges for social studies in the future. Here is where that overworked word "respect" found in social studies curricula becomes a necessity as an adjunct to tolerance. Perhaps social studies can be a healing element for Canadian society. As John F. Kennedy said, "If we cannot now end our differences, at least we can help make the world safe for diversity."[1]

Holocaust Studies

In the early 1960s I wrote an article on teaching about the Holocaust. It was inspired by my grade 8 students' interest in the Eichmann trial. Eichmann was a key person responsible for scheduling the roundup and transportation of Jews to the death camps during World War II. He was thwarted only in Budapest by Raoul Wallenberg and his team of Swedish diplomats' heroic actions.[2] The article dealt with how to make the large number of people killed in the Holocaust understandable to youngsters. No professional journal would publish it or even send it out for evaluation.[3] Editors sent me kindly letters saying that the Holocaust was a past event that was best left in the past. By the early 1970s things started to change dramatically as Holocaust deniers began to spew their fabrications. I became aware of this

when one of my university students asked how we knew that six million Jews were murdered. I replied that we obtained this information from the evidence presented at the Nuremberg War Tribunal, the demographic statistics from before and after World War II, and additional eyewitness testimony.

In the 1980s the public in Canada and internationally became aware of what was known as the "Keegstra affair." Jim Keegstra, a teacher in Eckville, Alberta, was teaching neo-Nazi doctrine to his students, including inciting hatred against Jews and promoting Holocaust denial. This incident was followed in the international press when Keegstra, who was also the mayor of Eckville, went through three trials and eventually was convicted of promoting hatred.[4] Unfortunately history repeated itself in that no Christian church issued a public condemnation of Keegstra's teaching when it happened. Indeed, even the Alberta Teachers' Association found itself severely criticized for its handling of the matter and ultimately amended its code of ethics to deal with such situations.[5]

During that time the National Council for the Social Studies began to promote Holocaust studies, and numerous issues of the journal *Social Education* dealt with this topic. *Canadian Social Studies* devoted the Summer 1995 issue to it, and both journals have continued to publish articles and book reviews on the topic. Recently Parliament unanimously legislated a national Holocaust commemoration day whose date is determined annually by the lunar Jewish calendar. A large body of classroom resources and Internet URLs dealing with the Holocaust[6] is now available.

Voices in the Curriculum

Whose voices are heard in the social studies curriculum, particularly with regard to the teaching of history, has been a long-standing issue.[7] Today one hears voices that were ignored in the past, such as those of women, minorities, and Aboriginal peoples. But to what extent do teaching materials include a sincere reflection of such peoples' concerns rather than a nod to political correctness? In 1998 the desire for a social studies curriculum that would reflect their own people led the Treaty 8 Tribal Council to commission the University of Alberta's Department of Elementary Education to work with them to produce a grades 1–6 social studies curriculum for use in reserve schools.[8] The provincial social studies curriculum was used as a template and the parallel First Nations' curriculum allows the teacher to meet the requirements of the provincial curriculum while using Treaty 8 examples and resources.

Not very many people, if any, seem interested in whose voice is reflected in the economics curriculum. Why is this important? In a capitalist, democratic society knowledge of the way the economy operates underlies the financial power structure. It is the gateway to economic independence and financial success. But very often the voice that is heard is that of big business or government seeking trained workers for the local economy. There is nothing wrong with job training, but it must not be at the expense of teaching young people about the practical elements of the economy: how to make money with money, how to invest for profit, how to function as an entrepreneur—in short, how to be among the movers and shakers who make the economy work. The reason for teaching economic literacy is not to develop a new generation of robber barons but to encourage students to become economically educated individuals who know how to take chances and mobilize the necessary elements to make their ideas happen. This curriculum objective goes beyond the fine work of such organizations as Junior Achievement and current secondary economics courses. It should begin at the elementary level and continue through secondary education. So whose voice is this? It is the future voice of the children in our schools who will benefit from this approach, both those who will be the authors of economic creativity and those who will be the front line workers to make it happen. It is also the voice of a nation seeking economic stability and continuous employment from a cadre of knowledgeable entrepreneurs and professionals.

Technology

When I started teaching, state of the art classroom technology consisted of overhead projectors, slide and film projectors, spirit duplicators, and mimeograph machines. Today's technology was that era's science fiction. The explosion of information technology has spawned an emphasis on technological literacy in the curriculum, with an emphasis on educating students to be proficient in operating and applying programs for speed and efficiency in problem-solving and creative endeavours. Keeping up with technological change and making the technology work for us is important, but where do we draw the line so that we continue to function as independent human beings not dependent on technology? Can we even do this? I do not propose that we return to Thoreau's *Walden,* since I don't think that is possible, but technology massages us into dependence. What starts as a novelty becomes a necessity. And this is the conundrum: with technology the quality of life is improved, but society becomes irrevocably changed.

What is needed is a curriculum emphasis on values in a technological society that complements training for technological literacy. Students need to consider questions about the appropriate uses of technology, they need to develop the ability to criticize technology, and above all they need to learn to apply technology in a moral manner. These three items are *sine qua non.* They are critical because with technology comes power. Never before have so many people had so much capacity to do so much damage—not merely locally, but worldwide. How do we control this new personal power? Only by fostering a value system that users of technology bring with them in operating the technology. A technological society requires a moral worldview for its own survival and well-being. Are our schools, businesses, professionals, and governments ready to implement and live by such values? If people can envision something, it can probably be created, and human vision is limitless. Without a moral foundation, our technological creativity can be our own undoing.

What of the Future?

What will the social studies curriculum be like as the twenty-first century progresses? To speculate at this time is to try to second-guess how society will develop, the social trends that will occur, the events that will transpire, the technology that will develop, the discoveries that will be made, and the willingness of people to place themselves at risk for the well-being of humanity.

What may occur surpasses our wildest dreams. You need only reflect on what someone might have written in 1904 about the future of society and education in the twentieth century to imagine the potential for what could happen by the end of the twenty-first. So I shall speculate as a dreamer and let my mind run free.

First, humanity will begin to colonize our solar system both on Mars and in habitat modules. Propulsion systems will move spaceships at the speed of light and physicists will be exploring how to exceed the speed of light. More deep-space probes will be sent out until the speed of light is exceeded and then human exploration of deep space will begin.

The genetic code for aging will be discovered and humans will have greatly extended life spans (of biblical proportions and possibly greater). This will result in social considerations affecting birth control, resource use, education, employment, and personal relations. It might result in marriages for set terms as well as marriages for life, although the current propensity for divorce seems to have already made this a moot point. Genetically based diseases will be successfully treated and cancer will be a thing of the past.

Miniaturization and robotics will be a major factor for replacing missing organs and limbs, with neural links to the brain to produce normal feelings and actions. This will complement genetic regrowth of replacement parts for the body, which will replace transplants from other persons. Robotics in the home will provide numerous conveniences, but robotics in the workplace will cause widespread unemployment and a glut of inexpensive manufactured items that few will be able to afford. We may see a trend towards labour-intensive professions and service industries to offset this problem, along with government employment programs of a similar nature.

The so-called "Star Trek transporter," the electronic-molecular movement of people and cargo, will become a reality.[9] All forms of current transportation will become obsolete, along with support elements such as highways, traffic signals, airports, cargo terminals, harbour facilities, rail lines, and various fuels and their assorted industries. The exception will be recreational use of older transportation technologies for competition and hobbies. New transportation technologies will affect the nature of cities, national boundaries, commerce, and crime. To envision such impacts, think of how the automobile and the airplane developed associated industries and changed our society.

This new century will see human rights tested to their limits. Technology can control as well as liberate. Even now global positioning satellites allow the tracking of any human being anywhere on the surface of the earth. Brain implant technology will foster mind control and the regulation of ideas and behaviours. While using this technology for dealing with criminals would be of value, such technology in the hands of a dictator gives new meaning to the term "absolute power." Democracies will see a tug-of-war between security agencies and human rights advocates for appropriate uses of such technology. Special legislation will be passed and the courts will be called on to interpret and enforce the use of these technologies, a trend we are already seeing with regard to security legislation.

Implications for Social Studies Curriculum

The social studies curriculum of the twenty-first century will need to educate young people to become responsible citizens capable of dealing with mechanical and biological technology developments and who are able to guide and control them for social betterment. Such citizens must be alert to the implications technology can have not only for our survival, but also for our humanity, lest we merge with technology rather than keep it as our servant. The danger is heightened because once technology makes a social impact and establishes itself, there is no going back. There must be thorough criticism and informed decisions by those who will be affected. Preparing students for this is a mandate for social studies educators for the twenty-first century.

The twenty-first century will indeed offer challenges and prospects for social studies educators.

Edmonton, 2003

Endnotes

1. See T. McConnell, "Telescope," *Edmonton Journal,* November 23, 2003, D2 for this quote attributed to John F. Kennedy.

2. For an article about Raoul Wallenberg and a sensitivity game for the secondary level dealing with how Wallenberg and his heroic team rescued Jews, see M. Fishbein, "Raoul Wallenberg, Human Rights Hero: A Role Model for Students and Social Studies," *Canadian Social Studies* 26 (1992): 102–106; and J.M. Kirman, "Raoul Wallenberg in Budapest," in ibid., 107–109.

3. It was originally published in a major New York City Jewish newspaper as "Teaching Gentile Students about a Jewish Tragedy," *The Jewish Press*, June 7, 1963, 2, and was eventually published in a revised form as "Giving Meaning to the Large Numbers of Holocaust Victims," *Canadian Social Studies* 29 (Summer 1995): 149.

4. The history and ramifications of this incident are discussed in D. Bercuson and D. Wertheimer, *A Trust Betrayed* (Toronto: Doubleday Canada, 1985).

5. A discussion of the role of the Alberta Teachers' Association in the "Keegstra affair" can be found in J.M. Kirman, "James Keegstra and the Eckville High School Incident," *The History and Social Science Teacher* 21 (1986): 209–213.

6. The Canadian Social Studies Super Site at www.ualberta.ca/~jkirman has two excellent comprehensive URLs about the Holocaust, with portals to other sites in the "Human Rights" section. They are "A Teachers' Guide to the Holocaust" and "United States Holocaust Memorial Museum."

7. An excellent book that will provide many insights into the issue of voices in the history curricula of Canada is George H. Richardson, *The Death of the Good Canadian: Teachers, National Identities, and the Social Studies Curriculum* (New York: P. Lang, 2002).

8. This curriculum was initiated as a commemoration project for the centennial of the signing of Treaty 8, June 21, 1899. The grade 1 segment was published as B. Conners and P. Shields, "The Treaty No. 8 Centennial Curriculum Development Project: Grade 1" (Edmonton: Treaty 8 Tribal Council, 2001).

9. This concept is not fantasy. In 1975 I was a member of a National Council for the Social Studies consulting group for the National Aeronautics and Space Administration on how to teach about Skylab. At the Marshall Space Flight Center in Huntsville, Alabama, we were addressed by Dr. Von Tiesenhausen, Director of Payload for the moon project. The question of such means of transport was raised with him. His answer was that it was theoretically possible, but we didn't have the technology for it yet.

Part 1

Contextual Challenges and Prospects

Teaching is often described as a solitary activity. Indeed, many teachers seem to prefer it that way, often saying things like, "Once I shut my classroom door I can do what I like." As much as teachers sometimes might prefer to escape the world of administrators, parents, colleagues, and the public, it is not really possible. For teaching, as Catherine Cornbleth pointed out, takes place in a number of overlapping contexts that extend through the education system and well beyond.[1] The purpose of this book is to introduce you to some of those contexts and how they have shaped and continue to shape policy, curricula, and teaching in the field of social studies education. For example, in addition to what goes on behind the doors of individual classrooms, Kathy Bickmore and Alan Sears make it clear that the organization and culture of the school play key roles in students' understanding of social concepts and processes; Penney Clark shows that the Canadian social studies community is not isolated but influenced by developments in the United States and the wider international community; and Ken Osborne and Stéphane Lévesque demonstrate that discussion about the nature of social studies education, both in English Canada and Québec, has been shaped by much wider societal debates about the kind of nation—or nations—we want and the characteristics of citizens necessary to build them.

We think it important to introduce you to the wider contexts of the field of social studies education for several reasons. First, and most pragmatically for those of you in pre-service university programs, knowledge of the current state of the field across the country may help you get a job by allowing you to demonstrate a significant depth and range of understanding of the challenges and prospects in social studies education.

Second, such knowledge will help you make well-grounded choices about what and how you are going to teach. As a number of the chapters point out, while there are fixed social studies curricula across Canada, all of these allow for considerable leeway in choosing the content on which to focus, as well as approaches for teaching that content. Shields and Ramsay, along with several others, make the point that the organizational framework for social studies curricula has shifted from a focus on the specific content to be taught to a focus on much broader student outcomes, including attention to the development of conceptual understanding, the learning of skills and processes, and the development of values and dispositions. Outcomes such as these provide a clear end point but little direction for getting there.

For example, Patricia Shields and Doug Ramsay point out that by the end of grade 6, students in Atlantic Canada are expected to be "able to identify and explain the rights and responsibilities of individual citizens in a local, national and global context." We could imagine approaching this particular outcome through a historical study of the evolution of human rights and responsibilities, as might be advocated by Ken Osborne; a study of how legal systems enshrine rights, as Wanda Cassidy might suggest; or a look at human rights as they relate to specific communities such as First Nations or ethnic minorities, as proposed by Jeff Orr and Manju Varma-Joshi. In fact, a comprehensive approach to addressing this outcome might involve a combination of all these and more. Furthermore, a teacher's responsibility to make decisions does not stop at selection of content but must also include choices about teaching frameworks and techniques. Does achieving this same outcome lend itself to using situated learning as outlined by Andrew Hughes and Alan Sears, or a critical thinking approach as described by Linda Farr-Darling and Ian Wright? Perhaps it will require some sense of conflict resolution processes as described by Kathy Bickmore, because we know human rights have often evolved and developed as the result of struggle and conflict. How should student progress towards this outcome be assessed? Drawing on John Myers' chapter, is it best to use tests, essays, or some form of performance assessment?

These are just some of the decisions you will be making in the context of your own classroom. Whether you are aware of it or not, these choices will flow from what you believe about what children should learn and how they can best learn it. It is our view that professional beliefs and choices like these ought to be informed by a solid grounding in the field.

The third reason for introducing you to the wider context in which social studies operates is that we hope you will examine your own ideas, values, and beliefs about social studies and how it should be taught. In their chapter on situated learning, Hughes and Sears make the point that students come to any new learning situation not as blank slates but with a complex cognitive structure including ideas and beliefs related to the area under study. Similarly, we know you come to the teaching profession with definite ideas about what teaching is and what it should be. You have, after all, considerable experience as students and probably some experience as teachers in a variety of settings. A key purpose of this book is to engage you in reflection and, perhaps, reformula-

tion of your thinking about social studies education. All the authors contributing to this collection bring to bear their own background and experiences. These have shaped their beliefs about the nature of social studies and how students should learn about the world in which they live. These beliefs are substantiated by appeal to higher order values concerning views of human nature, what qualifies as an educated person, what counts as truth, and what sort of society is desirable. We hope that engaging the ideas, beliefs, and values explicitly or implicitly endorsed by the authors might cause you to reflect on your own thinking about social studies education and push you to reconsider and reshape your own ideas, beliefs, and values where appropriate.

The fourth reason for addressing the wider context is that we hope over time you will play a role in shaping these contexts. Penney Clark and Stéphane Lévesque trace the evolution of social studies in English Canada and Québec, and Ken Osborne provides a detailed overview of a debate that has been at the centre of that evolution—the balance between teaching social studies as an integrated subject or focusing on the discipline of history. It is clear in each of these chapters that many factors, groups, and individuals have played a role in the development of Canadian social studies, including social studies teachers. Over the course of your careers many of you will serve on curriculum committees, join professional organizations, and assume leadership positions within the education system. Some of you will write chapters in books about social studies and teach in university programs to prepare social studies teachers. (All of the authors in this book began their careers as classroom teachers of social studies, most with no idea they would end up where they are now.) In these roles you will be called on to participate in discussions and debates about what social studies curricula and teaching should look like beyond your own classrooms. You will play a role in deciding what shape the field will take; this is a key part of the professional responsibilities of educators. Again, your beliefs about the nature and purpose of social studies and the contribution it makes to developing an educated person will guide your participation at this level, and it is our view that those beliefs ought to be firmly rooted in a comprehensive knowledge of the field, including its history, contemporary trends, and its body of research knowledge. This book is designed to provide a beginning to developing that knowledge.

This first section is designed to introduce you to the key contexts of social studies education over the past century or more. As you read the chapters, consider the following questions:

1. What is the current shape of social studies curricula across Canada? Are there similarities across jurisdictions? What are the key differences?

2. How did curricula come to be what they are? What forces have played a role in shaping them?

3. What theoretical or research base underlies various approaches to social studies curricula and teaching? What beliefs undergird these theories and research bases?

4. Does the current organization of curricula make sense? What alternatives might be proposed? Where would you position yourself in current debates in the field, say between teaching social studies as an integrated subject or as separate disciplines (such as history, geography, economics, and so on)?

5. Should citizenship education be the central focus of social studies? If so, what kind of citizens do we want to produce?

6. Who has played a role in shaping social studies curricula over the years? Who should play a role?

Answering these questions is a step towards formulating your own vision of the challenges and prospects in teaching social studies.

Endnote

1   Catherine Cornbleth, *Curriculum in Context* (London: Falmer, 1990).

CHAPTER 1

The Historical Context of Social Studies in English Canada

Penney Clark

When examined historically, what is striking about social studies in English Canada is its consistent reliance on American models. Since its inception in the 1920s as a school subject in this country, the major movements that have affected social studies education in the United States have, in turn, shaped social studies curricula across Canada. These American models have not been adopted wholesale; instead they have been incorporated into education in uniquely Canadian fashion. Since Canadian provinces and territories have autonomy over education, and therefore over curriculum development, some consequent variation among provincial social studies curricula has occurred.[1]

American influence can be detected in the major social studies curriculum trends, which have paralleled those in the United States; in the American textbooks chosen for use in university-level teacher-training courses; in the number of American speakers invited to Canadian teachers' conventions; and in the American references used to lend legitimacy to provincial social studies curriculum guides and programs of study.

Canadians have not responded uniformly to the American influence. On the one hand, some people have welcomed it and have expressed gratitude for what seem to be scraps from the American table. One of these was the editor of the British Columbia social studies journal *Exploration,* who said upon returning from a National Council for the Social Studies convention in Cleveland: "It is typical of American generosity that Canadians should be invited to

learn at first hand the results of American investigations."[2] On the other hand lies rejection of this influence, expressed in references to "home-grown products;"[3] in the establishment of the Canada Studies Foundation; in support for the development of a Canadian educational publishing industry; and in emphasis during the 1970s and 1980s on Canadian national, regional, and local topics and issues in provincial curricula. However, in some sense, even these developments can be attributed to American influences, since without a perceived threat to Canadian culture, the need for such identifiably Canadian products would not have been so great.

This chapter is primarily concerned with curriculum at a policy level, rather than curriculum as interpreted in the classroom. While we must recognize that "reform advocated is not necessarily reform accomplished,"[4] our knowledge about the forces that shape social studies curricula at the classroom level is still woefully inadequate. This chapter will include some discussion of textbooks that have been used to interpret social studies curricula to students, as recognition that such textbooks have, at times, become the de facto curriculum.

Progressive Influences

Social studies is "an American invention."[5] The formal introduction of social studies into the secondary curriculum in the United States occurred with the publication in 1916 of *The Social Studies in Secondary Education,* the final report of the Committee on Social Studies of the Commission on the Reorganization of Secondary Education.[6] This report marked the first popular use of the term "social studies" to refer to an interdisciplinary approach combining history, civics, and the social sciences. This term was first used in curriculum documents in the western provinces of Canada in the 1920s and was introduced in Ontario in 1937.

Social studies curricula in Canada were organized around an "expanding horizons" approach. A typical topic sequence within this framework begins in the primary grades with self and family, moves on to neighbourhood and local community, and then to other communities. In the upper elementary grades, topics begin with students' own provinces and expand to include Canada as a whole, historically and geographically, then to other cultures around the world, and finally to ancient civilizations. Secondary grades look at history, geography, and government of Canada, and then move on to world history and present-day global political, economic, and social relationships. American Paul Hanna has been credited with the articulation of this approach in the 1950s, although the model itself was evident by the early 1900s.[7]

The introduction of social studies in Canada was associated with the child-centred focus promoted by the progressive education movement in the United States. The 1930s saw Canadian provincial department of education officials, curriculum developers, and Normal School instructors embrace features of the American progressive education movement. During this decade, major curricular revision reflecting this progressive philosophy occurred across the country. Saskatchewan, in 1931, was the first province to begin this process, followed by Nova Scotia in 1933, Alberta and British Columbia in 1936, Ontario in 1937, and Manitoba, New Brunswick, and Protestant Québec over the next three years.

The new child-centred approach implied correlation of subject matter around the needs and interests of the child. Emphasis was on the "whole" child who would "grow, physically, emotionally and spiritually, as well as mentally . . . growth is total, not partial."[8]

Curricula were activity-oriented, with a focus on group investigations, which were intended to promote cooperation, communication, and democratic decision-making skills. These group investigations were usually called "enterprises" in the elementary curriculum, a term taken from the British *Hadow Report* of 1926. Social studies formed the "core of the curriculum. . . . Since an enterprise is a series of purposeful activities revolving about one central theme, the relationship between Social Studies and enterprises can easily be appreciated."[9] At the secondary level this approach found expression in programs referred to in different provinces as core curriculum, life adjustment curriculum, or a block program consisting of an integration of social studies with language arts and the humanities.

There are a number of indications of the high degree of influence the American progressive education movement had on curriculum revision in Canada at this time. For instance, in the social studies section of the 1936 *Alberta Programme of Studies for the Intermediate School*,[10] the developers include an extensive quote from "The Tentative Course of Study" for the state of Virginia, essentially providing a definition of social studies, as well as a list of teaching suggestions adapted from leading American social studies educator Harold Rugg's *Teacher's Guide to the Social Studies* series. Of a list of twenty books provided as references in the 1936 Alberta document, all are of American origin. *The Journal of Education* in Nova Scotia published a number of articles by American progressive educators, including W.H. Kilpatrick, with the intention of helping teachers deepen their understanding of the tenets of progressivism. In setting out the curriculum revision stages in British Columbia, the Minister of Education, G.M. Weir, specified that one task of the developers was to formulate fundamental principles based on the theories of prominent American educators such as Franklin Bobbitt, David Snedden, and George S. Counts, as found in Harrap's *The Technique of Curriculum Making,* a guide that was widely used at the time.[11] Weir also advised that developers be familiar with the "seven cardinal principles" first laid out in the famous report of the Commission on the Reorganization of Secondary Education, set up in 1915 by the National Education Association in the United States.[12]

Members of the (American) Progressive Education Association came to speak at Canadian teachers' conventions. These included Hilda Taba, who was later to become so influential in social studies curriculum development, and Harold Rugg, author of *Man in a Changing Society,* a series of social studies texts that was said to have "affected the curriculum of more schools throughout the country [Canada] than any other single publication."[13]

A writer in the *Alberta Teachers' Association Magazine* indicates the attitude of Canadian teachers towards this American influence:

> The 1939 Easter Convention is over, and if there is one regret that lingers, it is that all the teachers in Alberta could not have been there. . . . The central feature of the convention, of course, was the invading host of American educators (nine of them) to put before us the aims, doctrines, practices, and hopes of the Progressive Education Association of the United States. . . . This they did, and they did it in a way to win in conspicuous degree the respect and confidence of everyone.[14]

American educators came to Canada to teach Enterprise Education summer school courses. One of these educators, Lillian Gray, provided a course outline that is said to have served as the basis of the 1940 revision of the Alberta curriculum.[15] Just as American educators came to Canada to teach courses, many Canadian educators took graduate courses in the United States. It is estimated that 1,097 Canadian teachers attended Teachers' College, Columbia University, between 1923 and 1938.[16]

The Enterprise in Theory and Practice, written by Donalda Dickie in 1940,[17] was a reference book on instruction, using the ideas and methods of progressive education. The "bible of the activity program in Canada,"[18] as it has been called, cites a number of American thinkers and lists a number of American examples of activities and enterprises.

Concerns about American cultural domination were prevalent during this period and are evident in a certain reluctance to acknowledge the American influence on curriculum. According to George

Tomkins, "Canadian educators displayed characteristic political sagacity in ascribing progressive ideas to British, rather than American, influences."[19] This is evident in the choice of the term "enterprise" from the British *Hadow Report* of 1926 over the term "project" from W.H. Kilpatrick's project method, even though the British report itself drew on American progressive sources. (Kilpatrick defined a project as "a wholehearted, purposeful activity proceeding in a social environment.")[20] It is also evident in the frequent use of the phrase "home-grown products,"[21] intended to convey the message that, although admittedly influenced by American ideas, curricula and materials had a Canadian twist.[22]

Many American ideas came directly from the United States to various parts of Canada. However, there was also a great deal of cross-pollination among educators in different Canadian provinces. For instance, the British Columbia Department of Education invited J.H. Putman, a progressive educator from Ontario, to join with British Columbian G.M. Weir to conduct the province's *Survey of the School System,* published in 1925.[23] Reform leaders such as Donalda Dickie, H.C. Newland, Stanley Watson, and H.B. King were frequently called upon to speak at teachers' conventions and contribute articles in teacher journals of provinces other than their own. Dickie's *The Enterprise in Theory and Practice* was used as a manual in Normal Schools in various parts of the country and was referred to frequently in provincial teacher journals. According to Alberta's H.C. Newland, the Ontario curriculum revision of 1937 involved wholesale plagiarizing of his own province's revision of the previous year.[24] New Brunswick acknowledged its debt to the "principles and methods which had proven successful in the western provinces and Ontario"[25] when it launched its new curriculum in 1939. American thought affected Canadian social studies curricula in two ways: by direct influence, and through interprovincial activity, since so many of the ideas travelling across provincial borders were American in origin.

Great Britain was another influence, both in the proportion of provincial social studies curricula devoted to study of Britain's geography and history, and in attitudes towards Britain found in textbooks. Approved textbooks, additional ad hoc materials sent to schools, and the patriotic activities in which students engaged combined to create an intellectual and social milieu that encouraged and promoted a sense of Canadian citizenship that was wrapped up in an enveloping allegiance to Great Britain and its empire, and the ideals for which it stood.[26]

The image prevalent in the texts is one of pride in Canada's increasing independence as a nation, juxtaposed with allegiance to Great Britain and the British Empire. In the widely used *History of Canada for High Schools* by Duncan McArthur, Britain's relationship with Canada is likened to that "of a fond parent to a full-grown son, proud of his attainments, willing to give aid and counsel, but placing on his shoulders complete responsibility for his conduct."[27]

Some of the extensive emphasis on Canada's relationship to Great Britain and the power and benevolence of the British Empire in textbooks and other materials may have been an attempt to counteract the reality of American cultural influence.[28] A 1930 cross-Canada survey of 1,288 grade 12 students found that 28 percent of students in Victoria and Vancouver read no English periodicals at all (40 percent was the cross-country average). American publications were widely read by students. American radio programs were preferred to Canadian, with the seven most popular programs all of American origin. Students voted overwhelmingly for American movies over British. It is interesting to note that they received their highest preference rate in Victoria, "a city referred to in tourist literature as 'a bit of old England.'"[29]

The "Structure of the Disciplines"

As Edith Deyell, an education professor at the University of British Columbia, pointed out, social studies was in a state of "ferment,"[30] in both Canada and the United States during the 1960s. Many considered it to be a school subject that had lost its focus, and called instead for an emphasis on history and geography as separate disciplines.

The 1950s had ushered in a period of strong

public debate across Canada regarding the effectiveness of progressive education. This debate coalesced around Hilda Neatby's aptly titled missive, *So Little For the Mind: An Indictment of Canadian Education* (1953), a scathing condemnation of progressive education in Canada. Neatby, a history professor at the University of Saskatchewan, questioned the intellectual aimlessness of progressive education.[31] She declared that the enterprise approach "as carried out by the average, harried, uninspired teacher, can be the dullest, most stereotyped, least stimulating way of teaching imaginable." She lamented the fact that social studies was "taught not only without the classic distinctions between geography, history, and politics, but also without the logical arrangement of place, time, and causation ordinarily considered to be inherent in these disciplines." She described social studies as "the truly typical part of the progressive curriculum with its obsession for indoctrination." This was because "everything is, of course, subordinated to the innumerable aims and attitudes which the teacher, in theory, must ever bear in mind."[32] The example she used was the British Columbia social studies curriculum for junior high school, with its ten powers, skills. and right habits of study, its eleven right ideals and attitudes, and fourteen desirable abilities, all to be developed by social studies.[33] In typical Canadian fashion, the response was to set up Royal Commissions to study the situation. In fact, half the provinces—British Columbia, Alberta, Saskatchewan, Manitoba, and Prince Edward Island—followed this path in 1959 or 1960.

The international political climate provided support for those who questioned the progressive tone of North American school curricula. The so-called Cold War between East and West was at its height. The launching of the Russian satellite Sputnik in 1957 aroused American concern about Soviet superiority in the realms of science and technology. As a result, the teaching of science, as well as other subjects, in American schools, was widely criticized as the reason for the United States falling behind the Soviets. Because official Canadian education documents also espoused a progressive philosophy, they too fell under this criticism from Neatby and others.

Published amid this climate of concern about education, Jerome Bruner's brief book, *The Process of Education,* took the American education scene by storm in 1960. According to Bruner, the goal of education was to give students "an understanding of the fundamental structure of whatever subject we choose to teach." By structure, Bruner meant the concepts and techniques of inquiry peculiar to a particular discipline. Bruner's second contention was that the basic ideas at the heart of the disciplines are simple enough for students at any level to grasp; therefore, we should not delay presenting students with these ideas but must develop ways to present them in forms that students can understand most easily. Bruner's third major point was that intuitive thinking had been undervalued in favour of analytic thinking, and he concluded that as far as history was concerned, inductive discovery was more fruitful than deductive presentation by the teacher. These three themes were based on Bruner's conviction that "intellectual activity anywhere is the same, whether at the frontier of knowledge or in a third-grade classroom." The major implication of these beliefs was that rather than simply presenting students with the findings of a discipline, they should become miniature scientists and use scientific inquiry techniques to make discoveries themselves.

The decade after the publication in 1960 of *The Process of Education* was marked in the United States by massive federal government funding for curriculum projects, particularly in science and mathematics. Several social studies projects were also funded. Bruner's declaration that "any subject can be taught effectively in some intellectually honest form to any child at any stage of development"[34] strongly challenged those who took on the task of developing new social studies materials based on the structures of the social science disciplines. The projects developed during this period were, in many respects, exemplary. Instead of simply giving students answers, they asked them questions that encouraged them to work with and think about the information provided. They used a multimedia approach that both presented information in appealing ways and catered to different learning styles and abilities. The varied instructional strategies included reading booklets,

viewing film loops, taking part in games and simulations, and building models. While there is little data available as to the extent these projects were used in Canada or how effective they were, those best known here, according to Tomkins, were Bruner's *Man: A Course of Study,* Edwin Fenton's *Social Studies Program for Able Students,* and publications of The High School Geography Project.[35] Two Canadian geography educators, Ronald Carswell and Angus Gunn, worked on The High School Geography Project.[36]

Man: A Course of Study[37] attempted to teach anthropological concepts and methods of inquiry to children. This program was very controversial in the United States and proved to be somewhat controversial in Canada as well. Certainly, controversy raged in Calgary in 1971, when a class of grade 7 students wrote to the Calgary Zoological Society objecting to the inadequate space provided for the baboons in the zoo. The letters followed a field trip to the zoo in order to compare animal and human behaviours, an activity intended to help students answer a major organizing question from *Man: A Course of Study,* "What is human about human beings?"[38]

In Canada the new era was marked by increased emphasis on history and geography as separate disciplines within social studies. This trend is reflected in the curriculum and instruction course in elementary social studies at the University of British Columbia, where the course title in the 1962-63 school year—"Curriculum and Instruction in Elementary Social Studies"—was changed to "Curriculum and Instruction in History and Geography" at the start of the next year. It is interesting to note that by the 1974–75 school year the title again referred to social studies—the encapsulation of an era.

Many new Canadian curriculum materials appeared on the scene, although they tended to be textbooks rather than the elaborate programs developed in the United States. History materials emphasized the use of primary sources, as students were encouraged to become miniature historians. The two-volume *Making Canadian History,* authorized for use in secondary schools in Ontario and British Columbia, had students use original source documents in order to engage in the tasks of historians. The text begins:

> You are presented with an opportunity to work this year as the historian works. This book supplies you with some of the evidence of past events as seen by eyewitnesses. . . .
>
> At the beginning we have provided you with the kinds of questions that the historian asks of his pictures, maps, and eyewitness accounts. We expect you to "read the evidence," and to draw your own conclusions.[39]

Collections of primary resource facsimiles in what were called Jackdaw kits were popular. These collections, intended to facilitate commonly studied topics such as Confederation, contained copies of such historical documents as newspaper articles, letters, deeds, price lists, fur-trading tokens, tickets, photographs, and posters.[40] While the immediate model for the Jackdaw kits was British,[41] the climate that led to their widespread use was created by American influences. History textbooks with a more traditional format, such as the widely used *Challenge & Survival*,[42] contained excerpts from historical documents interspersed with standard textbook prose.

While the climate for the fostering of a discipline-centred social studies arose from developments in the United States, the actual impetus for a discovery approach to geography education came from British sources, most specifically in the person of Neville Scarfe, who is considered by some to have been the leading world figure in geography education at the time.[43] Scarfe arrived from Britain in 1951 to take the position of dean of education at the University of Manitoba. After investigating the status of geography education in Canada, Scarfe concluded that, especially in western Canada, it was treated as only a minor part of social studies. It received more attention in the eastern provinces, where it had status as a separate subject.

Scarfe accused certain commonly used textbooks of "murder[ing] geography by their method of presentation."[44] Scarfe and other British geographers originally introduced British geography texts to Canada. However, in 1963, Scarfe co-authored *A New Geography of Canada* with two Canadian geographers, George and Doreen Tomkins. Other Canadian geography texts published during this period were *Canada: A Regional Geography* by George Tomkins and Theo Hills, and *Discovering Our Land* by Doreen Tomkins.[45] All of these Canadian texts used a discovery approach that involved students in the use of maps and other data sources in order to draw conclusions. According to Tomkins, Scarfe's use of discovery methods predated the influence of Bruner.[46] Tomkins also points out that the revival of geography in Canadian schools preceded *The High School Geography Project,* which was an attempt to re-establish a school subject that was in almost total eclipse at the secondary level in the United States. Therefore, it seems that the American structure of the disciplines approach reinforced and encouraged a trend that was already present in geography education in Canada during the 1960s.

The influence of the structure of the disciplines movement was also evident at the level of provincial curricula. Design for Learning, a 1962 assessment of all social science curricula in Ontario, made explicit reference to it, and, according to Northrop Frye, the editor of the report, Bruner's ideas permeated the thinking behind the entire investigation.[47] British Columbia secondary school curriculum guides during this period continued to use the term social studies, but as an umbrella for discrete courses in history and geography, each constituting half a year's work.[48] A definitive list of concepts that "form the framework which unifies the field . . . and gives meaning to the factual content of the discipline"[49] was provided for history and for geography in the 1968 British Columbia secondary social studies curriculum guide.

The structure of the disciplines approach can also be seen in textbooks written by Canadian university educators and used in faculty of education social studies curriculum and instruction courses during the 1960s and early 1970s. Text monographs such as *Teaching the Subjects in the Social Studies*[50] and *Teaching History and Geography: A Source Book of Suggestions* exemplified this approach. The latter text states that "a major purpose of the social studies [is] that elementary school children should begin to learn the thinking patterns, or structure, of the social sciences."[51] Texts that were collections of readings, such as *Teaching for Tomorrow*, edited by John Lewis, and Geoffrey Milburn's *Teaching History in Canada,* also reflected this view.[52]

Another American influence during this period was the work of Hilda Taba and her colleagues in Contra Costa County, California. Taba's text, *Teachers' Handbook for Elementary Social Studies*,[53] was used in Canadian university social studies curriculum and instruction courses during the 1970s,[54] her colleagues were invited to speak at Canadian conferences,[55] and her texts, published by Addison-Wesley, were authorized for primary social studies in several provinces. Taba identified a number of "key concepts." The 1973 Ontario history curriculum used this approach (although unacknowledged in the curriculum guide) in its identification of such concepts as "change, diversity, order, individualism, the common good, worth of the individual, concern for others, dignity of labour, tradition, and culture" as being "central to the human experience."[56] Another of Taba's recommendations for organizing social studies curricular content was what she called the "spiral" curriculum: returning at different grade levels to certain major concepts at increasingly abstract levels and in ways that were further from students' direct experience. For instance, the concept of interdependence could be dealt with in terms of the family, services in a community, trade among nations, and so on. This approach soon found its way into some Canadian provincial social studies curriculum documents. In the 1978 Alberta curriculum, the spiral approach was applied to thirteen concepts—human needs, identity, values, perspective, inquiry, interaction, influence, social change, adjustment, environment, institution, power, and resources—from the primary grades through to the end of the secondary program.[57] (This curriculum does not acknowledge Taba, although the previous 1971 curriculum, which uses the same approach, had done so.) The Ontario curriculum also referred to the spiral curriculum.

Edwin Fenton's inquiry approach enjoyed some prominence in Canada during this period.[58] Fenton, proceeding from Bruner's belief that students should use the methods of inquiry of the disciplines just as scholars do, developed an inquiry model that he intended to be explicitly taught. According to Ken Osborne, the practical result of Fenton's work was to encourage the treatment of the disciplines as a series of problems.[59] Osborne points to the influence that this approach had on the direction taken by Ontario's sociological Man In Society course, which was organized around social problems rather than a formal outline of sociology as a discipline. Fenton's approach was a first step towards the use of inquiry procedures for dealing with social issues, an approach that became prominent in Canada in the 1970s. This trend will be discussed later.

Upon his return from the 1966 National Council for the Social Studies Conference in the United States, a Canadian educator declared, "If you were to ask me, at this moment, what is new in social studies, I would reply, 'Read Bruner and Fenton.'"[60] Just as the American Progressive Education movement had done, Bruner's structure of the disciplines approach provided a rallying point for change in the Canadian social studies curriculum. This approach soon appeared in provincial curriculum documents and texts used in school classrooms, as well as in courses for the training of teachers. Canadian social studies continued to be "made in America."

Canada Studies

George Tomkins, co-director of the Canada Studies Foundation, proclaimed in 1972 that "Canadian Studies has begun to take its place with politics, sex and sport as a staple of cocktail party conversation."[61] Although this bit of hyperbole may only have been true for the circles in which Tomkins travelled, Canadian studies was certainly of wide concern at the time.

If Hilda Neatby's *So Little for the Mind* was the landmark publication for Canadian social studies in the 1950s and Bruner's *The Process of Education* in the 1960s, there is no doubt that A.B. Hodgetts' *What Culture? What Heritage?* enjoyed this status in the 1970s. This publication was a direct result of concern about American cultural domination and loss of Canadian identity. The National History Project, of which this book was the final report, was a two-year, comprehensive survey of history and civic education across the country, carried out at the time of Canada's centennial celebration. It generated an unusual degree of interest, making "publishing history in Canadian education as a best-seller that appealed alike to professional educators, the media, academia, and a broad spectrum of the lay public."[62] It also sparked debate in at least one provincial legislature[63] and was widely covered in the media. A history teacher and textbook author, Hodgetts concluded that civic education in Canada was in a dismal state. Regarding the teaching of Canadian history, he decided that "we are teaching a bland, unrealistic consensus version of our past: a dry-as-dust chronological story of uninterrupted political and economic progress told without the controversy that is an inherent part of history." He called for radically new approaches to Canadian studies in which students would no longer be "bench-bound listeners" but would be encouraged "to discover a real and vital Canada for themselves."[64] In a later book, *Teaching Canada for the '80s*, Hodgetts and his co-author, Paul Gallagher, argued for "a cooperative and systematic nation-wide effort to improve the quality of studies of Canada in Canadian schools."[65]

Hodgetts proposed a national Canada Studies Consortium that would be interprovincial in nature, independent of any government or existing agency, and run from a series of regional centres. "Its exclusive purpose," he argued, "should be to develop and distribute Canadian Studies materials and teaching strategies for use in elementary and secondary schools."[66] The Canada Studies Foundation was formed in 1970, with Hodgetts as its first director, and continued until 1986. The foundation sponsored projects in every region of the country, produced over 150 publications, involved 1,300 teachers and other educators in curriculum development, and provided in-service education for 30,000 teachers.[67] Curriculum development projects were organized in three groups: the Laurentian Project in Ontario and Québec; Project Atlantic Canada, involving each of the Maritime provinces and Newfoundland-Labrador; and Project Canada West, involving the four western provinces.

A profusion of Canadian social studies materials appeared during the 1970s and 1980s. At the same time as curriculum projects were being developed under the auspices of the Canada Studies Foundation, provincial curricula showed increased emphasis on Canadian studies, and materials were required to support these topics. Increased attention was paid to the encouragement of Canadian publishing. During the 1970s and 1980s, nearly every province took on various projects to develop materials for classroom use. Alberta, with the financial resources of its Heritage Trust Fund at hand, invested the most money in such projects. In 1977, $8,387,000 was invested in its Alberta Heritage Learning Resources Project. The objectives of the project were:

> To provide additional Canadian content learning resources for the language arts, social studies, and science curricula of Alberta schools.
>
> To provide an outlet for the talents of editors, authors, illustrators, graphic artists, and film producers from Alberta and other parts of Canada.
>
> To utilize the provincial capabilities for publishing and printing with the clear recognition that the volume, quantity, and timeliness of the projects may require assistance beyond provincial boundaries.[68]

Alberta, with several publishing companies producing social studies resources at this time, was very supportive of small local educational publishers.[69] Prince Edward Island developed resource books and kits on the province's history, and distributed an essay collection called *Readings in Prince Edward Island History*[70] to schools. The introduction of the Maritime Studies program in the 1980s also encouraged local publishers, as did the ongoing development of materials suitable for use in all three Maritime provinces. Newfoundland had a grade 9 history text, *Canada Since Confederation: An Atlantic Perspective*.[71] In British Columbia, a contract for an elementary school social studies series was awarded to Douglas & McIntyre (Educational), a local publisher, in 1982.

These materials were provided to elementary schools in British Columbia and also found a market across Canada.[72]

A Canadian company, Fitzhenry and Whiteside, published many popular social studies materials during the 1970s and 1980s. Its Growth of a Nation series of historical booklets, [73] written by Canadian authors, was authorized in every province.[74] In addition, subsidiaries of large American publishing companies produced many materials written by Canadian authors suitable for social studies curricula. In Search of Canada, published by Prentice-Hall in 1977, is an example of one such text that was used widely in Canada.[75]

Tomkins has pointed out that "it can be argued that foreign or external influences on the Canadian curriculum have been at least as great for the negative responses they have evoked as for the positive contributions they have made."[76] The formation of the Canada Studies Foundation and the proliferation of social studies materials both under its auspices and those of provincial government departments of education, as well as the increased emphasis on Canada in provincial curricula, were reactions against the potential (and actuality) of American cultural domination. While the reaction itself could be considered negative, the results were positive. "Made in America" took on a distinctly Canadian aspect.

Social Issues and Values Education

By the mid-1970s the "structure of the disciplines" movement as such was over in both Canada and the United States, although it seems safe to say that aspects of it have been retained. The approach has been subject to a lengthy list of criticisms. Most recently, writers in the American social studies journal The Social Studies have criticized it for an overreliance on knowledge objectives and inquiry procedures from the social science disciplines while ignoring the needs and interests of students and societal problems; materials that were too sophisticated for the students; its failure to involve typical teachers in material development; ignorance of the "hidden curriculum" of gender, social class, ethnic, and religious issues; the logistical complexity of many of the projects; a failure to bridge the cultural gap between the researcher and the real world of teaching, which involves large classes, multiple preparations, and often hostile students; and naïveté regarding the politics of curriculum development, including textbook adoption methods and the influence of publishers.[77] Many of these criticisms are valid in Canada. Certainly, here as in the United States, the social studies tide turned towards an emphasis on values education and social issues in the 1970s.

Once again, Jerome Bruner signalled the new emphasis in social studies education, this time on teaching students to examine their own values and to become active decision-makers by working through issues of both social and personal concern. It was a 1971 article entitled "The Process of Education Revisited" that heralded this change:

> I believe I would be quite satisfied to declare, if not a moratorium, then something of a de-emphasis on matters that have to do with the structure of history, the structure of physics, the nature of mathematical consistency and deal with it rather in the context of the problems that face us.[78]

Bruner referred to such American social problems as poverty, racism, the unpopular war in Vietnam, and the extent to which schools had become "instruments of the evil forces in our society."[79] Osborne pointed out that Canada, too, had a "crisis of values"[80] at the time, with the October crisis of 1970, new societal concerns such as sexism, the stirring of discontent among Native peoples, and a breakdown in federal/provincial relations.

The response in Canada, as in the United States, was to change the orientation of provincial social studies curricula and classroom materials. Max van Manen and Jim Parsons identify four new program types by which many Canadian social studies curricula could be categorized through the 1970s and into the 1980s. These are social reconstruction and reflective awareness, moral education and valuing processes, environmental education and social problems approach, and Canada studies and citizenship education, all of which have a social issues component.[81]

Van Manen and Parsons describe the aim of social reconstruction and reflective awareness as "the development of an active critical awareness on the part of all citizens to the need for social change towards a more just and equitable social world order."[82] As examples of this approach, they point to black studies, women's studies, and Third World or development studies courses that were regularly offered in Ontario.

They divide the moral education and valuing processes program type into two approaches. The first, the moral reasoning approach, was based on the work of Lawrence Kohlberg at Harvard, and was intended to move children up systematically from lower to higher stages of moral reasoning. According to Osborne, many social studies theorists saw the improvement of moral reasoning as a valuable goal and the use of Kohlberg's dilemmas as a useful teaching strategy, but they did not use his stage theory or concern themselves unduly with the detailed analysis of moral reasoning that he advocated.[83] The second approach was that of values clarification, which was based on a three-stage model (choosing, prizing, acting) developed by Louis Raths, Merrill Harmin, and Sidney Simon in their 1966 book, *Values and Teaching*, published in Columbus, Ohio.[84] The values clarification approach encouraged students to choose their own system of values. This model has been described as "extraordinarily influential"[85] in the development of the 1971 Alberta social studies curricula, Experiences in Decision Making, for elementary schools, and Responding to Change, for secondary.[86] It formed the basis of the social studies curriculum in Alberta from 1971 until it was revised in 1978 (in interim form). The 1971 Alberta curriculum emphasizes that its approach was based unequivocally on the model by Raths et al., providing a version of the model in the curriculum guides and even going so far as to inform the reader that copies of the book *Values and Teaching* were available through the Alberta Education School Book Branch. This curriculum was always controversial among Alberta educators.[87] The Downey Report, an

assessment of the extent to which this curriculum was actually implemented, concluded that most social studies teachers either did not agree with or did not understand the intents and methods of the values clarification approach upon which the curriculum was based.[88]

Van Manen and Parsons describe the environmental education and social problems approach as one that focuses on local problems as well as larger issues such as overpopulation, pollution, and resource depletion. The Canada studies and citizenship education program type deals with issues of particular concern to Canadians, as has been discussed previously.

In practice, most Canadian social studies curricula could not be clearly identified as one or another of these program types. Rather, they are a blend of two or more types, with varying degrees of emphasis. The 1981 Alberta social studies curriculum is an example of such a blend of approaches. It contained elements of the social reconstruction and reflective awareness, the environmental education and social problems, and Canada studies and citizenship education program types. This curriculum defined social studies as "the school subject in which students learn to explore and, where possible, to resolve, social issues that are of public and personal concern."[89] The content for each grade was organized around three major issues (two in grades 11 and 12) and the curriculum encouraged teachers to help students become involved in real-life applications of the decisions they reached related to these issues. While issues were said to be related to local, provincial, national, and world situations, the emphasis was on Canada, with actual time allocation to Canada studies representing about 60 percent of total prescribed content.

Two influential groups of American social studies educators had been at work on projects dealing with approaches to social issues throughout the 1960s, when the focus elsewhere had been on social science education. One group, at Harvard University, was led by eminent social studies scholars Donald Oliver, James Shaver, and Fred Newmann. *Teaching Public Issues in the High School*, by Oliver and Shaver, consisted of materials focusing on controversial issues and student decision-making.[90] Another group, at Indiana University, consisting of Shirley Engle and Frederick Smith, with their graduate students, Byron Massialas, C. Benjamin Cox, and Jan Tucker, conducted work on the concept of citizenship education as reflective inquiry. Members of this group published a number of books and articles supporting this approach to social studies teaching.[91]

The Canadian Critical Issues Series (also known as the Public Issues Program),[92] developed at the Ontario Institute for Studies in Education, was modelled on the Harvard Teaching Public Issues in the High School Project. As Osborne puts it, the Harvard Social Studies Project was "transmogrified into a Canadian context."[93] Two of the developers of the Canadian program described the intent of the program as follows:

> Basically the program has two goals. The first is to enable students to gain an understanding of the society in which they live through the active discussion of its major social conflicts. The second, which in practice is inseparable from the first, is to enable students to acquire those skills necessary for the analysis, discussion, and resolution of such conflicts or issues.[94]

Units of this program dealt with such topics as Canadian-American relations, French Canadian separatism, police methods, and the status of women in Canadian society.

The Canada Studies Foundation sponsored such issues-oriented materials as its Public Issues in Canada: Possibilities for Classroom Teaching, developed at the University of British Columbia in the 1980s.[95] This set of materials includes booklets such as *The Quality of Work Life*, *A Multicultural Experience*, and *Free Trade*. The Atlantic Centre of the Canada Studies Foundation published a set of booklets under the title Understanding the Canadian Environment,[96] that examine Canada's physical, cultural, and political environment. This series includes such titles as *Canada: Challenges in the Development of Resources*, *Canada: Human Rights: Foundations for Freedom*, and *Canada: Human Rights and the Law*. All of these resources provided students with case studies

of current Canadian social issues for analysis and discussion. Students were expected to explore the various perspectives on these issues and come to a decision as to their own positions. These materials, too, are a combination of several of van Manen and Parson's program types.

Throughout the 1970s, in spite of little official attention to the United States in Canadian social studies curricula and strong attention to the development of Canadian textbook publishing, the American influence remained pervasive. For example, use of American social studies methods texts for the training of future teachers continued as before. Both *Social Studies for Children in a Democracy* by John Michaelis and Hilda Taba's *Teacher's Handbook for Elementary Social Studies*[97] were popular choices. Canadians who chose to attend graduate school outside the country usually did so in the United States.[98] A 1976 review of social studies literature published during the previous decade reveals conceptions of such topics as concepts, inquiry, and discovery that are almost entirely derivative of American sources.[99] Canadian scholars discussed American issues in Canadian locations and drew upon a largely American body of literature.

This "Made in America" influence contributed to a commonality in Canadian provincial social studies curricula. A 1982 survey of the social studies curriculum in every province, carried out by the Council of Ministers of Education, revealed that the common focus was now on inquiry approaches, with a goal of providing "students with the knowledge, skills, values and thought processes which will enable them to participate effectively and responsibly in the ever-changing environment of their community, their country and their world."[100] However, this emphasis on inquiry has been interpreted differently across the country. To demonstrate this point, here are definitions of social studies from curriculum guides of the 1980s for the provinces of British Columbia, Alberta, Nova Scotia, and Ontario. The first three provinces used the term social studies from the primary grades through to the secondary. Ontario had a program called Environmental Studies in the elementary grades, which was developed locally, while in the secondary grades, courses were offered as history and contemporary studies or geography.

> The curriculum continues British Columbia's traditional reliance on history and geography . . . as the prime organizers of knowledge and learning activities in Social Studies. (British Columbia)[101]

> Social studies is the school subject in which students learn to explore and, where possible, to resolve, social issues that are of public and personal concern. (Alberta)[102]

> Aims . . . to provide students with a wide variety of skills and to expose them to a variety of content relating to geography, history and other social studies aspects, both about Canada and other areas of the world. (Nova Scotia)[103]

> Will help students understand their own and other societies, become active participants in their education and their society, and develop both self-confidence and concern for the welfare of others. (Ontario History and Contemporary Studies)[104]

It is clear from these definitions that provincial interpretations of the school subject often called social studies have differed. Some provinces make it clear that their social studies program is based in the social science disciplines, particularly history and geography. Others place much more emphasis on social-inquiry skills.

Renewed Emphasis on Citizenship

The 1960s witnessed a change of focus from the citizenship concerns that were previously evident in social studies, to more academic concerns with an emphasis on the social sciences. In the 1970s there was another shift, this time to moral issues and values education. The Canadian Studies emphasis, a phenomenon unique to Canada, also took place during the 1970s. Osborne points out that "Canadian Studies in some ways combined the attention to academic rigour of the sixties, the counter-theme

of public issues, and the seventies' interest in values, as it presented a highly eclectic face to the world."[105]

The 1980s saw a renewed emphasis on citizenship, this time viewed through the lens of political education. This interest is evident in monographs on the topic, such as Osborne's *The Teaching of Politics: Some Suggestions for Teachers*.[106] A component of this political education is social action. The work of Fred Newmann and his colleagues at the National Center on Effective Secondary Schools at the University of Wisconsin-Madison was influential in this regard.[107] Newmann urged students to develop "environmental competence"[108] and engage in social action as the natural outcome of considering public issues. The 1981 Alberta curriculum incorporated this notion with the seventh step of its inquiry model, "applying the decision," which encouraged students to "create a plan of action to apply the decision (e.g., work for an improved school or classroom environment; provide services to a community group on a close interpersonal basis; or participate actively in a political process).[109] However, the 1988 junior high social studies curriculum dropped the social action component of its predecessor, endorsing instead what it called "responsible citizenship." This form of citizenship, as described in curriculum documents, includes critical and creative thinking, as well as problem-solving and decision-making, but without the final step of acting on one's decisions.[110]

It is interesting to note that while Alberta took the notion of social action further than any other province in the early 1980s, it then went against the tide. While Alberta began to back away from this notion, other provinces were incorporating it into their curricula. The 1985 Manitoba curriculum, for example, referred to community involvement such as volunteer work with the elderly or participation in a political campaign.[111] Newfoundland referred to a "need for a shift in emphasis from passively learning knowledge in favour of an active acquisition and utilization of knowledge."[112] The Common Curriculum of Ontario included participation in service activities in the home or school community, as well as activities related to global and/or environmental issues.[113]

Several scholars writing in this period note a

decline in separate history courses and a greater emphasis on social studies, with its interdisciplinary focus.[114] This decline of history began with the trend away from Bruner's disciplinary emphasis in the 1970s.

During the late 1980s and early 1990s social studies received increasing skills emphasis, particularly in history. For example, Bob Davis points out in *Whatever Happened to High School History?* that Ontario's History and Contemporary Studies program

> includes the teaching of both "attitude and cognitive" skills in its aims. Thirty-two of the 65 pages of the book are devoted to skills, one 11-page chapter being entitled Development and Growth in Cognitive Skills, and guideline appendices A to D contain detailed charts about what skills are to be taught, at what streamed level and in what courses.[115]

The 1970s and 1980s also saw a focus on curriculum materials. As newspaper headlines such as "Slanted Textbooks" and "Tell It the Way It Was"[116] attest, in the late 1960s there was a great deal of public interest in the way in which Canada's changing social reality was portrayed in school textbooks. During the next two decades a multitude of studies tried to determine whether and in what ways texts were biased towards particular societal groups. The ultimate purpose of these studies was to remove texts from provincially approved lists if they were deemed to be too biased for student eyes. These studies were usually sponsored by provincial human rights commissions, provincial departments of education, or groups such as Native organizations, which had particular concerns regarding the depiction of their constituents. A landmark study in this regard was *Teaching Prejudice*, Garnet McDiarmid and David Pratt's 1971 study of 143 Ontario authorized social studies textbooks.[117]

As a result of such studies, each province developed social awareness criteria for use in assessing potential resources before they receive authorization status. The intention is to authorize only those materials accurately depicting the racial and ethnic plu-ralism of Canada and showing people of both genders and of various races, ethnic groups, ages, and abilities, including older people and people with disabilities, all making positive contributions to Canadian society, past and present. *Race, Religion, and Culture in Ontario School Materials*, developed by the Ministry of Education in Ontario in 1981,[118] is an example of a document that incorporates such criteria. Alberta's "tolerance and understanding" criterion is another example.[119]

In the 1980s and the early 1990s, although Canadian scholars remained attuned to American thinking, they began carving out their own areas of contribution to social studies theory. A 1984 examination by Geoffrey Milburn of theme issues of *The History and Social Science Teacher*, the national social studies journal, reveals original contributions to areas such as working-class history, multiculturalism, the relevance of ancient history, economic education, quantitative methods, human rights, social science techniques, moral education and social studies, and values education.[120] Milburn also refers to major monographs such as those of Bennett on organizing Canadian history, Paula Bourne and John Eisenberg on social issues, Kieran Egan on educational development, Donald C. Wilson on Canadian studies, J.A. Ross and F.J. Maynes on problem-solving, and Dean Wood on multiculturalism.[121]

While the 1980s witnessed a shift away from a single-minded reliance on American sources, U.S. materials remained in use, particularly in faculties of education. Articles in *The History and Social Science Teacher* often made reference to American sources. American textbooks such as *Social Studies for Children* by John U. Michaelis, *Children and Their World* by David A. Welton and John T. Mallan, and *Social Studies in Elementary Education* by John Jarolimek[122] continued to be used in social studies curriculum and instruction courses in faculties of education. As Tomkins pointed out, such "influences are no doubt extremely variable, largely informal and probably non-measurable but they cannot be discounted."[123]

Re-emergence of History Education

Current trends of note are a renewed interest in the place of history in the curriculum, a continuation of the citizenship education momentum identified earlier, and new regional curriculum initiatives in western and northern Canada and the Atlantic region. Of these, the most dominant is the re-emergence of history education.

Vigorous debates about the place of history in the school curriculum were front and centre at the turn of the twenty-first century. They were sparked by the publication in 1998 of eminent historian J.L. Granatstein's provocatively titled *Who Killed Canadian History?*[124] This widely read polemic pointed to various killers, including university historians who narrowed their focus to gender, labour, regional or local history rather than the broad sweep of Canadian history; provincial departments of education that mandated interdisciplinary social studies instead of history courses, and advocated a parochial regionalism; interest groups that managed to insert their narrow agendas into the curriculum; and the federal government, which failed to mandate national standards for history education.

Granatstein acknowledged "some small signs that history is beginning to make some impact on the public consciousness."[125] Perhaps the first hint that these small signs were going to become an avalanche was the 1999 national conference, Giving the Past a Future, organized by the McGill Institute for the Study of Canada. This event, which attracted some 750 university historians and education faculty members, school history teachers, and Ministry of Education curriculum specialists, as well as archivists, curators, and publishers, was the first national conference on the teaching of Canada's history. A second national gathering, the Giving the Future a Past conference in Winnipeg in 2001, followed this conference.

It was at these conferences that the issue of national standards came to the fore. Those in favour of standards, such as Rudyard Griffiths of the newly formed Dominion Institute, argued on the basis of the value of a national history curriculum in promoting a strong national identity and sense of citizenship. Those opposed argued for a "critical disciplinary history," intended to give students a rational approach to dealing with conflicting historical accounts through developing their own interpretations based on thoughtful examination of evidence.[126]

The establishment of the Historica Foundation in 2000 is another signal that the place of history in the school curriculum is becoming more secure. This privately funded foundation has sponsored several initiatives such as the increasingly popular Heritage Fairs Program, well-attended summer institutes for teachers, and the production of a website with history lesson plans. Two other developments of interest are the CBC/Radio Canada millennium film project, *Canada: A People's History*, which is used extensively in schools, and the establishment by Peter Seixas in 2001 of the Centre for the Study of Historical Consciousness in the Faculty of Education at the University of British Columbia, which is attracting history teachers as graduate students.

Citizenship education continues to be the stated purpose of social studies in provincial curriculum documents. Social studies scholars Gerald Clarke, Andrew Hughes, and Alan Sears, at the University of New Brunswick, have been active in citizenship research and student assessment both nationally and internationally. The newly created Citizenship Education Research Network (CERN), comprised of curriculum scholars from across the country, has held a series of forums on issues around citizenship education in Canada. This work may in time have a direct impact on curriculum reform.

Since the mid-1990s, curriculum revision has taken place in every province. Regional curriculum initiatives have been mounted in the Atlantic region and among the western provinces and the territories. The Atlantic region has experienced greater success, perhaps due to a longer history of joint provincial curriculum initiatives. New Brunswick, Nova Scotia, Prince Edward Island, and Newfoundland united to develop *The Foundation for the Atlantic Canada Social Studies Curriculum*, a project that began with the establishment of the Atlantic Provinces Education Foundation (APEF) in 1995.[127] They have since jointly developed new curricula for grades K–

9 based on this document. They offer a grade 9 course called "Atlantic Canada in the Global Community."

The experience of the Western and Northern Canadian Protocol for Collaboration in Basic Education has been more contentious with regard to social studies than for its projects in other curricular areas. This collaboration was based on an agreement signed in December of 1993 by the Ministers of Education of British Columbia, Alberta, Saskatchewan, Manitoba, the Yukon Territory, and the Northwest Territories, with Nunavut joining in 2000. Over the course of the project, British Columbia and Alberta withdrew from direct involvement. Thus, the final 2002 document, the *Common Curriculum Framework for Social Studies, Kindergarten to Grade 9* credits only the other jurisdictions for their "cooperative efforts,"[128] although all are acknowledged as holders of copyright.

Curriculum development based on the *Common Curriculum Framework* has been inconsistent. British Columbia produced a new K–11 curriculum in 1997 and 1998, without reference to the work of what was then called the Western Protocol.[129] The Yukon Territory uses the British Columbia curriculum, "modified and enhanced to meet Yukon needs."[130] In 2002, Alberta adopted a consultation draft based on the *Common Curriculum Framework* document to guide its future curriculum development. This province expects its major revisions to be completed by 2006.[131] The Northwest Territories has developed its own K–9 curriculum based on the *Common Curriculum Framework* document, and uses the Alberta grades 10–12 curriculum, with some locally developed options. It also has a grade 10 course called Northern Studies, which is a graduation requirement. Nunavut uses the Northwest Territories K–9 curriculum, the Alberta 10–12 curriculum, and the Northwest Territories' Northern Studies course. Saskatchewan, like British Columbia, chose not to wait for the WNCP to complete its work, producing new curricula throughout the 1990s. Manitoba is currently engaged in major curriculum revision based on the *Common Curriculum Framework* document.[132]

Ontario, meanwhile, has carried on independently, replacing its short-lived *Common Curriculum:*

Policies and Outcomes, Grades 1–9, 1995 with new courses. This province has retained its emphasis on social studies in grades 1 to 6, and history and geography in grades 7 and 8. Mandatory courses in grades 9 and 10 and optional grade 11 and 12 courses are offered under the umbrella term Canadian and World Studies.

One common feature of these new curricula has been critical thinking. The Critical Thinking Consortium in British Columbia has taken this the furthest, with its Critical Challenges Across the Curriculum Series. Most of the booklets developed in this series support the social studies curriculum. Titles include *Snapshots of 19th Century Canada, Critical Challenges in Law and Government: Canada's Constitutional Crisis—A Simulation*, and *Critical Challenges in Social Studies for Upper Elementary Students.*[133]

Social studies educators in this country remain without a strong national network. There is no national organization of social studies teachers. Nor is there a national conference. However, the journal *Canadian Social Studies* continues to provide a forum for exploration of topics of interest, albeit on the web rather than in print form, as in the past. It is published three to four times annually, with George Richardson at the University of Alberta as its current editor, and includes contributions from both classroom teachers and university educators.

There are currently four Canadian social studies methodology textbooks used in the training of preservice teachers, all of which are favoured over American texts: *Elementary Social Studies: A Practical Approach*, by Ian Wright from UBC; *Elementary Social Studies*, by Joseph Kirman at the University of Alberta; an edited collection by Roland Case from Simon Fraser University and Penney Clark from UBC called *The Canadian Anthology of Social Studies: Issues and Strategies for Teachers*; and the book from which the current volume has evolved, *Trends & Issues in Canadian Social Studies.*[134] Canadian educators of social studies teachers seem eager to use Canadian rather than American materials in this period.

Conclusion

Ironically, although history is an important component of social studies, the history of social studies education in Canada has not received a great deal of attention. This study has used broad strokes to paint a picture of its development in Canada from its inception to the early years of the twenty-first century. American social studies thought has affected Canadian curricula from the progressive education movement of the 1920s through the structure of the disciplines and the Canada Studies movements, continuing on through the social issues and values education influences, to the citizenship emphasis of the 1980s. In the 1990s, social studies curricula began to be more uniquely Canadian.

The many social studies texts and other curriculum materials written by Canadian authors have always mitigated these influences somewhat. The numerous materials developed by the Canada Studies Foundation may have provided the impetus for the present emphasis on materials written by Canadian authors. However, it is more likely that the societal conditions that spawned the foundation also resulted in the perception of a need to encourage Canadian educational publishers and authors. It seems particularly important to develop Canadian-made resources in social studies because citizenship goals and Canadian content are dominant themes in the curriculum.

The opportunity for interaction offered by the national social studies teachers' journal, *Canadian Social Studies*, has also encouraged the generation of uniquely Canadian ideas. This journal has continued to struggle along under several guises over the years because of a strong commitment among Canadian social studies educators to provide a national forum for exchange of ideas.

Michael Katz, in discussing the Canadian educational experience, once said "simple notions of direct borrowing will not suffice."[135] In examining the influence of American ideas and products on social studies education in Canada, one cannot overlook the ways in which Canadians, to fit their own unique circumstances, have adapted American sources. George Tomkins made the point that American models and strategies have been useful in Canadian curriculum and materials development, whereas the direct importation of American materials has not.[136]

Canadians have always found American influences on Canadian curricula somewhat abhorrent. This complaint, made in 1919, is typical: "All of our up-to-date information practically comes to us from the United States. We use the bulletin of the United States Bureau of Education to know what is going on in the western provinces even."[137] It is as if we have "held our noses and voted 'yes'" to American educational ideas, just as we were advised to do in our 1992 national referendum. British sources have been much more palatable than American. Hence, in the 1930s, it was acceptable to receive American progressive ideas through the vehicle of the British Hadow Report. It was also acceptable for many years to use a geography textbook that referred to France as "our neighbour across the channel."[138]

It is impossible to entirely avoid the American influence on social studies education in Canada. Instead, Canadian social studies educators have chosen to benefit from the dollars and energy put into social studies education in the United States by taking the models and strategies that seem useful, adapting them to the Canadian context, and discarding the rest, while at the same time working to develop and share uniquely Canadian ideas.

Endnotes

1   The Yukon has used the British Columbia social studies curriculum and the Northwest Territories has used Alberta's. Nunavut has used both the Northwest Territories' and Alberta's. There is some room for local curriculum development in the territories.

2   Bernard G. Holt, "The National Council for the Social Studies Convention at Cleveland," *Exploration* 7 (June 1967): 1.

3   William E. Hay and A.B. Stettler to Dr. H.C. Newland, Edmonton, AB, 19 June 1936, in *Topics in the History of Education in Western Canada: A Skill Centred Approach*, ed. R.S. Patterson (Edmonton: Publication Services, Faculty of Education, University of Alberta, n.d.).

4   Hazel Whitman Hertzberg, *Social Studies Reform: 1880–1980* (Boulder, CO: Social Science Education Consortium, 1981), xi.

5   Hazel Whitman Hertzberg, "Social Studies Reform: The Lessons of History," in *Social Studies in the 1980s: A Report of Project Span*, ed. Irving Morrissett (Alexandria, VA: Association for Supervision and Curriculum Development, 1982), 5.

6   National Education Association of the United States, Com-

mission on the Reorganization of Secondary Education, Committee on Social Studies, *Social Studies in Secondary Education; A Six-year Program Adapted both to the 6-3-3 and the 8-4 Plans of Organization* (Washington, DC: Government Printing Office, 1916).

[7] For a discussion of this approach, see James E. Akenson, "Historical Factors in the Development of Elementary Social Studies: Focus on the Expanding Environments," *Theory and Research in Social Education* 15, no. 2 (1987): 155–171; Paul Hanna, "Society—Child—Curriculum," in *Education 2000 AD*, ed. Clarence W. Hunnicutt (Syracuse: Syracuse University Press, 1956); and for a Canadian critique of this approach, see Kieran Egan, "John Dewey and the Social Studies Curriculum," *Theory and Research in Social Education* 8, no. 2 (1980): 37–55.

[8] H.C. Newland, "Report of the Supervisor of Schools," in *Thirty-sixth Annual Report of the Department of Education of the Province of Alberta* (Edmonton: King's Printer, 1941), 12.

[9] Department of Education, Alberta, *Programme of Studies for the Elementary School* (Edmonton: King's Printer, 1941), 56.

[10] Department of Education, Alberta, *Programme of Studies for the Intermediate School and Departmental Regulations Relating to the Grade IX Examination* (Edmonton: King's Printer, 1936), 34, 36.

[11] G.M. Weir, "The Revision of the Curriculum," *The B.C. Teacher* XIV (April 1935): 21.

[12] Jean Mann, "Progressive Education and the Depression in British Columbia," (master's thesis, University of British Columbia, 1978), 180–188.

[13] "Guest Speaker at Easter Convention," *The ATA Magazine* 21 (March 1941): 4.

[14] C. Sansom, "A Friendly Convention," *The ATA Magazine* 19 (May 1939): 2.

[15] R.S. Patterson, "The Canadian Response to Progressive Education," in *Essays on Canadian Education*, ed. Nick Kach et al. (Calgary: Detselig, 1986), 74.

[16] W.W. Brickman, "William Heard Kilpatrick and International Education," *Educational Theory* 16 (1966): 20.

[17] Donalda James Dickie, *The Enterprise in Theory and Practice* (Toronto: W.J. Gage, 1940).

[18] Nancy Sheehan, "Education, the Society and the Curriculum in Alberta 1905–1980: An Overview," in *Schools in the West: Essays in Canadian Educational History*, ed. Nancy M. Sheehan, J. Donald Wilson, and David C. Jones (Calgary: Detselig, 1986), 44.

[19] George S. Tomkins, *A Common Countenance: Stability and Change in the Canadian Curriculum* (Scarborough, ON: Prentice-Hall, 1986), 194.

[20] William H. Kilpatrick, "The Project Method," *Teachers College Record* 19 (1918): 330.

[21] Hay to Newland, *Topics in the History of Education in Western Canada*.

[22] Mann, "Progressive Education and the Depression in British Columbia," 14.

[23] J.H. Putman and G.M. Weir, *Survey of the School System* (Victoria: King's Printer, 1925).

[24] Cited in Tomkins, *A Common Countenance*, 198.

[25] Fletcher Peacock, "Director of Educational Services Report," in *Annual Report of the Department* (Fredericton: King's Printer, 1944), 8.

[26] For a discussion of imperialism as a form of Canadian nationalism, see Carl Berger, *The Sense of Power: Studies in the Ideas of Canadian Imperialism, 1867–1914* (Toronto: University of Toronto Press, 1970).

[27] Duncan McArthur, *History of Canada for High Schools* (Toronto: W.J. Gage, 1927), 484.

[28] This point is made by Stamp with regard to the observance of Empire Day in Ontario schools. See Robert M. Stamp, "Empire Day in the Schools of Ontario: The Training of Young Imperialists," *Journal of Canadian Studies* VII (August 1973): 370.

[29] Henry F. Angus, ed., *Canada and Her Great Neighbour: Sociological Surveys of Opinions and Attitudes in Canada Concerning the United States* (Toronto: Ryerson Press, 1938), 370.

[30] Edith Deyell, "Ferment in the Social Studies: Where Will It Lead?" *Canadian Education and Research Digest* 4 (March 1964): 56.

[31] Neatby's conclusions were based on an examination of provincial Department of Education documents such as curriculum guides, programs of study, and reading lists. Sutherland has shown that classroom practice differed substantially from the tenor of these progressive documents, remaining as formal in the 1950s as it had been in the 1920s. See Neil Sutherland, "The Triumph of 'Formalism': Elementary Schooling in Vancouver from the 1920s to the 1960s," in *Vancouver Past: Essays in Social History*, Vancouver Centennial Issue of *BC Studies*, ed. R.A.J. McDonald and Jean Barman (Vancouver: UBC Press, 1986), 175–210.

[32] Hilda Neatby, *So Little for the Mind* (Toronto: Clarke, Irwin, 1953), 179, 162–163.

[33] Department of Education, British Columbia, *Programme of Studies for the Junior High Schools* (Victoria: King's Printer, 1948).

[34] Jerome Bruner, *The Process of Education* (Cambridge, MA: Harvard University Press, 1960), 11, 14, 33.

[35] George S. Tomkins, "The Social Studies in Canada," in *A Canadian Social Studies*, 2nd ed., ed. Jim Parsons, Geoff Milburn, and Max van Manen (Edmonton: University of Alberta, 1985), 19.

[36] See Angus M. Gunn, ed., *High School Geography Project: Legacy for the Seventies* (Montreal: Centre Educatif et Culturel, 1972) for a listing of publications of this project.

[37] Jerome Bruner, *Man: A Course of Study* (Cambridge, MA: Education Development Center, 1968). A version of MACOS called Steps to Our Social World was developed by the Toronto Board of Education in the 1970s. John Myers, consultant, Toronto Board of Education, personal communication, June 1993.

[38] Kathy Dueck, Frank Horvath, and Vic Zelinski, "Bev Priftis' Class Takes On the Calgary Zoo," *One World* XVI (Summer 1977): 7–8.

[39] Neil Sutherland and Edith Deyell, *Making Canadian History*, Book 1 (Toronto: W.J. Gage, 1966), vi.

[40] These were often published by Clarke Irwin. See advertisement, *Canadian Journal of History* 3 (July 1963): 35–36.

[41] Geoffrey Milburn, "The Social Studies Curriculum in Canada: A Survey of the Published Literature in the Last Decade," *Journal of Educational Thought* 10 (1976): 216.

[42] H.H. Herstein, L.J. Hughes, and R.C. Kirbyson, *Challenge and Survival: The History of Canada* (Scarborough, ON: Prentice-Hall, 1970).

[43] Tomkins, *A Common Countenance*, 397.

[44] Neville V. Scarfe, "The Teaching of Geography in Canada," *The Canadian Geographer* 5 (1955): 4.

[45] Neville V. Scarfe, George S. Tomkins, and Doreen Tomkins, *A New Geography of Canada* (Toronto: W.J. Gage, 1963); George S. Tomkins and Theo L. Hills, *Canada: A Regional Geography* (Toronto: W.J. Gage, 1962); and Doreen Tomkins, *Discovering Our Land* (Toronto: W.J. Gage, 1966).

[46] George S. Tomkins, "School Geography in Canada: An Historical Perspective," in *Canadian Geographic Education*, ed. R. Choquette, J. Wolforth, and M. Villemure (Ottawa: University of Ottawa Press, 1980), 3–17.

[47] Northrop Frye, ed., *Design for Learning* (Toronto: University of Toronto Press, 1962), 8–16.

[48] Province of British Columbia, Department of Education, Division of Curriculum, *Secondary School Curriculum Guide, Social Studies* (Victoria: Queen's Printer, 1968), 13.

[49] Ibid., 11.

[50] Evelyn Moore and Edward E. Owen, *Teaching the Subjects in the Social Studies: A Handbook for Teachers* (Toronto: Macmillan, 1966).

[51] Francis G. Hardwick, with Edith Deyell, J. Neil Sutherland, and George S. Tomkins, *Teaching History and Geography: A Source Book of Suggestions*, 2nd ed. (Toronto: W.J. Gage, 1967), i.

[52] John Lewis, ed., *Teaching for Tomorrow: A Symposium on the Social Studies in Canada* (Toronto: Nelson, 1969); and Geoff Milburn, *Teaching History in Canada* (Toronto: McGraw-Hill, 1972).

[53] Hilda Taba, *A Teacher's Handbook to Elementary Social Studies: An Inductive Approach* (Don Mills, ON: Addison-Wesley, 1967).

[54] Charles Curtis, interview by author, 20 November 1992, Vancouver. John Harrison, interview by author, 20 November 1992, Vancouver.

[55] Pat Hardy, "The Contra Costa County Social Studies Project," in *Conference on the New Social Studies* (Vancouver: B.C. Teachers' Federation, 1967), 18–28.

[56] Ontario Ministry of Education, *History: Intermediate Division* (Toronto: Author, 1973), 5.

[57] Alberta Education, *1978 Alberta Social Studies Curriculum: Interim Edition* (Edmonton: Author, 1978), 11–13.

[58] Edwin Fenton, *Teaching the New Social Studies in Secondary Schools: An Inductive Approach* (New York: Holt, Rinehart & Winston, 1966).

[59] Ken Osborne, "A Consummation Devoutly to be Wished: Social Studies and General Curriculum Theory," in *Curriculum Canada V: School Subject Research and Curriculum/Instruction Theory*, Proceedings of the Fifth Invitational Conference on Curriculum Research of the Canadian Association for Curriculum Studies, ed. Douglas A. Roberts and John O. Fritz (Vancouver: Centre for the Study of Curriculum and Instruction, University of British Columbia, 1984), 91.

[60] Holt, "The National Council for the Social Studies Convention at Cleveland," 2.

[61] George S. Tomkins, "And Just What Is the Canada Studies Foundation?" *The B.C. Teacher* 52 (March 1972): 212.

[62] George S. Tomkins, "The Canada Studies Foundation: A Canadian Approach to Curriculum Intervention," *Canadian Journal of Education* 2 (1977): 5.

[63] John N. Grant, "The Canada Studies Foundation: An Historical Overview," in *The Canada Studies Foundation*, ed. John N. Grant, Robert Anderson, and Peter L. McCreath (Toronto: The Canada Studies Foundation, 1986), 11.

[64] A.B. Hodgetts, *What Culture? What Heritage? A Study of Civic Education in Canada* (Toronto: OISE Press, 1968), 24, 45, 121.

[65] A.B. Hodgetts and Paul Gallagher, *Teaching Canada for the '80s* (Toronto: OISE Press, 1978), vi.

[66] Hodgetts, *What Culture? What Heritage?*, 118.

[67] Grant, *The Canada Studies Foundation*, 29.

[68] Alberta Education, *The Alberta Learning Resources Project* (Edmonton: Author, 1978), quoted in Rowland Lorimer, "Publishers, Governments, and Learning Materials: The Canadian Context," *Curriculum Inquiry* 14 (Fall 1984): 292.

[69] It is interesting to note that one of these small firms, although since purchased by Thomson Learning, published a geography textbook that was recommended by the National Geographic Society and is currently selling in the United States.

[70] Harry Baglole, ed., *Readings in Prince Edward Island History* (Charlottetown: Department of Education, 1976).

[71] Richard Howard, Sonia Riddoch, and Peter Watson, *Canada Since Confederation: An Atlantic Perspective* (Toronto: Copp Clark, 1976).

[72] Carol Langford and Chuck Heath, eds., *Explorations: A Canadian Social Studies Program for Elementary Schools* (Vancouver: Douglas & McIntyre [Educational], 1983–1985). The educational division, which was created as a result of this contract, has since been disbanded. The materials produced are currently being marketed by a large central Canadian company, Nelson Canada.

[73] Daniel R. Birch, ed., *Growth of a Nation* Series, 18 vols. (Toronto: Fitzhenry & Whiteside, 1974–86).

[74] Stan Garrod, interview by author, 4 December 1992, Vancouver.

[75] Ronald C. Kirbyson, *In Search of Canada*, 2 vols. (Scarborough, ON: Prentice-Hall, 1977).

[76] George S. Tomkins, "Foreign Influences on Curriculum and Curriculum Policy Making in Canada: Some Impressions in Historical and Contemporary Perspective," *Curriculum Inquiry* 11 (1981): 158.

[77] See, for example, Edwin Fenton, "Reflections on the 'New Social Studies,'" *The Social Studies* 82 (May/June 1991): 84–90; Byron G. Massialas, "The 'New Social Studies'—Retrospect and Prospect," *The Social Studies* 83 (May/June 1992): 120–124; Peter B. Dow, "Past as Prologue: The Legacy of Sputnik," *The Social Studies* 83 (July/August 1992): 164–171; Marion J. Rice, "Reflections on the New Social Studies," *The Social Studies* 83 (September/October 1992): 224–231; Barry K. Beyer, "Gone but Not Forgotten—Reflections on the New Social Studies Movement," *The Social Studies* 85 (November/December 1994): 251–255; and William D. Rader, "The Elementary School Economics Project at the University of Chicago," *The Social Studies* 86 (March/April 1995): 85–90.

[78] Jerome Bruner, "The Process of Education Revisited," *Phi Delta Kappan* 53 (July 1971): 21.

[79] Ibid., 20.

[80] Osborne, "A Consummation Devoutly to be Wished," 95.

[81] Max van Manen and Jim Parsons, "What Are the Social Studies?" in *A Canadian Social Studies*, rev. ed., ed. Jim Parsons, Geoff Milburn, and Max van Manen (Edmonton: University of Alberta Faculty of Education, 1985), 2–11.

[82] Ibid., 6.

[83] Osborne, "A Consummation Devoutly to be Wished," 97.

[84] Louis E. Raths, Merrill Harmin, and Sidney B. Simon, *Values and Teaching: Working with Values in the Classroom* (Columbus, OH: Charles E. Merrill, 1966), 30.

[85] Milburn, "The Social Studies Curriculum in Canada," 222.

[86] Alberta Education, *Experiences in Decision Making* (Edmonton: Author, 1971); and Alberta Education, *Responding to Change* (Edmonton: Author, 1971).

[87] See Hugh Lytton, "A Critique of a Value-oriented Social Studies Program," *Canadian Journal of History and Social Science* 8 (Winter 1973): 47–52.

[88] L.W. Downey Research Associates Ltd., *The Social Studies in Alberta—1975: A Report of an Assessment* (Edmonton: Alberta Education, 1975).

[89] Alberta Education, *1981 Alberta Social Studies Curriculum* (Edmonton: Author, 1981), 1.

[90] D. Oliver and J. Shaver, *Teaching Public Issues in the High School* (Boston: Houghton Mifflin, 1966).

[91] See Byron G. Massialas and C. Benjamin Cox, *Inquiry in Social Studies* (New York: McGraw-Hill, 1966); and Frederick R. Smith and C. Benjamin Cox, *New Strategies and Curriculum in the Social Studies* (Chicago: Rand McNally & Co., 1969).

[92] John Eisenberg and Malcolm Levin, eds., *Canadian Critical Issues* Series (Toronto: OISE Press, 1972–1981).

[93] Osborne, "A Consummation Devoutly to be Wished," 95.

[94] Paula Bourne and John Eisenberg, "The Canadian Public Issues Program: Learning to Deal with Social Controversy," *Orbit* 6 (December 1975): 16–18.

[95] Donald C. Wilson, ed., *Public Issues in Canada: Possibilities for Classroom Teaching*, 14 vols. (Vancouver: Faculty of Education, University of British Columbia, 1984–1988).

[96] Stephen Penney and Robert Dwyer, *Understanding the Canadian Environment* (Agincourt, ON: Canada Studies Foundation, 1984).

[97] John U. Michaelis, *Social Studies for Children in a Democracy: Recent Trends and Developments*, 4th ed. (Englewood Cliffs, NJ: Prentice-Hall, 1968); and Taba, *A Teacher's Handbook to Elementary Social Studies*.

[98] C.K. Curtis of the University of British Columbia received the 1978 Exemplary Dissertation Award from the American National Council for the Social Studies for his work on citizenship education for slow learners. He received his doctorate from Utah State University.

[99] Milburn, "The Social Studies Curriculum in Canada."

[100] Council of Ministers of Education, Canada, *Social Studies: A Survey of Provincial Curricula at the Elementary and Secondary Levels* (Toronto: Author, 1982), 4.

[101] British Columbia, Schools Department, Curriculum Development Branch, *Social Studies Curriculum Guide: Grade Eight–Grade Eleven* (Victoria: Author, 1985), 3.

[102] Alberta Education, *1981 Alberta Social Studies Curriculum*, 1.

[103] Council of Ministers of Education, *Social Studies: A Survey of Provincial Curricula*, 57.

[104] Ontario Ministry of Education, *Curriculum Guideline: History and Contemporary Studies* (Toronto: Queen's Printer, 1986), 5.

[105] Osborne, "A Consummation Devoutly to be Wished," 87.

[106] Ken Osborne, *The Teaching of Politics: Some Suggestions for Teachers* (Toronto: The Canada Studies Foundation, 1982).

[107] See Chuck Chamberlin, "Citizenship as the Goal of Social Studies: Passive Knower or Active Doer?" *Canadian Social Studies* 26, no. 1 (Fall 1991): 23–26.

[108] Fred Newmann, *Education for Citizenship Action* (Berkeley, CA: McCutchan Publishing, 1977), 157. See also R.A. Rutter and F. Newmann, "The Potential of Community Service to Enhance Civic Responsibility," *Social Education* 53 (1989): 371–374.

[109] Alberta Education, *1981 Alberta Social Studies Curriculum*, 9.

[110] Alberta Education, *Junior High Social Studies Teacher Resource Manual* (Edmonton: Author, 1988).

[111] Manitoba Education, *Social Studies: K to 12 Overview* (Winnipeg: Author, 1985), 12.

[112] Government of Newfoundland and Labrador, Department of Education, Division of Program Development, *A Curriculum Framework for Social Studies: Navigating the Future* (St. John's: Author, 1993), 3.

[113] Ontario Ministry of Education, *The Common Curriculum, Grades 1 to 9, Working Document* (Toronto: Queen's Printer, 1993).

[114] See R.C. McLeod, "History in Canadian Secondary Schools," report to the Canadian Historical Association, *Canadian Historical Review* 63 (December 1982): 573–585; Bob Davis, *Whatever Happened to High School History? Burying the Political Memory of Youth: Ontario, 1945–1995* (Toronto: James Lorimer, 1995); Ken Osborne, "'I'm Not Going to Think How Cabot Discovered Newfoundland When I'm Doing My Job': The Status of History in Canadian High Schools," paper presented to the annual meeting of the Canadian Historical Association, Calgary, AB, June 1994; and Ken Osborne, *In Defence of History: Teaching the Past and the Meaning of Democratic Citizenship*, Our Schools/Our Selves Monograph Series, no. 17 (Toronto: Our Schools/Our Selves Education Foundation, 1995).

[115] Davis, *Whatever Happened to High School History?*, 63.

[116] "Slanted Textbooks," *Toronto Telegram*, 18 January 1967, 6; and "Tell It the Way It Was," *Toronto Daily Star*, 15 October 1968, 6.

[117] Garnet McDiarmid and David Pratt, *Teaching Prejudice: A Content Analysis of Social Studies Textbooks Authorized for Use in Ontario* (Toronto: OISE Press, 1971).

[118] Ontario Ministry of Education, *Race, Religion and Culture in Ontario School Materials* (Toronto: Author, 1981).

[119] Alberta Education Curriculum, "Teacher Reference Manual for Learning Resources Identified as 'Unacceptable' or 'Problematic' during the Curriculum Audit for Tolerance and Understanding" (Edmonton: Alberta Education, 1985).

[120] Geoffrey Milburn, "Alternative Perspectives—Social Studies and Curriculum Theory in Canada: A Response to Ken Osborne," in *Curriculum Canada V*, 126–127.

[121] Paul W. Bennett, *Rediscovering Canadian History* (Toronto: OISE Press, 1980); Paula Bourne and John Eisenberg, *Social Issues in the Curriculum* (Toronto: OISE Press, 1978); Kieran Egan, *Educational Development* (New York: Oxford University Press, 1979); Donald C. Wilson, ed., *Teaching Public Issues in a Canadian Context* (Toronto: OISE Press, 1982); and J.A. Ross and F.J. Maynes, *Teacher's Guide to Ethnic Studies* (Toronto: OISE Press, 1978).

[122] John U. Michaelis, *Social Studies for Children: A Guide to Basic Instruction*, 10th ed. (Englewood Cliffs, NJ: Prentice-Hall, 1992); David A. Welton and John T. Mallan, *Children and Their World: Strategies for Teaching Social Studies*, 4th ed. (Boston: Houghton Mifflin, 1992); and Walter C. Parker and John Jarolimek, *Social Studies in Elementary Education*, 10th ed. (Upper Saddle River, NJ: Prentice-Hall, 1997). Note: Previous editions were written by Jarolimek as sole author.

[123] Tomkins, "The Social Studies in Canada," 26.

[124] Jack L. Granatstein, *Who Killed Canadian History?* (Toronto: HarperCollins, 1998).

[125] Ibid., 49.

[126] Desmond Morton, "Teaching and Learning History in Canada," in *Knowing, Teaching, and Learning History: National and International Perspectives*, ed. Peter N. Stearns, Peter Seixas, and Samuel Wineburg (New York: New York University Press, 2000), 51–62; and Peter Seixas, "The Purposes of Teaching Canadian History," *Canadian Social Studies* 36, no. 2 (Winter 2002), http://www.quasar.ualberta.ca/css/Css_36_2/.

[127] Departments of Education, New Brunswick, Newfoundland and Labrador, Nova Scotia, and Prince Edward Island, *Foundation for the Atlantic Canada Social Studies Curriculum* (Halifax: Nova Scotia Education and Culture, English Program Services, 1999).

[128] Western Canadian Protocol for Collaboration in Basic Education, *The Common Curriculum Framework for Social Studies: Kindergarten to Grade 9* (Winnipeg: Manitoba Education, Training and Youth, 2002), iii.

[129] British Columbia Ministry of Education, Skills, and Training, *Social Studies K to 7: Integrated Resource Package* (Victoria: Author, 1998); ———, *Social Studies 8 to 10: Integrated Resource Package* (Victoria: Author, 1997); ———, *Social Studies 11: Integrated Resource Package* (Victoria: Author, 1997).

[130] Government of Yukon, Department of Education, http://www.education.gov.yk.ca (accessed October 8, 2003).

[131] Alberta Learning, *Social Studies Kindergarten to Grade 12 Consultation Draft* (Edmonton: Author, August 2002); ———, *Report on Consultations: Alberta Social Studies Kindergarten to Grade 9 Program of Studies Consultation Draft* (Edmonton: Author, 2003).

[132] Manitoba Education and Youth, *Kindergarten to Grade 8 Social Studies: Manitoba Curriculum Framework of Outcomes (Draft)* (Winnipeg: Author, 2003).

[133] Ruth Sandwell and Mark Woloshen, *Snapshots of 19th Century Canada* (Victoria: British Columbia Ministry of Education, 2002); Phyllis Schwartz and Aric Hayes, *Critical Challenges in Law and Government: Canada's Constitutional Crisis—A Simulation* (TC²—The Critical Thinking Cooperative and Field Relations and Teacher In-Service Education, Faculty of Education, Simon Fraser University, 1998); and John Harrison, Neil Smith, and Ian Wright, *Critical Challenges in Social Studies for Upper Elementary Students* (TC²—The Critical Thinking Cooperative and Field Relations and Teacher In-Service Education, Faculty of Education, Simon Fraser University, 1999).

[134] Ian Wright, *Elementary Social Studies: A Practical Approach to Teaching and Learning*, 5th ed. (Toronto: Prentice-Hall, 2001); Joseph M. Kirman, *Elementary Social Studies: Creative Classroom Ideas*, 3rd ed. (Toronto: Prentice-Hall, 2002); Roland Case and Penney Clark, eds., *The Canadian Anthology of Social Studies: Issues and Strategies for Teachers* (Vancouver: Pacific Educational Press, 1999); and Ian Wright and Alan Sears, eds., *Trends and Issues in Canadian Social Studies* (Vancouver: Pacific Educational Press, 1997).

[135] Paul H. Mattingly and Michael B. Katz, eds., *Education and Social Change: Themes from Ontario's Past* (New York: New York University Press, 1975).

[136] George S. Tomkins, "Foreign Influences on Curriculum and Curriculum Policy Making in Canada," 157–166.

137 H.T.J. Coleman, *Report of the National Conference on Character Education in Relation to Canadian Citizenship* (Winnipeg: King's Printer, 1919), quoted in Patterson, "The Canadian Response to Progressive Education," 72.

138 George W. Cornish, *Canadian Geography for Juniors*, British Columbia ed. (Toronto: J.M. Dent, 1927).

CHAPTER 2

Social Studies Across English Canada

Patricia N. Shields and Douglas Ramsay

Attempting to characterize social studies education across English Canada can be as complex and challenging as trying to capture the essence of what it means to be a Canadian. Social studies curricula across Canada have gone through a period of considerable change over the past few years, with programs implemented in Ontario and British Columbia, those under development in Alberta and Manitoba, and through common curriculum framework projects such as the Western Canadian Protocol and the Atlantic Common Framework.

An overview of social studies that relies on curriculum documentation, however, results in a different picture than one created through a reflection on the attitudes and concerns of social studies educators across Canada. The curriculum change and implementation process that has occurred in regions and provinces across Canada has not been without its challenges, and those are reflected in what some social studies educators have expressed as serious concerns about the future of social studies curriculum. The "terrain of social studies education has changed dramatically in the last decade, and not for the better," writes George Richardson.[1] These words reflect common concerns that are rooted to some degree in the ambiguity that has always characterized social studies as a subject area; however, they are more recently coming to the forefront as concerns related to issues such as the displacement of social studies in the school curriculum, the lack of training and background of many teachers who are placed into social studies positions, decreased sup-

port in professional development, and gaps in resources that support the curriculum.

This chapter attempts to provide an overview of current social studies curricula across English Canada, as well as observations arising from two recent projects involving social studies teachers across the country who were asked to provide comments on challenges and issues facing them as they make decisions about how they teach the subject.[2] These two perspectives provide a context from which to consider the current state of social studies curriculum and issues arising from its implementation. To this end, this chapter has been organized into three sections:

- The identity crisis of social studies

- An overview of social studies curriculum across English Canada

- Challenges in teaching social studies

The concerns reflected in articles, research, and resources for social studies, as well as those reflected in the media,[3] present an array of questions and issues about the nature of social studies: Should social studies be treated as a distinct subject or abandoned in favour of a more focused, disciplinary approach to the teaching of history and civics, and to a lesser extent, geography and the social sciences? What is the purpose of social studies curriculum, what is taught, and how is it organized across Canada? What are some current issues that influence the way social studies is taught? These questions provide a focus for this chapter and can provide a perspective from which to examine memories of your own social studies experiences, as well as different approaches to social studies curriculum.

The Identity Crisis of Social Studies

Social studies education is, in some ways, in a state of crisis. This crisis is reflected in debates over what students know and do not know, and the culpability of the educational system in preparing or not preparing students to be knowledgeable citizens. In an increasingly public discourse, the debate over whether or not civic and historical knowledge is taught effectively is getting a large share of media attention. In a less public space, the crisis of social studies exists in the support, time, training, and resource gaps that exist for teachers of social studies courses which, in turn, can affect what and how students are taught.

Social studies has been, and remains, a contentious subject area, perhaps more so than any other subject in the school curriculum. There is no single, consistent definition of social studies, although the National Council for the Social Studies (NCSS) in the United States, the largest professional organization of social studies educators in North America, describes it as "the integrated study of the social sciences to promote civic competence."[4] Social studies education has also been described as a subject area in the throes of a continual identity crisis that was grounded by key works of the first half of the twentieth century and largely influenced by American conceptions of the subject area.[5] Some argue that social studies curriculum continues to be based to a large extent on traditional assumptions about society[6] and the way students learn about the world around them, even though society and societal attitudes have undergone tremendous economic, political, and social change.[7] However, others recognize that changes have occurred in social studies curriculum development, both in terms of the way knowledge is viewed and how curriculum is developed.

A telling sign of the confused identity of social studies is reflected in the preponderance of American literature often cited in Canadian social studies articles and documents, and the extent to which Canadian social studies education is influenced by American research and social education trends. The Atlantic Provinces Education Foundation (APEF) common framework document acknowledges the strong influence of the 1994 NCSS standards document in its development.[8] One example is an increasing trend towards addressing the moral and ethical aspects of social education, which is resulting in greater attention being paid to the role of character education in social studies and other curricula. Many available materials and resources on character education are American, and they are often offered as "canned" programs that provide little more than a recitation of skill development activities without meaningful and relevant contexts for Canadian students.

While definitions of social studies reflected in Canadian curricula differ from each other to some extent, they all reflect the inter- or multidisciplinary nature of the subject area and the goal of teaching citizenship. The Western Canadian Protocol's Common Curriculum Framework for Social Studies defines social studies as an interdisciplinary subject that draws upon history, geography, economics, law, political science, and other disciplines for "the study of people in relation to each other and to their world. Social studies helps students become active and responsible citizens within their communities, locally, nationally, and globally, in a complex and changing world."[9] The new Alberta social studies program adds the term "issues based" to its definition of social studies as an interdisciplinary subject, and emphasizes "the role of critical inquiry in fostering understanding and involvement in practical and ethical issues that face communities and humankind."[10] The Foundation for the Atlantic Canada Social Studies Curriculum describes social studies as a subject area that

provides coordinated, systematic study [drawing on] disciplines such as anthropology, economics, geography, history, political science, psychology, sociology, as well as appropriate content from the humanities, mathematics, and the natural sciences.[11]

Attempts to develop a common curriculum in Canada

The process of social studies curriculum development itself has changed. In 1998, the Western Canadian Protocol was established to develop a common social studies curriculum for the four western provinces and, at that time, two territories. The Western Canadian Protocol (WCP) project in social studies was modelled after similar curriculum development projects in language arts, mathematics, and science. The most significant aspect of this project was the formation of teams that included both francophone and Aboriginal representatives, an approach unlike any other curriculum development process in North America. This attempt to develop a common western Canadian curriculum has not been entirely successful, with first British Columbia, then Alberta withdrawing from the development process. The remaining provinces and territories—Manitoba, Saskatchewan, the Northwest Territories, Yukon, and Nunavut—have varying timelines for, and commitments to, the implementation of the foundation in new social studies programs of studies. Even though Alberta withdrew from the WCP project, it has had substantial impact on the development of the new social studies curriculum. The Atlantic Provinces Education Foundation, initiated in 1995, has been more successful in efforts to develop a common curriculum, and this program is currently being implemented in the Atlantic provinces at the grades 1, 2, and 7 levels. This common framework allows for substantial variation in provincial implementation. Although the APEF project has been successful in implementing common curriculum standards across the four Atlantic provinces, a primary driving force behind the commitment to do so has been linked to resource needs, particularly the ability to attract publishers' interest in a larger market base for customized resource development.

The issue of national standards

The Council of Ministers of Education in Canada (CMEC) has, at various times and levels of engagement over the past number of years, visited and re-visited the issue of national standards, or common outcomes, in citizenship education. Like the Western Canadian Protocol for Social Studies, however, projects that attempted to establish national standards for citizenship education have been abandoned as a result of lack of consensus over what these standards should involve, as well as concern over maintaining education as a provincial mandate and responsibility. Various educationally based not-for-profit organizations have taken a vocal stance on the need for national standards or common outcomes in citizenship and history education, yet not all of these organizations are enthusiastic about situating history education within a social studies framework.[12]

The issue of whether or not national standards in social studies, history, or citizenship education can be developed remains contentious. In this sense, Canadian social studies education differs from that in the United States. Various national standards documents that delineate common outcomes in history, geography, economics, and civics have been developed in the United States. In addition to these discipline-focused standards, a social studies standards document was developed by the National Council for the Social Studies. It is important to note, however, that the NCSS social studies standards have not been without influence on the development of social studies curricula across Canada. The move towards organizing curriculum around strands and themes is reflected in the new Manitoba and Alberta curricula, as well as in the Atlantic provinces social studies common framework. It is also, to a lesser extent, reflected in the organizers used across British Columbia's K–11 social studies curriculum. Ontario's curriculum remains more discipline-centred, with history and geography topics used as organizers. Canadian social studies curricula in the western and Atlantic provinces and the territories have shifted from topical organizers to conceptual organizers, and like the NCSS standards, emphasize citizenship, identity, diversity, and multiple perspectives. The NCSS social studies standards are organized to incorporate learning experiences from many disciplines and are designed to serve three purposes:

- to serve as a framework for social studies program design from kindergarten through grade 12 (K–12)

- to function as a guide for curriculum decisions by providing student performance expectations in the areas of knowledge, processes, and attitudes

- to provide examples of classroom activities that will guide teachers as they design instruction to help their students meet performance expectations

The framework of the standards consists of ten themes incorporating fields of study that roughly correspond with one or more relevant disciplines (see chart below). These ten themes are reflected in the strands, themes, and organizers present in current and developing Canadian social studies programs.

Organizing social studies curriculum

In Canada, a traditional "expanding environments"[13] approach is still prevalent throughout most provincial and territorial social studies curricula: moving from family and community in primary grades through to province and nation in upper elementary grades and national and global in junior high grades. For example, history is typically introduced first at the family and community level, next at the provincial or territorial level, and then at the national level. This is changing somewhat as more recently developed social studies curricula reflect the understanding that younger students are capable of learning about national and global concepts and topics. There is increasing diversity across provincial and territorial curricula as the grade levels increase. Junior high curricula differ more among provinces and territories than elementary grade curricula do.

The social studies programs under development and implementation in the Atlantic provinces and Alberta present general and specific outcomes centred on conceptual organizers (strands) and skill and process areas. These outcomes provide benchmarks to be achieved by a particular stage, replacing the repetition of knowledge, skills, or attitude objectives that occurred in a more traditional spiralling curricular structure that reinforced the same objectives at different grade levels. While general outcomes are used to delineate both content and process—what students are expected to know and be able to do when they have completed a grade—specific outcomes identify the components of knowledge, skills, values, and attitudes that students are expected to demonstrate within a grade or level. Outcomes at a grade level represent learning about all or most of the conceptual organizers, and a broader framework[15] is typically used to identify benchmarks at key grade levels—typically grades 3, 6, 9, and 12 (see chart on page 42). The new Alberta social studies program adds inquiry questions as indicators of the knowledge, skills, and attitudes embedded in a specific outcome. For example, a specific outcome from the grade 6 curriculum that expects students to "demonstrate an understanding of the fundamental principles of democracy" does so by requiring students to:

> [E]xplore and reflect on the following questions and issues:
>
> - What is democracy (i.e., justice, equity, freedoms, representation)?
>
> - What are similarities and differences between direct and representative democracy?
>
> - What are the rights and responsibilities of citizens living in a representative democracy?

NCSS CURRICULUM STANDARDS FOR SOCIAL STUDIES IN THE UNITED STATES[14]

NCSS Themes

I	Culture
II	Time, continuity, and change
III	People, places, and environments
IV	Individual identity and development
V	Individuals, groups, and institutions
VI	Power, authority, and governance
VII	Production, distribution, and consumption
VIII	Science, technology, and society
IX	Global connections
X	Civic ideals and practice

EXAMPLES OF BENCHMARK OUTCOMES FROM THE FOUNDATION FOR THE ATLANTIC CANADA SOCIAL STUDIES CURRICULUM[16]

	Citizenship, Power, and Governance	Culture and Diversity
Grade 3	Identify examples of their rights and responsibilities as citizens.	Identify some characteristics unique to one's self and other characteristics that all humans share.
Grade 6	Identify and explain the rights and responsibilities of individual citizens in a local, national, and global context.	Describe the influences that shape personal identity.
Grade 9	Identify and explain persistent issues involving the rights, responsibilities, roles, and status of individual citizens and groups in a local, national, and global context.	Explore the factors that influence one's perceptions, attitudes, values, and beliefs.
Grade 12	Analyze major issues involving the rights, responsibilities, roles, and status of individual citizens and groups in a local, national, and global context.	Analyze the factors that contribute to the perception of self and the development of a worldview.

- How does Canada's justice system help protect your democratic and constitutional rights?[17]

Citizenship as a rationale for teaching social studies

Views of citizenship are changing within social studies curricula. The emphasis on responsibility and accountability that dominated the language of social studies and citizenship education in the late 1980s and early 1990s has shifted back to one more associated with activism and concerned with social and political participation. This marks a return to a view more common in the social studies curricula in the 1970s, particularly in Alberta. Although the concept of responsibility is still present in social studies curricula, more recent programs centre on multiple understandings and perspectives around citizenship and identity. The Western Canadian Protocol project has in many ways influenced a shift to a new social studies curriculum that is more fluid and cognizant of multiple and overlapping understandings and conceptions of the act of being a citizen. Although the new curriculum is not a panacea for clearly defining the role of citizenship education

in social studies programs, the public debate over the developing WCP curriculum has brought the perspectives of Aboriginal and francophone citizenship education to a more public place for many teachers in the western provinces.

The goals and rationales for teaching social studies in Canadian schools are explicitly centred on the teaching of citizenship, as described in a 1998 document by the British Columbia Ministry of Education:

> The overarching goal of social studies is to develop thoughtful, responsible, active citizens who are able to acquire the requisite information to consider multiple perspectives and to make reasoned judgements. The Social Studies K to 11 curriculum provides students with opportunities as future citizens to critically reflect upon events and issues in order to examine the present, make connections with the past, and consider the future.[18]

Although citizenship goals are central to all Canadian social studies programs, these goals do not centre only on knowledge-based outcomes. Ontario's social studies curriculum is centred on teaching for informed citizenship, but also focuses on the skills and processes that encourage success in the world of work:

> The focus of teaching and learning in the social studies, history, and geography curriculum is on the development of essential knowledge and skills. Students must develop a thorough knowledge of basic concepts that they can apply in a wide range of situations. They must also develop the broad-based skills that are vital to success in the world of work: they must learn to evaluate different points of view and examine information critically to solve problems and make decisions on a variety of issues.[19]

The Ontario social studies curriculum, like those in most other jurisdictions, focuses on critical thinking and considering multiple perspectives. Most curricula agree that inquiry skills are a central part of teaching for effective and active citizenship, and consideration of social issues is important as a framework around which to organize instruction.

Increasing attention is being paid in the curriculum development process to the role of process in teaching for citizenship. Original conceptions of citizenship education in the context of social studies programs focused almost exclusively on knowledge-centred outcomes related to civics, history, and geography. As the public discourse of citizenship shifted to issues such as human rights, language, nationalism, globalization, equality, and multiculturalism, discussions of what should be taught as part of citizenship education became more concerned with the concept of inclusion—how to teach for tolerance, develop respect for diversity, and entrench antiracism and equality programs in school curricula. More recently, social studies goals reflect the understanding that strategies such as inquiry, the use of literature to evoke emotional connections, and the use of case studies to develop knowledge, skills, values, and dispositions can be employed in teaching active citizenship.[20]

Although the "public persona" of citizenship education has gained exposure in recent years, there is still much debate, and often widely conflicting views, as to what constitutes citizenship education and exactly how it should be represented in school curricula. Social studies has frequently been described as the traditional "home" of citizenship education,[21] yet there is growing awareness of the role of citizenship education in other subject areas. A discrete citizenship education course is offered in Ontario, and there are indications that other Canadian provinces are considering the same type of approach to provide a stronger focus on the goals of citizenship education.

Citizenship is commonly stated as the raison d'etre of social studies education, but very little is actually known about what goes on in Canadian social studies classrooms to teach for citizenship. The last major study of teaching practice in social studies was A.B. Hodgetts' 1968 report on civic education in Canada. This report stated that a passive, transmissionist model of teaching prevailed in Canadian social studies classrooms and that very few students learning about citizenship were engaged in active, participatory activities.[22]

An Overview of Social Studies Curriculum Across English Canada

One of the primary challenges in trying to construct a national picture of the social studies curriculum in English Canada is that provinces and territories take different approaches to how social studies is structured and defined as a subject area.[23] Canadian curriculum documents tend to associate disciplines of social studies with fields of knowledge—history, geography, economics, law, philosophy, political science, anthropology, and other social sciences.

The Atlantic provinces and the current Alberta program base the organization of their curricula on what can be described as a multidisciplinary approach—one that explicitly identifies the disciplines of social studies but makes connections among them. For example, in the New Brunswick grade 8 social studies program, "Atlantic Canada in the Global Community," the disciplines, "especially anthropology, economics, geography, history, law, political science, and sociology"[24] are incorporated into five key themes: Physical Setting, Culture, Economics, Technology, and Interdependence. Issues and topics are used as organizational structures to connect disciplines such as history and politics to contexts that are relevant and meaningful for adolescent students. Alberta's current social studies curriculum separates the disciplines by focusing on them as topics within grade levels, but it emphasizes the need to make connections among them. In grades 4 and 5, the current Alberta program has students focus first on a topic centred on geographic concepts and understandings (Alberta: Its Geography and People; Canada: Its Geography and People) and then on a topic focused on periods in history (Alberta: Its People in History; Early Canada: Exploration and Settlement).[25]

British Columbia, the Yukon, and Saskatchewan take more of an interdisciplinary or integrated approach to social studies—albeit not a uniform one—tending to implicitly address the disciplines in a format that is based on key themes or topic areas. For example, British Columbia's social studies curriculum is organized around themes that repeat at each grade level from kindergarten to grade 10: Applications of Social Studies; Society and Culture; Politics and Law; Economy and Technology, and Environment.[26] Saskatchewan focuses more than any other province on integration between subject areas, and social studies philosophy and rationale statements centre on six common essential learnings that cross all subject areas: Independent Learning; Personal and Social Values and Skills; Critical and Creative Thinking; Communication; Numeracy; and Technological Literacy.[27] These common essential learnings are "incorporated into social studies teaching as perspectives which influence how social studies is taught . . . and are to be taught and evaluated as part of the social studies courses."[28]

Ontario takes a more explicitly discipline-based approach, focusing on history and geography. Social studies in Ontario is delivered at the elementary level as an "umbrella" course that covers history and geography topics; however, there is also a separate definition of social studies that identifies a primary purpose of elementary social studies as encouraging students to "examine and understand communi-

ties."[29] The Northwest Territories organizes its social studies outcomes around strands that are associated with developmental levels rather than grade levels. Further variation in the way social studies is approached across Canada arises because social studies is compulsory from K–12 in Alberta whereas in other provinces Canadian history or discipline-based courses such as geography or world history are taught at the senior high level. In most provincial and territorial curricula, history tends to be implicitly emphasized over geography.

How learning outcomes and objectives are written in provincial curriculum documents also varies. For example, some curricula identify separate knowledge, skill, and attitude objectives, while others identify outcomes that are performance-based, identifying what students should both know and be able to do. British Columbia uses prescribed learning outcomes that focus on both content and process. Critical thinking is reinforced as a key element of social studies programs. Inquiry is a key element across many provincial curricula, and is consistently linked to critical thinking and consideration of multiple perspectives. In the current Alberta program, specific inquiry steps and models provide the basis from which students study topics. The models are linked to critical and creative thinking and are meant to be adapted according to topics, disciplinary emphases, and the needs of students. Although other provincial and territorial curricula do not always explicitly identify such step-by-step models, similar processes are implicitly evident in their social studies programs (see chart on page 45).

All provinces and territories structure curriculum outcomes using assumptions about what is developmentally appropriate for students. Skills objectives tend to move from an emphasis on identification, description, and comparison in the primary grades towards more complex skills involving synthesis and evaluation in the upper elementary and secondary grades. There is some crossover among these skill levels at different grade levels.

"Softer" social studies concepts, such as story,[30] the importance of identity in the context of citizenship education,[31] and the concept of belonging have gained importance in the social studies curriculum.

PROBLEM-SOLVING AND DECISION-MAKING MODELS IN THE 1990 ALBERTA SOCIAL STUDIES PROGRAM OF STUDIES[32]

A Model for Problem-Solving	A Model for Decision-Making
Understand the question/problem	Understand the issue
Develop research questions and procedures	Develop research questions and procedures
Gather, organize, and interpret information	Gather, organize, and interpret information
Develop a conclusion/solution	Think of alternatives
	Make a choice
	Take action (if feasible and desirable)

The importance of using a narrative approach in the development of historical thinking is reflected in the 1993 Newfoundland and Labrador social studies framework.[33] Although "narrative" as both a research methodology and a way of presenting information has influenced the use of storytelling as a valid approach to teaching in social studies, "story as concept" is also evident in the new Alberta social studies curriculum; its inclusion has been strongly influenced by the Aboriginal emphasis on story and the oral traditions of Aboriginal cultures. The vision of the WCP Common Curriculum Framework document reflects an approach to social studies curriculum that emphasizes more emotively laden concepts such as "heart" and "spirit." It states:

> The Common Curriculum Framework for Social Studies K–12 will meet the needs and reflect the nature of the 21st century learner and will have the concepts of Canadian citizenship and identity at its heart. It will be reflective of the diverse cultural perspectives, including Aboriginal and Francophone, that contribute to Canada's evolving realities. The Framework will ultimately contribute to a Canadian spirit—a spirit that will be fundamental in creating a sense of belonging for each one of our students as he or she engages in active and responsible citizenship locally, nationally, and globally.[34]

Neither Alberta nor Manitoba has retained the references to the concepts of "heart" and "spirit" in the present versions of their new social studies programs; however, story and voice as both concepts and approaches to teaching are central to many of the outcomes of these two programs.

The discussion of provincial curricula that follows provides an overview of the key approaches to social studies that each province and territory takes. Although teachers out of necessity focus primarily on the specific curriculum that they must teach, reflecting on the various approaches to social studies curriculum can provide insight into ways of teaching and issues arising from the implementation of a social studies program in your classroom.

Social studies in British Columbia

Social studies in British Columbia is organized around five interrelated curriculum organizers that are consistent from kindergarten through grade 10.[35] These organizers reflect a belief that social studies should be interdisciplinary in nature, and they include an organizer that focuses on process as opposed to content. The organizers are: Society and Culture; Politics and Law; Economy and Technology; the Environment; and Applications of Social Studies. This last organizer reflects the importance of providing students with a framework of developmental skills and processes that will be used throughout the curriculum. It emphasizes an inquiry process similar to the Alberta model presented in the chart above. In grade 11, the British Columbia social studies curriculum focuses on Skills and Processes, along with Social, Cultural, Political, Legal, Economic, and Environmental issues.[36] At the grade 12 level, discrete courses are offered in B.C. First Nations Studies, Comparative Civilizations, Geography, History, and Law.

New curriculum in Alberta, Manitoba, and the Territories

In Alberta, Manitoba, and the territories, new curricula retain much of the vision and framework established by the Western Canadian Protocol project. Although Alberta withdrew from the project to develop a provincial program in 2001, its new program of studies, like those of Manitoba and the territories, centres on concepts of citizenship and identity in Canadian and global contexts. The Manitoba curriculum presents outcomes inclusive of Aboriginal, francophone, and other cultural perspectives, emphasizing the need for students to participate actively as citizens and members of communities and to make informed and ethical choices when faced with the challenges of living in a pluralistic democratic society.[37] The curriculum outcomes address knowledge and attitudes focused on Canada, the world, the environment, and democracy, along with a skills and competencies goal centred on critical thinking and inquiry.[38] Thematic strands provide the basis for the general learning outcomes in the K–8 social studies curriculum (see chart below). As do Ontario and British Columbia (at the grade 12 level), Manitoba departs from an integrated social studies program in senior secondary grade levels, offering courses in Canadian Studies, Geographic Issues, Social and Political History, Western Civilization, World Geography, and World Issues. The grades 9 through 12 curricula are currently under review, with new programs slated for implementation from 2005 through 2008.

Although the Northwest Territories and Nunavut generally use Alberta programs of study, the Northwest Territories currently offers a distinct elementary social studies program and a civics program at the junior secondary level. Nunavut, at the time of its division from the Northwest Territories, approved curriculum from both the Northwest Territories and Alberta. Nunavut is developing new programs for its schools, and within social studies is currently developing a grade 8 module on archaeology that falls within the framework of the Western and Northern Canadian Protocol outcomes.[39] Yukon uses the British Columbia curriculum, modifying it to meet its needs.

The new Alberta social studies program reflects some departures from traditional social studies approaches, placing more explicit emphasis on concepts related to active citizenship, democracy, and participation.[40] This curriculum incorporates multiple approaches to learning and recognizes the importance of diverse perspectives in learning contexts. The student's evolving sense of citizenship and identity is at the centre of all learning experiences in this program. Like Manitoba's new curriculum, Alberta's is organized around thematic strands that are linked to interdisciplinary areas reflected in each grade. Both of these new programs have been developed using a consultative process involving review and feedback by teachers and other interested parties as new drafts

KINDERGARTEN TO GRADE 8 SOCIAL STUDIES, MANITOBA CURRICULUM FRAMEWORK OF OUTCOMES[41]

Theme	General Learning Outcome
Identity, Culture, and Community	Students will explore concepts of identity, culture, and community in relation to individuals, societies, and nations.
The Land: Places and People	Students will explore the dynamic relationships of people with the land, places, and environments.
Historical Connections	Students will explore how people, events, and ideas of the past shape the present and influence the future.
Global Interdependence	Students will explore the global interdependence of people, communities, societies, nations, and environments.
Power and Authority	Students will explore the processes and structures of power and authority, and their implications for individuals, relationships, communities, and nations.
Economics and Resources	Students will explore the distribution of resources and wealth in relation to individuals, communities, and nations.

of the programs were released. The Alberta program incorporates elements that support current work on historical thinking and the critical analysis of history,[42] as well as an explicit emphasis on technology skills and processes.

Social studies in Saskatchewan

In Saskatchewan social studies is defined as "a study of people and their relationships with their social and physical environments."[43] Throughout the Saskatchewan curriculum there is an emphasis on the integration of Indian and Métis content and perspectives.[44] The Saskatchewan social studies program also explicitly identifies an approach to resource-based teaching and learning. This means that, particularly at elementary grade levels, no primary resources are identified for teachers; rather, numerous resources and instructional approaches are suggested for classroom use. This places decisions about implementation primarily with the classroom teacher, *and* it creates an implicit emphasis on locally developed resources and programs. Although Saskatchewan has stayed involved with the Western Canadian Protocol project, it is still using the 1995 social studies curriculum at the elementary level, more recently updated curricula at the junior levels, and more dated curricula at the senior levels.

Ontario social studies

Ontario's approach to social studies at the elementary level is unique in Canada. From grades 1–6, its program is organized around two primary themes: Heritage and Citizenship, and Canada and World Connections, relating to history and geography respectively (see chart below). The program then separates into distinct history and geography courses for grades 7 and 8. The Ontario program's approach to teaching and learning is similar in both course structures, with knowledge and skills outcomes organized around curriculum expectations and achievement levels. While Ontario's social studies program is similar to other provinces' programs in emphasizing the importance of inquiry, critical thinking, and research, it also outlines the importance of "habits of mind" in attitude development.[45] However, achievement levels identify four areas of knowledge and skill development in social studies, history, and geography.[46]

Common curriculum in the Atlantic provinces

The Foundation for the Atlantic Canada Social Studies Curriculum for Grades K–9 is the most successful attempt to coordinate a social studies program among various provinces. Developed cooperatively, this curriculum provides a framework for social stud-

THE ONTARIO CURRICULUM IN SOCIAL STUDIES GRADES 1–6; HISTORY AND GEOGRAPHY GRADES 7 AND 8[47]

Grade	Heritage and Citizenship Strand	Canada and World Connections Strand
One	Relationships, Rules, and Responsibilities	The Local Community
Two	Traditions and Celebrations	Features of Communities Around the World
Three	Pioneer Life	Urban and Rural Communities
Four	Medieval Times	The Provinces and Territories of Canada
Five	Early Civilizations	Aspects of Government in Canada
Six	Aboriginal Peoples and European Explorers	Canada and Its Trading Partners
	History	Geography
Seven	New France	The Themes of Geographic Inquiry
	British North America	Patterns in Physical Geography
	Conflict and Change	Natural Resources
Eight	Confederation	Patterns in Human Geography
	The Development of Western Canada	Economic Systems
	Canada: A Changing Society	Migration

ies programs in New Brunswick, Nova Scotia, Prince Edward Island, and Newfoundland and Labrador. Each province can adopt its own implementation schedule and customize its curriculum. The APEF curriculum standards emphasize social studies that is multidisciplinary, integrative, active, and experiential, drawing on the humanities, social sciences, and pure sciences.

As with other revised provincial social studies programs, the APEF document emphasizes effective citizenship as a primary goal of social studies. It contends that social studies must embody the main principles of freedom, equality, human dignity, justice, rule of law, and civic rights.[48] The social studies curriculum promotes students' growth as individuals and as citizens of Canada and an increasingly interdependent world. Again, consistent with present thinking about the need to give students multiple perspectives, the APEF curriculum provides opportunities for students to explore multiple approaches that may be used to analyze and interpret their own world and the world of others. Similar to other Canadian social studies programs, the APEF framework is organized around (1) conceptual strands, (2) processes, and (3) attitudes, values, and perspectives. Attitudes, values, and perspectives outcomes are integrated with conceptual strands and processes throughout the curriculum.

Decisions about what is taught in social studies

The political nature of the curriculum revision and development process has influenced decisions about what is taught as well as how it is taught. Demands to increase history content, to "disciplinize" social studies curricula, and to focus more explicitly on citizenship education have resulted in a curriculum development process that has generally been contentious and slow in moving to completion and implementation. In contrast, in Ontario over the past few years there has been relatively rapid development and implementation of new social studies, civics, history, and geography curricula. Both processes have caused some degree of frustration among teachers.

Although mandated curriculum essentially dictates what is taught in social studies across Canada, ultimate decisions about what is taught and how are made in the classroom. For many elementary teachers, the need to deal with literacy drives the content and resources used in social studies units, as well as affecting the priority that social studies receives.[49] The prominence of literacy skills and mathematics in standardized tests has resulted in less time being allotted to social studies curriculum, as well as an increased demand to address social studies topics in the context of language arts instruction. The underlying message is that social studies has less value, and therefore deserves less instructional time, than the other core subject areas. Some elementary generalists choose to replace aspects of mandated curriculum in order to respond to pressing needs and crises in their classrooms. For example, some teachers decide to address social and emotional issues that affect behaviour in the classroom and school, and omit topics that they perceive to be far removed from students' realities. Many teachers also describe critical issues in their social studies classrooms that involve the diverse and changing needs of the student populations they teach. Some teachers discuss the need for curriculum that addresses the diverse multicultural nature of student populations and that recognizes social factors that influence student views and experiences.

Challenges in Teaching Social Studies

The demographic of the teaching population is changing as the wave of early retirement incentives in recent years has affected the number of experienced teachers in Canadian classrooms, with younger teachers starting to form the majority. This factor, combined with the state of curriculum change in social studies, necessitates a critical look at some issues facing social studies teachers and the challenges that many of them deal with in implementing their curriculum.

Approaches to teaching

Although social studies curricula across Canadian provinces and territories generally purport an active, progressive approach to teaching methodology, the extent to which this actually happens is in question. Indeed, research indicates that many beginning teachers who build a commitment to more active, progressive teaching approaches during their pre-service years are strongly influenced by more traditional methods that they themselves experienced as students in their school years. Often they end up adopting and continuing to use these types of pedagogical approaches in their own teaching.[50]

Funding challenges

Many of the teachers we talked with over the past two years overwhelmingly agree that the challenges they are facing in their social studies classrooms have occurred as a result of funding cutbacks and lack of resources. There is an increasingly sharp distinction between "have" and "have-not" districts and jurisdictions across Canada. Economic and social conditions affect choices that teachers make about what and how to teach, and are leading to greater inequalities in the educational landscape.

There is an assumption that students can use the Internet as both a primary and secondary way to learn, especially for research projects, but in reality there are still serious gaps in availability and access to computers in schools and school districts. There are also serious discrepancies between those students who have computers in the home and those who do not. Significant inequalities exist between provinces in terms of the priority on financial support for social studies teaching, resource development, and purchasing new resources. Teacher access to computers is a problem in some school districts.[51] This problem is compounded by an increasing trend towards development of digital resources.

Lack of current and relevant resources

Although new curriculum implementation may foster a plethora of resource development initiatives, there are still gaps and issues that exist in resource support for social studies curriculum. The teachers we talked with frequently commented on the extent to which they have had to develop or adapt their own resources. Teachers of some grade levels in the Atlantic provinces have had to deal with severely dated resources and little support for technology integration. Teachers in many other areas of Canada, although able to access more resources, have had little opportunity for sustained professional development that helps them use these resources effectively. Teachers consistently commented on the need for curriculum and resources that address diverse student backgrounds, experiences, and ability levels, and the need to provide strategies and approaches that deal with the socioeconomic diversity and multicultural realities of today's classrooms. The need for current and relevant resources is, in many ways, a financial issue; however, it also reflects a changing reality in the classroom and a more explicit recognition of the need to support an increasingly diverse student population.

As a consequence of dealing with decreased funding, increased class sizes and curriculum demands, standardized testing pressures and decreased value placed on the relative importance of the social studies curriculum, many social studies teachers express the need for a "recipe book" approach to resource development. New resources must provide everything that is needed to meet curricular outcomes, as well as lay out the steps and strategies to do so. There is an increasing expectation that resources should provide multimedia components or references to easily locate and access them. Visual tools and organizers, cooperative learning strategies, geographic tools, and assessment strategies were frequently cited as important elements of effective resources. From a logistical point of view, more than a pedagogical one, teachers want resources that provide flexibility and choice. Curriculum outcomes that cover diverse topics within a single grade, combined with the reality of split-grade classrooms and lack of funding to purchase enough sets of resources for each classroom, means that teachers must look for ways to share resources and arrange schedules in order to implement the curriculum.

Many teachers we interviewed emphasized the importance of addressing literacy concerns and the need to ensure that resources address differing ability levels, student interests, and experiences. The diverse backgrounds from which students come need to be recognized and valued in both the curriculum development process and in the resources and training developed to support its implementation.

Displacement of social studies curriculum

One of the critical challenges teachers confront in implementing a social studies curriculum in some classrooms is its displacement by overriding social and economic factors. For example, a teacher in an elementary school in Nova Scotia discussed using social studies time to teach about bullying because of problems that the school is experiencing with this issue. Teachers in various areas of Canada with whom we discussed challenges in teaching social studies commented on the need for support to help them address the needs of a multicultural student population, particularly with students for whom English is a second language. In this context, social studies curriculum is sometimes displaced with instruction that focuses more on literacy and reading skill development, rather than on social studies concepts.

As discussed earlier, the administration of standardized testing in language arts and mathematics, particularly at the primary grade levels, has resulted in some teachers feeling pressured to increase time spent on those subjects so that their students do well in provincial assessment exams. Available budgets sometimes get allocated to resources for literacy or mathematics instead of social studies, or there is more emphasis on social studies resources that are literacy-based.

Decisions about the grade levels in which standardized tests are administered, and to what end they are used, have had a strong impact on what and how much social studies to teach. Alberta is the only province in Canada that administers provincial standardized assessment in social studies, with the exception of some senior grade level exit examinations in more discipline-based courses in other provinces. In Alberta, provincial social studies achievement examinations are administered at the grades 6 and 9 levels, and a provincial diploma examination at the grade 12 level. The lack of a provincial achievement examination in social studies at the grade 3 level, however, has created the same pressures that teachers in other provinces experience, resulting in a decreased emphasis on social studies at the primary level.

Some teachers who participated in our research felt that they needed to use their social studies time to deal with increasing demands on their time from other school or systemic initiatives. This has led to a perceived need by some teachers to "kill two birds" in teaching social studies, using integrated approaches that allow them to teach social studies outcomes while teaching other subject areas, particularly language arts. However, not all of these social studies teachers explicitly addressed reasons for using curriculum integration beyond its effectiveness as a time-saving device.

Lack of background and training

Increasing numbers of teachers who are teaching social studies courses are not trained in the disciplines of social studies, or as social studies specialists. This creates serious challenges as social studies curriculum becomes more complex and multifaceted. If teachers are to present multiple perspectives and ensure that students are exploring various historical, cultural, and social views and experiences, it is critical to provide them with multiple sources and background information on curriculum content.

Demands of overloaded curriculum

Although social studies curriculum has moved in what some would describe as more meaningful and relevant directions, some teachers questioned the move to an outcome-based curriculum and the depth of content expected of students. They expressed concern over the lack of scope and sequence in outcome-based program development and about the age-appropriateness of content for some students.

Many of these teachers have taught social studies curriculum based on the traditional expanding environments model, an approach that has a clearly defined scope and sequence. Some of these teachers have developed their own scope and sequence charts from new programs that are more outcome-centred, attempting to fit a new program into the more familiar structure provided by traditional approaches to organizing curriculum. This scenario highlights the fact that teacher resources and professional development activities that support new programs must provide support for teachers in understanding how to implement and assess new rationales and philosophical bases.

Some teachers questioned their ability to cover content expectations in the time allocated for implementation of social studies programs. This factor contributes to the recurring requests for "recipe book" approaches to resource development and background information components that we heard. While most teachers recognize the value of an inquiry-based approach to teaching social studies, many are reluctant to approach controversial issues or to carry the inquiry model forward into social action.[52] Recent curriculum drafts from both Alberta and Manitoba address teaching controversial issues in social studies classrooms, and the emphasis on social action that was prevalent in the 1970s has resurfaced in discussions of the importance of social studies education. However, time concerns are often cited as a rationale for being unable to fully implement the intent of a particular program of study.

Best practices in social studies teaching

What are best practices in social studies education? While current research points out the necessity and benefit of considering brain-based research, cooperative learning approaches, performance-based assessment strategies, and multiple learning styles and intelligences, the teachers with whom we talked typically identified best practice in social studies education that came from the embodied knowledge they have gained from their practice. The best practice they identified is consistent with many current trends in research, but the implementation of such practice seems to depend primarily on available resources. If resources provide structures and strategies for implementing proven methodologies with students, then teachers will use and apply them. On the other hand, teachers also talked frequently about the need or the pressure to construct their own resources. Whether or not these resources reflect best practice is difficult to ascertain; however, once these resources are in place, many teachers seem reluctant to stop using them when new and substantially different curriculum and resources are to be implemented.

Many teachers know that effective social studies methodology includes the use of strategies and activities that reflect active engagement and participation in learning. The teachers with whom we talked sometimes struggle with social studies concepts and topics that they feel are too conceptually difficult, too far removed from the experiences of the students they teach, or lacking currency. There seemed to be tacit agreement across the field that making social studies relevant for students is best accomplished through active, participatory approaches to learning, using projects, field trips, simulations, literature, learning centres, guest speakers, storytelling, and integrated learning approaches. Performance-based and formative assessment strategies were most often identified in conjunction with best practice in social studies; however, some teachers also expressed a need for resources such as blackline masters and workbooks to facilitate and assess skill development. Discussions about best practice often reflected a constructivist stance to learning; that is, teachers repeatedly reinforced the necessity of engaging students with content, and conversely were concerned about perceived curricular blocks to doing so.

The influence of the official social studies curriculum on best practice is unclear. Although the teachers with whom we talked sometimes associated programs of study directly with the activities they implement in their classroom, rarely did they explicitly identify these programs as a source of professional knowledge or learning. Awareness of the program of study varied; some of these teachers use it as the foundation for everything they do and others have not even looked at it. A key source of learning for many of these teachers as they develop their practice seems to be their own background and personal experience, as well as those professional development experiences that have had a profound impact on their teaching.

Conclusion

How curriculum is implemented often differs from what is presented in official curriculum documents. Implementation is influenced by social, economic, and political pressures and issues as well as by choices about strategies and resources that teachers make. Although conceptually social studies curricula across Canada have shifted to be more inclusive and considerate of multiple perspectives and the pluralistic nature of Canadian society, the approach to content has remained relatively static. That is, the expanding environments approach to content sequencing and discipline-based content organizers or themes continue to be used. More recently developed social studies curricula have been influenced by renewed interest in the nature of effective, participatory citizenship, increased recognition that such citizenship is multifaceted, the teaching of history and, to a lesser degree, geography as distinct subjects, and a more explicit focus on human rights and globalization. Through public consultations, various organizations and interest groups are more directly involved than in the past in the curriculum development process. There is an increased demand to address assessment and to provide effective support to deal with standardized provincial examinations. Critical thinking, inquiry, and research skills are consistently emphasized in social studies programs today.

Although teaching for citizenship remains a focus for social studies curricula, more attention is being paid to what that focus means to different Canadians, and there is an increasingly critical examination of how to teach for that goal.[53] The Manitoba Curriculum Framework (2003) states:

> The concept of citizenship takes on meaning in specific contexts and is determined by time and place. Diverse notions of citizenship have been used in the past and are

being used in the present, for both good and ill. Throughout much of history, citizenship has been exclusionary, class-based, racist, and sexist. In Canada, for instance, First Nations parents were forced to send their children to residential schools in the interests of citizenship.[54]

Therefore citizenship does not always have a positive connotation, and more inclusive understandings of citizenship should take these perspectives into account.

As Alan Sears stated in *Trends and Issues in Canadian Social Studies,* "Social studies is a field that is controversial at many levels."[55] Perhaps in no other subject area do so many facets of society get involved in the curriculum development and implementation process and have something to say about what should, or should not, be taught. Our experiences with the debate around the development of the Alberta curriculum, as well as our experiences with teachers participating in two survey projects across the country, have taught us that the nature of social studies reflects the complexities of what it means to be Canadian, and that social studies is a product of that very dialogue and debate. We continue to grapple with how the multiple visions and beliefs that make up Canada can be represented in what we teach to our students. Our research has also reaffirmed for us that there are many social studies teachers in classrooms across this country who are committed to continuing that dialogue in order to meet the many challenges they face and still teach to their own visions of what social studies education should be about.

Endnotes

1. George Richardson, "Casualties of War," *Canadian Social Studies* 37, no. 2 (Winter 2003), http://www.quasar.ualberta.ca/css/Css_37_2.
2. Observations have been drawn from a marketing study commissioned by Nelson Learning, which was conducted by the authors in the spring of 2001, and from a pilot study commissioned by Historica on the teaching of history in social studies and history curriculum, which was conducted by the authors in the spring of 2002. The Nelson Learning study involved elementary through high school teachers from vari-

ous provinces and asked them to reflect on and discuss their perceptions of issues and challenges involved in teaching social studies curriculum. The Historica study involved teachers from each province and two territories in focus groups and asked them to reflect on the experience of teaching Canadian history.

3 For an example of an article that discusses the use of media and polls to further the public debate around the issue of social studies versus history courses, see P. Clark, "Engaging the Field: A Conversation with Rudyard Griffiths," *Canadian Social Studies* 37, no. 1 (Fall, 2002), http://www .quasar.ualberta.ca/css/Css_37_1/ARrudyard_griffiths.htm.

4 Task Force on Standards for Teaching and Learning in the Social Studies, "A Vision for Powerful Teaching and Learning in the Social Studies: Building Social Understanding and Civic Efficacy," *Social Education* 57, no. 5 (1993): 213.

5 Penney Clark, in her chapter in this volume, argues that social studies is primarily an American invention and discusses the American influences on Canadian social studies curriculum. Perry Marker points out that the 1916 report of the National Education Association Committee on Social Studies in the United States "produced a tremendous impact on social studies curriculum" and "the scope and sequence of courses that, some 85 years later, still defines the contemporary social studies curriculum." This scope and sequence established the expanding environments approach to social studies education that is still prevalent today. See Perry Marker, "Thinking Out of the Box: Rethinking and Reinventing a Moribund Social Studies Curriculum," *Theory and Research in Social Education* 29, no. 4 (2001), 741.

6 Marker, "Thinking Out of the Box," 734. Marker argues that the social studies curriculum has remained static and discipline-bound, especially in history, even though society is unrecognizable from what it was when the subject area of social studies began.

7 For a description of the origins of social studies curriculum, see Robert D. Barr, James L. Barth, and S. Samuel Shermis, "Emergence of the Social Studies" in *Defining the Social Studies*, no. 51 (Washington, DC: NCSS Bulletin, 1977).

8 Atlantic Provinces Education Foundation, *Foundation for the Atlantic Canada Social Studies Curriculum* (Halifax: Nova Scotia Education and Culture, 1999), 1.

9 Western Canadian Protocol for Collaboration in Basic Education, *Common Curriculum Framework for Social Studies: Kindergarten to Grade 9* (Winnipeg: Manitoba Education, Training and Youth, 2002), 5.

10 Alberta Learning, *Social Studies Kindergarten to Grade 12 Validation Draft* (Edmonton: Author, May 2003), 1.

11 Atlantic Provinces Education Foundation, *Foundation for the Atlantic Canada Social Studies Curriculum*, 2.

12 For an example of a not-for-profit group that uses extensive marketing and media-based strategies to promote an educational mandate, see the website for the Dominion Institute at www.dominion.ca. The Dominion Institute has advocated

for the need to have distinct history courses that are not taught within the context of an integrated social studies course, and has been critical of the history components of some provincial social studies programs. Other organizations and foundations that have advocated some form of national framework are the Historica Foundation and Citizenship Matters.

13 This approach involves teaching the curriculum in increments or in a developmental sequence that begins with examples from the local environment and expands outward from there. For a concise discussion of this approach, see R. McKay and S. Gibson, *Reshaping the Future of Social Studies* (Edmonton: Alberta Learning, 1999).

14 From the National Council for the Social Studies website, www.socialstudies.org (accessed May 13, 2003).

15 Social studies frameworks have been produced for both the Atlantic Provinces Education Foundation social studies program and the Western Canadian Protocol for Collaboration in Basic Education, and are referenced in this chapter.

16 Atlantic Provinces Education Foundation, *Foundation for the Atlantic Canada Social Studies Curriculum*, 16–19.

17 Alberta Learning, *Social Studies Kindergarten to Grade 12 Validation Draft*, 73.

18 See, for example, British Columbia, Ministry of Education, Skills, and Training, *Social Studies K to 7: Integrated Resource Package* (Victoria: Author, 1998), 1.

19 Ontario Ministry of Education and Training, *The Ontario Curriculum Social Studies Grades 1 to 6; History and Geography Grades 7 and 8* (Toronto: Author, 1998), 2.

20 P. Shields with D. Ramsay, "Components of Citizenship Education: Initiating Action" (report in author's possession). This unpublished report on citizenship education in English Canada was submitted to the Western Canadian Protocol for Social Studies team and the Canadian Council of Ministers.

21 Alan Sears and Andrew S. Hughes, "Citizenship Education and Current Educational Reform," *Canadian Journal of Education* 21, no. 2 (1996): 123–142.

22 A.B. Hodgetts, *What Culture? What Heritage? A Study of Civic Education in Canada* (Toronto: OISE Press, 1968).

23 The content of social studies curriculum and how it is organized continues to be contentious. Traditional conceptions of social studies include a focus on the academic disciplines—history, geography, civics or political science, sociology and anthropology—while non-traditional conceptions of social studies embrace a curriculum organized around social problems and issues, with social science and humanities disciplines providing the context for examples and insights.

24 New Brunswick, Department of Education, Educational Programs and Services Branch, *Atlantic Canada in the Global Community Grade 8* (Fredericton: Author, 1998): 1.

25 Alberta Learning, Curriculum Branch, *Social Studies Program of Studies: Elementary Schools* (Edmonton: Author, 1990).

26 British Columbia Ministry of Education, Skills, and Train-

ing, *Social Studies K to 7: Integrated Resource Package* (Victoria: Author, 1998); ———, *Social Studies 8 to 10: Integrated Resource Package* (Victoria: Author, 1997).

27 Saskatchewan Education, *Social Studies: A Curriculum Guide for the Elementary Level* (Regina: Author, 1995), http://www.sasked.gov.sk.ca/docs/elemsoc/intro.html (accessed November 18, 2003).

28 Ibid.

29 Ontario Ministry of Education, *The Ontario Curriculum Social Studies*, 2.

30 The inclusion and increased attention given to story as both an instructional strategy and a concept is illustrated in many curriculum documents and frameworks. In the NCSS standards, a necessary skill for an "excellent" social studies program is the student's ability to develop and present "policies, arguments, and stories."

31 For a perspective on reactions to developing curriculum and a discussion on the link between the concepts of citizenship and identity, see Alberta Learning, *Report on Consultations: Alberta Social Studies Kindergarten to Grade 9 Program of Studies Consultation Draft* (Edmonton: Author, 2003), 3, http://www.learning.gov.ab.ca/k_12/curriculum/bySubject/social/report.pdf (accessed June 27, 2003).

32 Alberta Learning, *Social Studies Program of Studies*, B2.

33 Government of Newfoundland and Labrador, Department of Education, Division of Program Development, *A Curriculum Framework for Social Studies: Navigating the Future* (St. John's: Author, 1993), 35, http://www.gov.nf.ca/edu/sp/Frameworks/soc_studies/chap3.PDF (accessed June 27, 2003).

34 Western Canadian Protocol, *Foundation Document for the Development of the Common Curriculum Framework for Social Studies: Kindergarten to Grade 12* (Winnipeg: Author, February 15, 2000), 5.

35 British Columbia Ministry of Education, *Social Studies K to 7*; ———, *Social Studies 8 to 10*.

36 British Columbia Ministry of Education, *Social Studies 11: Integrated Resource Package*.

37 Manitoba Education and Youth, *Kindergarten to Grade 8 Social Studies: Manitoba Curriculum Framework of Outcomes* (Winnipeg: Author, 2003), 3.

38 Ibid., 4–5.

39 Some curriculum documents are provided on the Nunavut Department of Education website, which can be accessed at www.gov.nu.ca/education/eng.

40 Alberta Learning, *Social Studies Kindergarten to Grade 12 Validation Draft*.

41 Manitoba Education and Youth, *Kindergarten to Grade 8 Social Studies,* 12–13.

42 See Peter Seixas, "The Purposes of Teaching Canadian History," *Canadian Social Studies* 36, no. 2 (Winter 2002), http://www.quasar.ualberta.ca/css/Css_36_2/ARpurposes_teaching_canadian_history.htm for a discussion on the need to encourage students to assess and analyze his-

torical interpretations. See also Peter N. Stearns, Peter Seixas, and Samuel Wineburg, eds., *Knowing, Teaching, and Learning History: National and International Perspectives* (New York: New York University Press, 2000).

43 Saskatchewan Education, *Report of the Social Sciences Reference Committee* (Regina: Author, 1984), 1.

44 Saskatchewan Education, *Indian and Métis Education Policy from Kindergarten to Grade 12* (Regina: Author, 1995), 2.

45 Ontario Ministry of Education, *The Ontario Curriculum Social Studies*, 3.

46 Ibid., 10.

47 Ibid., 6.

48 Atlantic Provinces Education Foundation, *Foundation for the Atlantic Canada Social Studies Curriculum* (Halifax, Nova Scotia Education and Culture, English Program Services, 1998), 1.

49 The discussion that follows reflects opinions and statements made by a number of social studies teachers who participated in the Nelson Learning marketing study and the Historica study referenced earlier in this chapter.

50 See, for example, S. Veenman, "Perceived Problems of Beginning Teachers," *Review of Educational Research* 54, no. 2 (1984): 143–178; and Alan Sears, "Buying Back Your Soul: Restoring Ideals in Social Studies Teaching," *Social Studies and the Young Learner* 4, no. 3 (1992): 9–11.

51 Informal interviews with teachers in various areas of Canada revealed that not all teachers have access to an email account and that teachers have widely varying levels of Internet access.

52 K. Osborne and J. Seymour, "Political Education in Upper Elementary School," *International Journal of Social Education* 3, no. 2 (1988): 63.

53 For a discussion of the traditional "masculine" understanding of citizenship in social studies content, see Jennifer Tupper, "The Gendering of Citizenship in Social Studies Curriculum," *Canadian Social Studies* 36, no. 3 (Spring 2002), http://www.quasar.ualberta.ca/css/Css_36_3/ARgendering_of_citizenship.html.

54 Manitoba Education and Youth, *Kindergarten to Grade 8 Social Studies*, 9.

55 Alan Sears, "Social Studies in Canada," in *Trends and Issues in Canadian Social Studies*, ed. Ian Wright and Alan Sears (Vancouver: Pacific Educational Press, 1997), 34.

CHAPTER 3

History and Social Studies in Québec

An Historical Perspective

Stéphane Lévesque[‡]

The more complex society becomes, the more we must rely on the study of history to understand its present, and ultimately, to participate, as responsible citizens in a democracy, in defining its future.—Task Force on the Teaching of History[1]

Introduction

Like other Canadian provinces, Québec has undergone profound changes since the current history and social studies programs were implemented in the early 1980s. Increased immigration, cultural pluralism, human rights, globalization and its technologies, Québec national recognition, and, on the international stage, violent ethnic conflicts along with religious fundamentalism have, to varying degrees, intensified the need for greater historical and civic understanding of the peoples, values, cultures, and religions that shape Québec and Canadian society.

It is in this context that the Minister of Education, following the recommendations of the Estates General on Education (1995), appointed a task force on the teaching of history and social studies in

Québec schools in the mid-1990s to "return national and world history to its rightful place as a fundamental discipline in the education of young people in Québec."[2] Following public hearings and meetings with various educational and history specialists, the task force presented its final report to the Ministry of Education (Ministère de l'Éducation du Québec [MEQ]) in 1996. The 78-page report subsequently served as the cornerstone for developing the new history and geography programs now being implemented in Québec schools. With its new curriculum, Québec will soon be the first province to have history and geography, along with the formal addition of "citizenship education," as compulsory core subjects throughout the whole of the public school system. The newly implemented elementary curriculum clearly reinforces the notion that citizenship education is a fundamental goal of education in general, and history and geography in particular. As the document puts it,

> ces disciplines constituent les fondements de l'apprentissage de la vie dans une société pluraliste. L'éducation à la citoyenneté s'intègre aux apprentissages propres à la géographie et à l'histoire. Il s'agit cependant d'un apprentissage complexe auquel tous les programmes d'études doivent contribuer....[3]

Yet the notion of citizenship is complex and thus contested, particularly in a multicultural and multinational state such as Canada. Legitimated

[‡] I am grateful to professors J. Donald Wilson at the University of British Columbia and Kevin Kee at McGill University for their insightful comments and suggestions on drafts of this manuscript.

concepts, such as nation, state, and democracy, and "official" stories of the national past often conflict with the views and beliefs held by national and cultural minorities. This situation is also intensified by the regional nature of public education in Canada as dictated in Article 93 of the British North American Act (BNA Act). For example, when the former Québec Minister of Education introduced the educational policy statement of her ministry in 1997, she expressed the new changes in these terms:

> [T]he choices that are expressed in this policy statement reflect what Québecers expect from their schools….These choices, which are largely consistent with those being made in most Western countries with respect to the curriculum, also take into account the particular cultural context of Québec.[4]

Following this statement, we can argue that if the subject of social studies in English Canada has consistently relied on American models since its creation in the 1920s,[5] Québec history and geography have, for various political, historical, and educational reasons, historically followed similar but at times different Canadian educational paths. More specifically, this chapter will look at the historical development of history and social studies in francophone Québec from 1867 to date, as found in policy documents, curricula, textbooks, and other educational materials. It will then consider the latest developments in history and geography in light of the ongoing educational reform, keeping in mind that policy and curricular reforms do not necessarily translate into successful pedagogical practices as found in the classroom. To paraphrase Neil Sutherland, history tells us that past educational reforms that took place outside the classroom often had very little effect on what went on behind its door.[6]

History and Geography from 1867 to the 1920s

From the creation of New France in the seventeenth century until the mid-nineteenth century, education was very much a local concern in French Québec.

Because, at that time, most people did not attend school, they were not affected by the political and educational concerns during that period. In fact, Québec would have to wait until 1943 to have compulsory schooling, even though Liberal Premier Honoré Mercier suggested it as early as 1892.[7] This critical situation led to exceptionally low elementary and particularly high school attendance, and poor literacy skills among francophones. Jean-Pierre Charland reports, for instance, that enrolment for francophone Québecers between age five and nineteen was below 50 percent until the twentieth century. More appalling, almost 30 percent of adult francophones were illiterate, unable to read a plain letter (compared to only 7 percent in English-speaking Ontario).[8] But, the growing public debate about education in the twentieth century—particularly during the Quiet Revolution in the 1960s, which led to the creation of a public Ministry of Education—has served to increase the significance of public education in Québec and, by the same token, the teaching of history and citizenship.

Yet, as in English Canada, history and geography in Québec have not always received full consideration in past reforms, nor have these subjects adequately met the needs of democratic citizenship. It might be important to note from the outset that in keeping with French European traditions, Québec only recently adopted social studies as a subject, at the elementary level only. Until the late 1960s, history and geography were the dominant disciplines in both elementary and high schools. Interestingly, after intense criticism from historians and several elementary social studies teachers during the 1995–1996 educational reform, the new curriculum marks a clear return to the original approach to citizenship with greater focus on history, rather than social studies.

Following the creation of the Ministry of Public Instruction (Ministère de l'Instruction Publique) in 1867, which was dismantled in 1875 by the dominant influence of *ultramontane* Catholic leaders who strongly believed in the supremacy of the Church over the state and opposed the creation of one public committee to govern both English (Protestant) and French (Catholic) education in the province, the first official programs were implemented in 1872–1873 at the elementary level.[9] Geography and history programs focused explicitly on religion and modern civilization (Western Europe and Canada). At the core of these programs was religious history ("histoire sainte") followed by the history of (French) Canada, from New France to the Dominion of Canada, and some preliminary notions of world geography. "Canadian history," Geneviève Jain rightly notes in her analysis of education and Canadian identity in Québec from 1867 to 1914, "occupied a very small place in the curriculum. It was taught in the schools only after religious history."[10] Furthermore, unlike current curricula, the initial history and geography programs offered very little content for analysis, thus suggesting that local teachers were left alone with often minimal knowledge, skills, and materials to teach their subjects.

It is generally agreed by historians of education that the main purpose of history/geography until the 1920s was the rigid inculcation of religious, moral, and patriotic beliefs in French Canadians, with particular focus on the "heroic" character of their French ancestors (e.g., Dollard des Ormeaux, Madeleine de Verchères, Mgr de Laval) and the visible protection of the "Divine Providence" in the survival of the French Canadian nationality. The program of 1898, for instance, mentions that students will learn the history of Canada from the French Regime (grade 5) to the English domination (grade 6), followed by Church history up to the Crusades (grade 7) and from the Crusades to modern days (grade 8).[11] References to patriotism and religious faith are more explicitly found in the Québec teachers' manual of 1905, which states in its rationale that teachers must cultivate the love of the homeland, the attachment to traditions and institutions, and a respect for *our* beautiful language and religious faith. As the manual put it, "[L'enseignant doit] cultiver chez les élèves le patriotisme, l'amour du sol natal, l'attachement aux traditions et aux institutions nationales, le respect de notre belle langue et de notre foi religieuse."[12]

Textbooks that supplemented the programs followed a conventional chronological account of Canada and Catholicism, dwelling on those "great figures" (heroes, martyrs, saints) so prominent in the geography and history of French Canada. F.X. Toussaint's textbook on the history of Canada, approved by the Conseil de l'Instruction Publique, makes explicit in its preface of 1890 that the role of history is to acknowledge the great achievements of Canadian expansion with explicit reference to Canadian patriotism. As Toussaint put it:

> Aujourd'hui cette confédération compte HUIT provinces, et de plus un immense territoire capable de former plusieurs royaumes! Elle a franchi les Montagnes Rocheuses à pas de géant, et reculé ses bornes jusqu'au Pacifique! Un cours d'Histoire du Canada doit noter ces agrandissements prodigieux; l'instituteur canadien a le devoir de les mettre sous les yeux de ses élèves. Une leçon d'histoire nationale est une leçon de patriotisme.[13]‡

Similar patriotic and expansionist references are also found in the first Canadian history textbook produced by prominent French Canadian historian F.X. Garneau in 1856. This textbook is particularly interesting not only because of the nexus of ideas about French Canadian survival ("survivance") and the religious character of the Canadiens,[14] but also because of the official approval of the Catholic council included in the preface of the 1861 edition. In the first paragraph, we can read that teachers and the clergy were impatiently waiting for a (French) Canadian textbook that could be used in class to counterbalance European exploits by advancing the epic story of a Catholic people in the young country of Canada.

> Les chefs d'institutions se plaignaient, avec raison, de l'anomalie qu'il y a d'enseigner aux enfants du sol, l'histoire des peuples éloignés et des nations éteintes jusque dans ces particularités les plus minutieuses, et de leur taire toutes ces aventures chevaleresques, ces événements héroïques, cette grande et religieuse épopée qui s'est déroulée

‡ An unofficial English translation of this and subsequent French quotations is found in the Endnotes for this chapter.

autour du berceau de la jeune famille canadienne et qui lui sert comme d'une auréole de gloire.[15]

This nation-building approach to history and geography was very much focused on the survival of the French Canadian nationality and the clerical ideologies that made this "église-nation" unique in Canada.[16] English Canada was treated as a separate imperialist nation, with a different language, culture, and religion. First Nations were simply portrayed as savages ("sauvages") who had to be colonized. And ordinary people, including women, were generally ignored, though some mention was made in the textbooks of a few female heroes such as Marie de l'Incarnation and Madeleine de Verchères. The understanding of the Canadiens by the French Canadian élite during the period might be best symbolized by the views expressed by Abbé Laflèche, one of the most brilliant Québec *ultramontanes*, who wrote in 1866:

> The providential mission of the Canadian people is essentially religious: it is the conversion to Catholicism of the poor faithless people who inhabit this country, and the extension of the Kingdom of God by the formation of a nationality that is above all Catholic.[17]

In terms of learning, very few documents of the period offer evidence of teaching methods and student learning in history and geography. Yet, as Charland argues in his analysis of education in nineteenth-century Québec, given the authoritative role of the clergy, the poor training of teachers, and the shortage of teaching resources, we can speculate that the focus was very much on the repetitive inculcation of a series of chronological events and figures found in textbooks (when available) perceived by the élite of the time as significant for the development of (French) Canada. Supporting this view, the superintendent of Public Instruction, Boucher de la Bruère, prepared in 1898 a project for a pedagogical conference that school inspectors had to disseminate to their teachers in which he made explicit references to the teaching of history and the necessity of countering "false" historical accounts and

presenting the "exact" facts about their nation, culture, and institutions. He also stressed the necessity of viewing history as progress for the Canadiens.

> To do well, it is necessary to think of history in the elementary school as the national subject, par excellence; that is, to give it the task of making the country known and loved, … to make the students understand the main workings of the social and administrative organisms in areas that they can comprehend and about which there is an opportunity to combat errors, prejudices, and widely held false beliefs; to get them to love the present and honor the past, to inject at the same time a sense of progress and respect for national traditions.[18]

One of the few progressive inspectors of the time, critical of rote learning, also had this to say about the teaching of history and geography in 1891:

> Tout le mal provient de la méthode suivie; la mémorisation joue un rôle trop grand dans toutes les écoles; on retrouve des cartes mais l'on ne s'en sert pas ou sans résultat pratique. Il en est ainsi de l'histoire du Canada. On trouve un bon nombre d'élèves en état de réciter de mémoire tout le petit volume qu'on leur a mis entre les mains; mais ils ne sont pas nombreux parmi ces mêmes élèves ceux qui peuvent faire un résumé intelligent des premiers essais de colonisation ou des principaux faits de l'administration de nos premiers gouverneurs français.[19]

The teachers' manual of 1905 also offers some evidence supporting the views expressed above by inspector Lévesque. In the teaching strategies section, the document suggests that history/geography teachers should not neglect any of the proposed methods offered, which included the systematic use of oral lectures accompanied by summative assessments integrated in the textbooks, blackboard notes and maps, synoptical reviews, and basic explanations of unknown names, dates, and events. The manual goes on to suggest that lectures must be carefully supported by repetitive exercises that are meant to "engrave" important notions in the minds of the pupils.[20] In a parallel manner, Thérèse Hamel notes in her historical analysis of teachers in French Québec (1836–1939) that increasingly programs of this period included explicit concentric teaching methods, moving from the known to the unknown, that left teachers with very limited ability to deviate from the prescribed approaches or to encourage students to be active in their learning. As she puts it :

> Dans cette optique, les programmes deviennent de plus en plus explicites et précis, ne laissant rien au hasard des situations pédagogiques éventuelles. L'enseignant, véritable maître d'œuvre, y devient le transmetteur d'une culture centrée sur l'apprentissage d'un bagage défini de certaines connaissances jugées essentielles aux générations futures.[21]

As these last examples suggest, school history and geography during this period can be understood as subjects of both public and religious interests. In the eyes of the clergy and the Québec political elite, they had become too important to be left to parents or private initiatives.

History and Geography from the 1920s to the 1950s

While most English Canadian provinces had officially implemented public education systems by the 1920s, along with some progressive educational philosophies, Québec was still relying heavily on the clergy to govern education. Yet, some Québec educators and political leaders were interested in trying to reform the religious education system in place since 1875. Efforts were made in the early twentieth century by a group of professional leaders, led by the journalist Godfroy Langlois who founded La Ligue de l'Enseignement in 1902. George S. Tomkins notes that one member of the Ligue, Gaspard de Serres, later became a member of the federal Robertson Royal Commission on Industrial Training and Technical Education of 1910, which

served as a blueprint for implementing the so-called "New Education" in Canadian education and showed the necessity of reforming provincial curricula to adapt to changing economic needs.[22]

Influenced by European and North American progressive educational reforms, which also put greater emphasis on the development of the "whole child," history and geography programs in Québec slowly adapted to the educational changes that had already been taking place elsewhere. The history program of 1923, for instance, introduced the idea of adapting history to the psychological and physiological development of the child. Teachers were counselled to use simple storytelling methods (biographical) with junior levels and to move to more analytical history ("explicatif") with senior levels. The program of 1938 goes further by mentioning that good pedagogy must be effective and interesting for students. Lectures must involve vivid storytelling accompanied with individual readings in class, and teachers' explanations to clarify historical concepts such as cause and effect and historical continuity. Focus was no longer exclusively on the mastering of historical narratives but increasingly on the development of "intelligence" (what the program refers to as a "philosophy of history").

Perhaps the most progressive program of the period is the one of 1948 which is entirely structured around Canadian themes ("approche thématique"): "Chez les Indiens, les missionnaires sont venus" (grade 1), "Les français s'établissent au pays des indiens" (grade 2), "Ils ont fait notre pays" (grade 3), "Découvreurs et pionniers" (grades 4-5), "L'épopée canadienne" (grades 6-7).[23] It is also noted that history and geography should be introduced in alternate years from grade 4 to grade 7. Teachers are encouraged to use more active teaching methods adapted to their students, favour individual and group work, and allow for individual readings other than the textbook (in silence!) when deemed possible. The program also includes overall and specific outcomes.

> On fournira autant que possible les sources de renseignement supplémentaires au manuel. On favorisera les lectures libres; on consacrera à l'histoire certaines heures de

lectures silencieuses. On recourra à des procédés actifs et créateurs. Tenant compte des différences individuelles, on laissera une certaine liberté dans les lectures, les activités ou les entreprises. On encouragera les entreprises libres par groupes, confiant par exemple à diverses équipes le soin de recueillir la documentation sur tel ou tel sujet d'étude, avec l'ambition de communiquer à leur camarades les résultats de leurs recherches.[24]

Roy, Gauthier, and Tardif believe that this program was largely influenced by child-centred approaches suggested by the Comité permanent des éducateurs de Québec in 1942 chaired by the Père George-Henri Lévesque, founder of the School of Social Sciences at Laval University and co-chair, with Vincent Massey, of the Royal Commission of National Development in the Arts, Letters, and Sciences (1950). The report of the committee makes reference to new developments in educational psychology (stages of mental development) and their impact on teaching and learning in school. In his analysis of school programs in Québec, Jean Plante also points to changes in the suggested pedagogies found in the "manuels pédagogiques" (pedagogical manuals) for pre-service teachers from the turn of the century to the 1950s. While in the 1900s manuals consistently justified their approaches with reference to the "mission providentielle" of educators and the authoritative role of the clergy, manuals of the 1950s no longer refer to a moral authority to legitimate their instructional actions. As Plante puts it, "les [sic] justification doit [dorénavant] être construite selon des procédés d'argumentation fort élevés."[25] Hamel comes to similar conclusions, suggesting that for the first time the pedagogical manual of Roland Vinette (1948) "[tient] compte de l'enfant en tant que sujet de son apprentissage, et se penche sur sa façon de comprendre, d'étudier et d'assimiler les enseignements donnés."[26]

Yet saying that Québec history and geography programs of this period more or less embraced notions of the New Education reform taking place in English Canada and elsewhere in North America is not to say that history and geography were

supportive or closer to the historical, political, cultural, and religious views of English Canadians. The original vision of a binational state that transcended provincial attachment, now defended by vocal leaders such as abbé Lionel Groulx who kept the clerico-nationalism flame, was still very much dominant in both the structure of the programs and the content of the textbooks. The "progressive" Canadian history program of 1948, for instance, states that the overall goals are:

> [Faire] connaître les principaux événements qui ont marqué l'évolution de notre peuple; [l']histoire de notre patrie et de ceux qui l'ont faite ce qu'elle est aujourd'hui. L'enseignement de cette matière doit faire ressortir les traits distinctifs qui donnent à notre histoire son relief particulier, son caractère propre: le but apostolique en même temps que national poursuivi par les découvreurs, les fondateurs, les organisateurs de notre pays; la pureté de nos origines canadiennes-françaises; le caractère religieux, moral, héroïque et idéaliste de nos ancêtres; la lutte constante contre des difficultés de toutes sortes; la protection visible de la Providence sur la survivance de notre nationalité.[27]

History teaching was very much in tune with the religious-nationalist views expressed by the clerical élite. One Québec commentator described the situation of history teaching in Québec during the 1940s in the report produced by the royal commission co-chaired by Père George-Henri Lévesque in the following terms:

> L'historien s'est servi de l'histoire pour y chercher une leçon de fierté nationale, de fidélité aux principes pour lesquels les ancêtres ont tant combattu, de résistance aux attaques, conscientes ou non, contre leur nationalité. Sous la plume de nos auteurs, l'histoire enseigne à conserver le mode de vie française et catholique, donne des exemples de courage et de ténacité qui constituent toujours une inspiration.[28]

During the same period, abbé Arthur Maheux

of Laval University also accused French and English Canadian history textbooks of fostering division and hatred. In his Canadian Historical Association Presidential Address of 1949, he claimed:

> Our text-books in Canadian history have followed [French and British] trends for a long time. They have been nationalist text-books. They have imbued the young with the idea that the French and English in Canada are widely separated along cultural lines. In this way we have created a wall between the two main Canadian groups."[29]

Similar comments were expressed by other critics of the programs, including Jean Bruchési, under-secretary to the province of Québec.[30]

In fact, analysis of textbooks clearly indicates that Canadian history focused exclusively on the development and survival of the "habitants" (Canadiens) in North America with little understanding of English Canadians, even those in the province of Québec. In the grades 8–9 Canadian history textbook, *Mon Pays: Histoire du Canada*, the intent is to follow the path of our ancestors who built this country: beautiful and vast, Catholic and French. This goal is reflected in the following patriotic poem from Ferland:[31]

> Canada! Canada! Toi que le ciel protège,
> Toi qui, sous ton manteau de verdure ou de neige,
> Dans l'ombre de tes bois verdoyants ou jaunis,
> Sur les bords de ton fleuve aux grandes eaux sereines,
> Du sommet de tes monts et du sein de tes pleines,
> Es pour le Canada le plus beau des pays,
> Gloire à Toi! Gloire à Toi!

The grades 11–12 history textbook, *Mon pays, synthèse de l'histoire du Canada*, goes even further by explicitly separating the French and English Canadian "races" and condemning intermarriage which, in its view, weakens the cultural and national survival of the Canadiens. The French Canadian seigneurs, the author argues, "courtisaient le vainqueur, en lui livrant [leurs] fils et [leurs] filles."[32] Gérald Filteau supported this conclusion in his textbook, *La civilisation catholique et française au Canada*:

> Ces races composantes sont, au Canada, la française et l'anglaise. Et c'est parce que nous, d'origine française, nous ne voulons pas de fusion de notre race avec l'autre, qu'il nous arrive encore de nous appeler nous-mêmes 'Canadien-français.' "[33]

This state of affairs in Québec history remained virtually unchanged until the 1960s, when drastic changes in political, cultural, and educational matters for the so-called "Québécois" emerged. Kenneth McRoberts observes:

> The 1960s were marked by an open dialogue and debate about the nature of Canada....Francophone and anglophone Canadians confronted, in a way they never had before, their fundamentally divergent conceptions of Canada. The trigger for that process was, of course, developments in Québec.[34]

From the 1960s to the 1990s: Thirty Years of "Progress"

The election in 1960 of the Liberal party of Jean Lesage, under the slogan "Maîtres chez nous," precipitated long-needed social, economic, and educational reforms seen by the emerging national-liberal elite as necessary to catch up with ("rattraper") English Canadian and Western liberal trends. Honouring its electoral promise, the Lesage government created in 1961 a Royal Commission of Inquiry on Education, known as the Parent Commission after the name of its chair, Mgr Alphonse Parent of Laval University. In 1963, the Commission published its first report, dealing primarily with the control and organization of the education system. It recommended the creation of a secular Ministry of Education that would be the source of authority for both private and public education and both francophone and anglophone schools. It also recommended the appointment of a Superior Council of Education (Conseil supérieur de l'éducation) to advise the Minister of Education and to act as a means of communication between the public and the government. Following most recommendations of the Parent Commission, in 1964 the government passed the famous Bill 60, which established for the first time since 1875 a Ministry of Education. One member of the Commission, Guy Rocher, later argued that Bill 60 and the reform of education that followed constituted nothing less than the core of the whole Quiet Revolution. As he put it:

> À cette époque-là, la réflexion sur la réforme de l'enseignement se trouvait à toucher la fine pointe du changement social, économique et culturel qui marquait ce qu'on appelait déjà "la Révolution tranquille". C'est vers l'enseignement que l'on se tournait surtout, parce qu'on croyait que pour changer la société, édifier un Québec nouveau, il fallait rebâtir le système d'enseignement de nouvelles assises. On croyait volontiers que le système d'enseignement avait une grande influence sur l'avenir économique et culturel d'une nation.[35]

Following Bill 60, the Parent Commission presented other recommendations dealing with the programs of studies, the organization of public and private schools, and post-secondary education (including the creation of CÉGEPs). According to the Parent Commission, education, and more specifically teaching, was to aim at individual instruction, overall development of the child, and the stimulation of creativity among students. Overall, the Parent Commission adopted features of neo-progressive educational reforms taking place in English Canada and the United States, but maintained deep concern for economic, political, and social changes going on in Québec life.[36] The Ministry of Education later put it in these terms:

> Partout on a compris que la société d'au-

jourd'hui, et plus encore celle de demain, pose à l'enseignement des exigences sans précédent. Pour que la civilisation moderne progresse, ce qui est pour elle condition de survie, il est devenu nécessaire que tous les citoyens sans exception reçoivent une instruction convenable et que le grand nombre bénéficie d'un enseignement avancé. On peut donc dire que la crise de l'enseignement s'inscrit dans le cadre d'une vaste crise de civilisation.[37]

Despite some controversies (especially with the clergy) and slowdowns in the implementation of the recommendations, the reform of education represented a revolutionary project for the modernization of Québec society. As far as the teaching of history/geography was concerned, the Parent Commission recommended from the outset that history be dissociated from the traditional nationalist-religious justification and focus on the scientific study of the past using historical documents.

> [T]he first aim in the teaching of history is not the development of a civic, patriotic or religious conscience. This confusion can only be harmful to history, to patriotism and to religion. The teaching of history aims to develop the human mind by the objective and honest study of the past, based on documents.[38]

The reform also sought to bridge the gap between English (Protestant) and French (Catholic) systems of education in Québec and, at the same time, to standardize Québec history programs with a positivist view of history as an "objective" social science that could unify English- and French-speaking students.

> The teaching of history in the Province of Québec has been the object of many criticisms. One of the main problems is the separation between the Protestant element, mainly English speaking, and the Catholic element, in majority French speaking. If history is a science aiming at an objective

interpretation, it is difficult to understand why it is taught from two extremely different perspectives, as it is actually [the case]. . . . As for the history of Canada, it is understandable that the French students study in greater detail the French regime, and the English students the events since 1760. But both groups have everything to gain from a good knowledge of the whole history of Canada, and the main lines of the programme could be the same for all.[39]

The Parent Commission was not alone in deploring the contemporary situation between French and English Canadians. At the federal level, the Liberal government of Lester B. Pearson actively sought to accommodate the aspirations of the Québécois by making all Canadians more conscious, and also more respectful, of Québec historical views and demands. Central to this federal effort was the Royal Commission on Bilingualism and Biculturalism, the so-called B&B Commission, created in 1963 and chaired by André Laurendeau and Davidson Dunton. The mandate of the commission was to:

[I]nquire into and report on the existing state of bilingualism and biculturalism in Canada and to recommend what steps should be taken to develop the Canadian federation on the basis of an equal partnership between the two founding races, taking into account the contribution made by other ethnic groups to the cultural enrichment of Canada and the measures that should be taken to safeguard that contribution.[40]

At the request of the B&B Commission, a study of history education in English Canada and Québec was undertaken by Marcel Trudel and Geneviève Jain. Although the original plan was to survey the objectives of the various teaching institutions, as well as provide an analysis of official courses of study, the study was restricted to "a comparative study of Canadian history textbooks in use across the country."[41] As might be expected, the comparative study of Trudel and Jain painted a bleak picture of Canadian history as found in textbooks in use in French and English Canada. Two groups of textbooks, concluded the two authors, are distinguishable:

[O]ne consisting of the English-language textbooks and the French work by Charles, considers that history is above all a field of study intended to give the future citizens a political and social education; the other, composed of French-language books, aims to inculcate a moral education.[42]

While English textbooks focused on citizenship, French (Catholic) ones, except for brother Charles' book La Nouvelle France, turn out to be "a catechism lesson or a grandiloquent sermon."[43] French textbooks were not only written in epic poetry, like heroic literature, but also focused essentially on their own national-religious "survivance" in Canada. English textbooks, on the contrary, presented a less emotional view of Canadian history with greater focus on pan-Canadian developments and the roles of (British) Europeans and immigrants.

Still, English textbooks ignored by and large the "Canadiens," their culture, language, and religion, either by portraying them as an old-fashioned rural society or by abstaining from critical analysis, preferring to focus on the great achievements of British Canadians. Supporting this view of the "infantilization of French Canadians," one English Canadian commentator educated in the period, who once visited Québec in the early 1960s, argues:

as a product of the [English] Canadian school system. . . . I expected to encounter a quaint, rustic society, less sophisticated than my own but much more fun-loving and emotional.[44]

With this lamentable state of affairs, Trudel and Jain concluded that historians urgently needed to be persuaded to take more interest in school textbooks and seriously help develop materials "conforming as closely as possible to recognized historical standards."[45] If both authors believed it would be totally unrealistic to look for one single interpretation that English and French Canada would accept, they nonetheless recommended to the B&B

Commission that schools no longer impose one national narrative that is held to be self-evident or learn from different historical accounts of the same country.

Moving from textbook analysis to classroom teaching and learning, A.B. Hodgetts came to similar conclusions in his comparative study of civic education in 1968. In all areas studied, Hodgetts' study pointed to stultifying teaching methods, bored students, a dearth of good materials published about Canada, and an excess of textbooks that offered bland consensus versions of Canadian history. He found that "much of the standardized Canadian history taught in these schools [was] antiquated and fundamentally useless."[46] Not only were French and English Canadian courses "trapped within the confines of political, constitutional or military history,"[47] but they did not make any attempt to relate the events of the past to the problems and concerns of the present time. Perhaps the most problematic finding was that students in English and French Canada (Québec) were presented a totally different understanding of Canadian culture and heritage. Hodgetts argued that "Canadian studies in the schools of both linguistic communities do so little to encourage a mutual understanding of their separate attitudes, aspirations and interest."[48]

Following the publication of the Parent Report, all existing history and geography programs were modified to reflect new social, political, and also pedagogical developments in Canadian and Québec society. Indeed, the report strongly recommended that public schools urgently adapt to modern psychological developments that place the child at the centre of his/her learning; a situation that the Parent Commission believed was lacking under the religion-dominated school system.[49]

At the elementary levels, the Ministry of Education reorganized all history and geography programs to include aspects of other social sciences under the subject of social studies ("sciences humaines") as found elsewhere in English Canada and the United States. The Ministry believed that social studies were more appropriate, at the junior levels, "to the observation of *reality* from a physical, historical, social or human point of view."[50] Clearly

in tune with the intellectual approaches proposed a few years earlier by scholars such as Jerome Bruner, inquiry methods were privileged for accomplishing this humanistic goal. To that purpose, the Ministry of Education published a social science teaching guide in which the following inquiry model was proposed: (1) research: student observes, questions, and inquires; (2) critique: student classifies, discusses, and compares data; (3) synthesis: student puts together his/her work and communicates his/her conclusions to colleagues.[51]

At the high school levels, the Ministry approved the implementation of a new course, Introduction to History, designed to initiate students to the approach of the discipline. Teachers were also encouraged to rely on chronology, autobiography, local history, and the study of other (American) civilizations. Similarly, the History of Canada course was entirely revamped after strong criticism that the teaching of history was not only negligible but also irrelevant to students. In 1970, the course Histoire du Canada 41 was created with greater emphasis on social, political, and constitutional historical events of the twentieth century. With the redefinition of French Canadian nationality as a modern liberal identity focused more exclusively on Québec, a growing number of separatists predictably advocated a more nationalist history in school in the 1970s.[52] Roy, Gauthier, and Tardif argue, however, that Québec society was in a sweeping period of modernization that was meant to expand Québécois' horizons, not to return them to obsolete nationalist views of Québec. As such, there were strong objections to make "national history a patriotic history."

> Le Québec de la Révolution tranquille se voulait une société ouverte sur le monde. On ne pouvait donc plus se permettre d'utiliser l'histoire dans une perspective bassement patriotique. Il fallait, au contraire, se servir de cette discipline pour former des citoyens éveillés à la chose publique et ouverts sur le monde.[53]

All the educational changes emerging from the Quiet Revolution that took place in the late 1960s and

1970s eventually culminated in a policy statement and plan of action published in 1979 on which the current history, geography, and social studies programs are based.[54] In 1981–1982, a set of new programs was once again implemented at the elementary and high school levels with much greater emphasis on learning outcomes (outlined in general, intermediate, and specific objectives). Social studies was designed not so much to teach historical thinking but to help students develop their comprehension of the social, geographic, economic, and historical realities of the world in which they live—a shift from the original Brunerian thinking of the 1960s.

> Ce programme s'inscrit dans une perspective de développement de la conscience individuelle et collective des enfants du cours primaire. Il leur propose un cheminement d'exploration progressive du monde, cheminement qui les amènera, à partir de leur vécu, à prendre conscience des dimensions géographiques, historiques et culturelles du réel et qui les incitera à s'engager à leur mesure et à leur manière dans le présent et le devenir de la société.[55]

The pedagogical approach recommended by the Ministry is inductive; teachers are facilitators of students' active learning. They must be familiar with the appropriate resources (not only textbooks) and be able to stimulate students' inquiry, problem-solving, and interaction with their milieu (through map readings, first-person accounts, local visits, speakers, and so on). Assessment is increasingly formative, with strong emphasis on the prescribed learning outcomes detailed in the program. The learning outcomes are based on cognitive-process orientations; that is, how students not only master knowledge but develop their various thinking and problem-solving skills. For Hensler, Raymond, and Elbaz, who analyzed this social studies program, each proposed activity "doit permettre la réalisation de plusieurs types d'apprentissages: acquisition de connaissances, habiletés, attitudes, techniques."[56]

Unlike at the elementary levels, history and geography have remained the dominant subjects at the high school levels. Two geography courses (general geography in secondary I [grade 7] and geography of Québec and Canada in secondary III [grade 9]) and two history courses (one general history in secondary II [grade 8] and one history of Canada and Québec in secondary IV [grade 10]), along with an elective world history course in secondary V [grade 11] developed in the mid-1980s, account for the bulk of history/geography taught to Québec high school students. While both secondary I geography and secondary II general history courses build on the content of social studies (at the elementary levels), by introducing students to the methods of the disciplines and developing a sense of belonging to the broader global community, history/geography of Québec and Canada focus more explicitly on the environment and communities of Québec and Canada, along with greater emphasis on disciplinary approaches. In its rationale, the history of Québec and Canada (translated for the English school system) states:

> The History of Québec and Canada course focuses on an understanding of the evolution of Québec society within the Canadian, North American, and Western contexts. It attempts to answer in a special way the questions which the pupil is asking himself about the society to which he belongs.[57]

Then it goes on to describe the suggested pedagogical approach focused on students' own learning environment:

> The study of history should help the pupil to answer questions about the present. Actual events as well as the surrounding environment confront him with a vast amount of information that he must learn to decode. History earns its rightful place in the educational process by stimulating questions in the pupil's mind, using local history of current problems.[58]

Following the previous curricular changes that emerged from the Parent Commission, history and geography programs no longer stress the recitation and memorization of facts. Rather, they help develop, through a variety of recommended teaching approaches and learning activities, the intellectual skills necessary for understanding the disciplines. In his analysis of the secondary IV history program, Christian Laville argues that the proposed pedagogy "does not emphasize recitation, but rather learning by practice. Teachers regularly look for problem-solving and inductive capacities, especially with young students."[59] Yet, Roy, Gauthier, and Tardif are much more critical of the current history programs, suggesting that the considerable amount of historical information and detailed outcomes found in the program (whole history of Québec and Canada in one year) coupled with a culminating provincial examination at the end of the year do not lend themselves easily to child-centred approaches suggested by the Ministry. As they put it:

> Le problème que l'on peut envisager ici est le suivant: comment peut-on couvrir l'ensemble des objectifs du programme tout en laissant les élèves progresser par eux-mêmes. . . .Plusieurs enseignants seront tentés de recourir à un enseignement de type magistral afin de voir l'ensemble du programme…[60]

The Latest Reform: Teaching for Citizenship

The implementation of the current Québec history, geography, and social studies programs has not gone uncontested. In the 1990s, the teaching of history and geography was being called into question by various authorities, including teachers themselves. The situation was exacerbated by failed constitutional negotiations, which were meant to officially bring Québec back into the 1982 Constitution, and by the 1995 referendum on Québec sovereignty. As in another era, increased pressure came from both sides (Québec and Canada) to put forth a "national" curriculum, or at least some kind of national standards that would provide a shared vision of history and identity for both Québécois and Canadians.[61] In Québec, a number of vocal organizations (e.g., La Société St-Jean-Baptiste) and commentators (including scholars) strongly criti-

cized, not without reason, the current history programs for their Québec or anti-Québec nationalist tones, depending on the perspective adopted.[62] Monique Nemni, for example, claimed that programs, and particularly prescribed history textbooks, continued to have a nationalist rationale by explicitly selecting or omitting significant events of Québec's national past (e.g., FLQ crisis and the War Measures Act of 1970), thus reinforcing the Parti Québécois nationalist agenda.[63] All these comments pushed the Task Force on Curriculum Reform (1997), which immediately followed the Task Force on the Teaching of History, to conclude that the question of nationalism divides Québec, but schools, and particularly history programs, cannot avoid the issue altogether in an "education for democratic citizenship."[64] So the task force asked the following questions:

> How should history be dealt with? The history of a nation centers around certain defining moments, which unify the perspective from which history is presented: American independence, the French Revolution, German unification. Why? Because the history of these countries seeks to answer the question of identity: What does it mean to be American? What does it mean to be French? What does it mean to be German? In Québec, the relative importance assigned to various defining moments changes according to how the following questions are answered: What does it mean to be Canadian? French Canadian? English Canadian? From Québec? Given this difficulty, either Québec history is neglected, or else it becomes over-specific. In both cases, there is a tendency to reduce the place of history teaching within the curriculum.[65]

Following these remarks, the task force recommended without delay that history, along with citizenship education, receive a more prominent place in the curriculum, not so much as a nation-building tool but rather to help students from increasingly different ethnic backgrounds develop the skills needed to successfully integrate into society and actively participate in its democratic future.

Others, particularly members of ethnic minorities, legitimately questioned the current employment equity policies in the teaching profession (especially with regard to Québec cultural communities) and the inclusiveness of programs still structured essentially around the historicity of French and English Canadian, and to a certain extent Native peoples.[66] Both task forces (history and curriculum) made some reference to this critical state of affairs. As a result, the government policy statement on intercultural education that followed in 1998 recognized:

[T]here is at present no citizenship education course to encourage students to participate actively in the community and help them develop a civic spirit that is attuned to a pluralistic society. The programs that treat this question do not cover it adequately. The focus on diversity is limited, and has not been generalized within the curriculum. The result is that students from other cultures have difficulty recognizing themselves in certain learning content, which may have a negative effect on their sense of belonging.[67]

Parallel to these criticisms and policy changes, some scholars, influenced by recent socio-constructivist developments in history and civic education and educational psychology in Europe and the United States, have paid increased attention to current teaching methods and students' own understandings in history.[68] Moving out from the shadow of behaviorism, these researchers have questioned not only the teaching approaches taken by history teachers but also made more explicit the necessity of taking into account what students bring to the classroom and what they take out with them when they leave school. Robert Martineau, for example, found in his study of high school history students that most of them continue to hold very instrumental views of history equated to factual recall, and to perceive history as of little use outside the classroom.[69] Not surprisingly, he linked students' negative attitudes to the type of teaching they were receiving in class. This teaching, he reported, is largely dominated by traditional lectures and textbook lessons, and geared towards the final provincial examinations, which essentially evaluate historical knowledge.[70] Other researchers, such as Jocelyn Létourneau and Stéphane Lévesque, have reported that despite more inclusive and less nationalist programs and resources, most francophone students still adhere to a Québec nationalist historical narrative, which gives pride of place to the survival and accomplishments of Québécois.[71] In both cases, however, it is not entirely clear whether these students have developed their nationalist views of Canada's past in or outside the classroom, as many factors, including the media, influence their thinking.[72]

It is in this context that the Ministry of Education implemented in 2000–2001 its new constructivist curriculum entitled Programme de formation de l'école québécoise, first at the elementary level and then at the high school level.[73] It is intended that by 2006 both elementary and high school level students will be following the new curriculum, which is centred around essential disciplinary learning and cross-subject learning ("compétences transversales"). History and citizenship education, and to a lesser degree geography, have been given a crucial role in the development of both disciplinary and cross-subject learning. More specifically, Québec students will be required to take history, geography, and citizenship from grade 3 to grade 10, which will make Québec the first province to put such heavy emphasis on citizenship education.[74]

From an historical perspective it is ironic to observe that less than forty years ago studies found that while English Canadian education systems had put greater emphasis on citizenship education, Québec was still very much focused on the inculcation of moral and religious values. Today, Québec has drastically changed its approach to history, officially making citizenship education one of its educational priorities throughout the entire public school system, a first for Canada. The recent terrorist attacks and military campaigns on the international stage only reinforce the necessity of making citizenship education a priority.[75] Claude Corbo at Université de Montréal, who chaired an earlier task force on elementary and high school learning, recently concluded that the terrorist attacks of September 11, 2001 make it clear that twenty-first-century students can no longer graduate with a limited social, historical, and civic understanding of the communities in which they live.

> [L]es événements survenus à New York et à Washington, le 11 septembre 2001, confèrent une pertinence accrue [à la nécessité d'assurer, par l'éducation, la préservation et l'épanouissement des valeurs qui nous définissent]. D'une part, il faut, par un curriculum accordant plus d'importance à l'univers social (géographie, histoire, éducation à la citoyenneté), fournir aux jeunes des moyens de comprendre des enjeux sociocritiques très complexes. . . . D'autre part, il s'impose de les rendre capables progressivement de confronter des enjeux collectifs de nature économique, social et politique dont la complexité rend les solutions simplistes invalides sinon dangereuses.[76]

All these developments, both domestic and international, have certainly not facilitated the work of educators. Québec history teachers, as Jon Bradley observes, must now deal with a host of both epistemological and pedagogical issues that can have an impact on their ability to teach for democratic citizenship.[77] Yet Québec has for the first time in Canadian school history taken the lead. The present challenge, as it was some thirty years ago, is for both French and English Canadian educators to learn from each other and develop shared conceptions of citizenship that will best advance democracy.[78]

Endnotes

[1] Task Force on the Teaching of History, *Learning from the Past* (Québec: Gouvernement du Québec, 1996), 3.

[2] Ibid., ix.

[3] Ministère de l'Éducation du Québec, *Programme de formation de l'école québécoise: éducation préscolaire et enseignement primaire* (Québec: Gouvernement du Québec, 2001), 165.

[4] Pauline Marois, quoted in Ministère de l'Éducation du Québec, *Québec School on Course: Educational Policy Statement* (Québec: Gouvernement du Québec, 1997), 3.

[5] See Penney Clark, "'Home-Grown Product' or 'Made in America'?: History of Social Studies in English Canada," in *Trends and Issues in Canadian Social Studies*, ed. Ian Wright and Alan Sears (Vancouver: Pacific Educational Press, 1997), 68.

[6] Neil Sutherland, "The Triumph of 'Formalism': Elementary Schooling in Vancouver from the 1920s to the 1960s," in *Children, Teachers, and Schools in the History of British Columbia*, ed. J. Barman, Neil Sutherland, and J.D. Wilson (Calgary: Detselig, 1995), 119.

[7] See Louis-Philippe Audet, "Society and Education in New France," in *Canadian Education: A History*, ed. J.D. Wilson, R.M. Stamp, and L.P. Audet (Scarborough, ON: Prentice-Hall, 1970), 70–85.

[8] Jean-Pierre Charland, *L'entreprise éducative au Québec, 1840–1900* (Ste-Foy: Presses de l'Université Laval, 2000), 349, 381.

[9] This is not to say, however, that history and geography were not taught in "common schools" before 1872. As found in the analysis of Simon Roy, Clermont Gauthier, and Maurice Tardif, *Évolution des programmes d'histoire de 1861 à nos jours* (Ste-Foy: Cahiers du LABRAPS, 1992), teaching history was vital to the preservation of a French Canadian identity in Québec throughout the nineteenth century. Yet, as there was no ministry of education, the development of history programs was essentially left to school board administrators and teachers.

[10] Geneviève Jain, "Nationalism and Educational Politics in Ontario and Québec: 1867–1914," in *Canadian Schools and Canadian Identity*, ed. A. Chaiton and N. McDonald (Toronto: Gage), 51.

[11] Département de l'Instruction Publique, *Code scolaire de la province de Québec* (Québec: Dussault et Proulx Imprimeurs, 1899).

[12] Département de l'Instruction Publique, *Manuel de l'instituteur catholique de la province de Québec* (Montréal: Beauchemin, 1905), 102.

[13] F.X. Toussaint, *Abrégé d'histoire du Canada à l'usage des jeunes étudiants de la province de Québec* (Québec: Librairie Langlais, 1923), 3. [*Translation*: Today this confederation has eight provinces and a territory the size of many kingdoms! It has crossed the Rockies and pushed its limits to the Pacific Ocean. A history course must mention these prodigious developments. Canadian educators have the duty to present them to their students. A national history lesson is a lesson in patriotism.]

[14] For a good discussion of the construction and (distinct) evolution of the French Canadian (*Canadien*) identity, see the works of Michel Brunet, *Canadians et canadiens* (Montréal: Fides, 1954); ———, *La Présence anglaise et les Canadiens* (Montréal: Beauchemin, 1964); Léon Dion, *Nationalismes et politique au Québec* (Montréal: Hurtubise HMH, 1975); Arthur I. Silver, *The French-Canadian Idea of Confederation, 1864–1900* (Toronto: University of Toronto Press, 1982); Paul-

André Linteau, René Duroché, and Jean-Claude Robert, *Québec: A History, 1867–1929* (Toronto: Lorimer, 1983); and Kenneth McRoberts, *Misconceiving Canada: The Struggle for National Unity* (Toronto: Oxford University Press, 1997).

15 F.X. Garneau, *Abrégé d'histoire du Canada depuis sa découverte jusqu'à 1840* (Québec: Librairie Langlais, 1865), iii. [*Translation*: School principals complain, not without reason, about the inconsistency of teaching Canadian-born children the history of foreign people and of faded nations in every detail, while remaining silent about the chivalrous adventures, heroic events, and glorious and religious epic of our young Canadian family.]

16 For a more detailed historical analysis of the "église-nation" in French Québec see Ramsay Cook, *Canada, Québec and the Uses of Nationalism,* 2nd ed. (Toronto: McClelland & Stewart, 1995), 85–97.

17 Abbé Laflèche, quoted in Cook, *Canada, Québec and the Uses of Nationalism,* 89.

18 Boucher de la Bruère, quoted in Jain, "Nationalism and Educational Politics in Ontario and Québec," 51.

19 Inspecteur Lévesque, quoted in Charland, *L'entreprise éducative au Québec,* 235–236. [*Translation*: The major problem comes from the methods employed; memorization is still playing a dominant role in schools. We find maps but they have little application or use in the classroom. The same can be said of Canadian history. We can easily find students who can aptly recite their entire textbook but few can actually make an intelligent review of the early settlements or the actions of the first French governors.]

20 Département de l'Instruction Publique, *Manuel de l'instituteur catholique de la province de Québec,* 50.

21 Thérèse Hamel, *Un siècle de formation des maîtres au Québec, 1836–1939* (LaSalle, QC: Hurtubise HMH, 1995), 311 (emphasis in the original).

22 George S. Tomkins, *A Common Countenance: Stability and Change in the Canadian Curriculum* (Scarborough, ON: Prentice-Hall, 1986), 116. As Tomkins notes, the New Education, a term originally coined in the United States in the late 1860s by scholar Charles W. Eliot and later popularized by Frances W. Parker, came to replace the "old" education that focused on the memorization of abstract subjects. The new pedagogical goals were to make students more active in their learning and to help develop the "whole child," the moral, the mental, and the physical. This movement led to the development, by the turn of the century, of new subjects (manual training, domestic science, agriculture, health, and physical education) that were seen as necessary for supporting the aims of the New Education.

23 See Roy, Gauthier, and Tardif, *Évolution des programmes d'histoire de 1861 à nos jours,* 135.

24 Comité catholique du Conseil de l'Instruction Publique, *Programme d'études des écoles élémentaires: 1959* (Québec: Gouvernement du Québec, 1959), 495–496. [*Translation*: Teachers must, as much as possible, include extra references and resources. Free reading time should be favoured; in history a certain amount of time should be allocated for personal reading. Teachers should use active teaching approaches taking into consideration individual abilities and learning styles. Group work and inquiry projects should be encouraged, as well as students demonstrating the ability to effectively communicate research findings.]

25 Jean Plante, "Évolution dans l'élaboration des programmes d'études au Québec," *Curriculum in Canada in Historical Perspective* 6 (May 1979): 29.

26 Hamel, *Un siècle de formation des maîtres au Québec,* 309.

27 Comité catholique du Conseil de l'Instruction Publique, *Programme d'études des écoles élémentaires,* 481. [*Translation*: Make students aware of the key events that define the evolution of our people, the history of our native land, and of those who contributed to what it is today. The teaching of this subject must stress the distinctive character of our unique history; the apostolic and national goals followed by our explorers, settlers, and leaders; the purity of our French Canadian origins; the religious, moral, heroic, and idealistic character of our ancestors; the constant fight against adversity; the visible protection of providence for the survival of our nationality.]

28 Claude Bilodeau, "L'histoire nationale," in *Royal Commission Studies: A Selection of Essays Prepared for the Royal Commission on National Development in the Arts, Letters, and Sciences* (Ottawa: King's Press, 1951), 217. [*Translation*: The historian has used history for patriotic lessons, obligations to ancestors, and the survival of their nationality. With their pen, authors present a history that promotes the respect of a distinct French and Catholic way of life, and gives examples of courage and strength.]

29 Abbé Arthur Maheux, "A Dilemma for Our Culture" (Ottawa: CHA/SHC report of the annual meeting, 1949), http://www.cha-shc.ca/bilingue/addresses/1949.htm.

30 Jean Bruchési, "L'enseignement de l'histoire du Canada" (Ottawa: CHA/SHC report of the annual meeting, 1952), http://www.cha-shc.ca/bilingue/addresses/1952.htm. Bruchési was also very critical of the ability of teachers to teach history given their educational training. In 1952, as president of the CHA/SHC, he claimed, "les meilleurs programmes et les meilleurs manuels ne vaudront à peu près rien entre les mains d'un maître incompétent." Quoted in Ken Osborne, " 'Our History Syllabus Has Us Gasping': History in Canadian Schools—Past, Present, and Future," *Canadian Historical Review* 81, no. 3 (September 2000), 429.

31 Guy Laviolette, *Mon Pays: Histoire du Canada* (La Prairie, QC: Procure des Frères de l'Instruction Chrétienne, 1954), 5.

32 Hermann Plante and Louis Martel, *Mon pays, synthèse d'histoire du Canada,* 3rd ed. (Québec: Éditions du Pélican, 1963), 201.

33 Gérald Filteau, *La civilisation catholique et française au Canada* (Montréal: Centre de Psychologie et de Pédagogie, 1960), 457.

34 Kenneth McRoberts, *Misconceiving Canada: The Struggle for National Unity* (Toronto: Oxford University Press, 1997), 31.

35   Guy Rocher, *Entre les rêves et l'histoire: Entretiens avec G. Khal* (Montréal: VLB Editeur, 1989), 47–48. [*Translation:* During that period, the reform of education was touching on social, economic, and cultural changes that defined what was already called the "Quiet Revolution." We explicitly looked at teaching because we believed that in order to change society, to create a new Québec, we had to rebuild the entire education system from its foundations. We honestly thought that the education system was a key influence on the future of the nation.]

36   J. Donald Wilson, "From the Swinging Sixties to the Sobering Seventies," in *Precepts, Policy and Process: Perspectives on Contemporary Canadian Education*, ed. Hugh A. Stevenson and J. Donald Wilson (London, ON: Alexander, Blake, 1977), 32.

37   Ministère de l'Éducation du Québec, *Une histoire de l'éducation au Québec* (Québec: Gouvernement du Québec, 1989): 49. [*Translation:* Everywhere we have understood that today's and even more so tomorrow's society poses unprecedented challenges for teaching. In order for civilization to progress, and survive, it is necessary that all citizens, without exception, receive public education and as many as possible have access to higher education. We can say that a crisis in education is part of a larger crisis of civilization.]

38   *Royal Commission of Inquiry on Education in the Province of Québec* (Québec: Gouvernement du Québec, 1965), 142.

39   Ibid., 140–141. For a broader discussion of the role of history in the shaping of "Canadians" during the period, see Ken Osborne, *In Defence of History: Teaching the Past and the Meaning of Democratic Citizenship*, Our Schools/Our Selves Monograph Series, no. 17 (Toronto: Our Schools/Our Selves Education Foundation, 1995), 66–67.

40   Royal Commission on Bilingualism and Biculturalism, *Preliminary Report* (Ottawa: Queen's Printer, 1965), 151.

41   Marcel Trudel and Geneviève Jain, *Canadian History Textbooks: A Comparative Study* (Ottawa: Queen's Printer, 1970), xi.

42   Ibid., 123.

43   Ibid.

44   Daniel Francis, *National Dreams: Myth, Memory, and Canadian History* (Vancouver: Arsenal Pulp Press, 1997), 88.

45   Trudel and Jain, *Canadian History Textbooks*, 132.

46   A.B. Hodgetts, *What Culture? What Heritage? A Study of Civic Education in Canada* (Toronto: OISE Press, 1968), 19.

47   Ibid., 20.

48   Ibid., 34.

49   See Conseil supérieur de l'éducation, *Rapport annuel, 1987–1988 sur l'état et les besoins de l'éducation: Le Rapport Parent 25 ans après* (Québec: Gouvernement du Québec, 1988), 52–53.

50   Ministry of Education, quoted in Task Force on the Teaching of History, *Learning from the Past*, 10.

51   See Ministère de l'Éducation du Québec, *Diverses approches dans l'enseignement des sciences humaines à l'élémentaire* (Québec: Gouvernement du Québec, 1973), 8–9.

52   For a more detailed analysis of the influence of nationalist views on Québec school history, see Eric Bédard, "Parti québécois et l'enseignement de l'histoire," *Bulletin d'histoire politique* 5 (1997): 38–47.

53   Roy, Gauthier, and Tardif, *Évolution des programmes d'histoire de 1861 à nos jours*, 164. [*Translation:* The Quiet Revolution was meant to open society to the world. So we could no longer accept utilizing history for a purely patriotic mission. On the contrary, we had to use the discipline to create enlightened citizens open to public affairs and to the world.]

54   Ministère de l'Éducation du Québec, *L'École québécoise: énoncé de politique et plan d'action* (Québec: Gouvernement du Québec, 1979).

55   Ministère de l'Éducation du Québec, *Programme d'études: Primaire, sciences humaines*, 3. [*Translation:* In keeping with a perspective of individual and collective development, this program favours a learning progression, based on lived experiences, which will make students aware of the geographic, historical, and cultural dimensions of their society and its future.]

56   Hélène Hensler, Danielle Raymond, and Freema Elbaz, *Analyse comparative et critique des nouveaux programmes d'études du primaire* (Sherbrooke, QC: Éditions du CRP, 1986), 12.

57   Ministère de l'Éducation du Québec, *Secondary School Curriculum: History of Québec and Canada, Secondary 4* (Québec: Gouvernement du Québec, 1983), 16.

58   Ibid.

59   Christian Laville, "History Taught in Québec Is Not Really that Different from the History Taught Elsewhere in Canada," *Canadian Social Studies* 31 (Fall 1996): 23.

60   Roy, Gauthier, and Tardif, *Évolution des programmes d'histoire de 1861 à nos jours*, 201. [*Translation:* The problem we can anticipate is as follows: how can teachers cover the entire curricular objectives while allowing students time to progress and learn at their own pace. . . .Many teachers will be tempted to use teacher-centred lectures to meet the objectives. . . .]

61   For examples of works dealing with "national" history in Québec, see Micheline Dumont, "Pour sortir de l'ambiguïté," *Bulletin d'histoire politique* 5 (1997): 16–29; Jack L. Granatstein, *Who Killed Canadian History?* (Toronto: HarperCollins, 1998); Robert Comeau and Bernard Dionne, eds., *À propos de l'histoire nationale* (Sillery, QC: Presses Universitaires du Septentrion, 1998); John Meisel, Guy Rocher, and Arthur Silver, *Si je me souviens bien/As I recall: Historical Perspectives* (Montréal: Institut de Recherche en Politiques Publiques, 1999); Gérard Bouchard, *La nation au futur et au passé* (Montréal: VLB, 1999); Jocelyn Létourneau, "L'avenir du Canada: par rapport à quelle histoire?" *Canadian Historical Review* 81 (June 2000): 230–259; Michel Venne, ed., *Penser la nation québécoise* (Montréal: Québec Amerique, 2000); and Gérard Bouchard, *Genèse des nations et cultures*

du nouveau monde (Montréal: Boréal, 2000).

62 See, for instance, the arguments presented by René Durocher, "L'enseignement de l'histoire du Québec et du Canada: Peut-on faire les deux en même temps?" (working paper, McGill Institute for the Study of Canada, Montréal, 1996), 29–33; Louis Lafrance, "Des étudiants sans histoire," *Le Devoir*, October 22, 1996, B1; Josée Legault, "Histoire d'exister," *Bulletin d'histoire politique* 5 (1997), 13–15; Claude Richard, "Des manuels d'histoire incomplets et partiaux," *Le Devoir*, January 15, 1997, A8; and Monique Nemni, "Canada: The Case of the Vanishing Country," *Cité Libre* 26 (June 1998): 61–71.

63 For a comparative analysis of Québec and Ontario history textbooks, see Winifred Braunsch, "A Comparative Study of Canadian History Textbooks: Ontario and Québec in 2001" (master's thesis, University of Western Ontario, 2001).

64 The notion of teaching citizenship received increased attention in Québec education in the late 1990s. Following the Estates General on Education (1995), the Conseil supérieur de l'éducation (CSE) published a special report in 1998 in which the members explicitly advised the minister to put forth a plan of action for citizenship education. The CSE reported that pluralism, civic apathy, changing identities, globalization, and Québec's particular context force Québec society to revisit its education objectives and put greater emphasis on teaching and living citizenship in school. See CSE, *Éduquer à la citoyenneté: rapport annuel* (Québec: Gouvernement du Québec, 1998). During the same period, a small number of Québec scholars also intensified their research on citizenship education. See Marie McAndrew and Caroline Tessier, "L'éducation à la citoyenneté en milieu québécois: situation actuelle et perspectives comparatives," *Canadian Ethnic Studies* 29 (1997): 58–81; Brian Young, "L'éducation à la citoyenneté et l'historien professionel: quelques hypothèses," in *À propos de l'histoire nationale*, ed. R. Comeau and B. Dionne (Sillery, QC: Presses Universitaires du Septentrion, 1998), 57–64; Robert Martineau and Christian Laville, "L'histoire: voie royale vers la citoyenneté?" *Vie pédagogique* 109 (December 1998): 35–38; and Christian Laville, "Histoire et éducation civique: échec notoire, solution simple," (paper presented at the Citizenship 2020/Citoyenneté 2020 conference, McGill Institute for the Study of Canada, October 2000). More recently, a number of Québec scholars and graduate students have presented research papers at the annual meetings of the Citizenship Education Research Network (CERN), a pan-Canadian group of interested researchers, policy-makers, practitioners, and stakeholders in citizenship education. The papers can be accessed at http://canada.metropolis.net/research-policy/cern-pub/index.html.

65 Task Force on Curriculum Reform, *Reaffirming the Mission of Our Schools* (Québec: Gouvernement du Québec, 1997), 34–35.

66 For a more extensive discussion on intercultural education, pluralism, and education in Québec, see Fernand Ouellet, ed., *Les institutions face aux défis du pluralisme ethnoculturel* (Québec: Institut québécois de recherche sur la culture, 1995); France Gagnon, Marie McAndrew, and Michel Pagé, eds., *Pluralisme, citoyenneté et éducation* (Montréal: Harmattan, 1996); Marie McAndrew, "De l'interculturel au civique: 20 ans d'approche québécoise," in *Diversité humaine. Démocratie, multiculturalisme et citoyenneté*, ed. L.K. Sosoe (Ste-Foy: Presses de l'Université Laval, 2002), 537–540; and Guy Bourgeault and Cynthia Hamel, "Diversité ethnoculturelle et profession enseignante: état de la situation à l'Université de Montréal et éléments de problématique," in *L'intégration des minorités visibles et ethnoculturelles dans la profession enseignante: Récits d'expériences, enjeux et perspectives*, ed. D. Mujawamariya (Montréal: Éditions Logiques, 2002), 29–45.

67 Ministère de l'Éducation du Québec, *A School for the Future: Policy Statement on Education Integration and Intercultural Education* (Québec: Gouvernement du Québec, 1998), 12.

68 For European and North American examples, see Jacqueline Costa-Lascoux, "L'enfant, citoyen à l'école," *Revue française de pédagogie* 101 (1992): 71–78; François Audigier, *L'éducation à la citoyenneté* (Paris: Institut National de Recherche Pédagogique, 1999); ———, "School Disciplines, Social Representations, and the Construction of the Didactics of History, Geography, and Civics," *Instructional Science* 27 (1999): 97–117; Peter N. Stearns, Peter Seixas, and Samuel Wineburg, eds., *Knowing, Teaching and Learning History: National and International Perspectives* (New York: New York University Press, 2000); Samuel Wineburg, *Historical Thinking and Other Unnatural Acts: Charting the Future of Teaching the Past* (Philadelphia: Temple University Press, 2001); and Linda Levstik and Keith Barton, *Doing History: Investigating with Children in Elementary and Middle Schools* (Mahwah, NJ: Lawrence Erlbaum, 2001).

69 Robert Martineau, *L'histoire à l'école: matière à penser* (Montréal: L'Harmattan, 1999).

70 See also Martineau's critical comments on Québec textbooks and learning guides in Mireille Jobin, "Les cahiers d'exercices en classe: l'histoire de quelques dérives," *Vie Pédagogique* 124 (September/October 2002): 20–23.

71 Jocelyn Létourneau, "De la mémoire historique des jeunes franco-québécois d'héritage canadien-français," *CHA/SHC Bulletin* 28.3 (2002): 1–2; and Stéphane Lévesque, "Journey into the World of the School: High School Students' Understandings of Citizenship in B.C. and Québec," (doctoral dissertation, University of British Columbia, 2001).

72 For an interesting perspective on the position(s) and influence of the Québec press and intellectuals on Canadian history, see the inside story of Mark Starowicz, the man behind the CBC/SRC series "Canada: A People's History," in his *Making History* (Toronto: McClelland & Stewart, 2003). Starowicz argues, based on his experience, "nowhere in this country is the subject of history more volatile than in Québec. But as the hostility in Radio-Canada and the press mounted, the

more amazed I became at the defensiveness. . . . The very
act of doing a history of Canada meant that we were twisting
it to suit some federalist fiction" (p. 315).

73 Ministère de l'Éducation du Québec, *Programme de formation
de l'école québécoise*.

74 See also Jean-François Cardin, "The Construction of History
Curriculum in Québec: Lessons for Canada" (lecture, Visiting
Scholars Program, Centre for the Study of Historical
Consciousness, University of British Columbia, June 6, 2002).

75 For a more detailed analysis of Canadian school history and
terrorism, see my article " 'Bin Laden Is Responsible; It was
Shown on Tape': Canadian High School Students' Historical
Understanding of Terrorism," *Theory and Research in Social
Education* 31 (2003): 51–81. See also the special editions of
Social Education 65 (December 2001) and *Canadian Issues/
Thèmes Canadiens* (September 2002).

76 Claude Corbo, "Les enjeux essentiels d'une réforme scolaire
annoncée," *Vie pédagogique* 121 (November/December 2001):
8–9. [*Translation*: The attacks of September 11, 2001 in New
York and Washington, DC, increased the necessity of
preserving our public education and the values that define
it. On the one hand, we need a curriculum with greater focus
on social education (history, geography, citizenship) so as to
teach students the complexities of current issues. On the
other hand, we must engage students in the critical study
of complex economic, social, and political problems that
render the adoption of simple solutions invalid, if not
dangerous.]

77 Jon G. Bradley, "The Teaching of History in Québec," CHA/
SHC *Bulletin* 28.1 (2002): 19.

78 For a similar, more recent argument, see Michael Ignatieff,
"The History that Matters Most," in *Great Questions of Canada*,
ed. R. Griffiths (Toronto: Stoddart, 2000), 7–24.

CHAPTER 4

History and Social Studies: Partners or Rivals?

Ken Osborne

Introduction

In this chapter I examine the debate that has been waxing and waning since at least the 1920s over whether we should teach history as a discipline in its own right or blend into an interdisciplinary social studies that draws on all the social sciences. To do so I examine what seem to me to be the five main claims and counterclaims made on either side of the debate. Though I write as a supporter of history and therefore a critic of social studies, I have tried to examine the arguments as dispassionately as I know how. As often as not, the debate is more an exchange of slogans than a reasoned investigation of the issues. In what follows, I have tried to avoid the former and concentrate on the latter in the hope that, regardless of which side of the divide readers choose to join, they will do so knowing what the argument is all about.

Broadly speaking, there are three conceptions of social studies. One sees it as a purely administrative label embracing history, geography, and perhaps other subjects such as economics or sociology, all taught separately as single disciplines. In the late 1960s, for example, I was social studies department head in a Winnipeg high school but the department taught only history and geography courses, except for one world problems course that was largely a combination of the other two subjects. We treated the term "social studies" as a timetabling and reporting convenience and nothing more. The second con-

ception sees social studies as "the social sciences simplified for pedagogical purposes," usually taught in some integrated form and organized around themes, such as technology, democracy, human rights, and many others.[1] The third sees social studies as an interdisciplinary subject in its own right, "the integrated study of the social sciences and humanities to promote civic competence."[2] These last two conceptions are the subject of this chapter.

The question of whether or not history is preferable to social studies, or vice versa, has long been contentious, but it has assumed a renewed importance with today's heightened interest in citizenship education. In addition, the current wave of curriculum development exemplified in the Western Canada Protocol for Social Studies, the Atlantic Canada Social Studies Curriculum, and the revision of the history curriculum in Québec, all discussed elsewhere in this volume, gives it practical as well as theoretical significance. It has assumed particular vehemence in the United States, where projects to define national standards in history, geography, and civics conspicuously ignored social studies, with the result that the struggle between defenders of social studies and advocates of the traditional disciplines have become part of the culture wars over the shape of American education.[3]

The question also runs through current debates over the state of history in Canadian schools, with some commentators blaming the rise of interdisciplinary social studies for what they see as the elimination of history from school curricula.[4] In Canada, social studies displaced history from the early grades in the 1930s, but, except for Alberta, which made social studies the core of its curriculum through high school early on, it was not until the 1970s, under the influence of the so-called "new social studies" in the United States, that it began to reshape the secondary school curriculum, first in the form of interdisciplinary courses in Canadian Studies and then courses in contemporary issues and the social sciences.[5] Today the momentum seems to lie not with history or geography, but with social studies. At the moment (2003), there is a disjuncture between overall statements of curricular purpose, which increasingly speak the language of interdisciplinary social studies, and actual courses of study, which often remain based on history and geography, especially in the high schools, but this seems likely to change as curriculum development proceeds and social studies gains in popularity. A few years ago, only Alberta organized its K–12 curriculum in the form of interdisciplinary social studies. Today, only Québec and to some extent Manitoba are not planning to do so, while curriculum documents across Canada increasingly borrow from the version of social studies promoted by the National Council for the Social Studies in the United States.

The question thus arises: Are history and social studies partners or rivals? This chapter explores this question by examining five claims that, in various forms, recur at regular intervals on either the history or social studies side of the debate. Limitations of space have forced me to omit much detail and many references, and many of those I include are American rather than Canadian.[6] This, however, reflects the reality that until very recently the debate has been largely based in the United States, although it has had consequences for Canada, where curriculum development in social studies has largely followed American models. Though I write as a supporter of history, I do not, unlike some of history's defenders, see social studies as inherently flawed. There are persuasive arguments for teaching social studies, and in a perfect world we should no doubt teach both social studies and history. However, curricula are already overcrowded and there is simply not enough time to teach everything we think we should be taught. As a result, curriculum development entails making tough choices. This being so, my choice is for history. All things being equal, I believe that history, properly organized and taught, offers a better education than does interdisciplinary social studies. It is, in my view, a better preparation for citizenship and a better vehicle for the attainment of that informed, constructive skepticism that is the goal of liberal education.

Claims and Counterclaims

Historians' criticisms of social studies can be summarized as follows. One, social studies lacks conceptual and philosophical coherence and so cannot serve as the foundation of an intellectually cohesive curriculum. Two, social studies is too oriented to the study of current affairs and contemporary problems and does not do justice to the past. Three, social studies does not pay enough attention to the teaching of historical thinking and the value of a broad understanding of the past. Four, social studies is more an exercise in socialization than education and takes an unduly passive and functionalist view of citizenship. Five, social studies is based on a faulty theory of learning and takes too limited a view of what students can do.

Defenders of social studies stand these objections on their head. They argue that, one, history is often little more than a pointless coverage of quickly forgotten information, a mind-deadening recital of one-damned-thing-after-another that bores most students and serves no useful intellectual or social purpose. Two, they see history's concern with the past as obstructing attention to the present, and maintain that an understanding of the past is educationally useful only to the extent that it helps us understand the present and shape the future. Three, they note that many history courses do not in fact teach students to think historically, that the value of historical thinking can be exaggerated, and that in any case the elements of it that matter are included in social studies. Four, they point out that social studies is the only subject in the curriculum that takes education for citizenship as its explicit goal and that citizenship is central to the health of democracy. They also maintain that social studies is no more an exercise in socialization than is history, which has often been taught as an instrument of nationalist, racist, sexist, or other propaganda. Five, they insist that social studies does not underestimate students' capabilities and in fact pays more attention to students' needs and interests than does history.

Claim 1: Social studies lacks conceptual and philosophical coherence and so cannot serve as the foundation of an intellectually cohesive curriculum.

From its beginnings in the early 1900s, critics of social studies have attacked what they variously call its incoherence, its ambiguity, and its unrealistic ambitiousness. In recent years the most eloquent spokesperson for this line of argument has been Kieran Egan at Simon Fraser University, who some twenty years ago wrote of social studies, "[C]onceptually, it lacks the logical and psychological principles necessary to give it a coherent structure."[7] Seeing in social studies an "erosion of education," Egan described its aims as consisting of "vacuous generalities" of "mind-numbing vagueness" distinguished by their "ideological innocence."[8] Moreover, its organization is "so confused that it tries to work with conflicting principles of content selection."[9] The result, according to Egan, is that the social studies "has not worked, does not work, and cannot work."[10]

Most defenders of social studies reject these and similar charges. Writing in 1939, Edgar Wesley argued that social studies had a "fortunate and clarifying effect" and provided "a clearer conception of the function and responsibility of the schools with respect to their social obligations." He also reminded teachers that history alone was not an adequate foundation for a curriculum and that the social sciences must not be ignored.[11] On the other hand, some social studies advocates acknowledge their subject's "ambiguity, inconsistency, and contradiction," going so far as to call it "a schizophrenic bastard child."[12] Some see this as a strength not a weakness, a sign of the dynamism of social studies: "Because the present is always changing and because there are as many futures as there are possibilities, social studies will never be static; instead it will remain the dynamic domain of the becoming."[13] Others see it less positively and over the years have offered various remedies, arguing that decision-making, or the analysis of social issues or concepts, should form the organizing thread that holds social studies together. However, according to one social studies theorist, "The history of efforts to reform social studies is replete with false starts, curricular fads, blind alleys, and heroic efforts amid ongoing theological conflicts over what should be taught in schools."[14] Historians see this weakness as inherent in the very concept of social studies and thus beyond remedy. From its beginnings, they maintain, social studies has been a concept in search of a definition.[15]

The current official (in the sense that it is endorsed by the National Council for the Social Studies in the United States) definition of social studies is as follows:

> Social studies is the integrated study of the social sciences and humanities to promote civic competence. Within the school program, social studies provides coordinated, systematic study drawing upon such disciplines as anthropology, archaeology, economics, geography, history, law, philosophy, political science, psychology, religion, and sociology, as well as appropriate content from the humanities, mathematics, and natural sciences. The primary purpose of social studies is to help young people develop the ability to make informed and reasoned decisions for the public good as citizens of a culturally diverse, democratic society in an interdependent world.[16]

Even a cursory reading of this statement reveals some ambiguities. It is not clear, for example, whether social studies is an of amalgam of its component disciplines, as suggested by such words as "integrated" and "coordinated," or simply draws upon them as needed while leaving them intact. Moreover, in drawing not only on the social sciences, but also on the humanities, and even on mathematics and the natural sciences, social studies comes close to embracing the whole curriculum. Nor are the ten "strands" that accompany the definition uniquely social. "Individual development and identity," for example, which constitute one of the strands, are as well served by literature as by the social sciences, while "science, technology and society" obviously have as much to with science as with social studies.

Similarly, the goal of "civic competence" is something to which every subject contributes, as does the so-called hidden curriculum of schooling. The definition equates civic competence with "the ability to make informed and reasoned decisions for the public good," but this raises as many questions as it answers. Making such decisions, no matter how reasoned and informed, is likely to entail conflict, especially in a "culturally diverse, democratic society," but the definition avoids this reality. Instead, it conveys an impression of free and equal citizens working harmoniously together, united by a shared vision of the public good, as though society were simply a town-meeting writ large. And it is not at all clear what the final phrase of the definition adds to the goal of civic competence: just what are the curricular implications of living in an "interdependent world"?

Finally, the definition's emphasis on civic competence as the "primary purpose" of social studies draws attention to the absence of any other goals. The definition is silent, for example, about such things as intellectual development, cultural literacy, the widening of students' horizons, the enlarging of any sense of alternatives and choices, a sense of connectedness with the past, an informed awareness of heritage. As important as it is, there is more to education than citizenship and more to citizenship than civic competence.

Even so, argue advocates of social studies, there is no other subject in the curriculum that takes the teaching of citizenship as its explicit goal. Few people would deny that the health of democracy depends on a flourishing civil society, the informed participation of citizens in public life, and their commitment to democratic principles and values. Moreover, democratic citizenship has to be learned—and therefore taught. However, to say that every subject teaches citizenship runs a very real risk that no one

teaches it, as science teachers concentrate on science, mathematics teachers on mathematics, and so on, especially when schools are told to emphasize the teaching of basic skills and prepare students for the world of work. This is why, for example, England has recently installed citizenship as a compulsory subject in its school curriculum.[17] Citizenship is, of course, a much contested word, as described elsewhere in this volume, but, at the very least, it requires that citizens possess the necessary knowledge, skills, and values to play an informed role in public affairs in ways that are consistent with and reinforce democratic principles. Thus, citizenship education is essential and social studies is, above all, the subject that consciously sets out to deliver it. As supporters of social studies see it, history does not provide a sufficient basis for citizenship education, which must incorporate elements of such subjects as sociology, law, economics, political studies, and other social sciences. In an ideal world, they continue, we could perhaps teach both medieval history and the basic principles of economics, but, since choices must be made, it is more important that citizens have at least a minimal understanding of economic concepts than of the feudal system.

The ambiguities that exist in general definitions of social studies do not necessarily exist in specific programs within social studies, some of which have displayed a high degree of conceptual coherence and intellectual rigour. Examples include Harold Rugg's *Man and His Changing Society* program of the 1920s and 1930s; the Harvard Social Studies Project of the 1960s and 1970s; and the *Man: A Course of Study* program of the same period.[18] There is not space to describe them here but, whatever one thinks of their educational value, there can be little doubt of their theoretical strengths. Nor can it be doubted that they worked. In fact, they worked so successfully that in the 1940s Rugg's *Man and His Changing Society* program and in the 1960s the *Man: A Course of Study* curriculum were shut down by cultural conservatives afraid of their success.[19] Such programs, however, are the exception, not the rule, and many social studies programs, as they are taught, leave much to be desired. According to one survey of the field, "The belief among social studies educators that social studies should focus on problems confronting the society . . . makes the social studies susceptible to the inclusion of any topic that can be termed a 'problem.'" The result is that social studies is especially "susceptible to topical fads promoted by well-meaning advocates."[20]

Defenders of social studies observe that history has been no more immune to topical fads than any other subject, including social studies. Over the years special interest groups and policy-makers alike have taken control of history for their own ideological purposes. A century or so ago policy-makers installed history in the school curriculum, not because they valued the study of the past for its own sake, but because they saw history as a means of instilling patriotism and nationalism in the young—which is why H.G. Wells held history teachers largely to blame for the chauvinistic nationalism that he saw as responsible for World War I.[21] Today's history educators disagree about whether or not to teach national history; about what comprises national history; about the balance of local, regional, national, and global history that should be taught; about whether to teach history chronologically or in some other way; about whether there is one agreed-on version of the past that all students should learn; about the balance among political, social, and other forms of history; about the proper balance between historical knowledge and historical thinking; and other such curricular questions.

Peter Seixas has described three orientations to history education which, he suggests, might be fundamentally at odds with each other. They are the traditional "single best story" approach found in most curricula and textbooks; the "disciplinary" approach, which emphasizes historical method and historical thinking rather than the coverage of subject matter; and the "postmodern" approach in which students neither learn the one best story nor evaluate different accounts of the past in order to see whether such a story is possible, but instead examine "how different groups organize the past into histories and how their rhetorical and narratological strategies serve present-day purposes."[22] In short, history today seems to be as muddled and incoherent as social studies is said to be.

Whatever history once was, historians have for some years been describing it as in a state of crisis, "the gravest perhaps since the emergence of history as an organized profession about a hundred years ago," one historian wrote recently.[23] Old ideals of objectivity are called into question; social, cultural, and other historians explore new paradigms; narrative history is challenged by other forms of synthesis; established periodizations are overturned; new criteria of significance are constructed; specialization leads to fragmentation; postmodern self-awareness puts established modes of historical practice under the microscope. As one historian has recently observed, "As the discipline has expanded, embracing new historical themes far from what used to be taken as the essence of the curriculum, and with a marked defensiveness prompted by the gnawing of self-doubts created by postmodernist philosophies, it has become ever less clear and more open to dispute precisely what that discipline is, what a university syllabus should comprise, and what purpose history serves."[24] According to another historian, by the 1980s, "As a broad community of discourse, as a community of scholars united by common aims, common standards and common purposes, the discipline of history had ceased to exist."[25] If social studies lacks coherence, so, it seems, does history.

It seems to me, however, that there is an important difference between the two alleged crises. The crisis of social studies arises from its weaknesses, which social studies theorists spend more time analyzing than seeking to remedy.[26] The crisis of history, on the other hand (and not all historians see it as a crisis), arises from its strengths, as new conceptualizations of the discipline, new research methods, and new findings enlarge its scope and open up previously ignored areas of human behaviour. It is true that not all historians see this growth in positive terms. Apart from those who worry over what they see as the fragmentation and over-specialization of history and the erosion of any agreed narrative of the past, there are those who take issue with what they describe as "victimology," "compensatory" history, or "black arm-band" history. They use these pejoratives to label such fields as women's history, Native history, Black history, working-class history, and other forms of history-from-below, which they see as concentrating on the negative aspects of the past and exposing the abuses of the nation state, rather than celebrating its triumphs. Such criticisms are misguided, however. They ignore the reality that the old national narratives were often partial and biased accounts of the past that left out whole areas of the human experience.[27] The work of social historians, with their opening up of aspects of the past that were previously known only to specialists, if known at all, has enormously enriched both our understanding of the past and our ability to make it interesting to students. What traditionally minded historians see as history's crisis is better seen as its golden age. To the extent that there is a crisis in history, it is a product of the discipline's vigorous and apparently uncontrollable growth, a sign of health, not of decline. The crisis of social studies, by contrast, is one of doubt and confusion, a sign of its search to escape from a pedagogical dead end.

Nonetheless, the growth of history has undoubtedly complicated the task of curriculum development. The old history was clear about its educational aims. The new history is much more confused. It offers no clear guide for the selection of content or even the definition of aims and objectives. As the experiences of the National History Curriculum in England and the National History Standards in the United States have shown, curriculum development in history can be a political and pedagogical minefield.[28] There have been, and are, coherent programs within the discipline of history, as in social studies, ranging from Fred Morrow Fling's source-method in the early 1900s, to Edwin Fenton's new history in the 1960s, and Britain's School Council 13–16 Project more recently, but their existence should not obscure the reality that in many instances history in the schools has been as intellectually barren as social studies is claimed to be by its critics.[29]

Claim 2: In its emphasis on current affairs and contemporary problems, social studies does not do justice to the past.

To this accusation defenders of social studies reply that it describes a virtue, not a fault, since the whole point of social studies is to help students understand the world in which they live. Moreover, they observe, historians' interest in the past is usually the product of a wish to make sense of the present. They further point out that social studies does not ignore the past, but concentrates on those aspects of the past that help explain the present.

Historians argue that this selective approach to the past ignores its "otherness," its very past-ness, by seeing it only as the seedbed of present trends. From the historian's perspective, what is important about the past is its difference from the present. As one history educator put it years ago, "But if we seek to understand what the past was, and how the present grew out of it, our fundamental question must be not what matters *now* but what mattered *then*. . . ."[30] Admittedly, historians are not unanimous on this point; some emphasize continuity, others emphasize change. All, however, try to see the past on its own terms. One of the more persuasive arguments in defence of history is that it enables us to see through the conventional wisdom of the present by showing us times and places where things were done differently. As historians see it, to view the past only in terms of its relevance to the present or to study only those aspects of the past that help make sense of the present is to blunt history's challenge to society's taken-for-granted assumptions, to ignore the roads not taken, the alternatives not pursued in the past. It turns history into a story of winners whose influence we can trace into the present, and losers, who in the well-known words of historian E.P. Thompson, are thereby subject to "the enormous condescension of posterity."[31]

Historians argue that delving into the past to explain the origins of isolated topics (this month Confederation, next month immigration, and so on) destroys its coherence and prevents students from seeing how different lines of development—social, political, intellectual, economic, and so forth—interact over time. We understand a phenomenon in the past not by isolating it from its context and seeing how it affects the present, but by connecting it with other phenomena proceeding simultaneously with it. An understanding of the past requires attending to context and chronology, to seeing the events of the past as episodes in a continuing drama. Years ago, the influential history educator Henry Johnson described this as "development," arguing that the social studies approach to the past prevented students from seeing how development, which he insisted was very different from progress, took place historically. In his view, "the historical idea of development," together with historical method, should be "the controlling aim of school instruction in history."[32]

Historians also believe that the concentration of social studies on contemporary problems and issues will not properly prepare students for citizenship, even though this is the central objective of social studies education. What is important today might not be important thirty years from now and, to the extent that citizenship education means preparing students for an unpredictable future, programs organized around current issues might not prepare students for the issues they will face as adult citizens. The best way to prepare for the future is to understand the past.

Defenders of social studies are not persuaded by such arguments. They believe that social studies can be just as effective as history in teaching students about the "otherness" of the past and about alternatives to our taken-for-granted assumptions. To study alternatives to Canada's current political system, for example, we do not have to go back to Athens and Sparta, to medieval monarchy, or to the French Revolution. We can look instead to other political systems currently in existence. And if the goal is to develop in students a wider awareness of the diversity of human behaviour and culture, then anthropology is at least as useful as history. Defenders of social studies agree that to understand the present we must know something about the past, but insist that, since we cannot teach the whole of the known past, we have to select those aspects of it that seem most important, and this means concentrating on those topics that help us better understand the present and plan for the future. Thus, why not begin with the present and work back into the past as needed? Such a procedure would be more interesting and intelligible to students, most of whom are more interested in the present than the past anyway. It is also consistent with the long-standing peda-gogical principle of moving from the known to the unknown. Indeed, some historians write history this way, employing a reverse chronology that moves from the present backwards into the past.[33]

Whatever their approaches to chronology, historians argue that to concentrate on contemporary issues shortchanges the young and distorts the past. If children do in fact live in the present, this is all the more reason to stretch their thinking by introducing them to the past. In these historians' view, to use the past only as a source of case studies for use in the present obscures the interaction of change and continuity over time, and destroys any sense of history as an ongoing narrative, however provisional and contested, linking past, present, and future, while also obstructing the development of the historical consciousness that is so crucial to citizenship and human understanding. Students can learn about selected aspects of the past from a social studies course, but only history can give them a sense of the sweep of human experience over time, an understanding of how human beings have sought to come to terms with each other and with their environment, and an informed awareness of the wide range of human behaviour.

Claim 3: Social studies does not pay enough attention to the teaching of historical thinking and the value of a broad understanding of the past.

For the past hundred years, historians have seen historical thinking and historical method as central to the teaching of history. Few went as far as Fred Morrow Fling, who in the 1890s declared method to be more important than subject matter and argued that the "study of proof" should be the centrepiece of any history curriculum, but all agreed that the study of history involved more than memorizing facts.[34] They wanted history to be an "educational" and not simply an "informational" subject. In the 1890s, historians saw history's educational value in terms of the development of what they variously called historical thinking, historical mindedness, historical culture, the historical outlook, and the historic sense. Today they are more likely to speak of historical consciousness. Whatever the term, it comprises a basic familiarity with historical method and a way of looking at the world that is historically informed. For historian Mary Sheldon Barnes, the historic sense was "the sense by which we enter into the life of universal man (sic)." In her words:

> Wherever man has lived, we feel and know; our personality is widened by the personality of ages and races; until we run back for thousands of years, and out into thousands of souls; and equipped with this wider personality, this new environment of intellectual and spiritual existence, we find ourselves able more deftly and certainly to understand the present and foresee the future.[35]

Historical mindedness includes the ability to think in terms of development over time; to balance causes and effects; to detach oneself from the preoccupations of the moment; to situate the present in the context of the known past and the unknown future; to see the world as others see it; to accept that change and continuity are constants in human life; to appreciate the contingency of the present and the malleability of the future; and, above all, to see beyond the conventional wisdom of one's time and place — all of which depend, not only on an understanding of history as a discipline, but also on the possession of a broad historical knowledge that social studies, by definition, cannot deliver. Social studies can and often does include some study of the past. It can teach some of the elements of historical method. It cannot teach students to be historically minded, since this demands a familiarity with the broad sweep of the past and an ability to see it historically, which only the study of history can provide.

Defenders of social studies see things differently. In their view, a good social studies course can effectively introduce students to the idea of alternative futures, give them a sense of the contingency of the present, and illuminate its links with the past. They observe that history, especially in its more Whiggish versions, has often been used not just to explain, but to justify the present and that, no matter how hard they might try, historians cannot escape the assumptions and preoccupations of their own times, so that, as the philosopher Benedetto Croce famously observed, all history is in a sense contemporary history.

The National Council for the Social Studies includes "time, continuity, and change" as one of the ten "thematic strands" of social studies, though it defines it rather narrowly as the study of "the ways human beings view themselves in and over time."[36] The NCSS also speaks of the importance of "historical perspective," but confines it largely to questions of personal identity, defining it as the capacity to answer such questions as:

> Who am I? What happened in the past? How am I connected to those in the past? How has the world changed and how might it change in the future? Why does our personal sense of relatedness to the past change? How can the perspective we have about our own life experiences be viewed as part of the larger human story across time? How do our personal stories reflect varying points of view and inform contemporary ideas and actions?[37]

The NCSS formulation centres social studies on the experience and concerns of students. Historians concede that this emphasis on the personal might be a necessary pedagogical strategy in order to make the past real and intelligible to students who, by definition, are lacking in maturity and experience. They deny that it should shape the goals of history education. Most historians would argue that the educational function of history is to move us out of our personal frame of reference. The question is not, "How am I connected to those in the past?" but rather, "What does the past tell us about the range and variety of human behaviour, about what it means to be human?" By contrast, social studies focuses on the experience and concerns of students. This has been a preoccupation of social studies ever since its establishment as a school subject by the influential 1916 American report, *Social Studies in Secondary Schools,* with its argument that curricula should be organized around students' "present life interests" on the assumption that "children live in the present and not in the past. The past becomes educational to them only as it is related to the present."[38]

For historians, this is too restrictive a view. They value history for its ability to take us beyond our present life interests, to enlarge our sense of identity by introducing us to the life interests of others, past and present, and so help us think more deeply about what we might otherwise take for granted. History certainly can be and has been used to enhance personal and group identity, thus becoming not a critical assessment of the past but a self-congratulatory and exclusionary pride in heritage. Nationalism thrives on a selective approach to history, designed to celebrate the glories of the allegedly national past. Properly taught, however, history helps us to step outside our identity and heritage and to re-imagine them. It shows them to be historical constructs and makes them subjects of investigation rather than causes for celebration.[39]

The NCSS concepts of time, continuity, and change do not do justice to the richness and complexity of history. They describe an obvious reality that any child soon recognizes: time passes, some things change, some things stay the same. The challenge for the historian is to apply the concepts of continuity and change to specific historical phenomena. How revolutionary were the French and Russian Revolutions, for example? To what extent did they perpetuate features of pre-revolutionary society and to what extent did they break from it? And if change occurred, change for whom? For men? For women? For elites? For people at large? If the concepts of continuity and change are to mean anything, they must be applied to concrete historical phenomena, otherwise they are banal statements of the obvious. But to study such phenomena, especially with school-age students, involves much more than clarifying the extent to which they exemplify continuity and change. The most effective way to study continuity and change is not to focus on them as discrete concepts but to embed them in a rich and informative body of historical content that covers a large enough sweep of history to reveal their operation over a series of historical phenomena.

More fundamentally, history is more than a few concepts, no matter how comprehensive. It is the story of humanity's attempts to cope with the world in which it finds itself. The primary reason for studying history is to see how human beings have sought to cope with the problems they faced and so to enlarge our view of what it means to be human. Defenders of history see their subject as indispensable to self-knowledge and therefore to citizenship. In their view, the only way to understand what human beings are capable of, for good or ill, is to see what they have done. Advocates of social studies reply that historical knowledge is not the only way to achieve this and that all the social sciences have something important to teach us. In the words of one social studies theorist: "A discipline-based approach is inadequate for conscious development of the well-rounded synthesis needed for quality decision-making and active social participation."[40] This is obviously why time, continuity, and change form only one of ten strands in the NCSS definition of social studies, with others dealing with culture, environment, governance, economics, and other social phenomena.

Viewed through the lens of social studies, the world is too complex to be understood only through history, and the social sciences are too important to be crowded out of the curriculum by a single discipline. For the historian, however, most social science concepts (for example, gender, class, culture, and the like) can be best taught at the school level in the concrete context of history. Citizens will inevitably learn about their society once they know how to read and think. What they will not construct for themselves is the historical consciousness that comes from the systematic study of history, which most people will encounter only in school.

Claim 4: Social studies is more an exercise in socialization than education and takes an unduly passive and functionalist view of citizenship, teaching students to conform to what exists rather than to question it.

In the opinion of historian Diane Ravitch, admittedly no friend of social studies, the creators of social studies cared "more about socializing students than about encouraging intellectual growth and independent thinking."[41] There can be little doubt that the original 1916 social studies report saw social studies as a socializing subject designed to make each student a "thoroughly efficient member" of society.

Indeed, social studies began as an attempt to teach Native and African Americans to accept their place in a racist society. Its creator, Thomas Jesse Jones, saw history as an irrelevance, even a threat, to this task, and transferred his approach to the education of working-class and immigrant children who, he feared, might grow up to be a threat to the established social order. Better that such children should learn about the functioning of their local community than about the history of the struggle for social justice. Citizenship, and therefore social studies, was defined in terms of its contribution to social efficiency, not to challenging conventional wisdom.[42]

This emphasis on socialization is still to be found in some versions of social studies. Given the close connection between social studies and education for citizenship, it can hardly be otherwise. Citizenship entails an acceptance of an existing order, and any society depends upon a sense of common understanding and shared values, and therefore on the socialization of the young. This, after all, is why governments instituted compulsory public schooling in the first place. Democracies, however, also depend on citizens who are willing to question conventional wisdom, to follow conscience rather than custom, so that education for democratic citizenship must contain an element of counter-socialization. As philosopher Richard Rorty puts it, "You have to describe the country in terms of what you passionately hope it will become, as well as in terms of what you know it to be now. You have to be loyal to a dream country rather than the one to which you wake up every morning."[43] In short, both socialization and education are necessary to the health of democracy. The question is where to strike the balance between them. One early version of social studies spoke not of socialization but "social reconstruction." The economic crisis of the 1930s persuaded some social studies advocates that fundamental social reform was necessary, that the schools could and should build a new cooperative social order, and that social studies was the key to producing the critically minded, activist citizens needed to achieve this.[44] The social reconstructionists never overcame the depoliticized child-centredness of their progressive education allies and by the Cold War 1950s many of them en-

dorsed a conformist "life-adjustment" curriculum, but they pioneered a commitment to social justice and activist citizenship that remains alive in social studies. However, there is no empirical evidence that social studies is more effective than history in producing democratic citizens.

Defenders of social studies accurately point out that history has often been used as an instrument of socialization. Despite historians' commitment to scientific history, history quickly became an instrument of nationalist, ideological, and other forms of propaganda. Few went as far as French historian and educationist Ernest Lavisse did, with his admonition that "if the pupil does not come away with a vital memory of our national glories ... if he does not become a citizen imbued with a sense of duty and a soldier who loves his rifle, the teacher will have wasted his time," but the spirit embodied in his words lay not far beneath the surface of much history teaching.[45] History education was intended to buttress the established order, not to question it. It is misleading, therefore, to accuse social studies of being a vehicle of socialization, when history itself has so often been used more as an instrument of socialization than of education.

At the same time, history can be used to counter nationalist and other myths and to challenge accepted assumptions. History is a critical discipline that historicizes conventional wisdom and thus reveals its contingency. Accepted truths are shown to be socially constructed; traditions are shown to be invented; nations turn out to be imagined communities; heritage is revealed to be an ideological construct.[46] As described by historian J.H. Plumb, the uncritical "past" is undermined by critical "history."[47] But, respond the supporters of social studies, if history can do this, so can social studies. It is not a question of critical history versus uncritical social studies. Neither subject is inherently critical or conformist. Everything depends on how they are taught.

Claim 5: Social studies is based on a faulty theory of learning and takes too limited a view of what students can do.

Social studies is based on the belief that students learn best from the concrete realities of their immediate environment and personal experience. This is why in the 1930s Canadian provinces dropped history from the early grades and replaced it with the "expanding horizons" approach of social studies, where children begin by studying their local surroundings before slowly moving out into the wider world.[48] Only a few years ago, some researchers, including some historians, suggested that history was not a suitable subject even for high school students, since its subject matter was too remote from their experience.[49] Such research, however, at best showed only what students did in certain circumstances, not what they might do when taught appropriately, and there were researchers who showed that students could do far more than was usually expected of them.[50] Today, researchers are demonstrating that when taught creatively, even elementary students can handle history in more sophisticated ways than was once believed.[51] Moreover, as Kieran Egan has long pointed out, even young children can think beyond the concretely immediate. In their own lives, as in their stories, they encounter such abstractions as fear, anger, trust, courage, and a range of other experiences, not to mention dinosaurs, monsters, and other unreal phenomena, ranging from Thomas the Tank Engine to Harry Potter.[52]

Before the 1930s, schools taught history even in the early grades. No one expected young children to study it as a formal discipline, but they learned about the past in age-appropriate ways, usually through stories. Educationists believed that this served several purposes. It was a way of learning to read and write. It gave students general knowledge. It taught them that there was a past that was different from the present and that it was interesting. It laid a foundation for later, more systematic work. It introduced them to some basic questions of existence, of distinguishing right from wrong, fairness from injustice, and other such dichotomies. From the 1930s on most provinces dropped this approach to the past and replaced it with the expanding horizons approach of social studies, in the belief that this was more accessible to young children and therefore a better preparation for citizenship. In recent years, some jurisdictions, most notably California, have reintroduced history in the early grades, but, for the most part, social studies remains in place. Schools remain convinced that the here and now of social studies is more appropriate to the early grades than the long ago and far away of history.

There are traces of the here-and-now learning theory of social studies in the secondary grades also. It speaks not of expanding horizons but of "relevance." Students, it claims, are more interested in what they have to learn, and learn it more effectively, when they see its relevance to their own lives. It is easier, therefore, to teach current issues than history. It seems likely that teachers were attracted to social studies because they believed that students would find it more interesting than history. This might explain, in part, why social studies entered Canadian high school curricula in the 1970s. The elimination of provincial examinations and the relaxation of curriculum controls coincided with a rapid increase in high school enrolment. The result was that teachers were faced with more and more students who they too easily judged to be non-academic and therefore unlikely to find history interesting, so they turned to social studies instead. History failed to shake off its image as a university-oriented, and often dull, subject that had little to offer non-academic students who were thought to lack the cultural capital and the motivation to endure it.

In large part, history's defenders had only themselves to blame. In failing to make their subject interesting, they opened the door to what seemed to be more attractive rivals. Social studies has sometimes been pedagogically more adventurous than history, though it has had its share of pedestrian teaching, while history has often remained confined to the textbook and worksheet and other such didactic techniques.[53] Some social studies advocates see didactic teaching methods as inherent in the very nature of history, with its reliance on the mastery of factual information. A more contemporary criticism holds that history's defenders are for the most part politically and culturally conservative and wedded to didactic teaching. In the words of one critic:

> [A]dvocates of a disciplines-based approach to social studies tend to think of knowledge gain as the test of learning, while advocates of a reflective approach tend to emphasize thoughtfulness and social criticism.[54]

What such patently false antitheses ignore is that history is no less reflective and socially critical than social studies, and that history's defenders are to be found on the political left as well as the right, and even those on the right generally favour a reflective pedagogy.

The irony is that by the end of the 1920s there was general agreement on what it meant to teach history well. First, depth was preferable to coverage, so that it was better to teach a few topics in detail than many topics more superficially. Second, topics should be treated as problems to be explored (not solved) rather than facts to be memorized. Third, students must range far beyond the textbook. Fourth, they must work with primary sources. Fifth, learning must be seen as an active process, engaging students in a variety of different experiences, all designed to promote thought and imagination. Sixth, students must undertake some genuinely original research. Seventh, the history classroom must become a "laboratory," with books, maps, documents, pictures, and other resources being the equipment and open-ended problems serving as the experiments. Eighth, students must understand and use the elements of historical method, approaching history not only as the story of the past but as a form of disciplined inquiry so that they learned to think historically. Ninth, history was the record of all aspects of life in the past—social, economic, and intellectual, as well as political and military. Tenth, history should embrace relevant findings from all the social sciences.[55]

In any event, most teachers lacked the necessary training, lacked resources, faced onerous working conditions, and so were unable to overcome the tradition in which they themselves had been taught, where history was the memorization of names and dates. This approach to teaching history was reinforced by having compulsory examinations that were primarily fact-based—examinations whose pass and failure rates served as indicators of teachers' competence. Given these circumstances, when curriculum requirements were relaxed in the 1970s, it is not surprising that imaginative teachers sometimes took the opportunity to shake off what seemed like the dead hand of history to embrace the opportunities offered by interdisciplinary social studies.

Conclusion

Where, then, does this discussion leave us? Of the five claims and counterclaims examined above, the first seems to me to give a clear advantage to history. Unlike social studies, history's crisis (if indeed it exists) is one of growth, not stasis, and as an established discipline it represents what psychologist Howard Gardner has called one of "the most important cognitive achievements of human beings." As Gardner puts it, we need to know the "understandings of the disciplines . . . if we are to be fully human, to live in our time, to be able to understand it to the best of our abilities, and to build upon it."[56] The second and third claims also seem to me to give the advantage to history, though I can see how a supporter of social studies might think otherwise. The fourth claim applies equally well to both history and social studies, but it seems to me that history, despite the ways it has been used to promote ideological and other prejudices, is potentially more educative than social studies. Despite its emphasis on active citizenship, there is no evidence that social studies in fact promotes it more effectively than does history. To quote two American social studies theorists, "If social studies is intended to increase voter participation and respect for law, it appears to be failing."[57] The fifth claim rests on empirical evidence that undermines the social studies contention that students are too immature to understand history, though the fact that they can understand history does not necessarily entail the conclusion that they should therefore study it.

The choice between history and social studies is more a matter of educational philosophy than it is of empirical data. We cannot usefully argue about history and social studies in the abstract, treating them as absolutes whose contours are definitively fixed. Everything depends on the particulars of specific curricula. A good social studies course, well taught, is preferable to a poor history course, poorly taught. For that matter, it is preferable to a good history course if that course is taught badly.

This said, my loyalty still lies with history. The quality of historical-mindedness seems to me so crucial to making the most of our lives as human beings and to fulfilling the obligations of democratic citizenship that we must not neglect any opportunity to develop it in the young, especially when, for most of us, it is only in school that we are likely to acquire it. We can learn about the past in a thousand ways, but much of what we learn will be partial or incomplete or just plain wrong. It will be history as entertainment or propaganda, not as understanding. Only in school are most people likely to learn about the past systematically, acquiring understanding as well as knowledge, gaining some awareness of the discipline as well as the subject matter of history, while also developing a sense of connectedness that helps us locate ourselves in a continuum of past, present, and future. To quote H.G. Wells, a self-declared fanatic about the importance of history:

> I cannot think of an education as even half done until there has been a fairly sound review of the whole of the known past, from the beginnings of the geological record up to our own time. Until that is done the pupil has not been *placed* in the world.[58]

Wells' belief that an informed understanding of history is essential to locating ourselves in time and place, without becoming the prisoner of either, works at two levels, the national and the global. Both are important. We live in a world of sovereign states and our lives are shaped to a considerable extent by the kind of state in which we live. For a state to function effectively it needs to retain the support of its citizens, especially if it has any claim to being democratic. Citizens are bound together, in large part, by a sense of belonging to a common country. In Canada, where differing definitions of national identity exist, this process can be especially complicated. Officially bilingual and multicultural, geographically huge, regionally and culturally diverse, federally governed, situated next door to the world's superpower, Canada is not a nation-state in any conventional sense. More than most countries, Canada is engaged in a continuing debate about the kind of country it is and wants to be. To participate in this debate in any meaningful way, Canadian citizens need to be historically informed. This does not mean that we must teach one officially authorized version of national history. Nor does it mean that we must

reinvent the old nation-building history to which some commentators want us to return. It is possible to combine Peter Seixas' three conceptions of history education that I referred to earlier in this chapter. There is a single story in the sense of a bare-bones chronology, beginning with the thousands of years of First Nations' history, moving on to the establishment of French Canada, the arrival of the British, and so on. We can subject this to what Seixas calls a disciplinary approach by applying methods of historical analysis to it, examining who is saying what about the past, testing for proof, and generally deploying the principles of historical method. We can even, should we choose, raise a postmodern banner and investigate how this history has been and is used and whether one version of Canada's past is possible or perhaps even desirable. In this way we are teaching history, not heritage, and certainly not myth. Equally important, we are introducing students to the continuing conversation that characterizes Canada's public life and equipping them to participate in it as citizens.

A similar argument can be made for teaching world history. It has become a truism to say that we now live in a global village, but there is one sense in which it is not yet an accurate description of the world in which we live. In the typical village everyone knows everyone else. But we know very little about our fellow villagers and their histories. A sense of global citizenship depends upon a sense of membership in a global community, and this depends in turn upon a sense of a common history that has affected us all. As with Canadian history, this does not mean teaching an officially approved, feel-good version of the past. Rather, it means appreciating how men and women have tried to shape their lives over the thousands of years of human history. It means seeing ourselves as the heirs of the past and the stewards of the future, which in turn means seeing the whole of history as our inheritance. To turn again to H.G. Wells: "We have lost touch with history. We have ceased to see human affairs as one great epic unfolding. And only by the universal teaching of universal history can that epic quality be restored."[59] Historical mindedness is our strongest defence against those who claim to know history but seek to use it to their own advantage. At the same time it reveals to us a world of choices and alternatives of which we might otherwise remain unaware. As I used to tell my students, "You may not be interested in history, but history is certainly interested in you." What they did not know could hurt them—and a lot of other people.

For me, this is the central message of Orwell's *Nineteen Eighty-Four,* which is a disturbing meditation on the power of history. What makes the novel truly terrifying is not Big Brother or the thought police but the fact that most people did exactly what the party wanted, no questions asked. They were malleable because they knew no history and, knowing no history, had no sense of connectedness with anything outside the here and now of the party and its dictates, no grounds to question what they were told, no realization that things could be other than what they were. What made the novel's central character, Winston Smith, so dangerous to the party was that he had a glimmering of historical knowledge, a suspicion that the past had been different from the present and that, therefore, the future could be different again. In his defence of postmodern approaches to history, Keith Jenkins recently observed that he was "optimistic about living in a world 'without histories' if what passes for history, however imagined, is a block to the imagining of things that, in the name of emancipation and empowerment, are altogether more relevant and to the point."[60] However, few of us favour a history that blocks our ability to imagine alternatives to what we might otherwise take for granted. Indeed, historical understanding is our best guarantee that we will imagine them. If anyone wants to know why history matters, they need only read *Nineteen Eighty-Four.* In an ideal world we should no doubt teach both history and social studies but, since there is not time in the curriculum to do so, we have to make some tough choices. Mine is for history.

Endnotes

1   Edgar B. Wesley and Stanley P. Wronski, *Teaching Social Studies in High Schools* (Boston: Heath, 1964), 3.

2   National Council for the Social Studies, *Expectations of Excellence: Curriculum Standards for Social Studies* (Washington, DC: NCSS, 1994), vii.

3   Richard W. Evans, "Is Social Studies Dying? Reflections on Educational Reform," *International Journal of Social Education* 7, no. 2 (1992): 89–99; and Diane Ravitch, "From History to Social Studies: Dilemmas and Problems," in *Challenges to the Humanities,* ed. Chester E. Finn, Diane Ravitch, and P. Holley Roberts (New York: Holmes & Meier, 1985), 80–95.

4   Jack L. Granatstein, *Who Killed Canadian History?* (Toronto: HarperCollins, 1998). For a general survey of the Canadian history debate, see Ken Osborne, "'Our Syllabus Has Us Gasping': History in Canadian Schools—Past, Present, and Future," *Canadian Historical Review* 81, no. 3 (September 2000): 404–435; and ———, "Teaching History in Schools: A Canadian Debate," *Journal of Curriculum Studies* 35, no. 5 (2003): 585–626.

5   Ken Osborne, "'To the Schools We Must Look for the Good Canadian': Developments in the Teaching of History in the Schools since 1960," *Journal of Canadian Studies* 22, no. 3 (1987): 104–126; A.B. Hodgetts and Paul Gallagher, *Teaching Canada for the '80s* (Toronto: OISE Press, 1978); Bob Davis, *Whatever Happened to High School History? Burying the Political Memory of Youth: Ontario, 1945–1995* (Toronto: James Lorimer, 1995); and Amy von Heyking, "Selling Progressive Education to Albertans, 1935–53," *Historical Studies in Education* 10 (1998): 64–84.

6   For the American debate, see Michael Whelan, "History and the Social Studies: A Response to the Critics," *Theory and Research in Social Education* 20, no. 1 (1992): 2–16; and ———, "Reaction and Response," *Theory and Research in Social Education* 20, no. 3 (1992): 313–350.

7   Kieran Egan, "John Dewey and the Social Studies Curriculum," *Theory and Research in Social Education* 8, no. 2 (Summer 1980): 37.

8   Kieran Egan, "Social Studies and the Erosion of Education," *Curriculum Inquiry* 13, no. 2 (1983): 195.

9   Ibid., 196.

10 Ibid., 195.

11 Edgar B. Wesley, "Reading Plans for Social Studies Teachers," in *Inservice Growth of Social Studies Teachers,* ed. B.W. Phillips (Washington, DC: NCSS, 1939), 119.

12 Robert D. Barr, James L. Barth, and S. Samuel Shermis, *Defining the Social Studies,* no. 51 (Washington, DC: NCSS, 1977), 1.

13 H. Robert Brady, "The Nature of Social Studies and the Problem of Definition," *International Journal of Social Education* 8, no. 1 (1993): 19.

14 Richard W. Evans, "Is Social Studies Dying?", 89. For specific reform efforts, see Shirley H. Engle, "Decision-making: The Heart of Social Studies Instruction," *Social Education* 24, no. 7 (1960): 301–304, 306; Maurice P. Hunt and Lawrence

E. Metcalf, *Teaching High School Social Studies* (New York: HarperCollins, 1955); Fred M. Newmann, *Clarifying Public Controversy* (Boston: Little, Brown, 1970); and Richard W. Evans, "Teaching Social Issues: Implementing an Issues-centered Curriculum," in *The Social Studies Curriculum: Purposes, Problems, and Possibilities,* ed. E. Wayne Ross (Albany: State University of New York Press, 2001), 291–309.

15 See Donald O. Schneider, "History, Social Sciences, and the Social Studies," *Social Education* 53, no. 3 (1989): 148–154; Alberta M. Dougan, "The Search for a Definition of the Social Studies: A Historical Overview," *International Journal of Social Education* 3, no. 3 (1988/89): 13–36; and Ian Wright, "Just What Sort of Question Is 'What Is Social Studies?' and How Do We Go About Answering It?" *International Journal of Social Education* 13, no. 1 (1998): 66–76.

16 National Council for the Social Studies, *Expectations of Excellence,* 3.

17 Terence H. McLaughlin, "Citizenship Education in England: The Crick Report and Beyond," *Journal of Philosophy of Education* 34, no. 4 (2000): 541–570; and Bernard Crick, "Education for Citizenship: The Citizenship Order," *Parliamentary Affairs* 55 (2002): 488–504.

18 Murry R. Nelson, "The Development of the Rugg Social Studies Materials," *Theory and Research in Social Education* 5, no. 3 (1977): 64–83; Donald W. Oliver and James P. Shaver, *Teaching Public Issues in the High School* (Boston: Houghton Mifflin, 1966); and Jerome S. Bruner, *Toward a Theory of Instruction* (Cambridge, MA: Harvard University Press, 1966), 73–101.

19 Peter Dow, *Schoolhouse Politics: Lessons from the Sputnik Era* (Cambridge, MA: Harvard University Press, 1991); N.T. Bagenstos, "Social Reconstruction: The Controversy over the Textbooks of Harold Rugg," *Theory and Research in Social Education* 5, no. 3 (1977): 22–38; and Ellen Boesenberg and Karen S. Poland, "Struggle at the Frontier of Curriculum: The Rugg Textbooks Controversy in Binghamton, New York," *Theory and Research in Social Education* 29, no. 4 (2001): 640–671.

20 Gerald Marker and Howard Mehlinger, "Social Studies," in *Handbook of Research on Curriculum: A Project of the American Educational Association,* ed. Philip W. Jackson (New York: Macmillan, 1992), 836.

21 Herbert G. Wells, *Travels of a Radical Republican in Search of Hot Water* (Harmondsworth, UK: Penguin Books, 1939).

22 Peter Seixas, "Schweigen! die Kinder! or, Does Postmodern History have a Place in the Schools?" in *Knowing, Teaching, and Learning History: National and International Perspectives,* ed. Peter N. Stearns, Peter Seixas, and Samuel Wineburg (New York: New York University Press, 2000), 19–37.

23 Theodore S. Hamerow, *Reflections on History and Historians* (Madison: University of Wisconsin Press, 1987), 3.

24 Ian Kershaw, "Behind the Screen: How Television Trumpets and Trivializes History," *Times Literary Supplement* no. 5215, March 14, 2003, 16.

25 Peter Novick, *That Noble Dream: The "Objectivity Question" and the American Historical Profession* (Cambridge, MA: Cambridge University Press, 1988), 628. For less alarmist surveys of the state of history, see Joyce Appleby, Lynn Hunt, and Margaret Jacob, *Telling the Truth about History* (New York: Norton, 1994); Richard J. Evans, *In Defence of History* (London: Granta, 1997); George Iggers, *Historiography in the Twentieth Century: From Scientific Objectivity to the Postmodern Challenge* (Hanover: Wesleyan University Press, 1997). A postmodern response can be found in Keith Jenkins, *Why History? Ethics and Postmodernity* (London: Routledge, 1999). For the educational implications of what some see as the crisis in history, see Peter Seixas, " 'Parallel Crises': History and the Social Studies Curriculum in the U.S.A.," *Journal of Curriculum Studies* 25, no. 3 (1993): 235–250; and Peter Seixas, "Schweigen! die Kinder! or, Does Postmodern History have a Place in the Schools?" in *Knowing, Teaching, and Learning History: National and International Perspectives,* ed. Peter N. Stearns, Peter Seixas, and Samuel Wineburg (New York: New York University Press, 2000), 19–37.

26 For two surveys that reveal the philosophical disarray and pedagogical inertia of social studies, see Gerald Marker and Howard Mehlinger, "Social Studies," 830–850; and Peter Seixas, "Review of Research on Social Studies," in *Handbook of Research on Teaching,* 4th ed., ed. Virginia Richardson (Washington, DC: American Educational Research, 2001), 545–565.

27 For examples of these debates, see Arthur M. Schlesinger, Jr., *The Disuniting of America: Reflections on a Multicultural Society* (New York: Norton, 1991); Lawrence W. Levine, *The Opening of the American Mind: Canons, Culture, and History* (Boston: Beacon, 1996); Daniel Francis, *National Dreams: Myth, Memory, and Canadian History* (Vancouver: Arsenal Pulp Press, 1997); J.L. Granatstein, *Who Killed Canadian History?* (Toronto: HarperCollins, 1998); Eric Foner, *Who Owns History? Rethinking the Past in a Changing World* (New York: Hill & Wang, 2002); and Stuart MacIntyre and Anna Clark, *The History Wars* (Melbourne: Melbourne University Press, 2003).

28 Gary B. Nash, Charlotte Crabtree, and Ross E. Dunn, *History on Trial: Culture Wars and the Teaching of the Past* (New York: Knopf, 1977); Linda Symcox, *Whose History? The Struggle for National Standards in American Classrooms* (New York: Teachers College Press, 2002); and Robert Phillips, *History Teaching, Nationhood and the State* (London: Cassell, 1998).

29 For the classic Canadian description of pointless history teaching, see A.B. Hodgetts, *What Culture? What Heritage? A Study of Civic Education in Canada* (Toronto: OISE Press, 1968). See also Fred Morrow Fling, *Outline of Historical Method* (Lincoln, NE: Miller, 1899); Edwin Fenton, *Teaching the New Social Studies in Secondary Schools: An Inductive Approach* (New York: Holt, Rinehart & Winston, 1966); and Schools Council 13–16 Project, *A New Look at History* (Edinburgh: Holmes & McDougall, 1976).

[30]   Henry Johnson, *The Other Side of Main Street: A History Teacher from Sauk Centre* (New York: Columbia University Press, 1943), 247.

[31]   Edward P. Thompson, *The Making of the English Working Class* (Harmondsworth, UK: Penguin, 1968), 13.

[32]   Johnson, *The Other Side of Main Street,* 255.

[33]   Examples include Geoffrey Barraclough, *An Introduction to Contemporary History* (London: Watts, 1964); and Norman Davies, *Heart of Europe: A Short History of Poland* (Oxford: Oxford University Press, 1984).

[34]   For Fling, see his "One Use of Sources in the Teaching of History," *The Historical Outlook* 1, no. 1 (1909), reprinted in *The Social Studies* 85, no. 5 (1994): 206–210.

[35]   Mary Sheldon Barnes, *Studies in Historical Method* (Boston: Heath, 1896), 47.

[36]   National Council for the Social Studies, *Expectations of Excellence,* 22.

[37]   Ibid.

[38]   David W. Saxe, *Social Studies in Schools: The Early Years* (Albany: State University of New York Press, 1991), 223, 234.

[39]   See, for example, James W. Loewen, *Lies My Teacher Told Me: Everything Your American History Got Wrong* (New York: Simon & Schuster, 1995); David Lowenthal, *Possessed by the Past: The Heritage Crusade and the Spoils of History* (New York: The Free Press, 1996); Eric Hobsbawm, *On History* (London: Weidenfeld & Nicolson, 1997); and Daniel Francis, *National Dreams: Myth, Memory, and Canadian History* (Vancouver: Arsenal Pulp Press, 1997).

[40]   Evans, "Teaching Social Issues," 294.

[41]   The Ravitch quotation occurs in Symcox, *Whose History?,* 71.

[42]   Michael B. Lybarger, "Origins of the Modern Social Studies, 1900–1916," *History of Education Quarterly* 23 (1983): 455–468; W.H. Watkins, *The White Architects of Black Education: Ideology and Power in America, 1865–1954* (New York: Teachers College Press, 2001), 98–117.

[43]   Richard Rorty, *Achieving Our Country: Leftist Thought in Twentieth-Century America* (Cambridge, MA: Harvard University Press, 1998), 101.

[44]   George S. Counts, *Dare the Schools Build a New Social Order?* (New York: John Day, 1932); C.A. Bowers, *The Progressive Educator and the Depression: The Radical Years* (New York: Random House, 1969); William R. Stanley, "The Radical Reconstructionist Rationale for Social Education," *Theory and Research in Social Education* 8, no. 4 (1981): 55–79; and M.E. James, *Social Reconstruction through Education: The Philosophy, History, and Curricula of a Radical Idea* (Norwood, NJ: Ablex, 1995).

[45]   Pierre Nora, "Lavisse, The Nation's Teacher," in *Realms of Memory: The Construction of the French Past,* ed. Pierre Nora (New York: Columbia Press, 1997), 181.

[46]   Eric Hobsbawm and Terence Ranger, eds., *The Invention of Tradition* (Cambridge, MA: Cambridge University Press,

1983); Benedict Anderson, *Imagined Communities: Reflections on the Origin and Spread of Nationalism* (London: Verso, 1991); and Patrick J. Geary, *The Myth of Nations: The Medieval Origins of Europe* (Princeton: Princeton University Press, 2002).

[47]   J.H. Plumb, *The Death of the Past* (London, Macmillan, 1969).

[48]   Leo W. LeRiche, "The Expanding Environments Sequence in Elementary Social Studies: The Origins," *Theory and Research in Social Education* 15, no. 3 (1987): 137–154; Roger A. Baskerville and F. William Sesow, "In Defense of Hanna and the 'Expanding Horizons' Approach to Social Studies," *Theory and Research in Social Education* 4, no. 1 (1976): 220–232. For a critical view, see Diane Ravitch, "'Tot Sociology': Or Whatever Happened to History in the Grade Schools?" *American Scholar* 56 (1987): 343–354.

[49]   For a summary of this research, see Ken Osborne, "Some Psychological Concerns for the Teaching of History," *History and Social Science Teacher* 11 (1975): 15–25. See also Samuel Wineburg, *Historical Thinking and Other Unnatural Acts: Charting the Future of Teaching the Past* (Philadelphia: Temple University Press, 2001), 28–60.

[50]   Martin Booth, "Skills, Concepts and Attitudes: The Development of Adolescent Children's Historical Thinking," *History and Theory* 22 (1983): 101–117; Denis Shemilt, "Adolescent Ideas about Evidence and Methodology in History," in *The History Curriculum for Teachers,* ed. C. Portal (Lewes, UK: Falmer, 1987), 39–61; and Martin Booth, "Ages and Concepts: A Critique of the Piagetian Approach to History Teaching," in ibid., 22–38.

[51]   See, for example, Jere Brophy and Bruce VanSledright, *Teaching and Learning History in Elementary Schools* (New York: Teachers College Press, 1997); Linda Levstik and Keith Barton, *Doing History: Investigating with Children in Elementary and Middle Schools* (Mahwah, NJ: Lawrence Erlbaum, 2001); Samuel Wineburg, *Historical Thinking and Other Unnatural Acts: Charting the Future of Teaching the Past* (Philadelphia: Temple University Press, 2001); Suzanne M. Wilson, "Research on History Teaching," in *Handbook of Research on Teaching,* 4th ed., ed. Virginia Richardson (Washington, DC: American Educational Research Association, 2001), 527–544; and Bruce VanSledright, *In Search of America's Past: Learning to Read History in Elementary School* (New York: Teachers College Press, 2002).

[52]   Kieran Egan, *Educational Development* (New York: Oxford University Press, 1979); ———, *Primary Understanding: Education in Early Childhood* (New York: Routledge, 1988); and ———, *Romantic Understanding: The Development of Rationality and Imagination, Ages 8–15* (New York: Routledge, 1990).

[53]   For a recent study of history teaching in Québec that illustrates this point, see Robert Martineau, *L'histoire à l'école: matière à penser* (Montréal: L'Harmattan, 1999).

[54]   Evans, "Teaching Social Issues," 292. For an example of history as social criticism, see Harvey J. Kaye *"Why Do Ruling Classes Fear History?" and Other Questions* (New York:

St. Martin's, 1996).

55 See, for example, Mary D. Sheldon, *Studies in General History* (Boston: Heath, 1885); Mary Sheldon Barnes, *Studies in Historical Method* (Boston: Heath, 1896); Fred Morrow Fling and Howard W. Caldwell, *Studies in European and American History: An Introduction to the Source Study Method in History* (Lincoln, NE: Miller, 1897); Fred Morrow Fling, *Outline of Historical Method* (Lincoln, NE: Miller, 1899); American Historical Association, *The Study of History in Schools: Report to the American Historical Association by the Committee of Seven* (New York, Macmillan, 1902); Charles D. Hazen et al., *Historical Sources in Schools: Report to the New England History Teachers' Association by a Select Committee* (New York: Macmillan, 1902); M.W. Keatinge, *Studies in the Teaching of History* (London: A&C Black, 1910); James Harvey Robinson, *The New History* (New York: Macmillan, 1912); Henry Johnson, *The Teaching of History in Elementary and Secondary Schools* (New York: Macmillan, 1915); John Adams, ed., *The New Teaching* (London: Hodder & Stoughton, 1919); Herbert G. Wells, *The Story of a Great Schoolmaster* (New York: Macmillan, 1924); and Henry Johnson, *The Other Side of Main Street: A History Teacher from Sauk Centre* (New York: Columbia University Press, 1943).

56 Howard Gardner, *The Unschooled Mind* (New York: Basic Books, 1991), 11.

57 Marker and Mehlinger, "Social Studies," 844.

58 Herbert G. Wells, *The Salvaging of Civilization* (New York: Macmillan, 1921), 153.

59 Ibid., 112–113.

60 Keith Jenkins, *Re-thinking History* (London: Routledge, 2003), xix.

CHAPTER 5

In Search of Good Citizens

Citizenship Education and Social Studies in Canada

Alan Sears

Introduction: Citizenship as a Central Purpose for Education

Ken Osborne ends an excellent recent article on citizenship education in Canada with the argument that "citizenship seems to have vanished from the educational agenda."[1] While Osborne might be right in the substantive sense, he is most definitely not right when it comes to rhetoric. Across Canada, preparation for democratic citizenship is widely acknowledged as a central goal for public schooling. The Province of British Columbia, for example, recently published a policy document titled *The Graduation Program 2004*, which includes a section outlining the desired attributes of the B.C. graduate "in the areas of intellectual, human and social, and career development."[2] Citizenship is front and centre as a key goal of public schooling according to this document, which says, in part:

> In their human and social development, graduates should achieve:
>
> • The knowledge and skills required to be socially responsible citizens who act in caring and principled ways, respecting the diversity of all people and the rights of others to hold different ideas and beliefs.
>
> • The knowledge and understanding they

need to participate in democracy as Canadians and global citizens, acting in accordance with the laws, rights and responsibilities of democracy. . . .[3]

At the other end of the country, the Atlantic Provinces Education Foundation identifies citizenship as one of six "Essential Graduation Learnings."[4] Lest we think this focus on citizenship as a central goal for public education is exclusive to English Canada, the Ministère de l'Éducation du Québec contends "the ultimate goal of elementary education is to prepare students to participate actively in society by playing a constructive role as citizens."[5]

Ministries of education in Canada are not alone in identifying education for citizenship as central to the educational enterprise. The Canadian Teachers' Federation (CTF) claims that 75 percent of teachers support the idea "that the role of public education is to provide a well-balanced general education to prepare children for life and to assume the responsibilities of good citizenship."[6] The CTF itself has long supported education for democratic citizenship as a central goal for public education and has recently renewed that commitment through the launch of the program Living Democracy: Renewing Our Vision of Citizenship Education.[7]

Even beyond the education community there appears to be wide support for the idea that schools ought to focus considerable attention on preparing democratic citizens. Twenty years ago, George Tomkins argued "the goal of 'citizenship' probably comes closer than any other to identifying the purpose that Canadians have usually believed the social studies should serve, even though they might not agree on what a 'good' citizen (or a good Canadian) is."[8] More recently a series of public opinion surveys in Canada demonstrated support for a wide range of purposes for public schooling, "but the two dominant goals emerging from such polls are preparing students for the world of work and preparing them for citizenship."[9]

It is not only in Canada where citizenship education is touted as a key aspect of schooling. The editors of a book looking at current approaches to citizenship education in twenty-four countries write, "It is clear . . . that a review and rethinking of civic education is taking place not only in post-communist countries and those with a short recent history of democracy but also in well-developed and longstanding democracies."[10] Indeed, the language of democratic citizenship and citizenship education is showing up in the policies and curricula of jurisdictions as diverse as Australia, Russia, Colombia, and Singapore—some of which one might be reluctant to call democratic.

This wide and general acceptance of preparation for democratic citizenship as a fundamental purpose of public education, however, belies considerable confusion and debate in the field around several key questions including:

• What do we mean by citizenship and citizenship education?

• What do we know about where young people are relative to the knowledge, skills, and dispositions necessary for effective citizenship?

• What are the best ways to educate citizens?

• What can be done to strengthen citizenship education in Canada and elsewhere?

In the remainder of this chapter I will turn to these questions, not so much to provide answers as to introduce the range of thinking, practice, and debate in each area.

Citizenship and Citizenship Education as Contested Concepts

I often begin presentations on citizenship education by asking participants to engage in a short exercise. I divide them into small groups and instruct each group to design a job advertisement for the "Ideal Canadian Citizen." We talk for a minute about what typical job ads contain, including a description of the ideal candidate's educational background, personal qualities, skills and experience, and then I set the groups to work with poster paper and markers to write their ads. When completed, the advertisements are posted around the room to provide a jumping-off point for our discussion. Inevitably someone objects to the word "ideal," but I point out that job advertisements shoot for the perfect candidate and selection committees take the person who comes closest to that target, with the best mix of education, experience, and personal qualities. A typical ad emerging from this activity looks like the one below.

While each ad is unique in wording and emphasis, overall they are usually very similar in substance. The participants' first impression is that there is obviously wide agreement on the qualities of good citizenship, but then I begin to ask questions about

---

WANTED—THE IDEAL CANADIAN

The person we are looking for:

Has a love for Canada

Obeys the law

Knows Canadian history and geography

Is bilingual (French/English)

Is open-minded and tolerant of difference

Is a critical thinker

Is a good public speaker

Has lived in or travelled to various parts of
    the country

Has a record of involvement with the community

Loves hockey

the various criteria they have identified, pushing them to think beyond the surface. I have done this activity dozens of times over several years with groups of people ranging from elementary school students through graduate students to members of a local Rotary Club. One of the most common criteria identified across this wide range of groups is, "A good citizen obeys the law." I then ask, Was Mahatma Gandhi a good citizen of India? How about Martin Luther King, was he a good citizen of the U.S.? Or Nelson Mandela, a convicted terrorist, is he a good citizen of South Africa? How about Emmeline Pankhurst, who went to jail twelve times in 1912 for her part in suffragette protests (many of which involved the destruction of property) of British laws against women's suffrage, was she a good citizen of Britain? Closer to home, how about Louis Riel, leader of the Métis Rebellion in Western Canada, or Louis Joseph Papineau and William Lyon Mackenzie, leaders of the Rebellions of 1837 in the Canadas, were they good citizens? Or protesters arrested at the Asia-Pacific Economic Cooperation (APEC) summit in Vancouver in 1997, or at the Summit of the Americas in Québec City in 2001, are they good citizens? Most of the historic figures mentioned above are now, at least in the mainstream, considered heroes, with monuments erected in their honour, movies made of their lives, and streets, airports, and other public areas named after them. Nelson Mandela was considered such a good citizen by the parliament of Canada that he was made an honorary citizen of this country in November 2001, only the second individual to receive that honour. Emmeline Pankhurst was identified by *Time* magazine as one of the 100 most influential people of the twentieth century. *Time* placed her in the category "Heroes and Icons," which it described as "twenty people who articulated the longings of the last 100 years, exemplifying courage, selflessness, exuberance, superhuman ability and amazing grace."[11] It is interesting to note that joining Mrs. Pankhurst on that list of twenty are several others who fell afoul of the law in various countries including Rosa Parks, Che Guevara, Muhammad Ali, and Andrei Sakharov.

On reflection, most participants begin to back away from the contention that a good citizen always

obeys the law, acknowledging that it is sometimes not only appropriate but even necessary for democratic citizens to break the law. The crunch comes, however, when I ask how we decide when it is appropriate and necessary to break the law, or if are there any limits to what a good citizen should do to challenge an unjust law. This is where the veneer of consensus begins to wear thin. Some participants quickly come to the conclusion that it is never appropriate to use violence against people or property in support of a political cause, but others, in the tradition of Mackenzie, Pankhurst, and Mandela, argue that sometimes injustice is so great, and the powers that be so resistant to change, violence is the only recourse.

If we push beyond the surface, this kind of complexity and difference of opinion exists around virtually every one of the criteria identified for good citizenship. When we say, for example, good citizens are open-minded and tolerant, does that mean open to anything? Tolerant of any lifestyle or cultural practice? What about the practice of infibulation, better known as female genital mutilation? Some parents in Canada wish to subject their daughters to this procedure, arguing it is part of their culture, what does it mean to be tolerant in this case?[†]

As a democratic society we enshrine constitutional protection for free speech, but what about those who deny the Holocaust, contending it has been greatly exaggerated as part of a Jewish conspiracy to undermine Western Christian civilization? Should we protect their speech? Does it make a difference who they are? What if one happens to be a teacher who consistently expresses such views in the public square, in books, newspaper articles, or speeches? Should he or she be fired? What about the Jewish children in their classrooms, schools, and communities, aren't these children and their families entitled to some protection as well?

When we say a good citizen should know the history and geography of their country, what exactly

---

† In Canada and most Western democracies this practice has recently been made illegal (1995 in the U.S.; 1997 in Canada), but there is evidence it continues to be practised by some.

do we mean? One of the most public educational debates in Canada over the past ten years or so has been over exactly that question. Some people, including some well-known historians, contend that Canadian history, as it has been taught in schools, has been effectively put to death by social historians, social scientists, and teachers infected with fuzzy thinking about what it is young citizens should learn about their country. Many from those groups, however, argue, with some evidence, that school history has been dominated by a bland, consensus version of political and military history, which avoids controversial subjects and is never connected to the lives and experiences of the people studying it.[12]

My point is this: while there is considerable consensus that preparation for democratic citizenship ought to be a central goal of public education, there is very little real consensus around what we mean by a "good" citizen. Most policy documents or public opinion surveys treat citizenship superficially, assuming we all understand the concept the same way. With most groups of people, even those from similar backgrounds, it does not take much probing to demonstrate that any apparent consensus about the meaning of good citizenship does not run very deep. This is as true for those developing educational policy and programs as it is for the students in my classes or the general public. In North America the school subject of social studies has been the part of the curriculum most directly charged with the responsibility of educating citizens and, even here, there is little agreement about what this should mean. Writing about social studies in a major research handbook on education, Marker and Mehlinger point out:

> the apparent consensus on behalf of citizenship education is almost meaningless. Behind that totem to which nearly all social studies researchers pay homage, lies continuous and rancorous debate about the purposes of social studies.[13]

The debate about what constitutes good citizenship continues, in part at least, because citizenship is a contested concept. The idea of contested concepts is rooted in the premise that there are some concepts inevitably mired in continual disputes about

their proper use. These disputes do not arise because the people involved are arguing about different concepts to which they have mistakenly given the same name, but because the internal complexity of the concept makes for disputes that "are perfectly genuine: which, although not resolvable by argument of any kind, are nevertheless sustained by perfectly respectable arguments and evidence."[14] Most writers hold a concept of citizenship that contains the same elements: "knowledge, skills, values, and participation,"[15] but there is wide disagreement about the role, nature, and relative importance of each element.

Disputes about citizenship arise not only because it is an internally complex concept, but also because it is a normative one. Normative concepts often fail to command a universally shared definition not only because of their complexity but also because they "describe from a moral point of view."[16] They are, in fact, appraisive in that they involve making judgements about what is better and best. Those who speak of educating for citizenship are not so much concerned with the narrow legal definition of citizenship as with some normative sense of good citizenship.

A group of researchers at the University of Montreal developed a conceptual framework to illustrate some of the constituent and competing elements of citizenship in liberal democracies. Figure 1 provides an illustration of how these elements interact.

In this model the vertical axis deals with citizens' sense of belonging. Most feel some sense of attachment to the national state but also derive a sense of belonging and citizenship from their connection to cultural or social groups within the nation (subnational) or to organizations that extend beyond the nation (supranational). Several political theorists have written about the multinational nature of the Canadian state.[17] Kymlicka argues that Canada contains at least two "national minorities," the Québécois and First Nations. Unlike more recent immigrant groups, these peoples existed as organized groups with defined territory as well as social and political institutions before the Canadian state was formed. For the most part, members of these communities continue to see themselves as citizens of those entities as well as citizens of Canada. As Charles Taylor points out, this is essentially the two-level model of citizenship being worked out in the European Union [EU] where people are both citizens of their particular member country and, by virtue of that, citizens of the EU.[18]

In fact, people do not have to be members of national minorities to feel a sense of divided loyalties. Prominent Canadian historian Desmond Morton examines the persistent difficulty Canada has had establishing an overarching sense of national identity among its citizens, particularly when compared with its closest neighbour, the United States. Morton agues: "Canadian citizenship has had to coexist with loyalties to old homelands, newer provinces, or nations within and protected by the federal state, specifically *la nation canadienne française*."[19]

Recent research demonstrates that young Canadian citizens locate themselves on different places along this sense-of-belonging axis, with some feeling the tug of nation most strongly while others more closely identify with their province or region.[20] Indeed, most citizens in a democracy would not locate themselves at either extreme of the axis but at some point along it.

The horizontal axis in the model represents the tensions between the rights that allow citizens in a democracy to be free of the encumbrance of others to pursue "life, liberty, and happiness," to use an American phrase, and the obligation for democratic citizens to participate in their society. One writer asks the question this way: Are we to be idiots or citizens?[21] For the ancient Athenians, an idiot was a completely private person, cut off from all others, while the citizen took up his obligation to help shape and run society. The latter necessarily meant giving up some individual liberty in the service of others and the wider community, but such were the obligations of citizenship. There is great debate today about the forms of participation in which citizens should engage and even greater concern about signs of growing citizen disengagement. The latter is seen most clearly in declining voting rates among young citizens almost everywhere in the world. Voting is often seen as the most basic way in which citizens can and should participate in their own governance.[22]

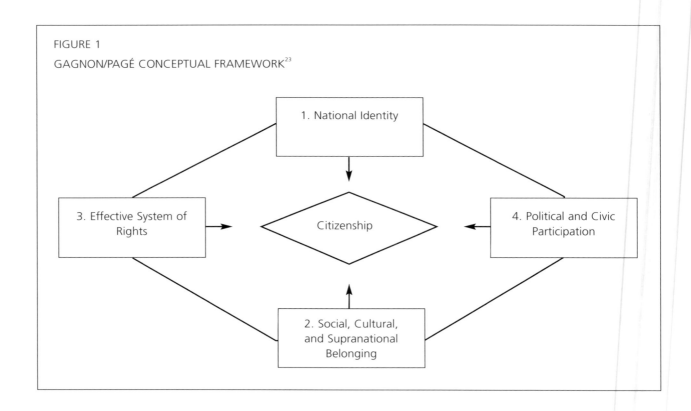

FIGURE 1

GAGNON/PAGÉ CONCEPTUAL FRAMEWORK[23]

1. National Identity

3. Effective System of Rights

Citizenship

4. Political and Civic Participation

2. Social, Cultural, and Supranational Belonging

Citizens sometimes choose to not participate in their societies for a wide range of reasons, including: cynicism about the political process and political actors; low sense of personal efficacy or agency; feelings of exclusion due to race, gender, or class; narrow definitions about what counts as citizen participation; and personal preferences. Recent research indicates a trend away from participation in traditional political activities—voting; joining political parties; running for office—and towards what is alternatively called private or non-conventional modes of participation, including various forms of community-based activism and service.[24] Even then, much research documents fairly low levels of participation in both so-called conventional and non-conventional activities. Recent initiatives in citizenship education have been largely focused on addressing this perceived alienation from participating in civic life. Many, it seems, locate themselves towards the left-hand side of the horizontal axis, focused more on maintaining their rights to private life rather than on their contribution to the civic community. This has been of great concern to policy-makers and citizenship educators.

What the model demonstrates is that citizenship is a complicated idea, affected by many factors, including where a person finds his or her sense of belonging and the degree to which he or she is engaged with the civic culture. The varying degrees of force exerted by all of the polls on the model will pull individual citizens to different points on the scale and lead them to see their citizenship differently at various times in their lives and in different contexts.

All of this, of course, complicates the enterprise of educating citizens. The programs we design and implement for citizenship education are going to depend on the kind of citizen desired. For most of our history in Canada (at least outside Québec), there has been a great desire to educate citizens with a deep sense of attachment to the nation state vis-à-vis provincial, cultural, or ethnic identities. A number of attempts have been made to use the education system to help create the kind of overarching national myths that seem to sustain the strong sense of national unity in the United States. Before World War II, these myths were grounded in attachment to

the British Empire and the celebration of Canada's connection with all things British. With the weakening of the empire after the war, attention turned to creating home-grown myths to garner the loyalty of Canadians. History and social studies curricula in schools have been the main designated purveyors of these attempts at creating a national consciousness, but other extra- and co-curricular vehicles have been used as well, such as school assemblies and ceremonies to commemorate Empire Day, Remembrance Day, or Flag Day. The federal government, which has no constitutional role in education but has obvious interests in strengthening national unity, creates educational materials and sponsors a number of programs designed to foster a common sense of being Canadian. [25]

Current curricular goals with respect to national identity tend to be vague. *The Common Curriculum Framework for Social Studies: Kindergarten to Grade 9* published as part of the Western Canadian Protocol for Collaboration in Basic Education states that it "will ultimately contribute to a Canadian spirit—a spirit that will be fundamental in creating a sense of belonging for each one of our students as he or she engages in active and responsible citizenship locally, nationally and globally."[26] It is unclear exactly what this "Canadian spirit" consists of, but this does represent one of the few explicitly stated goals for national identity in contemporary Canadian curricula, which tend to focus on more generic goals of good citizenship such as active participation, critical thinking and decision-making.

In terms of the participation of ordinary citizens in public life, there is considerable evidence that citizenship and citizenship education in Canada have traditionally been constructed in more elitist and passive terms than in many other democracies, particularly the United States. In other words, between elections Canadian citizens have largely been expected to leave the shaping of the county to political elites.[27] In the past, citizenship education in Canada has, for the most part, reinforced this elitist conception of democratic citizenship.[28] Curtis, for example, points out that from the earliest years of public schooling in Canada West (Ontario) in the nineteenth century, "education was centrally concerned with the making of political subjects, with subjectification. But these political subjects were not seen as self-creating. They were to be made by their governors after the image of an easily governed population."[29]

Studies of more contemporary times have also described practice in citizenship education that is largely consistent with an elitist conception. In his landmark study of civic education in Canada, Hodgetts wrote about the "bland consensus version of history"[30] that dominated Canadian social studies classrooms. History teaching of this type focused almost exclusively on political and military matters, avoided matters of controversy, did not make any connection to the present, and emphasized the memorization of, among other things, "nice, neat little acts of parliament."[31] As Osborne writes, "the combination of curricula, examinations, textbooks, and pedagogy that prevailed before 1968, even when it was successful, served to produce a particularly conservative kind of citizenship."[32] While there is evidence that Hodgetts' research methodology had serious flaws, other studies have lent support to the argument that an elitist conception of citizenship education has dominated Canadian social studies, and several studies make the case that citizenship education in Canada has often been used to attempt to impose a narrow view of national culture on all students.[33]

Although citizenship education in Canada has generally been consistent with the elitist conception, in recent years there has been a move along the continuum to a more activist conception, at least in terms of official policy and mandated curricula. In her 1989 study, Masemann found that "the main ideology of citizenship education is the importance of citizen action and participation."[34] Sears and Hughes demonstrate that this trend has continued, arguing:

> Officially at least, good Canadian citizens are seen as people who are: knowledgeable about contemporary society and the issues it faces; disposed to work toward the common good; supportive of pluralism; and skilled at taking action to make their communities, nation, and world a better place for all people.[35]

They are careful to point out, however, that classroom practice is often different from officially mandated policy and there is considerable circumstantial evidence that citizenship education in Canadian schools maintains its essentially conservative character.

In sum, citizenship is a complex and contested concept and people use it to mean a wide range of things. Approaches to citizenship education naturally flow from these ideas about what constitutes a good citizen. In the past, Canadians, at least those responsible for shaping educational policy and programs, have generally held passive and conservative ideas about what constitutes good citizenship (i.e., good citizens are loyal to the nation state and vote every four years or so) and consequently citizenship education programs in schools have been designed to produce this kind of citizen. An examination of curriculum and policy documents in Canada indicates that in recent years the conception of good citizenship has shifted to emphasize active engagement in public issues. Indeed, a large measure of consensus exists across educational jurisdictions not only at the level of general educational goal statements but also at the level of specific citizenship goals of the intended curriculum. In all provinces and territories the goal of citizenship education is to create knowledgeable individuals committed to active participation in a pluralist society.[36] If there is general agreement that this is the goal of citizenship education, it seems to me that a fundamental question we need to answer before planning programs is: What do we know about where young people are relative to the knowledge, skills, and dispositions necessary for effective citizenship? We will turn to that question now.

Young People as Citizens

The degree to which activity in the field of citizenship education around the world seems to be driven by a sense of crisis about the state of young citizens is striking. Citizens, particularly young ones, are described as ignorant—they do not know even the basic information necessary to function as citizens; alienated—they feel cut off from the political life of their societies, which they see as pervaded by dishonesty and corruption; and agnostic—they do not believe in the values necessary to undergird democratic citizenship.

The Civics Expert Group in Australia coined an interesting phrase, "civic deficit," to capture the idea of pervasive ignorance among the citizenry. The researchers reported that studies they commissioned "revealed a high level of ignorance about Australia's system of governments and its origins."[37] The British Advisory Group on Citizenship also used the language of deficit to describe British citizens' knowledge of their country's history and system of government.[38] In Canada, the Dominion Institute reminds us every July 1 and Remembrance Day that Canadians are disturbingly ignorant of basic facts of Canadian history, government, and contemporary culture, although wealthy Canadian families and foundations have poured millions of dollars into curriculum projects intended to "reclaim" a lost Canadian identity.[39]

In a more academic vein, eminent professors Michael Bliss and Jack Granatstein wonder about the "Sundering of Canada" and *Who Killed Canadian History?*[40] Peter Mansbridge, perhaps English Canada's best-known journalist, summed up the attitude well in a lecture at the Centre for Canadian Studies at Mount Allison University when he said, "Our ignorance is appalling."[41] In Canada and the rest of the world, this mantra of the ignorant citizen has been used to support calls for increased curricular attention to the knowledge of citizenship, particularly the study of national history and politics.

More compelling perhaps than the crisis of ignorance is the crisis of alienation. Carole Hahn, reporting on survey data collected in 1986 and again in 1993 from students in four European countries (Denmark, Germany, the Netherlands, and England) and the United States, outlines generally high levels of cynicism and disengagement from the political process.[42] Similarly, the authors of a significant international study write that "countries find themselves with increasing numbers of adolescents who are disengaged from the political system,"[43] and the British Advisory Group on Citizenship cites reports in that county that speak of a "potentially explosive

alienation" from the institutions of government.[44] In Canada, "voter turnout has declined in three straight federal elections," reaching a record low in the last one.[45]

Several explanations have been advanced to explain this alienation from politics, including high youth unemployment and bad personal experiences with attempts to influence the system.[46] A key reason advanced is disillusionment with corrupt or dishonest politicians. Hahn reports that in 1993 in four of the five countries she studied, less than 25 percent of students said that politicians could be trusted and in the fifth country (Denmark), only half said they could be trusted. She goes on to write, "Everywhere perceptions of honesty declined by about 20 percent from 1986 to 1993."[47] Interview data she collected indicates that media reports of political scandals were a major contributor to this decline. It is not only in the West where the practice of politics is linked to the growth of alienation among citizens. In summing up the situation in Japan, William Cummings writes, "Postwar school education has taught young people to value the democratic process. But postwar politics has been less than enthralling. Thus it would seem that apathy is common among young people and apparently increasing."[48] In Britain and elsewhere, "a coherent and sequential programme of citizenship education" is seen as the solution, at least in large part, to the crisis of alienation.[49]

In addition to the dual crises of ignorance and alienation, one finds in the literature great concern about the lack of commitment to the values of citizenship. I call this the crisis of agnosticism: citizens do not believe in democracy. There is wide agreement that democratic citizenship requires a commitment to certain values or dispositions. In other words, to be a democratic citizen it is not enough to know about democracy, one must believe in democracy as well.

Carole Hahn examined the level of commitment among the students she surveyed in Europe and the U.S. to certain democratic rights. In particular she looked at support for free speech and a free press. What she found was consistent with other work in the field in that it indicated that the students expressed a high degree of support for these rights in the abstract, but when applied to particular situations involving the freedom of groups that the students did not like, the levels of support for their right to express themselves or publish articles in the press declined significantly. Hahn contends that this equivocation about some of "the core principles of individual liberty and respect for all" is cause for concern and is not well-addressed in citizenship education programs. She writes that her school visits in the five countries suggested to her "that educators have not given much deliberate attention to developing in students the capacity to extend fundamental freedoms and basic civil rights to groups that are the most disliked."[50] Because of the crisis of agnosticism, there is a growing focus on developing the values of democratic citizenship in citizenship education programs.

The concern about ignorant, alienated, and agnostic citizens is driving a flurry of activity in citizenship education around the world.[51] In Canada this has led, among other things, to the development of a compulsory grade 10 civics course in Ontario and the requirement that high school students in that province complete forty hours of "community involvement activities" in order to graduate.[52] However much these claims of serious deficit in the knowledge, skills, and dispositions of young citizens ring true, in reality we know very little about what students in Canada know or can do, or how they feel about citizenship.

Close examination reveals that the empirical evidence for the crisis of ignorance facing citizenship and citizenship education is rather thin. Ian McAllister, an Australian political scientist, writing about the so-called new "civics deficit" in his country and elsewhere, argues:

> Ever since mass opinion surveys first began to be used in the 1940's they have consistently shown that most citizens are anything but knowledgeable about politics. The majority know little about politics and possess minimal factual knowledge about the operation of the political system.[53]

In his recent work Ken Osborne makes similar points with regard to historical knowledge in Canada, knowledge that is often regarded as foundational for informed citizenship. While scholars such as Bliss and Granatstein contend there has been a significant decline in knowledge of the history of Canada as a whole, Osborne argues that the evidence does not support this. He demonstrates the lack of historical knowledge among the Canadian population is not new but has been of concern to educators and policy-makers for 100 years or more, and has precipitated at least four previous crises of ignorance in the field of history education.[54]

What about the second element of the crisis, the alienation of citizens from civic participation? By many of the traditional measures—voting rates, numbers of young people joining political parties, levels of trusting politicians and public institutions—there certainly seems to be cause for concern around the world in both established and emerging democracies.[55] A key indicator of this alienation is a serious decline in voting rates. In Canada, for example, voter turn-out reached a record low of 61 percent in the federal election of 2000. The same pattern is being experienced in democracies around the world, and the evidence suggests that the most significant decline is among younger voters.[56] While much of the rhetoric in the citizenship education community attributes this decline to growing cynicism among young people, closer examination of the evidence indicates a much more complex situation. In fact, surveys of young people in Canada indicate "they are no more cynical than older Canadians."[57]

David Buckingham points out that there is a much more positive way of reading young people's disengagement from political processes. That is, young people have good reason to be alienated from a system that does not take them seriously. Perhaps the deficit is not with the young people, he suggests, but with a political system not open to real consultation and effective participation.[58] Hahn's interviews with young people in Britain seems to confirm this, as these young citizens often identified not being listened to or taken seriously by politicians as a key factor in their alienation. Similarly, the Centre for Research and Information on Canada suggests that structural elements such as Liberal Party hegemony, the permanent voters' list and the first-past-the-post system of election might all contribute to voter disaffection. They argue that young people are no more alienated than their parents but are less likely to vote out of a sense of duty.[59] One could argue that attitude is a positive one for democracy in the long run.[60] It is interesting to note that, while Hahn found students largely alienated from the formal political process, she did not find them alienated from all forms of participation. They were very willing to participate in community-based activities where they could see themselves making a difference.[61] A recent study asked a representative sample of fourteen-year-olds in twenty-eight countries about the kinds of civic activities they intended to participate in as adults, and the results indicate that these students are more positively disposed to participation than is evident in recent surveys of adult participation in Britain and the United States.[62] Madeleine Gauthier surveys recent research on the participation of youth in Québec and concludes that, while there is a definite shift away from participation in traditional party politics, there are clear signs that a new political generation is active and shaping its own sense of what it means to be civically engaged. She writes:

> Despite commonly-held opinions, modern young people are far from apathetic. They are active at various levels of involvement in community life, although political partisanship is often suspect, even sometimes by those who officially belong to a political party.[63]

In looking at longitudinal data from across advanced industrial democracies, Dalton argues that, while "there is clear evidence of a general erosion of support for politicians"[64] and formal political processes, one "response to popular dissatisfaction has been a move toward participatory democracy."[65] In early 2003, protests against a war in Iraq brought millions into the streets worldwide. While reports indicate these protestors were from a wide range of ages and social classes, there were many young people concerned enough to join and, in many cases, organize the rallies.[66]

What of growing concerns about an apparent lack of belief in certain fundamental democratic values? Is it true that young citizens in particular lack such basic dispositions as respect for diversity, open-mindedness, or commitment to the common good? While news reports of rising xenophobia evidenced in racially motivated attacks on foreign workers and ethnic minorities in Europe and the United States, or of fights between black and white students at a Canadian high school, might lead one to conclude there is a serious deficit of democratic values among the young, careful scrutiny demonstrates the situation is not that simple. Hahn reports, for example, that the European and American students she surveyed and interviewed were very concerned about racism in their societies. So much so, in fact, that they supported limiting the public speech and access to the press for members of identified racist groups.[67] While one might argue that willingness to support the suppression of basic rights for some groups is evidence of low levels of commitment to certain democratic values, it does, however, demonstrate that many young people are indeed concerned about respecting ethnocultural diversity. A British Council conference on citizenship education heard from secondary school students and teachers about student-initiated programs to promote human rights, counter racism, and develop pan-European understanding. In several cases students had worked with public authorities and advocacy groups, such as Amnesty International, to organize workshops and conferences for their peers on issues related to human rights and diversity.[68] In Canada, historian and nationally syndicated columnist Gwynne Dyer has written and lectured widely about how multicultural and immigration policies have largely been successful in making Canada into a more diverse, tolerant, and stable society.[69]

All of this is not to dismiss concerns about the ignorance, alienation, and agnosticism of young citizens but simply to say we really do not know much about where students in Canada, or elsewhere in the world, are in relation to our citizenship goals for them. Almost forty years ago A.B. Hodgetts directed a nation-wide study of civic education in Canada that included observation in hundreds of classrooms, surveys of thousands of students and teachers, and careful analysis of textbooks and other teaching materials.[70] Hodgetts' report examined student knowledge and attitudes, pedagogical practice, the quality of teaching materials, and teacher training. Despite methodological difficulties, the report became widely accepted as the baseline for social studies teaching and learning in Canada, and its recommendations, particularly the establishment of the Canada Studies Foundation, had a significant impact on social studies curricula, materials, and teaching.

Since 1968, however, there has been no systematic, large-scale effort to evaluate civic education in Canada either by academic researchers or through provincial or national testing programs. Small-scale, sporadic studies have been reported in the academic literature but by and large these have been uncoordinated and therefore have failed to provide the basis for a reliable body of knowledge.[71] Testing programs, where they exist, are largely focused on the knowledge covered in particular courses or programs and are only tangentially related to the situated knowledge of citizenship as described above. There is virtually no effort to assess the skills or dispositions of citizenship on a wide scale. In recent years the Dominion Institute has commissioned several surveys of Canadians' knowledge related to history and citizenship. The results of these surveys have been widely reported in the popular press and have been used as part of a lobbying campaign for more and better history and social studies education in Canadian schools, but again, only factual information is being tested, with little attention to context. This testing is certainly not consistent with the sort of citizenship knowledge described in curricula and policies across the country. Some very promising research has begun over the past several years but it is far too early to make sweeping policy and curricular recommendations from this work and it is clear that there is a range of ways in which young people understand their citizenship and a one-size-fits-all approach will probably not work.

Educating Citizens

The prevailing ideology of citizenship education found in contemporary Canadian curricula tends towards an activist or participatory conception of citizenship. What appears to be clearly associated with this activist/participatory ideology is a commitment to a pedagogy of active learning.

Curriculum documents generally include suggestions for teachers on appropriate teaching and learning strategies. Ministry/department of education guidelines include teaching strategies ranging from direct instruction through interactive and indirect instruction to independent study and experiential learning. In 1991 Saskatchewan Education identified forty-six specific instructional methods as elements in these general strategies.[72] They are reproduced in Newfoundland's 1993 *Curriculum Framework for Social Studies* and again in the 1998 curriculum guide *Atlantic Canada in the Global Community,* a joint enterprise of the four Atlantic provinces (see Table 1). None of the methods emphasizes the "chalk-and-talk" and "question-and-answer" methods that Hodgetts identified as the dominant instructional approaches. Of course, the methods identified here constitute a broad repertoire of teaching/learning activities that includes, but is not limited to, the interests and concerns of citizenship education.

The Newfoundland and Labrador *Curriculum Framework for Social Studies,* in addressing the issue of teaching/learning approaches, says "there is no one best method, rather, there is a method which, in a particular situation, for a definite purpose, at a specific grade level, with certain resources available, will be effective."[73] No doubt this is so, but there is little specific direction to the teacher concerning how to match the method with the situation, purpose, grade level, and resources. Invariably, the teaching suggestions or recommended activities or sample teaching strategies encountered by teachers in curriculum guidelines are presented as choices from which they might select some or none, according to their professional judgement. Specific learning experiences are never mandated, nor are any particular learning strategies. Indeed, very little is expressed by way of preferred methods except a vague commitment to support those that require more active learning on the part of students. "These are only suggestions and ideas that can be adapted and modified for different situations and needs,"[74] a Saskatchewan teacher's guide states. Certainly the implication in all of the guidelines is that teachers should choose whether to employ a strategy, when to employ it, and how to employ it.

What is abundantly clear is that the ministries/ departments are reluctant to give firm direction on the matter of teaching and learning strategies in areas that are normally associated with citizenship education. An exception to this lies in the growing approval of learning activities that involve young people in direct participation in and experience of life in the community. Often this takes the form of volunteer work with social service agencies, in the belief that such experience will contribute to the development of a commitment to voluntarism. Apprenticeship-like experiences in the realms of business and politics are also popular; again, the presumption is that the direct experience of participation will help foster a commitment to participation in the life of the community, however defined. The recent report of the Conseil supérieur de l'Éducation (CSE) places special emphasis upon extracurricular initiatives in

Québec, such as student involvement in student councils, youth parliaments, community involvement, and the work of international associations such as Solidarité Tiers Monde.[75]

This faith in "service learning" as a vehicle for developing citizenship is showing up in educational jurisdictions across North America with many, including Ontario, requiring certain levels of community service for high school graduation. Rahima Wade and David Saxe, in their review of the literature on service-learning, point out that these programs typically focus on four key outcome areas: academic development—students will learn something about the issues in their communities and develop academic skills; social and personal development—students will develop a sense of altruism (commitment to the common good) as well as heightened self-esteem; political efficacy—students will believe that they can participate effectively, that they can make a difference; and future participation—students will grow into adults who are more likely to be participating citizens.[76]

In June of 2002 the McGill Department of Po-

TABLE 1

POSSIBLE TEACHING/LEARNING APPROACHES

Direct Instruction	Interactive Instruction	Indirect Instruction	Independent Study	Experiential Learning
Explicit teaching	Debates	Problem-solving	Essays	Field trips
Drill & practice	Role playing	Case studies	Computer assisted instruction	Conducting experiments
Structured overview	Panels	Inquiry	Reports	Simulations
Mastery lecture	Brainstorming	Reading for meaning	Learning activity packages	Games
Compare and contrast	Peer practice	Reflective discussion	Correspondence lessons	Focused imaging
Didactic questions	Discussion	Concept formation	Learning contracts	Field observations
Demonstrations	Laboratory groups	Concept mapping	Homework	Role playing
Guides for reading, listening, viewing	Cooperative learning groups	Concept attainment	Research projects	Synectics
	Problem-solving	Cloze procedures	Assigned questions	Model-building
	Circle of knowledge		Learning centres	Surveys
	Tutorial groups			
	Interviewing			

litical Science sponsored a workshop titled "Citizen-ship on Trial: Interdisciplinary Perspectives on the Political Socialization of Adolescents."[77] This event brought together political scientists, social theorists, and educators from Canada, the United States, and Europe to share research relating to young people and citizenship. A number of the presentations dealt with evidence of the relationship between youth involvement in community organizations and later civic activity. All presenters argued that the relationship between community involvement when young and later civic engagement is very complex. There is clear evidence that those who are engaged in civic activity as young people are more likely to be engaged as adults, but there is no evidence that this is a cause and effect relationship; it may simply indicate the personality traits of those individuals who choose to participate.[78] The citizenship education community needs to stay connected to this growing body of work and engage in discussion and debate with colleagues in political science.

The truth is that while there is a growing body of research knowledge about children's learning and how to foster that learning through teaching, not much of what we know has been systematically applied to the specific context of citizenship education. Preliminary work has begun but much more needs to be done. The research of Carole Hahn and the International Association for the Evaluation of Educational Achievement (IEA) indicates, for example, what appears to be a correlation between classrooms in which important social issues are discussed and investigated in a climate of openness and debate, and greater student knowledge and engagement.[79] This is helpful information but needs to be pushed further so that we can begin to understand the specific kinds of issues and pedagogical approaches that will foster growth towards good citizenship.

It is important to think about pedagogy not only in terms of the delivery of lessons in the classroom but also in terms of the context in which those lessons are delivered. Despite the fact that every educational jurisdiction in Canada states in policy and curricula that schools are places for the development of democratic citizenship and that students ought to learn to be involved and to confront difficult social and public issues, schools are often not very democratic places for either students or teachers. There is evidence, for example, that teachers resist dealing with critical issues in the classroom and that schools often discipline students who seek, in relatively benign ways, to express concern about policies or practices.[80] In the words of student David Brand, who was disqualified from participating in a school event because he protested his school's requirement that all students watch a daily program of news provided by the Youth News Network, "School is not the place to have an opinion."[81]

In spite of platitudes about preparing students for democratic citizenship, the attitude of educators often seems to be consistent with that expressed by Gene Hackman's character in the movie *Crimson Tide*. Hackman, playing the captain of a nuclear submarine, says to his first officer, "We are here to defend democracy, not practise it." Too often citizenship education in schools is sterile and removed from real issues—it is designed to teach about democracy, not practise it. When this is the case, students "learn lessons different from the ones taught in their social studies class about exercising one's democratic rights."[82]

Conclusion: The Way Forward

I began this chapter with Osborne's suggestion that citizenship is not a high priority on the educational agendas of ministries of education or the public across Canada. It is clear that at the level of rhetoric this is not true: there is lots of talk in policy and curriculum documents about citizenship as a central goal for schooling in general and social studies education in particular. A look below the surface, however, demonstrates Osborne is clearly right: technical and vocational concerns have been driving the educational ship over the last number of years and social studies is a low priority in educational jurisdictions around the world.[83] This is particularly clear in the level of attention given to the subject in provincial and national testing programs where it is virtually non-existent (Alberta is the only province to regularly test social studies on a province-wide basis), as well as in curriculum reform initiatives, which generally see social studies lagging well behind work in literacy, mathematics, science, and technology.

In my view, some of the blame for the decline of citizenship as a real priority for schooling can be laid squarely at the feet of those of us who work in the field of citizenship education. We are often not clear about what it is we mean by good citizenship, how it can be effectively taught, and how we can assess student progress towards it. A review of the public education system in Ontario argues, "Policies introduced over the past seven or eight years were developed and enacted without much demonstrable attention to empirical evidence about what would improve teaching and learning."[84] While this report is commenting on educational reform across the board, the same claim could be made about reform in citizenship education over time and across jurisdictions: it is often driven more by hype and personal agendas than by evidence and thoughtful deliberation.[85] If we want citizenship education to be taken seriously, it is incumbent on those of us in the field to provide a knowledge base to support reform. Some of this work has begun. The recent IEA study, for example, has provided a broad overview of the intended curriculum in citizenship education in many parts of the world as well as a sense of the civic knowledge, skills, and attitudes of fourteen-year-olds in twenty-eight countries.[86] Carole Hahn also provides interesting comparative data about civic education programs and students' knowledge, skills, and values in Europe and the U.S.[87] The data set for the IEA study is massive (90,000 students from twenty-eight countries were surveyed) and the analysis of that data is still at the preliminary stages. Much more work can and should be done with this data to address more specific and complex questions.

A recent survey conducted with first-year anglophone and francophone college and university students in several regions of Canada has also produced some interesting results. The survey sought to investigate several areas related to citizenship: where these students find their sense of belonging (to the nation, province or local area); what their attitudes are to diversity; and what their level of civic engagement is (both at the time of the survey and projected into the future). Again, the survey data is in the early stages of analysis but it clearly shows a number of types, which vary according to province, linguistic background, gender, and so on.[88]

Along with this large-scale survey work it is essential to build a more qualitative body of knowledge about the ways students think and feel about citizenship. There is a growing body of constructivist work on students' thinking in social studies, but it is very much in its infancy, particularly compared with work in science or mathematics.[89] This kind of work is necessary to fill out and extend the kind of knowledge large-scale studies like the IEA Civic Education study provide. For example, the IEA study has very positive results related to students' acceptance of diversity. When asked if immigrants should have the opportunity to keep their own language, for example, 77 percent of the students agreed or strongly agreed. On the question of being able to keep their own customs and lifestyle, 80 percent agreed or strongly agreed, and 81 percent felt immigrants should have the same rights as everyone else.[90]

Overall, the authors of the report on the research conclude, "Attitudes toward immigrants are generally positive."[91] While this might appear to be good news, it strikes me that much closer examination is necessary. All of the questions about immigrants on the IEA survey were posed in the abstract, with no implications for respondents. It is easy to say immigrants ought to be able to keep their own language and cultural practices and exercise the same rights as everyone else if there is no implied or actual accommodation required on the part of other citizens. What if, however, immigrants begin to demand government services in their own languages, raising the costs for those services and the tax burden for everyone; would the responses remain so positive? Accommodation, after all, is where the rubber hits the road with regard to diversity. A key question is: To what degree are citizens willing to accommodate diversity even when it costs them something materially or socially? The IEA study does not answer this question, but it needs to be addressed. The Citizenship Education Research and Development Group at the University of New

Brunswick and others are engaged in programs of phenomenographic research to get at the structure of young citizens' thinking about ideas such as respect for diversity, dissent, political participation, and privacy. It is hoped this kind of work will expand on other quantitative and qualitative work about young people's thinking in the social realm.

These are examples of some of the work being done that has the potential to build a knowledge base for reform in the field of citizenship education. This is a good beginning but it is just a beginning. Much more needs to be done. Some years ago Marker and Mehlinger reviewed research in social studies education for a major research handbook and concluded that most of the published literature was not empirical in nature but was concerned with advocating one approach or another with little or no basis in evidence.[92] Similarly, it seems to me that too much energy and print in the field of citizenship education has been given over to cult-like mantras about both what is wrong with citizenship education and how it can be fixed. Educational scholars in the field have a responsibility to provide deeper analysis about both areas to help, in the words of Janice Gross Stein, move the public conversation "from cult to analysis."[93]

Endnotes

[1]   Ken Osborne, "Public Schooling and Citizenship Education in Canada," in *Educating Citizens for a Pluralistic Society*, ed. Rosa Bruno-Jofré and Natalia Aponiuk, special issue, *Canadian Ethnic Studies* 32, no. 1 (2000): 40.

[2]   British Columbia Ministry of Education, *The Graduation Program 2004* (Victoria: Author, 2003), 3.

[3]   Ibid., 3–4.

[4]   Atlantic Provinces Education Foundation, *The Atlantic Canadian Framework for Essential Graduation Learning in Schools* (Halifax: Author, n.d.), 6–11.

[5]   Ministère de l'Éducation, *Education in Québec: An Overview* (Québec: Gouvernement du Québec, 2001), 5.

[6]   Denis Wall, Marita Moll, and Bernie Frose-Germain, "Living Democracy: Renewing Our Vision of Citizenship Education," *Canadian Teachers' Federation* (December 2000): 6.

[7]   Ibid.

[8]   George S. Tomkins, *A Common Countenance: Stability and Change in the Canadian Curriculum* (Scarborough, ON: Prentice-Hall, 1986), 15.

[9]   Kenneth Leithwood, Michael Fullan, and Nancy Watson, *The Schools We Need: Recent Education Policy in Ontario, Recommendations for Moving Forward* (Toronto: OISE Press, 2003), 5. See also Charles Ungerleider, *Failing Our Kids: How We Are Ruining Our Public Schools* (Toronto: McClelland & Stewart, 2003), 29–34.

[10] Judith Torney-Purta, John Schwille, and Jo-Ann Amadeo, eds., *Civic Education Across Countries: Twenty-four National Case Studies from the IEA Civic Education Project* (Amsterdam: IEA, 1999), 30.

[11] "Heroes and Icons," *Time,* http://www.time.com/time/time100/heroes/index.html.

[12] For a comprehensive review of this debate see Ken Osborne, "'Our History Syllabus Has Us Gasping': History in Canadian Schools—Past, Present, and Future," *Canadian Historical Review* 81, no. 3 (September 2000), 404–435.

[13] G. Marker and H. Mehlinger, "Social Studies, " in *Handbook of Research on Curriculum: A Project of the American Educational Association*, ed. P.W. Jackson (New York: Macmillan, 1992), 832.

[14] W.B. Gallie, *Philosophy and Historical Understanding* (London: Chatto & Windus, 1964), 158.

[15] Marker and Mehlinger, "Social Studies," 835.

[16] W.E. Connolly, *Terms of Political Discourse* (Lexington, MA: Heath, 1974), 24.

[17] See, for example, Charles Taylor, *Reconciling the Solitudes: Essays on Canadian Federalism and Nationalism* (Montreal: McGill-Queen's University Press, 1993); Will Kymlicka, *Finding Our Way: Rethinking Ethnocultural Relations in Canada* (Toronto: Oxford University Press, 1998); and W. Kaplan, ed., *Belonging: The Meaning and Future of Canadian Citizenship*, (Montreal: McGill-Queen's University Press, 1993).

[18] Taylor, *Reconciling the Solitudes*, 182.

[19] Desmond Morton, "Divided Loyalties? Divided Country?" in *Belonging*, 54.

[20] Michel Pagé and Marie-Hélène Chastenay, "Citizenship Profiles of Young Canadians," *Canadian Diversity* 2, no. 1, (Spring 2003): 36–38.

[21] Os Guiness, "Tribespeople, Idiots, or Citizens? Religious Liberty and the Reforging of American Public Philosophy," in *Social Education* 54, no. 5 (1990): 278–286.

[22] I have written extensively of these concerns in "The Cult of Citizenship" (paper presented at Reimagining Citizenship as an Interdisciplinary Curriculum, A CSSE Pre-conference, Dalhousie University, Halifax, Tuesday, May 27, 2003). See also Centre for Research and Information on Canada, *Voter Participation in Canada: Is Canadian Democracy in Crisis?* (Montreal: Author, October 2001); Pippa Norris, ed., *Critical Citizens: Global Support for Democratic Governance* (Oxford: Oxford University Press, 1999).

[23] France Gagnon and Michel Pagé, Conceptual Framework for An Analysis of Citizenship in the Liberal Democracies, vol. 2: Six Approaches to Citizenship in Six Liberal Democracies (prepared for Multiculturalism Directorate and Citizen Participation Directorate DG, Citizens' Participation and

Multiculturalism and Strategic Research and Analysis (SRA) Directorate DG, Strategic Planning and Policy Coordination, Department of Canadian Heritage, May 1999), 126.

24 See, for example, Norris, *Critical Citizens*; and Judith Torney-Purta et al., *Citizenship Education in Twenty-eight Countries: Civic Knowledge and Engagement at Age Fourteen* (Amsterdam: IEA, 2001).

25 See, for example, Alan Sears, "'Scarcely Yet a People': State Policy in Citizenship Education, 1947–1982," (doctoral dissertation, University of British Columbia).

26 Western Canadian Protocol for Collaboration in Basic Education, *The Common Curriculum Framework for Social Studies: Kindergarten to Grade 9* (Winnipeg: Manitoba Education, Training and Youth, 2002), 3.

27 R. Bothwell, "Something of Value? Subjects and Citizens in Canadian History," in *Belonging*, 25–49; P. Resnick, *The Masks of Proteus: Reflections on the Canadian State* (Montreal: McGill-Queen's University Press, 1990); and S.M. Lipsett, *Continental Divide: The Values and Institutions of the United States and Canada* (New York: Routledge, 1991).

28 Alan Sears, "Social Studies as Citizenship Education in English Canada: A Review of Research," *Theory and Research in Social Education* 22, no. 1 (1994): 6–43; Ken Osborne, "'Education is the Best National Insurance': Citizenship Education in Canadian Schools Past and Present," *Canadian and International Education* 25, no. 2 (December 1996): 31–58; and Alan Sears and Andrew Hughes, "Citizenship Education and Current Educational Reform," *Canadian Journal of Education* 21, no. 2 (1996): 123–142.

29 Bruce Curtis, *Building the Educational State: Canada West, 1836–1871* (London, ON: Althouse Press, 1988), 102.

30 A.B. Hodgetts, *What Culture? What Heritage? A Study of Civic Education in Canada* (Toronto: OISE Press, 1968), 24.

31 Ibid.

32 Ken Osborne, *In Defence of History: Teaching the Past and the Meaning of Democratic Citizenship*, Our Schools/Our Selves Monograph Series, no. 17 (Toronto: Our Schools/Our Selves Education Foundation, 1995), 21.

33 George S. Tomkins, "The Scandal in Canadian Studies," (ERIC Document ED044335, 1969). See also Sears, "Social Studies as Citizenship Education."

34 V. Masemann, "The Current Status of Teaching About Citizenship in Canadian Schools," in *Canada and Citizenship Education*, ed. K. McLeod (Toronto: Canadian Education Association, 1989), 29.

35 Sears and Hughes, "Citizenship Education and Current Educational Reform," 134

36 Ibid.; and A. Sears, G. Clarke, and A. Hughes, "Canadian Citizenship Education: The Pluralist Ideal and Citizenship Education for a Post-modern State," in *Civic Education Across Countries*, ed. Torney-Purta, Schwille, and Amadeo, 111–135.

37 Civics Expert Group, *Whereas The People . . . Civics and Citizenship Education* (Canberra: Australian Government Publishing Service, 1994), 132.

38 Advisory Group on Citizenship, *Education for Citizenship and the Teaching of Democracy in Schools* (London: Qualifications and Curriculum Authority, 1998), 14.

39 See, for example, Rudyard Griffiths, "A Culture of Forgetfulness in a Country with Much to Remember: Military Heritage," *National Post*, November 11, 2000, B04; and Julie Smyth, "Ignorance of Our Own History Shames Canadians, Survey: Onus Placed on Schools, Wide Support for Tougher Standards," *National Post*, September 10, 2001, A1.

40 Michael Bliss, "Privatizing the Mind: The Sundering of Canadian History, The Sundering of Canada," *Journal of Canadian Studies* 26, no. 4 (1991/92): 5–17; and Jack L. Granatstein, *Who Killed Canadian History?* (Toronto: HarperCollins, 1998).

41 Peter Mansbridge, *Canada's History: Why Do We Know So Little?* (Sackville, NS: Centre For Canadian Studies, Mount Allison University, 1997), 7.

42 Carole Hahn, *Becoming Political: Comparative Perspectives on Citizenship Education* (Albany: State University of New York Press, 1998); ———, "Citizenship Education: An Empirical Study of Policy, Practices and Outcomes," *Oxford Review of Education* 25 (March–June, 1999): 231–250.

43 Torney-Purta, Schwille, and Amadeo, *Civic Education Across Countries*, 14.

44 Advisory Group on Citizenship, *Education for Citizenship*, 16.

45 Centre for Research and Information on Canada, *Voter Participation in Canada*, 4.

46 Torney-Purta, Schwille, and Amadeo, *Civic Education Across Countries*; and Hahn, *Becoming Policital*.

47 Hahn, *Becoming Political*, 29.

48 William K. Cummings, "Education for Democracy in Japan and Asia," in *Can Democracy be Taught? Perspectives on Education for Democracy in the United States, Central and Eastern Europe, Russia, South Africa, and Japan*, ed. Andrew Oldenquist (Bloomington, IN: Phi Delta Kappa Educational Foundation, 1996), 215.

49 Advisory Group on Citizenship, *Education for Citizenship*, 16.

50 Hahn, *Becoming Political*, 175.

51 This activity is discussed in more detail in Sears, "The Cult of Citizenship."

52 Ontario Ministry of Education and Training, *High School Diploma Requirements* (Ontario: Queen's Printer, 2004), http://www.edu.gov.on.ca/eng/document/brochure/stepup/high.html (accessed August 11, 2003).

53 Ian McAllister, "Civic Education and Political Knowledge in Australia," *Australian Journal of Political Science* 33, no. 1 (March 1998): 7.

54 Osborne, "'Our History Syllabus Has Us Gasping,'" 404–435.

55 See, for example, Hahn, *Becoming Political;* and Torney-Purta, Schwille, and Amadeo, *Civic Education Across Countries*; and Norris, *Critical Citizens*.

56 Centre for Research and Information on Canada, "Voter Participation," 4; Kent M. Jennings and Laura Stoker, "Genera-

tional Change, Life Processes, and Social Capital" (paper presented at Citizenship on Trial: Interdisciplinary Perspectives on the Political Socialization of Adolescents, McGill University, Montreal, June 20–21, 2002); and Dietlind Stolle and Marc Hooghe, "Preparing for the Learning School of Democracy: The Effects of Youth and Adolescent Involvement on Value Patterns and Participation in Adult Life" (paper presented at Ibid.).

57 Centre for Research and Information on Canada, *Voter Participation*, 1.

58 David Buckingham, "Young People, Politics and News Media: Beyond Political Socialization," *Oxford Review of Education* 25 (March–June, 1999): 171–175.

59 Centre for Research and Information on Canada, *Voter Participation*.

60 Hahn, *Becoming Political*.

61 Ibid.

62 Torney-Purta et al., *Citizenship Education in Twenty-eight Countries*; Geraint Parry and George Moyser, "More Participation, More Democracy?" in *Defining and Measuring Democracy* 36, Sage Modern Politics Series, ed. David Beetham (London: Sage Publications, 1994):44–62; and National Center for Educational Statistics, *1996 National Household Education Survey: Adult Civic Involvement in the United States* (Washington, DC: U.S. Department of Education, Office of Educational Research and Improvement, 1997).

63 Madeleine Gauthier, "The Inadequacy of Concepts: The Rise of Youth Interest in Civic Participation in Québec" (paper presented at Citizenship on Trial), 10.

64 Russell Dalton, "Political Support in Advanced Industrial Democracies," in *Critical Citizens*, 63.

65 Ibid., 76.

66 Robert D. McFadden, "Threats and Responses: Overview; From New York to Melbourne, Cries for Peace," *The New York Times*, February 16, 2003, http://ww.newyorktimes.com/.

67 Hahn, *Becoming Political*, 138.

68 There were several presentations of this nature at the British Council Conference Education for Citizenship: Preparation in Schools for Full Participation in Democracy in Adult Life (London, October 10–15, 1999).

69 See, for example, Gwynne Dyer, "He Saved His Country," *Moncton Times and Transcript*, September 30, 2000, D11; ———, "Demographic Changes Are Helping to Ease the Threat of Separatism," *Fredericton Daily Gleaner*, December 14, 1998, A6.

70 Hodgetts, *What Culture? What Heritage?*

71 Sears, "Social Studies as Citizenship Education."

72 Saskatchewan Education, *Instructional Approaches: A Framework for Professional Practice* (Regina: Author, 1991), 51.

73 Government of Newfoundland and Labrador, Department of Education, *A Curriculum Framework for Social Studies: Navigating the Future* (St. John's: Author, 1993), 61.

74 Saskatchewan Education, *History 20, World Issues: A Teacher's Activity Guide* (Regina: Author, 1994), 1–6.

75 Conseil supérieur de l'Éducation, *Éduquer à la citoyenneté: rapport annuel* (Québec: Gouvernement du Québec, 1998).

76 Rahima C. Wade and David W. Saxe, "Community Service—Learning in the Social Studies: Historical Roots, Empirical Evidence, Critical Issues," *Theory and Research in Social Education* 24, no. 2 (1996): 333.

77 Information about the 2002 conference, including the program and papers, can be accessed at http://www.youthconference.mcgill.ca/.

78 Dietlind Stolle and Marc Hooghe, "Preparing for the Learning School of Democracy" (paper presented at Citizenship on Trial).

79 Hahn, *Becoming Political*; Torney-Purta et al., *Citizenship Education in Twenty-eight Countries*.

80 See, for example, Alan Sears and Mark Perry, "Beyond Civics: Paying Attention to the Contexts of Citizenship Education," *Education Canada* 40, no. 3: 28–31.

81 David Brand, "The High Cost of Speaking Out in School," http://www.straightgoods.com/item323.asp (accessed April 27, 2000).

82 Charles Ungerleider, *Failing Our Kids: How We Are Ruining Our Public Schools* (Toronto: McClelland & Stewart, 2003).

83 Torney-Purta, Schwille, and Amadeo, *Civic Education Across Countries*.

84 Kenneth Leithwood, Michael Fullan, and Nancy Watson, *The Schools We Need: A New Blueprint for Ontario, Final Report* (Toronto: OISE Press, 2003), 18.

85 Sears, "The Cult of Citizenship."

86 Torney-Purta, Schwille, and Amadeo, *Civic Education Across Countries; and* Torney-Purta et al., *Citizenship Education in Twenty-eight Countries*.

87 Hahn, *Becoming Political*.

88 Pagé and Chastenay, "Citizenship Profiles."

89 For recent examples, see Jere Brophy and Janet Alleman, "Primary-Grade Students' Knowledge and Thinking About the Economics of Meeting Families' Shelter Needs," *American Educational Research Journal* 39, no. 22 (Summer 2002): 423–468; and Jere Brophy, Janet Alleman, and Carolyn O'Mahony, "Primary-Grade Students' Knowledge and Thinking About Food Production and the Origins of Common Foods," *Theory and Research in Social Education* 31, no. 1 (2003): 10–50.

90 Torney-Purta et al., *Citizenship Education in Twenty-eight Countries*, 203.

91 Ibid., 105.

92 Marker and Mehlinger, "Social Studies," 830–851.

93 Janice Gross Stein, *The Cult of Efficiency* (Toronto: Anansi, 2001), 192.

Part 2

Content Challenges and Prospects

The chapters in Part 1 attest to the fact there is significant debate about the meanings of social studies and citizenship education. This conversation continues in Part 2 where the authors explore what content should be included in social studies. As several chapters in Part 1 make clear, history and geography have formed the traditional core of social studies instruction. Even among advocates of these disciplines, there is a considerable range of views about just what history and geography to teach. For example, Peter Seixas advocates a particular approach to teaching history with the central objective being the development of historical thinking. Others, such as Jack Granatstein, have challenged this, contending that learning specific historical content should be the central purpose of teaching the subject. Wanda Hurren argues that school geography should borrow from contemporary research and trends in academic geography and take a much more critical stance than has been the case in the past.

As Penney Clark and Ken Osborne make clear, social studies education in most Canadian jurisdictions has moved away from an exclusive focus on history and geography to include attention to a much wider range of content areas. Sometimes these show up in the curriculum as separate disciplines such as law, economics, or political science, but most often they appear as part of an integrated social studies approach organized around themes or issues. Jeff Orr makes the case, for example, that Native Studies works much better integrated into compulsory so-

cial studies courses than as a separate area of study where it is often marginalized. Wanda Cassidy argues in favour of teaching "law related education," as opposed to law per se, and she situates LRE squarely within an integrated social studies curriculum. George Richardson shows how various conceptualizations of globalization have provided a focus for integrated social studies, and Lisa Loutzenheiser, Manju Varma-Joshi, and Kathy Bickmore demonstrate that issues related to gender, race, and ethnicity cut across disciplinary lines. It is clearly the case that images are part of every subject area and, according to Walt Werner, they need to be critically analyzed to the same extent that other authors ask us to be critical of print media.

All these authors have particular conceptualizations of their fields and where they fit in social studies education. These can be traced back and linked to the conceptions of social studies outlined in Part 1. All argue their subject matter is not only worthy of curriculum inclusion, but essential to a comprehensive social education. Again, as teachers you will have to make choices about what to teach and how to teach it. In teaching about confederation, for example, will you focus on developing historical empathy for the particular actors involved; celebrating a great national achievement; examining the legal division of powers between provinces and the federal government; exploring the exclusion of women, Aboriginal people, and minority groups from the process; or setting it in the global context of nineteenth-century nation-building? It is easy to respond with "all of the above," but the truth is, limited time and resources are going to force you to make choices. The authors in Part 2 present powerful arguments for going in particular directions.

As you read these chapters consider how you would answer the following questions:

1. How are the authors' conceptions of their subject matter related to the conceptions of social studies and citizenship education presented in Part 1?

2. Could Ken Osborne (Part 1) argue that all the subjects discussed here are better dealt with through history than through social studies? Why or why not?

3. How is the development of each subject area discussed here linked to the more general history of social studies and citizenship education as outlined by Penney Clark, Alan Sears, and Stéphane Lévesque in Part 1?

4. How are the subjects discussed here dealt with in present social studies curricula as described by Patricia Shields and Douglas Ramsay in Part 1?

5. What unique contribution can each type of subject matter make to social studies education?

6. Are the subjects related to each other? If so, how are they related?

7. Should each subject area be included in the social studies curriculum? If so, how should they be included and in which grades? If not, what subject(s) should receive priority?

8. Given the context in which you teach or will be teaching, what possibilities and constraints are there for including the various subject areas in your social studies curriculum?

CHAPTER 6

Teaching Historical Thinking

Peter Seixas and Carla Peck[‡]

To clarify the goals of teaching history in the schools, we begin by presenting three scenarios involving young people's encounters with history outside of school.

For entertainment, two teenaged friends go to a film dealing with a historical topic, perhaps Pearl Harbor. They are swept into the cinematic portrayal and emerge at the end, one saying to the other, "How could people have thought that way back then?"

A family from eastern Canada visits Victoria's Royal British Columbia Museum. Walking through the "school" in a reconstruction of a turn-of-the-twentieth century mining town, the parents encourage the ten- and twelve-year-olds to imagine what it must have been like for settlers in early British Columbia. "I'm glad I didn't have to go to that school," says one.

A thirteen-year-old girl, reading Karen Cushman's *Catherine, Called Birdy*,[1] a fictional novel about a girl in thirteenth-century England, exclaims to herself, with a shock of recognition, "She feels exactly the way I do about being cooped up by my parents!"

Historical film, historical reconstructions, and historical fiction are all designed to sweep their audiences into an apparent past. When successful, the audiences imagine, as do the people mentioned above, that they are experiencing history as histori-

cal actors experienced it, that they have a direct window into what the past looked like, felt like, and what it meant. How can school history possibly compete with these media?

In this chapter, we will argue that school history has a different objective, and that it should come at history from an entirely different angle. While these genres aim to sweep students in, school history should provide students with the ability to approach historical narratives critically—precisely not to be "swept in." That is, a good history curriculum would prompt students to ask of cinematic and fictional accounts of the past, as well as their textbooks' and teachers' accounts, who constructed this account and why? What sources did they use? What other accounts are there of the same events or lives? How and why do they differ? Which should we believe?

The ability to confront historical accounts critically, however, is not all that should be aimed for in the school history curriculum. On the positive side, students need also to begin to be able to offer accounts of the past that they have good reason to believe. This is an enormously complex process, of course, and some readers will stop right here and say, "Leave that to the historians! We're lucky if students even learn a few historical facts." We would argue, however, that young people do have images of the past in their minds, and that in their more thoughtful moments they do sporadically, incompletely, and often inaccurately, attempt to figure out what the past might mean for them and for their futures. The job of history education is to work with

[‡] Carla Peck revised the original version of this chapter, written by Peter Seixas for *Trends and Issues in Canadian Social Studies*.

these fragments of thinking and develop them so that students have a better basis upon which to make sense of their own lives. That is, we need to teach students to think historically. In part because history in Canada is taught largely within the context of social studies, we have done all too little thinking about what "thinking historically" really means.[2]

Consider the following two quotes, which seem, on first glance, to be pointed in two diametrically opposite directions:

The past is never dead, it's not even past.
—William Faulkner[3]

The past is a foreign country: they do things differently there.—L.P. Hartley[4]

What might these quotations tell us about how to think about our relationship to the past? Faulkner points to the fact that the past suffuses every part of our lives; it is embodied in our streets, buildings, our schools, our personalities, our government, and our ideas. Indeed, it is embodied in our own bodies; our civilization's scientific legacy was injected into my arm in the form of a tetanus shot yesterday. A hernia scar is a legacy of the relatively recent past, while my genetic inheritance is the legacy of generations. The past shapes everything we are, everything we do. The past is, as Faulkner said, not even past.

On the other hand, as Hartley reminds us, the past is "a foreign country." The past may be so different, that it's different in ways that we don't even imagine. Not only did people experience a radically different external world, but the whole structure of their feelings and thoughts was different. Their reasons for doing things were radically different from our own. At every step of the way, then, as we try to know the past, we need to ask ourselves whether we are anachronistically imposing our own frameworks of meaning upon people from another time.

If Faulkner is right, then we need to know a lot about the past to know who we are (individually and collectively) in any deep way. If Hartley is right, then finding out about the past is no easy matter. We think they are both right. Taken together, they show us how big and important and difficult a problem it is to think historically. Perhaps the only thing

that is more difficult is to teach students to do so.

Basically, we have two ways of knowing about the past: traces and accounts. (We believe "traces" and "accounts" capture the important differences more clearly and comprehensively than the more commonly used "primary" and "secondary" sources.) Both are problematic for reasons that we will explain.

Traces include documents both official and public (such as the British North America Act) and unofficial and private (such as a teenager's journal entry). They also include relics, such as the *Enola Gay*, the plane now lodged in the Smithsonian Museum in Washington, DC, which dropped the atomic bomb on Hiroshima. Traces cannot be read simply or directly. They don't tell us what happened in so many words. They must be contextualized and analyzed. We use them as bases for inferences. They offer only a starting point to reconstruct what happened and why and what it all means. Furthermore, they change over time. The meanings of words in documents change over time, often in subtle and slippery ways. Physical artifacts decay, unless they are preserved or restored. But then the preservation and restoration become traces of a later period, embedded with ideas about how we think things should have looked or felt. Furthermore, artifacts can mislead us, if placed in contexts different from those of the lost worlds they once inhabited.

Accounts include narratives and explanations of what happened in the past. Storytellers, journalists, filmmakers, grandmothers, textbook writers and novelists—as well as historians—all create accounts of the past. Once again, we can't read them simply or directly. Unlike traces, they do tell us what happened in so many words, but we cannot necessarily believe them. They change over time, so that an account of the Northwest Rebellion written for Canadian school children in 1893 looks very different from one published in 2003.

Despite all of these problems, traces and accounts are all we have to work with as we try to know about the past, the past we need to know in order to know who we are. How do we do it? That is, what do we do when we think historically? In the next section of the chapter, we explore six problems that are central to historical thinking.[5] These are all implicit in the history lessons we present in school. But so much of history instruction is caught up in teaching "the facts" that we often let students fend for themselves in the crucial tasks of making sense of the information that we present. By defining the kind of sense-making that is particular to understanding the past, it becomes possible to make it an explicit part of history curriculum and assessment. Only then can we start to piece together the problem of what might count as advancement in historical thinking.

Elements of Historical Thinking

Significance

We can't teach everything that happened in the past, nor can a historian write about everything that happened in the past. In choosing what to teach and what to write about, teachers and researchers make distinctions between the historically significant and the historically trivial. Students, too, must be able to distinguish the significant from the trivial. But what makes an event or a trend or a person historically significant? The answer is not straightforward. In confronting various fragmentary historical traces and accounts, we undertake a process of sifting and drawing of relationships to make sense of the past. But what kind of relationships do we draw? Significant events and people may be those that have the greatest impact on people and our environment over the longest period of time. Thus World War I, the French Revolution, and the great political, economic, and military leaders would count as the most significant. But, by these criteria, the entire corpus of social history, "history from the bottom up," women's history, and labour history, which have occupied the bulk of professional historians' time and energy over the past thirty years, might be discounted as trivial. Such criteria would not allow much time for the study of as sparsely populated a country as Canada, let alone the regional or local histories that command the focus of historians, teachers, and students.

Clearly these criteria, alone, are not adequate. "Significance" is about a relationship not only among events and people of the past, but also about the relationship of those events and people to us, in the present, who are doing the historical thinking. Defining historical significance involves organizing events in a narrative that will show us something important about our position in the world. Like each of the elements of historical thinking, nobody can make much headway on historical significance if they do not already "know" a fair amount of history. On the other hand, "knowing" a lot of historical facts is useless without knowing how they fit together and why they might be important.

Epistemology and evidence

What accounts of the past should we believe, on what grounds, and with what reservations? When students read the historical novel, *Copper Sunrise,* how should they approach its portrayal of the end of the Beothuk? When they read their social studies textbook's account of the Riel Rebellion, should they have a different stance towards the things it says? When they hear a grandmother tell about her experiences in the Japanese occupation of Hong Kong, what should they believe? Public media are filled with conflicting historical accounts and interpretations of what they mean: Native land claims, the experiences of the inmates in residential schools, the role of Canadian soldiers and the Canadian air force in World War II, to name a few from Canadian history. Students need to develop abilities to assess these accounts and ask questions such as, "What are the problems with these accounts?" and "Shall I take them as is, or do they need revision?"

All of us rely selectively on the knowledge of experts, but young people's choices of which historical authorities to believe may be more or less warranted. They may rely uncritically on those whom they take to be experts, express generalized skepticism, or be able to articulate criteria for distinguishing reliable from unreliable authorities. Shortly after the film *Dances with Wolves* came out, I (Peter) interviewed a small sample of students after they watched several segments from it. They expressed a variety of reasons for believing the film's account of historical events: (1) the film's conformity to their understanding of human nature; (2) the familiarity of the depiction of the historical characters; (3) the film's compatibility with school history accounts; (4) the fact that it was a recent film; (5) the technical sophistication of the film; and (6) the emotional impact of the film. Students need to learn which of these grounds are better to rely on than others.

Students also need to be able to use traces. At the most elementary level, students can read traces only directly as information, that is, without questioning authenticity or reliability. At a more advanced stage, students may learn to use the words of even an unreliable witness as a basis for inferences about thought, motivation, and action in the past.

Continuity and change

Understanding change over time is central to historical thinking. Yet such understanding also relies on certain assumptions of continuity. For instance, if we talk about religion changing over time, we assume a relatively constant conceptual category, religion, within which the change takes place. At a certain point, the change may be profound enough that the same category is no longer appropriate for naming the phenomenon we wish to describe.

The interaction between the concepts of change and continuity raises a host of problems for students' historical thinking. Even when they consider profound change in one aspect of social, political, or economic life, students may assume much more continuity in other aspects of life than is warranted. For instance, a student looking at the technological development of photography (an example of what the British call "development studies") may fail to consider related changes in the purposes of photography, in the availability of photographs and camera equipment, or in various peoples' modes of "reading" photographs. Highlighting any example of change in the foreground may inadvertently contribute to a set of ahistorical assumptions about the background to the change. Yet the more is brought into the changing foreground, the more complex the picture becomes.

Individuals' direct experience of historical change is relevant to their conceptualization of change and continuity. Age is clearly a significant factor in such experience. A sixty-year-old in twenty-

first century North America has simply lived through more historical change than has a ten-year-old, and is likely to have more direct experience with how fundamentally things can change. But age is not the only factor in contributing to such historical experience. One's historical location is also significant. A person who lives through a war or a coup d'état, who experiences the ramifications of a technological innovation, who immigrates to a new country or who sees the impact of demographic change on a neighbourhood has a different experience of historical change from one who lives in traditional stability. Those who have lived through social instability may be more sensitive to the nuances of profound historical change. Teaching these nuances to students with diverse backgrounds requires attention to their different experiences.

Progress and decline

The issue of progress and decline adds an evaluative component to the issue of continuity and change. As things have changed, have they improved? They may do so in a number of different areas. Thus, we may speak of progress as technological, economic (in terms of standards of living), political (in terms of democratic participation and representation), moral (in terms of protection of human rights, or humane treatment more generally), environmental, scientific, spiritual, and so on. Each of these aspects of progress implies certain standards by which to evaluate change over time.

Most history textbooks (as well as most of the work of academic historians, until very recently) assume an underlying framework of historical progress. In Canadian history textbooks, a major component of progress is the development of Canadian constitutional autonomy. It is difficult to contemplate how one avoids nihilism and despair without some sense of the possibility of historical progress. Yet one need not look far in popular culture today to see that the idea of progress is under siege. Paul Kennedy coined the term "declinism" to describe the phenomenon.[6] *The New Yorker* listed fourteen books published in the last two years whose titles take the form, "The End of _____," including, among others, the future, education, reform, innocence, affluence, the victory culture, and evolution.[7] And they do not even include Francis Fukuyama's widely discussed 1992 meditation on "the end of history."[8]

How do students orient themselves in what appears to be a complex moment in historical time? How does this orientation help to frame their historical knowledge, and conversely, how might historical knowledge help to orient them better? And what should we do with our progress-based history textbooks?

Empathy (historical perspective-taking) and moral judgement

People in the past not only lived in different circumstances (in terms of, for example, technology, shelter, and political institutions), but also experienced and interpreted the world through different belief systems. When students confront the differences of the past, however, they may naturally (and mistakenly) assume that people living in different circumstances nevertheless thought in ways essentially similar to themselves. The error of "presentism" is a failure to realize how much they don't know about the past. Two aspects of our intellectual relationship with peoples different from ourselves are empathy and moral judgement.

Empathy, or historical perspective-taking, is not, in this context, an affective achievement. Rather, it is the ability to see and understand the world from a perspective not our own. In that sense, it requires "imagining" ourselves into the position of another. However—and this is crucial—that "imagining" must be based firmly on historical evidence if it is to have any meaning. Exercises that ask students to imagine being a medieval knight or a "fille du roi" make no sense unless they are based on a rich base of information about the fundamental structures and processes of everyday life during those times. Moreover, student writing and performance based on such exercises need to be assessed with an eye to anachronistic, presentist imposition of their own, twenty-first-century worldview upon the worlds of the past.

Paradoxically, this ahistorical presentism is sometimes used by historical novelists, filmmakers, and, alas, history teachers. These architects of historical accounts may attempt to make their characters "come alive" for their contemporary audiences by giving them familiar behaviours, motivations, assumptions, and conventions from their own culture. The resulting anachronisms are pervasive in the popular media. Thus after watching Native people discuss how to handle the white intruder in *Dances with Wolves*, one student said revealingly, "You get a sense that these are real people and they're trying to deal with a real problem, as opposed to just a 'bunch of Indians.'" What made the film so "real" for him? "I could see very easily a bunch of white people talking about almost exactly the same thing. . ." The power of the film came, then, from rendering Natives of 1863 familiar, like "white people" today. This student responded "empathetically" to the historical account that presented the "other" as fundamentally like himself. After all, we "understand" someone's actions if we believe that, facing similar circumstances, we would do the same. The paradox of empathy, then, is that it involves an effort to confront difference, which, at every turn, tempts us to impose our own frameworks of meaning on others.

Moral judgements in history pose similar kinds of problems. We make judgements by understanding historical actors as agents who faced decisions, sometimes individually, sometimes collectively, which had ethical consequences. Moral judgements require empathetic understanding, that is, an understanding of the differences between our moral universe and theirs, lest they be anachronistic impositions of our own standards upon the past. That having been said, meaningful history cannot entertain a relativism that disallows our condemnation of brutal slave-holders, enthusiastic Nazis, and marauding conquistadors. Exactly as with the problem of historical empathy, our ability to make moral judgements in history requires that we entertain the notion of an historically transcendent human commonality, a recognition of our humanity in the person of historical actors, at the same time that we open every door to the possibility that those actors differ from us in ways so profound that we perpetually risk misunderstanding them.

Historical agency

The problem of historical agency is a way of thinking about historical causation. The concept of agency, however, focuses the historian on relationships of power. Who makes historical change, and in what ways are their efforts constrained by the social, political, and economic structures in which they find themselves? Historian Jill Ker Conway describes her own "passion to understand the deterministic forces which constrained human freedom of the will." She continues, "I'd seen those deterministic forces overwhelm my rural family, and needed to understand for myself to what extent human action is free."[9]

In the past thirty years, historians have sought ways to understand the historical agency of relatively powerless groups. Labour historians, women's historians, and other social historians have attempted to take their subjects out of the textbook "sidebars" into the centre of history, and not simply as victims. How did they actively shape their lives, their cultures, and the course of history, as they operated within the constraints of their social and historical positions?

To what extent do young people have such a democratic sense of historical causation? How do they view their own relationship to social change? Do accounts of the past in which significance is located only among elites have an impact upon students' own sense of agency? Some of the most virulent arguments about history curriculum have involved assertions about the psychological impact of history on marginalized groups. Proponents of women's, ethnic, and working-class history claim, plausibly, that their histories would offer students a chance to see themselves as active forces for historical change; opponents, of course, may fear exactly that. How young people in a variety of social and historical situations understand their own life activity as a part of historical change is, then, an important consideration in thinking about the way we present the past.

Some Comments on Recent Research

As Ken Osborne has shown, there is a long history of Canadian debates about historical thinking in the history curriculum.[10] But a significant new body of history education research has accumulated over the past decade, exploring how students work with these problems. In many respects, it has the characteristics of any young field of research: it is vibrant, changes quickly, and still has much room for growth. Key texts in the field include the three volumes of the *International Review of History Education;*[11] the collection edited by Peter Stearns, Peter Seixas, and Sam Wineburg, entitled, *Knowing, Teaching and Learning History: National and International Perspectives;*[12] Sam Wineburg's *Historical Thinking and Other Unnatural Acts: Charting the Future of Teaching the Past;*[13] and Linda Levstik and Keith Barton's *Doing History: Investigating with Children in Elementary and Middle Schools.*[14]

Recent research on students' understanding of historical significance is, for the most part, concerned with how and why students ascribe significance to particular people and/or events from the past.[15] Students from varying ethnic groups and/or social contexts have been shown to understand historical significance in differing ways. Research on students' use of and ways of thinking about historical evidence has produced fairly consistent findings.[16] Perhaps the single most important conclusion is that the claim that young children are unable to work with evidence to construe a picture of the past appears to be untrue. Nevertheless, students' ability to work with evidence does not come naturally: it develops as an outcome of systematic teaching. Barton's work and that of Foster and Yeager also indicate that students are more adept at working with evidence orally, as opposed to providing written accounts.[17]

Barton has conducted much of the recent, albeit limited, research on students' understanding of continuity and change. In a comparative study involving students from the United States and Northern Ireland, Barton found that students' understanding of historical change differed significantly.[18] These differences, moreover, were strongly tied to differences in curriculum, and were rooted in deep differences between social, cultural and political contexts. Whereas American children tended to describe change as a story of their nation's progress, attributable to canonical individuals in their society, children in Northern Ireland tended "to describe change in terms of societal institutions and group processes."[19] Den Heyer found that American students generally linked agency and progress, and located the sources of historical change in "great men" (and sometimes women) who saw something wrong within their society and decided to make a change, rather than in social movements.[20] Again, national context and social location may account for variation in these ideas.

Peter Lee and Ros Ashby, building on a long tradition of British history education research, found that many students relied on "deficit theories"—that people from the past simply were not smart enough or did not know enough to act differently or to choose a different course of action—to explain the actions of people from the past.[21] There were glimpses of hope on issues of historical empathy, however. Some of the second-graders "behaved as if they believed that even puzzling institutions like the ones in the tasks could be made intelligible by understanding how people saw their world".[22] While this type of thinking was more typical of older students, the authors advise "how mistaken it would be for teachers to have low expectations of younger children."[23]

In the Classroom

If these issues and problems are as central to historical thinking as we argue, then they are probably already present, though perhaps submerged and unarticulated, in many of the best history classrooms. This chapter can be seen as a contribution towards bringing them to the surface, towards making them a central part of our history teaching. In order to help that process, we offer the following questions and exercises as a starting point.[24] They are not intended as lesson plans but as a way to start thinking about applying these ideas in the classroom. The bracketed suggestions are intended to serve as examples, and teachers may substitute alternative topics appropriate to their particular classrooms.

Significance

1. List four significant events in your own life. Why did you choose these? Write an autobiography using only these events and transitions between them. Now list four different significant events from your life. Write another autobiography using only these four and transitions among them. How are the two stories of your life similar? How are they different?

2. Draw a diagram showing the most significant events in your family's history from [the birth of your grandparents] to [the present]. Why did you choose these? Ask another member of your family to do the same exercise. How are they different?

3. Make a poster showing four significant events in the history of Canada. Be prepared to defend your choice of events to the class.

Epistemology and evidence

1. Examine a historical artifact. What do you think this is? What makes you say so?

2. What do you think [the artist, the photographer] wanted people to think when s/he [painted, took] this picture? How do you know?

3. How could we find out about what it was like in [schools 100 years ago]?

4. Which of these sources best shows how [radicals] were thinking about [the Family Compact] in [1837]?

5. What seems to be the director's purpose in the film [*Black Robe, 1492, The Ballad of Crowfoot*]? How did that purpose shape the story?

Continuity and change

1. Examine two or more photographs of the same street scene from different eras. What has changed? What has remained the same?

2. Examine a historical artifact. Why is this no longer in use? What do we use now instead? How does the change make our lives different?

3. Arrange the following [quotations, pictures, etc.]

in the order of the dates when they occurred. Explain why you ordered them in this way.

4. Conduct a development study of particular topics, for example, clothing, transportation, health, war, schooling. Different groups of students can research different topics and compare rates of change, progress (see below), causes of, and impediments to change.

Progress and decline

1. Have things progressed (i.e., improved) since the time [pictured, written about] here? In what ways yes? In what ways no? For whom?

2. Do you think things were better when [children were strictly disciplined; monarchs had absolute power]? Why?

3. How did the changes in [child labour laws] improve the lives of [children]?

Empathy (historical perspective-taking) and moral judgement

1. What did the author of this document think about [slavery]?

2. Write a response to [the coming of the railroad] from the perspective of [the Blackfoot].

3. How were the beliefs of [the Catholic clergy in New France] different from our own?

Historical agency

1. Which groups of people [have been/are/will be] most responsible for bringing about [equal political rights/social equality/economic security]?

2. Have there been people who have changed many other people's lives? Who? How?

3. What conditions helped [Nellie McClung] make a difference? What conditions made it harder for [Nellie McClung] to make a difference?

Conclusion

What we have proposed here is a radically different approach to history education than what is currently embedded in social studies curriculum documents. Thinking in social studies is too often defined in terms of generic "critical thinking" or "information processing" approaches. Following that line of reasoning leaves only "the facts" about the past as anything specifically historical. The argument here is that historical thinking involves certain distinct problems that cannot be collapsed into a more generic "critical thinking." We have attempted to show that students' social, political, and historical orientation requires confronting these problems. Students simply cannot get their bearings without grappling with these issues. Educators moan that too many social studies classrooms are dominated by rote memorization, mainly of historical facts. We have attempted here to define a richer vision of what students and teachers might strive towards.

Endnotes

1. Karen Cushman, *Catherine, Called Birdy* (New York: Clarion, 1994).

2. However, see Thomas C. Holt, *Thinking Historically: Narrative, Imagination, and Understanding* (New York: College Entrance Examination Board, 1990).

3. William Faulkner, *Requiem for a Nun* (New York: Random House, 1951); 92.

4. Quoted in David Lowenthal, *The Past Is a Foreign Country* (New York: Cambridge University Press, 1985), xvi.

5. Another version of these ideas appears in Peter Seixas, "Conceptualizing the Growth of Historical Understanding," in *Handbook of Education and Human Development: New Models of Learning, Teaching, and Schooling*, ed. David Olson and Nancy Torrance (Cambridge, MA: Blackwell, 1996).

6. Paul Kennedy, *The Rise and Fall of the Great Powers: Economic Change and Military Conflict from 1500–2000* (New York: Random House, 1987).

7. *The New Yorker* 71, no. 42 (December 25, 1995/January 1, 1996): 9–10.

8. Francis Fukuyama, *The End of History and the Last Man* (New York: Free Press, 1992).

9. Jill Ker Conway, *True North: A Memoir* (New York: Vintage, 1995), ix.

10. Ken Osborne, "Teaching History in Schools: A Canadian Debate," *Journal of Curriculum Studies* 35, no. 5 (2003): 585–626.

11 Alaric Dickinson et al., eds., *International Yearbook of History Education*, International Review of History Education, vol. 1 (London: Woburn Press, 1995); James F. Voss and Mario Carretero, eds., *Learning and Reasoning in History*, International Review of History Education, vol. 2 (London: Woburn Press, 1998); and Alaric Dickinson, Peter Gordon, and Peter Lee, eds., *Raising Standards in History Education*, International Review of History Education, vol. 3 (London: Woburn Press, 2001).

12 Peter N. Stearns, Peter Seixas, and Samuel Wineburg, eds., *Knowing, Teaching, and Learning History: National and International Perspectives* (New York: New York University Press, 2000).

13 Samuel Wineburg, *Historical Thinking and Other Unnatural Acts: Charting the Future of Teaching the Past* (Philadelphia: Temple University Press, 2001).

14 Linda Levstik and Keith Barton, *Doing History: Investigating with Children in Elementary and Middle Schools* (Mahwah, NJ: Lawrence Erlbaum, 2001).

15 See, for example, Dario J. Almarza, "Contexts Shaping Minority Language Students' Perceptions of American History," *Journal of Social Studies Research* 25, no. 2 (2001): 4–22; Keith Barton, "'You'd be Wanting to Know about the Past': Social Contexts of Children's Historical Understanding in Northern Ireland and the USA," *Comparative Education* 37, no. 1 (2001): 89–106; Keith C. Barton and Linda S. Levstik, "'It Wasn't a Good Part of History': National Identity and Students' Explanations of Historical Significance," *Teachers College Record* 99, no. 3 (1998): 478–513; Terrie Epstein, "Deconstructing Differences in African-American and European-American Adolescents' Perspectives of U.S. History," *Curriculum Inquiry* 28, no. 4 (1998): 397–423; ———, "Adolescents' Perspectives on Racial Diversity in U.S. History: Case Studies from an Urban Classroom," *American Educational Research Journal* 37, no. 1 (2000): 185–214; ———, "Racial Identity and Young People's Perspectives on Social Education," *Theory into Practice* 40, no. 1 (2001): 42–47; Linda S. Levstik, "The Well at the Bottom of the World: Positionality and New Zealand [Aotearoa] Adolescents' Conceptions of Historical Significance" (paper presented at the annual meeting of the American Educational Research Association, Montreal, April 1999); Peter Seixas, "Historical Understanding Among Adolescents in a Multicultural Setting," *Curriculum Inquiry* 23, no. 3 (1993): 301–325; ———, "Students' Understanding of Historical Significance," *Theory and Research in Social Education* 22, no. 3 (1994): 281–304; ———, "Mapping the Terrain of Historical Significance," *Social Education* 61, no. 1 (1997): 22–27; and James Wertsch, *Voices of Collective Remembering* (New York: Cambridge University Press, 2002).

16 See, for instance, Keith Barton, "'I Just Kinda Know': Elementary Students' Ideas about Historical Evidence," *Theory and Research in Social Education* 25, no. 4 (1997): 407–430; Stuart J. Foster and Elizabeth A. Yeager, "'You've Got To Put Together the Pieces': English 12-year-olds Encounter and Learn from Historical Evidence," *Journal of Curriculum Supervision* 14, no. 4 (1999): 286–317; Peter Lee and Rosalyn Ashby, "Progression in Historical Understanding among Students Ages 7–14," in *Knowing, Teaching, and Learning History*, 199–222; Bruce VanSledright, "Confronting History's Interpretive Paradox while Teaching Fifth Graders to Investigate the Past," *American Educational Research Journal* 39, no. 4 (2002): 1089–1115; Samuel Wineburg, "Making Historical Sense," in *Knowing, Teaching and Learning History*, 306–326; and ———, *Historical Thinking and Other Unnatural Acts.*

17 Barton, "'I Just Kinda Know'"; Foster and Yeager, "'You've Got To Put Together the Pieces.'"

18 Keith Barton, "A Sociocultural Perspective on Children's Understanding of Historical Change: Comparative Findings from Northern Ireland and the United States," *American Educational Research Journal* 38, no. 4 (2001): 881–913.

19 Ibid., p. 896.

20 In "Between Every 'Now' and 'Then': A Role for the Study of Historical Agency in History and Social Studies Education," *Theory and Research in Social Education* (forthcoming), Kent den Heyer draws largely on Keith Barton, "'Bossed Around by the Queen': Elementary Students' Understanding of Individuals and Institutions in History," *Journal of Curriculum and Supervision,* 12 (Summer 1997): 290–314; ———, "A Sociocultural Perspective on Children's Understanding of Historical Change," 881–913; ———, "'Oh, That's a Tricky Piece!': Children, Mediated Action, and the Tools of Historical Time," *The Elementary School Journal* 103, no. 2 (2002): 161–185; Ola Halldén, "On the Paradox of Understanding History in an Educational Setting," in *Teaching and Learning in History*, ed. Gaea Leinhardt, Isabel L. Beck, and Catherine Stainton (Hillsdale, NJ: Lawrence Erlbaum, 1994), 27–46; ———, "On Reasoning in History," in *Learning and Reasoning in History*, 272–278; and Peter Seixas, "Historical Understanding Among Adolescents in a Multicultural Setting," 301–325.

21 Peter Lee and Rosalyn Ashby, "Empathy, Perspective Taking, and Rational Understanding," in *Historical Empathy and Perspective Taking in the Social Studies*, ed. Ozro Luke Davis, Jr., Elizabeth A. Yeager, and Stuart J. Foster (Lanham, MD: Rowman & Littlefield), 21–50. See also Christopher Portal, ed., *The History Curriculum for Teachers* (London: Falmer, 1987).

22 Lee and Ashby, "Empathy, Perspective Taking, and Rational Understanding," 37.

23 Ibid.

24 Our thinking in these exercises has been shaped by Tim Lomas, *Teaching and Assessing Historical Understanding* (London: The Historical Association, 1990).

CHAPTER 7

School Geography and Academic Geography

Spaces of Possibility for Teaching and Learning

Wanda Hurren

For the purposes of the following discussion of geography education, a distinction is made between *school* geography—the teaching, learning, and research that is associated with pre-K–12 classrooms, and *academic* geography—the teaching, learning, and research associated with geography departments on university campuses. School geography has been studied in classrooms across North America since the beginnings of public education. Occasionally a subject in its own right within some school districts (especially at the secondary level), school geography is most often taught under the interdisciplinary umbrella of social studies.

Educators make decisions regarding what to teach in school geography lessons based on scholarship in both school geography and academic geography. While this chapter will highlight some basic aspects of school geography, the major focus will be on three established areas of current scholarship within academic geography, namely, *critical, cultural,* and *feminist* geography. How these areas might enrich school geography will also be explored. The premise of this chapter is not that school geography should change completely in order to mime academic geography; rather, it is that spaces of possibility open up for enriching school geography by attending to current scholarship within academic geography.

Judging by enrolment across Canada, it appears that school geography as a specific subject area is not popular. In the cases where provincial ministries of education were able to provide statistics on annual enrolments for social studies offerings at the secondary level,[1] geography courses had the lowest enrolments. These low enrolments could be a result of several factors: insufficient numbers of staff available to teach a variety of social studies; unqualified staff teaching in the area of geography; subject area hierarchies regarding course offerings and selections; and the underlying assumption that history is more rigorous, social studies is softer, and geography is not useful.

At the elementary school level, we can assume that all students have some exposure to geography through social studies curricula. While geography is not often labeled as a unit of study, many required units of study within provincially mandated social studies curricula include a geography component in terms of skills and content.

An earlier examination of teacher resource materials by this author (provincial curriculum materials, teacher education textbooks, and commercially produced teaching resources)[2] indicates that school geography is constructed within these documents in the following ways:

- As a set of tools and skills necessary for the geographically literate person and to manage the earth. Human beings are, in general, removed from the world, and it is assumed that our role is to "manage" the world. Typical listings for geographical skills, abilities, attitudes, and knowledge include such items as interpreting maps and globes, locating places on maps and globes, working with scale and distance, appreciating the relationship between the natural environment and lifestyles, and learning to see relationships between and among climate, landforms, vegetation, and population distribution.[3]

- As a set of two separate geographies related and connected to each other: physical and human, and each of these geographies is referred to in a language of "systems."

- As a subject that is spoken and written about largely in "physical" terms—features of landscape, regions, map skills, location-finding, distribution of resources and people, and size and structure.

Teacher resource materials for school geography generally define geography in terms of gaining the knowledge and skills necessary for decision-making and problem-solving with regard to issues of environmental and system sustainability and for the purposes of examining local, national, and international events. Teaching latitude and longitude are often listed as the first steps in teaching about location, and there are numerous activities that require students to adopt a bird's-eye view. A focus on map skills was evident in the majority of resources examined. This focus on map skills or how to use an atlas is evident in current initiatives such as the *National Geography Challenge,* a competition promoted by the Canadian Council of Geography Educators. Memorizing facts and figures is the emphasis in this challenge, and contestants come with a plethora of information gleaned for the most part from atlases: place names, capital cities, political boundary lines, population statistics, physical features, national exports and imports, world trade involvement, and so on.

A definition of geography taken from academic geography, and one that would seem useful for school geography, is explained by Canadian geographer and researcher Derek Gregory.[4] He encourages us to think of geography as a discourse (rather than discipline) that can be used for making sense of spaces and places in our everyday living. Thinking about geog-

raphy as a discourse would involve thinking about how it is we write about, read about, talk about, and think about geography, and this definition includes a recognition that these various discursive activities help to shape our notions of the world. If we write about the world in a "map skills" sort of way, that will determine our understanding of the world. If we study literature and short stories from various locations around the world as geographical texts, we will understand the world in another way.

This notion of geography as a discourse requires us to recognize geography as something being constructed even as we take part in various discursive practices, rather than as a discipline already established with a complete set of facts that just need to be learned. Conceiving of geography as a discourse and paying attention to current scholarship within critical, cultural, and feminist geography has the potential to move school geography beyond map skills to a critical questioning of the world around us.

Traditional school geography begins with the study of local spaces in earlier grades and moves to the study of more global spaces in later grades, with an inherent hierarchical structure in place that privileges the study of the "world out there" and larger world issues over local and regional phenomena. Current scholarship within academic geography acknowledges that what happens in our own backyards requires study and understanding. Renewed attention is placed on geographical phenomena occurring in the everyday world around us, less attention is placed on faraway lands, and caution is exercised against the exotic appeal of studying locations far from home. Academic geography recognizes that the boundary between local and global is not distinct, and that sophisticated study of the local milieu is necessary in any attempt to study global phenomena. Transposing this perspective to school geography would require the study of both local and global phenomena at both the elementary and secondary levels.

In the following discussion, three areas of scholarship within academic geography—critical, cultural, and feminist—are treated as separate categories. While it is useful to separate these categories for the purpose of introducing the ideas in this chapter, in real-life situations, these three categories merge and intersect. For example, a study of gender and race and the use of community recreation spaces would most likely be informed by all three of these areas of scholarship. The Ideas for School Geography section included at the end of the discussion of each area of scholarship follows current trends in academic geography, emphasizing activities in the everyday world of students. The suggested ideas can be adapted for study at any grade level.

Critical Geography

All lines on a map, we must acknowledge, are imaginary; they are ideas of order imposed on the sloshing flood of time and space.—Janette Turner Hospital[5]

When teaching social studies curriculum courses, I ask teacher education students to recall their elementary and secondary geography education, and to write down the first memory that comes to mind. The majority of students list "colouring maps" as their first memory. Many students can recall with great detail the various colours they used for certain countries (British Commonwealth nations were often coloured pink), states, provinces, and regions. Map skills are a prominent and important component of classroom geography.

The critical attention to mapping that is evident within academic geography is a development that would serve to enrich school geography. Including projects that require students to question what has been taken for granted about maps and to examine how maps are used to overpower or mislead would add a critical edge to the teaching of map skills. Analysis and critique of the uses and abuses of maps in (Western) society, and an exploration of the historical traditions of geography and mapping are also examples of projects that would incorporate a critical geography component within school geography. While both school geography and academic geography are often split into physical and human geography, critical geography calls this very split into question, arguing that these two areas are themselves human and socially determined constructions and

as such are open to further constructions and deconstructions. One prominent aspect of critical geography is the deconstructive nature of the work undertaken within this area of scholarship.

Deconstructive projects that pay close attention to the constructed nature of language and text—the "graphy" part of geography—and the material relationship between these entities and our notions of reality are common aspects of scholarship undertaken within critical geography. Critical geography adheres to the poststructural perspective that it is not just *what* we write about the world that is important, but also *how we write about the world*. Maps are one of the main textual formats or structures employed and created within geography, and within critical geography, the language and (taken-for-granted Western) traditions of mapping are examined for their role in constructing certain understandings of the world.

Alan Morantz takes a critical stance as he examines the maps and stories and traditions associated with mapping in Canada. He notes that maps are used "to seduce motorists and exploit consumers, [they] are a form of identity for small-town burghers, and a means of creative expression and recreation."[6] In his desire to make us all more aware of the power of maps, he warns us that maps "are windows on worldviews, assumptions and dreams. They are mirrors of the best and worst in human nature."[7]

Denis Wood and John Fels read a North Carolina state highway map and remind us that "there is nothing natural about a map. It is a cultural artifact, an accumulation of choices made among choices, every one of which reveals a value,"[8] even though a map is typically assumed to be neutral and non-political, especially a tourist map like the state highway map of North Carolina. Woods and Fels assert that most maps are used to possess, legitimate, and name. This claim is one well worth discussing in school geography classrooms.

Working with the *Nova Scotia Scenic Travelways Map for Doers and Dreamers,*[9] it is easy enough to see how the geographical area featured in a tourist map is constructed a certain way (for example, as "wilderness" or as a "scenic" route, or as an area of "abundant hiking trails") by the map-makers to suit their (commercial) purposes. It is also easy to see that a certain type of tourist is desired. In general, the desired map readers/tourists would be able-bodied (handicap access information is not provided regarding hiking trails or wilderness areas or look-out spots), young (the majority of photographs accompanying tourist maps depict young, physically active people), with access to private vehicles or funds for rental vehicles. There is no information included regarding public transportation routes and timetables, except for car/ferry schedules. Photographic inserts of tourists and local people at various venues around the province feature white, young, physically active people. Judging from the images accompanying the map, we are asked to believe that around every corner there is a young, energetic fiddler, and the sun is always shining in Nova Scotia.

J.B. Harley, a prominent critical geographer, contends that maps are about texts and knowledge and power.[10] Harley acknowledges the colonial power of maps, and notes the way Europeans were able to "draw lines across the territories of Indian nations without sensing the reality of their political identity."[11] Referencing the pin and paper map battles that generals have been able to fight totally removed from the bloody battlefields, Harley notes, "While the map is never the reality, in such ways it helps to create a different reality."[12] Even today we witness, and, it might be suggested, take part in these battles when we tune in to television stations and receive mapped images of updates on the war in Iraq. We view maps that portray the boundary lines of countries, with red stars often used to indicate battle areas and major cities. The rest of the territory on the maps is usually empty—clean and white, giving consumers of television news the notion that warring areas are for the most part isolated "starred" areas. Using a star to mark a battlefield or where gunfire has been occurring is a way of tidying up the messiness and bloodiness of war.

Further evidence of this "different reality" created through the selective use of map images was apparent in the recent news coverage of the death of two Canadian soldiers in Afghanistan. Two soldiers were killed and several injured when a land mine exploded under the vehicle in which they were trav-

elling. When the news broke, most television news coverage included a map image of clean white territory with one star or dot to indicate the location of the explosion. Viewers were presented with the news that soldiers are indeed killed in their peacekeeping efforts, and at the same time, they were presented with a neat and tidy map image. Maps depicting areas where buried land mines were suspected, or where buried land mines had exploded, were not made available. The selective use of map images in effect downplayed the danger and expense (in terms of human lives and military equipment) of Canada's peacekeeping efforts in Afghanistan.

Ideas for school geography

Display a variety of maps in the classroom that take into account purposes for mapping apart from political boundaries and capital cities. Examples of atlases and maps to include:

- A map of "Downunder," which displays the world with the northern and southern hemispheres reversed. Australia is at the top of the map, and Canada is at the bottom. By calling into question what is taken for granted, engage students in discussing how the world is represented on maps and why the prime meridian is located in Greenwich, England.

- Maps of the local community, the school layout, hiking trails, tourist maps, road and highway maps, maps of the ocean floor, maps of the night sky, and so on.

- Atlases that present information not usually found in an atlas are useful to explore with students. For example, the *State of Women in the World Atlas* (includes maps depicting locations throughout the world for plastic surgery, breast augmentation, rape victims, and equal opportunities for women), or the *State of War and Peace Atlas*.

- David Turnbull's book *Maps Are Territories* displays maps from around the world and mapping traditions from various groups of people around the world. Students will see the many ways in which people communicate location.

Cultural Geography

certain spaces = certain identities—Natter and Jones[13]

Current scholarship within cultural geography pays close attention to social theory and explores the relationships between spaces and identities of groups and individuals. Poststructurally, neither space nor identity is seen as a static entity. Each is always in process: space changes over time (who uses the space, how it is used), and identity changes over time (often as a result of the particular spaces we inhabit or frequent). Within this growing area of scholarship, the work of Henri Lefebvre is influential, and his notion that "space is at once result and cause, product and producer" informs inquiries into space and identity.[14] Groups and individuals are considered to be both producers of space and produced by spaces. An example of the dialectical relationship between spaces and identities can be seen in a study presently being conducted in three Western Canadian public secondary schools.[15] This study is exploring relationships between how students use the social spaces in their school and how they negotiate their identities. For example, as producers of space, a group of high school students claims a space in the parking lot as their area to hang out, and it becomes a designated space noted by others. An example of student identities being produced by space is a group of students who have become known as "tough" and "smokers," even if they do not smoke cigarettes, because they hang out in the area that has become known as the smoking area in their particular high school.

The environmental determinism perspective present in school geography promotes the idea that the physical environment determines settlement patterns, movement, and exploration. Within cultural geography, this perspective is called into question. Current social theories taken up within academic geography recognize the role of power, knowledge, and human agency in settlement patterns, movement, and exploration. For example, studies undertaken through a worldwide organization known as Metropolis, which studies migration around the world, illustrate that immigrant and refugee populations are involved in a process of simultaneous segregation/congregation.[16] Immigrant groups are often left little choice regarding where they might settle in a new location because of the services they require. School board policies regarding the location of schools providing English language instruction often result in immigrant and refugee populations settling in an area where a designated ESL program is located. Segregated ethnic areas begin to develop. At the same time, immigrant and refugee families choose to settle in locations where people from similar ethnic backgrounds have settled in order to feel a sense of familiarity with customs and language. This results in a process of congregation, and illustrates that the cultural and social environment has much more of an impact on where immigrant and refugee groups settle than does the physical environment.

Examining a local community's use of recreational spaces would be a project for school geography that would attend to social theories, and this type of study can be undertaken at any grade level with adaptations. For example, where a golf course is located in a community (is it on prime real estate?) and who uses the course (gender, race, age, ethnicity) illustrates how space and identity are closely linked. It also illustrates how certain identities have more agency and power than others in determining how certain spaces are produced.

Golf courses are often located in aesthetically pleasing surroundings, or, if these surroundings do not exist, they are constructed. As a result, the space taken up for golf courses is most often considered to be prime real estate in a community. As a graduate student, I studied at the University of British Columbia in Vancouver, Canada. The campus is located on the edge of a peninsula and the views of the ocean, Pacific Spirit Park, and the coastal mountains are breathtaking. Affordable housing close to campus or on campus is very limited and was a constant concern for students and families, yet a nine-hole golf course took up prime space just within the gates of the campus. I often walked alongside the golf course and met golfers crossing the road from one fairway to the next. Most of these golfers were men over the age of twenty-five.

Exploring the locations and uses of community football and soccer fields and hockey arenas is another community recreation project within school geography that would make use of social theory and spatial practices of groups and individuals. Ice rinks are constructed on many prairie school grounds during the winter months. Often there are two rinks constructed—one with boards and lights for night skating/hockey games, and one without lights and a basic frame of 2" x 4" lumber for general skating. Asking students to observe at these locations and make note of how these ice spaces are used and by which groups and individuals would encourage students to pay attention to notions of identity, power, and space.

Ideas for school geography

With adaptations for various grade levels, students could take note of:

- Which spaces on the playground or within the school are considered to be the best, or "prime real estate," why they are the best, and which students use these spaces.

- Where various programs are located within the school (or school district) and which students (according to gender, race, age, sexual orientation, ability, grade level) make use of these programs (e.g., shop, day care, special education programs, English language programs, French language programs, fine arts programs).

- Which areas of the school are "open use" areas during lunch hours (e.g., the gymnasium) and which students (according to gender, race, age, sexual orientation, ability, grade level) make use of these facilities.

Feminist Geography

. . . I promised to show you a map you say but this is a mural
then yes let it be   these are small distinctions
where do we see it from is the question
—Adrienne Rich[17]

Some of the strongest questioning and critique of how geography has been constructed comes from the area of scholarship defined as feminist geography. In the above discussions of mapping traditions and space and identity, feminist scholarship has also been drawn upon. Issues of gender, race, ethnicity, ability, and access are those taken up within the scholarship of feminist geography. These same issues are taken up within critical and cultural geography. A major contribution of feminist geography has to do with epistemology—how we come to know things through the study of geography.

Embodied ways of knowing are acknowledged within feminist geography. While much of what occurs in both school geography and academic geography takes place from an aerial perspective and a disembodied bird's-eye view is encouraged, feminist geography attends to bodies in spaces and places. Work within feminist geography attempts to remind us of embodied experiences. This is often achieved through attention to the local, personal, and situated nature of our lives. Kathleen Kirby discusses the way maps separate subjects and space, and how they also present a mediating space between subjects and space. She believes that mapping has excluded ways of negotiating space that take into account ground-level perspectives (the "mural" effect) and the lived everydayness of bodies in spaces. Maps carry with them the danger of removing us from the realities of spaces and places. They tend to clean things up, erasing any messiness or discriminating practices or social injustices associated with particular places.[18]

Although John Dewey's reasons were primarily functional—he noted how children become fidgety if they have to sit for long periods of time without actively engaging their bodies in a learning experience—Dewey espoused the value of paying attention to the body in educational endeavours.[19] Embodied knowing is a form of knowing that, while we all make use of it, is often given minimal attention in schooling. It is a way of knowing that takes account of what we know through the senses of taste, touch, smell, hearing, sight, intuition, and emotion. While these senses seem to be in opposition to rational thought processes, it is recognized that they inform our rational knowing, and vice versa.

An inclusive approach to the study of geography requires that educators provide opportunities for students to experience the world through as many approaches as possible. While some students are challenged through rational, linear, disembodied thought processes, other students are challenged through the tactile senses, using their bodies to take in and process information. Embodied approaches to learning require getting down to "ground level" whenever possible in the study of location. For example, while it is often not possible to be on the Arctic tundra, or to hear and feel the roar of a pounding surf in the classroom, it is possible to experiment with temperature and moisture on a small scale, and to incorporate audio resources (audio-recorded soundscapes, world music examples, and so on) in the study of regions.

Embodied knowing is employed when we focus on local lived experiences of spaces and places or when we encourage the sensual while learning about places and spaces. This can often be accomplished through language that calls forth embodied responses—most often in the form of poetic language and music. Again, the recognition of embodied ways of knowing in geography allows for more inclusive approaches to learning about the world. While some students and teachers will be familiar with these approaches, others will not have been exposed to these ways of knowing and may find their thought processes enhanced by incorporating information through the senses.

Within school geography, taking a field trip is a useful way of acknowledging and making use of embodied ways of knowing. For example, as well as studying maps of the area to be explored, when students are in the space, encourage them to take ten minutes alone and think about how it feels to be there. Comments about the smell, the temperature, or the wind are usually made by students who are taking note of their own bodily senses. This provides an added dimension of knowing about the particular space.

Ideas for school geography

To acknowledge the personal and local experiences within the study of location, and to reinforce the idea that we take in valuable geographical information about a location through our bodies as well as our minds, try the following:

- ask students to make note of the feelings, memories, sounds, smells, and "gut feelings" or intuitive thoughts they experience as they walk through a variety of locations (e.g., a shopping mall, a local park, a local gym, a school hallway, a fast food restaurant)

- distribute maps of the school or school grounds and ask students to choose a location on the map that has significance for them, and choose a colour for that location. Have them describe why they chose that colour, using poetic or expository writing

- ask students to choose a place on a map and write about a conversation they overheard or an experience they had in that place.

Spaces of Possibility for Teaching and Learning

Why study geography? In general, any curriculum has the overall goal of helping students make sense of self and the world and exposing them to various possibilities open for being in the world. Geography as a subject area is certainly implicated in any attempt to understand the world. Recent curricular imperatives directed at learning about globalization and sustainability find a comfortable home in geography, though not exclusively. Environmental studies, world literature studies, and some of the natural sciences also address these imperatives. Typically included within the realm of the social studies, school geography is a subject area that also holds possibilities for achieving the overall goals of social studies: considering and understanding multiple perspectives, encouraging critical thinking, and making connections between past, present, and future.

Geography presents unique opportunities for understanding a multitude of aspects related to where we/others are at in the world. Whether it is for world peace, economic gain, sustainability, human interest, community study, or promoting feelings of nationalism, the teaching of school geography must continue to evolve. Both school geography and academic geography create opportunities for enriching our understandings of the spaces and places we experience in the world—and how those spaces and places affect who we are and how we experience the world.

Resources for Teachers

Hurren, Wanda. *Line Dancing: An Atlas of Geography Curriculum and Poetic Possibilities.* New York: Peter Lang, 2000.

Lutz, Catherine, and Jane Collins. *Reading National Geographic.* Chicago: University of Chicago Press, 1994.

Monmonier, Mark. *How to Lie with Maps.* Chicago: University of Chicago Press, 1996.

Monmonier, Mark. *Drawing the Line: Tales of Maps and Cartocontroversy.* New York: Henry Holt, 1995.

Morantz, Alan. *Where Is Here? Canada's Maps and the Stories They Tell.* Toronto: Penguin Books, 2002.

Seager, Joni. *The State of the Women in the World Atlas.* New Edition. Toronto: Penguin Books, 2002.

Turnbull, David. *Maps Are Territories: Science Is an Atlas.* Chicago: University of Chicago Press, 1989.

Endnotes

1   Statistics were available from Alberta, Saskatchewan, Ontario, and Newfoundland.

2   Adapted from an overview of the state of geography curriculum within the Canadian context, in Wanda Hurren, *Line Dancing: An Atlas of Geography Curriculum and Poetic Possibilities* (New York: Peter Lang, 2000).

3   Examples are based on information provided in British Columbia Ministry of Education, Skills, and Training, *Social Studies K to 7: Integrated Resource Package* (Victoria: Author, 1998), www.bced.gov.bc.ca/irp/irp.htm; and Saskatchewan Education, *Social Studies: A Curriculum Guide for the Elementary Level* (Regina: Author, 1995), www.sasked.gov.sk.ca/docs/social.html.

4   Derek Gregory, *Geographical Imaginations* (Cambridge, MA: Blackwell, 1994).

5   Janette Turner Hospital, *Isobars* (Baton Rouge: Louisiana State University Press, 1990), 1.

6   Alan Morantz, *Where Is Here? Canada's Maps and the Stories They Tell* (Toronto: Penguin Books, 2002), xiv.

7   Ibid., xv.

8   Denis Wood and John Fels, "Designs on Signs/Myth and Meaning in Maps," *Cartographica* 23, no. 3 (1986): 65.

9   Nova Scotia Tourism and Culture, *Scenic Travelways, Map for Doers and Dreamers* (Halifax: Author, 2003).

10   J.B. Harley, "Deconstructing the Map," in *Writing Worlds: Discourse, Text and Metaphor in the Representation of Landscape,* ed. Trevor Barnes and James Duncan (New York: Routledge, 1992), 231–247.

11   Ibid., 246.

12   Ibid., 247.

13   W. Natter and J. Jones, "Identity, Space, and Other Uncertainties," in *Space and Social Theory: Interpreting Modernity and Postmodernity,* ed. G. Benko and U. Strohmayer (Oxford: Blackwell, 1997), 141–161.

14   Henri Lefebvre, *The Production of Space* (Cambridge, MA: Blackwell, 1991), 142.

15   Wanda Hurren, "Spatial Practices and Ethnocultural Diversity in Public High Schools: Students Negotiating Spaces and Identities" (longitudinal study, 2001–2004, funded by the Social Sciences and Humanities Research Council of Canada and the Prairie Centre of Excellence for Research on Immigration and Integration).

16   L. Ahnstrom, "Ethnic Residential Segregation/Congregation and Social Distinction: A Conceptual Framework for Causal Analysis" (paper presented in Workshop 5, Divided Cities: Best Practices for the Social Inclusion of Ethnic Minorities in Local Communities, 4th International Metropolis Conference, Washington, DC, December 1999).

17   Adrienne Cecile Rich, *An Atlas of the Difficult World: Poems, 1988–1991* (New York: W.W. Norton, 1991), 6.

18   Kathleen Kirby, "Re: Mapping Subjectivity: Cartographic Vision and the Limits of Politics," in *Body Space,* ed. Nancy Duncan (New York: Routledge, 1996), 45–55.

19   John Dewey, *Democracy and Education* (New York: The Free Press, 1916).

CHAPTER 8

Law and Social Studies

Preparing Students for Citizenship

Wanda Cassidy

Most social studies teachers, when they think about teaching their subject, don't think about teaching law. Law is the purview of lawyers, who possess the knowledge and disseminate the information for a fee. Social studies is viewed as history and geography, current affairs, multiculturalism and citizenship, and maybe a little sociology and anthropology.[1] Even with an interdisciplinary conception of social studies, law usually is not part of the equation. Perhaps this is to be expected, as undergraduates preparing to be teachers have little opportunity to take a law course or be exposed to formal law content in their studies. Law is something one studies in a post-graduate program, in preparation for becoming a lawyer.

Yet if one examines the mandate of social studies education, the curriculum guides and required resources, at both the elementary and secondary levels, legal content is very much evident in both overt and covert ways. In fact, it is the position of law educators that social studies cannot be adequately taught without attention to law.[2] So, how can this be? What do we mean by law content? Why aren't teachers aware of these expectations, and how can they be expected to teach law if they have little knowledge of the subject themselves and have had no exposure to formal law courses?

These questions will be addressed as this chapter unfolds. Examples will be provided as to ways that teachers of social studies can address legal content, and teach it in engaging ways, even without the benefit of going to law school.

What Do We Mean by Law Education in Social Studies?

Part of the reason why social studies teachers balk at the idea of teaching law is that they see law in a narrow way. Law is something that we confront when we sign an agreement to purchase a car or home. Or, we encounter the legal system if called for jury duty, or to fight a traffic ticket, or to seek remedy in Small Claims Court for money owed. We might think of law when faced with a landlord/tenant dispute, or when wrongfully dismissed from a job, or when our neighbour's barking dog keeps us up all night. These more practical issues of life seemed far removed from the expectations of social studies education. But this is not the kind of law that social studies education subsumes. The kind of legal content that should be addressed in social studies courses goes far deeper and is more far-reaching than these issues, which are better addressed in a Consumer Education or a Personal Planning course. The kind of legal content being suggested in this chapter extends into the very heart of what we mean by living in a democracy, the values and principles we hold dear in Canadian society, and the hopes and dreams we have for our world.

Although over the past century there has been some debate about the priorities social studies education should have, Lybarger[3] quotes one of the founders of social studies when he says that, since its inception, social studies has been in pursuit of "all manner of efforts to promote human betterment." The organization that founded social studies says that social studies offers:

> . . . peculiar opportunities for the training of the individual as a member of society . . . a sense of the responsibility of the individual as a member of social groups, and the intelligence and the will to participate effectively in the promotion of the social well-being . . . a sense of membership in the world community with all the sympathies and sense of justice that this involves.[4]

Some knowledge of the law and its role in society and in a democracy is paramount to fulfilling these ambitions.

Law education in social studies is intimately intertwined with investigating the nature of citizenship, people's rights and responsibilities, social justice issues, personal and citizen empowerment, the values and beliefs that undergird our democracy, environmental issues, planning decisions, historical events and their ramifications, conflict resolution, world order, and so on.

In order to distinguish this kind of education about law from the kind of law lawyers study, proponents call it "law-related education" or LRE. This is education about law, or the relationship of law to the workings of society, not the fine details, facts, and procedures of law, which lawyers must learn in order to practise their profession.

History of Law-related Education

The law-related education movement in North America began in the 1960s and grew out of a variety of simultaneous events and initiatives. In the United States, several educators were concerned that the civics curriculum taught to students was too stodgy, too pedantic and archaic to engage the youth of the nation. Attempts to inculcate character and American values were not working. Course content was non-controversial, yet law-related issues were dominating the American scene.[5]

America was undergoing a massive social upheaval, with the hippie movement, anti-Vietnam war demonstrations, the women's movement, and the civil rights movement. Surveys done with students in school showed very little understanding of the American Bill of Rights, even after students completed American government and social studies courses. Like many educational reform initiatives, the law-related education movement was born out of crises and a call for change.[6] A new and fresh way of teaching the U.S. Constitution, the Bill of Rights, and American values was needed.

In the 1960s and early 1970s, the National Council of the Social Studies (NCSS) teamed up with the Civil Liberties Education Foundation and the American Bar Association to develop a program for teaching the Bill of Rights and for better educating American teachers in law-related concepts and ways of teaching law to students in school. Today, the Division for Public Education of the American Bar Association spearheads and coordinates the law-related education movement in the United States. Dr. Mabel McKinney-Browning, director of this program, comments:

> Throughout its history, law-related education has provided a substantive direction for the study of civics in schools. Law serves as the "glue" which connects the elements of civic education: politics, government, history, public policy and civic participation. The hallmarks of law-related education programs are the emphasis on real-world experiences, cooperative and participatory learning opportunities and substantive interactions with a broad range of legal and community resources.[7]

In Canada, the law-related education movement did not take its cues from the United States. Unlike social studies education, which was an American export adopted in Canada, the movement to advance LRE in schools sprang from different roots. In the early 1970s, the Canadian public began to clamour for increased access to the law, which, in prior decades, had become the purview of the legal profession. This grassroots movement to demystify the law and increase access by the general public was fuelled by a number of key statements made by Canada's Chief Justice and other prominent jurists.[8] They decried the state of legal knowledge among the Canadian public, including young people. Further, Canada was being bombarded with American television shows, which conveyed a false impression of our legal system. In a society that claimed ignorance of the law as no excuse for illegal behaviour, the state of Canadians' knowledge of the law was seen as dismal. "To make Canadians more legally literate" became a key goal of the Canadian Bar Association. They, along with law foundations and provincial and federal governments, determined to support the development of organizations or societies to improve the state of legal literacy among the adult population in Canada.[9] As a result, almost every province and territory in Canada initiated a program to advance public legal education.

In the process of establishing these programs for the general public, the lens also shifted to the dearth of legal knowledge in schools and the inadequate training in law for teachers. In British Columbia, for example, the Ministry of the Attorney General authorized a provincial survey of the Law 11 course, an elective under the social studies umbrella. The results shocked the legal community and government policy-makers.[10] Teachers were teaching this law course as part of their social studies assignment, but without any legal knowledge or opportunity to increase their knowledge. The textbooks were inaccurate and several years out of date. No outside resources were available to support the curriculum. No in-service or pre-service teacher education programs were available. As a result, teachers were bumbling along, and students' access to accurate, appropriate and sound legal education was woefully absent. This scenario repeated itself across Canada.[11]

A 1977 interview with then-Chief Justice of Canada Bora Laskin became a rallying cry for increased attention to the needs of students in schools, and of teachers who taught law-related curricula. Justice Laskin said,

> I'm very much concerned about the lack of education in the legal process in our schools, up to and including university. It's very im-

portant to have a citizenry which is socially literate and social literacy to me involves some appreciation of the legal system. There isn't a single act that any government can do that does not have to find its source in the legal system. . . . I hope that our educational authorities will pay attention to this.[12]

Soon, most of the organizations set up to improve the legal literacy of the public also focused their attention on the needs of school children and their teachers. Workshops in substantive law and teaching methodology were provided to teachers. Curriculum materials to support legal content were developed and distributed for a minimal fee to schools. Newsletters providing current legal information and resource information were disseminated. Lawyers were paired with teachers and came into classrooms. Court-watching programs were established. In some provinces university credit courses in law education were developed and offered to teachers and prospective teachers.[13]

While the impetus for the LRE movements in the United States and in Canada stemmed from somewhat different sources, the means through which LRE was promoted in schools was similar: workshops, curriculum resources, legal updating services, lawyer-teacher partnerships, and court-watching programs. Similarly, social studies education was viewed as the most logical home for education in law. While the Canadian movement initially called itself "legal education in schools," it quickly adopted the American term, "law-related education," as this more accurately reflected the broad goals and also could be distinguished from education for lawyers.

Social studies teachers in Canada, particularly at the secondary school level, were fairly well served by LRE programs from the early 1980s to the early 1990s. This was an era where funding was relatively easy to obtain, where government encouraged grassroots initiatives, where the legal community rallied behind programs in law education, and where Ministries of Education and school boards supported more "innovative," holistic programs like LRE. Teachers of the law elective had opportunities to upgrade their knowledge of law, purchase moderately priced classroom materials, borrow videotapes on legal issues, contact a central source for information on guest speakers or community resources, conduct field trips with students to local courthouses, and have their legal questions answered by legal experts. Even elementary teachers were beginning to enroll in courses and access programs in law-related education, and curriculum materials and resources were being developed to support their needs.

The LRE programs across Canada served this need for teachers, and although some provinces and territories had better-developed and more extensive programs, social studies teachers in most areas of the country had access to information. This wealth of services across Canada has unfortunately changed, and social studies teachers today no longer have access to the same level of support. Funding has been cut back and many programs have been eliminated, or curtailed substantially.[14] Yet, the mandate of social studies education remains the same, and knowledge of law continues to be an integral part of this mandate.

The next section discusses how law education is interconnected with social studies curricula. The chapter concludes with a discussion of how teachers can address the law dimension of curricula, even when external sources of support have been reduced.

The Converging Goals of Social Studies and LRE

When we examine the grand purposes of social studies education, we see that the goals are lofty and intimately tied into preparing individuals for participation as active and informed citizens, furthering the goals of democracy, and preparing future generations to contribute to making the world a better place.[15] Social studies education is about more than the development of cognitive understanding of Canadian history, world events, geographic settlement, or honing such skills as mapping, identifying bias, or producing a cogent essay. Social studies education is rooted in the Progressive Movement of the early 1900s, where schools were to reflect "the needs of existing community life . . . improving the life we have in common so that the future shall be better than the past."[16]

Law is intricately woven into the tapestry of these big ideas. Law is not a static system of rules, developed on high by a few and passed down to citizens without input or redress. Law in a democracy is meant to reflect the values, mores, and hopes of the society at large. The law intersects with the range of fundamental principles Canadians hold dear: justice, fairness, freedom, peace, equality, equity, caring, multiculturalism, pluralism, responsibility, obligation, neighbourliness, due process, privacy, consent, and the common good.

As ideals and beliefs change and develop, so does (or should) the law. Often there is a tension between existing law and where society wants to go, but this tension and debate about these differing conceptions is fundamental to an open and responsive society. The Canadian constitution and the Charter of Rights and Freedoms set down fundamental principles, freedoms, rights, and responsibilities upon which our society is based. These principles were evident in the Canadian common law tradition, reiterated in general terms in the 1963 Canadian Bill of Rights, and now are enshrined in the constitution. Moreover, Canada is guided by the rule of law, not the arbitrary rule of dictators or of those who happen to have the authority or money.

The law in Canada is designed to give people, ordinary Canadians, voice and power. People help shape laws, are involved in changing laws, and help implement laws. One jurist used the analogy that "law is the glue" that binds people together. Others have used the phrase "Law is the mirror of society,"[17] a reflection of what is important in a society. But law is more than a passive binding ingredient, or a reflective mirror; it is also a tool that can shape and direct the way society should go. It can be activist and proactive. Citizens informed about the nature of law and the purpose of law, and who are skilled in the tools of law, can influence society for good.

Law can also act as a catalyst for problem-solving or for balancing competing and conflicting rights and obligations. Passing laws or using legal means to resolve a dispute doesn't necessarily bring about long-term solutions to problems (in fact, it can sometimes exacerbate a problem). However, using the law wisely can be one means to provide a positive and fair solution to a given personal or societal problem. Mahatma Ghandi, one of the world's great peace-makers, and a lawyer by profession, saw law as a means to a greater purpose, that of "entering man's hearts" and bringing people together. After a particularly gruelling but successful arbitration hearing, Ghandi says:

> Both (parties) were happy over the result, and both rose in the public estimation. My joy was boundless. I had learnt the true practice of law. I had learnt to find out the better side of human nature and to enter men's hearts. . . . The lesson was so indelibly burnt into me. . . . I lost nothing thereby—not even money, certainly not my soul.[18]

Social studies education was designed from the outset to get at these big issues of what it means to live together in a democracy, of working together to build a respectful and responsible community, of bringing together various cultures and peoples into a common whole, of giving the young the tools and insights to help create a better world. Knowledge of the law, its concepts, working principles, and procedures is key to fulfilling these aims.

Informed social studies teachers need to pay attention to law when tackling these fundamental purposes of social studies education. Not to do so does a disservice to students and to the curriculum.

Incorporating Law-related Education into Social Studies

Law-related education can be incorporated into social studies in several ways:

- by addressing the overt law content in the curriculum in innovative and engaging ways

- by teasing out and developing the legal perspective or dimension of a topic (where the law content is covert)

- by using law-related procedures and methodologies to address the higher order and critical thinking objectives of social studies education

- by integrating law-related concepts and issues when examining and cultivating the attitudinal objectives of the social studies curriculum

- by modelling and incorporating law-related concepts and principles into the informal curriculum of the classroom and school

Each of these strategies is discussed in turn below.

Overt law content

An examination of social studies curricula reveals some overt law content. For example, both elementary and secondary school students study government and political processes; this includes law-making, law-enforcing, the role of the judiciary, the Charter of Rights and Freedoms, the constitution, elections and voting, and citizen rights and responsibilities. Both younger and older students have opportunities to study the history of First Nations and Aboriginal peoples, and the acts of government that relegated them to second-class status. Students learn about the founding of the West and the special powers given to the railroad, the land provisions offered to European immigrants, and the discriminatory policies against other potential immigrants. By the time a student graduates from high school, he or she will have learned about the Chinese Head Tax, the Conscription Act, the creation of the League of Nations and the United Nations, the War Measures Act, Bill 101 in Québec, the Indian Act, Canada's more recent multicultural policies, the North American Free Trade Agreement, the Kyoto Protocol, and other legislation that has shaped the history and development of Canada. These topics of study provide overt opportunities to examine law and its importance to Canada, past, present, and future.

Yet these topics are not the source of most of the rich opportunities for law-related education in social studies. An examination of other units of study shows that many have a legal angle or perspective that should be addressed in order to cover the topic adequately. These topics, however, require the teacher to have a "law-related lens." In other words, the curriculum guide does not specifically state that a given law or the legal perspective should be studied. Rather, the topic lends itself to a multidisciplinary examination where the legal perspective is key. The legal angle here is implicit.

Implicit legal content

In grade 3, for example, rather than merely examining the roles and responsibilities of different members of the community (mayor, police, firefighter, letter carrier, and so on), teachers can engage students in a local community issue related to a topic of interest to this age group (for example, littering, saving an indigenous frog, adding a stop sign near the school, improving the standards for keeping pets). Any issue that involves helping to improve the community means engaging with the law. For example, discussing important social values, exerting one's right to input as a citizen, influencing those in power, helping to change a law or passing a new law, or engaging in the process of making a collective decision to take a certain action.

Law-related education, even at the elementary level, involves much more than simple knowledge of legislation or of one's rights. It involves using information to affect positive change and moves students beyond mere knowledge of what exists to an understanding of the principles of justice and fairness, and to critical judgement of what is and what could be.[19]

Another example from the elementary curriculum is the study of Aboriginal peoples. A one-dimensional examination would have students learn how Aboriginal people used the environment for food, shelter, and tools, and would expose students to some of the tensions that arose from interactions with European settlers. By adding a law dimension, students would begin to look at the societal values and beliefs at the time, the resulting discriminatory practices, and how values and beliefs change over time and result in new policies, legislation, and practices. Similarly, differing beliefs about the environment and its use between First Nations peoples and the dominant culture could be examined, historically as well as in the present. By employing a "law-related lens," teachers adopt an issue-based approach that examines values, beliefs and mores, policies and practices.

The secondary curriculum provides many opportunities for law-related education. For example, women such as Nellie McClung and Irene Murdoch challenged the laws of the day to give women more rights. The history of immigration to Canada cannot be fully discussed without attention to legislation that barred certain groups, gave preference to others, charged fees to some, and sent others to remote locations. The opening of the West was tinged with legal issues: property rights, First Nations displacement, fur trading, building of the railway, immigration policies, timber rights, and so on. Issues of war and peace are tied to economic policies, world trade, and racist practices. Land use decisions cannot be adequately addressed without attention to zoning issues, societal values, environmental concerns, and policy priorities.

Any current event is closely interconnected with the law. In fact, an interesting activity is to ask students to circle everything in the local newspaper that is connected with law. An initial identification might only reveal the obvious—a police arrest, a civil suit, a business merger, a new piece of legislation. But as one probes further, students see that almost everything in the paper is connected with law. Consider, for example, the repatriation of Haida artifacts from an American museum; childhood obesity and the decision to ban fast foods from school cafeterias; tobacco advertising; confrontations between loggers and environmentalists; the establishment of a new national park; closing the borders to beef exports; E coli contamination and water purity; charges of human rights violations in Iraq; insider trading; sweat shops and the production of goods; and war criminal trials at the world court. Social studies teachers addressing current events must, of necessity, teach law-related education.

Law methodologies and higher-order thinking

Another way that law-related education enhances the teaching of social studies is through the use of the methodologies associated with law. Case studies, mock trials, moot appeals, and mediation are processes that can be employed to teach social studies content, as well as foster the higher order and critical thinking objectives.

THE CASE STUDY

Legal cases are decisions recorded by judges after hearing a case in court. Each case summarizes the relevant facts leading up to the issue(s), outlines the arguments presented by both sides, lists the precedent cases used by each side to support their case, and records the decision of the judge along with reasons for the decision. This process of analysis is similar to the inquiry method in education:[20] identify the key issue(s) to be decided; examine the data and collect pertinent information; weigh the different perspectives being presented; examine past situations or decisions that might be similar and help in this decision; make a decision and justify it with valid reasons.

In social studies education, we want students to be able to separate out important and relevant facts from extraneous information, we want them to see an issue from more than one perspective, and when a conclusion is reached, we want them to be able to give good reasons for the choice made. The legal case model provides a frame for developing these kinds of thinking processes in students. The topic for the case analysis need not be a legal issue. The process could be applied to an examination of a historical issue (for example, "Did the Industrial Revolution represent progress?"), a current event (for example, "Is hosting the 2010 Winter Olympics worth the expense?"), or a topic relevant to one's community (for example, "Should dogs be allowed to run free in parks?"). Teachers can write the scenario or draw upon articles from the press. Students investigate the issue, using traditional library research, the Internet, and other sources. They then follow the steps in a case analysis, either orally as a role play, using a debate format where both sides are argued, or as a written text, similar to what a judge would write.

THE MOCK TRIAL

The legal system relies on the trial as the last resort in resolving disputes and as a vehicle to determine if someone accused of a criminal offence is guilty and should suffer consequences. The trial process—a mock trial or role-played trial—provides a mechanism for ferreting out the issues of an event and presenting them in an engaging way for participants. Characters or events from history can be "tried" or "re-tried," with each student playing a role (prosecution or defence, the accused, the key witnesses, the court personnel, the media, the jury). Social studies classes have re-tried Louis Riel, put Chief Poundmaker on trial, tried King Louis the XVI, and tried Martin Luther, to mention a few examples.[21] Through this vehicle, students also hone skills of argumentation, oral presentation, active listening, and analysis. Because they work together in small groups, the success of their efforts is due in large part to the extent to which they work cooperatively and support one another. Creative abilities are also enhanced as students prepare costumes, develop their dramatic skills, and prepare innovative media reports of the events. Even elementary students are able to undertake trials; for example, a children's story or fairy tale can become the basis of a trial, thereby integrating language arts with law-related education.[22]

Simulations and role play are known for their success in bringing issues to life, engaging students emotionally, fostering cooperative learning, and allowing for individualization of expression.[23] The mock trial and the moot appeal are two excellent examples of simulations that engage students and teach curriculum content and cognitive processes in effective ways.

THE MOOT APPEAL

The moot appeal is based on the format of the appeal process in the court system. Here students argue points of law in two teams (the appellant and the respondent) before a panel of judges who read factums (documents), listen to concise arguments, ask probing questions, and arrive at a majority written decision. This legal process provides another vehicle for social studies teachers who wish to examine in depth an important historical or current issue, and who wish to foster higher-order thinking processes. The moot appeal of Roncerelli vs. Duplessis[24] is one example of a moot appeal based on the real trial of the former premier of Québec, M. Duplessis. This appeal examines the issues of freedom of religion, freedom of association, the right to bail, the rule of law, the authority of elected officials, and the responsibility of civil servants. These are issues Canadians face today, and the moot appeal is one way to effectively engage students in the process of examining them.

MEDIATION

Mediation processes are being relied upon more and more in legal circles and by the general public as a way to resolve disputes. In mediation people come together and proceed through a give-and-take process towards a mutually acceptable solution. Mediation processes encourage listening, flexibility, other-directedness, empathy, and compromise—important attributes within a social studies context. Using an historical or current issue, identifying the various perspectives (or roles) students might play, the mediation is carried out as a role play. The First Nations' sentencing circle is a form of mediation being used today to hear the impact of crime on all parties involved and to establish a fair sentence. The process of the sentencing circle, which requires listening, compromise, and a fair resolution of a problem, might also be used by social studies teachers as a means to encourage students to arrive at a fair and just solution to an important societal issue.

Attitudinal objectives and legal concepts

While the attitudinal objectives of social studies education often get less play than the cognitive or skill-based objectives, social studies, since its inception, has been about preparing young people to thoughtfully and activity participate in society and help improve the human condition. Scott[25] notes that this vision includes preparing students to be "caring, reflective, and proactive adults." The "social" in social studies denotes this objective. The American document that created social studies as an area of study states that social studies should provide opportunities for young people to:

> (gain) an appreciation of the nature and laws of social life, a sense of responsibility of the individual as a member of social groups, and the intelligence and the will to participate effectively in the promotion of the social well-being.[26]

Social studies policy documents in Canada make reference to teaching students to "tolerate differing views . . . [be] willing to participate in society . . . show respect for others . . . be concerned for the welfare of others."[27]

Law-related education is all about issues, about competing values, about what is paramount in society, about how people should be treated, about what is meant by the common good, about the relationship between minority and majority rights, about the kind of society people want to have and the challenges they face in getting there. Law-related education in social studies (legal topics, the law-related perspective, legal methodologies) can provide a natural vehicle whereby important citizenship attributes may be addressed and cultivated in students.

Law and the informal curriculum

This discussion of law-related education would not be complete without a discussion of the importance of the informal curriculum in the teaching of social studies and role LRE must play here. More and more, social studies educators are coming to realize that what the teacher does in the classroom, the processes for dealing with disputes, the degree of input the students have in class decisions, the level of respect from teacher to student, the fairness of marking procedures, the kind of community that is created in the classroom and the school, all teach powerful lessons to students.[28] There is real discontinuity in learning if the teacher teaches about democracy yet runs an autocratic classroom. Or, if students learn about the value of due process and a fair hearing in the Charter of Rights and Freedoms, yet have no voice when it comes to disciplinary matters or settling a dispute. What messages about inclusivity or respect for diversity are being conveyed by a teacher who spends all her time with the able students or the English-speaking students while ignoring those students struggling with the curriculum or the language? Where are the messages about the common good when the teacher fails to cultivate an environment where all students have an opportunity to learn, where students listen to each other and help each other succeed?

The challenge for teachers who incorporate law-related education into social studies is that students start learning about their rights, about fair procedures, about the values and beliefs upon which our law and society are based, and then they start asking questions and challenging the status quo. For teachers who value control, "ignorance of the law" may be the preferred route. But for teachers committed to the ideals of social studies education, knowledgeable students can open up a new and fresh way of being in the classroom. Student empowerment need not mean teacher dis-empowerment, but rather mutual and shared responsibility for the betterment of all. Rights in law are always counterbalanced with responsibilities and obligations. We cannot expect students to fulfill the social studies citizenship objectives upon graduation unless we provide them with opportunities to grapple with issues, think through obligations, and practise citizenship throughout their school years, both inside and outside the classroom.

Teachers can incorporate LRE into the informal curriculum of their classrooms in many different ways. One simple way is to take some time at the beginning of each school year to discuss with students what makes for a respectful, safe, and open working environment for all, and then to jointly establish classroom rules that reflect these principles. These rules can be modified from time to time as new issues arise or if one or more of the rules don't seem to work in the best interests of all. In doing so, teachers will find that students are amazingly insightful about what makes for a good classroom.

Another way to incorporate LRE is for teachers to establish a fair process for dealing with disputes, giving all parties the opportunity to speak in a non-

threatening setting before someone (perhaps the teacher) who listens and makes a fair decision, or asks the parties involved to come to a mutually agreed upon solution (as one would do in a mediation.) Whitley notes in her thesis that when she first came to her former school, the principal's attitude was "there was no problem if he did not see it, and if he dealt with a problem, it was permanently fixed. There was no discussion with the children involved. He would get the teacher's perspective and pronounce his edict."[29] She goes on to explain how this approach caused a lot of hurt among students, parents, and staff, which needed to be healed. Listening to students and giving them voice can take more time than a quick decision from on high, yet it is time well taken as students see conflict resolved in peaceful, responsible, respectful, and just ways.

Zukerman[30] notes in her study of democratic classrooms that the whole school benefits from spreading the power to students, by giving students authority to make important decisions rather than relegating them to planning hot dog day or an upcoming school dance. The school becomes productive and students feel engaged. The school becomes a community of learners, rather than merely a place where students come to learn.

The book *The Moral Life of Schools*[31] is replete with examples of how teachers, even in the first five minutes of each class, communicate powerful messages to students about their value as individuals, about what is important to learn, about trust, about listening, about respect and caring. The messages of the informal curriculum cannot be underestimated in shaping students' understanding of democracy, justice, and law.

Current Challenges Facing Law-related Education

At the start of this chapter, I mentioned that teachers are often intimidated by law, and perhaps more so at the notion of teaching law. Although law-related educators argue that the kind of law social studies teachers are asked to teach is not the fine details and facts of law that is the purview of lawyers, this message has difficulty getting out and being received. There are not enough purveyors of this message to reach a majority of teachers, the curriculum guides don't articulate the law-related perspective, and teachers already feel overwhelmed by other obligations in the curriculum.

The kind of law that law-related educators are promoting fits naturally and seamlessly into the content of the social studies curriculum across Canada, and with the higher-order thinking and citizenship attribute objectives. But to address legal topics or to incorporate the legal perspective or legal methodologies, teachers require a legal lens to see these curriculum opportunities and to massage the curriculum accordingly. This requires education on the part of teachers, and since the mid-1990s there have been fewer and fewer opportunities for teachers to take courses in LRE, attend in-service or pre-service workshops, or access appropriate curriculum resources.[32]

Law-related educators have debated removing the word "law" from their efforts when dealing with teachers, and substituting it with less intimidating words like "citizenship" or "social justice," yet these new words don't fully reflect the intent or breadth of the movement, and appear dishonest.

The loss of funding and the decline in programs supporting teachers in LRE initiatives is an ongoing challenge. While there are still programs operating in most provinces and territories aimed at the general public and at particular groups (e.g. First Nations, people with low incomes, new immigrants), few resources are allocated to benefit schools.[33] In the last couple of years, greater attention has been given to producing web-based information and resources for teachers and students. Using the Internet, information can reach a relatively wide audience relatively inexpensively.[34] Some websites are geared specifically to social studies teachers (for example, www.lawconnection.com), yet many teachers are not aware of this service, or they do not immediately see the relevance to their teaching.

In the United States, the American Bar Association (ABA) acts as a clearinghouse and facilitator for programs in support of LRE in schools. The ABA has funds to do this, whereas the Canadian Bar Association has a different mandate and far fewer financial resources. Recently, program staff still active in public legal education in Canada have begun to think again about the needs in schools and the support they might offer teachers and students. However, their financial resources are limited.

Given this situation, many of those who work in LRE have chosen to do quality work with teachers on a limited scope, letting the message of the importance of LRE to social studies and the innovative ways of teaching it be spread classroom to classroom, teacher to teacher, school to school. This bottom-up approach to educational change in social studies may be the most effective anyway, in the long run, given current implementation research.[35] Certainly those social studies teachers who have been exposed to the value of law-related education are highly committed to this approach and have become strong advocates for LRE in social studies.

Further research is needed to determine the extent to which the overt legal content of the curriculum is being addressed, as well as the extent to which the legal perspective and legal methodologies are being incorporated.[36] The benefit is there for social studies education and for the development of knowledgeable, proactive citizens.

Endnotes

[1] Carl Bognar, Wanda Cassidy, and Pat Clarke, *Social Studies in British Columbia: Results of the 1996 Provincial Learning Assessment* (Victoria: Ministry of Education, 1997).

[2] Margaret Ferguson, "Law-related Education in Elementary and Secondary Schools," in *The Canadian Anthology of Social Studies: Issues and Strategies for Teachers*, ed. Roland Case and Penney Clark (Burnaby: Faculty of Education, Simon Fraser University, 1997), 67–73; Shelby Sheppard, "Facing an Issue through Critical Thinking and Decision Making in Social Studies," in *Let's Talk About Law in Elementary School*, ed. Wanda Cassidy and Ruth Yates (Calgary: Detselig, 1998), 151–169.

[3] Jones cited in M. Lybarger, "The Historiography of Social Studies: Retrospect, Circumspect, and Prospect," in *Handbook of Research on Social Studies Teaching and Learning*, ed. J. Shaver (New York: Macmillan, 1991), 3–15.

[4] National Education Association of the United States, Commission on the Reorganization of Secondary Education, Committee on Social Studies, *Social Studies in Secondary Education; A Six-year Program Adapted both to the 6-3-3 and the 8-4*

Plans of Organization (Washington, DC: Government Printing Office, 1916).

[5] For further discussion, see Mabel C. McKinney-Browning, "Educating for Civic Participation: Law-related Education in the United States," in *Let's Talk About Law in Elementary School*, 31–40.

[6] Ibid., 31.

[7] Ibid., 33.

[8] See, for example, Ron Ianni, "Reflections on the State of Public Legal Education in Canada," *Canadian Community Law Journal* 3 (1979): 3–11.

[9] For further discussion, see proceedings from the first national conference, "Legal Education for Canadian Youth," in *Law vs. Learning: Examination for Discovery*, ed. W. Crawford (Ottawa: Canadian Law Information Council, 1981); and Gail Dykstra, "Public Legal Education: The Canadian Approach," in *Understanding the Law: A Handbook on Educating the Public*, ed. Robert S. Peck and Charles J. White (Chicago: American Bar Association, 1983), 29–38.

[10] See discussion in Wanda Cassidy, "Law-related Education in Canada: Yesterday and Today," in *Law vs. Learning*, 25–36.

[11] Ibid.

[12] The Honourable Mr. Bora Laskin, Chief Justice of the Supreme Court of Canada, *Maclean's* 90 (February 21, 1977): 9.

[13] Wanda Cassidy, "Law-related Education: Promoting Awareness, Participation and Action," in *Weaving Connections: Education for Peace, Social, and Environmental Justice*, ed. Tara Goldstein and David Selby (Toronto: Sumach Press, 2000), 297–322.

[14] See J. Beaufoy, "A Plea for Better PLEI," *Canadian Lawyer* (February 1999): 27–30; Cassidy, "Law-related Education: Promoting Awareness"; and Lois E. Gander, "The Changing Face of Public Legal Education in Canada," *News and Views on Civil Justice Reform: Canadian Forum on Civil Justice* 6 (Summer 2003): 4–8.

[15] Gerald Marker and Howard Mehlinger, "Social Studies," in *Handbook of Research on Curriculum: A Project of the American Educational Association*, ed. Philip W. Jackson (New York: Macmillan, 1992), 830–851; K. Scott, "Achieving Social Studies Affective Aims: Values, Empathy, and Moral Development," in *Handbook of Research on Curriculum*, 357–369.

[16] John Dewey, *Democracy and Education* (New York: The Free Press, 1916).

[17] S.M. Waddams, *Introduction to the Study of Law* (Toronto, Carswell, 1987), 1–24.

[18] M.T. Ghandi, "An Autobiography: The Story of My Experiments with Truth," in *The Western Idea of Law*, ed. J.C. Smith and D.N. Weisstub (Toronto: Butterworths, 1983), 87.

[19] Wanda Cassidy, "Why Teach Law in the Elementary Classroom?" in *Let's Talk About Law*, 19–30.

[20] Bruce Joyce and Marsha Weil, *Models of Teaching*, 5th ed. (Boston: Allyn & Bacon, 1996).

[21] See, for example, Charles Hou and Cynthia Hou, *The Riel Rebellion: A Biographical Approach* (Vancouver: Tantalus Research, 1984) and other real-life historical mock trials produced by the Law Courts Education Society of British Columbia.

[22] Examples can be found in Wanda Cassidy and Ruth Yates, *Once Upon a Crime: Exploring Justice Through Storybook Mock Trials and Conflict Resolution Activities* (Toronto: Emond Montgomery, 2004); Heather Gascoigne, "Learning Law Through Story Drama" in *Let's Talk About Law*, 71–87; Bev Price, "Legal Dilemmas in Multicultural Stories," in *Education 448, Course Reader* (Burnaby: Simon Fraser University Distance Education); and J. Norton, "The State vs. the Big Bad Wolf: A Study of the Justice System in the Elementary School," *Social Studies and the Young Learner* 5, no. 1 (1992): 5–9.

[23] See, for example, Joyce and Weil, *Models of Teaching*; Ruth Yates, "Experiencing Law Through Games and Simulations," in *Let's Talk About Law*, 131–150.

[24] Ruth Yates, Wanda Cassidy, and Michael Manley-Casimir, *A Case for Canada: Student Manual* (Toronto: Copp Clark Pitman, 1991).

[25] Scott, "Achieving Social Studies Affective Aims," 25.

[26] National Education Association, *Social Studies in Secondary Education*.

[27] Discussed in Bognar, Cassidy, and Clarke, *Social Studies in British Columbia*, 93–108.

[28] See, for example, P.W. Jackson, R. Boomstrom, and D. Hansen, *The Moral Life of Schools* (San Francisco: Jossey Bass, 1993); and Christie Whitley, "Building Citizenship, Democracy, and a Community of Learners Within a Context of a Restorative Justice Model" (master's project, Simon Fraser University, 2002).

[29] Whitley, "Building Citizenship," 8.

[30] S. Zukerman, "Democratic Student Involvement at the School Level: A Case Study of an Elementary School Council" (master's thesis, Simon Fraser University, 1997).

[31] P. Jackson, R. Boostrom, and D. Hansen, *The Moral Life of Schools*.

[32] British Columbia is the only province that offers university credit courses that are geared specifically to meeting the needs of teachers in law-related education. The University of British Columbia offers two courses and Simon Fraser University offers four courses; SFU's courses are offered on campus and through Distance Education. The Legal Studies Program in the Faculty of Extension at the University of Alberta does some programming for teachers and provides useful web-based information.

[33] A few provinces, through their public legal education organizations, still offer limited services to teachers, in particular British Columbia, Alberta, and Saskatchewan. Recently the national Public Legal Education and Information (PLEI) formed a committee to look for ways to foster LRE in schools, even in the era of limited funds. In British Columbia, a report funded by the Ministry of the Attorney General resulted in greater coordination among groups working in public le-

gal education and fostered a renewed interest in LRE. See Pat Pitsula, *Review of the Role of Public Legal Education in the Delivery of Justice Services* (Vancouver: Ministry of the Attorney General, 2003).

[34] The two websites most appropriate for Canadian teachers interested in learning more about law and ways to teach LRE to children are the Legal Studies Program site at the University of Alberta, www.acjnet.org, and a joint site of the Centre for Education, Law and Society at Simon Fraser University and the Law Courts Education Society of British Columbia, www.lawconnection.ca.

[35] See, for example, Elliott Eisner, "Educational Reform and the Ecology of Schooling," and Dennis Sparks and Susan Loucks-Horsley, "Five Models of Staff Development for Teachers," in *Contemporary Issues in Curriculum*, ed. Allan Ornstein and Linda S. Behar-Horenstein (Boston: Allyn & Bacon, 1999), 403–415 and 295–319.

[36] Little research has been done in the areas of public legal education and law-related education in schools. This is because those involved in programs are on the front lines of service delivery and focused on this objective. In the past five years, research has become more of a priority, yet funding continues to be a challenge.

CHAPTER 9

Global Education and the Challenge of Globalization

George Richardson

The earth [is] man's home.— New Canadian Geography[1]

Exploring . . . interdependence broadens students' global consciousness and empathy with world conditions.—Alberta Learning[2]

The statements above, the first published in 1899 and the second extracted from the current Alberta social studies curriculum, are separated by more than one hundred years, yet they both indicate that teaching about the world has always occupied an important position in social studies education. However, what has been called world studies, international education, or, more currently, global education, has continually evolved along with Canada's status as a nation and its perceived role in international affairs. From an early emphasis on Canada's membership in the British Empire and subsequently in the Commonwealth, through its UN involvement, its increasingly important relationship with the United States, to its post-Cold War participation in a complex matrix of organizations and agreements such as NAFTA, the WTO, the G-8, and the Kyoto Protocol, the content and purposes of global education have changed with the times.[3]

In many ways the prominent position assigned to global education stems from the traditional and widely used "expanding horizons" model of social studies. According to this model, the ideal structure of social studies is one that gradually leads students from knowledge of local contexts to progressively wider and more sophisticated understandings of self and community.[4] A model that uncritically situates global education as a culminating focus of the discipline has been questioned,[5] but there are also significant questions about what is meant by the term "global education" and about the role it should play in social studies. These questions have been made all the more urgent by the growing debate over the effects of globalization. In what follows I will argue that our understanding of global education has changed in response to different ways of viewing the world and that globalization—a phenomenon that brings with it its own particular worldview—has emerged as a force that presents significant challenges to the meaning and role of global education in schools.

Questions of Perspective: The Development of Global Education

In order to understand the current position of global education within the broader discipline of social studies, and why globalization represents such a problematic force, some sense of how global education has changed over time is needed. Looking at its history, it is possible to identify a number of shifts in perspective that have characterized how global education has been imagined in curriculum and schooling. These different "imaginaries"[6] do not represent a linear process—in many cases they overlap and intersect—but each has its own understanding of the purpose of global education, its own worldview, and its own value structure.

First perspective: The imperial imaginary

As indicated above, global education has always been a part of social studies, but for much of the twentieth century in Canada, as in other nations, learning about the world was primarily a function of the development of nationalism and national pride.[7] Students studied the world as much to establish the distinctness of their own nation as they did to gain insights into the history and culture of other nations. In Canada, in particular, the nationalistic orientation of world studies was framed by Canada's membership in the British Empire and subsequently in the Commonwealth.[8] Thus students learned about the world from British—and fundamentally imperial—perspectives. For example, as late as 1945 teachers in Ontario were still being reminded to "lead the pupil to see that he has duties and responsibilities towards his family, his school, his community, his province, the Dominion of Canada and the British Empire."[9] Until 1971, in a unit titled "Nationalism in the Modern World," Grade 12 students in Alberta were taught "the nationalism of various peoples of the Empire was the dynamic creation of the modern Commonwealth."[10] In both curricula, we see a worldview in which national identity was subsumed under the imperial connection, Canada was seen as acting in the world within the comforting and legitimizing confines of the British Empire, and learning about the world was an act of division in which students were encouraged to separate Empire from non-Empire and, more broadly, West from non-West.

In an analysis of the degree to which global education was (and to some degree continues to be) framed as a discourse of imperialism, it is useful to draw on some aspects of post-colonial scholarship. Briefly, post-colonial theory represents a vigorous re-examination of the history and legacy of Western colonialism in terms of the cultural and social consequences imperialism had for the colonized nation and the colonial power.[11] One of its most significant contributions has been to tie colonialism and the racist view of the world upon which it was grounded to the process of national identity formation in the West.[12] As post-colonial scholarship indicates, the function of the imperial imaginary for learning about the world was twofold. On one hand it was firmly grounded in developing Western nationalism. Thus Canada strengthened its own identity and occupied a privileged status in the world because of its continuing ties to the power and influence of Britain and the Commonwealth. On the other hand, its purpose was ideological, and the act of dividing the world into the West and the "foreign" and "less-advanced" non-West was a process directed at demonstrating the technical, cultural, and moral superiority of the West for the purposes of justifying imperialism.[13] From the imperial imaginary, the non-West or, as successive post-World War II social studies curriculum described it, the Third World or the Developing World, was used as a marker against which the West measured its own progress and established its own sense of identity, while the development of nations in the non-West was measured on the basis of the degree to which they westernized their economic and political institutions.[14]

Although it is possible to trace the imperial imaginary well into the present, in the post-World War II period, three alternative understandings of world studies were also developing. Essentially, these three ways of knowing the world revolved around differing perspectives on the interaction of nations. The first of these, the bipolar imaginary, held that the post-World War II world was characterized by a binary division of the globe into competing political and economic systems, the second, the multipolar imaginary, emphasized that the world after 1945 was one in which multilateralism and interdependence held sway; while the third, the ecological imaginary, stressed the importance of attending to cultural difference while underscoring the complexity and interconnectedness of all life forms.

Second perspective: The bipolar imaginary

In some respects, the bipolar imaginary was one that mirrored the imperial division of the world that characterized global education for most of the twentieth century, but in this case, the split was structured around ideological divisions and embedded in the Cold War. From a Cold War perspective, the world was divided into Communist and non-Communist spheres, and a key aim of social studies courses was to develop knowledge about Communism in order to better understand the methods and motives of a rival system. A second, and complementary aim for studying the communist world was to reinforce the inherent "rightness" of the democratic, capitalist system. Typically, social studies curricula of the Cold War era emphasized the values of individualism as opposed to collectivism, nationalism as opposed to internationalism, and confrontation as opposed to cooperation. Social studies curricula were particularly concerned with transmission of knowledge about the two systems, and the world itself was seen as a kind of forum or arena in which the rival powers competed for influence. Few aspects of social studies escaped being drawn into this Cold-War perspective. For example, global issues such as economic development, international relations, and human rights were seen within the context of the struggle for ideological dominance, and students writing standardized exams in social studies were frequently asked to compare the advantages and disadvantages of the two systems—with the expected result being a conclusion that liberal democracy and capitalism were far superior to the communist alternative. One representative example of the bipolar imaginary can be drawn from the 1955 Ontario Grade 12 World History curriculum. In the introduction to a unit of study entitled "The World since 1945," students were reminded, somewhat apocalyptically, that the post-war period had been characterized by "the release of atomic energy, the violent clash of ideologies [and] the fear of stalemate." These statements set the context in which students examined such specific topics as "Democracy vs. Communism" and "Democracy, our way of thought and life."[15] Critics of the bipolar perspective stressed that it limited students' understanding of the world to a simplistic binary relationship in which both sides of the conflict were reduced to the level of caricature and in which emerging global issues such as environmental degradation, population growth and the growing poverty gap between the North and the South were all but ignored.[16]

Third perspective: The multipolar imaginary

In sharp contrast to the bipolar imaginary was the view that held that the aim of world studies was to emphasize the inter-reliant nature of the world's peoples and nations. Related to the creation of the United Nations and Canada's post-war status as a rising middle power, the multipolar perspective emphasized the values of international cooperation, multilateralism and interdependence. Development education emerged from the multipolar imaginary of the 1960s, as did the idea that advances in telecommunication and international travel were producing a new world culture. Such a view—perhaps best characterized by Marshall McCluhan's notion that the world was becoming a global village—typifies many global education texts still in use today.[17] This perspective, coupled with emphasis on values education during the same period, produced a growing focus on activism. Global education appeared to have as its primary function raising students' consciousness of the interdependent nature of the world and of the social, political, and economic inequities that exist, with a view to taking action to raise the standard of living and quality of life in the developing world.[18] Typical of the social studies curriculum of the day was this idealistic statement from the 1971 Alberta social studies curriculum:

> In keeping with the basic tenets of democracy, the new social studies invites free and open inquiry . . . by actively confronting value issues, students will . . . deal not only with the "what is" but also with the "what ought to be.[19]

Given its focus on activism, it is not surprising that this period gave rise to extracurricular organizations such as UN and Amnesty International clubs that could be seen as a natural extension of the themes and issues then emerging in social studies classrooms.

A critique that has emerged around the multipolar imaginary is that, in some respects, it merely substituted one kind of singular view of the world (the global village) for the imperial view that held that the West was a political and economic model for the rest of the world. Constructed around a fundamentally nineteenth-century understanding of the moral obligation of the West to "make the world right," advocates of the one-world approach to social studies often tended to ignore or gloss over issues of cultural difference and conflicts in values in pursuit of a monological understanding that suggested that beyond superficial differences, the world's peoples were essentially one.[20] Thus, when applied to the notion of global education, the multipolar imaginary was framed in terms of promoting a particularly Western sense of agency and mission among students. These twin aims are perhaps best exemplified by the following extract taken from the 1981 Alberta social studies curriculum:

> If the world's problems belong to all of us and if we place our hope for a more peaceful and tolerant future in the hands of our young people, we must ensure that they understand the world they live in and accept the challenge of finding new and innovative solutions to the problems faced by people around the world.[21]

Despite its failings, one of the lasting effects of development education and the multipolar imaginary was to shift the discourse of social studies from knowing about the world to an emphasis on living in the world. The chief characteristic of this shift was that global education became much more oriented towards processes—that is, developing the skills and attitudes that would lead to active engagement—than it was with the transmission of knowledge. For example, as opposed to learning about differences in standard of living between the North and the South, process-oriented education stressed the need for students to ask critical questions about

the reasons for the disparity, to suggest possible solutions to the problem, and to evaluate the probable outcomes of the solutions they suggested.

The shift from a paradigm that viewed global education as transmission of knowledge about the world to one that suggested that students take a much more participatory and activist stance towards addressing global issues required two key elements to make it work. The first was a resource infrastructure that provided new curriculum materials and access to the international connections that could make those materials relevant by providing students with different opportunities for activism. The second element was a fundamental shift in pedagogy that suggested that teachers should act as facilitators in the learning process while it encouraged students to become actively engaged in their own learning. In the 1980s and early 1990s, the Canadian International Development Agency (CIDA) funded a series of Global Education Centres across the country. The purpose of these centres was to foster "global awareness among teachers, to assist them in finding curriculum opportunities, materials and techniques to nurture their students' will as well as their skills, to deal with global issues."[22] Although in the late 1990s these CIDA-funded centres typically fell victim to federal and provincial budget cuts, they were instrumental in providing the resources and opportunities for teachers and students to develop new understandings of the world and of the possibilities of global education.

In terms of the changes in teaching that were necessary to develop the participatory, activist ethos on which the multipolar imaginary was based, teachers emphasized the importance of group activities, cooperative learning, role play, and simulation in developing students' sense of agency and of the interconnectedness of global society. This shift away from direct instruction can perhaps best be seen in two examples, one drawn from a widely used text from the period, the other from the Saskatchewan curriculum. Published in 1988 with the aid of CIDA funding, *Global Teacher, Global Learner* was a resource book of strategies, techniques, and projects designed to help teachers and students "become global."[23] For its authors, Graham Pike and David Selby, the purpose of global education was to engender a shift in consciousness and perspective through which students were able to "develop the social and political skills necessary for becoming effective participants in democratic decision-making at a variety of levels, grassroots to global."[24] One example of the cooperative and empowering pedagogy characteristic of the development of the multipolar imaginary can be seen in an exercise excerpted from Pike and Selby's text. In the "Woolly Thinking" exercise, students were encouraged to pick one topic from among a list that included "the arms race, environmental pollution, human rights violations, or resource depletion." Students then had to negotiate with other students to identify as many possible connections between topics as they could. The connections were signified by coloured wool yarn stretched between students. The aim of the exercise was "to offer a potent visual symbol of the interlocking/systemic nature of contemporary global issues."[25]

The teaching activities suggested for the 1994 Saskatchewan Social Studies 20, History 20: World Issues course had a similarly participatory structure. As a culminating exercise "intended to give students an opportunity to make decisions about the world issues they have studied: human rights, population, environment, wealth, and world governance," students were encouraged to participate in a simulation in which they acted as members of a UN commission charged with addressing such issues as disarmament, Third World debt, and human rights violations. The purpose of the simulation was broader than learning about the global issues noted above; its intent was to provide a forum "to discuss these issues as a set of interacting problems, many of which have to be settled at the international level."[26]

Fourth perspective: The ecological imaginary

In the early 1990s, at the same time that many social studies curricula were focused on developing the multipolar imaginary, another shift in emphasis took place that was grounded in an ecological understanding of the complexity and interdependence of all life forms. The ecological imaginary combined environmentally based concerns for the survival of the planet with an increasing emphasis on the importance of cultural diversity and multiple perspectives on such issues as development, trade, and power relations between North and South nations.[27]

From an ecological stance, global education became increasingly concerned with a shift in values and was characterized by an emphasis on the need to teach students to acknowledge and respect diverse points of view on global issues.[28] Part of this move towards diversity reflects a conscious attempt on the part of social studies scholars to step beyond the traditional division of the world that separated West from non-West. These scholars argued that throughout its association with social studies, global education carried with it an insidious form of cultural homogenization.[29] Thus under the guise of the notion that fundamentally "we are all the same," global education tended to trivialize cultural differences, devalue non-Western cultures, and privilege Western ways of knowing. As John Willinsky asked, "What more will it take to break the colonizing hold of the other, especially when the other is in some sense oneself?"[30] From an ecological and cultural awareness perspective, global education concerned itself particularly with the ways in which students could be brought to view the world through the eyes of other nations and other cultures. This particular approach stressed that global education needed to be "transformative" in that it would cause students to re-examine their own values and beliefs with the aim of engendering "world mindedness"—a more holistic understanding of the world and a disposition towards taking action to address global problems and issues.[31] From a transformative perspective, global education stressed the importance of interconnections, perspectivity, caring, and alternatives, and students were encouraged to ask such questions as, "Why should we care?" and "How could things be different?"[32]

Typical of the ecological imaginary is this statement from the current Nova Scotia grade 12 course, Global History:

As dwellers within and citizens of the global village, students must learn about their global neighbours and their cultural diversity, about rights, responsibilities, equity, justice, about landscapes and environments, about interdependence, and how all of these have roles in their past, present, and future.[33]

The same ecologically grounded sense of the complex and interdependent nature of existence can be seen in the Saskatchewan grade 11 World Issues course. Organized around such concepts as "integration" and "dialectic," the course outline notes "individuals [need] to be a part of a larger whole in order to meet their physical, social, and human needs. Humans cannot develop and express their humanity outside of a human society.[34]

The pedagogies that are used to teach the ecological imaginary are not fundamentally different from those associated with the multipolar imaginary. In both cases, there is a strong emphasis on activity-based learning and extensive use of such strategies as role-playing, simulations, and brainstorming.[35] There are, however, two characteristics that differentiate the pedagogy of the ecological imaginary from the teaching approaches that are typical of the multipolar imaginary. The first is an increasing emphasis on the need for interdisciplinary approaches to appreciate the complex and interconnected issues that face the world community.[36] The 1994 Saskatchewan Social Studies 20 and History 20: World Issues course reflects this emphasis as follows:

> The issues facing the world do not have simple clear solutions. Rather they are multifaceted, ambiguous situations requiring choices among contradictory and conflicting values which can only be evaluated by presenting and discussing various viewpoints on an issue.[37]

The second distinguishing characteristic is an acknowledgement that it is critical to view social studies in general and global education in particular from the context of multiple perspectives. As the 2003 consultation draft for the new Alberta social studies program indicates:

> Critically examining multiple perspectives among local, national and global issues de-velops students' understanding of citizenship and identity and the interdependent or conflicting nature of individuals, communities, societies and nations.[38]

Teaching strategies that seek to incorporate multiple perspectives into global education will need to incorporate the development of what David Selby terms "perspective consciousness."[39]

Fifth perspective: The monopolar imaginary

More recently, there has been a return to a more monopolar view of the world in which global education is tied to neo-liberal constructs of the "world as a market." Thus with the 1991 collapse of the Soviet Union and the end of the Cold War came a renewed emphasis on economic expansion in which students were encouraged to acquire and develop the skills and knowledge necessary to make themselves and their nations more competitive in the emerging global market. The value structure inherent in this approach stresses individualism, competitiveness, and self-reliance, while it encourages students to look at the world as a single culture in which the dominant organizing principal is consumerism.[40]

Typical of the values that underpin the "world as competitive market" approach to global education are two excerpts from recent Ontario and Alberta curriculum documents. In Alberta, the stated aim of the social studies curriculum is "to equip students with the knowledge and skills necessary to function in the society in which they must ultimately find their place."[41] In Ontario, the Ministry of Education notes that the aim of the grades 9 to 12 program of studies, introduced in 2000, is to ensure that

> graduates from Ontario secondary schools are well prepared to lead satisfying and productive lives both as citizens and individuals and to compete successfully in a global economy in a rapidly changing world.[42]

The Challenge of Globalization

It is in light of the last two imaginaries that we come to the impact of globalization on global education. The radical disjunction between developing perspectivity and world-mindedness on one hand and preparing students to compete in the global economy on the other, suggests that global education is in the midst of a struggle between two competing ideologies. Before examining this struggle and the ways in which globalization represents a challenge to global education, it is important to establish an understanding of the phenomenon of globalization. Because it represents a broad series of effects, globalization is not always easy to define, but in general, the phenomenon has three characteristics. Economically, globalization is characterized by the free flow of goods and capital and the rise of consumerism on a global scale. Politically, globalization has challenged the sovereignty of nation states and raised significant questions about what it means to act as a citizen in a globalized world. Culturally, globalization has led to the loss of cultural diversity and a corresponding increase in cultural homogeneity.[43]

As already noted, traditionally global education tended to stress learning about the world over encouraging students to become active agents prepared to address global issues of social, economic, and political significance. With knowledge transmission as its primary emphasis, global education assumed a stable world that could be known, and was based on the belief that knowledge itself was sufficient to prepare students to act as responsible global citizens. As such, global education proceeded from an overwhelmingly Western point of view that privileged reason, transparency, and universalism over grounded local perspectives that emphasized the close emotive connections between communities and their cultural and physical environments. But the separation between the Western and non-Western worlds that was the basis for much of what students studied in global education is no longer such a convenient binary separating "us" from "them." The effects of globalization can be seen in Canada as well

as in such "developing" nations as India, Nigeria, and Indonesia that typically were the focus of global education courses. Because its impact is global, and because we are all subject to its influence, globalization presents three very specific challenges for global education. I will explore these challenges in the following subsections.

First challenge: Transmission or transformation

In many social studies classrooms, the emphasis on knowledge transmission that remains the primary focus of global education is maintained at the expense of the idea that global education could be transformative. Transformative education suggests that the purpose of global education is twofold: questioning students' existing understandings and perspectives with the aim of developing a new sense of world-mindedness, and empowering students to become active participants in addressing issues that impact the global community.[44] In some ways this choice between content and process is not new and has always been at the heart of the tensions that lie within social studies in general and global education in particular. However, I would argue that globalization represents a unique challenge that demands a reorientation of global education towards transformative education.

Given that it has profound and truly global effects, ranging from unregulated flows of capital to monoculturing and deforestation on a planetary scale, globalization is a phenomenon that demands that students do more than study its consequences; they also need to formulate an informed response to the impact globalization is having on their lives, the lives of others, and on the planet in general. While developing this response clearly requires knowledge about globalization, it also requires a sense of agency and a disposition to act that can only emerge from an understanding that students are fully implicated in the challenges globalization presents. This kind of understanding does not emerge from content knowledge; it is the product of a transformative process in which students are encouraged to critically examine their own perspectives on such issues as free trade and consumerism, and, on the basis of their examination, suggest courses of action to address these issues.

Second challenge: Single or multiple perspectives

As I have argued, global education has generally reinforced Western views of the world while it has tended to discount the worth of non-Western perspectives. This structure of privilege is rendered particularly problematic by globalization.

In its effects globalization has tended to ignore national boundaries and traditional dividing lines between the "developed" and "developing" worlds. In doing so, it has promoted a single worldview that in many respects resembles the imperial imaginary discussed earlier. But this worldview differs from the imperial imaginary in two significant ways, both of which present challenges to the current structure of global education. The first problematic aspect of globalization is its tendency to diminish local and national cultures in favour of a culture of decontextualized global consumerism. In this aspect, it is as much a challenge to nations like Canada (and, for example, its cultural industries) as it is to nations in the developing world. The second aspect, its neo-liberal emphasis on de-regulation, free trade, and free flows of capital, presents as much a problem to Canada (and, for example, public education and public health care) as it does to other nations around the world.

In response to these challenges, global education needs to re-examine its traditional "single perspective approach" and emphasize that there are multiple perspectives on such issues as development, governance, and trade. In terms of the impact of globalization, a multiple-perspective approach has two key benefits. First, it can be a point of interrogation and resistance to the cultural homogenization that is characteristic of globalization. Second, a multiple-perspectives approach encourages students to examine and step out of their own cultural locations in order to develop what Hannah Arendt terms the habit of "learning to imagine the other."[45] To the degree that global education promotes imagining the other,

it develops ethics of care, empathy, and appreciation of difference that are key aspects in countering the homogenizing tendencies of globalization.

Third challenge: national or global citizenship

The development of citizenship has long been the primary focus of social studies education.[46] In terms of global education in Canada, citizenship has typically been seen in two ways: first, as the civic responsibility to be an active and responsible member of the global community, and second, as an obligation to address inequities between the developed and developing world.[47] In both cases global citizenship is framed as a matter of national self-interest and almost exclusively tied to the civic structures of the nation state.[48] Thus students in Canada are urged to take up their responsibilities and obligations to address significant global issues such as international conflict, environmental degradation, or the protection of human rights as citizens of Canada rather than as citizens of the world. And where it is suggested that political action is necessary to bring about a needed change, it is through the nation and its foreign policy that action is accomplished. A good case in point is Manitoba's social studies curriculum for Senior 3, the last mandatory social studies course Manitoba students must take. Under a segment of the course titled "Canada's Involvement in International Affairs," students are asked the questions, "Why and how is Canada involved in international affairs?"; "How do other people and nations see us?" and "What is Canada's role as peacekeepers?"[49]

The questions are typical of those posed in other provincial curriculum documents, and although they do take up the question of the international civic responsibilities of nation states, they are also limiting in that they imply a field of action that effectively precludes the possibility of international responses to global issues. However, given the transnational realities of globalization, it is pertinent to ask whether global education would be better served by promoting global rather than national citizenship.

In some ways it is highly problematic to continue to endorse national citizenship in the context of global education. Because many of the issues that face the global community are international in scope and effect, it is uncertain what the actions of a single nation can do to address these concerns, and in the context of global education, the more frequently international issues are dealt with from national perspectives, the less opportunity students have to explore or develop other perspectives. A good example of this dilemma can be seen in the recent Kyoto Accord on climate change. While it may be useful to have students discuss and analyze Canada's decision to ratify the accord, it is also pertinent to ask whether a nationally based analysis works against the development of an emergent sense of the collective responsibilities of global citizenship.

On the other hand, the notion of global citizenship presents its own pedagogic challenges, and significant issues arise when we attempt to speak of "global citizens" and a "global civic community." For example, the meaning of such terms as "citizenship" and "citizen" are very much contested—even when we use them to refer to national contexts.[50] This uncertainty is only compounded when citizenship is placed in international contexts—particularly given the fact that there are no global civic structures capable, in any real sense, of functioning as a world government.[51] While it is clear that many Canadian curricula have the intent that students should think and act as global citizens, it is equally clear that the term "global citizen" carries substantially different meanings in different provinces. For example, in Ontario, the Canadian and World Studies program implemented in 2002 is structured around helping students develop "the knowledge, skills, and values they need to become responsible citizens and informed participants in Canadian democracy," and to "help them to perceive Canada in a global context and to understand its evolving role in the global community."[52] In British Columbia, the 1997 Social Studies 11 course indicates that as a result of completing the course:

> Students become familiar with the rights, responsibilities, and practice of Canadian and global citizenship. They also develop an awareness of global problems with a view to identifying personal roles, as Canadians and as global citizens, in determining solutions.[53]

Finally in Manitoba, where the existing World Studies curriculum dates from 1990 and is in the process of being revised, global citizenship is framed as a set of responses to such questions as:

> What is Canada's role in and involvement with the United Nations, NAFTA, NATO, NORAD, the Commonwealth? What role does Canada play in world peacekeeping efforts? What are the major challenges facing the people of the Developing World? How are Canadians helping to meet these challenges through various government and non-government programs?[54]

A further complication in attempting to incorporate global citizenship into different curricula is the thorny problem of civic allegiance. Citizenship education has typically been organized to promote patriotism and loyalty to the nation state;[55] global citizenship could well call this allegiance into question if a conflict arises between what are perceived to be the interests of the nation and those of the world as a whole. Questions of definition, structure, and allegiance that arise when we speak of global citizenship have led prominent Canadian political scientist Will Kymlicka to note, "globalization is undoubtedly producing a new civil society, but it has not yet produced anything we can recognize as transnational democratic citizenship."[56] Speaking of the political changes that have emerged since the collapse of the Soviet Union, Canadian writer and political philosopher Michael Ignatieff raises much the same concern, observing, "Though we have passed into a post-imperial age, we are not in a post-national age, and I cannot see how we will ever do so."[57] Yet despite these significant difficulties, many scholars have maintained that without a turn to world citizenship, students will not develop the imaginative capacity to see beyond the constraints of the nation and challenge the dominant narrative of globalization.[58]

Other scholars argue that it is critical to develop world citizenship because contemporary understandings of citizenship as bound to the national structure of parliaments, parties, and regular elections are increasingly circumscribed and made irrelevant by extra-national organizations such as the G-8, the WTO, and the World Bank.[59] The challenge of globalization raises the issue of whether social studies, and more specifically global education, can imagine a civic fabric on a global scale in which students can see themselves acting as informed and empowered global citizens.

Conclusion: The Struggle for Global Education

In the previous section I have attempted to lay out some of the challenges globalization presents to global education. In this final section I will discuss current ideological struggles that make global education very much a contested ground. As noted earlier, in broad terms the struggle is between two very different global imaginaries with quite dissimilar perspectives on globalization. The first is grounded in an ecological awareness of the fundamental interrelatedness of all aspects of the Earth and of the importance of physical and cultural diversity. From this perspective, the purpose of global education is to help students develop a sense of connectedness, empathy, and an appreciation for diversity and difference, and globalization is seen as an essentially negative force.[60] The second perspective is founded on neo-liberal economic ideas that suggest that despite superficial differences, individuals have fundamentally the same wants and needs, and that by serving their own self-interest, ultimately the interests of the planet are also served. From this perspective, the purpose of global education is to help students develop the knowledge and skills that will allow them to be competitive and successful in the global arena, and globalization is seen as an essentially positive force.[61]

By using brief examples drawn from the Alberta social studies program, it is possible to see how these two imaginaries act as competing discourses within a single curriculum, and the degree to which they represent different visions of the purpose of global education. Thus, on the one hand, the curriculum indicates:

> Students will be expected to develop an appreciation of the diversity that exists in the world, an appreciation that different perspectives exist on quality of life [and] an awareness and appreciation of the interdependent nature of the world.[62]

On the other hand, it is noted that in the face of a rapidly changing world, students must become

> Self-motivated, self-directed problem solvers and decision makers who are developing the skills necessary for learning and who develop a sense of self-worth and confidence in their ability to participate in a changing society.[63]

The opposing themes of interdependence and autonomy that the above passages highlight stand as evidence of the ideological tensions existing within global education. When coupled with the complexities globalization presents, it is clear that global education is at somewhat of a crossroads in its evolution. Caught between learning *about* the world and learning to live *in* the world, the specific challenge global education faces is how best to prepare students to act as informed, caring, and active participants in a globalized world.

Endnotes

[1] *New Canadian Geography* (Toronto: W.J. Gage, 1899), 38.

[2] Alberta Learning, *Social Studies Kindergarten to Grade Twelve* (Edmonton: Author, August 2002), 7.

[3] Roland Case, "Promoting 'Global Attitudes,'" *Canadian Social Studies* 30, no. 4 (Summer 1996): 174–177; Robert Fowler and Ian Wright, eds., *Thinking Globally about Social Studies Education* (Vancouver: Research and Development in Global Studies, Centre for the Study of Curriculum and Instruction, University of British Columbia, 1995); William Gaudelli, *World Class: Teaching and Learning in Global Times* (London: Lawrence Erlbaum, 2003); Merry M. Merryfield, "Moving the Center of Global Education: From Imperial World Views that Divide the World to Double Consciousness, Contrapuntal Pedagogy, Hybridity, and Cross-Cultural Competence," in *Critical Issues in Social Studies Research for the 21st Century*, ed. William B. Stanley (Greenwich, CT:

Information Age Publishing, 2001), 150–179; Graham Pike and David Selby, *In the Global Classroom: Book One* (Toronto: Pippin, 1999); and Walt Werner and Roland Case, "Themes of Global Education," in *Trends and Issues in Canadian Social Studies*, ed. Ian Wright and Alan Sears (Vancouver: Pacific Educational Press, 1997), 176–194.

4   Kieran Egan, *Children's Minds, Talking Rabbits and Clockwork Oranges: Essays on Education* (New York: Teachers College Press, 1999); Joe L. Kincheloe, *Getting Beyond the Facts: Teaching Social Studies/Social Sciences in the Twenty-first Century*, 2nd ed. (New York: Peter Lang, 2001); Alan Sears, "Social Studies in Canada," in *Trends and Issues*; and George S. Tomkins, "The Social Studies in Canada," in *Canadian Social Studies*, ed. Jim Parsons, Geoff Milburn, and Max van Manen (Edmonton: University of Alberta Faculty of Education, 1983), 12–30.

5   Egan, *Children's Minds*.

6   I draw on the work of David G. Smith for the notion of a "global imaginary," which "pertains less to any characteristic of the world in its ordinary condition than to what certain people *imagine* that condition to be." See David G. Smith, "Globalization and Education: Prospects for Postcolonial Pedagogy in a Hermeneutic Mode," *Interchange* 30 (1999): 3–4.

7   George H. Richardson, *The Death of the Good Canadian: Teachers, National Identities, and the Social Studies Curriculum* (New York: Peter Lang, 2002); ———, "A Border Within: The Western Canada Protocol for Social Studies Education and the Politics of National Identity Construction," *Revista Mexicana de Estudios Canadienses* Numéro 4, (Otono, 2002): 31–46; ———, "The Love that Dares Not Speak Its Name: Canadian Identity and the Alberta Social Studies Program," *Canadian Social Studies* 31, no. 2 (Winter 1997): 138–144.

8   John Willinsky, *Learning to Divide the World: Education at Empire's End* (Minneapolis: University of Minnesota Press, 1998).

9   Ontario Ministry of Education, *Courses of Study: Grades 9 and 10 Social Studies and History* (Toronto: Author, 1945), 10.

10 Alberta Education, *Senior High School Curriculum Guide 1955* (Edmonton: Author, 1955), 125.

11 See, for example, Ingrid Johnston, *Re-mapping Literary Worlds: Postcolonial Pedagogy in Practice* (New York: Peter Lang, 2003); Robert J.C. Young, *Postcolonialism: An Historical Introduction* (London: Blackwell, 2001); and Chris Tiffin and Alan Lawson, eds., *De-scribing Empire: Post-colonialism and Textuality* (London: Routledge, 1994).

12 See, for example, Homi K. Bhabha, *Nation and Narration* (London: Routledge, 1990); and Partha Chatterjee, *The Nation and Its Fragments: Colonial and Postcolonial Histories* (Princeton, NJ: Princeton University Press, 1993).

13 Merryfield, "Moving the Center of Global Education"; and Willinsky, *Learning to Divide the World*.

14 Edward Said, *Culture and Imperialism* (New York: Knopf, 1993); Christine Sleeter, "How White Teachers Construct Race," in *Race, Identity and Representation in Education*, ed. Cameron McCarthy and Warren Crichlow (New York: Routledge, 1993), 157–171.

15 Ontario Ministry of Education, *Courses of Study: Grades 11 and 12 World History* (Toronto: Author, 1955), 16.

16 For a brief discussion of the Cold War's impact on the worldview of social studies curriculum, see Gaudelli, *World Class*, 4–5.

17 See, for example, Robert Harshman and Christine Hannell, *World Issues in the Global Community* (Toronto: John Wiley & Sons, 1989); and E. Alyn Mitchner and R. Joanne Tuffs, *One World* (Edmonton: Reidmore Books, 1989).

18 Werner and Case, "Themes of Global Education," 177–178.

19 Alberta Education, *Programs of Study: Social Studies* (Edmonton: Author, 1971), 32.

20 Merryfield, "Moving the Center of Global Education," 180–181.

21 Alberta Education, "Global Education in Alberta's Schools," *Curriculum News* (1989), 8.

22 Earl Choldin, "An Experiment in Professional Development," *The ATA Magazine* (May/June 1989), 26.

23 Graham Pike and David Selby, *Global Teacher, Global Learner* (London: Hodder & Stoughton, 1988).

24 Ibid., 35.

25 Ibid., 141.

26 Saskatchewan Ministry of Education and Training, *Social Studies 20 and History 20: World Issues Activity Guide* (Regina: Author, 1994), 3.

27 David Selby, "Global Education: Towards a Quantum Model of Environmental Education," *Canadian Journal of Environmental Education* 4, (1999): 125–141; Werner and Case, "Themes of Global Education," 178.

28 Roland Case, "Key Elements of a Global Perspective," *Social Education* 51, no. 6 (1993): 318–325.

29 Merryfield, "Moving the Center of Global Education," 186; George Richardson, "Two Terms You Can (and Should) Use in the Classroom: Cultural Homogenization and Eurocentrism," *Canadian Social Studies* 35, no. 1 (Fall 2000), www.quasar.ualberta.ca/css.

30 Willinsky, *Learning to Divide the World*, 157.

31 David Selby, "Global Education as Transformative Education," www.citizens4change.org (accessed May 20, 2003).

32 Werner and Case, "Themes of Global Education," 178.

33 Nova Scotia Department of Education, *Global History Grade 12* (Halifax: Author, 2003), 4.

34 Saskatchewan Ministry of Education and Training, *Social Studies 20 and History 20: World Issues*, (Regina: Author, 1994), 2.

35 See, for example, David Selby, "Kaleidoscopic Mindset: New Meanings within Citizenship Education," *Global Education* (June 1994): 20–31; and Walt Werner, "Starting Points for Global Education," *Canadian Social Studies* 30, no. 4 (Summer 1996): 171–173.

36 See, for example, George Richardson and David Blades, "So-

cial Studies and Science Education: Developing World Citizenship through Interdisciplinary Partnerships," *Canadian Social Studies* 35, no. 3 (Spring 2001), http://www.quasar.ualberta.ca/css; P. Kubow, D. Grossman, and A. Ninomiya, "Multidimensional Citizenship: Educational Policy for the 21st Century," in *Citizenship for the 21st Century: An International Perspective on Education*, ed. John J. Cogan and Ray Derricot (London: Kogan Page, 1998), 115–133.

37 Saskatchewan Ministry of Education and Training, *Social Studies 20 and History 20: World Issues*, 2.

38 Alberta Learning, *Social Studies Grades 10–12 Program of Studies Consultation Draft* (Edmonton: Author, 2003), 1.

39 Pike and Selby, *In the Global Classroom: Book One.*

40 John McMurtry, "Twelve Questions about Globalization," *Canadian Social Studies* 37, no. 1 (Fall 2002), www.quasar.ualberta.ca/css.

41 Alberta Learning, *Social Studies: Kindergarten to Grade Twelve,* (Edmonton: Author, 2002), 1.

42 Ontario Ministry of Education, *The Ontario Curriculum, Grades 9 to 12: Program Planning and Assessment* (Toronto: Author, 2000), 1.

43 Nicholas C. Burbules and Carlos Alberto Torres, eds., *Globalization and Education: Critical Perspectives* (New York: Routledge, 2000); David Geoffrey Smith, "A Few Modest Prophecies: The WTO, Globalization and the Future of Public Education," *Canadian Social Studies* 35, no. 1 (Fall 2000), www.quasar.ualberta.ca/css.

44 Merry M. Merryfield, "Pedagogy for Global Perspectives in Education: Studies of Teachers' Thinking and Practice," *Theory and Research in Social Education* 26, no. 3 (1998): 342–379; David Selby, "Education for the Global Age: What Is Involved?" in *Thinking Globally about Social Studies Education*, 1–17.

45 Hannah Arendt, *Between Past and Future: Eight Exercises in Political Thought* (New York: Penguin Books, 1968), 241.

46 Ken Osborne, "Citizenship Education and Social Studies," in *Trends and Issues*, 39–67; and Alan Sears, "In Canada Even History Divides: Unique Features of Canadian Citizenship," *International Journal of Social Education* 11, no. 2 (1996/97): 53–67.

47 E. Starr and J. Nelson, "Teacher Perspectives on Global Education," *Canadian Social Studies* 28, no. 1 (Fall 1993): 12–14.

48 Werner and Case, "Themes of Global Education," 177.

49 Manitoba Education and Youth, *Senior 3: Canada—A Social and Political History* (Winnipeg: Author, 1988), 7.

50 Ken Osborne, "Education for Citizenship," *Education Canada* 38, no. 4 (Winter 1998/1999): 16–19; and Alan Sears and Mark Perry, "Beyond Civics: Paying Attention to the Contexts of Citizenship Education," *Education Canada* 40, no. 3 (Fall 2000): 28–31.

51 Gaudelli, *World Class,* 165.

52 Ontario Ministry of Education and Training, *The Program in Canadian and World Studies* (Toronto: Author, 2000), 3.

53 British Columbia Ministry of Education, Skills, and Training, *Social Studies 11: Integrated Resource Package* (Victoria: Author, 1997), 3.

54 Manitoba Education and Youth, *Senior 4: World Issues* (Winnipeg: Author, 1990), 5.

55 See, for example, Walter Feinburg, *Common Schools/Uncommon Identities: National Identity and Cultural Difference* (New Haven, CT: Yale University Press, 1998); and Eamonn Callan, *Creating Citizens: Political Education and Liberal Democracy* (Oxford: Oxford University Press, 1997).

56 Will Kymlicka, *Politics in the Vernacular: Nationalism, Multiculturalism, and Citizenship* (London: Oxford University Press, 2001), 326.

57 Michael Ignatieff, *Blood and Belonging: Journeys into the New Nationalism* (Toronto: Viking, 1993), 9.

58 See, for example, Mark Kingwell, *The World We Want: Virtue, Vice, and the Good Citizen* (Toronto: Viking, 2001); Martha C. Nussbaum, *Cultivating Humanity: A Classical Defense of Reform in Liberal Education* (Cambridge, MA: Harvard University Press, 1997); and George Richardson et al., "Fostering a Global Imaginary: The Possibilities and Paradoxes of Japanese and Canadian Students' Perceptions of the Responsibilities of Global Citizenship," *Policy Futures in Education* 1, no. 2 (2003): 402–420.

59 McMurtry, "Twelve Questions about Globalization"; Graham Pike, "Globalization and National Identity: In Pursuit of Meaning," *Theory into Practice* 39, no. 2 (2000): 64–73; Smith, "A Few Modest Prophecies"; and Audrey Osler and Kerry Vincent, *Citizenship and the Challenge of Global Education* (Stoke-on-Trent, UK: Trentham Books, 2002).

60 Joel Spring, *Education and the Rise of the Global Economy* (Mahwah, NJ: Lawrence Erlbaum, 1998); and J.C. Couture, "Global Issues and Activated Audiences," *Canadian Social Studies* 35, no. 1 (Fall 2000), www.quasar.ualberta.ca/css.

61 David Geoffrey Smith, "The Specific Challenges of Globalization for Teaching and Vice Versa," *Alberta Journal of Educational Research* 46, no. 1 (2000): 7–26.

62 Alberta Learning, *Social Studies Kindergarten to Grade Twelve* (Edmonton: Author, 2002), 1.

63 Ibid.

CHAPTER 10

Understanding Multiculturalism in the Social Studies Classroom

Manju Varma-Joshi

In discussions regarding cultural pluralism, it can be argued that Canada has a lot to be proud of. The ratification of the multicultural policy in 1971 made Canada the first country to officially promote ethnocultural diversity. Today the country's approach to diversity is supported by a broad federal legislative framework and addressed in a wide range of policies.[1] Whereas the primary question in diversity debates used to be, "Is ethnocultural pluralism part of the Canadian national identity?", the need for social cohesion and equal representation has changed the question to, "How is such diversity part of the Canadian national identity?" Because of their positions as public institutions, schools have certainly had a primary voice in this new conversation, giving teachers the responsibility to try to answer the latter question. This, of course, has led to questions that educators have tried to answer with research, programs, curriculum changes, and sometimes, criticism.

Provincial departments/ministries of education have incorporated a multicultural perspective in varying degrees, sometimes as part of an overarching philosophy and sometimes as a distinct component of the social studies curriculum. For example, the Foundation for the Atlantic Canada Social Studies curriculum includes the following in its citizenship outcomes: ability to "determine the principles and actions of just, pluralistic, and democratic societies" and to "demonstrate understanding of their cultural heritage and cultural identity and the contribution of diverse cultures to society."[2] Combined with a public education campaign supporting cultural diversity (for example, the ever-so-popular Heritage Moments), it would appear Canada is providing adequate support for your people to live in and contribute to a multicultural society.

However, many people argue that this is not the case. Critics of multicultural and anti-racist education have labeled multicultural and anti-racist education as a fad, a response to political correctness, a waste of taxpayers' money, and a national threat. As Kymlicka and Norman point out, special attention to minorities' needs, which includes critiquing school curricula, has historically been perceived as a deterrent to a unified citizenry.[3] Specifically, multicultural education has been described as corrosive to social cohesion.[4]

Even multicultural advocates have voiced a share of the criticism. The multicultural policy has been disparaged as a "largely superficial window-dressing exercise"[5] that, despite good intentions, has failed to address the racist inequalities that exist in public institutions such as schools. In a stinging paper on Black youth in public schools, George Dei identified Black dropouts as "pushed-outs" because of their inability to survive a schooling system fraught with subtle inequalities and blatant racism.[6] Others directly question the purpose of multicultural education. John Mallea, for example, asks:

Do multicultural education policies assume knowledge will reduce prejudice and discrimination? Do they recognize and legitimize cultural differences while failing to deal with racism at the institutional, structural and individual level?[7]

A chorus of criticism does imply that many schools are unprepared, unqualified, and sometimes unwilling to address multicultural and anti-racist concerns in the classroom.[8]

With all of this uncertainty and critique, it is understandable why educators may approach multicultural education with trepidation. Fortunately, much of this apprehension can be alleviated with a clear understanding of multicultural education's objectives, sound pedagogical strategies, and a strong commitment to the continued enhancement of educational processes. It is my hope that this chapter will help future teachers begin to attain a grounding in the objectives and pedagogical strategies of multicultural education.

In the next section I respond to questions raised in conversations I have had with both experienced and pre-service teachers. Following the responses I offer some suggested teaching strategies.

Objectives and Strategies for Multicultural Education

What is multicultural education?

Multicultural education has taken on a variety of faces. In their description of multicultural education, Sleeter and Grant note that the pedagogy's initial focus was on helping culturally different children succeed in the mainstream culture. As multicultural education developed, it adopted a human communications approach aimed at helping people of different backgrounds establish a sense of shared humanity. The term multicultural education was also used to describe courses in which groups' histories and oppressions were examined. This would have included curriculum such as Black studies and Pacific Rim studies.[9]

Grant and Sleeter note that multicultural education changed in the 1970s when it donned a cloak of celebration. They describe the movement as a philosophy that "link[ed] race, language, culture, gender, handicap and, to a lesser extent, social class, working toward making the entire school celebrate human diversity and equal opportunity."[10] While many were content with this form of multicultural education, others argued that the pedagogy failed to discuss social inequalities and required an action component that could empower minorities to demand change.[11] This led to the next evolution of the pedagogy, in which some educators added the prefix "critical" to multicultural education to denote a study that examines the diverse factors in our society such as linguistics, economics, ability, age, and race and how such factors produce power relations, privilege, and systemic discrimination.[12] Anti-racist educators, on the other hand, went a different route and underlined the saliency of race as the primary concern for education.[13] Given the different camps, it is sometimes confusing to discern between multicultural, critical multicultural, and anti-racist education. For example, in his article, "Multiculturalism in Social Studies," Kehoe provides characteristics to distinguish between multicultural and anti-racist education.[14] These guidelines, however, are somewhat artificial as some of the key characteristics, such as critical thinking, are claimed by all groups. However, at the heart of each of these philosophies is the aim of developing schools that are safe and satisfying places for all students to learn.

Today, teachers pursing multicultural education must embrace certain key elements. First, teachers must realize that the pedagogy is as much about instruction as it is about content. In other words, simply providing material that exposes students to difference will not sufficiently decrease discriminatory attitudes or increase equal opportunities. Kehoe and Mansfield highlight this conclusion in their study on students' applications of human rights. After teaching high school students the basic human rights, the researchers asked students to consider human rights principles in reference to both majority and minority groups. Results indicated that students were less likely to advocate a universal right, such as the freedom of religion, when applied to a minority or Aboriginal individual.[15] In another study, Aboud notes that children who articulated strong prejudicial views either maintained or increased their views after interacting with multicultural texts.[16] In both cases, researchers argued that simply familiarizing students with difference is not enough; educators also need to have an understanding of how their students understand difference, and they must adjust delivery of the material accordingly. The influence of instruction is one of the reasons that the celebration approach, with its focus on content, has fallen under criticism.

Another vital component of multicultural education is reform. Kehoe argues that the primary goal of modern multicultural education "is to achieve equal opportunity for all people."[17] An impediment to this objective is the reluctance of educators and other school parties to examine the expectations and values articulated in the classroom. Overcoming this barrier means reconstructing multicultural education as a pedagogy that focuses on all forms of difference and discrimination and delivers knowledge with this recognition. This objective takes us beyond the formal curriculum and demands transparency in teachers' attitudes, school policies, and the hidden curriculum. Reform goes beyond the classroom teacher and principal and includes everyone from custodians who report racial graffiti in the washrooms to the cafeteria staff who are informed of cultural dietary constraints.

Married to the concept of reform is reflection. Both teachers and students must engage in reflection. This element of multicultural education can be discomforting because it insists that we examine our own biases and involvement in systemic discrimination. This in no way means that we are individual racists. However, our modes of operation sometimes help maintain a discriminatory system. Often systems are sustained not because of our actions but because of our inaction. An example of this would be not paying attention to whether or not social studies material provided accurate and current presentations of the different cultures in Canada.

Multicultural education is about practice. Introducing students to the academic content of discrimination, privilege, and power is important. However, students must also be able to translate such information into practice. Social studies teachers can help develop this skill by encouraging students to examine different perspectives of an historical event, engaging students in games where they must critically evaluate the impact of one group's behaviour and choices on other groups, and by constructing a classroom environment that parallels the values supporting the curriculum. Teachers who talk about the power of multiple voices but do not allow all their students equal opportunities to speak undermine the very tenets of multicultural education.

Multicultural education embodies empathy. As social studies teachers, one of our responsibilities is to educate students about the world. To become effective adult citizens in a hopeful and democratic society, our students need to be able to understand each other whenever possible. For the social studies teacher, this means going beyond geographical and historical information to providing students with a sense of perspective, interdependence, and responsibility. This means trying to understand the people with whom we share the world and appreciate our common humanity.

Finally, multicultural education must address all forms of discrimination. While this may seem common sense, a number of past multicultural programs have tended to overlook this aspect. Rather, they have dealt with minority groups' commonalities and/or their differences from the mainstream, or have highlighted cultural artifacts such as foods and festivals. Even when the pedagogy has paid attention to racism, efforts have been described as "counter-productive"[18] and likely to provoke racist behaviour.[19] This logic dictates that if racism does exist, silence will keep it at bay. Yet research has shown that students must discuss issues of racism and other forms of discrimination in order to begin to combat them.[20] Censuring uncomfortable words such as racism and hate is inappropriate. Multiculturalism that promotes diversity but does not recognize barriers is ineffective.

Isn't all this attention to diversity just another fad?

Educational concerns with diversity have always been part of the school dialogue.[21] Since schools were developed as a primary tool for citizenship training, the treatment of diversity has been a key issue. How schools have dealt with difference has depended on society's view of diversity. Conversely, how Canadians have perceived difference has been part of a legacy inherited from our schooling. This symbiotic relationship has led schools and society to comprehend difference through four broad reactions: destroy, assert, ignore, and celebrate.[22]

The earliest response to diversity was to attempt to eradicate it. School curriculum stressed obedience, conformity, and tradition; difference was seen as a threat to social cohesion and national security. Visible minority and Aboriginal children underwent different strategies to obtain the same result—destruction of difference and protection of the Canadian identity. Immigrant children encountered school policies that "stressed the virtues of cultural uniformity over cultural accommodation"[23] in the campaign to champion the purity of the Canadian identity over a cultural mosaic. The story is no better for our First Nations communities. Forced to attend residential schools, Aboriginal children endured a process of cultural eradication that ranged from changes in appearance and name to loss of language and religion. Lessons learned from such schools are vivid scars on the Canadian mindset, reminders of the damage that can come about when difference is feared and demonized.

The oppositional stance to eradication was the assertion of difference. In this mindset, difference is constructed as biological and immutable.[24] Different ethnocultural groups are collectively labeled as lazy, violent, or unintelligent, as if each member carries a gene that fosters the negative characteristic. Because these deficiencies are perceived as biological, schools were able to claim that they had to deal with these deficiencies in the way they saw best.[25] As a result, many Aboriginal, Black, immigrant, and poor children were streamed into modified programs where their chances of personal betterment were limited.

The third response to difference is to minimize it. This is achieved by ignoring difference as a factor in learning. This position is often articulated in the statement, "I don't see colour; why can't I treat all of my students the same?" This colour- or difference-blind approach is often married to the notion of meritocracy, the belief that everyone starts at the same level and those who work hard will succeed. While effort is certainly tied to success, lack of effort is not the only reason for failure. Do children who have breakfast every morning and computers in their bedrooms start at the same place as children who live in communities of poverty? Embedded in both of these philosophies is the notion that school is a neutral and bias-free place to learn; such is not the case. Both the formal and hidden curricula legitimize the needs, interests, and identities of the majority group. Both the difference-blind approach and meritocracy ignore the daily hurdles that visible minority students must endure. These hurdles can range from dealing with name-calling to encountering curricula or teaching strategies that do not validate your culture or acknowledge how systemic racism has affected your cultural group. Students do not benefit from a difference-blind approach but rather need to have their differences acknowledged and accommodated within the learning process. When dealing with individuals who come to a place with different realities and privileges (or lack thereof), equal treatment does not mean fair treatment.

The final response to difference is the popular food, festivals, heroes, and holidays approach. While this a valuable step towards understanding diversity, too many schools stop here. Students leave school able to describe Ramadan or quote "I have a dream," but are unable to explain the assets of cultural diversity or the mechanism of racism. The celebratory style also ignores the issue of accommodation. While it is easy to tolerate or celebrate difference, it is a more difficult task to accept difference that requires substantial personal or societal change. Accommodation is a vital part of multiculturalism, yet it is missing from each of the methodologies described above.

Because schools have held a clear voice on how difference should be considered, attention to diversity cannot be perceived as trendy or a fad. However, our response to difference is evolving. The current form of multicultural education endeavours to go beyond the former reactions to difference. It is a developing philosophy that both reflects and values the place of pluralism in the current citizenry and national identity.

Won't multicultural education divide the country?

The supposition that multicultural education is antithetical to citizenship is also not novel. In both Canada and the United States, critics of multiculturalism have accused the approach of being divisive. Neil Bissoondath's best-selling book, *Selling Illusions: The Cult of Multiculturalism in Canada*, condemns the federal government's multiculturalism policy as the cause of ethnic ghettoization, claiming that the policy encourages immigrants to stay within their own groups, thus fracturing the greater Canadian community. Himself an immigrant, Bissoondath argues that cultural heritage is best retained and practised in the privacy of individual homes and not within the public realm.[26] Bissoondath, however, conveniently overlooks the fact that the greater Canadian community has publicly prospered through diversity. Civic sectors ranging from the economy to the arts have been enriched by the official and public promotion of various cultures and traditions—the very aspects of diversity he argues should be kept in the privacy of the home.

Critics also finger multicultural education as a means of undermining a national body of historical knowledge. A commonly cited solution is the dismantling of multicultural education (and the policies that support it) and the imposition of a nationwide curriculum on all students.[27] Interestingly, suggestions for this type of curriculum rely heavily on the male Eurocentric position and tend to be devoid of the various voices of minorities, women, the poor, and other disadvantaged groups. For example, in his book *Who Killed Canadian History?*, Granatstein clearly identifies men as the makers of history and dismisses the voices of other identities (women, the

poor, minorities, etc.) as "distortions" of the past.[28] This stance eclipses the concept of multiple historical perspectives and allows for the perpetration of disempowerment of various minority groups.[29] In contrast, multicultural education champions the inclusion of voices that have traditionally been silenced. It is within a multicultural curriculum that students learn about Canadian issues such as historical racist policies, immigrant success stories, and the realities of First Nations peoples. Teaching about and learning from the various facets of our Canadian reality is not divisive. Inclusion does not threaten national unity, but a sense of isolation, frustration, and discontent can.

Multicultural education's focus on disclosing racism has also led to accusations of divisiveness. Neito speaks to this tendency in her identification of schools' avoidance in "bringing up potentially contentious issues in the curriculum in fear that doing so may create or exacerbate animosity and hostility among students."[30] This type of position supports the belief that discussions regarding systemic racism, past racist policies, and recognition of personal injustices will not only divide students but may even incite violence. The logic appears to be that if citizens are not informed of inequalities, they will not be equipped to recognize or refute them in their own lives. Yet the result is neither peace nor unity, but rather ignorance and disempowerment. Multicultural education wages war against the latter reality by presenting students with the lessons from our racist past and the strategies to recognize and attack present-day prejudices. Racism is confronted not in order to lay blame or provoke deeper hatreds but to encourage empathy, perspective-taking, and social peace.

Despite the flawed arguments of divisiveness, we cannot simply frame such criticisms as the rants of anti-multiculturalists. Many of the arguments cited above reflect a very real public unease about multiculturalism. In 1991, the Citizens' Forum on Canada's Future reported a strong societal belief that if the country was to remain united, citizens must learn to be Canadians first.[31] This tension between the recognition of minority rights and the promotion of a unified citizenry is an ongoing debate. As

Kymlicka and Norman point out:

> . . . defenders of minority rights have often been suspicious of appeals to some ideal of "good citizenship," which they see as reflecting a demand that minorities should quietly learn to play by the majority's rules. . . . Conversely, those who wish to promote a more robust conception of civic virtue and democratic citizenship have often been suspicious of appeals to minority rights, which they see as reflecting the sort of politics of narrow self-interest that they seek to overcome.[32]

At the heart of this debate lies another question: Is one unified image of the Canadian identity a prerequisite for national unity? Critics of multiculturalism would argue yes and provide dire predictions of ethic balkanization where minority groups cling to their separate cultures, shun a Canadian identity, and contribute to the disintegration of the country. But this prophecy has yet to materialize. Along with the growth of multiculturalism, immigrants are taking less time to acquire their Canadian citizenship,[33] and according to the last census report, "Canadian" is now the fastest growing ethnic group in the country.[34] The split between belief and reality is a key reason why teachers must encourage their students to consider facts rather than fears.

Why can't we all just be Canadian?

This is an interesting question because it begs another question: What is Canadian? A colleague of mine, and a Canadian social studies educator, often asks people to draw a reverse timeline charting when different groups have come to Canada. The line could look something like this:

He then asks the drawer to locate where on the timeline the Canadian identity began. Do we go back to the Russians, the Dutch, or all the way back to the Aboriginal population? The point is that the Canadian identity is not fixed and there is no magic spot in time where the Canadian suddenly appeared.[35] This does not mean that we do not have a popular image of the Canadian citizen. This image is consistently white, English, and Christian.[36] Is this what we mean when we say that we want people to be Canadian? Does such a claim discount all difference?

On a deeper level, the call to be Canadian is a fearful response to accommodation. It is a call that is evoked whenever a threat to Canadian tradition is perceived. I once had a conversation with a class of pre-service teachers regarding the inclusion of turbans as part of the RCMP uniform. I was struck by the negative feelings regarding this change. Many felt that the very essence of what is Canadian had been attacked. Several students described the RCMP uniform as a tradition and said that if groups do not want to respect this uniform, they should avoid this career choice. What I found ironic is that such feelings regarding the sanctity of tradition were coming from a group training to become teachers, a profession from which many within this group would have been excluded had changes not occurred. It is distressing that when minorities insist on changes, we use such terms as "special interest" or "accommodation," both of which suggest an obliging change for a small group of people. When changes are the result of the majority's desires, we call it progress. Therefore, we have had to accommodate changes in the RCMP but have progressed in the field of teaching. This mindset needs to be challenged. Traditionally, diversity has been seen as a challenge to the Canadian identity. Diversity is not a challenge to the Canadian identity; it is the Canadian identity.

| Aboriginal | French | British | Irish | Dutch | Germans | Russians | Europeans | Asians |

Do I have to think about multicultural education if my school and community are predominantly white?

While Canada does present itself as a multicultural country, visibly diverse locations still only dot our national map. The majority of Canada is still predominantly white. This demographic reality has left many mainly white schools believing that multicultural education is not a priority for their students. To assume that multicultural education is for diverse locations only speaks to several problematic assumptions.

The first assumption is that a room of all white students equals a monocultural classroom. This is false. An all-white classroom can be as multicultural as a classroom of visibly diverse students. From the beginning, multicultural education has been inaccurately framed as pedagogy for the culturally different. While the main priority is the inclusion of visible minority children, the philosophy does not ignore the diversity within the white population. Even if this diversity is minimal, is it not possible that the composition of the location can change in the future or that the students will move? As teachers, it is our responsibility to prepare students for as many future opportunities as possible. This includes providing them with the skills to deal with future changes and the ability to go beyond their own backyards.

The second notion impeding multicultural instruction in white schools is the impression that a minimum population of visible minorities is required to make multicultural education worthwhile. This supposition generates some very disturbing questions: Do ethnocultural groups require a critical mass before they can see themselves in the curriculum and school environment? Is equality a demographic issue? If only one child feels excluded, should educators take the time to help? How many students are needed before an effort to include them all is worth the trouble? By being aware of all children's needs for inclusion and recognition, no matter how few, educators can help alleviate current pressures and perhaps prevent future problems.

The last two assumptions usually go hand-in-hand. First, that multicultural education is only for visible minority children or for children who encounter visible diversity daily; secondly, that racism exists solely in locations with significant visible minority populations. Both attitudes frame the presence of visible minorities as the reason for racism and the recipient of subsequent multicultural programs. Consequently, schools with a low number of visible minority students tend to render cross-cultural education as a low- or non-priority issue. For example, in her study on predominantly white British schools, Tomlinson noted, "Schools with few or no minority pupils make little effort to revise their curriculum, or develop policies, and tend to dismiss multicultural education as . . . 'a very low priority' and 'not our concern.'"[37]

There is ample research to refute both assumptions. Cross-cultural understanding is not just for the minority child. White children need multicultural education so that they too are aware of different perspectives. Children who are educated in a curriculum that is confined by their own beliefs may fail to consider the inclusion of others. A recent study involving grade 4 and 5 students living in a mainly white community in Atlantic Canada illustrates this. The two-year exploration of the participants' ideas of the Canadian citizen found that the children did not include any characteristics of visible diversity. When asked to describe their image of the Canadian through a variety of methods, the students consistently depicted the Canadian as white, English, and Christian. For these students, the Canadian is a racialized, rather than nationalized, identity.[38] Because these students had not been exposed to contrary evidence, they assumed their worldview was the only reality.

Research has also shown that children in predominantly white locations not only hold prejudicial beliefs but also that such attitudes may be even more deep-seated than among their integrated peers. Ramsey makes this assertion in her study of preschool children's attitudes towards difference. After showing ninety-three white participants photographs of visible minorities, she reported:

White children in segregated settings have been found to be more biased against African-Americans than are their peers in integrated settings. . . .Because these subjects live in an all-White community and had virtually no previous contact with either African-American or Asian-American children, . . . [they] made more positive comments about SR [same race] peers than DR [different race] peers in the open-ended task. . . . [D]espite the lack of direct cross-racial contact, the children in this all-White community noticed racial differences.[39]

Nearly three decades earlier, Clark made similar observations. After comparing racial views between white children in urban and rural sections of Georgia and children attending an all-white school in New York City, Clark surmised:

Attitudes towards Negroes are determined chiefly not by contact with the Negroes but by contact with the prevailing attitudes towards Negroes. It is not the Negro child, but the *idea* of the Negro child that influences children (italics in the original).[40]

Today, Clark's contention holds legitimacy; however, now individuals have greater virtual or second-hand exposure to visible minorities through the Internet, television, music, and other forms of popular media. Because many of these sources are rife with racial stereotypes, there is an even greater need to balance these messages with a curriculum that exposes and challenges misinformation. Based on the available research, it appears that not only is multicultural education necessary for children living in mainly white locations, it may actually be more crucial than for students who witness diversity as part of their regular routine. Katz asserts that multicultural education is required everywhere:

Racism is manifested not only in the minority ghettos of the cities but equally in the White ghettos of the suburbs, in the South, in the North. Racism not only affects people of color but Whites as well; it escapes no one. It is a part of us all and has deeply infil-

trated the lives and psyches of both the oppressed and the oppressor.[41]

Recognizing the need for change does not mean it is easily attained. While attention to racism in white schools is growing in the United States and Britain,[42] except for a few studies, Canadian research in this area is still extremely limited.[43] Mainly white schools often import multicultural programs from cities such as Toronto or Vancouver. Because these programs were developed for a different environment, they often fail, reinforcing the myth that white schools do not need multicultural programs. The real issue here is the lack of relevance for the students. Students in a predominantly white location such as Sackville, New Brunswick, do not conceptualize difference in the same way that students in Toronto do. So why use the same approach for both schools? Because of the lack of attention given to multicultural education in predominantly white schools, very few curricula or programs exist to help interested teachers. For teachers working in mainly white locations, the question they need to ask themselves is, "How can I authentically engage my students in discussions on diversity when they do not experience it on a daily basis?"

The first step is to acquire an awareness of your students' current understanding of diversity. This means exploring their prior knowledge of and experience with diversity. Often we credit our students with a greater recognition of diversity than they actually have. A student teacher once asked me what a residential school is. Although surprised, I asked someone from the class to provide a short explanation. I discovered that several of my students were not sure how to describe such schools. What was especially astonishing was the fact that there had been substantial recent news coverage on residential schools and issues of compensation for abuse. What I thought to be mainstream information was not part of several of my students' prior knowledge. Either they were not aware of the current event or had not recognized it as important. Peck found similar results in her study on white children's understanding of diversity. Her middle-school participants were unfamiliar with stimuli referring to the Arab or Muslim culture despite the fact that events such as the Middle East conflict and the war on Iraq dominated all forms of local and national media.[44] In both cases, it was easy, but erroneous, to assume that the students knew more than they did.

Once a teacher understands the various levels of the conceptualization of diversity that exist in the class, a program can be designed to meet the special needs of the students. This requires going the extra mile and ensuring that the materials are appropriate and relevant. A few years ago I gave a talk regarding the use of multicultural materials in the classroom. Afterwards, a teacher from Amherst, Nova Scotia, approached me and expressed her frustration with what she had heard. She explained that her school had a small population of Black students and that she had tried very hard to engage all of her students in cross-cultural understanding. She went on to describe her discussions on slavery and the Underground Railroad. She had also spent a lot of time on Martin Luther King, Jr. during Black History Month. When I asked her if she taught about the local Black community, she said, "No." What followed was a compelling conversation on why she had ignored local sources, especially given that she lived in a town with one of the oldest indigenous Black communities in the country. We also talked about how the curriculum is limited to historical events such as slavery, which makes the Black culture appear fossilized and non-vibrant. Four years later, the same teacher emailed me. She had altered her program to reach her particular students and, even though this meant making some changes each year, she was pleased to let me know that she and the students were learning and enjoying the curriculum.

Regardless of location, multicultural education is for everyone. To designate multicultural education as a non-white issue distorts the Canadian reality. Also, as pointed out in the description of multicultural education, the pedagogy is not just about different ethnic groups; it is also about the various types of diversity that exist in all classrooms, even when everyone has the same colour face. To pursue multicultural education is to open your students to apparent and subtle forms of diversity. To not do so is to ignore the various facets of diversity that exist in your school and in Canadian society.

What is the hidden curriculum?

Educators often make the distinction between the formal curriculum and the hidden curriculum. The formal curriculum refers to the curriculum, outcomes, and expectations that each teacher is legally bound to follow. The hidden curriculum is the collection of unstated and/or normalized assumptions and attitudes that influence the school environment. The hidden curriculum includes everything from school policies to staff-student relationships to classroom design. For example, a school may have a zero-tolerance policy towards tardiness. Children who have no problems arriving at school on time would not even notice this rule. However, children who face certain barriers in the morning would be punished by this rule. Such barriers may include having to take care of oneself and siblings in the morning, having a job before school hours, or holding different cultural beliefs about time.

Often such rules are not even articulated. Studies have shown how teachers often fail to incorporate their students' cultural learning styles into their personal instructional strategies. This is not done on purpose, but rather because the students' cultural differences are not considered.[45] In the classroom, a teacher may prize initiative and reward students who always try to answer a question first. Success would then come slowly to a child whose cultural background does not value competition.

While the hidden curriculum is impossible to avoid, teachers can be aware of its influence. This means constantly questioning, "What messages am I sending out?" "How do I ensure the success of all of my students?" Confronting the hidden curriculum also means disrupting patterns that have become so normalized that they appear common sense. For example, we often assume that the interested parent is the involved parent. A teacher may assume that a parent who fails to attend parent-teacher interviews is uncaring or uninterested in his or her child's schooling. However, in many cultures the teacher holds a dominant social role and the parent may be respecting the teacher's role by not taking up the teacher's time. Or perhaps interviews are only held at night and the particular parent works at night, has other children to care for, or cannot afford the transportation to school. For children and parents not from the mainstream culture, the hidden curriculum can be confusing and detrimental to the students' success.

How do I avoid controversy?

Values education and the teaching of controversial issues are important elements of social studies. However, controversy in the classroom can be a very real concern for teachers, especially for those who are new in their careers. The image of a parent calling and objecting to something taught in our classroom can be daunting. Yet, controversy is part of the multicultural education DNA. Among other condemnations, critics have labeled multicultural education as divisive and open to complete cultural relativism (the belief that all cultural values and practices are acceptable). Teachers who wish to employ a multicultural perspective need to be aware of the possibility of controversy and be familiar with strategies for dealing with hot topics.

One reason that multicultural education is seen as controversial is that many issues around pluralism are rife with misinformation. At your next social gathering, bring up issues such as First Nations peoples and taxes, refugees, affirmative action, and bilingualism—and get ready to hear a room full of heated opinions. Now imagine such discussions in your classroom. These subjects can be especially difficult to discuss with children with limited experience and knowledge of the world. Moreover, students may already hold opinions on these topics based on what they have heard outside of school. Multicultural education facilitates the exploration of these and other contentious topics in a manner that actively confronts misinformation and challenges stereotypes. Questioning personal beliefs often involves a sense of cognitive dissonance that can be disconcerting for students, especially when that information opposes the thinking of other important people, such as parents. Teachers can contain students' feelings of inner controversy by providing them with ample credible resources and the skills to comprehend and challenge information.

Another reason that multicultural education can cause a stir is that it demands a level of accommodation. While most Canadians are supportive of allowing various ethnocultural groups to keep their cultural beliefs, their support wavers when it requires changes in personal or social spheres. An example of this would be the inclusion of heritage language programs in schools. While many would support immigrant children retaining their mother tongue, support has wavered when tax dollars are used to sustain the programs.[46] Similar concerns have arisen when schools have attempted to create Native studies or Black studies courses. Students may have their own challenges with accommodation due to conflicts with their own value systems. It is imperative that teachers explore such conflicts and not simply instruct students to change their views.

While it is easy to claim personal accommodation of difference, doing so is usually more complicated. Each year, my pre-service teachers learn this first-hand through a class assignment that examines the school calendar. I introduce the assignment by stating that the current school calendar is closely related to the Christian calendar. Most, if not all, of my students usually agree with this observation and sometimes even provide proof by identifying Christian-based school holidays. I then supply my students with twenty holidays based on different ethnic groups' special days. Placing them in groups, I ask them to create a school calendar that allows for ten holidays and reflects Canadian cultural diversity. This task always creates a sense of discomfort. However, it also generates interesting discussions regarding accommodation. In the debriefing session, students discuss how they chose their holidays and the difficulty they had with the process. Some express surprise at their own reluctance to change the calendar; other are shocked by the resistance of fellow group members. What is especially interesting is the influence that multicultural education can have on them. Students who do this exercise after learning about multicultural education employ different strategies than those who do the exercise as an introduction to the pedagogy. The former group asks questions about the different holidays, weigh their relative importance, and display deeper-level reasoning in devising their calendar. They exhibit the thoughtful accommodation that multicultural education helps to promote.

Multicultural education is about interrogating personal beliefs and exploring novel perspectives. Because this can be new and stressful for teachers and students, it is important to develop a respectful classroom environment where students feel safe in expressing their opinions. It also vital that you develop an atmosphere of excellence where opinions are not emotional outbursts but born from thoughtful and legitimate evidence. Creating such an environment takes time. A trained multicultural educator would never drop a controversial topic into the laps of students in an impromptu manner. Instead, the teacher would begin with uncomplicated issues and provide students with the time to gather information and develop an opinion. Only after their controversy-resolution skills are developed should students be given more complicated questions to consider.

Teaching controversial issues does not have to be a negative experience. In order to teach controversial issues in a positive way, a multicultural educator must have a sound understanding of multicultural pedagogy. This is not a philosophy that one can follow half-heartedly. Those who do so are often unable to explain their teaching strategies when confronted by other teachers or parents. A prepared and educated teacher can explain how bringing grey-area topics into the classroom can be extremely enriching for teacher and students. It is through discussion of controversial issues that we learn to think critically, judge arguments, weigh evidence, recognize differing points of view, form and defend thoughtful opinions, and articulate our positions. Students also learn that not everything has a right or wrong answer and that differing opinions can coexist. Certainly these are valuable skills that both teachers and parents would want today's youth to have.

Is it enough to acknowledge March 21, the International Day for the Elimination of Racism, and Black History Month?

Let's restate this question in reference to another topic. How would we respond to a teacher who said, "I acknowledge World Literacy Day; do I have to refer to books the rest of the year?" While the new question sounds ridiculous, the former occurs on a regular basis. Although March 21 and Black History Month are important parts of multicultural education, they are just that—parts. To concentrate on diversity issues solely within the confines of these special dates is to designate such issues as supplementary or special education. Banks calls this the "Contribution Approach," in which extra information is tagged on to a special day because it is not considered important enough to be part of the regular curriculum.[47] In my office, I have a poster that reads:

Q: If February is Black History Month and March is Women's History Month, what do we do the rest of the year?

A: Discriminate.

This tongue-in-cheek comment reveals the danger of limiting important diversity discussions to one particular moment rather than incorporating multicultural education as the mainstream education. Black History Month has in fact encountered a substantial amount of criticism from multicultural educators who claim that Black issues are only discussed during February and that the coverage is light and limited to feel-good issues.[48] So students may learn about Martin Luther King, Jr., but they do not discuss current-day inequalities.

Special days or months should be treated the same as other special dates, such as World Literacy Day. This time should be taken to highlight discussions and information to which the students have already been exposed. By making diversity issues part of the mainstream curricula, schools are implicitly stating that these issues are vital to the development of the student and society.

If I advocate multicultural education, do I have to accept everyone's opinions?

Absolutely not. Like any practice employed in the classroom, multicultural education insists on common sense. In past classes, I have had social studies pre-service teachers try to defend slavery and deny the Holocaust. In multicultural education, there are certain issues that I call non-negotiables. Topics fall into this category when society has amassed enough proof to support a particular argument. A common attack on this argument is that people once accepted the world being flat as truth. This supposition, however, was based on limited evidence. A wider exploration deflated this belief and brought on the realization that the world is round. In reference to issues such as slavery and the Holocaust, society has engaged in this further exploration. We are now aware of the dehumanizing conditions of slavery and experience repercussions that reverberate even today. We have progressed beyond the ability to justify the economic ownership of one human being over another. Similarly, we have abundant global proof, both primary and secondary, that the Holocaust happened. As multicultural educators, it is our responsibility to rage against philosophies that diminish the devastation that has been wrought by hate, racism, and brutality—and we must use these lessons to deter similar catastrophic events from recurring. Entertaining notions steeped in intolerance cannot be equated to providing perspective or balance. A balance of opinions is valuable when such balance contributes to a question that has yet to be answered. Some questions, like the fact of the Holocaust and the falsity of racial superiority, have been answered.

Refusing to entertain some attitudes does not mean that they will not be voiced in your classroom. It is important not to shut your students down by simply stating that an opinion is unacceptable. A response to such comments should actually occur before they are made. By this I mean that teachers need to be proactive by teaching students such skills as sifting fact from opinions and recognizing hate. Students can then gain their own competence in recognizing flawed and false assumptions and may internally counter them without ever mentioning them in the classroom. Students should also be taught how to deal with controversial comments when they are uttered. Students whose opinions are attacked may simply fall into silence, leaving unspoken beliefs to dangerously simmer. Learning to respond to different perspectives is an important element in change and a necessary skill to facilitate in your classroom.

Teaching strategies

Along with acquiring information, effective multicultural educators also need to be familiar with practical teaching strategies and hazards. The following list contains a few suggestions to get you started. While this list is far from complete, many of the ideas are easy to implement and complement a social studies curriculum.

Using multicultural children's literature is an excellent way to engage your students in issues of diversity. Literature exposes students to topics they may be unfamiliar with. Literature can also be risk-free in that students can talk through the characters in order to discuss their feelings. Students should be encouraged to critically discuss their thoughts on the story, the characters, and their actions. They should also talk about the unfamiliar or elements that they disagree with. Today teachers can find numerous books connected to social studies themes such as immigration, conflict-resolution, and historical events, and can easily connect them to the existing curriculum.

Multicultural associations, federal departments, and other agencies can provide material and guest speakers to help supplement your curriculum. For example, the Department of Canadian Heritage produces items such as posters, pins, and educational programs meant for free distribution to schools. The advent of the Internet has made materials from around the globe accessible. Take the time to familiarize yourself with other parties interested in multiculturalism and see what they have to offer your class. A word of caution: nothing is free; every group has an agenda. Be sure to critically evaluate material (perhaps with your class) before endorsing it.

Invite guest speakers to your classroom; they can provide both a real-life factor and differing perspectives. But be careful not to invite minority guest speakers to only speak on minority issues. In other words, try to bring in speakers from minority cultures when discussing mainstream issues such as the environment or careers. Also, do not expect your guest to speak for the entire ethnocultural group. Like the majority, minority groups host a variety of opinions and experiences. To expect your guests to represent their whole group discounts its diversity.

Recognize certain dates. As mentioned above, dates such as Black History Month should not signify the only attention to Black issues but they are important opportunities to highlight issues discussed throughout the school year.

Simulations are a fun and instructive way for students to experience the curriculum. Students can do such activities as set up a mock UN, re-enact past events or engage in simulation games. Ensure that simulations are age appropriate and that students are debriefed afterward and given an opportunity to express their feelings. Also, be sure that students are well informed before engaging in activities. For example, if you want to engage your students in a debate on immigration, give them time and resources to find credible information. This will avoid having students confusing their opinions with facts.

Always be sure to establish the context. A discussion on multiculturalism in Canada would not be served well with storybooks set in India and Africa.

Do not oversimplify groups. For example, Black Canadians come from a variety of experiences and countries. To assume that they are all African is false and provides a false view of history. Take the time to learn about the groups that you are teaching in your classroom.

Conclusion

In the area of social studies, one often encounters a debate around identifying the key subject matter in the discipline. I have heard some argue that history is the backbone of social studies, while others contend that it is geography or citizenship education.

Multicultural education should be perceived in a different way. The pedagogy is more like the tendons and sinews that support the backbone; it provides flexibility, strength, and direction.

Today multicultural education is seen as a teaching strategy, a curriculum design, and a school philosophy. It is a process of education for all students, not just for visible minorities. Multicultural education insists on a curriculum that provides a variety of explanations and possibilities. However, it also goes beyond the curriculum and permeates all aspects of the school environment, ranging from teacher-student relationships to instructional strategies and administrative policies. Moreover, multicultural education is not just a colour issue. The philosophy examines various forms of diversity including racial, linguistic, religious, class, and gender, as well as issues of differing abilities. Above all, multicultural education discloses all forms of discrimination and affirms diversity in its various manifestations. Multicultural education serves the entire Canadian community. The pedagogy is not just about helping newcomers enter the mainstream but also about altering the actual character of the mainstream. It affirms the position that diversity is not a challenge to the Canadian identity, it is the Canadian identity.

Endnotes

1. Government of Canada, Department of Canadian Heritage, www.pch.gc.ca.
2. Departments of Education, New Brunswick, Newfoundland and Labrador, Nova Scotia, and Prince Edward Island, *Foundation for the Atlantic Canada Social Studies Curriculum* (Halifax: Nova Scotia Education and Culture, English Program Services, 1999), 6.
3. William Kymlicka and Wayne Norman, *Citizenship in Diverse Societies* (New York: Oxford University Press, 2000).
4. Neil Bissoondath, *Selling Illusions: The Cult of Multiculturalism in Canada* (Toronto: Penguin, 1994).
5. Jim Cummins and Marcel Danesi, *Heritage Languages: The Development and Denial of Canada's Linguistic Resources* (Toronto: Garamond Press, 1990), 9.
6. George Dei, *Reconstructing 'Dropout': The Dynamics of Black Students' Disengagement from School* (Toronto: University of Toronto Press, 1997).
7. John Mallea, *Schooling in a Plural Canada* (Clevedon, UK: Multilingual Matters, 1989), 114.

8   Agnes Calliste, "Anti-racist Education Initiatives in Nova Scotia," *Orbit* 25, no. 2 (1994): 48–49; Jim Cummins, *Negotiating Identities: Education for Empowerment in a Diverse Society* (Sacramento: California Association for Bilingual Education, 1996); and Lisa Delpit, *Other People's Children: Cultural Conflict in the Classroom* (New York: The New Press, 1995).

9   Christine Sleeter and Carl Grant, *Making Choices for Multicultural Education: Five Approaches to Race, Class, and Gender* (Columbus, OH: Merrill, 1988).

10 Ibid., 28.

11 James A. Banks, *Multiethnic Education: Theory and Practice*, 3rd ed. (Boston: Allyn & Bacon, 1994).

12 Michael Apple, *Education and Power* (Boston: Routledge & Kegan Paul, 1982); and Henry Giroux, "Curriculum, Multiculturalism, and the Politics of Identity," *School Principal* 76 (1992): 1–9.

13 Calliste, "Anti-racist Education Initiatives in Nova Scotia"; and Dei, *Reconstructing 'Dropout.'*

14 John Kehoe, "Multiculturalism in Social Studies," in *Trends and Issues in Canadian Social Studies*, ed. Ian Wright and Alan Sears (Vancouver: Pacific Educational Press, 1997), 147–160.

15 John Kehoe and Earl Mansfield, "The Limitations of Multicultural Education and Anti-racist Education," in *Multicultural Education: The State of the Art*, ed. Keith A. McLeod (Toronto: University of Toronto Press, 1993), 3–9.

16 Frances E. Aboud, "The Acquisition of Prejudice in Young White Children" (paper presented at the annual meeting of the American Educational Research Association, Montreal, April 1999).

17 Kehoe, "Multiculturalism in Social Studies," in *Trends and Issues*, 148.

18 Sally Tomlinson, *Multicultural Education in White Schools* (London: B.T. Batsford, 1990), 11.

19 Ahmed Ijaz, "We Can Change Our Children's Racial Attitudes," *Multiculturalism* 5, no. 2 (1982): 11–17.

20 Manju Varma-Joshi, "Multicultural Children's Literature: Storying the Canadian Identity" (doctoral dissertation, University of Toronto, 2000).

21 See Paul Axelrod, *The Promise of Schooling: Education in Canada, 1800–1914* (Toronto: University of Toronto Press, 1997).

22 Helen Harper, "Difference and Diversity in Ontario Schooling," *Canadian Journal of Education* 22, no. 2 (1997): 192–206.

23 Paul Axelrod, *The Promise of Schooling*, 68.

24 Helen Harper, "Difference and Diversity in Ontario Schooling."

25 Ibid.

26 Neil Bissoondath, *Selling Illusions.*

27 Alan Bloom, *The Closing of the American Mind* (New York: Simon & Schuster, 1987); and Jack L. Granatstein, *Who Killed Canadian History?* (Toronto: HarperCollins, 1998).

28 Granatstein, *Who Killed Canadian History?*

29 Timothy Stanley, "Why I Killed Canadian History: Conditions for an Anti-racist History in Canada," *Histoire sociale/Social History* 33, no. 65 (2000): 79–103.

30 Sonia Neito, "Lessons for Students on Creating a Chance to Dream," *Harvard Educational Review* 64, no. 4 (1994): 403.

31 Spicer Commission, *1991 Citizen's Forum on Canadian Unity*, www.uni.ca/spicer/html.

32 Kymlicka and Norman, "Citizenship in Culturally Diverse Societies: Issues, Contexts, Concepts," in *Citizenship in Diverse Societies*, 1.

33 Will Kymlicka, *Finding Our Way: Rethinking Ethnocultural Relations in Canada* (Toronto: Oxford University Press, 1998), 1.

34 Canadian Press, "One in Four Cites 'Canadian' Ethnicity in Census," *2001 Canada Census: What the Statistics Say*, January 21, 2003, http://www.canada.com/national/features/census/index_jan2003.html.

35 I want to thank Dr. Alan Sears for this great illustration, which I've "borrowed" many times.

36 Varma-Joshi, "Multicultural Children's Literature."

37 Tomlinson, *Multicultural Education in White Schools*, 11.

38 Varma-Joshi, "Multicultural Children's Literature."

39 Patricia Ramsey, "The Salience of Race in Young Children Growing Up in an All-White Community," *Journal of Educational Psychology* 83, no. 1 (1991): 33.

40 Kenneth Clark, *Prejudice and Your Child* (Boston: Beacon Press, 1963), 25. Clark's use of the word Negro would today be problematic. However, it also demonstrates the evolving nature of multiculturalism and the need to continually critique our own terms and language.

41 Judy Katz, *White Awareness: Handbook for Anti-racist Education* (Norman, OK: University of Oklahoma Press, 1978), 4.

42 See Ramsey, "The Salience of Race in Young Children" and Tomlinson, *Multicultural Education in White Schools.*

43 See Carla Peck, "Children's Understanding of Ethnic Diversity" (master's thesis, University of New Brunswick, 2003); and Varma-Joshi, "Multicultural Children's Literature."

44 Peck, "Children's Understanding of Ethnic Diversity."

45 See Katherine Au, "Participation Structures in a Reading Lesson with Hawaiian Children: Analysis of a Culturally Appropriate Instruction Event," *Anthropology and Educational Quarterly* 11, no. 2 (1980): 91–115; and Delpit, *Other People's Children.*

46 Cummins and Danesi, *Heritage Languages.*

47 Banks, *Multiethnic Education.*

48 Ibid.; and Dei, *Reconstructing 'Dropout.'*

CHAPTER 11

Teaching Social Studies for Understanding First Nations Issues

Jeff Orr

Social studies is the subject through which we are most likely to perpetuate racism and stereotypes about First Nations peoples.
—Sherry Farrell-Racette[1]

Most Canadian social studies teachers of my generation grew up much as I did, in a sheltered world that privileged European middle-class values and knowledge systems. Although I entered my first teaching position armed with three university degrees related to social sciences and social studies knowledge, I was woefully ignorant of the issues and challenges important to Aboriginal peoples. I am thankful that my very first days of teaching occurred in a First Nations community and resulted in me falling flat on my face as a teacher. Nothing in my life experiences or my seven years of social studies university education seemed to prepare me for my work in teaching the issues of importance for the people of this Aboriginal community. I did not understand their world because I had not been forced to examine it—or examine my views on it.

Since then, my practice has been largely about learning to teach and teaching to learn what I did not know about Aboriginal peoples and other socially marginalized peoples. I am continually working to uncover my own biases and my white middle-class privilege. I am thankful that I fell hard and that I chose to pick myself up rather than run away or get defensive. What follows are some of my reflections on teaching for First Nations issues. I hope that by the end of this chapter I will have convinced you

of the crucial importance of being an advocate for Aboriginal peoples rather than simply teaching about Aboriginal knowledge through history or social studies. I believe our world needs more citizens who see the legitimacy of Aboriginal perspectives and better understand their complexity than I did when I was twenty-something.

Consider the following statements:

- "First Nations people get free education and they don't pay taxes. Now they are taking all the fish. This is unfair."

- "Aboriginals want compensation for the loss of their land. This all happened a long time ago. My ancestors did not get compensation when they were forced out of the Highlands of Scotland. I think they should forget this past and move on. My people did."

- "I don't need to know about Natives because none of them live around here. I think we are learning far too much about Natives and our own European heritage is getting forgotten."

- "Clinging to their Aboriginal language and culture is holding them back. I think they should move off of the reserve and get jobs like everyone else in Canada."

I have heard all of these statements in social studies classrooms. What would you do if a student of yours said one of these statements in your class? Would you ignore it? Would you challenge his/her thinking? What would it mean for your classroom in the short term and over the full academic year? Teachers' responses to such questions reveal both their beliefs about and understanding of topics relating to First Nations. Discuss your response to these comments with other social studies pre-service teachers. What do your responses mean for what and how you would teach? What implications do these comments have for re-thinking your own knowledge of Aboriginal peoples? What does your response say about your own beliefs and biases about Aboriginal peoples?

Overview

In this chapter, we will examine some of the key issues that are typical problem areas for social studies teachers when it comes to teaching for a deep and articulated understanding of Canadian and global Aboriginal issues.

- You will explore your beliefs about some of the major curriculum questions in relation to the teaching of Aboriginal peoples and issues.

- You will come to know how to consider the merits of appropriate and accurate materials and knowledge for teaching First Nations history and social studies.

- You will also identify some Aboriginal ways of teaching and learning that may enhance your teaching of all students.

AN ACTIVITY TO CLARIFY VALUES

This activity can be used with pre-service or in-service social studies teachers to clarify where you stand on the teaching of Aboriginal issues. As the instructor poses each of the following values statements, line up across the front of the classroom based on the degree to which you agree or disagree with the opinion expressed. The instructor will then ask you to fold the line so that those who most disagree can discuss their differences. A variation is to form the values line and split it in the middle and have the two ends of each line fold together and discuss their opinions.

Values Statements

1. Part of the role of our work in social studies is to clarify injustices against Aboriginal peoples and help students consider their stance in the decolonization process.

2. Topics relating to Aboriginal peoples should be taught in depth in separate Native studies classes, not in general social studies courses. There is not enough room in our social studies classes for this to be done well.

3. If we only teach First Nations issues as they occurred in the past, there is a danger we will stereotype Aboriginal peoples.

4. There is a great deal of diversity in Aboriginal peoples in Canada, and no one group or perspective speaks for all First Peoples. We must therefore help our students see the diversity of Aboriginal peoples and only then look for commonalities in historical and contemporary Aboriginal social studies issues.

5. Aboriginal perspectives are often in opposition to mainstream Canadian perspectives about nationhood. We must be careful to not promote separatist movements and stances in our teaching.

6. Teachers should work alongside Aboriginal organizations and people to portray diverse, accurate, and contemporary Aboriginal perspectives about historical and contemporary social, economic, cultural, and political orientations to social studies issues.

What impact does each of these statements have upon your teaching practice? Ultimately you must decide the degree to which you support each of these statements. In the next section of this chapter we will examine each statement from the perspective of teaching *for* First Nations issues rather than teaching *about* First Nations knowledge. Teaching *for* First Nations issues has as its central curricular goal that students will arrive at a deeper understanding of Aboriginal social issues. It is based on the premise that a main focus of teaching Canadian social studies is to develop students' ability and commitment to serve as citizen advocates for greater social justice and equity for Aboriginal peoples. Teaching *about* First Nations peoples takes the position that as social studies teachers we teach about Aboriginal peoples, with no emphasis on social justice and equity. It assumes that in a democracy competing perspectives should and will be brought forward and it is the individual's responsibility to sort through these competing perspectives.

I subscribe to the view that working for greater equity and support for diversity for Aboriginal peoples in our society should be inherent in teaching Canadian social studies. There is overwhelming evidence that we have not yet solved the problems of racism and inequity facing Canadian Aboriginal peoples. Nor have our curricula consistently represented Aboriginal knowledge with accuracy. For instance, a survey of 348 secondary students from across Canada published in 2002 by the Canadian Race Relations Foundation shows that 79.3 percent of these students disagreed or strongly disagreed that their schooling provided them with the opportunity to learn and understand Aboriginal issues.[2] While we need to remain open to ways of addressing social issues facing Aboriginal peoples, my approach to teaching social studies in relation to Aboriginal issues is focused on achieving a greater understanding of and respect for Aboriginal knowledge. I believe that the teaching of Aboriginal social studies issues can and should help students see that part of their role as citizens is to redress social inequities.

Six Major Curriculum Questions

In this section I will address six major curriculum questions in teaching for understanding First Nations issues.

Should Aboriginal social studies clarify injustices and help students learn their place in the decolonization process?

I believe that a major role of social studies teaching is to identify injustices experienced by Aboriginal peoples in an historical and contemporary context. Throughout history, there have been many instances of injustice against Aboriginal peoples, and the process of colonialism is still exerting an influence upon Aboriginal peoples. Decolonization in relation to Aboriginal peoples is the active political and social engagement process that involves citizen-students in working towards a society in which Aboriginal peoples' knowledge systems and social situations are validated and their social conditions are improved. Decolonization is evident when dominant Canadian society strives to eliminate the socioeconomic gap between First Nations persons and mainstream Canadians with regard to such social indicators as health, life expectancy, economic independence, education levels, and per capita percentages of incarceration.

The teacher who teaches *for* First Nations issues would see it as his or her role to situate these indicators in an historical, sociological, or political analysis and look at issues from a First Nations perspective. He or she would know and use the language of decolonization and would see colonialism as an explanatory framework for understanding the poverty and dislocation of contemporary Aboriginal societies. This stance would use the kind of statements that opened this chapter as a way to make visible how our society has served to perpetuate white, middle-class Eurocentric ways at the expense of Indigenous peoples.

RESOURCES

Important websites that explore Aboriginal perspectives and issues on health, criminal justice, and economic status are as follows: First Nations and Inuit Health Branch, http://www.hc-sc.gc.ca/fnihb-dgspni/fnihb/index.htm; Health Canada and Aboriginal peoples, http://www.hc-sc.gc.ca/english/for_you/aboriginals.html; Canadian criminal justice system, http://www.ccja-acjp.ca/en/; Correctional Service Canada, http://www.csc-scc.gc.ca/text/prgrm/correctional/abissues/links_e.shtml; and Assembly of First Nations, http://www.afn.ca/.

Should Aboriginal issues be taught as separate Native studies courses or as integral to all social studies?

Teaching Aboriginal studies as a separate subject has been practised in some provinces in Canada for some time. It may or may not be a good practice, depending on the way it is done and whether this is the only experience that students get with Aboriginal topics. First Nations topics can certainly be taught in more depth when teachers can devote all their class time to exploring Native studies. But many Aboriginal educators argue that this allows teachers of other social studies courses to spend little time on Aboriginal issues. It may allow teachers to say, "They will cover that in the Native studies courses." This may particularly be a problem in communities in which there are significant numbers of Aboriginal students. If separate Native studies courses are taken primarily by Aboriginal students, non-Aboriginal students may get little or no exposure to Aboriginal perspectives, and they may not study alongside Aboriginal students. In Saskatchewan and Nova Scotia, for example, students can choose Native studies, history, or social studies to fulfill their social studies credits.

I have found through my research and teaching that a distinctive Aboriginal worldview and perspective on social studies issues enriches all social studies classes because it creates rich opportunities for exploring multiple perspectives and values. Yet we must recognize that few teachers have been adequately prepared to bring this perspective to the social studies classroom on a regular basis. My own story is a good example of a teacher whose university background in mainstream history and other social studies disciplines initially limited my understanding of Aboriginal issues. When teachers have a limited understanding of Aboriginal issues, they tend to teach about First Nations peoples as an abstract perspective and often with little understanding of, or empathy for, how Aboriginal peoples might see the issues. So the first challenge for social studies teachers who come to their work with these limitations is to awaken to the need to expand their knowl-

edge. Only then can they educate themselves through reading and viewing resources written from Aboriginal perspectives and getting to know Aboriginal people.

REFLECTION

Explore your own first-hand encounters with Aboriginal people. In what social situations have you worked alongside and come to know Aboriginal people? How have these experiences shaped your understanding of Aboriginal cultures, social issues, and knowledge?

Take an inventory of the social sciences and humanities courses you took in university or high school. Identify the degree to which they raised some of the following subjects and issues. Rate your understanding of these six issues on a scale from one to ten, one being non-existent and ten being excellent. What will you do to increase your understanding of these areas?

1. The treaty-making processes, past and present, between Aboriginal peoples and the British and Canadian governments.

2. Aboriginal dislocations from traditional lands across Canada and their impacts upon Aboriginal communities.

3. Government and institutional social policies towards Aboriginal peoples in such areas as economic development, education, and language—and the societal and individual responses to these policies.

4. Historical and contemporary accounts of racist policies and practices in relation to Aboriginal peoples.

5. The diversity of Canada's fifty-plus Aboriginal linguistic communities and cultures.

6. Aboriginal contributions to Canadian and global societies in such fields as technology, politics, law, the arts, science, and agriculture.

What are the challenges and threats of teaching First Nations history in isolation from contemporary issues?

Historical understanding of Aboriginal peoples is extremely important because it allows us to come to a deeper understanding of social situations at particular points in time and often to see social changes and adaptations that have occurred across time. But what if the historical perspective is all that we teach? Many teachers would argue that you cannot teach history well without relating the events of the past to the present. Yet I have seen many instances where students are not provided with the opportunity to connect historical events affecting Aboriginal-Canadian relations to contemporary issues. This invariably results in the perpetuation of stereotypes.

What if historical information about Aboriginal societies is taught to students through historical details and there is no attempt to ask students to consider the chain of events that led from this distant past to the current state of affairs? Many students in Canada are never provided with the opportunity to explore and come to understand the reasons for differences between Aboriginal identities and cultures in the "contact" or early colonial era and current situations of these same cultural groups. This often leaves students with no means of analysis for understanding the impact of social dislocation, cultural change, and colonial assimilation upon Aboriginal communities. Students need to be given the educational tools to analyze the ways that social and historical forces such as colonialism, racism, and assimilation have shaped the contemporary situation of Aboriginal peoples, and to recognize the multiple ways that Aboriginal peoples have successfully resisted assimilation and kept their cultures vibrant and alive.

Activities that move back and forth between historical and contemporary issues and concepts affecting Aboriginal peoples can make for exciting learning experiences for students. Such activities can allow for in-depth understanding of the causes behind historical forces that have resulted in (1) changes to Aboriginal peoples' social and physical environment, (2) conflict and racism, (3) changes and adaptations of Aboriginal cultural identity, and (4) preservation and revitalization of Aboriginal cultures and societies. Moreover, historical analysis that continually returns to the social issues of the present challenges our pedagogy to be more aware of the relevance of history to contemporary society. We cannot afford to leave events in the past, as this can serve to stereotype Aboriginal peoples as being peoples of the past. We need to focus on the changes and adaptations that have resulted from colonialism and Aboriginal peoples' resiliency in the face of forces of cultural assimilation.

RESOURCES

Native Education Services Associates (NESA) has produced several handbooks of excellent experiential education activities that can be used to help students understand historical-contemporary linkages. See, for instance, the three-volume set of *NESA Activities for Native and Multicultural Classrooms* edited by Don Sawyer et al.[3] *This Land Is My Land* is an amazing picture book filled with stories and art about the historical and contemporary tensions George Littlechild and many western Canadian Aboriginal people have experienced.[4] It is one of the best picture books I have found for uncovering how Aboriginal peoples have responded to challenging social issues. See also the McGill First Peoples' Library online, http://www.mcgill.ca/fph/library/, for examples of materials and resources that bring together historical and contemporary understandings of First Nations peoples.

How do we represent both the diversity and commonalities of Aboriginal peoples?

There is so much to know about Aboriginal peoples that no one person can know it all. So do not feel that you should know the details about every group of Aboriginal peoples in Canada and beyond. I believe it is far more important that you share your questions and uncertainty about the complexity of cultural differences across Aboriginal societies. Assist your students to understand that there are proportionally as many differences across Aboriginal societies and nations as there are across the many European societies and nations. Canada's Aboriginal peoples speak about fifty different Aboriginal languages that were part of twelve distinctive language families at the time Europeans came to Canada. Many of these languages are currently in danger of extinction—a commonality that binds people together. Even within particular linguistic communities such as Cree or Mi'kmaw, there is incredible linguistic and cultural diversity.

Part of the challenge for us as teachers is to help our students understand that cultural diversity finds expression in relation to and because of complex dimensions of Aboriginal spiritual, cultural, economic, and social worldviews. Aboriginal peoples' cultural diversity has been shaped by urbanization, politics, physical geography, and economic context. Thus we do not have one archetypal Aboriginal identity nor do we have one vision or perspective that speaks for Aboriginal peoples, past or present. It is important, therefore, to challenge your students to re-examine social studies issues from the perspectives of a variety of Aboriginal peoples.

At the same time, there are some common experiences that bind Aboriginal peoples together culturally and politically. These commonalities are also important to explore so that students can see that commonalities and solidarities across Aboriginal societies past and present have been shaped by the ways that the dominant society has interacted with Aboriginal societies. Commonalities are evident when seen in relation to:

- differing Aboriginal and European worldviews on spiritual, educational, economic, social, political, and environmental matters

- European language and cultural pressures upon Aboriginal languages and cultures that continually threaten Aboriginal peoples with cultural assimilation

- complex social issues common to most Aboriginal communities that are a result of cultural dislocation, identity transformation, and colonial policies and practices

REFLECTION

Reflect on how distinctive features of specific Aboriginal linguistic communities, such as cultural values, spirituality, sense of place, and linguistic diversity, collide with stereotypical views of Aboriginal peoples.

RESOURCES

Olive Dickason's *Canada's First Nations: A History of Founding Peoples from Earliest Times*[5] is probably the most comprehensive reference for helping teachers who are interested in exploring the diversity of First Nations in Canada.

What should be our curricular stance with regards to Aboriginal views of nationhood and self-determination?

As Taiaiake Alfred has said:

> Indigenous peoples are by definition the original inhabitants of the land. They had complex societies and systems of government. And they never gave consent to European ownership of territory or the establishment of European sovereignty over them.[6]

How we discuss Aboriginal perspectives of nationhood depends on our understanding of Aboriginal views of self-determination and self-government in relation to our own views of nationalism. On one extreme we have a perspective of Aboriginal self-government that is little different from the current state of Canadian municipal politics. This is not far removed from the current Indian Act relationship between Aboriginal peoples and the Canadian government. These views are rooted in a weak sense of Aboriginal nationhood that does not acknowledge Aboriginal peoples' quest for self-determination within Canada. The municipal-based system would allow for a level of taxation that would contribute to fiscal autonomy and independence, which its proponents see as an advanced state of self-government. Both this view and the current Indian Act relationship are colonial forms of governance that do not view Aboriginal peoples as self-determining nations in the sense that many Aboriginal people see things.

Many Aboriginal peoples are calling for a very different relationship within Canada that is based on a desire to regain and/or strengthen control over life and being. It aims to discontinue the current colonial relationship in order to allow economic and political independence and social and cultural reconstruction to flourish. This does not mean that Aboriginal nationhood entails separation from Canada. We can learn a great deal from Aboriginal concepts of nationhood such as that of the Haudonosaunee (Iroquois Confederacy), which was articulated to the Dutch in the early 1600s. In this view of sovereignty, Aboriginal and European nations paddle their own canoes side by side in "friendship, equality and justice."[7]

This call for a more complex understanding of diverse nations within the Canadian state is shared by a number of non-Aboriginal scholars as well, most notably Will Kymlicka.[8] His work supports the Aboriginal notion of nations within nations, as he argues that "national minorities" such as Aboriginal peoples have had a long-standing presence within the Canadian state as a result of colonization. Kymlicka argues that because of the colonization experience of national minorities, their relationship to the state is very different from that of "polyethnic minorities" who are peoples who have arrived in Canada more recently and have joined the Canadian state voluntarily. Such understandings of governance are enriching and important for helping to present more balanced perspectives about competing struggles for sovereignty.

RESOURCES

Read such insightful books as Taiaiake Alfred's *Peace, Power, and Righteousness: An Indigenous Manifesto* or John Bird, Lorraine Land, and Murray Macadam's *Nation to Nation: Aboriginal Sovereignty and the Future of Canada.*[9] These books present Aboriginal self-determination and nationhood from the perspectives of Aboriginal peoples. Exploring First Voices at the local community level will also bring forward Aboriginal perspectives on nationhood. See also the Assembly of First Nations website, http://www.afn.ca/

for current issues related to sovereignty and treaty negotiations and links to a variety of First Nations.

Whose voices should be heard when teachers present perspectives about Aboriginal social studies issues?

Teachers who present perspectives that are written or voiced by Aboriginal organizations and people are more likely to portray accurate historical and contemporary Aboriginal perspectives about social studies topics. It is not always possible to get an Aboriginal perspective on every historical event but it is important to teach our students to ask, How would a particular Aboriginal community take up this issue?

Aboriginal issues should be explored when and where possible using First Voices perspectives. It is important to keep focused on diversity of perspectives and to work to uncover Indigenous perspectives on issues being discussed. I have found that the more I bring forth First Voices to speak out on Aboriginal social studies issues, the less likely I am to be positioned as speaking *for* Aboriginal peoples. If we speak *with* Aboriginal peoples we are engaging in decolonizing actions. Invariably, First Voices result in a deepened and more diverse range of perspectives on social studies issues.

There are several Aboriginal issues that are very sensitive for even the most knowledgeable non-Aboriginal teacher to teach. Aboriginal spirituality is an area that many teachers, both Aboriginal and non-Aboriginal, are uncomfortable with. It is my position that spirituality and religion have a place in the classroom. However, I feel we should teach *about* religion in schools rather than teach *for* religion in schools.[10] The Canadian Charter of Rights and Freedoms states that we have the freedom of choosing our own religion but that we do not have the right to impose our religion on others in schools. Therefore, I think it is important to remember that participation in religious ceremonies in schools is against the Charter of Rights. To allow Aboriginal smudge ceremonies and not morning prayers from the Bible or Koran is to privilege one form of religion over another. However, if we teach about as many religions as we can, we are more likely to understand about others' religions, which may reduce the fear and suspicion that so often comes with ignorance of other religions. Helping students understand the place of various Aboriginal ceremonies as part of Aboriginal spirituality is as important and valid as understanding why Christians follow the ritualistic traditions of the Holy Bible, or why meditation is important to Mahayana Buddhists. What is important in all cases is to work towards First Voices perspectives about spirituality that do not position you as the person responsible for interpreting and representing Aboriginal or other perspectives.

Some teachers fall into the trap of relying upon guest speakers who represent a particular Aboriginal organization or category of society to speak for all Aboriginal peoples. This is a compelling way to proceed because it may absolve the teacher of any responsibility for speaking out and getting him- or herself into controversy. While it is important to have guest speakers, they should not be relied upon as the only Aboriginal voices in our curriculum. Nor should this be used as an excuse for teachers to keep their own views silent.

RESOURCES

CBC Manitoba has produced an excellent five-part mini-series exploring the spirituality of Aboriginal peoples.[11] Accurate films that portray Aboriginal peoples in examining issues are always a useful way to bring First Voices into the classroom. One of my favourites is *Babikiueria,* a film produced by the Australian Broadcasting Corporation that shows the colonization experience in Australia as if it were done by Aborigines.[12] This film is a useful tool for interrupting the assumptions white middle-class learners bring to the examination of colonialism and difference. *Education As We See It* is another good film about residential schooling that is part of the National Film Board series *First Nations: The Circle Unbroken.*[13] This series explores many aspects of social issues in Canada from a First Nations perspective.

There are a number of interesting books written by Aboriginal peoples that allow for a close-up ex-

amination of historical issues. In the picture book *As Long as the Rivers Flow*, Larry Loyie describes his early life with his family on the land.[14] The book contrasts the Aboriginal way of learning with the residential school system experienced by many Aboriginal people. Theytus Books, Kegedonce Press, and Pemmican Publishers are Aboriginal publishing houses, and Purich Publishing also specializes in Aboriginal issues. The Department of Indian and Northern Affairs has produced "A Select Bibliography of Children's Books by and about Aboriginal Peoples for Ages 4–14."[15] *Reading Voices, Dan Dha Ts'edenintth'e*[16] contrasts Aboriginal and non-Aboriginal perspectives of the Yukon's past, providing an excellent example of a style of scholarship that places First Nations voices and perspectives alongside European voices. In 2003/04 the British Columbia Ministry of Education published a textbook and teacher's guide to support its B.C. First Nations Studies course for grades 11 and 12. The teacher's guide includes an extensive bibliography of books, films, websites, and other resources by and about Aboriginal peoples.[17]

Aboriginal Pedagogy Is also Good Social Studies Pedagogy

In this final section, I share three teaching strategies that have become a central part of my work in Aboriginal and social education. Aboriginal pedagogy is typically based around the culture of the circle. Talking circles, cooperative learning, and conversational storytelling approaches are three forms of pedagogy that I have found helpful in communicating that are in keeping with Aboriginal ways of knowing. I describe each in turn below.

Talking circles as one form of circular pedagogy

Aboriginal pedagogy is typically based around the pedagogy of the circle. Talking circles are a good way to begin to use the circle as part of your teaching. Talking circles strive to eliminate hierarchy and to demonstrate that everyone's ideas and feelings belong in the classroom. Talking circles teach the value of listening to and respecting the ideas and opinions of others. The leader/instructor uses a physical object such as a stone or stick to focus the circle. The rules are that the person holding the object is the only person with the right to speak. All other participants are responsible for listening. At the beginning of talking circles, I usually state the rules. I then pose a topic relevant to the particular social studies issue and say a few words that represent some of my opinions on this issue. I then pass on the object in a clockwise direction.

RULES OF THE TALKING CIRCLE

1. Only the person with the object can speak.

2. Participants are encouraged to speak, but if they do not wish to do so, they simply need to pass on the object around the circle.

3. Comments should be directed to the issue and not to what other people have said. By no means are participants permitted to comment positively or negatively about the words of others.

4. It is our responsibility to listen to the speaker.

5. What is said in the circle is meant for the participants of the circle only; it stays in the circle.

Sometimes it takes several trips of the object around the circle before participants have had their say. Sometimes people do not speak on the first time around and sometimes some people do not speak at all. The strategy is a good way to ensure that no one person dominates the topic under discussion. I typically use talking circles after people have had a common experience of a story or film on a topic about which they may have strong feelings.

The circle is a powerful pedagogical tool. The talking circle discussed here is but one of many ways that the circle can be used as a way to enact a pedagogical relationship. If you find this strategy compelling, you might want to explore some other strategies that draw upon the circle, such as inside-outside circle, community circle, story circle, fish bowl, web circle, and red stocking. All of these strategies use the environment and structure of the circle as a way to organize and construct knowledge. Some of these strategies focus on the sanctity and validity of the individual voice, as the talking circle does. Others use the circle more as a place for the social construction of meaning.

RESOURCES

The following are several useful resources that identify ways to use the power of the circle in teaching: *Cooperative Learning and Social Studies; Educating for a Change; Global Teacher, Global Learner*; and the *Mi'kmaq Studies 10 Teachers' Guide*.[18]

Cooperative learning

Many people will tell you that they learn best through collaboration. Much of our school system is based around individual and competitive approaches. Aboriginal teachers with whom I have worked usually have developed a wide range of cooperative approaches that they use with their students. Cooperative learning is not a new idea, but it is still poorly understood. Some educators see it as a way in which individuals can hide behind the work of others; others feel that too many discipline problems emerge when they have students working in groups. These teachers have not come to see the ways that the process of cooperation serves to teach about responsibilities as citizens in a caring democracy. Cooperative learning enhances academic learning, increases the pro-social skills of students, and can contribute to the reduction of prejudice and stereotyping. My approach to cooperative learning is rooted in the work of my colleague Joanne Tompkins, who has been an avid user of cooperative learning strategies since her early days of teaching in the North.[19] The process she has taught me differs from the group work that many teachers call cooperative learning because it ensures through five features of cooperative learning that relations of power are challenged and not re-inscribed in the group. The five features of cooperative learning are positive interdependence, individual accountability, group processing, social skills, and face-to-face contact. These are used as a pedagogical framework to organize and conduct cooperative learning.

Positive interdependence is the very heart of cooperative learning. The success of one is dependent upon the success and participation of all. Traditional Aboriginal societies thrived upon cooperation amongst people in ways not unlike how committees, volunteer organizations, teams, and music and arts ensembles function. All of these groups thrive when there is positive interaction among all members. When such groups fail to work together, the results are often disastrous. In cooperative learning we place great emphasis upon assessing and teaching students to learn through and for positive interdependence.

If students know they are *individually accountable* for their own learning during cooperative tasks, their learning is likely to be more meaningful. Students are encouraged to participate equally, to work at ensuring that they contribute to the well-being of the group, and to strive to contribute to the social and academic learning of the group. This accountability can be both a reflective individual and teacher/peer exercise. If students are held individually accountable, then cooperative learning contributes to their individual learning and growth.

By making the *group processing* of how well things are done as a group a priority, students are given the opportunity to consider ways to improve their group's functioning. Reflective experiences that students contribute to on a regular basis are encouraged.

A range of *social skills* should be explicitly taught to students so that they can learn their place as citizens, living responsibly and cooperatively with one another. They learn to communicate their feelings and thoughts to get beyond simply agreeing on everything. Some social skills we process and work on learning explicitly are encouraging, active listening, the art of good conversation, disagreeing, staying on task, pacing, negotiating, being acceptably assertive, following directions, elaborating, contributing ideas, asking questions, and summarizing.

If participants are asked to work *face-to-face* they have the opportunity to really engage with one another in relational ways. They often need to be shown how to work by arranging themselves in such a manner that they are physically and relationally connected to one another and able to fully engage in the act of communicating and participating.

RESOURCES

The most valuable resource I have found for integrating cooperative learning more fully in my practice is Tom Morton's book *Cooperative Learning and Social Studies*.[20] Morton, a Canadian social studies teacher, explores and explains twenty-four different cooperative learning strategies with social studies lessons and examples.

Teaching through storytelling

People have been using stories as a mode of teaching since time immemorial. First Nations people used stories as a way to pass down traditions and to educate their youth for many generations before Europeans brought formal schooling to North America. Stories continue to be a central part of Aboriginal knowledge systems and are still the best way we know to communicate our understanding of human experiences. I suggest two ways that stories can be used for constructing, representing, and re-constructing knowledge in ways that can create personal connections for students to history and social studies. The two techniques that I use most often are reading stories (particularly picture books) and having students tell and re-tell stories.

READ STORIES TO STUDENTS

One of the greatest breakthroughs for me as a social studies teacher came when I discovered that children's stories had a place in my social studies curriculum. I will share two children's stories that I have used that I believe have changed how my students look at history. One is on a First Nations theme and the other is a book that can be used to help students think about the place of their ancestors in history. *Pink and Say*, by Patricia Polacco, is a story in which Polacco re-tells a story about the American Civil war that was passed on in her family for a number of generations.[21] This story allows students to see the human side of history and to see that they too are descended from people who have had rich and important experiences and influences upon history. I use the book to have students recall possible events their own ancestors might have participated in in relation to history, to help them imagine the stories of these ancestors, and then to engage in their own re-tellings of the same events. George Littlechild's book *This Land Is My Land* is filled with very rich personal responses that Littlechild provides to some of his paintings.[22] His paintings and words portray such issues as residential schools, changing lifestyles, and social dislocation. This book allows students to understand how one First Nations man makes sense of the world in which he lives. It creates many possibilities for connecting painting or other forms of artistic representation with storytelling.

HAVE STUDENTS RE-TELL STORIES

Stories are also a good way for us to give meaning to our experiences and to give them some coherence. Re-telling stories has been a useful way for me to help my students construct their own meaning out of classroom events. One technique is individual talk such as the talking circle discussed earlier; a second is individual response journalling, and a third is collaborative talk.

Response journals combine elements of letter-writing and personal journalling in response to a particular topic or experience. I use this strategy to encourage students to write down their thoughts on various social studies issues that we are discussing in class. I strive to have students continually share stories and experiences that relate to the topic at hand. For instance, if we view a film, I often ask students to write their personal stories of how the film resonates with their own life experiences. I respond to them in writing and strive to have them delve more deeply into ways to link to their experiences by returning to their own stories.

Collaborative talk aims to have students build upon one another's construction of stories. Story circles gather students in small cooperative groups to come up with stories that reflect their collective understanding of events, concepts, or experiences. I

often have students work in small cooperative groups to build stories together. There are many alternative structures that can make space for this collaborative talk. The corners strategy is a useful way to get students to explore their thoughts in relation to possible interpretations of a particular historical or social issue.[23] For example, a teacher might pose a question such as "What have been the impacts of western treaties on society?" Some students might go to one corner of the room and tell stories of the impact upon the landscape; those in another corner might speak of the impact upon people of European ancestry who settled in the West; those in another corner could explore the impact upon Aboriginal societies, and a fourth group could tell stories of the impact upon the wider Canadian society. The inside-outside circle strategy allows students to listen to the stories of others and also to tell their own story a number of times to different individuals.[24] Individuals arrange themselves in two circles with equal numbers of participants. A smaller inner circle faces outwards and a second circle gathers around the inner circle and faces inwards. After individuals hear the story of one person and share their own story with this person, either the inside or outside circle is rotated so that participants get to hear others' stories and to hone their own story as they repeatedly share it with others.

Conclusion

Teaching social studies for understanding of First Nations issues can be a very enriching and rewarding experience for both students and teachers. This chapter has shared some dimensions of teaching First Nations issues that support a greater understanding of and commitment to First Nations peoples. I believe it is important that as teachers we strive to cultivate an informed citizenry who have explored and clarified their place in honouring, respecting, and advancing the place of Aboriginal peoples within Canadian society. I believe that all social studies teachers should develop awareness of their crucial role in this knowledge-construction process. The knowledge we allow into our classrooms and the pedagogy we use to explore and construct this knowledge can and will make the difference between teaching *about* or *for* First Nations issues.

Endnotes

1   Sherry Farrell-Racette, personal communication, Regina, Saskatchewan, April 1995.

2   Canadian Race Relations Foundation, Coalition for the Advancement of Aboriginal Studies, *Learning About Walking in Beauty: Placing Aboriginal Perspectives in Canadian Classrooms; A Report from the Coalition for the Advancement of Aboriginal Studies (CAAS) Presented to the Canadian Race Relations Foundation (CRRF)* (Toronto: Author, 2002), 102.

3   Don Sawyer et al., *The NESA Activities Handbook for Native and Multicultural Classrooms*, 3 vol. (Vancouver: Tillacum Library, 1984, 1991, 1993).

4   George Littlechild, *This Land Is My Land* (Emeryville, CA: Children's Book Press, 1993).

5   Olive Dickason, *Canada's First Nations: A History of Founding Peoples from Earliest Times*, 3rd ed. (Don Mills, ON: Oxford University Press, 2002).

6   Taiaiake Alfred, *Peace, Power, Righteousness: An Indigenous Manifesto* (Don Mills, ON: Oxford University Press, 1999), 58.

7   John Bird, Lorraine Land, and Murray MacAdam, eds., *Nation to Nation: Aboriginal Sovereignty and the Future of Canada,* new edition (Toronto: Irwin, 2002), xvii.

8   Will Kymlicka, *Multicultural Citizenship* (Oxford: Oxford University Press, 1995), 10–33.

9   Alfred, *Peace, Power, Righteousness*; and Engelstad and Bird, *Nation to Nation*.

10 See Lois Sweet, *God in the Classroom: The Controversial Issue of Religion in Canada's Schools* (Toronto: McClelland & Stewart, 1998).

11 Cheryl McKenzie, *Spirituality of Aboriginal Peoples*, 5-pt. CBC Radio series (Winnipeg, CBC Manitoba, 2001), http://www.winnipeg.cbc.ca/archives/spirituality/.

12 Geoffrey Atherden, *Babikiueria* (Sydney: Australian Broadcasting Corporation, 1986), filmstrip.

13 Gary Marcuse et al., *Education As We See It*, NFB series, First Nations: The Circle Unbroken (Toronto: National Film Board, 1993), filmstrip.

14 Larry Loyie with Constance Brissenden, *As Long as the Rivers Flow* (Toronto: Groundwood Books, 2002).

15 Karen Russell-Letourneau, "A Select Bibliography of Children's Books By and About Aboriginal Peoples for Ages 4–14," (Ottawa: Indian and Northern Affairs Canada, 2000), http://www.ainc-inac.gc.ca/pr/lib/bib/ack_e.html.

16 Julie Cruikshank, *Dan Dha Ts'edenintth'e: Oral and Written Interpretations of the Yukon's Past* (Vancouver: Douglas & McIntyre, 1991).

17 The *B.C. First Nations Studies* student text and teacher's guide are available from Government Publication Services in Victoria, BC, www.publications.gov.bc.ca/info.

18 Tom Morton, *Cooperative Learning and Social Studies* (San Juan Capistrano, CA: Kagan Cooperative Learning, 1996); Rick Arnold et al., *Educating for a Change* (Toronto: Between the Lines Press, 1991); Graham Pike and David Selby, *Global Teacher, Global Learner* (London: Hodder & Stoughton, 1988); and Jeff Orr, Joanne Tompkins, and Harold Shaver, *Mi'kmaq Studies 10 Teachers' Guide* (Halifax: Nova Scotia Department of Education, 1997).

19 See Joanne Tompkins, *Teaching in a Cold and Windy Place: Change in an Inuit School* (Toronto: University of Toronto Press, 1998).

20 Morton, *Cooperative Learning and Social Studies*.

21 Patricia Polacco, *Pink and Say* (New York: Philomel Books, 1994).

22 Littlechild, *This Land Is My Land*.

23 See Morton, *Cooperative Learning and Social Studies*, 49–54.

24 Ibid., 91–96.

CHAPTER 12

Gender and Sexuality in the Social Studies Curriculum

Bound and Un-determined

Lisa W. Loutzenheiser

Introduction

Gender and sexuality are everywhere in our high schools: regulation of the length of girls' skirts and tops and boys' sagging pants; graffiti announcing Mr. Johnson's sexuality; the age-old stereotypes of sexual promiscuity and healthy adolescent conquest; hockey players wearing jerseys to class on game day; court battles over books discussing sexual diversity; and omnipresent representations of men and women paired off into romantic couples. Yet, except for singular days and lessons, explicit explorations of their meanings are frequently missing.[1]

In my high school and teacher education courses, I request that students document the uses of gender throughout one particular day, asking them to note the various ways in which they encounter gender at play, or see it introduced in the hallways, lunchrooms, and classrooms they inhabit. In response, I am often asked what I mean by gender or sex, despite the fact that I never use the word sex. I reply that it is their definitions of gender, and the interactions of gender in their worlds, which hold the most interest for me.

In the next class meeting, there is a buzz as students enter the room. Simultaneously there is excitement, frustration, and reluctance, and it is clear that the exercise has been both stimulating and confounding. A student will often raise her hand, asking, "Well, what do I do if I didn't see any examples of sexism all day?" I respond by encouraging other students to share their examples of gender, eliciting details of who was involved and why the student noted that particular incident. However, I wonder why sexism is often the solitary focus. Their examples centre on girls and/or women, and I inquire about the silences surrounding the ways gender works with, and on, boys and men. Having reviewed their own encounters, I invite students to expand upon and explore the connections between gender and sexism. If no one makes the association, I push the dialogue by asking if there might be more to the analyses of gender than interrogating the observable sexism played out around them. Despite some confused looks, nods of acceptance, and uncomfortable silences, the exercise becomes a starting point for students.

I use this example to illustrate the numerous ways gender surrounds each moment of the day in schools, even when it is not directly addressed. Commonly, gender is narrowly understood as the way in which sexism is perpetuated on women by men, and while this occurs and needs to be deconstructed as such, to leave the dialogue there does not address the larger issues that gender encompasses. What I am arguing for is an uncovering of the assumptions that we, as educators and teacher educators, hold about gender, as this necessitates discussions of sexism, heteronormativity, and constructions of femininities and masculinities.

Heteronormativity will be discussed in detail later in the chapter; it is being used here as an understanding of the pervasive systemic assumption of heterosexuality as the norm. Michael Warner uses the term "heteronormativity" as the manner in which "heterosexual culture thinks of itself as the elemental form of human association, as the very model of inter-gender relations, as the indivisible basis of all community, and the means of reproduction without which society wouldn't exist."[2] Sumara and Davis also note that although "what constitutes experiences of heterosexuality are incredibly varied, there remains a generalized set of cultural myths about what constitutes the quintessential heterosexualized identity."[3]

Schools are fertile locations for both social change and stagnation of stereotypes. Knowledge production and the lapses and inclusions of gender and sex in teaching and learning demand thorough and complicated analyses, as do the inclusion and exclusion of gender and sexuality in curricula. Without such analyses, there is a risk of continuing and promoting gender-based stereotypes. The opportunities to develop nuanced understandings of the intersections and interdependencies of gender, sex, sexuality, and race are lost when each is considered in isolation. These conversations have particular salience in the classroom because ideals of democratic participation, citizenship, civil rights, historical accuracy, and social issues are laced throughout social studies curricula. This chapter is an invitation for teachers, particularly those in their early years, to complicate and blur singular identities, moving towards integrated approaches to discussions and critical analyses of gender and sexualities in the classroom, thereby encouraging a pushing beyond the "add-and-stir" or "focus on similarity" models of curricular and pedagogical change.[4]

I argue that in order to address and disrupt the multiple meanings of gender in the classroom, issues of gender, sex, sexuality, and heteronormativity must be addressed with ideologically specific and rigorous critical methods. Therefore, the challenge is not only to reveal the intersectionalities of gender, sex, sexualities, and heteronormativity, but also to dissect how these gendered devices intersect with and reinforce race, class, and sexualities in the social studies classroom.[5] Within these notions, gender includes *and* encompasses far more than the experiences of girls and women in schools and classrooms.

A central goal of this chapter is to question what is normal and normalized in schools and classrooms, particularly in relation to gender. Why do we line boys and girls up separately in many early grade classrooms? Why do we make curricular examples including pairings according to the perceived sex of a child? Why do we have a homecoming king and queen? In some ways, the answer, like the problem, is historically perpetuated: because it has always been done that way, or because that is what the majority of parents and students desire. Often what we do is a reaction to what the parents experienced and what they therefore assume their children ought to experience. Nevertheless, I wonder about how we might change the tenor of our classrooms so that what is named "normal" is called into question in ways that make more room for difference, rocking the boat of normalcy in ways that require our students to interrogate gender, sex, and sexuality—thereby employing the critical thinking that many argue is the linchpin of an engaged democracy. In the following sections, the interrelationship of the terms gender and sex will be addressed. A short discussion of the early and continuing efforts to address gender in the classroom will follow, as well as an analysis of the effects of curricular initiatives and silences. Impacts of the interrelationships between gender, sex, and sexuality and the regulatory role each plays between and amongst each other will also be explored. A case study will be presented of how theory might be used to complicate and unpack these issues in the classroom, opening up spaces for pedagogical and curricular integration and messiness.

Gendered Sex

Terms such as gender and sex are bandied about, but are seldom clearly defined, or when defined, are rarely positioned outside of binaries of boy/girl, male/female. Binaries can be identified as consisting of two separate elements considered in diametric opposition. Often sex is understood as the biological distinction between male and female, while gender is explained as a social construction. That is, gender is a performance of social norms understood to be either masculine or feminine in terms of their enactments, rather than the presentation of some "true" manifestation of masculinity or femininity. Some scholars have argued that sex is what we are born with and gender is what we gain or acquire.[6] Accordingly, masculinity and femininity take on meaning through the social, political, and historical contexts in which they are located.

However, the terms gender and sex remain ambiguous and contested; they are not easily distinguishable and some theorists argue that they ought not to be the subject of dichotomous or binary constructions.[7] Butler, for example, argues that it is impossible to separate gender from sex, sex from gender, and gender or sex from sexuality, and equally unworkable are attempts to fundamentally erase binary definitions that presume a primal biological sex.[8] Scholars, including Butler, are questioning the immutability of sex and gender categories, and argue that the categories and meanings of boy, male, female, man, woman, and girl are discursively constituted through both language and social interaction. That is, we are reliant upon understandings of language and its implications as unchanging in order to make meanings and sense of words, symbols, and the performance of words such as gender and sex. For example, if the word man is uttered, an image appears in the reader's mind. It might vary for individual readers but the language conjures up a representation, which in turn, places more meaning on the word and the gendered performance of the term. One way to work with these representations at the early grades is to ask students to look at an animated story and give examples of why the characters act like "girls" and "boys" and when they move outside those roles. Using Disney-type films is useful in the higher grades as they are often accessible to all students and can be used to prompt questioning about how and why the creators both work within stereotypical gender roles and make attempts to alter them.

Early Movements and Equity Arguments

When gender is spoken of in relation to schools, issues such as the inequities of attention and achieve-

ment are discussed, as are the loss of girls' self-esteem and the need for more positive role models in the curriculum.[9] Hurren and others in social studies have advocated a reworking of social education, acknowledging:

> Social studies as a subject area has been constructed by men . . . and the hierarchical framework that privileges public over private and implies that the study of the issues traditionally associated with men require a more sophisticated, mature learner/body than the study of self, family and community, issues traditionally associated with women.[10]

In Canada, curriculum changes focusing on girls and schooling began several decades ago. For example, in the 1970s, the Ontario Ministry of Education formed a women's committee on education that developed and offered workshops for teachers, students, and administrators, created new curriculum materials, and offered guidelines for screening curricula.[11] The focus on equity was, and remains, an important first step but often relies on oversimplified notions.

Additionally, many of the gains were dependent upon the tenor of the political climate and which political party was in power. Gaskell and Taylor argue that there was:

> Energetic grass-roots organising in the 1970s, which won some resources from the state, and support from some teachers' unions. Girls' achievement and participation gradually increased, the curriculum was revised, and understandings of gender became more sophisticated. But by the 1990s, the public visibility of the movement . . . had diminished. Increased awareness of differences among women meant that women's issues were subsumed under a broad umbrella of "social justice," and the problems of boys dominated the headlines.[12]

The increasing concern regarding boys' achievement was and is manifest through the "moral panic" about boys' literacy failures. There is a growing body of research focusing on boys' underachievement in literacy, which constructs them as the "new victims."[13] While issues of different literacy gains among male students are important, one must also be careful to critically read attempts to position boys as the "new girls" or boys' seeming underachievement as caused by the gains of girls.[14] Griffin and Reed argue that these moves depoliticize and ahistorize the debates concerning the achievement of boys and girls.[15] It is worth noting that these new concerns about literacy have only arisen as affluent, white male achievement and test scores have declined.[16]

In schools, assumptions of an evenly gendered space within the classroom or school signal that meritocracy can and will prevail. At times, this results in the needs of male and female students being viewed as if in competition, resulting in needs centring on gender being more easily universalized. The intersectionality of class, ability, race, and sexuality with gender concerns are often considered secondary, or are lost altogether because competition for limited resources is fierce.

Curriculum, Pedagogy, and the Politics of Masculinities

As stated above, within K–12 (and teacher education) social studies courses, curricular conversations and lessons focusing on gender have often centred on the experiences and histories of girls and women. While many young female teachers may analyze their personal experiences as being gender-bias free, they become less likely to do the same when policies and systems such as the treatment of Native women under the Indian Act, the exclusion of Indo-Canadian women from gaining citizenship, or the continued discrepancies of women's and men's wages are actively discussed. This can, again, be read as a conversation about female or women's oppression; however, a more nuanced reading might lend itself to understanding how masculinity, as we construct it in Canada, impacts how gender and sexuality are viewed and produced in curricula, in student and teacher bodies, and in policy.

In the classroom

There is a pattern to initial conversations about gender in my social studies methods courses. The experiences and attitudes of boys and men are universalized and personalized; the conversation becomes that of "all boys view women as sex objects" or "all men are sexist." The generalizing of male experience often compels one or two students (interestingly enough, these are usually women) to defend the actions of individual men. The absence and erasure of boys and men leaves their position as the norm marked, but unchallenged. In addition, the pressures brought to bear on boys and men who do not meet the societal definitions or gender role norms of authentic masculinity are left underexposed. Connell argues that masculinity is not stationary nor a linguistic or material given; rather, it is created, reinforced, and recreated as individuals and groups act and are acted upon. Male bodies, and those constructed vis-à-vis the male body, are acted upon by media and school structures that valorize a particular kind of maleness over those considered lesser or weak.[17]

However, rather than engaging in dialogues of equity and gender role stereotypes, or discussions of sexism to explore how boys have come to be seen as "real" boys (authentically masculine), the conversation in my classroom often takes an essentialist turn. The discussion becomes one in which men are discriminated against as well, often highlighting and equating the exploitation and objectifying of the male body in contemporary society to that which women are subjected. Within this type of conversation, the social positioning, as well as the pressure that the performance of masculinities places upon men and boys is not explored, nor is its impact on all genders and sexualities. This type of personalization at an individual level and the need to shore up the construction of maleness and masculinity as unproblematic occurs most often when the analysis remains focused on micro-level personal motivations and intent, rather than shifting to contextualizing and understanding issues and actions systemically. What might it mean to build pedagogies and curricula that interrogate the complicated nature of genders and masculinities in social studies classrooms? How do we create curricula that both invite an understanding of the powerful political, social, and historical positions of gender, and an exploration of how masculinities and femininities regulate all genders and sexualities? A fairly straightforward lesson to begin the process of deconstructing gender in elementary and secondary classrooms is to ask students to demonstrate who they think boys and girls or males and females are. In elementary classrooms, students can be asked to draw pictures of a typical girl and a boy, or draw pictures and use words to describe their pictures. At the secondary level, it can be quite helpful to move to students' notions of the "ideal" girl or boy. This is not to ask them to call out, draw, or write about the stereotypical ideal but their own very personal notion of what is the ideal male or female. The instructor can then lead the class in a discussion of why students chose their representations. I find it most helpful when working with grades 5, 6, 7, and sometimes 8 to ask students to write about their own gender or sex; this usually avoids the pre-teen tendency to write about the object of their affections or to focus on physicality. One way to extend the conversation is for teachers to show images from television, movies, animation, or print media that both confirm and confound the ideals that students have created. For some classes this will be enough to begin the processes of interrogating what is "real" or "authentic"; for others, a more explicated questioning will be needed.

Curricula, Pedagogies, and Gendered Misunderstandings

Even in an age when teaching for diversity and teaching for social justice are currently concerns within education, there has been a continuing lack of focus on gender, sex, and sexuality within social studies itself. Crocco notes:

> To date, while some attention has been paid to gender within social studies (e.g., Scott, 1995; Tetrault, 1987), a discourse about the links between gender and sexuality, mi-

sogyny, homophobia, and violence in our society has largely been missing.[18]

Similarly, Tupper notes:

> Gender and difference are not currently central questions in citizenship education, and understandings of what constitute citizenship appear to live within the boundaries of the nation state.[19]

In contemporary terms, curricular change in gender and social studies has most often been focused on add-and-stir and equity-focused models. These models leave overall teaching and learning goals and objectives the same but add a lesson here or there on top of the regular lessons. These add-on lessons are generally developed with a desire for curricular inclusion, with the belief that incorporating them will help students develop higher self-esteem, increased achievement, and educational equity. While increased representations of girls and women, particularly women of colour, exist in some classrooms, Noddings questions,

> What . . . does the addition of women into history texts as special coloured boxes, or increased pictures of First Nations bands mean if there is little or no critical explication or integration of the curriculum?[20]

Many argue that even add-and-stir is a step forward, and ought to be applauded; however, it does not push teachers or students to move beyond traditional understandings.

In this model, little of the curricular or pedagogical planning is changed; the unit or essential questions are not altered and the critical analyses of the roles of gender, race and/or sexuality can be left unexplored. It allows the schools, teachers, and school boards to tick off the gender and/or multicultural education box of curricular reform without altering the school culture and its explicit or hidden curricula. The paucity of integration and overreliance on one- or two-day lessons that are not tied to the rest of the curriculum result in a lack of depth of analysis in relation to the systemic, thereby "trivializ[ing] the history under examination."[21]

I am not arguing that there are no gains to be

made within or through equity arguments, or initial introductions of gender, sexuality, and sex into social studies curricula. However, I am suggesting that this ought not to be the only project engaging in discussions of how gender is, and ought to be, worked within social studies classrooms. The uneasiness expressed by some scholars, teachers, and researchers is that the political potency of the category "woman," or what some consider positive manifestations of differences between men and women, are lost. Somewhat conversely, I would argue that any complete removal of difference is impossible and undesirable. The important work within gender and sexuality is in the very difference that many who advocate gender equity seem to erase or overlook. I am advocating a move towards a greater understanding of who is included and excluded in the categories of woman and man, boy and girl, particularly as our understanding of these words and the meanings they produce change and develop.

A brief interlude on the regulatory nature of sex, gender, sexuality, and race

As noted above, when gender has been written up in the teaching of social studies or social studies methods, the focus has largely been on sex as an essentialized, dichotomized, and discrete category. There is a girl and a boy, and they (their meaning and manifestations) are thought to be relatively universal. That is to say, the experiences of all women and girls, or all boys and men, are believed to be predominantly the same regardless of specific context. Under this rubric, the project, then, is to understand what equal or equity means, and to strive to erase the differences. Accordingly, once the playing field is considered even, and girls and boys have the same advantages, it follows that those who ought to succeed will. This reliance on notions of a meritocracy as an organizing tenet negates the social, political, and historical differences apparent in living in Canada.

An organizing of gender as singular or universal also silences the ways that gender functions for both women and men, and that race, sex, and sexuality have a regulatory function upon each other. Writing about boys, Kimmel says, "As adolescents, we learn that our peers are a kind of gender police, constantly threatening to unmask us as feminine, as sissies."[22] If one thinks of a typical classroom, each day there is regulation of student and teacher sex, gender, and sexuality. Recently I heard a male teacher say to a female high school student who had physically reacted to verbal harassment by a male student, "Girls don't beat up boys, do they? That's just not right. Does a boy want a girl who is stronger than he is?" The young men in the room responded by hooting at the boy who had been bested by this girl, calling him a "fag" and a "sissy."

Epstein argues that readings of the body are unavoidably heterosexual or assumed to be heterosexual, because masculinity and femininity are intertwined, and thus, a "real" boy or girl is, and must be, assumed to be heterosexual.[23] In order to be considered authentically masculine, one must conform to certain gender ideals. A boy at the bottom of the student heap is considered less masculine; he is viewed as more like a girl than a boy and therefore not a man. One need only walk the hall of any school to understand that the insults of choice between boys and young men are "fag," "sissy," and "that's so gay." When a male does not conform to traditional gender role performances, he is assumed gay and this performance of gay (no matter the young person's sexual orientation) serves as a policing of the gender norms around him and to which he is expected to conform. The student is constructed as an "other" who is always held up as that which is not masculine. In these ways, gender and sex act as a regulatory agent for normed sexuality.

Butler argues that accepted constructs of sex and sexuality not only define the boundaries as a norm but function as part of a system or practice that both regulates what is normal in relation to gender, sex, and sexuality, and (re)produces what is acceptable through its very regulatory nature. What is male or female, in the ways that we think of as biological, becomes an ideal that can never be made real, but is articulated and circulated and re-articulated through bodies that attempt to, and are forced to, adhere to an impossible set of gender norms.[24] In the example above, the girl has been told that she has to be weaker than a boy if she wishes to be sexually attractive to a boy. Given the social norms that dictate what a "real" girl desires, according to social myth, she must perform her gender in such a way that reinforces and reproduces the heterosexual masculinity of the boy, simultaneously confirming the central importance of being wanted *by* a boy; that is, reproducing her own femininity.

The male in this story is denigrated as being "like a girl." The use of the word "fag" has little to do with whether the individual has gay experience; rather, it is a direct questioning of the boy's masculinity, and masculinity as part of a collective understanding. The boy is being called out as performing less than an authentically masculine role. The desire for authentic masculinity requires an effort

> to maintain a manly front over everything we do. What we wear. How we talk. How we walk. What we eat. Every mannerism, every movement, contains a coded gender language.[25]

These constructions of masculinity and femininity also regulate how race is performed and perceived. People of colour are an "other" against which gender propriety is measured. Either they are "less than," meaning not masculine or feminine enough, or they are

> simultaneously cast as hyper masculine, as sexually aggressive . . . thus black men were depicted as rampaging sexual beasts, women carnivorously carnal, and gay men as sexually insatiable. . .[26]

In similar ways, Asian Canadian men are represented as being asexual, and Asian Canadian women are often seen as exotic, submissive, and willing to please. Asian Canadian males are viewed as asexual because they are perceived as not conforming to how a (white) man would or ought to perform. If he is not in the image of this imaginary man, then he has to be placed outside of what is manly; that is, he is asexual. Women, on the other hand, are viewed as functioning and performing within a stricture of the object of men's desire. Women either conform to the Saint or Mother figure or become the hypersexualized Slut—the exoticized "other" who does not act how a good girl ought, which is wanting to be the object of the male gaze. In this light, the only norm against which one's gender and sexuality and their performance are measured is that of the normed dominant culture, which brings pressure to bear for gender (and through that racial) assimilation or conformity. If a racialized body is the ultimate gendered or sexualized "other," then its very existence polices what is outside the bounds of the norm. Again, the mythical but regulating norm is measured against the heteronormative, white, authentically male body. Within our classrooms, this speaks to pedagogies, school culture, and curricula.

Working with Difference and the Untidiness of Gender, Sex, and Sexuality

What might it mean to engage in a critical analysis of gendered norms, both in relation to what is occurring today, and in relation to the history and civics that are being taught? I agree with Tupper and Mouffe who call for a social studies pedagogy and curriculum that exposes the multiplicity of social relations that exist. Mouffe advocates an "articulation of an ensemble subject position, corresponding to the multiplicity of social relations in which it is inscribed."[27] One can look at social studies teaching and learning as an explicit discussion of how the multiple identities of students and teachers co-exist at any one time. This "ensemble of selves" constructs the place from which we come to understand history, geography, and other social education, as well as the relations between teachers and students, and students with each other. Often this "ensemble of selves" and positions is not taken up as part of designing, planning, or articulating teaching. If this messy space of multiple student and teacher identities and selves is acknowledged and utilized, then it is possible to look at the role of teaching as creating spaces that at the least make some room for differences as well as similarities. According to Tupper:

This means that when students engage in social studies content, they are exposed to a myriad of experiences in which the intersections of gender, race, class and culture all contribute to the experiences of citizenship. Since the way that we engage . . . depends upon the way in which we understand our own subjectivities . . . [28]

However, utilizing or inviting unessentialized categories of gender makes meanings and understandings messy and complicated. The end result of the knowledges created in this manner is often uncertain, and this can be difficult and scary for instructors. One example of an issue that is useful to disrupt the "naturalness" of biological sex in teacher education or secondary classrooms is to introduce an awareness of the existence of people who are intersex; that is, those who are born with "ambiguous" genitalia that cannot be categorized as identifiably male or identifiably female. An exploration such as this allows students to work with notions that if sex is not sex, might it be possible that sex, like gender, is both material and constructed, and "made" by discourse or language and its social contexts. That is, bodies become (authentically) male or female through the ways we understand physicality to be expressed and how gender is performed. Performativity is not an act or a conscious working (although it can be) of what it is to be male/masculine or female/feminine. Rather, it is within the relationship between the word "girl," and how we expect to "see" girl, and how a girl actually acts.

To return to the ideal male or female exercise, one might ask students if it is it possible to separate out which part is girl, and which part is the learned expression of girl? Which part is white, which part is a learned expression of whiteness? Or is it likely that what is female is constituted by the expression of this construction, which merely reinforces what girl or even female might be? These questions push students to formulate opinions of how the categories of girls and boys exist. Can we allow for an exploration of how gender is not male *or* female, but male *and* female, in addition to intersex, and the yet-to-be-named, future understandings of Self, Other and identity?

Engaging with intersectionality

How else might we explore the ways normative functions of gender, sex, and sexuality run through the history and politics of Canada? What messages do students receive from the texts that are used in social studies courses? How might students be aided in understanding a complex reading of gender as moving beyond curricular adding-on of the contributions of women (bracketed off into boxes here and there)? What is left as normative in the classroom? What is identified as normative, and how might students be encouraged to engage with the normative? When I was teaching at the high school level, a number of colleagues and I assigned students the task of exploring and engaging with the myriad points of view within their own class and from the perspective of the text. Students were asked to come up with criteria through which they felt they could better understand how race, sexuality, gender, and ability were discussed or ignored in the texts. In my class, I asked students to construct these criteria with a focus on intersectionality, as well as the area or areas that held the most interest for them. Students found designing criteria very difficult. They assumed that setting standards that they could call fair and unbiased, or inclusive, would be straightforward. In many of their minds, it was merely a matter of textbook authors having the desire to offer more inclusive and complicated accounts. Attempting to design their own criteria helped them to better understand why textbooks are constructed in a relatively constrained fashion. My colleagues and I encouraged students to present their criteria to their classmates for critical feedback. Student criteria ranged from simply "evidence of women's contribution," "attempting to address or acknowledge traditional silences in curriculum," and "examples of disrupting traditional male and female roles," to attempts to engage with intersectionality by utilizing "evidence of analysis that race and gender are interrelated," "understanding that local context impacts intersections and ramifications of policy concerning race and gender," and "applying mixed notions of male, female, gay, queer, not queer as important to understanding how history happens." They then applied their criteria to the section of the text with which we were engaged, as well as to their own and a peer's research paper. Lastly, students were required to select a section of the text and rewrite it following the standards they had set and incorporating their points of view and those of the other student whose paper they had read.

We found that students pushed their peers harder than we might have to carefully construct criteria that could be useful, and they avoided essentializing notions of gender and race. Students generally found that heteronormativity was not engaged in texts or peer research, and therefore even those who attempted to address the issues found themselves unable to apply the criteria. What might it mean to include an analysis of gender in social studies classrooms that takes into account the symbiotic, regulatory, and policing relationships of sexuality, sex, and heteronormativity?

Through Theory's Eyes—A Case Study of Reading of Sex and Gender through Sexuality

One method of reading texts, policies, and historical events in such a way as to problematize the "normal" is by utilizing a theory that invites an opening up of spaces where our common sense understandings of sex and sexuality, and the political, social, and historical relationships and contexts in which they function are left open, messy, and problematic. That is, we need to develop a theory that requires teaching and learning from the perspective that identities and gender are fluid and changing.

This understanding of self, whether that self is reader, researcher, teacher, or writer, requires an interrogation of both who that person is and how who she or he is influences the teaching, reading, writing, or historiography. Add to this the notion that the "who" of who you view that student, parent or colleague to be, or how they see themselves, is not stable and cannot be fixed as singularly woman, of colour, poor, student, archivist, teacher, and so on. The part(s) of one's identities forefronted on any particular day, or in any particular reading or performance, is variable and ever-changing. Now think

of a child sitting in a second grade classroom, a child who looks like most of the other children in the classroom. Her behaviour and actions mirror those of her peers. She is similar to them, but she also holds a significant part of who she is at home apart from her school self, because she has learned through the hidden and explicit curriculum that her family is unacceptable, different, odd, and fodder for teasing. While she is not only the child of parents who identify as lesbian, the fact that she does not have any positive inclusion of this self is in tension with the other identities which seem to "fit" with her peers. Yet there is nothing that she sees, hears, or experiences that offers spaces for the tensions of who she is to be positively addressed or reinforced in the school or classroom. The theory that I find so helpful in disrupting what is termed normal (in its many guises) across myriad areas, including gender and sex, is called "queer theory." I recognize the discomfort many readers may experience in entertaining a theory called "queer" theory. While the term "queer" has been used as a pejorative, and often raises a great measure of discomfort, I would suggest that theoretically and politically it has been reclaimed as a pedagogy and theory that dislodges the requirements of fixed identities such as gay or lesbian, and subsequently heterosexual.

I ask the reader to entertain the discomfort as a productive method of reading my pedagogical and curricular suggestions. If you wish to discard this out of turn is it useful to ask why. Perhaps it is appropriate to interrogate the discomfort, not as an avenue to talk about sex in the elementary classroom, but as an example of how gender functions within and amongst sexuality and sex. A theory that questions our common sense notions of what exists in relation to an acceptance of gender policing and sexuality might be fruitful for instructors at all levels.

I am arguing that queer theory offers readings of gender at an early age: questioning how this girl is positioned (Will she be gay or straight? Does she have (or need) male role models?), and how her experiences might be productively accepted as similar to and different from those of her peers. Understanding that sexuality and gender exist within their classroom might open up spaces for her peers to see an acceptance of fluid notions of self and family. Canadian curriculum theorists Brent Davis and Dennis Sumara state:

> Bridged to the work of curriculum theory, queer theory asks that the forms of curriculum and relations to pedagogy be appropriated as sites to interpret the particularities of the perceived differences among persons, not merely among categories of persons. "Queer" is not meant as a signifier that represents gay, lesbian, bisexual, and transgendered identities . . . so doing, the possibilities for what might count as knowledge are broadened—not just knowledge about sexuality, but knowledge about how forms of desire are inextricable from processes of perception, cognition and interpretation.[29]

Making use of queer theory in a social studies context invites an opening up of spaces where our common-sense understandings of gender, sex, and sexuality are left open, messy, and productively problematic. For teachers, the fluidity of selves demands this and affords a possibility of discussing sexuality as a site of social change in ways that demand the intersectionality of races, genders, and sexualities. The implementation of queer theory is not a call to speak to sex or sex acts in the classroom. Nor is queer theory a call for the classroom to *become* gendered and (hetero)sexualized. It is, rather, a tool to uncover and analyze how the classroom is already sexualized and heterosexualized.[30] No longer is the notion of who or what is gay, black, able, and so on fixed or universal. Daunting though it may be, queer theory also encourages interrogation of all categories around which we seem drawn to organize. It is the work of these theories to disrupt the uncritical usage of categories and labeling, and to require interrogation of when these constructions are useful and when they further stereotype or merely encourage a lack of complexity in favour of ease of understanding. That is, questioning the easiness of placing individuals, events, and solutions into established categories that make solutions and understandings more straightforward.

Employing queer theory and pedagogies points teachers and students towards fluid, partial, and decidedly queer notions of gender, race, class, sexuality, and (dis)ability. Pedagogies such as I am attempting to describe might also address the needs of queer students of colour and other marginalized students in different ways. That is, schools often assume/presume that queerly identified students are "othered" primarily based on their sexual orientation. A pedagogy such as I am advocating would acknowledge and explore the ways students cannot silence one identity in order to ultimately foreground another. As noted above, gender is regulated by and through sexuality and the fear of being labeled "other." Recognizing the usefulness of fluidity and the blurring of constructions requires that teachers interrupt the "normal" of heterosexuality; therefore gender and sex are called into question because normal is no longer a useful or singularly "real" construct.

By uncovering and questioning the "normal" and *why* we construct us/them, normal/abnormal within textbooks, other curricular materials, and discussions, we alter the pace of "normal" within classroom spaces. By questioning, for example, how heteronormativity functions, the power of heteronormativity is lessened and gender ideals become more open to disruption—and broader sets of behaviours and performances are deemed allowable.

I am supporting an approach to pedagogy based upon parallel and intersecting streams involving race, sexuality, class, gender, (dis)ability, and so on. Single issue conversations, such as having one day to speak to or read about gay, lesbian, and bisexual issues or one-shot inclusions of African Canadian, First Nations, Asian Canadian, and Indo Canadian perspectives are much easier than incorporating ongoing interrogations of how sex, sexuality, heteronormativity, and race are intertwined. Without creating pedagogical intersections, it is easy to utilize the tidier and more boundaried categorical identifications. That is, by falling back on the white/Black, gay/straight binaries we leave little room to make visible complicated renderings that can invite more complex understandings. Yet, there is often formidable resistance to working with race and sexuality independently, much less interconnectedly.

As instructors, we have to employ new techniques and engage in conversations that compel us and our students to work towards understandings of the interconnectedness of many identities. These constructions, as complex and untidy as they are to dissect, are helpful in encouraging multiple perspectives and multiple considerations of gender in social studies.

Endnotes

[1]   Margaret Smith Crocco, "The Missing Discourse About Gender and Sexuality in the Social Studies," *Theory into Practice* 40, no. 1 (2001), 66.

[2]   Michael Warner, ed., *Fear of a Queer Planet: Queer Politics and Social Theory*, Cultural Politics Series, vol. 6 (Minneapolis: University of Minnesota Press, 1993), xxi.

[3]   Dennis Sumara and Brent Davis, "Interrupting Heteronormativity: Toward a Queer Curriculum Theory," *Curriculum Inquiry* 29, no. 2 (1999): 193.

[4]   A more detailed explanation of "add-and-stir" is introduced in a later section. Suffice to say, add-and-stir models are those that insert multicultural curricular content into already established lessons without altering the purposes of the lessons or unit.

[5]   I am cognizant of the limitations of this list, in terms of both repeating the very categories I am attempting to blur and its omissions. The complex issue of disability, for example, is not addressed in this paper; therefore, I chose not to include it in the laundry list of oppressions.

[6]   Ann Oakley, *Sex, Gender and Society* (London: Maurice Temple Smith, 1972).

[7]   Deborah P. Britzman, *Lost Subjects, Contested Objects: Toward a Psychoanalytic Inquiry of Learning* (Albany, NY: State University of New York Press, 1998), and Judith P. Butler, *Bodies That Matter: On the Discursive Limits of "Sex"* (New York: Routlege, 1993).

[8]   Butler, *Bodies That Matter*; ———, *Gender Trouble: Feminism and the Subversion of Identity*, Thinking Gender Series (New York: Routledge, 1990).

[9]   Peggy Orenstein, *Schoolgirls: Young Women, Self-Esteem, and the Confidence Gap* (New York: Doubleday, 1994); and Myra Sadker and David Sadker, *Failing at Fairness: How America's Schools Cheat Girls* (New York: C. Scribner's & Sons, 1994).

[10]   Wanda Hurren, "Gender Issues within the Discursive Spaces of Social Studies Education," *Canadian Social Studies* 36, no. 3 (Spring 2002), www.quasar.ualberta/css/Css_36_3/ARgender_issues_within_the_discursive_spaces.html.

[11]   Jane Gaskell and Sandra Taylor, "The Women's Movement in Canadian and Australian Education: From Liberation and Sexism to Boys and Social Justice," *Gender and Education* 15, no. 2 (2003).

[12]   Ibid., 152.

[13]   Christine Griffin, "Discourses of Crisis and Loss: Analysing the 'Boys' Underachievement' Debate," *Journal of Youth Studies* 3, no. 2 (2000); and Elaine Millard, *Differently Literate: Boys, Girls, and the Schooling of Literacy* (London: Falmer, 1997).

[14]   Griffin, "Discourses of Crisis and Loss"; Lynn Raphael Reed, "Troubling Boys and Disturbing Discourses on Masculinity and Schooling: A Feminist Exploration of the Current Debates and Interventions Concerning Boys in School," *Gender and Education* 11, no. 1 (1999).

[15]   Ibid.

[16]   Christine Griffin, "Discourses of Crisis and Loss."

[17]   R.W. Connell, *The Men and the Boys* (Cambridge, UK: Polity Press, 2000).

[18]   Crocco, "The Missing Discourse About Gender and Sexuality," 66.

[19]   Jennifer Tupper, "The Gendering of Citizenship in Social Studies Curriculum," *Canadian Social Studies* 36, no. 3 (Spring 2002), www.quasar.ualberta/css/Css_36_3/ARgendering_of_citizenship.html.

[20]   Nel Noddings, "Social Studies and Feminism," in *The Social Studies Curriculum: Purposes, Problems, and Possibilities*, ed. E. Wayne Ross (Albany, NY: State University of New York Press, 1997), 59.

[21]   Ibid.

[22]   Michael S. Kimmel, "Masculinity as Homophobia: Fear, Shame and the Silence in the Construction of Gender Identity," in *Readings for Diversity and Social Justice: An Anthology on Racism, Sexism, AntiSemitism, Heterosexism, Ableism, and Classism*, ed. Maurianne Adams et al. (New York: Routledge, 2000), 215.

[23]   Debbie Epstein, "Keeping Them in Their Place: Hetero/Sexist Harassment, Gender and the Enforcement of Heterosexuality," in *Sex, Sensibility, and the Gendered Body*, ed. Janet Holland and Lisa Adkins (London: Macmillan, 1996); and Crocco, "The Missing Discourse About Gender."

[24]   Butler, *Bodies That Matter*.

[25]   Kimmel, "Masculinity as Homophobia," 216.

[26]   Ibid., 217.

[27]   Chantal Mouffe, "Feminism, Citizenship and Radical Democratic Politics," in *Feminists Theorize the Political*, ed. Joan W. Scott (New York: Routledge, 1992), 376, cited in Tupper, "The Gendering of Citizenship," 376.

[28]   Tupper, "The Gendering of Citizenship."

[29]   Sumara and Davis, "Interrupting Heteronormativity," 192.

[30]   Ibid.

CHAPTER 13

Education for Peace-building Citizenship

Teaching the Dimensions of Conflict Resolution in Social Studies[‡]

Kathy Bickmore

Peace in the twenty-first century is elusive and fragile indeed. New and recurrent patterns of conflict and violence, coupled with globalized mass communications, shake the very foundations of citizenship, and therefore of social studies education. Affluence, non-belligerence, non-dominance, and luck have protected Canada from experiencing a major act of war on our own soil in recent generations. Yet the September 11, 2001 terrorist assaults on the United States—and subsequent wars "of" and "on" terrorism in Afghanistan, Iraq, Israel/Palestine, and elsewhere—have made evident the eroding sense of security of citizens in "peaceful" nations, as well as the appalling insecurity endured by many other world citizens. Changes in the practice of war-making have made civilians, even children and those whose governments are supposedly not at war, targets more and more frequently. The perception of children as targets is not limited to political conflicts: news media are also saturated with reports of bullying, abductions, and murders of children. Spectacle-oriented global instant news technology and urbanized postmodern culture bring the news directly to young people, increasingly without buffers. Our small warring world keeps becoming more tightly knit together, and even children in relatively peaceful places like Canada cannot be unaffected. Recog-

nizing this problem, and facing it as a learning opportunity, is crucial if social studies is to be relevant and effective in the twenty-first century.

This chapter is about how social studies teachers can help young people to develop their capacities for building a more robust, democratic, stable peace in a world that includes global and local violence and terrorism. I will begin by explaining a few key terms, and then outline the challenges and opportunities that peace and conflict theory offers to social studies educators.

Conflict refers to disagreements or problems that emerge due to incompatible interests (wants and needs). Difference does not necessarily imply conflict: some differences are entirely compatible, adding diversity and vibrancy to community life. However, when fulfilling the wants or needs of one person or group seems to be at the expense of meeting somebody else's interests, then there is conflict. Conflict can be handled in myriad ways. It should not be confused with violence—the damaging manner in which some conflicts are handled. Violence often points to (underlying) conflict, but it is a symptom. Conflict resolution refers to the processes of seeking to understand conflicts and their sources and to non-violently resolve human problems (it is not merely the endpoint of dispute settlement).

Conflicts show us who we are. As young people grow up, they develop their sense of personal identity in relation to their agreements and disagreements with what others want, believe, and choose to do. Standing up for one's beliefs in the face of conflict-

[‡] Parts of a much earlier version of this chapter were published in "Canada and the World: One Year After 9/11," a theme issue of *Canadian Issues/Thèmes canadiens* (September 2002): 19–23.

ing pressures, in fact, can be a defining moment in a person's development.

Citizenship represents identity on a social scale—who are "we," with what groups and nations do I share common cause? Again, conflict is a key organizing principle. To act as a democratic citizen is to participate in expression, debate, and deliberation about different viewpoints—the balancing of different interests—to make joint decisions. For example, debates and deliberations about whether and how Canada should participate in the so-called war on terrorism, or about national and domestic security measures, involve citizens in both intra-national and international conflict management. Social studies must prepare young people to understand and to participate in managing these types of conflicts.

Conflict and conflict resolution have always been important in social studies. Critical thinking (the capacity to analyze and evaluate conflicting viewpoints, assumptions, or discrepant evidence) is deeply associated with the purposes of many academic subject areas, especially social studies.[1] Geographers, politicians, lawyers, political scientists, economists, historians, and sociologists are considered experts when they have the capacity to manage the various social conflict questions and problems relevant to their disciplines. But ordinary citizens are also involved in managing conflict: the inevitable conflicts and controversies that constitute democratic life. Openly discussing such conflicts and controversial issues in social studies classrooms generates more student interest, more knowledge of, and more intention to participate in citizen political activity.[2] Thus social studies, both as preparation for citizenship as well as for possible future work in social sciences, depends upon conflict resolution education. Conflict resolution education prepares students to recognize, interpret, and analyze conflicting interests, to develop and persuasively articulate viewpoints on conflictual questions, to listen to and reason thoughtfully about the viewpoints of others, to invent and evaluate solution options, and to employ conflict management and negotiation procedures.

Democratic governance and participation processes—ensuring equitable access and rights, regulating the exchange of resources, and other collective decision-making—are mechanisms for peaceful conflict resolution in that they are processes for moving towards joint decisions or problem-solving. Democratic deliberation and passionate debate, although they often do not result in simple agreements, are important ingredients of conflict resolution processes. Democratic structures provide procedural protections to enhance equitable and inclusive attention to diverse viewpoints in these processes. Democratization is an essential element of peace-building, and peace-building is an equally essential prerequisite for democracy.[3]

Paradoxically the modern nation-state was developed and consolidated through its monopoly on the use of force. In exchange for (real or imagined) security in the face of war and violent crime, citizens cede authority to states. The current threats of conflict polarization globally and domestically, terrorism, and violence threaten precisely because they operate within our communities and nation-states, highlighting the dilemma of how governments might maintain security without unduly repressing equity and freedom. Citizens negotiate, through governments, the rules by which rights and differences are mediated and regulated, attempting to balance security with inclusivity.[4] In short, peace is built upon active democracy and democratization, and thus upon informed citizenship; therefore education for peace-building is citizenship education. It is a key purpose of social studies to provide opportunities for young people to learn how to become competent participants in the effective and equitable management of conflict and violence in their societies.

Preparation to Handle the Dimensions of Conflict

Peace, to be real and sustained, requires vibrant activity, not absence of conflict. Among diverse human beings in complex and shifting environments, conflict (although not necessarily violence) is a constant. From peace and conflict theory we can derive four dimensions of conflict, all of them relevant to social studies education. The two most basic dimensions of any conflict are the substance of what the conflict is about—the differing wants and needs of stakeholders—and the relationship—the degree of (inter)dependence, power balance, and (dis)equilibrium among stakeholders.[5] Cutting across those two dimensions are the processes for managing conflict (prevailing practices and mechanisms that may be available to facilitate resolution), and the availability of resources (to fulfill stakeholders' wants and needs, to improve the relationship, and/or to facilitate the conflict resolution process itself).

Weakness in any of these four dimensions of conflict—a lack of capability to communicate about or reinvent the substance of the conflict to better meet participants' interests; discriminatory or fractured relationships; inaccessible or unfair conflict management processes; and/or scarcity or inequitable distribution of resources—tends to make conflict more frequent, intense, protracted, and harmful (see Figure 1). In these contexts, governments tend to rely heavily on coercive mechanisms—such as surveillance, police, and military—for keeping a minimal peace. An overreliance on coercive peacekeeping can be a threat to democracy because it sacrifices freedom and broad decision-making participation in exchange for social order.

Since in human life problems and disagreements are inevitable, societies and citizens prepare for peace by preparing to handle conflict justly and non-violently. Peace-building involves attention to each of the dimensions of conflict, as needed. A key dimension of peace-building is to create, implement, and make accessible an array of processes for handling conflicts—including legislatures, courts, security systems, unions and labour laws, facilitators and mediators, and more. Second, since healthy, reliable, balanced, democratic relationships—communication, engagement, and equitable interaction among individuals and social groups—are a key dimension of conflict resolution, repairing or nurturing those relationships is a key dimension of peace-building. Third, since so many conflicts are about wants and needs, mechanisms for developing, protecting, and justly distributing resources can ensure that more people's needs are met, more of the time, to prevent and de-escalate (reduce the scope of) many conflicts. Resources include those that sustain citizens' lives (including basics such as food and clean water), and those that help to manage the difficult conflicts that do occur (such as reliable sources of information and conflict resolution centres). Fourth, we can't predict

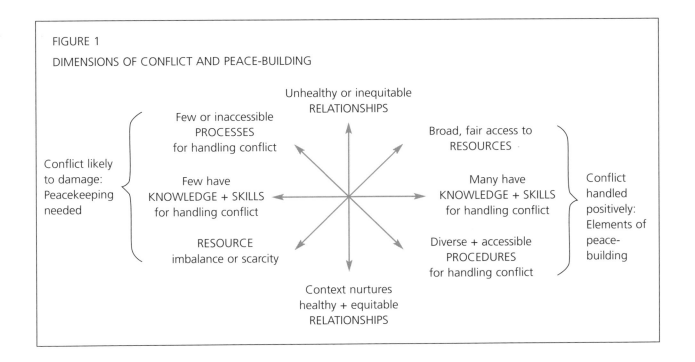

FIGURE 1

DIMENSIONS OF CONFLICT AND PEACE-BUILDING

the exact wants and needs at stake in every conflict, but we can ensure that citizens learn generalizable concepts, knowledge, and skills for understanding and communicating about conflict, so that they will have the capacity to understand and handle the conflicts that occur in their personal and political lives.

The content and skills of social studies have an extremely important contribution to make to all of these dimensions of peace-building. Social studies prepares young people to understand conflict and to recognize, use, evaluate, and facilitate conflict resolution processes; to understand and develop healthy and equitable relationships with diverse local and global neighbours; to competently manage questions of development, protection, use, and allocation of resources; and to analyze and communicate about interpersonal, social, and political conflicts.

Social Education for Peace-building Citizenship

People learn through experience, as much as through planned lessons. Thus in education for peace-building citizenship, learners' implicit awareness and competence are developed through modelling and practice as they participate in decision-making and problem-solving processes and in their relationships within and between the cultures, communities, and individuals around them. The roles, relationships, and approaches to conflict demonstrated in classroom and school discipline, in family and peer relations, and in popular culture are powerful socializers because they are pervasive, and because (by virtue of being implicit) they are often taken for granted, not questioned.

However, this powerful social context does not imply that social studies is unimportant. First, those implicit roles and relationships are practised in social studies class, as much as anywhere else. Second, explicit knowledge and skills for handling conflict are an essential complement and safety net for implicit learning through practice. Because human minds rely on language for understanding, practice without thoughtful naming and reflection would be uncritical, inaccessible, and not easily adapted to new

situations or needs. The lived curriculum of school discipline and governance, resource use, and human inclusion and exclusion educates hand in hand with the peace and conflict topics in the formal curriculum.

The formal curriculum, especially in social studies, provides the opportunity to develop autonomous competence in concepts and skills—to make sense of various kinds of conflict and violence, to develop awareness of alternative perspectives, and to choose and implement effective approaches to resolving such challenges. Peace-building citizenship education does not necessarily require adding a great deal of new curriculum content. It's more about clarifying and using the conflict-related learning opportunities that are already embedded in what and how we teach, including problem-posing and -solving processes, critical analysis of societal relationships and resource concerns, methods of inquiry, communication, and deliberation. The remainder of this chapter examines how social studies teaching might best build students' capacities for each of the four dimensions of peace-building in citizenship education.

Conflict Management Processes

The culture and regulations of any community, school, and classroom provide a pattern of opportunities, processes, and implicit knowledge for managing conflict, which make the difference in whether tensions escalate into violence. The array of possibilities for managing conflict and violence form a continuum from relatively short-term intervention approaches (peacekeeping) to medium-term dispute resolution approaches (peacemaking) to relatively long-term restorative and prevention approaches (peace-building). The continuum ranges from one-dimensional (peacekeeping alone) to increasingly multidimensional (peace-building, which tends to include peacemaking and some peacekeeping elements in a comprehensive whole). Peacekeeping (containment), peacemaking (resolution), and peace-building (problem-solving and restoration to alleviate underlying causes of violence) are all essential elements of making peace, in the world and in educational settings (see Figure 2). Peace-building is particularly well suited to the relatively safe and long-range time horizon of school environments. Unfortunately, it is also often the most ignored component of education for peace in schools.

Contrary to the impression given by the mass media, the incidence of violence among North American young people has not increased in recent years.[6] However, restrictive and punitive approaches to discipline in schools (peacekeeping) are increasingly prevalent.[7] Unfortunately, school discipline practices often disproportionately punish less-affluent and non-white students.[8] Similar racialized

biases in our formal legal system have been especially visible in anti-crime and counterterrorist security measures, especially since September 11, 2001.[9] Children learn about conflict management, obedience, and social differentiation from their experiences with these processes, in and out of school. Replacing punitive and inequitable discipline procedures with initiatives for student learning through participation in problem-solving—such as student governance, negotiation and deliberation opportunities, and conflict mediation—can improve students' capacity to handle differing viewpoints and their interest in engaging in school.[10]

Some of the most-studied conflict resolution

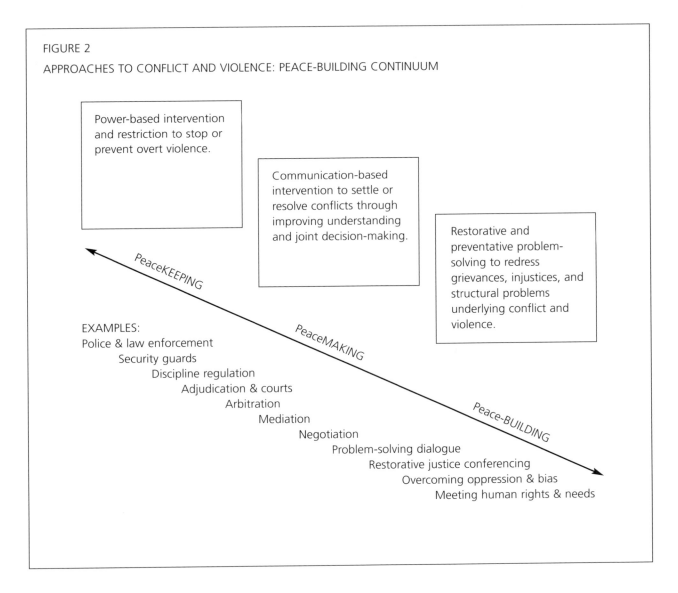

FIGURE 2

APPROACHES TO CONFLICT AND VIOLENCE: PEACE-BUILDING CONTINUUM

Power-based intervention and restriction to stop or prevent overt violence.

Communication-based intervention to settle or resolve conflicts through improving understanding and joint decision-making.

Restorative and preventative problem-solving to redress grievances, injustices, and structural problems underlying conflict and violence.

PeaceKEEPING

PeaceMAKING

Peace-BUILDING

EXAMPLES:
Police & law enforcement
Security guards
Discipline regulation
Adjudication & courts
Arbitration
Mediation
Negotiation
Problem-solving dialogue
Restorative justice conferencing
Overcoming oppression & bias
Meeting human rights & needs

education programs are alternative dispute resolution (peacemaking) procedures that complement discipline systems in schools. In most of these programs, a small number of students are trained as peer facilitators or mediators; the other students learn by observing and participating in this peer-facilitated negotiation process when they need help managing their own day-to-day conflicts. Where implemented equitably and fully enough to affect patterns of conflict management in the school, such programs have been shown to improve students' understandings of non-violent conflict resolution, their social conflict behaviour, and their constructive engagement with school.[11] Peer conflict mediation programs can reduce the absences and distraction from academic tasks that arise from unresolved disputes, and also encourage practice of academically relevant skills such as communication, paraphrasing, evaluating alternatives, predicting consequences, and problem-solving. Thus, well-implemented programs can be associated with strengthened academic achievement.[12] Peer mediation is neither sufficient as a sole approach to student conflict education, nor effective for every conflict, such as power-imbalanced harassment situations.[13] However, research demonstrates the valuable contribution of student participation in autonomous peer conflict management as part of a comprehensive peace-building education.

Other forms of self-governance that involve a similar range of conflict skills, such as class meetings and student government, would be similarly beneficial.[14] Beyond peer-facilitated conflict negotiation (mediation), other classroom strategies for handling interpersonal and community conflicts include peacemaking circles (also known as community or family group conferencing) and class meetings.[15] Some Canadian school boards offer some such active learning opportunities as part of the social studies curriculum; in other cases, these opportunities are extra-curricular (supported more informally by social studies teachers). In provinces such as Ontario, where budget cuts have precipitated curriculum narrowing and/or work-to-rule labour conflicts with teachers, the learning opportunities embedded in regular classroom activity and the for-credit curriculum stand a better chance of being sus-

tained and reaching a wider range of students. Alberta's current social studies curriculum for grades 4 and 6 expects students to learn to cooperate, respect others' viewpoints, and solve group problems; Saskatchewan's (1995 and 1999) curriculum for grades 1, 3, 5, 9 and 10 teaches the relationship among needs and wants, decision-making, and conflict resolution at personal and later at political levels.

Because the curricula embody many examples of meaningful human conflict, social studies classrooms are ideal settings to develop young people's understanding of key elements of conflict and their competence in identifying and applying conflict resolution choices. Practice for democratic peace-building does not necessarily mean complete practice of democracy. Teachers' expertise gives them special decision-making responsibility; therefore the classroom majority does not rule and the leader is not elected. Also, since school is compulsory, students cannot choose to participate or not.[16] Nonetheless, social studies classrooms can teach and offer regular opportunities for students to practise many of the roles and skills that are components of "civil peace"—thoughtful, equitable, non-violent analysis and decision-making in the context of diversity.[17] Such deliberations can involve interpersonal relations and discipline matters in the classroom community.[18] At least as important, however, students and teachers can examine the key conflicts and controversies of social and political life in the wide world—the subject matter and the raison d'être of social studies education.[19] As mentioned above, it is in the relatively few classrooms that include open and inclusive discussions of controversial issues that students develop knowledge, interest, and a sense of personal efficacy in citizenship participation.[20]

Multicultural, Anti-bias, and Global Education

Because the relationship among the participants influences conflict as much as does the substance of the dispute, conflicts with various people (e.g. one's nearest and dearest, a passing stranger, a powerful supervisor or bully, or someone from a misunderstood cultural background) evolve differently. Multicultural societies such as we have in Canada present unique opportunities for learning to (re)build resilient, equitable relationships across the boundaries of difference that often divide the world. It is not that we are one big, happy family: serious conflicts and inequities persist in Canada.[21] However, citizen action has created policies and community practices such as multiculturalism, hate crime sanctions, and the Charter of Rights and Freedoms that help to reshape our relationships, and to improve and ensure respectful coexistence.[22] For example, there were outbursts of hostile incidents against Arabs, Muslims, and Jews in Canada after September 11, 2001 and during the U.S.-led coalition's war with Iraq, but at the same time there was strong condemnation of such hateful actions, and some attempts at redress, from both ordinary citizens and those in authority.[23] Social studies content, inquiry, and interaction encourage students to become familiar with diverse peoples, cultures, and political perspectives, and to relate these to current, historic, and geographically distant human events and concerns, thus helping students to overcome the biases that are rooted in ignorance.

Key concepts for peace-building relationships that should be embedded in social studies teaching include bias, social construction of gender and ethnic/racial identities, and global (inter)dependence.[24] For example, British Columbia's 1998 social studies curriculum for grade 5 emphasizes concepts of fairness in relation to federal and provincial human rights and ombudsperson legislation. The Atlantic provinces' curriculum includes a culture and diversity strand, evidenced for example in Nova Scotia's grade 6 examination of multiculturalism in relation to settlement and grade 7 and 8 units on responsive government. Interactive pedagogies such as readers' theatre and simulations, combined with thoughtful preparation and debriefing of roles and concepts, can illuminate diverse perspectives and the interests that underlie them, sources of power, and opportunities for addressing inequity problems.

Public schools are among the first places where children work together and share public space with their diverse neighbours. It is a challenge, but also a strength, of social studies classes that they are most often heterogeneous (rather than segregated into unequal streamed classes). As such, they present particularly good opportunities for young people to learn to develop healthy, equitable, and inclusive relationships with people of different origins, religions, economic statuses, and cultural backgrounds.[25] Unfortunately, schools and classrooms are often organized in ways that actually encourage social competition, bullying, and exclusion.[26] To encourage respectful cooperative interaction and recognition of diverse abilities requires reorganization of the ways we do academic grouping and tasks, and training to facilitate students' cooperative learning work.[27] As with any other learning, students are more likely to talk and work together effectively when they are explicitly trained and held accountable for respectful cooperative interaction. Certain curriculum and teaching strategies also can effectively reduce bias and intolerance.[28] Schools and classrooms do not have a uniformly good record in nurturing peaceful relationships, but there is clear evidence that they can do so.

Relationship rebuilding requires practice, i.e. concrete action. Paradoxically, "feet first" behaviour change probably influences attitude change more often than "hearts and minds" attitude change causes behaviour change.[29] Simple contact is not enough, and in fact can reinforce prejudices and hostilities if interactions are not equitable and safe. However, well-designed programs of peace-building communication among members of conflicting groups can help them to unlearn hostility and prejudice, provided these experiences involve close, prolonged, and frequent contact, cooperation towards common goals, and equalized status among participants.[30] Rebuilding hurt relationships in the wake of the intolerance reawakened by war requires carefully sustained collaborative action. In order to create safe and effective educational opportunities for children, adults, too, must cooperate across the differences that have divided us.

Social studies for peace-building citizenship education examines human diversity, including particular global and local conflicts, their contexts, and their participants. Bland multicultural awareness of the contributions of people presented as "others" is not sufficient: building peace requires facing deep differences, felt enmities, and the roots of disagreements. For example, the 1998 British Columbia curriculum for grade 4 has students compare various Aboriginal and European perspectives on first contact and settlement. New Brunswick's 1983 social studies curriculum for grades 7 and 8 foregrounds conflicts over Aboriginal and other human rights, rebellion and revolution, discrimination, and suffrage in relation to understanding responsive government.

The particular problems and players in conflict will change in our students' lifetimes, but today's preoccupations nonetheless present concepts and skill-building opportunities that will be useful in the future. Overcoming ignorance and bias against Muslims, including the 18 percent of Muslims who are Arab, is important in its own right and as a currently relevant example of education for tolerance.[31] Perhaps the contradictions embodied in the Christian, Caucasian, and male identities of other terrorists—such as the boys who gunned down their peers in Taber, Alberta, and other schools; David Koresh of the Waco incident; Timothy McVeigh of the Oklahoma City courthouse incident; or various anti-abortion murderers—also deserve more thoughtful attention. Most Canadian provinces address such conflicts mainly in secondary grades. In addition to upper secondary courses in world issues and international politics, particular human rights and conflict concerns are also addressed in identity-based courses such as Aboriginal Studies (in many provinces), Holocaust Studies (New Brunswick), and African Canadian and Mi'kmaq Studies (Nova Scotia). This is a start, but if these key concepts were also previewed in elementary grades they would likely be more effective. Fairness is a particular interest of young children. Consistent and well-supported practice with questions of justice and dialogue across serious differences would give school meaning, as well as provide a foundation for cognitive and social/moral development. It is an ongoing process to develop understanding of the identities and viewpoints of unfamiliar others, nearby and across the world.

Development and Distribution of Resources

Resource scarcity, contamination of resources, and unfair exchange—whether local or global in scope—cause and exacerbate conflict and inhibit efforts at resolution. Education about development, protection, and exchange of resources is not sufficient for peace-building, but this awareness and capacity to analyze is a necessary condition. In Canada, as in other places that on average have high standards of living, many citizens are not very conscious of the world's rapidly increasing gap between the "haves" and "have-nots." Meanwhile, modern mass communications have made that gap appallingly obvious to those experiencing relative deprivation. There is no greater source of global conflict and violence than this resource gap and the ingenuity gaps it exacerbates.[32] Conflicts are often filtered through particular ideologies and identity interpretations, but underlying resource interests cause or exacerbate many of the most protracted social conflicts.[33] An important dimension of peace-building citizenship education is to help Canadian children understand twenty-first-century processes of global resource development and trade, and the poverty, disease, war, and terrorism that are the deadly consequences of the current inequitable exchange. Only awareness can unleash the creative ingenuity needed to overcome these problems in our fragile world system.

Geography and economics offer frameworks for examining questions of resources, development, and other conflicts rooted in space and/or capital exchange. For example, the question of where to locate a subway line or a landfill requires geographic and economic concepts such as population density, supply/demand, comparative advantage, and human/environment interaction. Particularly relevant in the wake of September 2001 and the Iraq war is knowledge about the geopolitics of global resources and trade, and especially our own energy consumption and oil interests in the Middle East. This subject is often inadequately covered, although the Atlantic provinces' 1998 grade 9 course, Atlantic Canada in the Global Community, and Quebec's 1988 Secondary V course on twentieth-century history do address contemporary geopolitics. Applying geopolitical concepts to examples of real conflict (and the associated democratic decision-making processes) gives them life and meaning.[34] Immigration and trade policies, pollution, and energy conservation likewise apply, develop, and make relevant the key ideas of economics and geography.[35] Geography skills such as thematic mapping and skills such as graphing and prediction, used in both geography and economics, also facilitate conflict analysis. Social studies aims to help even young students find their place in the physical and social world. For example, Ontario's 1998 curriculum for grade 2, Manitoba's 1982 curriculum for grade 4, and Newfoundland's 1978 curricula for grades 4 and 6 social studies expect children to understand similarities and differences in the ways communities around the world meet their needs. British Columbia's 1998 curricula for grades 6 and 7 encourage comparison of different political and cultural systems, and the associated social expectations such as gender roles.

Peace-building itself requires resources. The allocation of resources to basic education, as well as to peace-building citizenship education in particular, makes social inclusion and sustainable violence reduction possible.[36] In some Canadian provinces, including Ontario, such educational resources are still today denied to children whose parents' legal immigration status is unclear.[37] Such a denial deepens social divisions and puts our society, and these children most of all, at risk. School system quality (over-all opportunities) and equity (reduced disparity between most and least successful) are directly associated with reduced levels of violence.[38] Children learn what their society and government value by observing where tangible resources are placed and which learning resources are valued. In schools, resources for competitive assessment, regulation, enforcement, and punishment seem to outweigh those for pro-active relationship-building and problem-solving learning activities.

Knowledge and skills for handling conflict

Peace-building citizenship education will be best served by multiple guided opportunities in classrooms to model and encourage tangible practice of non-violent conflict management processes, healthy and equitable relationships, and development and fair distribution of resources. At the same time, citizens' capacity for such peace-building depends upon their development of awareness, understanding, and skills for making sense of conflict, violence, and alternatives. There is a continuous interdependence between problem-posing and problem-solving. As Freire states, "The unfinished character of [humans] and the transformational character of reality necessitate that education be an ongoing activity."[39] The development of conflict knowledge—in concert with new patterns of behaviour—is an important dimension of peace-building that belongs in the social studies classroom. Classroom lessons can and should face the real-life conflicts that make social studies worth knowing.

The content of social studies, especially politics and history, offers opportunities to engage students in practising for democratic peace-building citizenship through guided analysis and discussion of various examples of conflict. For example, history offers opportunities to systematically study different participants and viewpoints about intergroup relations and decision-making. Social studies curricula often address federalism and nation-building conflicts faced by John A. Macdonald or in the Québec Act; conflicts in settler-Aboriginal and settler-immigrant relations including the cases of Louis Riel and Oka; and domestic equity issues raised in the rebellions of 1837 or the Charter of Rights and Freedoms.[40] In addition, skills for peace-building are fostered by interpreting points of view in political cartoons or primary sources, researching interests underlying stakeholder claims, and practising persuasive advocacy writing. For example, students can create political cartoons about an historical issue or compare/contrast roles and issues between a current political cartoon and an historical conflict—thereby articulating and consolidating their understandings of alternate points of view, the meanings and uses of symbols, sources of power and persuasion, and so forth. Also, teachers can guide students' attention to the historical roots of contemporary conflicts, such as in British Columbia's 1997 grade 9 social studies curriculum and Alberta's 1990 grade 10 social studies curriculum, which discuss alternate solutions to issues.[41]

While it is true that schooling needs constantly to catch up with the world, there is already significant space for peace-building citizenship education in our formal curricula. For example, in the Ontario (1998) and British Columbia (1998) curricula, grade 5 children are expected to understand the rights and responsibilities of Canadians and how immigrants become Canadian citizens. By grades 7 and 8, Ontario children are expected to examine conflicting viewpoints regarding historical issues and to understand factors including social movements that contribute to change in society. There is even more opportunity to practise constructive conflict resolution concepts and skills in secondary social studies curricula. The problem, of course, is that the real conflicts that make social studies relevant are often ignored or buried in overloaded menus of fragmented and oversimplified detail.[42] This cannot be blamed on recent curriculum revisions; conflict continues to underlie the major topics in the social studies, and addressing multiple viewpoints about that conflict is a good way to make social studies content comprehensible and memorable. It is worth the risk to attach the key ideas and skills of the subject matter to explicit conflicts about which reasonable people have disagreed or continue to disagree, thereby giving students guided practice in the conflict analysis, communication, and resolution skills that are essential for citizenship.

Conflict resolution skills are a natural integration point between social studies and other curriculum areas (especially language and literacy), and between academic curriculum and students' own life experiences of conflict, inside and beyond the classroom. For example, British Columbia's 1998 social studies curriculum for grades 2–3 examines the influence of mass media on citizens' and students' own thinking; Alberta's 1990 curricula for grades 6 and 8 emphasize classroom and school decision-making processes and writing from multiple viewpoints; and Ontario's 1997 language arts curriculum for grade 5 expects children to present and justify their view-

points to specific audiences and to make judgements about an author's content and viewpoint. Nearly all literature plots involve some type of conflict, so reading and writing are natural places for conflict education. By about grade 7 in language arts, as well as social studies, students across Canada are expected to respond constructively to alternative ideas or viewpoints and to express opinions confidently but without trying to dominate. Ontario's 1998 Health and Physical Education curriculum's healthy living strand includes personal safety and conflict resolution skills; for example, describing exploitative behaviours in grade 1 and identifying challenges such as conflicting opinions in their relationships with family and friends in grade 4. At the interpersonal and relatively non-controversial level, conflict concepts and skills are easily integrated into the existing curriculum, in and across many academic subjects.

To really do peace-building citizenship education, however, we also need to find a little more space for the difficult questions—those that touch upon human fears, injustices, and struggles over problem-solving. There has long been a tradition of research and practice in social studies education that advocates and prepares teachers to effectively address exciting (controversial) public issues in the classroom, but admittedly this has represented the exemplary practice of relatively few teachers, not the norm.[43] It is ironic, actually, that cherished ideals such as peace and justice attract controversy and are therefore often avoided in classrooms. Here is where the well-established fields of peace and conflict studies have the most to offer, since their conceptual frameworks, mission, and experience are based on addressing conflict and controversy in constructive, respectful, and effective ways.[44]

Education about peace, education for peace, and peace through a democratic problem-posing process in education have long and somewhat separate roots in various contexts.[45] A large part of the early work in peace studies emphasized what Johan Galtung and others call "negative peace," i.e. the goal of reducing or eliminating overt violence, war, and militarism, especially at the national and international levels.[46] Current peace studies focus on the more comprehensive notions of "positive peace" and peace-building, including not only the absence of violence but also the alleviation of underlying problems through active mechanisms for resolving conflict, protecting human rights, repairing relationships, and ensuring justice.[47] Cross-cultural, anti-bias, and international development education, rooted in civil and human rights movements, are routinely woven into this more comprehensive understanding of positive peace-building education.[48] Much of this work emphasizes the importance of instilling values and attitudes such as empathy, compassion, respect for diversity, and non-violent intentions.[49] The question, of course, is how such values might be "caught" or taught without imposition.

The other crucial strand in peace-building citizenship education that has both separate and common roots with peace education is conflict and conflict resolution studies. While education for peace inevitably confronts conflict and its management, the converse is not necessarily true. There is a huge amount of conflict resolution education material that remains resolutely apolitical (i.e., seldom challenging prevailing political arrangements) and focused on interpersonal dispute settlement.[50] Perhaps because of this less socially and politically critical stance, and the attractiveness of dispute settlement (quelling disturbance) to those in power in schools and society, conflict resolution education has had more success in becoming broadly and explicitly implemented in curricula across North America than has comprehensive peace-building education. This is worth further study and reflection. On one hand, conflict resolution is a crucial component of peace-building citizenship education, with the potential to empower young people with the skills to think for themselves and to act on their own and others' behalf. On the other hand, to handle twenty-first-century peace-building challenges such as schools torn by bullying or societies torn by war, students need opportunities to learn about global and local social and political structures, agency, and us vs. them ideologies.[51]

Gender socialization is a key element of the culture of conflict and violence: much individual as well as military violence is perpetrated by males and wrapped up in assertions of masculinity and hetero-

sexuality.[52] Unfortunately so far, prevailing peace education and social studies materials typically give substantially less constructive attention to the challenges of sexism—and the broadening (positive) acceptance of non-violent masculinities—than they do to the (also essential and underexamined) matters of race, culture, and national origin.

It is paradoxical that most of the topics and skill-building expectations that could provide opportunities for peace-building citizenship education are already included in Canadian social studies curricula, but that the biggest challenge in achieving these goals probably involves teachers' knowledge and skills, not those of our students. To teach deeply enough about conflict and conflict resolution to facilitate peace-building citizenship development, teachers need a cushion of knowledge about the anatomy of conflict and the intricacies of world political relations. Above all, teachers need experience and comfort with handling the uncertainty and controversy that are inherent in studying relevant, exciting, unsolved human problems.

Conclusion

In this terrorist era, it is more crucial than ever for young people to recognize the inevitability of conflict and the choices and opportunities it presents for solving problems. This requires learning to identify and analyze the conflicts underlying violence. It is important to understand that conflicts present choices because they can be handled in many different ways. To try to explain a problem, or to seek alternate solutions, is not to excuse a violent act. Even when hurt feelings might make retaliation seem attractive, other responses are more likely to be effective in eliminating the sources of future atrocities. Peace-building citizenship education includes vocabulary, examples, and reflection on the ways conflicts may arise, evolve, escalate, and de-escalate, and on the ways participants, bystanders, advocates, third-party peacemakers, and institutional changes can help to move conflicts away from violence and towards resolution, in the often-implicit daily practice of discipline and human relations in school, as well as in explicit social studies subject matter.[53]

War, including terrorism, and the evolving national and international institutions for conflict management and security, have changed in recent decades. There is much to examine in the social studies in order to make sense of our consequent roles as citizens. It can be daunting to teach questions that have no clear answers, but there are indeed places to begin. Even the largest and stickiest transnational problems and human rights violations can be handled effectively by non-violent citizen action.[54] More than most citizens are aware, individuals are influenced by, and influential in, social institutions such as the state, the military, and the globalized business infrastructure. We make up those social structures, and we continue to transform them.

Peace-building citizenship education can help young people to develop the capacity to think, speak, and make decisions for themselves (while at the same time respecting others' viewpoints). Democracy and innovation depend upon this capacity. Canadian curriculum guidelines do not preclude this kind of active citizenship education, but they don't encourage, guide, or allocate resources to it to the extent that is needed. It would be better to integrate peace and conflict resolution education in social studies much more fully, and earlier, rather than waiting to figure out later that we have wasted energy and ingenuity by not asking the right questions.

Mikhail Kalashnikov, inventor of the infamous AK-47 automatic rifle, said years later: "I would prefer to have invented a machine that people could use and that would help farmers with their work: for example, a lawnmower." The same article quoted Albert Einstein, whose work assisted the development of the atom bomb, as saying: "If only I had known, I should have become a watchmaker."[55]

Recent terrorist incidents and war-making around the world have offered a wake-up call. We cannot protect our children by closing our eyes, avoiding controversy, hoping that wars will be fought far away and between professional soldiers. The fragile foundations of positive peace are already beginning to exist: our responsibility is to build on those foundations an education for peace-building citizenship that can give our young people the opportunity to create, together, a less violent world.

Endnotes

[1]   See Shirley H. Engle and Anna S. Ochoa, *Education for Democratic Citizenship: Decision Making in the Social Studies* (New York: Teachers College Press, 1988); N. Houser, "Negotiating Dissonance and Safety for the Common Good: Social Education in the Elementary Classroom," *Theory and Research in Social Education* 24, no. 3 (1996): 294–312; Ken Osborne, *Teaching for Democratic Citizenship* (Toronto: Our Schools/ Our Selves Education Foundation, 1991); and A. Sears, G. Clarke, and A. Hughes, "Canadian Citizenship Education: The Pluralist Ideal and Citizenship Education for a Postmodern State," in *Civic Education Across Countries: Twenty-four National Case Studies from the IEA Civic Education Project*, ed. Judith Torney-Purta, John Schwille, and Jo-Ann Amadeo (Amsterdam: IEA, 1999), 111–135.

[2]   Carole Hahn, *Becoming Political: Comparative Perspectives on Citizenship Education* (Albany: State University of New York Press, 1998); and Judith Torney-Purta et al., *Citizenship Education in Twenty-eight Countries: Civic Knowledge and Engagement at Age Fourteen; Executive Summary* (Amsterdam: IEA, 2001), www.wam.umd.edu/~iea/.

[3]   See, for example, Kenneth D. Bush and Diana Saltarelli, eds., *The Two Faces of Education in Ethnic Conflict: Towards a Peacebuilding Education for Children* (Florence, Italy: UNICEF Innocenti Research Centre, 2000); Larry J. Fisk, "Shaping Visionaries: Nurturing Peace through Education," in *Patterns of Conflict, Paths to Peace*, ed. Larry J. Fisk and John Schellenberg (Peterborough, ON: Broadview Press, 2000), 159–193; and D. Mousseau, "Democratizing with Ethnic Divisions: A Source of Conflict?" *Journal of Peace Research* 38, no. 5 (2001): 547–567.

[4]   Janice Gross Stein, *The Cult of Efficiency* (Toronto: Anansi, 2001).

[5]   A. Curle and M. Dugan, "Peacemaking: Stages and Sequence," *Peace and Change* 8, no. 2/3 (Summer 1982): 19–28; Roger Fisher and William Ury, eds., *Getting to Yes: Negotiating Agreement Without Giving In*, 2nd ed. (New York: Penguin Books, 1991; and L. Kriesberg, "Social Conflict Theories and Conflict Resolution," *Peace and Change* 8, no. 2/3 (Summer 1982): 3–17.

[6]   K. Brooks, V. Schiraldi, and J. Ziedenberg, *Schoolhouse Hype: Two Years Later* (Washington, DC: Justice Policy Institute and Children's Law Center, April 2000); and S. Jull, "Youth Violence, Schools and the Management Question: A Discussion of Zero Tolerance and Equity in Public Schooling," *Canadian Journal of Educational Administration and Policy* 17 (2000), www.umanitoba.ca/publications/.

[7]   Canadian Press, "Suspensions Soar in Schools: Critics Are Alarmed at Trend of Punishing Young for Minor Offences," Toronto *Star*, July 22, 2002, A3.

[8]   R. Johnston, "Federal Data Highlight Disparities in Discipline," *Education Week* 19, no. 41 (June 21, 2000): 3; and Jull, "Youth Violence, Schools and the Management Question."

9   See, for example, Canadian Press, "Canada Criticized Over Minorities: UN Committee Points to Treatment of Aboriginals, Others," Toronto *Star*, August 7, 2002, A9.

10 S. Adalbjarnadottir, "Fostering Children's Social Conflict Resolutions in the Classroom: A Developmental Approach," in *Effective and Responsible Teaching*, ed. Fritz Oser, Andreas Dick, and Jean-Luc Patry (San Francisco: Jossey-Bass, 1992), 397–412; and E. Sadowsky, "Taking Part: Democracy in the Elementary School," in *Learning for Life: Moral Education Theory and Practice*, ed. Andrew Garrod (Westport, CT: Praeger, 1992), 246–262.

11 C. Cunningham et al., "The Effects of Primary Division, Student-mediated Conflict Resolution Programs on Playground Aggression," *Journal of Child Psychology and Psychiatry* 39, no. 5, (1998): 653–662; and T. Jones, "Research Supports Effectiveness of Peer Mediation," *The Fourth R* 82 (March/April 1998): 1–27.

12 K. Bickmore, "Peer Mediation Training and Program Implementation in Elementary Schools: Research Results," *Conflict Resolution Quarterly* 20, no. 2 (February 2003): 137–160.

13 K. Bickmore, "How Might Social Education Resist (Hetero)sexism? Facing the Impact of Gender and Sexual Ideology on Citizenship," *Theory and Research in Social Education* 30, no. 2 (2002): 198–216; ———, "Conflict Resolution Education: Multiple Options for Contributing to Just and Democratic Peace," in *Handbook of Conflict Management*, ed. W. Pammer and J. Killian (New York: Marcel-Dekker Publishers, 2003), 3–32; E. Opffer, "Toward Cultural Transformation: Comprehensive Approaches to Conflict Resolution," *Theory into Practice* 36, no. 1 (1997): 46–52.

14 P. Avery, "The Future of Political Participation in Civic Education," in *The Future of the Social Studies*, ed. M. Nelson (Boulder, CO: Social Science Education Consortium, 1994), 47–52; N. Danielson, "Helping Pupils to Help Themselves: Pupils' Councils and Participation," in *Toward Democratic Schooling: European Experiences*, ed. K. Jenson and S. Walker (Milton Keynes, UK: Open University Press, 1989), 151–156; M. Hepburn, "Can Schools, Teachers, and Administrators Make a Difference?" in *Democratic Education in Schools and Classrooms*, no. 70, ed. M. Hepburn (Washington, DC: NCSS, 1983), 5–29; and R. Howard and R. Kenny, "Education for Democracy: Promoting Citizenship and Critical Reasoning through School Governance," in *Learning for Life*, 210–217.

15 A. Angell, "Nurturing Democratic Community at School: A Qualitative Analysis of an Elementary Class Council" (paper presented at the annual meeting of the American Educational Research Association, New York, April 1996); J. Goodman, *Elementary Schooling for Critical Democracy* (Albany: State University of New York Press, 1992); D. Moore, "Community Conferencing for Young People in Conflict," (2003), www.mediate.com/articles/mooreD1.cfm; and B. Taylor and G. Kummery, "Family Group Conferencing," *Educational Leadership* 54, no. 1 (September 1996): 44–46.

16 M.A. Raywid, "The Democratic Classroom: Mistake or Misnomer," *Theory into Practice* 15, no. 1 (1976), reprinted in *Theory into Practice* 26 (1977): 480–489.

17 R. Case and I. Wright, "Taking Seriously the Teaching of Critical Thinking," in *The Canadian Anthology of Social Studies: Issues and Strategies for Teachers*, ed. Roland Case and Penney Clark (Burnaby: Faculty of Education, Simon Fraser University, 1997), 179–193; J. Fein and R. Gerber, eds., *Teaching Geography for a Better World* (Edinburgh: Oliver & Boyd/Longman, 1988); and D. Perkins, "Paradoxes of Peace and the Prospects of Peace Education," in *Peace Education: The Concept, Principles, and Practices Around the World*, ed. G. Salomon and B. Nevo (Mahwah, NJ: Lawrence Erlbaum, 2002), 37–53.

18 A. Osler and H. Starkey, "Children's Rights and Citizenship: Some Implications for the Management of Schools," *International Journal of Children's Rights* 6 (1998): 313–333; and D. Schimmel, "Traditional Rule-making and the Subversion of Citizenship Education," *Social Education* 61, no. 2 (1997): 70–74.

19 D. Hess, "Discussing Controversial Public Issues in Secondary Social Studies Classrooms: Learning from Skilled Teachers," *Theory and Research in Social Education* 30, no. 1 (Winter 2002): 10–41.

20 Carole Hahn, "Empirical Research on Issues-centered Social Studies," in *Handbook on Issues-centered Social Studies*, ed. R. Evans and D. Saxe (Washington, DC: NCSS, 1996), 25–41.

21 See, for example, M. I. Alladin, *Racism in Canadian Schools* (Toronto: Harcourt-Brace, 1996); P. Baldwin and D. Baldwin, "The Portrayal of Women in Classroom Textbooks," *Canadian Social Studies* 26 no. 3 (Spring 1992): 110–114; and Canadian Press, "Canada Criticized over Minorities."

22 V. Strong-Boag, "Claiming a Place in the Nation: Citizenship Education and the Challenge of Feminists, Natives, and Workers in Post-Confederation Canada," *Canadian and International Education* 25, no. 2 (December 1996): 128–145.

23 See, for example, League for Human Rights of B'nai Brith Canada, *2002 Audit of Antisemitic Incidents*, www.bnaibrith.ca; L. Brown, "Schools Battle to Remain Clear of Hostilities," Toronto *Star*, September 21, 2001, A12; and K. Rushowy, "Schools Move to Quell Unrest in the Classroom," Toronto *Star*, September 14, 2001, A2.

24 See, for example, M. Merryfield and R. Remy, *Teaching about International Conflict and Peace* (Albany: State University of New York Press, 1995); and E. Boulding, *Building a Global Civic Culture: Education for an Interdependent World* (New York: Teachers College Press, 1988).

25 V.G. Paley, *You Can't Say You Can't Play* (Cambridge, MA: Harvard University Press, 1992).

26 E. Aronson, *Nobody Left to Hate: Teaching Compassion after Columbine* (New York: Worth Publishers, 2000); and T. Gordon, J. Holland, and E. Lahelma, *Making Spaces: Citizenship and Difference in Schools* (London: Macmillan, 2000).

27 E. Cohen and R. Lotan, eds., *Working for Equity in

Heterogeneous Classrooms (New York: Teachers College Press, 1997); and J. Oakes et al., "Detracking: The Social Construction of Ability, Cultural Politics, and Resistance to Reform," *Teachers College Record* 98, no. 3 (1997): 482–510.

28 P. Avery, J. Sullivan, and S. Wood, "Teaching for Tolerance of Diverse Beliefs," *Theory into Practice* 36, no. 1 (1997): 32–38; and K. Mock, "Holocaust and Hope: Holocaust Education in the Context of Anti-racist Education in Canada," in *The Holocaust's Ghost: Writings on Art, Politics, Law and Education*, ed. F.C. Decoste and B. Schwarz (Edmonton: University of Alberta Press, 2000), 465–482.

29 C. McCauley, "Head First versus Feet First in Peace Education," in *Peace Education: The Concept, Principles, and Practices Around the World*, 247–258.

30 W. Stephan, *Reducing Prejudice and Stereotyping in Schools* (New York: Teachers College Press, 1999); and N. Tal-Or, D. Boninger, and F. Gleicher, "Understanding the Conditions and Processes Necessary for Intergroup Contact to Reduce Prejudice," in *Peace Education: The Concept, Principles, and Practices Around the World*, 89–107.

31 K. Alavi, "At Risk of Prejudice: Teaching Tolerance about Muslim Americans," *Social Education* 65, no. 6 (October 2001): 344–348.

32 T. Homer-Dixon, *The Ingenuity Gap* (Toronto: Alfred Knopf, 2000).

33 C. Mukarubuga, "Rwanda: Attaining and Sustaining Peace," in *Peace Education: The Concept, Principles, and Practices Around the World*, 229–236; and M. Ross, *The Management of Conflict* (New Haven: Yale University Press, 1993).

34 See, for example, Fein and Gerber, *Teaching Geography for a Better World*.

35 See, for example, Energy Educators of Ontario, *Global Energy Issues* and *Canadian Energy Issues* (Toronto: Author, 1992); and Michael Klare, "The Geopolitics of War," in "War, Terrorism, and America's Classrooms," special issue, *Rethinking Schools Online* 16, no. 2 (2001/2002), http://www.rethinkingschools.org

36 Bush and Saltarelli, *The Two Faces of Education in Ethnic Conflict*.

37 A. Koehl, "Locked Out of the Classroom: The Children of Illegal Immigrants Are Being Denied the Right to Education and the Surprising Part Is that It's Happening Here in Ontario," Toronto *Star*, May 10, 2002, A25.

38 M. Akiba et al., "Student Victimization: National and School System Effects on School Violence in Thirty-seven Nations," *American Educational Research Journal* 39, no. 4 (Winter 2002): 829–853.

39 P. Freire, *Pedagogy of the Oppressed* (New York: Continuum, 1970), 72.

40 See, for example, Paul W. Bennett, *Rediscovering Canadian History* (Toronto: OISE Press, 1980); K. Bickmore, "Teaching Conflict and Conflict Resolution in School: (Extra-) Curricular Considerations," in *How Children Understand War and Peace: A Call for International Peace Education*, ed. Amiram

Raviv, Louis Oppenheimer, and Daniel Bar-Tal (San Francisco: Jossey-Bass, 1999), 233-259; K. Bickmore, "Conflicts Global and Local: An Elementary Approach," *Social Education* 66, no. 4 (May 2002): 235–238; and Melinda Fine, " 'You Can't Just Say that the Only Ones Who Can Speak Are Those Who Agree with Your Position': Political Discourse in the Classroom," *Harvard Educational Review* 63, no. 4 (Winter 1993): 412–433.

41 See also Hess, "Discussing Controversial Public Issues in Secondary Social Studies Classrooms."

42 L. McNeil, *Contradictions of Control: School Structure and School Knowledge* (New York: Routledge, 1986); and N. Houser, "Negotiating Dissonance and Safety for the Common Good: Social Education in the Elementary Classroom."

43 Fred M. Newmann, with the assistance of W. Donald Oliver, *Clarifying Public Controversy: An Approach to Teaching Social Studies* (Boston: Little, Brown, 1970); and Hahn, "Empirical Research on Issues-centered Social Studies."

44 D. Hicks, "Peace and conflict," in *Children and Controversial Issues*, ed. B. Carrington and B. Troyna (London: Falmer, 1988), 172–188; and William J. Kreidler, "Teaching Controversial Issues to Elementary Children," in *Elementary Perspectives: Teaching Concepts of Peace and Conflict*, ed. William J. Kreidler (Cambridge, MA: Educators for Social Responsibility, 1990): 229–236.

45 Fisk, "Shaping Visionaries: Nurturing Peace through Education," in *Patterns of Conflict, Paths to Peace*, 159–193.

46 Cited in B. Reardon, *Comprehensive Peace Education* (New York: Teachers College Press, 1988).

47 I. Harris, "From World Peace to Peace in the 'Hood: Peace Education in a Postmodern World," *Journal for a Just and Caring Education* 2, no. 4 (October 1996): 378–395.

48 R. Burns and R. Aspeslagh, "Peace Education and the Comparative Study of Education," in *Comparative Education Reader*, ed. E. Beauchamp (New York: Routledge/Falmer, 2003), 217–234; and Stephan, *Reducing Prejudice and Stereotyping in Schools*.

49 D. Bar-Tal, "The Elusive Nature of Peace Education," in *Peace Education: The Concept, Principles, and Practices Around the World*, 27–36; and Reardon, *Comprehensive Peace Education*.

50 W. Carruthers et al., "Conflict Resolution as Curriculum: A Definition, Description, and Process for Integration in Core Curricula," *The School Counselor* 43 (May 1996): 345–373; and Jones, "Research Supports Effectiveness of Peer Mediation," 1–27.

51 Aronson, *Nobody Left to Hate*; and Bush and Saltarelli, *The Two Faces of Education in Ethnic Conflict*.

52 M. Mills, *Challenging Violence in Schools: An Issue of Masculinities* (Buckingham, UK: Open University Press, 2001); and Boulding, *Building a Global Civic Culture*.

53 K. Bickmore, "Student Conflict Resolution, Power 'Sharing' in Schools, and Citizenship Education," *Curriculum Inquiry* 31, no. 2 (Summer 2001): 137–162.

54 P. Ackerman and J. Duvall, *A Force More Powerful: A Century*

of Nonviolent Conflict (New York: Palgrave Publishers, 2000), also on video (Washington, DC: WETA, 2000), http://www.pbs.org/weta/forcemorepowerful/; and C. Soudien, "Memory Work and the Remaking of the Future: A Critical Look at the Pedagogical Value of the Truth and Reconciliation Commission for Peace," in *Peace Education: The Concept, Principles, and Practices Around the World*, 155–161.

55 Guardian News Service, "Inventor of AK-47 Wishes He'd Made a Lawnmower Instead," quoted in *Globe and Mail*, June 30, 2002, A9.

CHAPTER 14

Towards Visual Literacy

Walter Werner

Just to see certain things: in the complexities of today's world that might be quite an achievement.—Roy Boyne[1]

A magazine editor wryly observed, "Analyzing everything that passes in front of us can be an exhausting business—not something to do all day and every day." And he is right. Each day brings hundreds of visual images speaking to current issues, collective memories, social identities, and personal desires. "But," he suggests, "it's worthwhile every so often to look slightly askance at the images which confront you."[2] This suggests a delightful task for social studies.

Visual literacy first finds its basis in concepts rather than teaching methods. Concepts provide tools for noticing new things, raising questions, making productive connections, and reading images in more thoughtful ways. But what ideas are useful? One source for relevant concepts is the multi-disciplinary literature on "visual culture," where writers examine the production, circulation, uses, and contextual interpretations of all types of images.[3] This differs from art history's traditional interest in those works thought to have special merit, focusing on the circumstances of their creation, their authors' intentions and patrons' desires, and their "inherent" aesthetic values. By contrast, visual culture does not limit itself to a privileged Western canon. It casts a broad eye across the visual spectrum, from museum displays to highway billboards, from monuments in the local park to photojournalism, from postcards to postage stamps, from Aunt Linda's picture album to Johnny's social studies textbook. The purpose is to understand changing meanings and uses of images across time and place, including "the work performed by the image in the life of a culture," and how "the aesthetic value of a work depends on the prevailing cultural conditions."[4] During the late nineteenth and early twentieth centuries, tourism to the Canadian Rockies was promoted through tinted photos, posters, and postcards that made a few places—such as Lake Louise, Mt. Rundle, the Three Sisters, and Moraine Lake—famous around the world. These images constructed an imaginary place of desire and unspoiled natural beauty. By the 1950s these iconic photographs were so widespread and recognizable that they came to stand for Canada itself, took on new purposes as collectibles, and were invested with changing aesthetic, nostalgic, and economic values. A visual culture perspective analyzes how they reflected the Canadian Pacific Railway's commercial interests and cultural practices, encouraged particular tourist expectations and stereotypes about Canada, and influenced the uses and meanings of national parks over time. A variety of concepts and theories could be brought to the task.

My purpose is to recommend six overlapping concepts for promoting visual literacy: multiple readings, viewer standpoints, rhetorical devices, intertextuality, power, and reflexivity.[5] This introductory cluster is illustrative rather than exhaustive, and does not imply an instructional hierarchy or sequence. Any one of the concepts provides a starting point for discussing commonplace images within textbooks, newspapers, or commercial posters. Because of space limitations, examples focus on still images rather than television, video games, and movies.

Mutiple Readings

"All items of visual culture, no matter what their medium or aesthetic quality, can be considered to be 'texts' that are subject to an endless series of 'readings'. . ."[6] The word "reading" is deliberately used because written and visual texts do not communicate on their own. Nor is there one intrinsic meaning embedded within a picture's design or subject matter, or its author's intentions, waiting to be uncovered through the correct reading. Elements and relationships within an image are interpreted through readers' purposes, values, and prior understandings. Meanings arise through these interactions.

Encounters that viewers have with an image are also shaped by milieu. In 1989 thousands of Chinese students in Tiananmen Square rallied around the Goddess of Democracy in front of the Great Hall of the People. After tanks crushed protestors and their symbol of hope for national reform on June 4, university students around the world placed replicas of the statue on their campuses. But these very different contexts gave rise to new meanings. As the Goddess travelled across cultural, political, and institutional contexts, and as time passed, it took on added local meanings mediated by the surroundings. At one Canadian university a scaled-down image sits amidst a tranquil setting of large plants, open space, and institutional furniture within the enclosed courtyard of a student union building, where individuals come to quietly read or nap, and small groups meet to eat lunches and chat. Although a plaque commemorates the demonstrators who died, the white statue now signifies support for ongoing democracy struggles around the world, and the aesthetics and social uses of the architecturally designed space speak more generally to the internationalization of campus life.[7] At another Canadian university a weathered replica sits at the busy intersection of sidewalks, next to

cafeterias, theatres, and a pub, where it is the frequent target of graffiti. Meanings are diverse for the thousands of students who pass each day, including those from China able to make connections to past events or invest it with their own personal memories and agendas. In similar ways, interpretations of textbook pictures are influenced by captions, placement in relation to surrounding texts, chapter storylines, teachers' off-hand questions, and ongoing classroom discussions. The quality of readers' attention also depends on whether images are viewed for personal interest or under the constraints and time pressure of assignments. Contextual factors influence how images are seen and understood.

There will always be a surplus of meaning arising from reader/text interactions. Let me briefly illustrate some possibilities. In June of 1940, a newspaper photographer snapped a black-and-white picture as hundreds of soldiers marched three abreast down a street in the town of New Westminster, British Columbia.[8] In the foreground is a young boy, his arm and fingers outstretched, running after a soldier who, without breaking rank, reaches back to him. A young woman, clutching her purse, hurries after the lad and strains to grab his other arm. After this photo was published in the local newspaper, it was picked up by an American magazine, and for the rest of the war hung in schools throughout the Vancouver area. Now it appears in social studies textbooks and popular literature,[9] where it can be read in overlapping ways:[10]

- *Empathetic readings* imaginatively enter into the desires and emotions expressed through the faces of the three main characters, and the outstretched hands that strain but do not touch. Shared human experience provides the common ground necessary for interpreting what this event meant to the participants at that moment in time.

- *Narrative readings* move beyond the picture's frame to its implied storylines. This frozen instant in time is animated through inferences about what led up to the moment (antecedents, causes, prior actions) and what will follow (consequences, next steps). There is the immediate drama of this event and the surrounding soldiers who witnessed it, as well as a larger story about the Duke of Connaught's Own Rifles marching to their ship en route to Europe.[11]

- *Editorial readings* infer the photojournalist's normative stance towards the subject matter. The image creates a sensitive and positive editorial judgement about the costs to those affected by Canada's war effort. Not only is a five-year-old (Warren) leaving his father (Private Jack Bernard), but on a larger scale, each of the hundreds of nameless soldiers, family members, and onlookers in the photograph is sacrificing personal relationships in support of a national cause. The image portrays this loss in a sympathetic and approving manner.

- *Instrumental readings* treat the picture as an information resource to be mined for facts about soldiers' uniforms, women's clothing and hairstyles, architectural styles, and so on. When placed alongside related pictures, it provides evidence about cultural practices and social hierarchies taken for granted at that time and place.[12]

- *Indexical readings* go beyond a narrow decoding of elements and symbols to the social attitudes,

political conditions, and institutional priorities that allowed the picture to have popular acceptance and wide circulation. It points to (i.e., serves as an index of) popular sentiments towards the war, and the photo's uses in the media and schools helped sustain patriotic support for those who were so engaged.

- *Aesthetic readings* appreciate and judge the work of this professional photographer on aesthetic criteria without having to know where and when the event occurred. Attention is given to the use of composition—shape, line, symmetry, movement, perspective, shading—for creating the tensions and mood that make this visual experience engaging and pleasurable.

- *Iconic readings* infer the broader collective determination that the picture came to represent across North America. An icon embodies or stands for something more abstract and beyond itself. Within the pages of a national magazine or hanging on classroom walls, this portrait of a child reaching out to say goodbye to a father put a human face to the ideal of determined service and patriotic sacrifice, just as other wartime images of a cigar-smoking Winston Churchill, or raising the flag at Iwo Jima, came to symbolize the goal of victory. Audiences read the photo as embodying a hopeful ideal that far transcends a brief moment in an obscure working-class town.

- *Oppositional and evaluative readings* critique (and even reject) how the event is portrayed (e.g., its silences, how the viewer is positioned), and the propagandistic uses of this emotionally laden content to stir nationalism, strengthen collective action, and discourage dissent and debate over war issues. Evaluation focuses on incongruities between "what is" and "what should be," the actual and the ideal. Judgements about this gap and how the image could be changed depend upon criteria brought to the image.

Many other readings are possible. The number is not the point. More important is a recognition that interpretation depends upon purpose and background knowledge. An uninformed viewer would see a bunch of uniformed men walking down a road past some watching women and a child.[13] Richness of meaning depends upon what is brought to the text, including some understanding of its subject matter (e.g., who are these soldiers, why are they marching, and where are they going?), immediate context (e.g., where and when was the photo taken, and for what purpose?), the larger social and political backdrop (e.g., what was Canada's war effort and what was the popular attitude towards it in 1940?), and subsequent uses to which the photo was put. Meanings are enlarged and become layered through the give-and-take of discussion.

The above readings are not equally applicable to all images. Few are iconic in the sense of embodying a broader cultural stereotype, and not all capture a moment from an ongoing narrative or provide enough information from which to infer local social and institutional values. Although romanticized paintings depicting the deaths of Wolfe and Montcalm in 1759 are difficult to read empathetically, they can be interpreted in other rich ways.[14] Indexically, they portray the artists' political allegiances, as well as the cultural and aesthetic sensibilities of eighteenth-century elites who commissioned memorializations of such events. They also provide iconic statements about the role of honour, loyalty, duty, hierarchy, and glory in war for the sake of empire. Narratively they depict a moment in time within a nested set of stories, from a small battle on the Plains of Abraham to the much larger narratives of France's loss of an important colony and shifting power relations within Europe. The choice of how to read an image depends on the type of image (e.g., political cartoon, historical painting, commercial, newspaper photo), the specifics of its subject matter, the contexts within which it is used, and the reader's purpose and knowledge. The onus lies on the interpreter to communicate purpose and provide evidence for inferences. Through group discussion, interpretations can then be judged on their appropriateness and supporting evidence. The goal is not to find one best interpretation. Rather, juxtaposing readings highlights the partialness and insightfulness of each, opens possibilities for enlarged

meanings, and makes the process of seeing more self-conscious.[15]

The teacher's role is to encourage multiple readings. This can be done by capitalizing on teachable moments, wondering out loud about the meaning of a picture in the chapter, raising a question or doubt about a caption, soliciting and offering counter-interpretations, and modelling the use of criteria for judging amongst different readings. This instructional sequence from description to judgement is illustrated in these general questions:

1. What is this image about?

2. What interpretations can be given?

3. What purpose and evidence supports each interpretation?

4. What interpretations are compelling, and why?

Viewer Standpoints

Images offer more than representations. They also place the viewer in a position from which to see and interpret that representation. To borrow a clumsy term, they "construct spectatorship" in a number of ways. Most obvious is the physical position that is offered. An image provides a perspective from which to look, including an angle of vision (e.g., I am placed off to one side, above, below, or directly in front of the image), and a field of view that may be panoramic or quite narrow. As well, there is a spatial relationship that sets me close, far away from, or in the midst of the portrayed event. This physical positioning implies a psychological position. Shoulder-to-shoulder placement with those in the picture offers an active role in the event, whereas a perspective of looking up at or down on the group suggests a more passive identification. I may be placed within the social circle as a friendly insider, as an observer curiously watching at a distance from the sidelines, or even as an unnoticed voyeur observing through a partially open window or door.

An image also provides viewers with a particular gaze—an attitude or emotional tone (e.g., empathetic, neutral, hostile), or a broader ideological stance (e.g., Eurocentric, patriarchal, ethnocentric, colonial, provincial, classist)—towards the portrayed event, group, place, or person. Tourist photos may look at individuals in respectful and sympathetic ways, or at worst, objectify "otherness" as exotic, cute, or helpless, reproducing stereotypes that tell more about the photographer's expectations than about the subject matter. A gaze may be designed to persuade an audience, as when international agencies involved in fundraising for relief projects use close-up pictures of hungry children to discomfort the viewer, engender guilt, and motivate action. An intimate view of human misery—starvation, disaster, poverty—may even implicate viewers in the broader conditions that produced that misery.

A standpoint is further provided through the ideal viewer that is assumed. For example, the long European tradition of painting female nudes primarily assumed a male audience that commissioned, painted, and owned these works.[16] Such paintings took for granted what connoisseurs believed and valued, what they expected to see, and where they were located socially and politically. Those excluded from this idealized standpoint would find the representations difficult to interpret or even offensive. Similarly, the ideal viewer of an X-ray negative is someone who is able to "see" through the lens of a medical discourse that provides the specialized classification systems and causal assumptions for making symptoms visible. Professional experience and language direct what is seen and how. The same image is mute and even inaccessible to an onlooker who lacks relevant concepts and expertise. When a social studies textbook provides a picture as historical or geographical evidence, this implies a reader who has the necessary background for seeing what this is a record of. There is much more to observation of distant events and places than naïve sight.[17] The photo and its placement within the chapter may also assume that readers share an ideology (e.g., national patriotism) or identity (e.g., based on social class, gender, ethnocultural affiliation, religious persuasion, regionalism).

Readers can, of course, resist the ways in which an image positions them, reject the particular gaze or assumed audience, and reposition themselves in other ways. Standpoints can be multiple and mobile. When I picked up the *Globe and Mail* and looked at a large colour photo of an Israeli bus wrecked by a suicide bomber, I found myself positioned about six metres from the side of the vehicle. My elevated and wide-angle observer standpoint looked over the heads of ten emergency workers, through the blown-out widows, and down at the bloody corpses of three women and two men still sitting in their seats.[18] This vivid gaze did not allow for academic distance and neutrality, but encouraged a curiosity that led to revulsion and anger. Some letters to the editor over the next two days rejected this standpoint as much too close and the look as disrespectful. They were shocked by the graphic and detailed view, offended that they were cast as curious gawkers of others' misfortune, and wanted to back away from the psychological and political stance afforded them. Other readers accepted the gaze as encouraging them to temporarily set aside larger contentious issues and empathetically feel for those who were on that bus. Critical readings recognize the physical and psychological positions offered to viewers, and contest/accept the way in which the event is portrayed with its implied storyline and politics. Standpoints can be made visible through classroom discussion around the following kinds of questions:

1. In what ways is the viewer positioned? (e.g., physical and psychological standpoints, the particular gaze, assumptions about ideal viewers)

2. What are the effects of viewer standpoints on interpretation? (e.g., who is included/excluded?)

3. Should this positioning be accepted? Why or why not?

Rhetorical Devices

Many images are designed to promote an opinion, provoke emotion, or encourage action (e.g., commercial ads, editorial cartoons, photojournalism, political posters, protest art). Although persuasion is accomplished through various types of rhetorical devices, only five are identified here: caricature, symbols, binaries, implied narratives, and analogies.

Caricature is usually the easiest to recognize. It

resembles the intended subject—the person, object, event, institution, group, or place—although the particular points of similarity are very selective in order to place the subject in a favourable or unfavourable light. A political cartoonist, for example, "focuses on an individual's unique physical characteristics and exaggerates or distorts them to make the person readily identifiable and to expose his or her vices and follies."[19] The cartoon fails if the resemblance is too simplified or distorted. But if successful, the communicative power of stereotype and exaggeration coaxes a viewer into making a judgement and taking a stand. Caricature has also been used for centuries to vilify imagined enemies; fear and hatred are aroused through representing "the other" as threatening or disgusting.[20] This practice was illustrated prior to the second war on Iraq when the *Globe and Mail* printed a quarter-page crude drawing of Saddam Hussein replete with animal snout and large canine teeth.[21] In photojournalism, caricature operates more subtly when the subject is caught in an unflattering pose or exaggerated gesture. Social studies textbooks are loaded with caricatures—drawings, paintings, cartoons, and photos—that convey opinions about prime ministers, monarchs, presidents, reformers, and sundry other leaders. These portraits are usually presented as rhetorically self-evident, as if young readers already recognize how manipulation works. Exceptions are noteworthy. In a grade 8 book, didactic captions anchoring official portraits of Charles I and Oliver Cromwell point out the artists' use of positive or negative exaggeration:

- This miniature, by the artist Samuel Cooper, shows Oliver Cromwell as he requested, "warts and all." This reflected Cromwell's Puritan views about the sin of vanity. Do you think this is an effective portrait? Was it painted to influence the way people thought about Cromwell and his program?

- Like all monarchs, King Charles I had one of the world's best painters do his portraits. This painting by Van Dyke shows Charles as he wished to be seen. What qualities does the painting suggest that Charles possessed? Is this a bet-

ter portrait than the one of Cromwell? Explain why or why not.[22]

These brief captions remind viewers that caricature provides selective details designed to encourage particular meanings. The point of this deliberate distortion is to praise (as in the two examples above), or more commonly, to satirize and ridicule.

A second group of rhetorical devices are *symbols* whose meanings are suggested through contextual usage within an image itself, or established by broader conventions that change over time. In the nineteenth century, the United States was represented by a motherly looking Mrs. Columbia, Canada by a robust Johnny Canuck or slight Miss Canada, and Britain by John Bull and St. George. These conventions have changed, whereas others still serve as effective shorthand (e.g., a flag represents a country, including its people, geography, history, values, state; a crown stands for a monarch or the monarchy; Ottawa's peace tower evokes the House of Commons; the dome of the American Capitol building symbolizes the legislative branch).

The use of *binary juxtaposition* brings together opposing elements in order to highlight competing values or ideas (e.g., rich/poor, dirty/clean, selfish/generous, unemployed/employed, old/young, individual/group, urban/rural, traditional/modern, hope/despair, present/future, up/down, and so on). Photojournalists commonly employ binaries to suggest editorial comment. For example, an iguana sunbathing on the black lava rocks of a Galapagos beach is backgrounded by a listing oil tanker that ran aground. The similar shapes of the iguana and the ship, and their above/below alignment, imply a relationship loaded with evaluative comment.[23] Such contrasts are designed to provoke emotion (e.g., discomfort, anger, guilt), nudge questions, and invite evaluation. Whether stark or subtle, though, binaries only work as viewers recognize and are willing to engage the oppositions.

Implied narratives are triggered when images suggest that there is a next step or consequence that flows from what is depicted. Most commercial ads imply that something desirable will happen in the future if the product is bought now; there is also the implicit warning that lack of action could result in an undesirable storyline. Visual elements may promise enhanced beauty or status, which in turn leads to romance, happiness, and other enviable ends. So new SUVs are pictured with young-looking individuals personifying desirable traits (e.g., adventuresome, seductive, dependable, tough-minded, sophisticated, wealthy), or linked with valued places (e.g., upper-class neighbourhoods, commanding mountain tops, gentle countryside, pristine wilderness, nostalgic family events). Meanings arise not from the separate elements (car, person, place) but through the unstated storyline that buying this vehicle helps achieve outcomes beyond the product itself. The rhetorical purpose is to produce desire, even though the viewer may know that the SUV is overpriced, unsafe, and environmentally unfriendly. "It proposes to each of us that we transform ourselves, or our lives, by buying something more," says John Berger. "This more, it proposes, will make us in some way richer—even though we will be poorer by having spent our money."[24]

Some of the most interesting devices are *analogies*.[25] A visual analogy implies that one thing is similar to another. Simple analogies set two elements side by side (above and below; foreground and background), thereby encouraging comparison between the juxtaposed parts. According to Walker and Chaplin, visual simile "is extremely common in advertising photography and generally operates within a single frame image via a juxtaposition of two items in such a way that a likeness between them is implied. For example, a cup of coffee and jars of coffee were shown in the foreground of an advert while in the background there were several famous works of art. This arrangement was a visual version of the proposition: 'Our brand of coffee is like a work of art.'"[26] The commercial product achieves meanings through association with something assumed to be good.

Analogies only work, though, as one is able to see and interpret the implied connection. They are activated by the cultural knowledge brought to them. The first political cartoon published in a North American newspaper (Benjamin Franklin, *The Pennsylvania Gazette*, 1754) presented a crudely drawn snake cut in eight, each piece accompanied by the initials of a colony. Although the caption ("Unite or Die") and the analogy are clear—the severed snake is like the eight colonies facing an important decision—the metaphor does not work for contemporary viewers because of Franklin's choice of a sliced-up snake. Viewers at the time, however, were able to call upon a cultural superstition—a severed snake had the ability to rejoin and live—that animated the analogy and encouraged interpretation.[27] The analogy's meanings do not lie in its component parts but in the viewer's ability to recognize and interpret the comparison, and this "seeing" depends upon what the viewer brings to it.

An agricultural analogy that appeared regularly in Canadian newspapers and magazines from the 1860s through the 1940s was that of a cow fed in one region (or city or province) and milked in another. A typical example is the 1915 cartoon drawn by Arch Dale for *The Grain Growers' Guide*,[28] reproduced on the next page. The cow represents a confederation characterized by regional economic inequalities. Hard-working farmers in the prairie provinces do the work of producing wealth that is unfairly "milked" by gleeful capitalists in eastern cities. Canadian readers over the past 150 years have had no difficulties understanding this analogy along with its symbolism, caricature, binaries, and implied narratives.

Political cartoons can be difficult to read when their analogies are taken from historical events or personalities, literary allusions, or cultural proverbs. They may then function as inside jokes between the artist and those readers able to pick up the subtle allusions. Brian Gable of the *Globe and Mail*, for example, frequently borrowed analogies from a range of sources such as Jewish and Christian scriptures (e.g., Noah's ark, four horsemen of the Apocalypse), Renaissance art (e.g., God and Adam reaching to one another in Michelangelo's *Creation* painted on the ceiling of the Sistine Chapel), British literature (e.g., Gulliver tied down by the Lilliputians in Jonathan Swift's *Gulliver's Travels*), historical events (e.g., storming of the Bastille), fairy tales and children's stories (e.g., "Little Red Riding Hood"), famous photographs and paintings of the twentieth century (e.g., Salvador Dali's *Time*, Rosenthal's 1945 *Iwo Jima*), proverbs, symbolic characters (e.g., Liberty, St. Peter), movies (e.g., *Sound of Music*), and TV shows (e.g., "The Simpsons"). To activate the analogies, though, one needs access to various literary, historical, and cultural memory banks.[29]

Because rhetorical devices are so pervasive, visual literacy includes recognition of how they highlight and hide meanings. Naïve and literal readings may accurately identify the represented object, person, place, or event, yet fail to understand how persuasion is at work and with what effects. A newspaper picture of the prime minister delivering a speech evokes a more sophisticated and interesting response when I realize that the photographer aligned the speaker's head in front of a light bulb (e.g., the halo effect implies that the speech was too earnest, sanctimonious, or hypocritical). But the figurative punch is lost on uninformed viewers. The following questions illustrate the broad instructional movement from recognition to interpretation and evaluation:

1. What rhetorical devices are used?

2. What meanings do these devices encourage?

3. Why are these devices effective or not?

Intertextuality

"The meaning of an image," notes an art critic, "is changed according to what one sees immediately beside it or what comes immediately after it."[30] Intertextuality is at work whenever an image is interpreted in the light of (through or against) another visual or written text. Common examples are the photograph and headline on the front page of a newspaper, images on adjacent billboards, or the graph, picture, caption, and written text on a magazine page. Each mini-text plays off—reinforces, supplements, counters, or subverts—and influences how the others are seen and understood. This blurring of boundaries mediates

THE MILCH COW

A 1915 political cartoon published in *The Grain Growers' Guide*. It suggests farmers in the prairie provinces do the work of producing wealth that is unfairly "milked" by gleeful capitalists in eastern cities.

and enriches meanings. Three forms of intertextuality are commonly encountered.[31]

Intertextuality across images operates when they are placed together (paired, sequenced, clustered) in the same location. Galleries group items as a way of encouraging visitors to notice nuance and tension facilitated through the associations. Within a cluster or montage, each piece serves as supportive foreground or contrastive background for interpreting the others. Similarly within textbooks, images are grouped on the same page and sequenced within a chapter. Whether the juxtapositions are seen as stark and contrastive, or complementary and mutually reinforcing, meanings are enriched as the reader notices each within the context of the others. For example, when a nineteenth-century photo of New Westminster—the small, rough and muddy capital of the crown colony of British Columbia—is set alongside the original pretentious map that was to guide the town's development, the uninspiring actuality is given richer meaning when seen in terms of the planners' grand intentions and the community's hopes for the future.[32] Sequences of images are often suggestive of a temporal storyline—before and after, then and now, antecedent and consequence—related to change and progress. Photos of the original gold rush town of Barkerville in the mid-1860s and as it is recreated today as a tourist site not only play on the then/now distinction, but also provoke questions about how "place" is radically redefined through changing purposes and uses over time.[33]

Intertextuality is evident *within* images that borrow symbols, themes or compositional elements from prior texts.[34] Political cartoonists, commercial advertisers, and photojournalists paraphrase famous images in creative and ironic ways. Two widely used sources previously mentioned are God and Adam reaching out to one another in Michelangelo's *Creation*, and Rosenthal's 1945 photo of the flag being raised at Iwo Jima. Visual quoting also occurs when characters or storylines are taken from famous historical events, literary and biblical texts, fairy tales and children's stories, movies, and TV shows.[35] The effects can be striking. Controversy arose when images and words selected from Martin Luther King,

Jr.'s "I have a dream" speech in Washington, August 28, 1963, cast him as a pitchman for cellphones and telecom networks.[36] One of these ads digitally removed the huge crowd in front of Mr. King to emphasize a rather different "connection" message: "For passion to inspire a nation it has to reach a nation. Before you can inspire, before you can touch, before you can empower, you must first connect. And for more people, more businesses, more countries around the world, that connection is made with Alcatel."[37] Viewers who lack background knowledge would be unable to recognize the visual quoting and its uses.

A third form of intertextuality is between image and word. Composite meanings arise as the two are integrated. In a grade 8 textbook, discussion of the Protestant Reformation is accompanied by a picture showing the ornate and rich interior of a sixteenth-century Vatican church; alongside the picture is a biblical quotation in Elizabethan English, "If thou wilt be perfect, go and sell that thou hast, and give to the poor, and thou shalt have treasure in heaven."[38] The reader is left to resolve the ambiguity or reject the implied contradiction. Invariably textbooks use captions to anchor images for two purposes. The primary purpose is to limit the indeterminacy of meaning by framing observation and controlling interpretation. This point was vividly illustrated when a magazine published eight portraits of Fidel Castro on the same page, each with a very different caption.[39] When words didactically state what the picture is about, the range of possible readings is narrowed, even to the point where the image simply serves to illustrate and reinforce the words; in such cases it is worth questioning the caption's authority. A second reason for anchoring the image is to disturb or counter its implied message. Here viewers are positioned as critics questioning the meaning of what is seen. This purpose is illustrated by comparing the use of captions within three textbooks, each containing a similarly styled painting of an Aboriginal trapper bartering with two European traders over the worth of his furs. The three captions state:

- This painting is titled "Dickering with the Factor" and it illustrates the relationship between the Native peoples and the fur traders. Which group benefited the most from trading?[40]

- Why do you think a Factor would want to have as wide a variety of goods as possible in his store?[41]

- In the Trading Room. A Native person has brought furs to the French at a trading post to trade for European goods.[42]

The first gently encourages readers to notice and question elements of unequal power evidenced within the drawing, whereas the other two captions accept the way in which it positions not only the three subjects, but also the viewer. Students can become even more aware of the role of captions when composing their own alternatives and comparing the different effects.

On the other hand, words do not always dominate. Images also influence how words are interpreted. For example, a photo gives authenticity and immediacy to a written account, providing the visual "proof" that makes the account seem obvious and even more compelling. Further, a strong image or set of images supplies a dispositional tone—an attitude or emotion—through which the written text is then read. It lends a sense of urgency to the discussion of an issue, and may even predispose readers to support a particular side.

The following questions illustrate how the concept of intertextuality can be introduced after students have read and discussed a textbook chapter:

1. What does this picture mean?

2. How are interpretations influenced by the picture's surroundings? (e.g., caption, paragraphs, sidebar text, another picture, graph, chart)

3. In what ways does the picture(s) influence how the surrounding paragraphs and images are read?

4. Why would you delete or add an image, change the location of images, or modify a caption within this chapter?

The Power of Images

Power does not reside within an image, but in its effects upon viewers. A powerful picture has consequences for what people believe and do. It influences their ideas and actions in at least two overlapping ways: surveillance and persuasion.

Modern surveillance serves security, enforcement, and archival purposes largely through passive means. This occurs when people monitor their own behaviour as a result of believing that electronic eyes may be watching and recording their movements within airports, banks, stores, parking lots, and along highways. Because they do not know where and when a camera may be present, they act on the assumption that they are seen, and the effect of this belief is self-regulation. Not surprisingly, for millennia similar effects were achieved through public displays of still images depicting rulers and deities whose eyes always observed. Some religious traditions venerated icons, commonly in the form of stylized portraits of saints who seemed to look directly back at the viewer.[43] When hung within a home, the painting invoked the presence of the saint whose constant gaze reminded the faithful of the larger truth that God's eye is omnipresent; those who were observed internalized the gaze of the observer and acted accordingly.

Similarly, as European empires spread across the world, portraits of monarchs were placed within classrooms, civic buildings, and prominent outdoor spaces not for aesthetic reasons, but to illustrate the presence of the imperial eye to oversee the farthest reaches of any colony. An interesting feature of twentieth-century totalitarian regimes was their widespread use of the ruler's gaze. Saddam Hussein's Iraq was an extreme example. His ubiquitous face overlooked public squares, major street corners, and places of work and leisure, and even appeared within homes, reminding citizens that all aspects of their lives were within the state's purview through the local eyes of party members. This consistent message of being watched had effects as citizens internalized the assumed surveillance.

A different example of surveillance through images lies in the multiple archival records many institutions file on their members, including photos for driver's licences, passports, security cards, job application forms, school yearbooks, as well as other forms of images from fingerprints to dental X-rays, all of which confer identity and serve official identification purposes. Such archives raise issues about privacy rights and legitimate uses for images, especially now that the camera's presence is so widespread and taken for granted; many jurisdictions place legal restrictions on taking close-up pictures of people on sidewalks, or using their images without permission.

The power of images is also demonstrated through their persuasion effects. During early years of the Cold War, newspaper pictures of nuclear tests and their aftermath convinced some people to build shelters or move from urban centres. And as already discussed, the power of rhetorical devices in commercial or political advertisements is to persuade viewers of an idea or action. An interesting ad by the Canadian Air Transport Security Authority depicts a briefcase as seen by an electronic scanner: keys, pens, cell phone, and notebooks are clearly visible, as well as what appears to be the thin edge of a knife or letter opener.[44] The caption says: "You see a briefcase. We see a big problem." By visually demonstrating to viewers that they are under effective airport surveillance ("the scanner clearly sees everything you carry"), the ad persuades travellers to notice what is in their briefcases before stepping up to the screen. If not, there is the open-ended threat of a "big problem." Whether or not the ad actually has the intended effect (i.e., power) depends upon the viewer's understanding of and reaction to the implied threat. Sometimes images have persuasion effects that are not intended, as when persistent media depictions of violence inspire readers to fear that rates of mugging, murder, and sundry mayhem are rising on city streets. Even a single image can have very real unintended consequences. For instance, a Canadian federal politician (Robert Stanfield) never lived down the negative impression created by a photo that caught him awkwardly fumbling a football during a ceremony at a CFL game; newspapers chose to publish that particular picture even though on the same occasion he also caught the ball successfully.[45]

Classroom discussion of power effects moves beyond conjecture to supportive evidence and evaluative criteria:

1. What are (or have been, or might be) the intended or unintended consequences of this image upon beliefs and actions?

2. What reasons or evidence support these claims?

3. On what criteria could these effects be evaluated? (e.g., fairness, respectfulness, legality)

Reflexivity

Viewing is loaded with expectations and assumptions. Images become accessible to the extent that they easily evoke memories and emotions related to the familiar. Those with broad community appeal connect widely to shared hopes, fears, and values. This is why most public images—billboards, outdoor statues, magazine pictures—are seen as friendly and non-problematic. They meet expectations. "[T]he statue of a local hero, usually a soldier, in a city park is a common example. It doesn't challenge our assumptions at all. Its very purpose is to reinforce our shared image bank of what soldiering is like."[46] Similar examples are found in battlefield paintings scattered throughout textbooks, showing soldiers in the expected poses of camaraderie, bravery, and stoicism. Such pictures are agreeable because they fit accepted stereotypes. Rarely are readers shown the mental breakdown, personal doubt, and brutality that go with soldiering. What viewers find (in)accessible and (dis)agreeable speaks to their own expectations and beliefs. In short, interpreters are autobiographically present in their interpretations. Seeing is largely a product of an individual's or group's prior experiences.

Another important truism is that seeing is situated in the cultural present.[47] Images are invested with meaning and used from the standpoint of the present, and as time goes on, these investments and uses change. Historical representations within the textbook cannot offer transparent windows into past events. They do not show what it was like then. Although they point to the past and make some aspects of the past present, they are always understood in the present through contemporary cultural resources (e.g., purposes, concepts, questions, predispositions) that are part of current discursive frames. When students look at an historical painting, they actively imagine a past event and enter into it through the sensibilities and interpretive tools available to them. All interpretation "has its origins in the contemporary circumstances of the interpretation."[48]

Reflexivity recognizes the interpreter. It is awareness that how we read and use visuals depends upon a prior outlook. As Michael Apples notes, "We must always be willing to read our own readings of a text, to interpret our own interpretations of what it means" in order to understand how our ethnocultural, social class, gender, religious, or other experiences may influence how we read the text, perhaps in unwarranted ways.[49] Classroom discussion of why we do or do not find an image recognizable and agreeable is a good place for introducing reflexivity. The following questions turn from text to interpreter:

1.   What are our reactions to this image?

     a. Why have we reacted in these ways?

     b. What do these reactions imply about what we take for granted? (e.g., our expectations, stereotypes, political values, social locations, past experiences)

2.   How are we using present experience to understand this image?

     a. Why should we be cautious about reading current events (or hopes, issues, values, practices) back into the past? Are there more appropriate ways to interpret this image?

     b. Why is it appropriate or not appropriate to use this image to justify a present event, action, or policy? To make the present appear better than the past?

The school's broad mandate promotes literacy in written, numerical, spoken, visual, kinesthetic, and musical forms of representation. Priority is rightly put on reading, writing, and speaking the word, but social educators also recognize that the social world is thoroughly visual, and that the visual shapes and carries the social. Issues, values and identities are promoted and contested through images, as are ideas about the past and future. Although visual literacy is part of social education, it need not be treated as one more addition to the overcrowded curriculum. Rather, at opportune moments one or more of the concepts discussed above can be used to re-examine a picture from a textbook or newspaper. Visual literacy is learned through the questions and counterinterpretations brought to the ongoing discussion and, where appropriate, by mentioning the underlying concepts. Over time students gain the tools for making visual experience more insightful, critical, and enjoyable.

Endnotes

1   Roy Boyne, "Fractured Subjectivity," in *Visual Culture*, ed. Chris Jenks (London: Routledge, 1995), 61.

2   Peter Stalker, "Can I Take Your Picture? The Strange World of Photography," *The New Internationalist* 18, no. 5 (1988): 6.

3   See, for example, Norman Bryson, Michael Ann Holly, and Keith Moxey, eds., *Visual Culture: Images and Interpretations* (London: Wesleyan University Press, 1994); Chris Jenks, ed., *Visual Culture* (London: Routledge, 1995); Stuart Hall, ed., *Representation: Cultural Representations and Signifying Practices* (Thousand Oaks, CA: Sage Publications, 1997); John Walker and Sarah Chaplin, *Visual Culture: An Introduction* (Manchester, UK: Manchester University Press, 1997); Nicholas Mirzoeff, ed., *The Visual Culture Reader* (London: Routledge, 1998); Jessica Evans and Stuart Hall, eds., *Visual Culture: The Reader* (London: Sage Publications, 1999); Irit Rogoff, *Terra Infirma: Geography's Visual Culture* (New York: Routledge, 2000); Liz Wells, ed., *Photography: A Critical Introduction* (London: Routledge, 2000); Gillian Rose, *Visual Methodologies* (Thousand Oaks, CA: Sage Publications, 2001); Richard Howells, *Visual Culture* (Cambridge, UK: Polity Press, 2003); and Amelia Jones, ed., *The Feminism and Visual Culture Reader* (London: Routledge, 2003).

4   Bryson, Holly, and Moxey, *Visual Culture*, xvi. The aesthetic value of an image is less intrinsic and more dependent on "what a culture brings to the work rather than on what the culture finds in it."

5   I do not trace the nuances, uses, and histories of these concepts as they travel across disciplines; see Mieke Bal, *Travelling Concepts in the Humanities* (Toronto: University of Toronto Press, 2002). Discussion of these concepts draws upon Walt Werner, "Reading Authorship Into Texts," *Theory and Research in Social Education* 28, no. 2 (2000): 193–219; ———, "Reading Visual Texts," *Theory and Research in Social Education* 30, no. 3 (2002): 401–428; and ———, "Reading Visual Rheto-

ric: Political Cartoons," *International Journal of Social Education* 18, no. 1 (2003): 81–98. Many other concepts are also necessary, such as representation, voice, absence/silence, mediation, and so on.

6   Walker and Chaplin, *Visual Culture*, 118.

7   R. Paul Dyck, "Goddess of Democracy," *Arch: The University of Calgary Alumni Magazine* (Spring 2002): 29.

8   Photograph by Claude P. Dettloff, "Wait for Me, Daddy: Private Jack Bernard, B.C. Regiment (Duke of Connaught's Own Rifles) Saying Goodbye to His Five-year-old Son Warren," June 1940, National Archives of Canada (C-038723), used by permission of Mrs. D. Joan Macpherson.

9   See, for example, Daniel Francis et al., *Canadian Issues: A Contemporary Perspective* (Toronto: Oxford University Press, 1998), 147; and *Globe and Mail*, November 6, 1999, D8.

10 Explanations and illustrations of these readings are found in Werner, "Reading Visual Texts."

11 Some images encourage viewers to recall a storyline borrowed from historical events or religious myths. A political cartoon of a leader with staff outstretched to the sea evokes the larger exodus narrative, but is lost on those do not understand the religious reference.

12 Peter Bourke, *Eyewitnessing: Uses of Images as Historical Evidence* (Ithaca, NY: Cornell University Press, 2001).

13 Similarly, as a letter to the editor noted, the Mona Lisa would be "just a picture of some woman smiling, or not," to someone without background knowledge. Letter to the editor, *Globe and Mail*, May 28, 2003, A14.

14 Daniel Francis, *The Imaginary Indian: The Image of the Indian in Canadian Culture* (Vancouver: Arsenal Pulp Press, 1992), 13–15.

15 This instructional process is illustrated well in Jennifer Pazienza and Gerald Clarke, "Integrating Text and Image: Teaching Art and History," in *Trends and Issues in Canadian Social Studies*, ed. Ian Wright and Alan Sears (Vancouver: Pacific Educational Press, 1997), 275–294.

16 John Berger, *Ways of Seeing* (London: Penguin, 1972).

17 Andrew Barry, "Reporting and Visualizing," in *Visual Culture*, ed. Chris Jenks, 52.

18 *Globe and Mail*, May 19, 2003, A1.

19 Charles Hou and Cynthia Hou, *The Art of Decoding Political Cartoons: A Teacher's Guide* (Vancouver: Moody's Lookout Press, 1998), 11.

20 War posters dehumanize soldiers and leaders on both sides. See, for example, Brett Silverstein, "Enemy Images: The Psychology of U.S. Attitudes and Cognitions Regarding the Soviet Union," *American Psychologist* 44, no. 6 (1989): 903–913; Sam Keen, "Looking at Ourselves Looking at Each Other," *Educational Leadership* 46, no. 4 (1989): 80–83; and Donald Robinson, ed., *As Others See Us* (New York: Houghton Mifflin, 1969).

21 Stephanie Nolen, "Saddam's Bark and Bite," *Globe and Mail*, November 16, 2002, F1.

22 Michael Cranny, *Crossroads: A Meeting of Nations* (Scar-borough, ON: Prentice Hall Ginn Canada, 1998), 41.

23 *Globe and Mail*, January 25, 2001, A10.

24 Berger, *Ways of Seeing*, 131.

25 Walker and Chaplin, *Visual Culture*, 119–125. The authors identify visual analogies referred to in this chapter.

26 Ibid., 120.

27 Stephen Hess and Milton Kaplan, *The Ungentlemanly Art: A History of American Political Cartoons* (New York: Macmillan, 1968).

28 Arch Dale, *The Grain Growers' Guide*, 1915, used by permission of the Glenbow Archives (NA-3055-24).

29 For a discussion of sources and types of analogies in political cartoons, see Werner, "Reading Visual Rhetoric."

30 Berger, *Ways of Seeing*, 29.

31 These three forms of intertextuality and the conventions used to activate them within textbooks are explained and illustrated in Walter Werner, "What Does This Picture Say? Reading the Intertextuality of Visual Images," *The International Journal of Social Education* 19 (forthcoming).

32 Michael Cranny et al., *Horizons: Canada Moves West* (Toronto: Prentice Hall Ginn Canada, 1999), 218.

33 Ibid., 222–223.

34 Walker and Chaplin, *Visual Culture*, 142.

35 Walter Werner, "On Political Cartoons: Visual Analogies, Intertextuality, and Cultural Memory" (paper presented at The Fading Image: Visual Culture and the Transformation of Memory conference, Centre for the Study of Historical Consciousness, University of British Columbia, May 16, 2003).

36 Scott Leith, "Did Martin Luther King Dream of Selling Cellphones?" *Globe and Mail*, March 30, 2001, M1.

37 *Report on Business Magazine* (April 2001): 60–61.

38 Michael Cranny with Graham Jarvis, *Pathways: Civilizations Through Time* (Scarborough, ON: Prentice Hall Ginn Canada, 1998), 276.

39 *The New Internationalist* 18, no. 5 (1988): 10.

40 Vivien Bowers and Stan Garrod, *Our Land: Building the West* (Toronto: Gage Educational Publishing, 1987), 126.

41 Cranny, *Crossroads*, 261.

42 Penney Clark and Roberta McKay, *Canada Revisited* (Edmonton: Arnold, 1992), 28.

43 The examples of religious and totalitarian surveillance are from Walker and Chaplin, *Visual Culture*, 106.

44 Advertisement for Canadian Air Transport Security Authority, *Report on Business Magazine* (June 2003).

45 Francis et al., *Canadian Issues*, 284.

46 Elizabeth Vallance, "The Public Curriculum of Orderly Images," *Educational Researcher* 24, no. 2 (1995): 6.

47 "Cultural analysis . . . is based on a keen awareness of the critic's situatedness in the present, the social and cultural present from which we look, and look back, at the objects that are always already of the past, objects that we take to define our present culture. Thus, it can be summarized by the phrase 'cultural memory in the present.' . . . This understanding is not based on an attempt to isolate and enshrine

the past in an objectivist 'reconstruction', nor on an effort to project it on an evolutionist line. . . . Instead, cultural analysis seeks to understand the past as *part of* the present, as what we have around us, and without which no culture could be able to exist." Mieke Bal, *The Practice of Cultural Analysis* (Stanford, CA: Stanford University Press, 1999), 1.

[48] Bryson, Holly, and Moxey, *Visual Culture*, xxvii.

[49] Michael Apple, *Democratic Education in a Conservative Age* (New York: Routledge, 1993), 60.

Part 3

Process Challenges and Prospects

Although it is impossible to have content without process and process without content, the distinction is a useful analytical tool if we remember that it is only analytical. In Part 2, many authors presented teaching techniques that complemented their conception of their subject areas. They talked about critical analysis, investigating the local community, role-playing, and talking circles. In Part 3, we look specifically at the pedagogy and processes in social studies that underlie the suggestions made in Part 2.

We have come a long way from when there were only a few teaching techniques and teachers relied upon chalk and talk and student reading of a textbook and answering questions based on what they had read. Mark Evans and Ian Hundey present several large frameworks, each providing a context for specific techniques teachers can use in the classroom. They provide examples in each category to show us how these overarching techniques can be put into practice. Andrew Hughes and Alan Sears follow with a chapter on situated learning, which is rooted in constructivism, one of the dominant learning theories. They provide research evidence to substantiate their suggestions and practical ideas to bring life to a complex topic.

Whatever it is that students learn they must either have prior knowledge of concepts or must learn the concepts that make sense of the material to be learned. For example, it is useless to teach about democracy without knowing what students mean by this, and if their meanings are unclear or incor-

rect, we must apply strategies to help them clarify the concept. Andrew Hughes introduces ideas for helping students grapple with concepts that are necessary for understanding the subject matter of social studies. Some of these strategies will involve critical thinking, and Linda Farr Darling and Ian Wright introduce us to this with special reference to building a community where critical thought is encouraged. Ann Sherman continues this dialogue when discussing how teachers can foster democratic citizenship and critical thinking in the elementary classroom.

Wherever there is social studies subject matter and citizenship education, there is the potential to confront conflict, as Kathy Bickmore demonstrated in Part 2. Andrew Hughes and Alan Sears use a conflict situation as the basis for their chapter on situated learning. The critical challenge category described by Mark Evans and Ian Hundey is another example where conflicts can occur regarding what to believe and what actions ought to be taken. All of the processes outlined here can be supported by the use of computers, and although the impact of computers is a topic worthy of study in the social studies curriculum, Sue Gibson points out that they can be used for much more than to help students obtain information and practice particular skills. Gibson argues that it is time to use computers in innovative ways, such as facilitating joint online projects between Canadian students and students on other continents.

All of what students do can be and often ought to be assessed. Like the explosion of teaching methodologies, there has been a corresponding one in assessment. No longer do we have to rely on the tried and often true methods of multiple choice, fill-in-the-blanks, and so on. Now there is a plethora of ways, including self-assessment, to determine what students have learned, how well they have learned, and how well they have thought about what they have learned. These assessment strategies are outlined by John Myers, who includes tips for how to design good assessments.

As you read these chapters, consider how you would respond to the following questions:

1. Are there any common elements in the teaching strategies outlined in these chapters?

2. What qualifies as good teaching?

3. What theories of learning are stated or implied by the authors? To which theory do you subscribe?

4. How does your background experience influence your use and acceptance of the teaching methods outlined here?

5. How do your ideas about what and how students should learn influence how you will assess students?

6. What qualifies as good assessment?

7. Which of the teaching methods do you think you will use? Why?

8. How do you think the context of the classroom/school/community in which you teach will influence how you will teach and assess students?

CHAPTER 15

Instructional Approaches in Social Studies Education

From "What to Teach" to "How to Teach"

Mark Evans and Ian Hundey

Earlier chapters in this book have explored the context and subject matter of social studies; this chapter initiates specific discussion about social studies instruction. Our underlying assumption is that the "what to teach" and the "how to teach" ought to be congruent and should not be separated or separable. Accordingly, what you have read in earlier chapters about the nature of social studies, its subject matter, and its curriculum organization will provide a backdrop for your understanding of instructional approaches dealt with in this chapter.

Overall, this chapter is intended to provide an introductory look at instructional approaches that are the result of disciplined and grounded inquiry, and that are of particular value to those involved in social studies education. The instructional approaches we describe and the instructional frameworks we explore provide a basis for building or expanding knowledge and competence in social studies teaching

Towards Instructional Expertise

Current research emphasizes the importance of teachers' expertise. A number of recent studies illustrate what Darling-Hammond has summarized:

> Teacher expertise is one of the most important factors in determining student achievement . . . that is, teachers who know a lot about teaching and learning and who work

in environments that allow them to know students are the critical elements of successful learning.[1]

Teachers are ultimately the people whose task it is to work creatively with their students and translate theoretical notions into practice. Teacher-shaped classroom and school events are the embodiment of the curriculum and provide the environment for effective learning. A critical element of teacher expertise is understanding of, and skill in, instruction.

Understanding of instruction has been greatly enhanced by substantive research and development work in recent decades. A variety of educators and education researchers offer a range of substantive evidence-informed instructional approaches that closely align instructional purposes and practices and attend to deep understanding.[2] Underpinning these works is a sense that instruction has become increasingly complex and ought to be approached in a way that respects the "relations between its elements: the teacher, the classroom or other context, content, the view of learning and learning about learning."[3]

When the authors of this chapter completed their teacher education methods courses in the 1960s and 1970s, they were introduced to a rather limited repertoire of instructional practices. Practices emphasized knowledge acquisition and comprehension supplemented by some attention to "higher order questioning techniques" and to "discovery" learning. We were introduced to social studies methods that included mini-lectures, demonstrations, question-and-answer activities, and document study. The use of audio-visual materials (tapes, films, and filmstrips) was promoted to appeal to different learning styles. The assessment approaches that we learned were mostly of a paper-and-pencil variety.

In contrast, university methods courses in social studies today typically aim at the development of a broad instructional repertoire or what Bennett and Rolheiser refer to as "instructional intelligence"— an understanding of instruction that involves not only technical competence but also an understanding of the theoretical and research underpinnings. This aim is further supported through other elements of teacher education programs that reflect a growing sense that a better understanding of the interacting factors affecting teaching and learning is crucial to a teacher's instructional effectiveness. Attention to this aim is also reflected in an increasing range of ongoing professional learning opportunities offered at faculties of education (and by school districts) for practising teachers.

Changes in social studies education have not been limited to faculty of education programs, of course. Indeed, in recent years there has been growing attention to thinking about teaching and learning in the social studies in schools. Recent reforms in curricula across Canada and initiatives on the part of social studies teachers have sparked new instructional approaches such as case-based learning, public issue research projects, cooperative learning structures, simulations, experiential and community-based learning activities, public information exhibits, youth forums, and Internet-based inquiries and linkages. Newly developed websites, texts, and resource materials provide a rich array of performance-based classroom ideas and activities. A cursory examination of these practices—and others—reveals the emergence of a range of sophisticated learning strategies that attends to deepened conceptual understanding; substantive public-issue investigation, from the local to the global; critical judgement and communication; building capacity for personal and interpersonal understanding; providing for community involvement and political participation; and authenticity—real-life themes, contexts, and performances.[4]

This increase in attention to instructional and assessment strategies employed by teachers in social studies—and in many other subjects—can be illustrated in a simple exercise. If you are an experienced social studies teacher, take a moment to write down all of the instructional approaches—including assessment instruments—used in your social studies classroom. If you are a beginning teacher, ask an experienced colleague to describe his or her instructional repertoire. A recent study on instructional integration asked four secondary teachers in four different subjects to do just that. The resulting lists ranged from eleven instructional approaches to over fifty.[5]

The emphasis on continuous development of teacher expertise and the increased attention to instruction has perhaps made the discussion of social studies instruction more complex than it might have been in the past. To make that discussion productive in this chapter, we offer sections that:

- explore the relationship of instruction to the overall social studies curriculum

- acknowledge some of the other instructional influences and choices facing a social studies teacher

- offer instructional frameworks that integrate strong theoretical foundations with a high level of practical value

Instruction and the Social Studies Curriculum

Various studies suggest that teachers' beliefs and understandings have a crucial effect on how they choose to teach.[6] One's beliefs and understandings about curriculum, the subject being taught, teaching and learning, characteristics of learners, the learning context(s), self, and how these factors interact are cited as important factors influencing one's instructional choices, and subsequently, one's impact.

To take one example, consider how teachers' views of the curriculum might influence instructional decisions. Teachers who view social studies as an integrated study will make different instructional choices from those who favour a discipline-specific curriculum. A teacher of integrated social studies might choose an instructional approach based on case studies that integrate past and present and involve issues related to geography, politics, and sociology. A subject specialist geography teacher might choose to engage in sustained field study to teach concepts associated purely with physical geography. A teacher of citizenship education who is encouraging "active citizenship" might choose to directly involve students in community action initiatives.

The organization of the curriculum also influences instruction. Most prescribed curriculum is organized in terms of a sequence of planning steps:

- objectives or outcomes or expectations
- teaching and learning strategies
- student activities
- resources
- assessment and evaluation
- transition to the next topic
- program review and modification

Teachers have been following this curriculum sequence, whether working through a formally organized curriculum or through a more informal process of step-by-step planning, as standard practice for years. Within this sequence, the objectives, outcomes or expectations stage, and available resources stage traditionally have influenced the choices made regarding teacher strategies and student activities. Recent emphasis on assessment and evaluation has led to a variation on this approach—starting the sequence from the end. "Backward design" means you start with the end in mind—"the desired results (goals or standards)—and then derive the curriculum from the evidence of learning (performances) called for by the standard and the teaching needed to equip students to perform."[7] The "end starting-point" usually takes the form of an assessment instrument or other culminating activity, where your students undertake a complex task to synthesize and demonstrate what they have learned. For example, if a unit of work in politics ends with a model par-

liament simulation, you start with this and ask yourself a series of questions. What will the students need to know and comprehend (enduring understandings) in order to undertake the simulation successfully? What skills will they need? What dispositions or attitudes need development?

Whether working through the curriculum forwards or backwards, you will constantly be making choices about instruction. Which instructional approaches best meet this set of learning intentions? Which resources will most effectively allow students to be successful in accomplishing these learning intentions? What assessment instrument(s) most effectively align with the learning intentions, the selected instructional approaches, and students' progress through the whole unit or course?

In recent years another curriculum consideration, curriculum reform, has strongly influenced instruction—both positively and negatively. In most provinces and territories, the social studies curriculum has been revised to become more descriptive and more prescriptive in terms of student outcomes. Clearly defined curriculum goals and intentions allow for clear understanding of the curriculum requirements, specificity of focus, and consistency in coverage from school to school and district to district. Precise expectations help answer the social studies teacher's question: What should I teach? The better curriculum documents offer support for another concern: How should I teach it?

Yet official curriculum goals—and ways to achieve those goals—can sometimes be at odds with what we know from the research about effective instruction. In some jurisdictions the sheer number of outcomes creates a curriculum overload that gets in the way of wise instructional choices. For example in Ontario, the curriculum for grade 5 (The Ontario Curriculum, Social Studies Grades 1 to 6) specifies forty-two specific expectations on two entirely unconnected topics: Early Civilizations and Aspects of Government in Canada. The grade 10 geography curriculum (The Ontario Curriculum, Canadian and World Studies, Grades 9 and 10) identifies seventy-three specific expectations, most involving multiple examples.

In other cases curriculum stipulations are viewed

as ill-conceived in that they do not reflect "good social studies," or "good history" or "good geography" in the minds of individual teachers or in the collective judgement of their colleagues. Some teachers recognize that even where the curriculum presents "good social studies," the requirements may not be suitable for a particular context: the community, the class (or some members of the class), the strengths and convictions of the teacher, or the available resources.

In summary, the curriculum shapes and at times limits instructional choices. At the same time there are other influences and issues that affect teachers' choices of instructional approaches.

Instructional Influences and Instructional Choices

A teacher's understanding of subject matter (e.g., facts and concepts and/or the ways and means by which knowledge is generated and established) may influence his or her instructional decisions. Consider the potentially different approaches to the teaching of history. If the teacher were to agree with historian Michael Bliss that "the main purpose of history teaching at practically every level below graduate instruction is to teach [knowledge] content,"[8] then the teacher might choose to emphasize key concepts, events, and turning points, and choose instructional approaches such as a lecture, a lecture linked to cooperative learning structures, a concept attainment activity, and/or Socratic teaching. If, however, the teacher were to agree with Peter Seixas that history must move beyond myth and heritage to deal with "complexity and uncertainty . . . with multiple causes, conflicting belief systems, and historical actors' differing perspectives,"[9] different instructional choices would be taken. Seixas' view of history might lead a teacher to emphasize the analysis of primary sources, conflicting interpretations, bias and objectivity in history, and use more constructivist-oriented instructional strategies such as inquiry and creative controversy. A teacher influenced by the increasing attention to popular history (e.g., television's "History Minutes" and "Canada: A Peoples' History" may be the best-known examples)

might agree with the history filmmaker who points to narrative as the way to "communicate to a non-specialist audience that isn't highly motivated to stick with your subject if they find it confusing or tedious."[10] Such a teacher might choose to teach through narrative techniques such as eyewitness stories, historical literature, and oral history projects. If a teacher had a strong commitment to exploring issues of equity and oppression in history, instructional choices again would be influenced. For example, a teacher might choose to address the neglect of women's experiences in many histories and emphasize the central roles that women played so students could understand:

> Women did not meekly sit by their spinning wheels or their cooking fires. They became leaders, doctors, artists, and award-winning writers; women defended forts, began newspapers, passed on military secrets, and rescued princes.[11]

Such a teacher might consciously decide to choose cases, narratives, and stories that highlight this perspective, and engage students in critical investigations and role-plays designed to provide insights into history from women's perspectives.

Teachers' understandings of teaching and learning also influence what instructional practices are used in the classroom. Teachers have varying understandings about how students learn. Some believe that their students arrive at school with certain abilities that continue to develop as they mature and learn. Others believe that experience is the basis of learning. Still others think that students construct their own knowledge based on personal and collaborative inquiries. Teachers also have varying understandings of specific types of instruction (e.g., discussion; simulations and role play; peer teaching; cooperative learning structures) and what is achieved through their use. Joyce and Weil with Calhoun, for example, outline a variety of models of teaching—situated in information processing, social, personal, and behavioural families—that are used by teachers for varying purposes.[12] Learning intentions often associated with social studies education (e.g., informed decision-making, critical thinking, ethical reasoning) are complex and multi-faceted. Choosing effective instructional practices from an expanding range and diversity of practices requires rather sophisticated levels of technical competence and theoretical understanding.

Student characteristics also influence a teacher's instructional choices. Factors such as attention to students' prior knowledge and ability, age and developmental factors, motivation, self-esteem, gender, cultural background, and/or socio-economic status may influence a teacher's choice of instructional strategies. Of particular interest is the increasing attention to issues of student diversity and inclusivity, and its implications for instruction. It is generally understood that instructional approaches have often attended to a dominant or mainstream culture, and therefore only to a portion of the learners. Instructional approaches that respond to the increasingly diverse backgrounds of all students in our classrooms need to be developed further. Choosing culturally responsive instructional approaches will require teachers to assess and adjust their instruction in response to the learning styles, beliefs, and experiences of their students. And, as Blair and Jones suggest,

> [this] does not involve a simple matching of instruction to cultural features but it is also a matter of adjusting and adapting instruction to meet the needs of all students. It requires a departure from familiar patterns of instruction and a willingness to utilize newer patterns.[13]

Choosing effective instructional practices is also influenced by contextual factors within the school and the community/communities where one teaches. There is enormous variation across teaching contexts. According to Turner-Bisset, some of the school-based contextual factors that influence a teacher's instructional choices are

> socioeconomic level of the catchment area; the type and size of school; the class size; the amount and quality of support teachers and other colleagues give to each other; the feedback teachers receive on their performance; the quality of relationships in the

school; and the expectations and attitudes of the head teacher.[14]

Context can provide important supports, but it can also be restrictive. For example, it can lead to teacher frustration and a sense of "deprofessionalization," which can leave classroom teaching and learning practices largely didactic and passive.

All of these factors—curriculum influences, teacher understanding of subject matter, views about how students learn, characteristics of individual students, cultural considerations, and the contexts within which teaching and learning take place—underscore not only the complexity of instructional choices you might make, but also the complexity of thinking about or designing instruction. One way to handle this complexity is to consider instructional frameworks that help you make effective instructional choices while also providing a context for reflection, discussion, and further learning about instruction.

Four Instructional Frameworks

What follows is an overview of four instructional design frameworks that respond to a complex and integrated understanding of instruction. These are overarching frameworks beyond the "expectation of the month." They represent approaches that are appropriate and useful no matter how the curriculum is organized or what the agreed upon purpose or focus of study is. Under these mega-frameworks an array of instructional strategies, instructional skills, and instructional concepts may be deployed and a wide array of assessment approaches may be utilized.

Furthermore, they provide varying perspectives upon which to make thoughtful instructional choices. No single framework can suit all circumstances involving the curriculum requirements, the make-up of a particular class, the strengths and preferences of a teacher, and the available resources. Your familiarity with multiple approaches will provide you with a solid grounding over the course of your career, make you more insightful about social studies curriculum issues and practices, and allow you to make decisions about how to teach from a broad and deep perspective.

In writing this chapter we were very aware that there are many models and frameworks to choose from. One colleague asked us why we weren't basing the chapter on *Models of Teaching*, which is perhaps the most umbrella-like of all frameworks and is studied widely at faculties of education. The answer to the question lies in the mega-qualities of that framework. With its elaborate examination of a range of teaching models, we felt that we could not do this framework justice in a single chapter. Nor did we want to put it forward as the sole framework, thereby suggesting that it was the answer to all instructional questions and the panacea for all instructional problems. We encourage you, however, to explore and come to appreciate *Models of Teaching*, which is referenced in the endnotes.[15]

We decided to focus on the following instructional frameworks:

- Dimensions of Learning Framework

- Story-Model Frameworks

- A Critical Thinking Framework

- Productive Pedagogies Framework

We selected these four because they are widely applicable across all social studies disciplines and topics; they have pedagogical integrity in terms of setting high standards for social studies learning; each has at least one unique feature that advances instructional sophistication; and they are the products of disciplined and grounded inquiry. It should be noted that the following descriptions are only introductions to these very complex instructional frameworks—introductions that we hope will stimulate your interest in investigating them further. We provide not only overviews of the four frameworks but sample applications that highlight the practical value of these models.

Dimensions of Learning Framework

Assisting students to acquire and integrate new information, construct meaning of new concepts, think

critically and creatively, and use complex reasoning processes in meaningful ways are just a few of the goals of learning associated with social studies curricula. The goals range from the specific and rudimentary to the comprehensive and complex and require a rather extensive instructional repertoire.

Dimensions of Learning offers an instructional framework for teachers that identifies a variety of teaching and learning activities and strategies that may be used when considering how to address this rich array of learning intentions. This framework is an extension of Marzano's work on cognition and learning described in *Dimensions of Thinking: A Framework for Curriculum and Instruction*[16] and research completed by the Dimensions of Learning Research and Development Consortium undertaken by the Mid-continent Regional Educational Laboratory (McREL) in the United States. The framework infuses a variety of evidence-informed instructional approaches with the primary intent of improving the quality of teaching and learning in various subject areas. A number of resources emerged from this initiative, ranging from texts that explain the framework's underpinning theory and research to classroom learning materials that provide practical applications.

Dimensions of Learning rests on five assumptions:[17]

1. Instruction must reflect the best of what we know about how learning occurs.

2. Learning involves a complex system of interactive processes that includes five types of thinking, represented in the five dimensions of learning.

3. The K–12 curriculum should include the explicit teaching of attitudes, perceptions, and mental habits that facilitate learning.

4. A comprehensive approach to instruction includes at least two distinct types of instruction: one that is more teacher-directed, and another that is more student-directed.

5. Assessment should focus on students' use of knowledge and complex reasoning processes rather than on their recall of information

The framework outlines five key dimensions.[18] For each of these dimensions, various instructional strategies are offered and suggestions are provided for integrating these strategies in ways that best respond to the learning intentions.

Dimension 1, *positive attitudes and perceptions about learning*, acknowledges the importance of using instructional strategies that both foster self-esteem and efficacy and nurture a safe and positive classroom climate.

- Helping students develop positive attitudes and perceptions about classroom climate

- Helping students develop positive attitudes and perceptions about classroom tasks

Dimension 2, *acquiring and integrating knowledge*, refers to the use of instructional strategies that encourage knowledge acquisition—acquiring new knowledge, knowledge retention, and integrating it (scaffolding) with the learner's prior knowledge in ways that help students make sense "of the new phenomena in light of existing beliefs and thought patterns" rather than accumulate facts.

- Declarative knowledge

- Procedural knowledge

Dimension 3, *extending and refining knowledge,* focuses on that dimension of learning that encourages students to think more critically and creatively about a social studies theme or issue. Instructional strategies that encourage various types of thinking such as comparison, classification, critiquing, inductive analysis, using evidence, and recognizing multiple perspectives are suggested.

- Comparing

- Classifying

- Abstracting

- Inductive reasoning

- Deductive reasoning

- Constructing support

- Analyzing errors

- Analyzing perspectives

Dimension 4, *using knowledge meaningfully*, refers to the dimension of learning that encourages students to use their knowledge in meaningful ways. Instructional strategies highlight ways in which students might demonstrate their capacity to investigate issues or problems that stand out in the social studies curriculum and/or are of personal interest, and by doing so, demonstrate their capacity to problem-solve, resolve conflict, make decisions, and so on.

- Decision-making

- Problem-solving

- Invention

- Experimental inquiry

- Investigation

- Systems analysis

Dimension 5, *productive habits of mind*, is concerned with one's personal approach to learning. Instructional strategies nurture habits viewed as important to various forms of thinking, in particular critical thinking, creative thinking, and self-regulated thinking.

- Critical thinking habits

    Be accurate and seek accuracy
    Be clear and seek clarity
    Maintain an open mind
    Restrain impulsivity
    Take a position when the situation warrants it
    Respond appropriately to others' feelings and level of knowledge

- Creative thinking habits

    Persevere
    Push the limits of your knowledge and abilities
    Generate, trust, and maintain your own standards of evaluation
    Generate new ways of viewing a situation that are outside the boundaries of standard conventions

- Self-regulated thinking habits

    Monitor your own thinking
    Plan appropriately
    Identify and use necessary resources
    Respond appropriately to feedback
    Evaluate the effectiveness of your actions

Marzano stresses that "the five dimensions of learning are not independent of one another" and ought to be used "in complex ways, not in one any set pattern." Learning "is a highly complex set of interactive processes that differ from person to person and from context to context."[19] Instructional strategies offered within this framework keep each of these dimensions in mind. Sample applications of the Dimensions of Learning Framework appear on pages 227 and 228.

Story-Model Frameworks

Stories are how we explain, how we teach, how we entertain ourselves, and how we often do all three at once. They are at the juncture where facts and feelings meet. And for those reasons, they are central to civilizations—in fact, civilization takes form in our mind as a series of narratives.[20]

Stories are at the heart of social studies. Social studies teachers use stories to help students conceptualize big pictures—e.g., the story of glacial retreat, the story of waves of migration, the story of developing rights and freedoms. They use the stories of interesting people, decisive actions, natural phenomena, and political breakthroughs to illustrate topics in social studies curricula. Teachers know that the elements of "story"—friction, drama, heroism, disaster, triumph, emotion, imagination, and commonalities among peoples—appeal to students and provide powerful tools for learning. Stories are how we make sense of the world and our experience.

Some educators have gone beyond the practice of using stories as part of their instruction to using "story" as the basis for planning curriculum and organizing instruction. They have done so to capitalize on the fundamental appeal of story and on the power of students' imagination. They see story-based planning as an authentic way to link student thinking to real-world stories and as a means for developing integrated or holistic curriculum.

Two educators in particular have explored the possibilities of story-models as a basis for curriculum and instruction. Susan Drake has proposed two approaches. The first, the "Journey of the Hero," is the basis for most stories throughout time and across cultures. The hero is called to adventure; he or she leaves the kingdom in search of this adventure. Ahead are the demons to be confronted, the dragons to slay (struggle). Finally, the hero slays the dragon, receives a reward, and returns to the kingdom where he or she must share the lessons of the journey.[21] You might see this journey-story as the basis for studying exploration or settlement, or the exploits of a political radical or civil-rights reformer.

More widely applicable to social studies and more familiar to social studies teachers is Drake's story-model for developing integrated curriculum.[22] This model involves the following steps for dealing with a topic or issue:

1. Identify why the present story is in a state of flux or change.

2. Identify the roots of the conflict by looking at the past or old story, identifying implicit values in this old story.

3. Explore the future through

    (a) the projected story (based on following the values of the old story);

    (b) the ideal story (based on ideal values).

4. Create a new story by integrating the necessary from the old story and the feasible from the ideal story.

5. Develop a personal story—a personal position or personal action plan for the new story.

You might best appreciate the possibilities for Drake's story-model by thinking through an example for a topic such as the development of a new housing project on fertile farmland; the redevelopment of an historic downtown; the logging of an old-growth forest; or the introduction of proportional representation in federal elections.

The other educator associated with a story model is Kieran Egan. Egan provides an alternative approach to outcomes-based planning and a counter view to the assumption that teaching must proceed from the concrete to the abstract. His Story Form Model proposes a framework that "draws on the power of the story form and uses that power in teaching."[23] More recently, Egan has offered a number of instructional frameworks appropriate for social studies: The Romantic Planning Framework; the Philosophical Planning Framework, and the Mythic Planning Framework. One of the authors of this chapter has had successful experiences working through the Mythic Planning Framework—in its former guise as the Story Form Model—with social studies students, and that model is presented below.

THE STORY FORM MODEL

1. Identifying importance

   What is important about this topic? What is affectively engaging about it?

2. Finding binary opposites

   What binary concepts best capture the affective importance of the topic?

3. Organizing the content into a story form

   First teaching event

   What content most dramatically embodies the binary concepts, in order to provide access to the topic? What image best captures that content and its dramatic contrast?

   Structuring the body of the lesson or unit

   What content best articulates the topic into a clear story form?

4. Conclusion

   What is the best way of resolving the conflict inherent in the binary concepts? What degree of mediation is it appropriate to seek? How far is it appropriate to make the structuring binary concepts explicit?

5. Evaluation

   How can one know whether the topic has been understood, its importance grasped, and the content learned?

As is the case with the other instructional frameworks presented in this chapter, the authors firmly believe that the best understanding comes through using the framework for a particular topic. A sample topic is presented on page 229, but we encourage you to work through one of your own (hint: start by identifying the "binary opposites" appropriate for your topic).

A Critical Thinking Framework

The term "critical thinking" has different meanings for different social studies teachers. For some it has meant the encouragement of healthy skepticism or academic rigour—often in regard to particular issues-based topics in the curriculum. For others, critical thinking has been viewed as one of the skills areas developed through the teaching of strategies such as problem-solving or decision-making. These perspectives have resulted in a limited view of critical thinking, relegating it to episodes in the curriculum and heightening tensions between teachers' concerns for covering the core content and their interest in critical inquiries. In recent years more comprehensive approaches to critical thinking have been proposed. In these approaches, critical thinking is seen as a fundamental element—the core—for social studies curriculum.

One of these more recent approaches provides a critical thinking perspective in terms of authentic experience:

> Promoting critical thinking at any level is not simply a matter of implementing a few strategies from a pedagogical cookbook—rather it is a way of life in the classroom.[24]

Making critical thinking "the way of life in the classroom" involves an ethic for critical thinking based on five principles:

Dimensions of Learning Framework

This framework assumes that the five broad dimensions of learning are being infused throughout the particular social studies course and that instructional activities and strategies being used are congruent with the focus of learning. In some cases, specific dimensions may be infused into a particular lesson or unit. In other cases, the various dimensions may be integrated to achieve more sophisticated learning outcomes. Two sample instructional approaches are provided below, reflecting this variation.

SAMPLE 1: RECOGNIZING POINT(S) OF VIEW ABOUT A CONTEMPORARY ISSUE

This sample addresses Dimension 2 of the framework, *acquiring and integrating knowledge.* This dimension identifies two categories of knowledge: declarative knowledge (i.e., facts, concepts, and generalizations students should know and understand about the subject) and procedural knowledge (learning skills and processes important to the subject that students should be able to demonstrate). This sample focuses on nurturing students' capacity to "recognize point of view," a type of procedural knowledge. While there are different approaches a teacher may take to develop various types of knowledge, Marzano encourages three instructional phases when learning procedural knowledge: constructing models, shaping, and internalizing.[25]

1. CONSTRUCTING MODELS

Phase one focuses on assisting students to think about rough steps they might use to recognize point(s) of view in a newspaper article or journal about a contemporary issue. Examples from students' and/or the teacher's experiences of how to do this should be provided, although students ought to be encouraged to construct their own approaches. One approach the teacher might offer students in this initial phase of recognizing point of view is to identify the subject being discussed and the author of the article; identify which aspects of the subject are emphasized by the author; identify any aspects of the subject that are downplayed by the author; and based on what has been identified in the preceding steps, describe the author's point of view. Students should be encouraged to discuss and refine their approaches, to develop a written or graphic representation (e.g., a flow chart) of the steps that they would use, and rehearse it in their minds. Discussion about this skill and its importance in their day-to-day lives should also be addressed in this phase.

2. SHAPING

Phase two involves students practising using their initial models and making refinements to—shaping—the models based on what works and what doesn't. A variety of articles with differing points of view on a particular contemporary issue should be provided for students to practise on. During this phase teachers may assist with the shaping process and address common errors and pitfalls. Some questions the teacher might ask are: Why can it be difficult to recognize point of view? What additional information would you need to understand the author's point of view better? and Why is it important for you to be able to recognize other people's points of view about contemporary issues? Students should be encouraged to again refine their initial representations and discuss when and where this skill may be used in their daily lives. Teachers should also be carrying out checks to ensure that all students understand the concept.

3. INTERNALIZING

Internalizing requires extensive practice and time. Curriculum decisions need to be made about those aspects of procedural knowledge that are truly needed and those that are of lesser importance. Based on these decisions, opportunities to practise need to be provided throughout the duration of a course (and across courses) if the selected skills and processes are to be internalized.

SAMPLE 2: INVESTIGATING A SOCIAL ISSUE

Investigation is central to social studies curricula and is used to explore deeper understandings of concepts; construct scenarios of historical events or situations where controversy or confusion exists; or clarify perspectives about a contemporary issue. Different dimensions of the framework are infused in a student investigation. To be sure, the selection of a relevant social issue, the support given to student learning, and the concern for student success in this investigation reflect Dimension 1, *positive attitudes and perceptions about learning.* Clearly new knowledge needs to be learned (Dimension 2, *acquiring and integrating knowledge*) and data collected need to be classified and analyzed (Dimension 3, *extending and refining knowledge*). As well, knowledge produced needs to be used meaningfully (Dimension 4, *using knowledge meaningfully*), and students need to reflect critically on the whole investigation process (Dimension 5, *productive habits of mind*).

For each dimension and stage of the investigation, various instructional activities and strategies need to be selected that will effectively respond to the targeted goals of learning. In this sample, using knowledge meaningfully through investigation will be highlighted. Below is a brief sketch of some of the stages to be included. Of course there are many variations and instructional decisions to be made at each stage.

1. UNDERSTANDING THE PROCESS AND PURPOSES OF INVESTIGATION

Phase one introduces students to the range of possible issues to be examined, different types of investigations, and the purposes of social investigation.

2. CARRYING OUT AN INVESTIGATION

Phase two introduces students to a process for carrying out an investigation and an opportunity to try out the process with a simple question. The following steps might be highlighted for an investigation being undertaken by students in a grade 9 social studies class:

- choose a topic and identify a central question for investigation
- develop a tentative plan to guide the investigation
- identify and locate appropriate learning resources (e.g., computer, print, visuals, people, community sites)
- assess information collected in light of the central question
- record main ideas in your own words and through diagrams, graphs, etc.
- review data collected and fill in any missing gaps through further investigation and discussions with peers and the teacher
- prepare final product and share what you've learned

This phase should also alert students to some of the challenges. For example, sometimes the focus of the investigation may be too complex or resources may not be readily available. In either case, assistance may be required during this phase to deal with challenges students anticipate during the investigation process.

3. PLANNING THE INVESTIGATION

This phase involves choosing a tentative topic, assessing what you already know about the topic, preparing a list of key questions to be investigated, and mapping out a general plan—including a timeline—for the investigation.

4. WORKING TOGETHER THROUGH THE INVESTIGATION

This stage involves locating and selecting appropriate learning resources, finding, assessing, and recording pertinent information related to the focus of the investigation. A variety of choices needs to be considered at this stage. What types of sources of information will be used? How many? How will notes be recorded? How will data be classified and organized?

5. COMMUNICATING THE FINDINGS OF THE INVESTIGATION

Phase five involves sharing the final product. The assignment requirements, the audience, the preparation time, and the format need to be considered at this stage. A variety of possible formats (bulletin board, radio broadcast, and/or a newspaper article) may be used to present the findings.

6. REFLECTING ABOUT THE INVESTIGATION PROCESS

This phase provides an opportunity for the teacher and students to identify and assess the main strengths and weaknesses of the investigation and how these understandings may be applied to future investigations.

The Story Form Model

SAMPLE: LAND USE—AN ABANDONED CANAL

1. Identifying importance

    This topic is important because it is an issue in the local community: What to do with an abandoned 100-year-old canal? The topic is affectively engaging because most of the students have played on the locks or along the canal banks.

2. Finding binary opposites

    Preservation vs. destruction

3. Organizing the content into a story form

    First teaching event

    The teacher presents an issue to the class: the old canal on the edge of town is to be destroyed because it is dangerous: the banks are crumbling and the railings around the locks have collapsed. The teacher records student reactions and then asks them to imagine alternatives to destroying the canal.

    Structuring the body of the lesson or unit

    Students explore three alternatives: (i) destroy the locks and fill in the canal; (ii) preserve it by making it safe and building a walking trail alongside; (iii) restore it and use it for boating. Working in groups, students consider criteria for assessing the alternatives: costs, public support, political support, technical complexities. They interview local politicians, conduct household and peer surveys, consult local historical and naturalist societies, and visit the community engineering office. They decide on one alternative and present their findings to the town council.

4. Conclusion

    Students discover that many community members see the canal as an attractive local feature and as a reserve for birds and fish, and they strongly oppose its destruction. The students also discover that it would be too expensive to restore the canal-locks for boating and that the modern water supply is not adequate. They conclude that the best alternative is to preserve the canal, make it safe, and build a walking trail alongside. The public supports this idea, and some town councillors do too. The costs are an issue, but the students plan to lobby provincial politi-cians and find sponsors to contribute to the preservation plan.

5. Evaluation

    The students submit their group analyses of the alternatives based on the criteria. As well, students individually submit written statements summarizing what they learned about their community and the political process, and about themselves.

    The teacher debriefs the episode in terms of student understanding of the binary opposites: Why should we try to preserve features of the natural or built landscape? What are the community tensions involved with preservation and destruction? Under what circumstances is it acceptable to destroy a local feature? What government processes are there for assessing such issues? What roles can citizens have?

1. Knowledge is not fixed, but always subject to re-examination and change.

2. There is no question which cannot, or should not, be asked.

3. Awareness of, and empathy for, alternative world views is essential.

4. There is need of tolerance for ambiguity.

5. There is a need for a sceptical attitude towards text.

Another recent approach for making critical thinking the "way of life in the classroom" is based on the straightforward proposition that "critical thinking is in some sense good thinking. It is the quality of the thinking, not the process of thinking, which distinguishes critical, from uncritical thinking."[26] This approach has been developed into an elaborate conceptual, curriculum and instructional framework within The Critical Thinking Consortium, a non-profit society consisting of twenty-one school districts, three universities, and several provincial associations in British Columbia. The consortium's materials define critical thinking as "the thinking through of a problematic situation about what to believe or how to act where the thinker makes reasoned judgements that embody the qualities of a competent thinker."[27]

This definition of critical thinking leads to a four-pronged approach to help students improve as critical thinkers:[28]

1. Building a community of thinkers within the school and classroom so that students frequently experience learning opportunities requiring critical thinking, engage in critical and cooperative dialogue with others in the community, critically examine their own work and that of their peers, and see their teachers as models who practise critical thinking and collegiality in learning.

2. Infusing critical challenges throughout the curriculum so that students are deliberately presented with problematic situations that require a critical thinking response. Four questions guide the choice of critical challenges: Does the task require judgement? Is the challenge meaningful to students? Does it reflect key subject components of the curriculum? Do students have the tools to address the challenge or can they be taught them in addressing it?

3. Developing the intellectual tools for critical thinking so that students have the knowledge, skills, and dispositions to respond to the critical challenges: background knowledge; criteria for judgement; critical thinking vocabulary; thinking strategies; and habits of mind.

4. Assessing students' competence in using the tools so that there is congruence between what is taught in promoting critical thinking and what is assessed and evaluated. The intellectual tools are the basis of the criteria for assessing students' work.

Educators in The Critical Thinking Consortium have been using this critical thinking/critical challenges approach for several years, and an ambitious program of publishing resources is underway. Sample social studies activities based on this four-pronged model may be viewed at https://public.sd38.bc.ca/RTRWeb/. You may best understand the value and potential of this approach by choosing a social studies topic and working through the framework yourself. An example of the Critical Thinking Framework appears on page 231. You are encouraged to develop your own application.

Productive Pedagogies Framework

Productive Pedagogies, like Dimensions of Learning, offers a comprehensive framework for thinking about classroom instruction. It highlights four broad dimensions: *intellectual quality; relevance; supportive classroom environment;* and *recognition of difference.* Productive Pedagogies is not a specific strategy but rather a way of thinking about instruction that attempts to respond empirically to two central questions: What classroom practices contribute to increased student learning for all students? And, What classroom practices contribute to more equitable student learning? The framework requires teachers

Critical Thinking Framework

SAMPLE: SETTLING THE WEST

1. Create a critical community

At the beginning of the school year the students and the teacher engage in a cooperative exercise to identify key focuses (e.g., a focus on understanding concepts like conflict and change, and a focus on finding local links for topics) and operating norms for their social studies classroom (e.g., question-raising is as important as question-answering, and respect for alternative points of view). In previous topics students have engaged in cooperative group activities such as "round table" and "three-step interview" to gain experience in sharing insights, listening to each other, and building on each others' ideas.

2. Provide a critical challenge

The critical question in this topic is: "Which three factors best explain why settlers moved West in the period 1880–1914?"

3. Teach the tools

- Background knowledge: Students gain knowledge about the factors for migration from texts, library resources, and the Internet. Factors include economic and political distress in emigrant homelands; attractions of a new life in the West; easier travel on new railways; free or cheap land; administrative organization of settlement; and personal or family factors. They review their understanding of the push-pull concept of migration learned in earlier classes.

- Criteria for judgement: With the teacher, students develop a list of criteria for deciding which factors would have been most compelling. For example, which factors offered the most physical/psychological comfort, which had the biggest financial implications, and which satisfied cultural aspirations of immigrants?

- Critical Thinking vocabulary: The class reviews such terms as *criterion, generalization, point of view,* and *multiple causation*.

- Thinking strategies: In-their-shoes activity. In groups, students consider the reasons for migrating westward from the points of view of eastern Canadian farmers; eastern Canadian industrial workers; western European industrial workers; central European farmers; Aboriginal and Métis settlers (moving from near-west to further west). Each group of students uses a chart to indicate the most compelling causes for migration for its particular migrants and justifies its ranking of the causes.

- Habits of mind: Students practise formulating and supporting a position and developing empathy for points of view and human circumstances that are different from their own.

4. Assess the tools

Following presentations from the groups, students individually assume the roles of members of groups other than their original ones. They write essays explaining, in their role, their new circumstances and their three main reasons for migrating to the West.

to think deliberately about what and how they are teaching, the learning styles and backgrounds of their students, and the contexts in which they are teaching. The framework includes twenty "productive pedagogies" believed to improve the quality of instruction. Of particular importance is attention to the "recognition of difference," a dimension often under-represented in other approaches.

The framework was developed for the Queensland, Australia, context by the Queensland School Reform Longitudinal Study (SRLS) Group, under the direction of Dr. James Ladwig and Professor Bob Lingard. Various educators and researchers in schools in Queensland and New South Wales, Australia, have been involved in aspects of its implementation, assorted research studies, and the development of a number of classroom resources.[29] Studies on the use of the Productive Pedagogies Framework have tended to be positive in terms of student learning and increased teacher familiarity with and use of a broader range of high-quality instructional approaches. The framework was influenced by Newmann's and Wehlage's work on "standards for authentic instruction," which emphasized three key criteria:

> Students construct meaning and produce knowledge, students use disciplined inquiry to construct meaning, and students aim their work toward production of discourse, products, and performances that have value or meaning beyond success in school.[30]

The following is an overview of the Productive Pedagogies Framework:

Dimension 1, *intellectual quality*, focuses on knowledge acquisition and knowledge-in-use. Underpinning this dimension is the belief that all students should be expected to demonstrate work of high intellectual quality. Instructional approaches are encouraged that require students to demonstrate deepened understandings and perform tasks that reflect higher-order thinking, problem-solving, and constructivist forms of thinking rather than the transmission of information. This approach is about engaging students in big ideas and complex understandings.[31]

- Higher-order thinking
- Deep knowledge
- Deep understanding
- Substantive conversation
- Knowledge as problematic
- Metalanguage

Dimension 2, *relevance*, emphasizes the need to ensure that the focus of learning is relevant to students and to themes or issues of significance outside the classroom. Instructional approaches are encouraged that help students examine real issues and real-world problems and make connections to their past experiences and background knowledge and the world beyond the classroom.

- Knowledge integration
- Background knowledge
- Connectedness to the world
- Problem-based curriculum

Dimension 3, *supportive classroom environment*, focuses on the importance of creating an inclusive learning environment that is respectful and attentive to the diverse learning needs of all students, particularly for students from disadvantaged backgrounds. Instructional approaches are encouraged that provide social support for students' achievement, academic engagement, and a high degree of self-regulation and direction.

- Student direction
- Social support
- Academic engagement
- Explicit quality performance criteria
- Self-regulation

Dimension 4, *recognition of difference*, an element often not addressed in other instructional approaches, focuses on the importance of valuing individual and cultural difference, in particular non-dominant cul-

Productive Pedagogies Framework

This framework assumes that the four broad dimensions of learning are being infused throughout the particular social studies course and that instructional activities and strategies being used are congruent with the focus of learning. As with the Dimensions of Learning Framework, an aspect of one dimension may be infused into a particular lesson or unit or various dimensions may be integrated into a lesson or unit to achieve more sophisticated learning outcomes.

SAMPLE: RIGHTS OF YOUTH FORUM

This sample highlights both Dimension 2, *relevance* ("connectedness to the world" and "problem-based curriculum") and the active citizenship element of Dimension 4, *recognition of difference*. This latter element addresses the growing attention to how active citizenship can be encouraged in the classroom and school in ways that move from more traditional and passive approaches to ones that are more transformative and active. Active citizenship within the Productive Pedagogies context acknowledges the importance of democratic engagement both in terms of participation and responsibility. A continuum of practice is provided that contrasts "minimalist" and "maximalist" representations. The sample below tends toward the maximalist end of the continuum.

1. THE FOCUS

This instructional strategy focuses on the rights of youth. It is a blend of a variety of instructional strategies including decision-making, group investigation, and role-playing. It highlights inquiry, critical reasoning, interpersonal conversation, decision-making, an understanding of how one's personal values affects one's response to public issues, and participatory literacies—all important capacities in the democratic process. Authenticity is a primary consideration in this strategy. The issue of youth rights is to be examined and considered in light of national and international rights legislation. Various perspectives and cases are explored and discussed. In this process, knowledge and understanding are deepened, higher-order thinking is undertaken, and substantive conversations take place—all elements of Dimension 1, *intellectual quality*.

2. RESEARCH GROUPS

Students establish small groups (3 or 4 students) and begin to establish research plans. Students locate and review relevant cases and sources of information in preparation for taking a position in a role play in an imaginary Rights of Youth Forum. Consideration of other perspectives, including their underlying values and potential public consequences, are explored. With Dimension 3, *supportive classroom environment*, in mind, the teacher has ensured that the students have gained appropriate skills in cooperative small-group learning and have the necessary social support, while he or she also encourages self-regulation.

In considering other perspectives, students are required to explore non-dominant cultural positions and to consider issues of exclusion and inclusion in terms of public consequences of these positions (Dimension 4, *recognition of difference*).

3. ROLE-PLAY

The role play is enacted within a real or imagined authentic context; the roles are based on each group's research and the stance taken in response to the issue of youth rights. A Youth Rights Forum could be held district-wide, involving students from schools across the district, or in the classroom as part of a "staged" nationally organized forum.

4. DEBRIEF AND PERSONAL ACTION

The research and role play are debriefed. Personal action may be taken (e.g., recommendations may be framed in a submission to the appropriate government department responsible for youth rights).

tural knowledge. Instructional approaches that attend to the recognition of differences and that "encompass inclusivity of non-dominant groups" are stressed.[32]

- Cultural knowledges
- Inclusivity
- Narrative
- Group identity
- Active citizenship

A sample application of the Productive Pedagogies Framework appears on page 233.

Conclusion

Instruction in its most comprehensive form uses—and is influenced by—different kinds of knowledge in various combinations. Teachers' perspectives on the knowledge content and the pedagogy of social studies affect what and how they teach. Highly competent teachers are able to apply a range of strategies that are appropriate for particular curriculum aims, diverse learner characteristics, and circumstances. They build up a complex instructional repertoire that incorporates and integrates understandings of the curriculum, subject matter, processes of teaching and learning, characteristics of learners, and the learning context(s). Attempting to build this instructional repertoire in the form of a thick cookbook of accumulated strategies can be a daunting exercise and may lead to instructional chaos.

The four instructional design frameworks provided in this chapter offer contexts for thinking about instruction in more holistic and integrated ways rather than seeing it as simply a collection of all known strategies. These frameworks, all the products of disciplined and grounded inquiry, attempt to respond to the complex and integrated understanding of instruction by providing navigational aids for social studies teachers. They provide varying perspectives within which reflection and discussion might take place, ongoing professional learning might be stimulated, and thoughtful instructional choices might be made to advance both theoretical

sophistication and technical know-how in the design and development of effective social studies instruction.

Endnotes

1 L. Darling-Hammond, "Teachers and Teaching: Testing Policy Hypotheses from a National Commission Paper," *Educational Researcher* 27, no. 1 (1998): 6.

2 See, for example, Barrie Bennett and Carol Rolheiser, *Beyond Monet: The Artful Science of Instructional Integration* (Toronto: Bookation, 2001); Bruce Joyce and Marsha Weil with Emily Calhoun, *Models of Teaching*, 6th ed. (Boston: Allyn & Bacon, 2000); Robert Marzano et al., *Dimensions of Learning: Teacher's Manual* (Alexandria, VA: Association for Supervision and Curriculum Development, 1997); Peter Mortimore, ed., *Understanding Pedagogy and Its Impact on Learning* (London: Paul Chapman, 1999); Rosy Turner-Bisset, *Expert Teaching: Knowledge and Pedagogy to Lead the Profession* (London: David Fulton Publishers, 2001); and Grant Wiggins and Jay McTighe, *Understanding by Design* (Alexandria, VA: Association for Supervision and Curriculum Development, 1998).

3 S. Hallam and J. Ireson, "Pedagogy in the Secondary School," in *Understanding Pedagogy and Its Impact on Learning*, 8.

4 M. Evans and I. Hundey, "Educating for Citizenship in Canada: New Meanings in a Changing World," in *Weaving Connections: Educating for Peace, Social and Environmental Justice*, ed. Tara Goldstein and David Selby (Toronto: Sumach Press, 2000).

5 B. Bennett, S. Anderson, and M. Evans, "Towards a Theory of Instructional Acquisition" (paper presented at the annual meeting of the American Educational Research Association, Chicago, 1997).

6 See, for example, J. Ireson, P. Mortimore, and S. Hallam, "The Common Strands of Pedagogy and Their Implications," in *Understanding Pedagogy and Its Impact on Learning*; and Turner-Bisset, *Expert Teaching*.

7 Wiggins and McTighe, *Understanding by Design*, 8.

8 Michael Bliss, "Teaching Canadian National History," *Canadian Social Studies* 36, no. 2 (Winter 2002), http://www.quasar.ualberta.ca/css/Css_36_2/Articles.

9 Peter Seixas, "The Purposes of Teaching Canadian History," *Canadian Social Studies* 36, no. 2 (Winter 2002), http://www.quasar.ualberta.ca/css/Css_36_2/Articles.

10 G. Allen, "Canadian History in Film: A Roundtable Discussion," *Canadian Historical Review* 82, no. 2 (2001): 333.

11 Susan E. Merritt, *Her Story: Women from Canada's Past* (St. Catharines, ON: Vanwell Publishing, 1994), vii.

12 Joyce and Weil with Calhoun, *Models of Teaching*.

13 Timothy Blair and Deneese Jones, *Preparing for Student Teaching in a Pluralistic Classroom* (Boston: Allyn & Bacon, 1998), 9.

14 Turner-Bisset, *Expert Teaching*, 17.

15 Joyce and Weil with Calhoun, *Models of Teaching*.

16 Robert Marzano, *Dimensions of Thinking: A Framework for Curriculum and Instruction* (Alexandria, VA: Association for Supervision and Curriculum Development, 1988).

17 Robert Marzano, *A Different Kind of Classroom: Teaching with Dimensions of Learning* (Alexandria, VA: Association for Supervision and Curriculum Development, 1992).

18 Robert Marzano et al., *Dimensions of Learning: Teachers' Manual*.

19 Robert Marzano et al., *Implementing Dimensions of Learning* (Alexandria, VA: Association for Supervision and Curriculum Development, 1992), 11.

20 Robert Fulford, "The Triumph of Narrative," in *Story Works: How Teachers Can Use Shared Stories in the New Curriculum*, ed. David Booth and Robert Barton (Markham, ON: Pembroke Publishers, 2000), 8.

21 Susan Drake, *Planning Integrated Curriculum: The Call to Adventure* (Alexandria, VA: Association for Supervision and Curriculum Development, 1993).

22 Susan Drake, *Developing an Integrated Curriculum Using the Story Model* (Toronto: OISE Press, 1992).

23 Kieran Egan, *Teaching as Story Telling: An Alternative Approach to Teaching and Curriculum in the Elementary School* (London: Althouse Press, 1986), 2.

24 A. Sears and J. Parsons, "Principles of an Ethic of Critical Thinking," in *The Canadian Anthology of Social Studies: Issues and Strategies for Teachers*, ed. Roland Case and Penney Clark (Burnaby: Faculty of Education, Simon Fraser University, 1997), 173.

25 Marzano, *Dimensions of Learning*, 49.

26 S. Bailin et al., "Conceptualizing Critical Thinking," *Journal of Curriculum Studies* 31, no. 3 (1999): 288.

27 Roland Case and LeRoi Daniels, *Introduction to the TC² Conception of Critical Thinking* (Richmond, BC: Rich Thinking Resources, 2003), https://public.sd38.bc.ca/RTRWeb/PDFdocuments/CCIntro.pdf, i.

28 Ibid.; see https://public.sd38.bc.ca/RTRWeb/.

29 New South Wales Department of Education and Training, "Productive Pedagogy," *inform* (March 2002), www.det.nsw.edu.au/inform/yr2002/mar/pedagogy.htm, 4.

30 F. Newmann and G. Wehlage, "Standards for Authentic Instruction," *Educational Leadership* 50, no. 7 (1993): 8.

31 New South Wales, "Productive Pedagogy," 2.

32 Ibid.

Additional References

Chalmers, H. *Integration of Productive Pedagogies and Principles of Effective Learning and Teaching*. Queensland, Australia: Department of Education, Ipswich District Office, 2000.

Egan, Kieran. "Planning Frameworks" in *The Educated Mind: How Cognitive Tools Shape Our Understanding*. Chicago: University of Chicago Press, 1997. Also available online at http://www.educ.sfu.ca/kegan/Frame.html.

Hill, Geof. "Reflecting on Professional Practice with a Cracked Mirror: Productive Pedagogy Experiences." Paper presented at the Australian Association for Research in Education conference, Brisbane, Australia, December 2002, http://www.aare.edu.au/02pap/hil02657.htm.

Newmann, Fred, and Associates. *Authentic Achievement: Restructuring Schools for Intellectual Quality*. San Francisco: Jossey-Bass, 1996.

CHAPTER 16

Getting the Idea

An Introduction to Concept Learning and Teaching in Social Studies

Andrew S. Hughes

Concepts without precepts are empty; precepts without concepts are blind.—Immanuel Kant

In 1848, Dominic O'Hara left his home in Donegal in Northwest Ireland and came to North America where he settled in Saint John, New Brunswick. Thousands of other Irish men, women, and children made similar journeys at that time, as they did before 1848 and since. Dominic's story consists of a unique set of facts. It is a singular instance, as indeed are the stories of all the others. And yet, they have enough in common that we can bind them together in the *concept* of migration. For the Irish, the concept becomes emigration; for Canadians it is immigration. For one, it explains the depletion of a population; for the other, its growth. The idea captures not just the movement of people but also the forces that pushed them and pulled them, their hopes and their fears, what they gained and what they lost. Furthermore, the concept is not limited to the Irish migrations. It is an equally valuable idea in understanding the successive waves of people coming to Canada from Eastern and Western Europe in the early part of the twentieth century, and more recently from the West Indies and Southeast Asia. Nor is it restricted to Canada. It is just as valuable a concept to Argentineans and Chileans, Americans and Australians.

When someone tells us that they are an "immigrant," they are communicating to us only a highly generalized and simplified version of their lived experience. It tells us nothing of the details of the life of the particular immigrant: the country of origin, the reasons for leaving, the attractions of the new country, the difficulties encountered, the related joy and heartbreak. And yet, there is between us sufficient commonality of understanding that the communication has meaning. Embracing countless separate instances into one category of experience constitutes the formation of a concept. In placing them in a single category we are focusing on their critical attributes, that is, the features that they must possess in order to be recognized as an instance of the concept. Think of the concept "river." Do you see in your mind's eye the Colorado coursing through the Grand Canyon? Or perhaps the broad Saint Lawrence below Kingston or Montreal? So different! And yet both vivid exemplars of the concept. When you think of the concept of "leader," do you imagine Genghis Khan or Gandhi or Wayne Gretzky? How can such diverse individuals share the same label?

In many ways, the work of scholars through the ages has been to create concepts that help us better understand our world. When physical scientists speak of an atom, a species, a toxin, they are employing concepts that become the lenses through which we can interpret particular aspects of the world. So are social scientists, historians, and philosophers when they employ concepts such as freedom, justice, persecution, and prejudice. As social studies teachers we help to initiate our students into the concepts of history and the social sciences. Our aim is to assist our students to develop a set of lenses through which to see and interpret their world. Of course, some lenses will colour the picture, some will distort it or blur it, and some will bring it into sharper focus. They have to be tested. In order to test them, our students have first to acquire them. And so, the challenge that confronts us as teachers is how best to help our students learn the important concepts that constitute part of the legacy of our disciplines.

Formal and Informal Learning

Can you recall watching children as they first encounter the idea "hot"? The baby is just mobile enough to be getting into trouble; asserting independence with uncertain steps followed by stumblings and tumblings. The parents' joy in watching the strivings for independence is tempered by a concern about injury and harm. The unsteady steps towards an open fireplace are greeted with virtual panic as the child is whisked into the safety of strong arms and a comfortable lap. A minute later, of course, the child is struggling to get down and once again embark on the journey of exploration. What to do? Open fireplaces, hot ovens, boiling pots and pans on stoves, scalding water in bathtubs are not sources of innocent amusement. Parents are torn between childproofing the world so that no harm can befall their child and the realization that they cannot guard against every eventuality. They sense that they have to help their child learn to cope with the world, and so teaching and learning about "hot" begin. Here, parents are first-class teachers. Can you see how they take on the task? Can you see the hot fireplace? Grasping the child securely, the parent settles down close to the fire. Holding the child by the wrist, the parent reaches out towards the open flames. There is no rush, no fear, no worry. It's *warm, nice*. Wrong message! Closer. Close enough to feel the potential pain and discomfort but not close enough to burn. The fire is hot, says the parent, it *burns*, it *hurts*. *Don't touch! Stay away! Danger!* On that first occasion, the process is repeated several times. The child who has barely begun to talk and walk experiences the concept "hot" with its potential for hurt and harm. The child even begins to label the world when the

parent again holds out the hand and says, "The fire is hot! What is it? That's it . . . it's hot." The wonderful thing about parents, of course, is that they are infinitely patient (most of the time). And so the episode with the fireplace is repeated again and again—as a game, as a time of being together, until the parent is confident that the child cannot only say that the fire is hot but also appreciate what it means. And then on to ovens and stoves, hot water pipes and scalding baths. The idea "hot" is confronted in its various manifestations. Without ever having heard of cognitive psychology, parents help with the transfer of learning. Of course, the story isn't finished and years later both parents and children learn that television shows and rock stars can be hot, as can designer jeans, not to mention chilies and chimichangas. In fact, they learn that what is hot is cool, but that's a different concept.

The parents in the above tale have helped their child learn the concept by steering him or her through various dimensions of learning. The first encounters with the concept promote the acquisition of basic information. Subsequent encounters, especially those in new situations, allow the student to extend and refine their knowledge of the concept. When children avoid potentially harmful situations, they are using their knowledge of the concept in a meaningful way.[1] Interestingly, the learning is facilitated by the warm, trusting relationship between parent and child, and the whole experience fosters a disposition to learn more. All of this might be called informal learning. This is learning that emanates from everyday life. It is a spontaneous type of learning. When the child goes to school and eventually studies the concept of "heat" in his science class, the initial understanding developed at his parent's knee will be extended and elaborated through a process of systematic instruction. This is what constitutes formal learning. Of course, what the child ends up knowing will be the result of both processes. As teachers we are responsible for the systematic instruction that contributes to formal learning.

When I confront my job as a social studies teacher, I sometimes think of the child, the parent and the open fire. I ask myself, How can I take my students by the wrist and hold them gently near the fire so that they begin to learn what "hot" is? But now, of course, the concept is not "hot"; it is freedom, justice, prejudice, discrimination, export, import, migration, emigration, immigration, balance of power, balance of trade, labour, capital, Communism, capitalism, tyranny, absolutism, fascism, equality, equity, rights, responsibilities, due process, terrorism, consensus, cooperation, coercion, self-determination. Each idea is one of literally hundreds of concepts that is important in seeing, interpreting, and judging the social world. Now the question becomes, How do my students learn the ideas of the social studies and how can I help them? I remind myself that it is not enough to show the caring and loving disposition of the parent who is content to intuitively pursue a process of trial and error. If I am to present myself as a professional teacher, then I need to know what constitutes best practice in helping students learn important concepts.

Good Books as Exemplars of Concept Teaching

One of the more interesting studies of an important social studies concept is to be found in Crane Brinton's book, *The Anatomy of Revolution*. In this work, Brinton examines the English, American, French, and Russian revolutions in an attempt to reveal what he calls "their uniformities"; that is, he explores what it is about each of these four unique historical episodes that allows us to lump them together in a category we call "revolution." He points out that, in common usage, the term revolution is one of the "looser words." It has become scarcely more than an emphatic synonym for "change." But, he continues, "we keep in the corners of our mind a much more definite meaning, *a kind of central tough core not eroded into the looser strata of meaning.*"[2] (emphasis mine) And so, in his work, Brinton sorts out the central tough core from the looser strata. Each of the great revolutions constitutes a case, an instance, an exemplar, a particular set of facts, personages, events, causes, and consequences that is unique to its own time and place. What they share makes up their uniformities, the tough core, the essential features, of revolution. In the language of concept

learning, we call these the critical attributes of the concept. Although Brinton infers the critical attributes of "revolution" from just four cases, he allows us to start to hypothesize about the key features of revolutions in general. We can even check out our ideas by applying them to new instances—Algeria, China, Cuba, Iran.

So what does Brinton set out to help his reader do?

- He wants to make sure that we do not use the term "revolution" as a "loose word"; we should attach the label only to those events that truly merit it. He wants to make sure that we do not apply it in an indiscriminate manner to events better understood as change, progress, revision. He wants to make sure that we see the difference between our casual everyday use of language that may refer to revolutions in fashion or music and the precision of meaning applied by the historian and the social scientist.

- He wants us to be able to distinguish between those events that are truly revolutionary, that exhibit the tough core of meaning and not just a passing likeness. This means sorting out the singularities, the details, the facts, the uniqueness of each situation and distinguishing them from the "uniformities"; that is, the characteristics that all revolutions share, their critical attributes.

- He wants us to develop a schema or mental picture for interpreting new situations so that we can determine whether or not they can be classified as truly "revolutionary."

- He wants us to be able to articulate our understanding of the concept so that we can share our perceptions and interpretations.

And this is just what we want our students to achieve when we are helping them learn the concepts of history and the social sciences. A generic set of aims that we could use for any concept might say that our students will be able to:

1. name or label correctly the phenomena they encounter; not use terms loosely or casually;

2. classify people, places, things, and events and distinguish them from that which is similar but different;

3. use conceptual schema to frame and interpret new situations;

4. articulate their understanding of ideas.

As Brinton does for "revolution," Orlando Patterson does for "freedom" in *Freedom: Freedom in the Making of Western Culture*,[3] and Riesenberg does for "citizenship" in *Citizenship in the Western Tradition*.[4] These are all works that give us a deeper insight into an "idea"—revolution, freedom, citizenship. Long after we have forgotten the details of the events that helped us form the idea, there will persist a legacy in the form of the concept. Long after the specific actions of Jacobins and Bolsheviks, Roundheads and even Sons of Liberty have faded from memory, the concept of "reign of terror" remains firmly etched in our consciousness as one of the critical attributes of revolution.

The Three Phases of Concept Teaching

In teaching concepts, as in most school teaching, it can be helpful to think of the process as consisting of three phases: the *pre-active*, the *interactive*, and the *post-active*. The pre-active phase consists of what we do as teachers before we actually meet with our students; we sometimes refer to it as preparation or planning. The interactive phase consists of what teachers and students do to move the learning along. This can often mean a dialogue between teacher and student in the classroom, but it can just as importantly mean an interaction with other students, with various learning materials, with the human and material resources encountered on a field trip. Post-active teaching comprises what teachers do after the period of student engagement. It often means reflecting on the processes and products of the student learning, determining how well the student is progressing towards grasping the concept.

Pre-active teaching

In this phase of our work as social studies teachers, we select the concept(s) to be taught, establish instructional goals, choose resources, and plan how to use them.

SELECTING CONCEPTS

Not long ago, I observed a student teacher conduct a lesson on Hammurabi's Code. Do you remember any of this? An eye for an eye, a tooth for a tooth; the first known record in history of laws being written down and publicly displayed; equality of treatment within social classes but not between them. The teacher wanted the students to "know the information." And they did! They had dutifully read the textbook and responded to the teacher's questions, listing the laws, even explaining them. Sadly, the teaching and learning remained at the facts level. There was no attempt to make the learning conceptual. I suspect that after the next quiz the students won't be able to say much at all about Hammurabi's Code. So, we might ask, "What could the teacher do to lift this learning to a conceptual level?" The first point is that there is no need to try and stuff things in where they don't fit! When we are dealing with subject matter, we need to ask, "What does it give us?"—just like a sculptor who says that the stone dictates the image. In the case of Hammurabi's Code, it gives a lot. It addresses issues of enduring relevance: equality before the law (or the lack of it); ignorance of the law being no excuse; protection from arbitrary treatment. Studying Hammurabi not only helps us learn something of the origins of these concepts, it provides a springboard to propel us into a consideration of their contemporary relevance. As a teacher, then, I want to be clear about my goals. To be sure, I want my students to know the facts, the information, but I also want them to be able to grasp the important concepts that help us interpret and understand the facts. The concepts that can be applied to Hammurabi's Code are not limited to it. They are transferable.

(Give yourself a test here. Consider some of the topics that you have to teach. What do they give you in terms of opportunities for conceptual learning? What are

the key concepts that can be explored? Try it for three or four different grade levels. This will mean reviewing student textbooks or curriculum guides.)

As an example, think of the "Our Community" unit that is often used in the early grades. Often we structure such a unit around a set of questions: How do people in our community make a living? Where do they live? What sorts of recreation facilities are there? What sorts of rules are there in our community? Each question provides interesting opportunities. Certainly we can imagine how our six- and seven-year-olds would generate all kinds of information about jobs, about apartments and houses (perhaps even homelessness), about swimming pools and soccer fields, about playing safely and not littering—all of it interesting and helpful information. Might we also direct them in learning something about equity and fairness in our community? Or possibly about rights and responsibilities? Or about voting and democracy?

Perhaps you think little kids can't deal with such abstract and complex concepts? Go to any playground in Canada and just watch kids play. Keep your eye out for a disagreement and listen carefully. In a short space of time, some child will say, "That's no fair," and a complex but short-lived discussion about what constitutes fairness will occur—perhaps the discussion that more than any other characterizes civilized society. The "no fair" statement is scarcely grammatical, but it embodies a nascent theory of justice to which virtually any four- or five-year-old can relate.

ESTABLISHING GOALS

You probably already make use of objectives when planning your teaching. In working with concepts, we can use a generic format for our objectives as demonstrated previously. Here is an illustration adapted to a specific concept. Let's imagine that we have been studying about the development of the British colonies in North America and are now at the years leading up to the Revolutionary War. This topic gives us the opportunity of learning about the concept of "representative government." I want my students to grasp the idea. But what does that mean? What do I want?

1. When my students encounter descriptions of systems of government, some of them representative and some of them not, they should be able to classify them correctly.

2. When my students identify a system of government as being representative, they should be able to explain how they reached their conclusion.

3. When they are dealing with systems of government, my students should be able to label them correctly as representative or non-representative.

4. My students should be able to describe the critical attributes of any system of government labelled "representative. "

If we use "representative government" as a prototype, we can abstract a general form to guide all concept learning.

Students will:

- correctly classify examples and non-examples of a concept

- propose or suggest instances or examples not previously encountered

- correctly apply the name or label

- offer a satisfactory definition of the concept

(Take a three-minute pause and try to apply the generic model to some of the concepts that you identified earlier.)

CHOOSING LEARNING EXPERIENCES

At this point, we need to think about the sorts of learning experiences that will help our students grasp the concept. We can experience concepts directly and indirectly. Sometimes people are the victims of crime. This direct experience can give them a deeper understanding of and a more intelligent insight into the concept of crime than when crime is experienced "at a distance." But it is not likely that we would suggest becoming a victim of a crime in order to better understand it. We might suggest interviewing victims or viewing a video of an interview with a victim and/or a criminal, or reading an article, and so forth. Do you notice how each choice seems to become more and more remote from the actual experience? Many of the ideas we learn in school cannot be learned directly, but many can. If we considered the ways of experiencing an idea to range from direct personal experience at one end of a continuum to vague abstract talk at the other, we can see that the potential for learning is considerably greater towards the direct experience end of things. When the direct experience is not available, then the alternative that is closest to it has to be considered. Sometimes the alternative will be interaction with someone who has direct experience; it can be a role play or simulation, a case study or a problem situation, even a poem or a song. Only for simple, straightforward, two-cent concepts is it best addressed with a couple of oral descriptions from the teacher. The techniques and strategies described in the different chapters in this volume need to become part of the repertoire that you use in selecting learning experiences, whether direct or indirect.

Now that we have selected the concept(s), established the goals, and selected the learning experiences, we need to think about precisely how to operationalize the plan, how to put it into action.

Interactive teaching

It's Monday morning. I have thought about what I want my students to learn (the goals) and I have assembled the tools and the raw materials that we are going to use (the experiences). Now I have to put them to use. It's a bit like setting out to build a boat. We have the blueprint, the raw materials, the tools that we will need for the various jobs, and we are ready to begin. What should we do first, second, etcetera? As teachers, we ask similar questions: "What is the best way of getting the idea across?" "What do I need to be able to do?" We have already selected what we consider to be good learning experiences; now we have to put our plans into action.

Often, in discussions about concept learning and teaching we will hear reference to deductive and expository teaching as opposed to inductive and inquiry teaching. What these labels distinguish between are two different sequences of concept learning.

Consider the following teaching episode. Ms. Smith has been pursuing with her grade 9 students a unit on the economic development of Canada. She decides that her students' general understanding of the topic would be greatly enhanced if they had a working knowledge of the concepts of supply and demand. Ms. Smith wants to see if her students have an intuitive understanding of the concepts involved; she wants to assess their prior knowledge. As it happens, there has recently been a rock concert in town that many of the students wanted to attend but missed because tickets sold out quickly. It also happens that many of them have had their first encounter with ticket scalpers. The students are able to tell Ms. Smith about scalpers and the "outrageous prices" that they demanded for tickets to the concert. Ms. Smith probes. How is it that they can command such high prices for tickets? Why would anyone pay the price? What would have happened to the scalpers if the promoters had moved the concert to a larger arena or added two additional performances? What would have happened if enough people just did not want to see the concert? So, if you were a scalper what would you have to think about? Of course, Ms. Smith will push beyond the concepts and ask whether scalping should be allowed. Do promoters have any responsibility? Should there be legislation about it?

What she will discover is that her students likely have a great deal of personal experience with the interaction of the concepts of supply, demand and price. With some cueing, if need be, they will tell her how these laws operate with respect to hockey or baseball cards, blue jeans, coveted records, and even marbles. There will be stories of scalpers stuck with tickets they could not sell outside the Sky Dome or B.C. Place, of the disappointment of missing a favourite team or a wished-for holiday gift.

This sort of exploration of prior knowledge is common to both deductive and inductive concept teaching. It advances from the proposition that in order to help someone learn something new, we have to find out what they already know. At this point, the deductive and inductive approaches diverge.

THE DEDUCTIVE/EXPOSITORY APPROACH

In the deductive sequence, the teacher would now simply indicate that the focus of the rest of the lesson would be on the concepts of supply and demand. She labels the concepts to be studied. She would emphasize that following this work the students will be expected to define the concepts of supply, demand, and price and explain how they interact. She would reinforce that the students must make good use of this learning opportunity to ensure that they can employ these concepts to analyze and interpret various economic events. All of this acts as a signal—pay attention, here is the topic, make sure that you focus on learning the relevant information.

Next comes the presentation by the teacher of clear, comprehensive yet succinct definitions of the concepts to be studied. Good definitions perform two important functions. First, they distinguish between the critical and non-critical attributes of the concept. For example, an automobile can be painted any colour or not painted at all. All automobiles have this attribute but it is not critical to their being an automobile, so it is not likely that a definition would have much to say about colour. On the other hand, all automobiles have a means of propulsion, but having a means of propulsion, while necessary, is not sufficient to define the concept. Trains, boats and planes also have means of propulsion. So, a second function of a definition is to be sufficiently precise to allow us to distinguish it from related concepts; for example, distinguish an automobile from a motorcycle or a bicycle, a train, or a plane. We need a definition that helps us see an automobile as a vehicle but helps us appreciate that not all vehicles are automobiles. (*Try it! Imagine that you have to provide a definition of an automobile to a visitor from another planet.*) Our definitions, then, of supply, demand, and price, have to be sufficiently precise that the student can identify each one's critical attributes and infer which attributes of particular examples of the concept are not critical.

The third stage in the deductive approach to concept teaching is the presentation of a number of exemplars and non-exemplars. These are selected in order to help demonstrate to the students the significance of the critical attributes in defining the concept. If we use the example of the automobiles again it might go something like this. Suppose we go to the local car show, if we live in a city. We might also visit it in cyberspace or we could simply use a set of interesting photographs. Let's look at our first exemplar. This should be a typical automobile. Let's have several students describe it for us—its colour, its size, its cost, how fast it can go, and so on. Let's look at another, but one that has a different colour, size, cost, and speed potential. The students have given detailed and accurate descriptions of the particular automobiles that they have examined. Now we ask them to refer back to the definition. We ask, What is it that makes each one of our exemplars an automobile?

Let's look at another example. What is it that all of the examples that we have looked at have in common? Their uniformities are what make them automobiles. Let's look at some non-examples: a motorcycle, a train, a plane. We cue the students by asking them to explain why these cannot be classified as automobiles. Then we make it a little more difficult. What about a three-wheeled or a six-wheeled automobile? How important is the number of wheels? What about a large enclosed vehicle steered with a wheel, that runs on tracks and is capable of carrying several passengers? Initially we would ask the students to explain whether our example matches the definition in order to be classified as an automobile. If they experience difficulty, we direct them to particular attributes and probe to determine if they are critical or non-critical.

The process is just the same with concepts such as supply, demand, and price, as well as other more abstract concepts that we employ to make sense out of our social world. Having defined the concept of supply, we will use a variety of exemplars to show its critical attributes. Initially, we might choose to focus on supply as the amount of a commodity or service available to a potential market. We can select our exemplars to show the situation when there is abundance and when there is scarcity. Then we can extend and refine our students' understanding of supply through exemplars that demonstrate the relationship of supply to ease of production, proximity to markets, competition, cost of transportation, profitability, and so on. Our non-examples will be selected to help distinguish supply from demand from price.

The fourth stage in concept teaching in the deductive method concerns how we monitor our students' learning. It addresses the question, How do you know if they know? This is the problem of evaluation. In your studies you have likely encountered the concepts of formative and summative evaluation. A good way of keeping the distinction in mind is simply to remember that when the chef tastes the soup, that is formative evaluation. When the customer tastes it, that is summative evaluation. What is the critical distinction? Motive. The chef tastes the soup in order to determine if there is some way of improving it; the customer has no way of making much of a difference so is judging the soup to be tasty or not tasty.

As we teach, we will want to keep track of what it is that is causing our students difficulty. Do they think that some non-critical attributes are critical? This would be the case if a student suggested that in order for a government to be considered totalitarian it would have to be communist; or if a student said that a vehicle had to have four wheels in order to be an automobile. In helping our students learn complex ideas we need to be aware of the sorts of difficulties and confusions that develop. Some of these we can try to anticipate; others we can learn about by asking experienced colleagues about the problems students typically have in learning certain concepts. Of course, we will discover some of the difficulties from our own direct experience working with our own students.

Sometimes learning specialists refer to the deductive approach as a *ruleg* approach; that is, it em-

phasizes proceeding from the definition (or rule) to the examples. On the other hand, the inductive approach is referred to as *egrule* since it emphasizes starting with the examples and proceeding to a rule or definition.

THE INDUCTIVE/INQUIRY APPROACH

In an inductive approach, the teacher makes use of the same resources as in a deductive approach: the concepts need clear labels; we need a comprehensive definition; we will need exemplars and non-exemplars; and we need to have worked out how we will monitor our students' learning. The difference lies largely in the sequence of learning events.

In inductive teaching we can begin (step 1) by exploring our students' prior learning just as we did in the deductive sequence, but then we get down to cases right away. The "cases" here are the examples that we want our students to work with (step 2). Let's pursue our example of supply and demand. We share with our students a newspaper article that reports on the devastating effects of a recent spate of very cold weather on the Florida citrus crop. (This is our first case or exemplar.) We can encourage our students to reflect on the information. What are the effects upon growers? workers? truckers? producers in California or Chile? What about effects upon us? Can you "see" the discussion in your mind's eye?

(Try another three-minute pause right now!) Close your eyes and imagine the questions that you might ask your students and the responses they might give. Can you see how the students will explore the facts of a specific instance but can also go beyond the information given to speculate about its relevance in a general sense?)

As teachers we listen carefully to the way in which students express their ideas. Do they show some sense of the concepts of demand, supply, and price? Are they using these terms or labels?

Of course, one exemplar or instance will not be sufficient to ensure that everyone has grasped the central idea. We will need some more exemplars. Each one has been selected so as to focus on one of the key concepts. Suppose we simply monitor the price of tomatoes or strawberries over the past year at the local supermarket. (We happen to have made up a table for this purpose or we might simply have

---

KEY STEPS IN THE DEDUCTIVE STRATEGY

1. Assess prior knowledge.
2. Clearly name the concept to be learned (along with common synonyms).
3. Present a definition.
4. Use exemplars and non-exemplars to reinforce the critical attributes in the definition.
5. Monitor student learning.

collected the local newspaper advertisements so that our students can make their own tables.) What do we notice? Are there patterns or trends? Which months produce the highest and lowest prices? How might we explain it? Is it similar at all to the issue of citrus fruit in Florida? We might introduce another example by discussing the time when parents camped out overnight in local school board offices to ensure that they would be first in line to sign up their children for the French immersion program. (The discomfort of camping out in the offices is part of the price that they are prepared to pay for the commodity where demand may exceed supply.)

Each of the instances puts the student in contact with the concepts at work in the real world. At this point they may not even be using the "correct" labels for the concept and they certainly have not learned any definitions by rote. But labels and definitions can also be important. Here we can ask our students to develop their own definitions and use the correct names (steps 3 and 4). From the examples above, our students will have learned something (but not everything) about the concepts of supply, demand, and price. One of the more interesting things that they might have learned about price is that it is not always monetary. As the students come up with their definitions, it is important to keep in mind that their definitions represent how they see the concept at this point in time. They will point to those attributes that they think important. As teachers, we will be observing to see if they have missed critical attributes of the concept or if they have included as critical attributes those that are not. We have to appreciate, of course, that our students' knowledge of the concepts is not fixed and static. It will grow and develop with further experience, with learning encounters that will further refine and extend their understanding of the concepts. We know, for example, that we are going to move on to shape and twist our students' understandings of supply, demand, and price when we begin to explore the dimensions of market and planned economies. For the time being, however, we are pleased to see how their understanding of the concepts is evolving.

Checking on their understanding is step 5 in the inductive process. This does not necessarily mean that it comes at the end. It is something we will have been paying close attention to all the way through. Keep in mind that when we are checking up on students' understanding of concepts, there are a number of standard or general approaches that we can use regardless of whether the teaching has been deductive or inductive. These closely parallel the goals or objectives that we set in the first place. First of all, consider the task that students almost always face to determine whether they "know" a concept. They are asked to give a definition. If they can do this correctly, does it mean they know the concept? Not necessarily! Maybe it does, maybe it doesn't. It is conceivable that students have simply learned a definition by rote in the expectation that they will be asked for a definition. So we need to explore some other ways of tapping into their understanding of the concept.

Let's use the example of "representative government." Suppose I present the students with descriptions of some actual governments, some of them representative and some not. The students' task is to pick out all of the instances of the concept. Or we can ask the students to classify the governments as representative or non-representative and give explanations for their choices. If a student gets even one wrong, it points to some sort of misconception that we might be able to correct. Or, I might ask students to identify some of the countries that have recently been in the news, indicating whether their systems of government are representative. The focus is on seeing what gives students trouble. The reason is so that we might help them better understand the concept.

Some of these strategies should be very familiar to you. Do you remember singing along with "Sesame Street?" "*One of these things is not like the others; one of*

CHECKING FOR CONCEPT UNDERSTANDING

Can students:

1   Give definitions?

2.   Classify examples and non-examples?

3.   Use the concept name correctly?

4.   Recognize new examples of the concept?

these things doesn't belong. Can you guess which one is not like the others by the time I finish this song?" The instructional designers at "Sesame Street" show some excellent examples of how they helped children and parents monitor just what and how much was being learned.

Notice in the above table the *egrule* pattern of the inductive strategy as opposed to the *ruleg* pattern of the deductive strategy.

KEY STEPS IN THE INDUCTIVE STRATEGY

1. Assess prior knowledge.
2. Use exemplars and non-exemplars to reinforce the critical attributes in the definition.
3. Clearly name the concept to be learned (along with common synonyms).
4. Encourage students to generate definitions.
5. Monitor student learning.

A BRIEF NOTE ON EXEMPLARS AND NON-EXEMPLARS

Both exemplars and non-exemplars are crucially important when we are learning concepts. For example, it is hard to get a clear idea of slavery if we do not consider things that are not slavery (non-examples). Obviously we can contrast slavery with freedom, but more appropriate non-examples might be serfdom or the concept of "indentured servant." If you doubt how important the exemplar/non-exemplar relationship is, try to teach someone what "heads" is without mentioning "tails," or what exports are without mentioning imports.

Post-active teaching

Silence creeps across the school at the end of the day. We have been working on understanding some important concepts. Each one of us has been trying to become more effective in our concept teaching. How are we doing?

As far as the students are concerned, I can re-construct their understanding from specific happenings in class—the examples they used; the explanations they gave; the observations they made; what they remembered and what they forgot. And I also have the products that they generated from the vari-ous tasks woven into the instruction. As I examine their work, as I reflect on what happened, I can sort out what is obviously clear to them and what is still unclear. My post-active reflection is leading me to pre-active planning as I begin to think about our next encounters—and the process begins over again.

But what about me? How did I do in my quest to get better at teaching concepts?

- Did I select a concept that flowed naturally from the specific subject matter that we are studying? Is it a concept that, once grasped, will illumi-nate the subject matter?

- Did I have a specific strategy for helping my students learn the concept (either *ruleg* or *egrule*) and did I follow it?

- Did my exemplars hit the mark? What about my non-exemplars?

- Did I monitor my students' learning from start to finish? Can I say with any confidence whether they got the idea?

In the cut and thrust of the busy school day, the opportunity for reflection can be lost. The observa-tions that might improve future lessons are uninten-tionally forgotten or simply crowded out of the teacher's busy agenda. This is where we deserve some time for ourselves. Children, parents, and adminis-trators get almost everything we have to offer, so we are not going to feel guilty about protecting a little professional time for ourselves. Now is the time to reflect and record, to note what to keep and repeat, what to change, and what to revise.

Postscript: Learning from Jugglers

Can you juggle? I mean like the people in the circus, with three or four balls or other objects. Try it! You can learn some things very quickly. For example, don't start with sharp knives or burning torches. If you can't do it with two, you won't be able to do it with three. If you practise faithfully on your own, you can get to be fairly proficient. If you practise under the watchful eye of a master, you can get to be pretty good. If you have talent and work hard, you can become a master. If you never have to give a performance, you lose all interest and take up bridge. What does this have to do with teaching concepts?

Developing skill in helping our students learn complex concepts is a significant accomplishment. It requires a strong interest and commitment to our profession; it demands a desire to reach a high level of professional expertise; it involves a willingness to put in great amounts of time and effort in the form of practice and reflection; and it stresses a recognition that pushing the limits of our own learning is seldom achieved without help. We need to look to our own teachers and mentors. But remember that good mentors can be hard taskmasters. When Mentor thought that Telemachus' desire to while away his time on Calypso's island was not the best use of his time, he physically launched him off the cliffs and into the sea.

Endnotes

[1] Robert Marzano, *A Different Kind of Classroom: Teaching with Dimensions of Learning* (Alexandria, VA: Association for Supervision and Curriculum Development, 1992).
[2] Crane Brinton, *The Anatomy of Revolution*, rev. ed. (New York: Vantage Books, 1965), 4.
[3] Orlando Patterson, *Freedom in the Making of Western Culture* (New York: Basic Books, 1991).
[4] Peter Riesenberg, *Citizenship in the Western Tradition: Plato to Rousseau* (Chapel Hill, NC: University of North Carolina Press, 1992).

Further Reading

Betres, J. "Cognitive Style, Teacher Methods and Concept Attainment." *Theory and Research in Social Education* 12, no. 2 (1984): 1–18.

Beyer, Barry K., and Anthony N. Penna, eds. *Concepts in the Social Studies*. Washington, DC: NCSS, 1971.

Martorella, Peter. *Concept Learning in the Social Studies: Models for Structuring Curriculum*. Scranton, PA: Intext Educational Publishers, 1971.

McKenzie, G.R., and J. Sayer. "The Effects of Test-like Practice and Mnemonics on Learning Geography Facts." *Theory and Research in Social Education* 14, no. 3 (1986): 201–209.

McKinney, C.W. et al. "The Effects of Ordinary and Coordinate Concept Nonexamples on First-Grade Students' Acquisition of Three Coordinate Concepts." *Theory and Research in Social Education* 15, no. 1 (1987): 45–50.

Stanley, W.B., and R.C. Mathews. "Recent Research on Concept Learning: Implications for Social Education." *Theory and Research in Social Education* 12, no. 4 (1985): 57–74.

Yoho, R.F. "Effectiveness of Four Concept Teaching Strategies on Social Studies Concept Acquisition and Retention." *Theory and Research in Social Education* 14, no. 3 (1986): 211–224.

CHAPTER 17

Critical Thinking and the "Social" in Social Studies

Linda Farr Darling and Ian Wright

Introduction

This chapter revisits the purposes and nature of critical thinking as an educational ideal, particularly in light of recent critiques from several philosophical perspectives. We argue that critical thinking, despite some rumours to the contrary, is alive and well in Canadian social studies curriculum documents and that it is worth exploring the directions in which the teaching of critical thinking may now be headed. The first part of the chapter reviews influential conceptions in the field; the second examines the critiques that attempt to modify those conceptions; and the third and fourth parts take up practical questions related to social studies teaching, first by looking at the intellectual and social virtues we are seeking to develop, and second by recommending some strategies for developing individual thinkers within critical communities of inquiry.

Critical Thinking As an Educational Ideal

Good thinking has long been a goal of social studies education in Canada. In 1929, grade 1 students of social studies in British Columbia were expected to "develop their growing ability to use good judgement";[1] in 1938, grade 5 students were supposed to "extend the means of acquiring knowledge of the world through an intelligent and critical use of graphs, maps."[2] In the 1960s, grade 10 students in Saskatchewan were expected to "present reasoned arguments."[3] More recently, teachers in Newfoundland are urged to "stress the development of students' ability to think reflectively, creatively and independently."[4] In 2003 in Manitoba, students were expected to "critically analyze Canadian public issues and take a rationally and morally defensible position on them."[5] Other contemporary provincial curriculum guides contain the same sorts of objectives as the 1998 Ontario curriculum, which states, "[students] must learn to evaluate different points of view and examine information critically to solve problems and make decisions on a variety of issues."[6] In a similar vein, the Alberta Social Studies 10-20-30 guide states, "students require a wide range of critical and creative thinking skills and strategies that they can apply to a variety of situations."[7] In British Columbia, critical thinking objectives are included in social studies curricula for each of the grades from K–7.[8]

Citizenship education as a rationale for critical thinking

That these sorts of objectives appear in most contemporary social studies curriculum documents is not surprising. The major rationale for teaching social studies is citizenship education and, if this is defined in light of liberal democratic theories, then citizens have to make decisions on questions of public policy. As Siegel states:

The democratic citizen requires a wide variety of the many things which education can provide. She needs to be well-informed with respect to all sorts of matters of fact; to grasp fully the nature of democratic institutions, and to embrace fully their responsibilities; to treat her fellow democrats as equal partners in political life, etc. She also needs to be able to examine public policy concerns, to judge intelligently the many issues facing her society; to challenge and seek reasons for proposed changes (and continuations) of policy; to assess such reasons fairly and impartially, and to put aside self-interest when it is appropriate to do so.[9]

Thus, the need for good thinking can be made on the basis of educating students for democratic life. To achieve this requires a conception of thinking that will lead to the characteristics identified by Siegel.

Several such conceptions have been formulated; to describe and analyze them all is beyond the scope of this chapter. Instead, we will outline those that pertain to critical thinking as we believe that this best captures what is required in social studies education.

Conceptualizations of critical thinking

The most prevalent conception is one in which students are taught certain skills that, once learned, are to be applied in fairly mechanistic ways. These skills can be taught through such procedures as problem-solving, inquiry, or decision-making, or through posing questions at the higher levels of Bloom's taxonomy.[10] Here, it is assumed that there are generic processes and that answering analysis, synthesis, and evaluation questions involves generic procedures, criteria, and standards. This is questionable. There are particular criteria and standards for ascertaining the appropriateness of answers in different contexts. For example, in a problem about the latitude and longitude of a location on a map, the criterion is accuracy; in a moral problem it is ethical acceptability. Even though there will be some broad similarities between the procedures used to solve both problems (for example, clarifying the question, using accurate information), there will also be significant differences. Similarly, evaluating the artistry of a painting, which requires the application of aesthetic criteria, is different from evaluating a moral action, where the application of ethical criteria is required. Further problems with the skills conception can be found in the work of Bailin et al. and Hare.[11]

Several scholars have outlined conceptions of critical thinking that are useful in the teaching of social studies.

ROBERT ENNIS

An extremely thorough list of the competencies and dispositions necessary for critical thought is found in the works of Robert Ennis.[12] He defines critical thinking as "reasonable reflective thinking that is focussed on deciding what to believe and do."[13] His list of components includes proficiencies in observing, inferring, generalizing, and so on; and dispositions such as being open-minded and sensitive to the feelings, level of knowledge, and degree of sophistication of others.[14] He claims that the rules and standards of critical thinking cross subject boundaries—they are generalizable. So, for example, the standards for judging the reliability of observation claims would be the same in history, science, or the courtroom (witness testimony). His conception is useful, as he outlines the complexity of what is required for critical thought. However, he has not applied his ideas in an instructional program, whereas Paul, Lipman, and Bailin et al. have.

RICHARD PAUL

Paul and Elder define critical thinking as:

> That mode of thinking—about any subject, content or problem—in which the thinker improves the quality of his or her thinking by skillfully taking charge of the structures inherent in thinking and imposing intellectual standards upon them.[15]

Paul argues that critical thinkers must view an issue objectively from the various perspectives of those whose interests are involved. He states that most problems are "multi logical," as they cannot be resolved within a single frame of reference. To identify and define any problem "depends upon some arguable choice among alternative frames of references."[16] Thus, the frames have to be tested using such standards as clarity, accuracy, relevance, significance, completeness, precision, depth, consistency, sound logic, and fairness.[17] He argues that these standards must be applied to the elements of critical thinking (purposes, questions, points of view, information, inferences, concepts, implications and assumptions), within a framework of intellectual traits (humility, autonomy, integrity, courage, perseverance, empathy, fair-mindedness, and confidence in reason).[18] To teach this approach, Paul and his associates have developed a series of handbooks, and they present workshops across the United States, and hold an annual conference in the summer.[19]

MATTHEW LIPMAN

In contrast to Paul, who argues for the infusion of critical thinking into all subject areas, Lipman argues that a separate philosophy course is necessary to teach critical thinking. He defines critical thinking as,

> Skillful, responsible thinking that facilitates good judgment because it (1) relies on criteria, (2) is self-correcting, and (3) is sensitive to context."[20]

His Philosophy for Children program has a central aim of helping students learn to think so that they become "more thoughtful, more reflective, more considerate and more reasonable individuals."[21] To attain this goal, students are taught to assess factual information, deal reflectively with the relationship between facts and values, and reason well in many curriculum areas including the social sciences. A series of books has been created for students from kindergarten to high school.

SHARON BAILIN, ROLAND CASE, JERROLD COOMBS, AND LEROI DANIELS

A recent conception of critical thinking has been developed by Bailin, Case, Coombs, and Daniels.

This conception was written for the Ministry of Education in British Columbia and was intended to make the teaching of critical thinking clear and manageable for teachers and curriculum developers. Critical thinking is defined as involving thinking through problematic situations about what to believe or how to act where the thinker makes reasoned judgements that embody the attributes of quality thinking.[22] It is viewed as having three dimensions: critical challenges—the questions, tasks, or problems that provide the impetus and context for critical thinking; intellectual resources—the background knowledge and critical attributes (standards and principles of rational thought, concepts necessary for critical thought, strategies useful for tackling challenges, and attitudes or habits of mind, such as fair-mindedness) drawn upon when responding to critical challenges; and critically thoughtful responses that embody all of the above. This conception has been applied in the development of a number of critical challenge books, some of which pertain directly to the social studies curriculum.[23] The series, like other curriculum materials designed to support the teaching of critical thinking, has both advocates and critics, some concerned with practical questions, others concerned with theoretical ones such as those explored in the next section.

Critiques of Critical Thinking

Although critiques of critical thinking range widely as to the scope of concern, at least two sets of criticism have particular relevance to trends in social studies education: feminist critiques, and critiques from social epistemology. This is so partly because these critiques have drawn our attention more directly to the relational aspects of critical thinking, and partly because the critiques have refined our view of what is required for any community of inquiry to flourish, including a community focused on political concerns. The latter brings us into the field of social studies education quite directly. There is some overlap (and also tension) between the reasons presented in these critiques as well as in their epistemological foundations, but for discussion's sake we will address them separately here, and follow with some remarks about the practical consequence of these critiques for social studies teaching and learning.

Feminist critiques

Some feminist critics claim that the conceptions of critical thinking that drive school practices are deficient in several important ways. We have turned to Blythe Clinchy as our spokesperson to represent an influential feminist perspective, one that she began to develop in her co-authored book *Women's Ways of Knowing*.[24] Clinchy believes that "there is something deeply wrong" about the enterprise of teaching critical thinking as a primary way of knowing, partly because it eclipses teaching about and through other modes of thought that have value. She sees girls and women in particular, struggling (often unsuccessfully) to fit into an educational system that elevates intellectual detachment and separation over attachment and connection to that which is to be learned. She notes that such an emphasis can place students in adversarial relationships to each other, where their primary mode of interaction is debate and intensive (and sometimes destructive) scrutiny of one another's views. Thus she calls critical thinking "separate knowing" and describes it as only one "kind of knowing" that is based on separating the knower from the known.

Critical thinking, or separate knowing, places a high value on the impartial, the impersonal, and the unbiased. Its purpose is to critique, judge, and compare. "Its primary mode of discourse is argument," she writes, and as powerful as argument is, there is another voice to which we ought to attend. This is the voice of "connected knowing."

> Connected knowers are not dispassionate, unbiased observers. They deliberately bias themselves in favor of what they are examining. They try to get inside it and form an imaginative attachment to it. The heart of connected knowing is imaginative attachment: trying to get behind the other person's eyes and "look at it from that person's point of view."[25]

Connected knowing has a primary mode of discourse, too, and according to Clinchy, that mode is narrative. Rather than asking, What evidence do you have to support that claim? the connected knower asks for the story behind the claim, or, What in your experience led you to that position? The connected knower seeks to sympathize with another view, rather than judge it; she becomes attached to it, at least in the short term. But even in her critique, Clinchy makes it clear that she does not want to abandon the teaching of critical thinking; she readily acknowledges that learning about criteria and standards in any given practice serves a number of educational purposes. "Without it, you couldn't write a second draft of a paper; without it, you are unable to marshall a convincing argument, or detect a specious one."[26] Nevertheless, without attention to connected knowing, she believes that much of what we do in schools limits the possibilities for bringing learners into a genuine and productive relationship with each other and with their learning.

Clinchy's views rest on certain epistemological beliefs about the nature of knowledge and truth that are expressed in a different way by Barbara Thayer-Bacon. Like Clinchy, Thayer-Bacon is concerned that critical thinking privileges individual epistemic agency and the separation of the knower from the known as well as "knowers" from each other. In her view, this is especially apparent in traditional assessment practices:

> Our traditional means of assessing students . . . tend to emphasize many things about knowledge: that knowledge is a product which can be measured and quantified, rather than viewing knowing as a process; that knowledge is separate from us as knowers, rather than understanding knowers and knowledge as intimately connected.[27]

For Thayer-Bacon, the answer is to reconceptualize critical thinking as "constructive thinking," a term she believes captures the relational and communal sides of learning to think well. For her, constructive thinking emphasizes knowing and caring about the persons with whom you are in relation and then building understandings together, thereby creating a community of learners who use their powers of imagination and intuition alongside their reason in order to engage in dialogue and inquiry. Emotions and affect are as central as the intellect to the flourishing of these learners and their communicative practices.

The perspectives of both Clinchy and Thayer-Bacon can be placed within an epistemological framework that questions, among other things, the "standard" view of rationality that some believe has informed most conceptions of critical thinking. The model critical thinker, in this view, is an independent and rather solitary epistemic agent, more logical than emotional, more detached than connected, and more interested in arriving at the truth (no matter the consequences) than in preserving relationships or contributing to the overall health of an epistemic community. He (and this critical thinker is often described as a male) is seen to be acting on the basis of universalizable principles rather than responding to the needs of concrete others.[28] That this description can result in more of a caricature than a portrait of a live, embodied, and complex human being has been pointed out by many theorists. Yet the caricature continues to haunt conceptions of critical thinking and the teaching practices that follow from them. And underneath the description of this lonely critical thinker, however exaggerated it may be, is an important and persistent worry about the very possibility of individual epistemic independence. This is the focus of the second set of critiques we examine.

Critiques from social epistemology

A reconstruction of feminist critiques of critical thinking yields some important insights about epistemic independence that to a partial extent parallel the views of several contemporary epistemologists. Given their radically different projects and commitments, we suspect that any similarity is unintended. The parallel is especially apparent when we look at the work of Schmitt and Foley, who bring to our attention the difficulty (if not the impossibility) facing any individual agent who attempts to judge the reli-

ability of testimony in matters where she or he is not an expert.[29] Very quickly, the individual will have to turn to others who are better qualified to assess knowledge claims. Even if we engage in solitary pursuits as researchers and questioners, when it comes to matters of justification, according to Goldman, we are always in the realm of the social.[30]

Since the sphere of expertise for any one person is necessarily quite limited, one's ability to make a sound judgement about the validity of another's knowledge claims is extremely restricted. Mostly we take on trust the testimony of other people, and in fact this is an entirely reasonable thing for human beings to do. We could not get through a day without relying on what we believe to be the authentic expertise of others. In other words, we need to act on the presumption of trust, unless we have compelling reasons to do otherwise. Our efforts to judge or measure reliability often focus on the reliability of the testifier, not the testimony. For example, consider the kinds of questions we are likely to ask of a witness: Is this person in a good position to know about this matter? Is she or he especially qualified in this particular domain? Does he or she have the requisite credentials? Is he or she reputable? There are also a number of psychological motivations for belief acquisition and revision, including our inclination to believe others who appear to "be like us" and therefore have prima facie credibility.

Most epistemologists would agree that our network of beliefs owes much of its structure, content, and potential for revision to the knowledge and understandings of others. The very existence of a single and solitary epistemic agent, or an independent critical thinker, is gravely in doubt, then, from the point of view of the feminist critic of critical thinking, or through the lens of the social epistemologist, though their world views may remain otherwise divergent.

The potential impact of the critiques

There is little in the critiques from feminists or epistemologists that cannot be, or has not been, satisfactorily countered by critical thinking theorists. All of the authors of the conceptions of critical thinking outlined in the opening section would readily agree that critical thinking involves abilities, concepts, bodies of information, and importantly, dispositions, including those that make relationships fruitful, even possible. They do not conceive of critical thinking outside of epistemic communities, and certainly do not deny the relational quality of good thinking. Barring the skills conception of critical thinking, these conceptions all contain dispositional and attitudinal components necessary for social engagement; all of them presume that critical thinkers display certain character traits essential to productive inquiry and discourse. Such traits as an acknowledgement of fallibility and a willingness to take others' arguments seriously are viewed as necessary for a critical thinker.[31] Some have argued that if this is the case, such thinkers as Newton and Darwin could not be called critical thinkers as they did not demonstrate such traits in their daily lives.[32] However, we believe, as do most critical thinking theorists, that it would be irresponsible to argue that the teaching of critical thinking can be divorced from character education. This inseparability has been discussed in numerous ways in the literature; we offer a brief illustration here.

One of the purposes of education is to get people to think critically in a fair-minded way and to act in accordance with certain ethical principles, in particular principles of respect and what Callan calls reciprocity.[33] Thus, critical thinking must be related to the overall type of person we want the educational system to develop, and to the sorts of intellectual and social virtues that are developed through engagement with others. Since any individual is necessarily part of one or more communities, including epistemic ones, then the educational task is to create the kind of community in which persons can flourish intellectually and socially, for their own sake as well as for the sake of the community. In any community of inquiry where the goal is the acquisition of true beliefs and their justification, these virtues will help move the inquiry forward while at the same time ensuring that principles of respect and reciprocity remain central.

All of this is standard fare for critical thinking theorists; it is somewhat surprising that its impact on educational practice has not been significant. Yet the recent critiques of critical thinking, such as those we examined above, may have begun to change that. We would argue that the critiques have played a key role in shifting the emphasis of the conversation about the teaching of critical thinking. They have shifted our attention from cultivating the individual as an autonomous critical thinker to cultivating a community of critical thinkers. Even the notion of autonomy has been the subject of recent review, with such educators as Tim Sprod suggesting that a more perspicuous conception is "communicative autonomy"; that is, the ability and inclination to fully engage with others in dialogue within a community.[34] If, as the critics of "traditional" critical thinking models tell us, we are compelled to view the relational sides of critical thinking as indispensable to epistemic as well as social goals (such as preparation for citizenship), then we are compelled to put into place teaching practices that will help students engage with others constructively. This will be indispensable to the success of the inquiry at hand and for public deliberations that will arise in the larger society. The best way to do this may well be to engage in the thoughtful, even painstaking construction of communities of inquiry in classrooms.

Constructing the Community of Inquiry: Preconditions

Constructing communities of students who work together and support each other's learning is a worthwhile, if challenging, educational project and one that directs our attention towards the cultivation of many sorts of virtues, including moral ones. Philosopher Linda Zagzebski has argued that intellectual virtues are the most important to cultivate for purposes of inquiry within a community, and in fact they are preconditions for meaningful exchange between people.[35] Though we ordinarily attend to virtues in classrooms, it is not often for the purposes of furthering and supporting intellectual growth. Teachers justifiably spend time helping young children cultivate virtues such as patience, kindness, and generosity towards others. But in the rush to create supportive and caring classroom communities, we may overlook the fact that along with these social virtues we emphasize, intellectual virtues need to be developed and practised, too. This is because the community ideal for the classroom is not simply a caring community, it's an inquiring one. Not only do we want students to cooperate with one another, we want them to take responsibility for questioning, deliberating, and making decisions about what they are learning on their own and with others.

Intellectual virtues in deliberation

In this portion of the chapter, we introduce three of the intellectual virtues (sometimes called habits of mind) required for the establishment and maintenance of a community of inquiry. Our intent is to further conversations that have been started about the best ways to conceptualize and construct learning opportunities that will maximize respectful, responsible, and productive deliberations in classrooms in which the notion of a community of inquiry has become a powerful metaphor for the social construction of understandings. One advocate for teaching intellectual or epistemic (truth-conducive) virtues is philosopher Alvin Goldman. Goldman explains the role of epistemic virtues in developing a community of inquiry, a place for public deliberations about what to believe or do that is based on the exchange of good reasons. He does this by citing rules that will help students understand what is required for communication that is trustworthy, responsible, and aimed towards justified, true beliefs.[36]

Goldman writes that this sort of communication reflects "epistemic responsibility" on the part of students. Teaching epistemic responsibility goes hand in hand with teaching moral responsibility, including respecting others' rights and freedoms, treating them fairly, and extending support when needed. In order to be responsible in an epistemic as well as an ethical sense, Goldman believes students need to learn the rules of argumentation. This is so they can engage in deliberations that refine understandings, extend inquiry, and broaden discussion to include as many perspectives as possible in seeking answers.

What are the rules of argumentation for speakers? First, a speaker should assert a premise only if she believes it and is justified in believing it (that is, she has good reasons for her position and can articulate them). Second, a speaker should only assert a conclusion she herself believes and that she believes is justified and supported by her premises. Finally, a speaker should restrict her statements to premises that her listeners would be justified in believing and present "support relationships" between premises and conclusions that her listeners are capable of appreciating. Justification appropriate to the audience is an essential consideration because it is "truth-conducive" and helps bring listeners into the circle of reason. Becoming responsible in an epistemic sense requires developing the intellectual virtues that will ensure deliberative communication is sincere, justifiable, and intelligible. Among these will be the intellectual virtues of:

- integrity
- reasonableness
- empathic understanding

These have also been identified by other scholars, notably Richard Paul and Linda Elder.[37]

Integrity in deliberation relates to trustworthiness. In a community of inquiry, we come to trust members who have proven themselves to be sincere in their speech and actions. A speaker who consistently asserts what she believes is true, earns the trust of other community members. Reasonableness relates to a speaker's ability and readiness to offer good reasons and adequate evidence in support of her position. She is justified in believing what she tells the group. She is also able to apply "reasonableness" to her assessment of other positions, judging their accuracy on fair and reasonable grounds.

Empathic understanding refers to the extent to which a speaker appreciates the point of view of another and can imaginatively step into his or her shoes. If she understands and appreciates the perspectives of those around her, she will work to make sure her communication can be correctly interpreted. As Goldman puts it, she will offer justifications that can be understood and appreciated by her listeners.[38]

Cultivating these virtues may well be a lifelong task. In particular, the third intellectual virtue mentioned here (empathic understanding) is dependent on a degree of intellectual sophistication beyond that of most young children. However, viewing these intellectual virtues as goals to work towards can enrich deliberations at even primary levels. Teachers can pay special attention to the quality of their own communication in light of these standards. By explicitly modelling these intellectual virtues in class discussions, teachers can begin to bring children into a public sphere where reasons are valued, truth and sincerity are prized, and diverse understandings are appreciated. In addition, there are particular sorts of deliberations in which children can engage that demand the exercise of integrity, reasonableness, and empathic understanding.

Theoretical foundations for building a critical thinking classroom

In order to do justice to the rationales and concerns with some contemporary definitions of critical thinking, we have to go beyond the "mere" teaching of criteria and standards and consider what environment is needed. This is because reasonableness, integrity, and empathy cannot be learned didactically, they have to be experienced and practised. Dewey made this point many years ago when he argued that citizenship education is best taught by students experiencing it in democratically run classrooms. He also argued that knowledge is best learned through active participation in inquiry processes.[39] Kohlberg argued that in order to advance morally, students need to participate in moral debate and ultimately be educated in just community schools.[40] The same arguments apply to instruction in critical thinking. How then do we build a classroom community that is conducive to critical thought and in which the three intellectual virtues we introduced are central?

We need to start with teachers, because they are the people who set the tone in the classroom. According to Sears and Parsons, teachers need to embrace the following principles: (1) knowledge is subject to change; (2) any question can be asked; and

(3) awareness and empathy for alternative points of view, tolerance for ambiguity, and skepticism of text are required.[41]

The same qualities need to be encouraged in students by providing a classroom environment conducive to their development. The overall classroom environment should be built on respect for students as beings with the capacity for thought, choice, and judgement.[42] Throughout, teachers should model this behaviour, be willing to admit they don't know everything, change their minds when necessary, point out alternative points of view and, whenever possible, tell students why the information they are learning is worth knowing and why they believe that the information students are learning is believable. This entails that teachers care about evidence, reasons, and their students. Much has been written about caring in education.[43] As with other emotions, we take it that there is a cognitive aspect.[44] Nussbaum argues that emotions are bound up with judgements:

> If emotion is not there, neither is that judgement fully there. . . . It means that in order to represent certain sorts of truths, one must respect emotions. It also means that to communicate certain truths to one's readers, one will have to write so as to arouse the reader's emotions.[45]

So it is with caring. We build an image of ourselves with the help of others, and we often build knowledge with others.[46] Thus, the groups we engage with and how we engage with them are crucial. Caring entails that we are "open to hearing others' voices more completely and fairly," in an atmosphere of "acceptance and trust, inclusion and openness."[47] These approaches are just as important when we deal with ideas. If we care enough, we ask questions about the soundness of the arguments we encounter, the facts with which we engage, and the concepts we and others use. We will need a classroom where there is a sense of common purpose, mutual trust and respect, cooperation, safety in risk-taking, and opportunities for reflection, dialogue, and taking on others' perspectives.[48]

How does this need differ from what is already done in some schools in the name of cooperative learning? Cooperative learning objectives include the development of communication skills, the creation of trust and respect between students, a lower fear of failure, the development of a commitment to learning, and the fostering of individual and group accountability.[49] Results indicate that many of these benefits can be realized.[50] Whereas we would agree that the objectives and results of cooperative learning are desirable, the conceptualization of it is not broad enough to encompass what we have in mind. Cooperative learning may engender trust and respect between students when they are inquiring into a social studies topic, but the product of their deliberations may be an answer that was predetermined by the teacher. Thus, there may be little or no critical thought. Similarly, the dispositions students are expected to act on may not be the subject of debate. Why should students not question the teacher's admonition that they should be tolerant of others' viewpoints?

Strategies for Building Communities of Inquiry in Classrooms

Although cooperative learning may well aid in the development of the virtues outlined above, we believe that more needs to be done in order to bring theory closer to practice. We need to build a classroom where discussion is encouraged in open-minded and fair-minded ways. We can do this in a number of ways.[51]

1. PRESENT MANY OPPORTUNITIES FOR STUDENTS TO THINK CRITICALLY

This can be carried out either through the teaching of complete units or lessons using critical challenges,[52] or by redesigning a regular lesson that focuses on a critical thinking problem or question,[53] or by inserting a critical thinking activity into a lesson. For example, in a lesson where students are examining the various aspects of the local community (e.g., government, recreation, health care, and so on), students could be asked which one is in most

need of improvement in their community. Or, if students were designing a poster to synthesize what they had learned about the community, they would develop and apply criteria for a good poster. In the upper grades, students who are studying the North-West Rebellion and Louis Riel could be required to argue whether they thought the execution of Riel was justified, or, as an assignment, they could write a letter to a newspaper arguing their position. As with the other strategies mentioned below, teachers must build slowly. Generally speaking, students are not used to thinking critically. They like to know the right answer, and it can be disquieting for them to realize that knowledge is often tentative and subject to change and that value judgements are not necessarily absolute.

2. TEACH STANDARDS OF CRITICAL THOUGHT

In order that students demonstrate integrity and present reasonable arguments, we have to teach the standards of critical thought.[54] It is not enough to present students with activities that call for critical thought if they do not know what would count as reasonable answers. Thus the activities presented in the Critical Challenge series, the lesson plans devised by Paul and his colleagues, and ideas that you will find in textbooks and other instructional materials are all useful.[55] For example, standards for the reliability of observation claims have been identified by Norris, and those for authority (expert) claims by Ennis.[56]

3. ASK QUESTIONS THAT ARE BEYOND THE LEVEL OF RECALL

One powerful question is to ask students how they know that something is true. In our experience, students usually look very perplexed and tell you that it was in their textbook. Here is the opportunity to ask how the textbook author(s) knew it was true and if students cannot give an answer, telling students that authors have evidence for their claims and, depending on the claim being questioned, explaining what evidence the author in question was probably using. When students become more sophisticated, we can make them aware that evidence may be suspect and textbooks may not contain the most up-to-date information. Further, we should note that the textbook author has a bias and that there may well be other ways of looking at the topic being studied. We would not expect students to grasp epistemological questions when the concept is first introduced. Just like everything else, we build on their previous exposure to such questions and give them ample opportunity to learn what might qualify as a reasonable answer to a particular question. And we need to persuade students that reasons matter. They cannot just say, "Well, it is just my opinion"; they need to justify their stances. And this requires that they learn and apply the criteria and concepts of critical thought.

Richard Paul has developed a set of questions that focus on reasons. These include:[57] What evidence did they use? How do they know that the conclusion is reliable? How are they using a particular term? For example, when students are talking about "family," in what sense(s) are they using the term? Here, we could note that "family" has different connotations to different people. In open-ended discussions, teachers can ask students whether they agree with another student's response. If they all agree, then ask why and, if different reasons are forthcoming, then ask whether any one reason is better than another. And if there is disagreement, ask students how this might be resolved. Asking questions is also something that students need to learn to do in order to have student-focused discussions. Students should also question themselves— how do I know this is true? Is this my best argument? Have I considered other points of view? This encourages reflection and what Lipman calls "self correcting thinking."[58]

To encourage empathic understanding we need to ask students to consider and reason from different points of view. Teachers should, when appropriate, ask other students whether they agree with a position taken by a classmate. This is not to undermine the initial student's response; it is demonstrate that other students can have other (or the same) views, and that these are worthy of being heard. If students agree with one another, it is worth knowing that there can be shared views. Even if there is

agreement, reasons might differ and the question of which reason(s) provide most weight can be considered. Students can also be asked to reason from a viewpoint other than their own. Students can also be asked to reason from a viewpoint other than their own. An idea here is to ask students to take a position on an issue and then have them provide the most powerful arguments they can think of against their initial position. Another idea is to have debate teams on a given issue and not tell the teams which side they will be arguing until fifteen minutes before the debate. However, the debate strategy can have the negative effect of suggesting that what matters is winning, not critical thought. Literature also helps in developing empathic understanding as students can hear stories about people who have different points of view than their own. Role-playing is also a valuable activity.

Conclusion

The evidence across Canada seems to be that despite our best intentions, not as much critical thinking occurs in the classroom generally, or in social studies in particular, as we think is warranted.[59] A number of factors contribute to this state of affairs. These include persistent confusion about the nature of critical thinking; lack of teacher education in critical thinking; the focus on content coverage only in the social studies curriculum; lack of good assessment devices; and the perceived tensions concerning actually teaching for critical thinking. (For example, misconceptions that before students can think critically they have to learn vast amounts of content, or that using Socratic methods will lead to classroom management problems, or that critical thinking will only benefit the superior student anyway). Further, there are organizational problems such as the move towards provincial exams in social studies, where the goal is to ascertain how much information students can remember, not how critical they are towards what they read or hear. Finally, there is the perennial worry that teaching for critical thinking is dangerous: for teachers because parents will disapprove, and for society because it might lead students to challenge authority or have subversive ideas.

However, despite the practical and political difficulties and the ongoing conceptual tensions, there have been some successful attempts to build communities of critical thinkers in social studies classrooms. In British Columbia there is The Critical Thinking Consortium (TC²), an organization that conducts workshops, designs materials, carries out research, and works to infuse defensible teaching of critical thinking into all areas of the curriculum.[60] In other provinces, there are also substantial efforts to put critical thinking activities into the social studies curriculum. It is still an uphill battle, but worth it if we want students to be thoughtful, open-minded, and respectful of persons and of the ethical and epistemic principles that guide the construction and practices of communities of inquiry. Our goal in this chapter has been to review some of the discussion that has gone on within and outside of social studies circles, and hopefully to enrich the critical conversations to come.

Endnotes

[1] Department of Education, British Columbia, *Programme of Studies for the Elementary Schools of B.C., 1928–29* (Victoria: King's Printer, 1929), 85.

[2] Department of Education, British Columbia, *Programme of Studies for the Elementary Schools of B.C., Bulletin 2, 1938* (Victoria: King's Printer, 1938), 9.

[3] Department of Education, Saskatchewan, *Program of Studies for the High School: Social Studies, Grade 10* (Regina: Queen's Printer, 1961), 6.

[4] Government of Newfoundland and Labrador, Department of Education, *Intermediate Social Studies Curriculum Guide Grade 7–Grade 9* (St John's: Author, 1988), 5.

[5] Manitoba Education and Youth, *Kindergarten to Grade 8 Social Studies: Manitoba Curriculum Framework of Outcomes* (Winnipeg: Author, 2003), 9.

[6] The Ontario Curriculum, *Social Studies Grades 1 to 6; History and Geography Grades 7 and 8* (Toronto: Author, 1998), 1.

[7] Alberta Learning, *Social Studies 10-20-30 Senior High* (Edmonton: Author, 2000), 1.

[8] British Columbia, Ministry of Education, *Social Studies K to 7: Integrated Resource Package* (Victoria: Author, 1998).

[9] Harvey Siegel, *Educating Reason: Rationality, Critical Thinking, and Education* (New York: Routledge, 1988), 60.

[10] Benjamin Bloom, ed., *The Taxonomy of Educational Objectives: Cognitive Domain* (New York: Longmans, Green, 1974).

[11] Sharon Bailin et al., "Common Misconceptions of Critical Thinking," *Journal of Curriculum Studies* 31, no. 3 (1999): 269–283; William Hare, "Critical Thinking as an Aim of Education," *Inquiry: Critical Thinking Across the Disciplines* 18, no. 2 (1998): 38–51.

[12] Robert Ennis, "A Taxonomy of Critical Thinking Dispositions and Abilities," in *Teaching Thinking Skills: Theory and Practice*, ed. Joan Baron and Robert Sternberg (New York: Freeman, 1987), 9–26.

[13] Robert Ennis, "Critical Thinking: A Streamlined Conception," *Teaching Philosophy* 14, no. 1 (1991): 7.

[14] Ibid.

[15] Richard Paul and Linda Elder, *Critical Thinking: Tools for Taking Charge of Your Learning and Your Life* (Upper Saddle River, NJ: Prentice Hall, 2001), xx.

[16] Richard Paul, "Dialogical Thinking: Critical Thought Essential to the Acquisition of Rational Knowledge and Passions," in *Teaching Thinking Skills: Theory and Practice*, 138.

[17] Richard Paul, A.J.A. Binker, and Marla Charbonneau, *Critical Thinking Handbook: K–3, A Guide for Remodelling Lesson Plans in Language Arts, Social Studies and Science* (Rohnert Park, CA: Center for Critical Thinking and Moral Critique, Sonoma State University, 1987).

[18] Paul and Elder, *Critical Thinking: Tools for Taking Charge of Your Learning and Your Life*, 49.

[19] For information on Foundation for Critical Thinking workshops and the annual conference, see http://www.criticalthinking.org.

[20] Matthew Lipman, *Critical Thinking: What Can It Be?* Resource Publication Series, no. 1 (Upper Montclair, NJ: Institute for Critical Thinking, Montclair State College, 1988), 1.

[21] Matthew Lipman, Ann Margaret Sharp, and Frederick Oscanyan, *Philosophy in the Classroom* (Philadelphia: Temple University Press, 1980). For more information about the Philosophy for Children program at the Institute for Critical Thinking at Montclair State University, go to http://chss2.montclair.edu/ict/.

[22] Sharon Bailin et al., *A Conception of Critical Thinking for Curriculum, Instruction and Assessment* (Victoria, BC: Ministry of Education, 1993), 4.

[23] See, for example, Tami McDiarmid, Rita Manzo, and Trish Musselle, *Critical Challenges for Primary Students*, ed. Roland Case and LeRoi Daniels (Richmond, BC: Critical Thinking Cooperative, 1996); John Harrison, Neil Smith, and Ian Wright, eds., *Critical Challenges in Social Studies for Upper Elementary Students* (Richmond, BC: Critical Thinking Cooperative, 1999); and Ruth Sandwell et al., eds., *Early Contact and Settlement in New France,* (Richmond, BC: Critical Thinking Cooperative, 2002; Victoria: Ministry of Education, 2002).

[24] Blythe Clinchy is co-author with Mary Belenky et al., *Women's Ways of Knowing*, 10th ed. (New York: Basic Books, 1997). The quoted material is from Blythe Clinchy, "Connected Knowing," in *Philosophy of Education: Introductory Readings,*

Rev. 3rd ed., ed. William Hare and John Portelli (Calgary: Detselig Enterprises, 2001), 187–196.

25 Clinchy, "Connected Knowing," 192.

26 Ibid., 191.

27 Barbara Thayer-Bacon, "Constructive Thinking," in *Philosophy of Education: Introductory Readings*, 203.

28 Seyla Benhabib, *Situating the Self: Gender, Community, and Postmodernism in Contemporary Ethics* (Cambridge, UK: Polity Press, 1992).

29 Frederick Schmitt, "Justification, Sociality, and Autonomy," *Synthese* 73 (1987): 43–85; and Richard Foley, *The Theory of Epistemic Rationality* (Cambridge, MA: Harvard University Press, 1987).

30 Alvin Goldman, *Knowledge in the Social World* (Oxford: Oxford University Press, 1997).

31 Siegal, *Educating Reason*.

32 Connie Missimer, "Where's the Evidence?" *Inquiry: Critical Thinking Across the Disciplines* 14, no. 4 (1995): 1–18.

33 Eammon Callan, *Creating Citizens* (Oxford: Calendon Press, 1997).

34 Tim Sprod, *Philosophical Discussion in Moral Education: The Community of Ethical Inquiry* (London: Routledge, 2001).

35 Linda Trinkaus Zagzebski, *Virtues of the Mind: An Inquiry into the Nature of Virtue and the Ethical Foundations of Knowledge* (New York: Cambridge University Press, 1996).

36 Alvin Goldman, "Education and Social Epistemology," in *Philosophers on Education: New Historical Perspectives*, ed. Amelie Oksenberg Rorty (London: Routledge, 1998), 439–451.

37 Paul and Elder, *Critical Thinking: Tools for Taking Charge of Your Learning and Your Life*, 4–19.

38 Goldman, "Education and Social Epistemology."

39 John Dewey, *Democracy and Education* (New York: Macmillan, 1916).

40 Dawn Schrader, ed., *The Legacy of Lawrence Kohlberg* (San Francisco: Jossey-Bass, 1990).

41 Alan Sears and Jim Parsons, "Towards Critical Thinking as an Ethic," *Theory and Research in Social Education* 19, no. 1 (1991): 45–68.

42 Siegal, *Educating Reason*.

43 See Barbara Thayer-Bacon, "Caring's Role in Epistemology: Fears of Relativism," *Inquiry: Critical Thinking Across the Disciplines* 17, no. 2 (1997): 20–31; and ———, "Caring Reasoning," *Inquiry: Critical Thinking Across the Disciplines* 19, no. 4 (1999): 22–34.

44 Matthew Lipman, "Caring as Thinking," *Inquiry: Critical Thinking Across the Disciplines* 15, no. 1 (1995): 1–13.

45 Martha Nussbaum, "Emotions as Judgments of Value," *The Yale Journal of Criticism* 5, no. 2 (1992): 210.

46 Anne Sharp, "Self-transformation in the Community of Inquiry," *Inquiry: Critical Thinking Across the Disciplines* 16, no. 1 (1996): 36–47.

47 Thayer-Bacon, "Caring's Role in Epistemology," 23.

48 Laurence Spittler, "Concepts, Communities and the Tools of Good Thinking," *Inquiry: Critical Thinking Across the Disci-plines* 19, no. 2 (2000): 11–26.

49 See, for example, Tom Morton, "Cooperative Learning in the Social Studies" in *The Canadian Anthology of Social Studies: Issues and Strategies for Teachers*, ed. Roland Case and Penney Clark (Burnaby: Faculty of Education, Simon Fraser University, 1997), 275–286; and John Meyers, "Cooperative Learning: Putting the 'Social' into Social Studies," in *Trends and Issues in Canadian Social Studies*, ed. Ian Wright and Alan Sears (Vancouver: Pacific Educational Press, 1997), 352–364.

50 Robert Slavin, "Research on Cooperative Learning: Consensus and Controversy," *Educational Leadership* 47 (1990): 52–55.

51 Roland Case and Ian Wright, "Taking Seriously the Teaching of Critical Thinking," *Canadian Social Studies* 32, no. 1 (Fall 1997): 18–19.

52 See sample Critical Challenges books listed in endnote 23.

53 See Paul, Binker, and Charbonneau, *Critical Thinking Handbook*.

54 Case and Wright, "Taking Seriously the Teaching of Critical Thinking."

55 See, for example, Ian Wright, *Is That Right? Critical Thinking and the Social World of the Young Learner* (Toronto: Pippin, 2002).

56 Stephen Norris, "Defining Observational Competence," *Science Education* 68, no. 2 (1984): 129–142; and Robert Ennis, *Critical Thinking* (Upper Saddle River, NJ: Prentice Hall, 1996), 58–66.

57 Paul and Elder, *Critical Thinking: Tools for Taking Charge of Your Learning and Your Life*, 124–127.

58 Lipman, *Critical Thinking: What Can It Be?*, 3.

59 Ian Wright, "Critical Thinking in the Schools: Why Doesn't Much Happen?" *Informal Logic* 22, no. 2 (2002): 93–113.

60 See endnotes 19 and 22 for more information about The Critical Thinking Consortium.

CHAPTER 18

Situated Learning and Anchored Instruction as Vehicles for Social Education

Andrew S. Hughes and Alan Sears

On Tuesday March 10, 1914 a Canadian woman, Mary Richardson, entered the British National Gallery on Trafalgar Square in London and made her way to a room containing one of the gallery's most important recent acquisitions, *The Rokeby Venus*. *The Guardian* newspaper from the following day furnishes an account of what happened next:

> The woman, producing a meat chopper from her muff or cloak, smashed the glass of the picture, and rained blows upon the back of *The Venus*. A police officer was at the door of the room, and a gallery attendant also heard the smashing of the glass. They rushed towards the woman, but before they could seize her she had made seven cuts in the canvas.[1]

A criminal record report from New Scotland Yard makes it clear that Mrs. Richardson had been involved in "similar outrages" including the breaking of plate glass windows and possibly arson.[2] Mary Richardson, however, did not see her behaviour as outrageous at all. Not when compared to what she saw as the oppression of women by the British government of the day. In explaining her actions in the case of *The Rokeby Venus* she wrote, in part:

> I have tried to destroy the picture of the most beautiful woman in mythological history as a protest against the Government destroying Mrs. Pankhurst, who is the most beautiful character in modern history. . . .

> Justice is an element of beauty as much as colour and outline on canvas. Mrs. Pankhurst seeks to secure justice to womanhood, and for this she is being slowly murdered by a Government of Iscariot politicians. If there is an outcry against my deed, let everyone remember that such an outcry is an hypocrisy as long as they allow the destruction of Mrs. Pankhurst and other beautiful living women.[3]

What do you think? Was Mary Richardson's act an "outrage" or a justifiable act of political protest? Can you think of other examples of civil disobedience? Is the destruction of property, particularly irreplaceable works of art, ever justified in making a political point? If so, under what circumstances? If not, what are people to do in the face of repression or exclusion from civic life? What would other political personages say about Mrs. Richardson? Imagine Gandhi, Nelson Mandela, Margaret Thatcher, George W. Bush. How might they have acted in similar circumstances? Are there political and social situations in Canada or elsewhere today that might justify acts of civil disobedience, including violence?

The story of Mary Richardson is a compelling example of a key concept or idea mandated for study in most social studies education curricula—the place of dissent, in particular civil disobedience, in a democracy. In Canada's western provinces, for example, students in grade 4 are expected to "evaluate diverse ways of dealing with conflict or the misuse of power and authority," and students in grade 6 are expected to "demonstrate willingness to take a stand against discriminatory practices and behaviours."[4] It is our contention that incidents such as that of Mary Richardson and *The Rokeby Venus* provide powerful springboards and contexts for instruction about important social ideas and concepts. It is an anchor and part of an approach called Situated Learning, which can foster deeper thinking about complex social ideas. In the remainder of this chapter we will provide an overview of how this approach can be used in social studies education. Mary Richardson and *The Rokeby Venus* constitute the anchor to which we attach much of our exploration.

Contested Concepts

Situated Learning is rooted in an approach to education called social constructivism, and particularly in the work of Russian psychologist and learning theorist Lev Vygostky.[5] Fundamental to this approach to teaching is the idea that knowledge is "a cultural product."[6] In other words, ideas and concepts do not have inherent meanings apart from those created and negotiated by people in particular contexts. Ideas, then, are complex and fluid and may mean different things to different people. Sometimes those differences exist across time or contexts, but often the same concept can be understood somewhat differently by people in the same time and place; that is, they can be contested. Let's take the idea of democratic government as "the consent of the governed," for example. Almost everyone would agree that rule by the people is a necessary condition for democracy, but there is wide disagreement about what precisely that means. One area of contention might be who should constitute the governed whose consent is required? In Ancient Athens, widely acknowledged as the first democracy, those included as citizens represented a minority of the total population: women, foreigners, and slaves, although certainly governed, were not asked for their consent. Mary Richardson's act of civil disobedience described above was a reaction to the exclusion of women from participation in their own governance in more modern times.

While in contemporary Canada a much larger percentage of the population is entitled to play a role in selecting those who govern, not everyone is included. Under the Canada Election Act voting is restricted to citizens over the age of eighteen who meet particular residency requirements. There are a number of organizations in Canada and elsewhere who feel that the age restrictions exclude younger people from legitimate participation in their own governance and argue that the voting age should be lowered.[7] Until quite recently the Election Act also excluded "every person undergoing punishment as an inmate in any penal institution for the commission of any offence."[8] That provision of the Act was challenged by one inmate who argued his constitutional right to vote ought to override that section of the Election Act. The Supreme Court of Canada agreed, and in May of 1993 ruled that the blanket stripping of the franchise from inmates was unconstitutional. In 1999, however, the Court upheld the amended Act ,which prohibited from voting only prisoners serving more than two years, ruling that was a more justifiable limitation on the constitutional right to vote.[9] The point is simply this: while all agree that in democracies citizens have a right to participate in their own governance, exactly who gets included is contested.

There is also disagreement about how citizens are to give their consent. In Canada the consent of the governed in generally obtained through the election of representatives to various levels of government. At the federal and provincial levels these representatives are selected using a "first past the post" electoral system that often leads to the election of individual representatives and whole governments with much less than 50 percent of the popular vote. In fact, it is rare in Canada to have a government elected with more than 50 percent of the popular vote. Some believe this system is at least partly responsible for growing voter apathy and consequent record low turnouts at the polls because the end results are not reflective of the will of the people.[10] Other jurisdictions, Italy and Israel for example, elect representatives proportionally, with parties getting seats based on the percentage of the popular vote they obtain. This often leads to minority and coalition governments but is seen by some as more fairly representing the choices made by citizens.

In most democratic jurisdictions representatives are chosen only at election time and the governed have no recourse but to wait for the next election if they are not happy with the representation they receive. This is not the case everywhere, however, as many people around the world recently found out as they watched the recall of the elected governor of California and his replacement with a prominent Hollywood movie star.

Throughout its history Canada has been reluctant to put policy and legislative decisions directly to the people in the form of referenda, only doing so three times at the federal level. This process is more common in provincial or municipal politics but is still quite rare. In the United States, however, referenda are quite common, particularly at state and local levels. In several high-profile cases they have been used by citizens' groups to significantly change public policy. The Canadian Alliance Party (integrated into the Conservative Party of Canada in late 2003) has argued that Canada needs more of this so-called direct democracy, and its official policy calls for "increased direct democratic responsibility through referenda and citizens' initiatives." The policy states, in part,

> We recognize there are issues so important to Canadians that direct public input is desirable. Therefore, we will introduce measures that allow citizens to initiate binding referenda. In addition, we will also seek the consensus of all Canadians through judicious use of national referenda, both on issues having significant implications for Canadian society and on proposed changes to the country's Constitution.[11]

Again, the consent of the governed is a necessary condition for democracy, but that consent can be and is obtained in a myriad of ways.

In our view, this same kind of complexity and fluidity exists for most important social concepts. Respect for diversity, for example, shows up as a goal in most social studies curricula. But how is that respect to be manifested and what, if any, restrictions should the state impose on diversity? In fact, we would contend that all democratic societies both protect diversity and limit it at the same time. In Canada, for example, people have the constitutional right to both diverse opinions and free expression. If, however, that expression includes promoting hatred of certain groups of people it might be deemed illegal. In considering the tensions between respecting and honouring diversity and maintaining social cohesion, several Québec writers pose a key question, "On what foundation can we argue that the State must sometimes impose limitations on recognition of diversity?"[12]

An Anglican Bishop in New Brunswick, in thinking about how the church is to deal with disputes over beliefs and practices, has called for Christians to exhibit "a generous orthodoxy."[13] By that he means an orthodoxy that is centred in core beliefs that are firm but recognizes some flexibility and variation in the ways people work those out personally and socially in different times and contexts. Similarly, most democratic societies are rooted in core principles or concepts such as the rule of law; the consent of the governed and the right to dissent; the common good; respect for diversity; the right to privacy; and equality—but individuals and societies understand and institutionalize these principles in a wide variety of ways.

A central premise of Situated Learning is that learners can construct sophisticated and complex understandings of these kinds of concepts. They can know the diverse ways in which particular concepts have been and are understood and operationalized and they can develop well-articulated views about the best way to understand and use them in their own context. For that to happen, learners must be touched in profound ways. Such learning must take place in a social context, take into account the prior knowledge learners bring to the situation, put them in active contact with a range of ideas different from the ones they hold, and stimulate reshaping and extension of their own ideas. Deep learning, then, cannot be abstract and remote; it must be embedded in situations in which the abstractions find tangible, visible, and public expression that can be put to the test.

Learning in a Social Context

In our approach to Situated Learning we use the term "situated" in two ways. First, we intend it to indicate that students are situated in "a community of learners"[14] and, second, that we can use situations to project students into discussions of the key elements of important concepts and ideas. We will say more about the second later but now will consider how a community of learners operates.

A community of learners

In our experience, rhetoric about constructivism and constructivist teaching is common among students in pre-service education programs. These students often say, "I want to establish a constructivist classroom." When we ask what they mean by that, the reply is something like, "I want to run a classroom where children construct their own knowledge." When pressed further about what such a class would look like, our students talk about avoiding lecturing and other forms of direct presentation in favour of techniques that emphasize discussion and activity. In our view these conversations demonstrate both an emergent understanding of constructivist theory as well as possible significant misunderstandings of it. It is true that constructivists call for classrooms that involve students in "meaningful, problem-based activities" and "task oriented dialogue with one another,"[15] and therefore our students' commitment to activity and dialogue is consistent with general constructivist approaches to instruction. However, the statement "I want to run a classroom where children construct their own knowledge" implies that it is possible for knowledge to be obtained without the processes of construction, and this is not consistent with the theory, which holds that all knowledge is constructed. Windschitl explains:

> Even when students are in what seems to be rote learning situations such as drill and practice, or in passive situations such as lecture classes, they are constructing knowledge because that is the way the mind operates.[16]

A second, and perhaps more important, misunderstanding implied in our students' comments is the simple equating of activity and discussion with quality learning. Windschitl calls this "naïve constructivism" which, he says, places "an inordinate amount of faith in the ability of children to structure their own learning."[17] He goes on to point out that exciting, hands-on activity in and of itself does not necessarily lead to quality learning. In fact, some of the research he reviews indicates that where "activities, as opposed to ideas, are the starting points and basic units of instruction," students might actually regress in their understanding of complex ideas rather than advance.[18]

If discussion and activity alone are not sufficient conditions for establishing a constructivist community of learners, what are the features of this kind of teaching? Drawing from the work of Windschitl and others, we would suggest the following:

- Constructivist teachers involve students in collaborative consideration of problems or issues that are focused on important ideas and/or processes; complex; and require original thinking and interpretation. The resolution of these problems will help in the acquisition of "concepts and principles fundamental to the theme under study."[19] In our own work we have focused on key ideas related to democracy, such as the consent of the governed and the right to dissent; privacy; respect for diversity; the common good; loyalty; due process; and equity. We have designed activities to help students develop more sophisticated understandings of these concepts. In recent years researchers in the field of history education have identified key ideas and processes related to historical understanding and have been exploring ways to help students develop these skill sets. Peter Seixas' chapter in this volume provides an excellent overview of some of this work.[20]

- Constructivist teachers extend the dialogue about themes and ideas being studied well beyond the classroom, connecting students to diverse contemporary and historical thinking about the questions being examined. They connect their students to a much wider world of ideas. In a landmark study of social studies education in Canada in the mid-1960s, A.B. Hodgetts and his colleagues visited classrooms across the country to look at teaching methods. In most cases they found students to be "bench bound listeners" not at all engaged in the study of important questions or issues.[21] In some cases, the researchers found classrooms more focused on the investigation of issues, but for the most part discussions in these classrooms were limited to what students already knew. Teachers did not provide reading or other sources of information about the questions nor did they push the students to support their claims with reasons or evidence. Hodgetts called what he saw "democratic idle talk."[22] We will have more to say about this later but, in our view, this kind of uninformed conversation may be a good place to begin a study but is not a good place to end one.

- Constructivist teachers balance the tension between accepting and honouring students' knowledge and creating a climate that pushes them to extend and refine what they know. This is a delicate balance indeed. We want students to feel free to contribute to discussions and class activities and, at the same time, we want to challenge what they have to say, to lead them to consider other points of view, to look broadly and deeply at evidence that might counter their views and cause them to change their minds. "One key for teachers who want to structure discourse in this way, is to convince students that they can defend a view or opinion without feeling they have to defend themselves."[23]

- Constructivist teachers use a variety of approaches to foster the development of more complex understandings in their students. Constructivist teaching is far more complex than simply designing activities that will engage students in dialogue about important ideas. Windschitle explains that teachers act as "conceptual change agent[s], mentoring apprentices through the zone of proximal development, and

supporting a community of learners."[24] The zone of proximal development is an idea that comes from Vygotsky. He suggested that learners' thinking could best be developed by teachers or mentors who pay close attention to what learners already know and then design instruction to move them on from there. In this process, sometimes called cognitive apprenticeship, "student tasks are slightly more difficult than students can manage independently, requiring the aid of their peers and instructor to succeed."[25] A number of specific teaching and learning strategies are associated with this approach, including mentoring, coaching, scaffolding, articulating, reflecting, and exploring.[26]

- Constructivist teachers recognize that assessing learning is a complex and collaborative process. In constructivist classrooms "assessment methods are as rich (complex) and interpretive (potentially subjective) as the learning activities themselves. . . . Such assessments include clinical interviews, observation, student journals, peer reviews, research reports, building of physical models, performances in the forms of inquiries, plays, debates, dances, or artistic renderings."[27] These kinds of assessment instruments require clear criteria or rubrics, which are best designed in collaboration with the students so they are clear on expectations. Too often, teachers keep the assessment process, particularly the criteria for success, a closely guarded secret, which strikes us as counterproductive. There is clear evidence that students achieve much better when they clearly understand what is expected of them and why.

It is true that constructivist teaching is rooted in dialogue and activity, but it is much more than simply that. Done well, it reflects careful planning and skillful practice. In sum, we argue that learning is most effective when students are situated in a carefully structured community of learners that collaboratively investigates important questions; explores a wide range of information and thinking related to these questions; challenges participants in a supportive way to examine and extend their own ideas about these questions; uses specific strategies to mentor the development of more complex thinking; and establishes clear and mutually understood criteria for judging progress. We will now examine another key aspect of Situated Learning, making use of the prior learning students bring with them to any new learning situation.

Paying Attention to Prior Learning

Constructivists hold that students come to any learning situation not as blank slates but with a range of prior knowledge and experience that is critical in shaping how they respond to new learning. This prior knowledge is described in a range of ways in the literature. For example, Driver and Easley identify three different types of conceptions students might hold about a given concept:

- *preconceptions*—ideas that are not yet understood

- *misconceptions*—what occurs when "correct" formal theories are taught, but are misunderstood

- *alternative frameworks*—occur when students develop their own concepts, outside of the accepted norm. These alternative frameworks are thought to be a product of imaginative efforts to explain, and they show common traits.[28]

Whatever form this prior knowledge takes, research in several disciplines has suggested it is persistent (resistant to change) and plays a key role in how students assimilate or accommodate new learning.[29] It is absolutely essential that teachers pay attention to it when planning for instruction. A fundamental principle of constructivist teaching in general and situated learning in particular is to begin where students are and help them to both construct new knowledge on that foundation and, where necessary, tear apart and reconstruct prior knowledge. An analogy might help to make this point. Think of students' prior knowledge or, as some would call it, cognitive schema, as a modular bookshelf. The supports and the shelves help to structure the pieces of

knowledge that are represented by the books on the shelves. As the person acquires new knowledge—new books—a number of things might happen. The knowledge might fit well with what they already know and that book slides neatly on the shelf beside the others. The knowledge might be something almost completely new and require a new shelf to accommodate it. Another possibility, however, is that the knowledge is related to that on one of the shelves but does not seem to fit. It is like getting an oversized book that will not slide neatly onto the shelf. In this case the learner has some options. He or she can do what many of us might do with the oversized book: set it aside for the time being, perhaps putting it on the coffee table. The learner decides not to deal with the new knowledge, at least not for now. Another possibility is to turn the book sideways and slide it on the shelf that way. In other words, not accept the knowledge in the way presented but manipulate it so that it fits. This often means distorting the knowledge, or creating or adding to misconceptions. In his book *Wonderful Life,* science writer Stephen J. Gould has an example that shows how some of the world's best scientists did this early in the twentieth century when they found a rich deposit of fossils that provided evidence countering much of what was believed about evolution. Instead of dealing with the implications of that evidence, the scientists manipulated it to fit accepted views of the evolution of life. It wasn't until much later, when other investigators took a second look, that accepted thinking began to change.[30]

Of course the last possibility for that oversized book is to pull some pins and adjust the shelves so it fits. This is hard work, however, and often means adjusting not only the books on the shelf in question but those above and below it as well. Most of us would rather put the book on the coffee table or turn it sideways. Eventually, however, the coffee table fills up or the sideways books begin to interfere with putting other books on the shelf and we have to do the tough work of making adjustments. In similar fashion, people resist changing their minds until they become uncomfortable with their current way of thinking, until too many things no longer seem to fit. Part of good teaching is finding out what students already know and creating the cognitive dissonance that will lead to the hard work of adding new shelves or adjusting existing ones. Windschitl describes this dissonance as "a puzzling even shocking experience that prompts . . . an extensive reconsideration of their ideas."[31]

There are two senses in which teachers can know how their students think. The first is the general sense. This has to do with knowing the students and something about their life experiences and the local world in which they live. Teachers need to listen to their students, value the knowledge they bring with them to school and try to understand their worldview. Part of skillful teaching is connecting the knowledge and experience of students to the wider world, and to do that, teachers need to know something about that knowledge and experience. Jamie Escalante is a famous example of a teacher who did just that. Peruvian-born Escalante started teaching at an inner-city Los Angeles high school in 1982, and his amazing success teaching math and science to previously disconnected and unmotivated students has been documented in a number of books and the popular Hollywood movie *Stand and Deliver*. Part of Escalante's technique was to demonstrate the connection between mathematics and the history and contemporary life of his mostly Latino students.

Escalante had the advantage of sharing a general cultural background with his students, but his specific experience as an immigrant to the United States was much different from theirs living in an inner-city ghetto. He had to work hard to know his students and connect their world to the ideas he was teaching in calculus. Teachers who want to be successful need to do the same. As Windshilt writes:

> In classrooms where teachers are unaware of students' interests and life experiences, they not only fail to build on local knowledge but essentially offer 'disinvitations' to participate in classroom discourse.[32]

Part of building a community of learners is structuring time for members to share the knowledge, interests, and values they bring to class with them. Teachers can also know something about students' thinking in a far more specific sense. We can know

something of what they think about the concepts and ideas about which we plan to teach. This can be done in two ways. The first is to design specific activities to uncover prior knowledge. Let's go back to the story of Mary Richardson. It is intended as a springboard for considering the idea of the place of dissent, particularly civil disobedience, in a democracy. Before getting to this story we use an activity for finding out what our students already know about these ideas. We begin by asking them to list the ways in which people try to influence their governments either to do something they are not currently doing or to change policies and practices already in place. After students have had a few minutes to create their own list, we move to a class brainstorming session and create a collective list on the board. It often looks something like the chart below.

WAYS TO INFLUENCE GOVERNMENT	
Vote	Damage or destroy property
Write letters	Bombing
Use the media	Walkouts
Join a political party	Sign petitions
Contact politicians	Hunger strikes
Demonstrations	Revolution/Coup
Strikes	Lobbying
Boycotts	

Following that, we ask the students to individually take the items on the list and complete the activity shown on the chart in Figure 1.

Finally, we ask students to gather in groups of four or five, come up with a group rating for each of the activities, and plot their responses on a graph such as the one in Figure 2. The level of appropriateness runs horizontally along the x axis and the level of effectiveness runs vertically along the y axis. You can see, for example, that these students rated voting as highly appropriate but not particularly effective, in contrast with bombing, which they felt was effective but not at all appropriate. Lobbying they found moderately appropriate and very effective.

Inevitably, there is a fair bit of variation within

FIGURE 1

RATING METHODS OF INFLUENCING GOVERNMENTS

Give each of the activities in the preceding chart a score for effectiveness and appropriateness based on the following scales:

Very Effective		Effective		Neutral		Ineffective		Very Ineffective
+4	+3	+2	+1	0	−1	−2	−3	−4

Very Appropriate		Appropriate		Neutral		Inappropriate		Very Inappropriate
+4	+3	+2	+1	0	−1	−2	−3	−4

For example, if you listed writing a letter to a newspaper as one of the ways in which citizens try to influence government you need to rank it on both scales. If you think it is not a particularly effective way to influence government you would rank it at −1 or −2 on the Effectiveness scale. If you think it is a very appropriate activity you would rank it at a +3 or +4 on the Appropriateness scale. So the final ranking for writing a letter to the newspaper might be −1,+4.

groups and among groups about how each item should be rated. The particular rating does not matter as the activity is designed to assess what students already know and think about issues of dissent and civil disobedience in a democracy. In this regard we think this activity works on a couple of levels. First, it provides a good idea of the range of their knowledge—how many different kinds of activities can they name and provide examples of? Second, it provides a preliminary indication of how they feel about particular methods of dissent. The activity also sets in motion consideration of dissent as a complex concept as students begin to encounter ideas different from their own in developing the group ratings.

This is just one example of an activity designed to get at the specific prior knowledge of students. There are many others ranging from simple brainstorming through more formal activities such as having students develop a position paper or make a poster illustrating particular points. In trying to assess the historical thinking of a group of high school students, Peter Seixas asked them to list the most significant events in world history and then present them in a chart or drawing indicating both their relative importance and their relationship to each other.[33] As a way of understanding how elementary students conceptualized what a Canadian is, Manju Varma-

Joshi asked a group of them to draw a picture of both a Canadian and an immigrant.[34] Both these activities were part of larger research projects on student thinking, but would be relatively easy for a teacher to employ in the classroom and provide valuable insight into the ideas students bring to these topics.

A second way to know something about the specific ideas students bring with them to class is to pay attention to the growing body of research in the field. While social studies has lagged behind other areas, particularly science and mathematics, in the development of a body of knowledge about students' conceptions of key ideas, important work has been and is being carried out.[35] As mentioned above, the field of historical thinking, or historical consciousness, is one where there has been considerable research over the past ten to fifteen years. From the work of Rosalyn Ashby and Peter Lee in Britain, to that of Sam Wineburg in the United States and Peter Seixas in Canada, just to name a few, we are beginning to know a fair bit about how children and young people understand things such as historical significance, the use of historical evidence, and how historians make judgements.[36] Any teacher wanting to effectively teach history needs to pay close attention to that work.

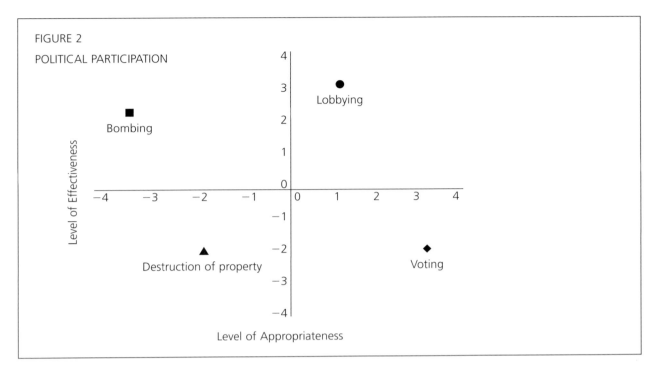

FIGURE 2
POLITICAL PARTICIPATION

This kind of research has been slower to be undertaken in the field of social studies. Brophy and Alleman, in surveying literature in the field, found:

Scholars concerned with curriculum and instruction have developed little information about topics addressed in K–3 social studies. There have been occasional surveys of knowledge about particular social studies topics (Guzzetta, 1969; Ratvich & Finn, 1987; U.S. Office of Education, 1995a, 1995b). However, these concentrate mostly on isolated facts such as names, places, or definitions, with reported findings limited to percentages of students able to answer each item correctly. To be more useful to educators, the research needs to probe children's understanding of connected networks of knowledge, analyze qualitative aspects of their thinking about such topics, and identify commonly held misconceptions.[37]

Brophy and his colleagues have made progress in addressing this gap in our knowledge by conducting major studies about how early elementary students understand some of the key ideas underlying most elementary social studies curricula. In particular, they have examined how these students understand the ways in which people in the United States meet their basic needs for food and shelter. The picture painted by these researchers is one of limited, spotty, and tacit knowledge, characterized by misconceptions and relatively low levels of sophistication. The implications of this research are profound. First and foremost, it is clear that "discovering valid prior knowledge that instruction can connect with and build upon" and "identifying misconceptions that need to be addressed" is a fundamental research goal and that curricular reform should not begin before these objectives are realized.[38]

Our own work, and that of graduate students and colleagues collaborating with us, has focused on mapping how children and young people understand key ideas related to citizenship, such as dissent; respect for diversity; and political participation.[39] Again, teachers who want to effectively teach social studies need to stay in touch with the growing body of work on students' ideas about the social world.

Anchoring Instruction in Situations

We said earlier that we use the term "situated" to indicate two things: that students are situated in "a community of learners" and that we can use situations to project students into discussions of the key elements of important concepts and ideas. We will now turn to a consideration of that second sense.

The story of Mary Richardson is one example of a situation that we use in this way. Often we begin by simply showing the painting and asking, What do you think this painting might have to do with democracy?[40] We move from there to presenting students with the story as relayed at the beginning of this chapter. In the context of having completed the activity on rating methods of dissent, we ask the students to rate what Mary Richardson did. Was it appropriate? Effective? In every group there is a range of opinions and usually a strong sense that they need to know more about the situation. They have questions such as, Who is the Mrs. Pankhurst referred to in both the newspaper account of the incident and Richardson's statement? What things had the suffragettes done before this to make their points? What had been the reaction of the government and the police? What were other groups and individuals doing to make the case for women's suffrage?

Again, the particular story of Mary Richardson and the suffragettes has an intrinsic interest but its true value lies in opening doors that allow the exploration of important democratic ideas of dissent and civil disobedience. Over the past several years we have been working with teachers in Canada and Russia to develop a number of such situations (which we sometimes call anchors or springboards) designed to lay bare elements of democratic living that are often contested and in conflict, and to engage students in the study of these. We have seen children from grades 3 through 12, with the guiding hand of their teachers, explore issues and ideas ranging from the value of a free press to the meaning of loyalty. The situation launches students into consideration of what democratic ideas have meant over time, in different contexts, and what they should mean in the here and now. To act as effective springboards for this kind of study, the stories should meet certain design specifications:

- They should be authentic. Most of the situations we have used, like the Mary Richardson story, are drawn from actual historical or current events. In our experience, contrived situations are often not nearly as compelling and interesting as actual ones. To paraphrase an old saying, "Truth is sometimes stranger, and often more interesting, than fiction." We do sometimes create fictionalized stories, but they are always rooted in actual events.

- They should be presented in a vivid rendering. The situations are used as springboards to launch students into the middle of a debate about the appropriate form of democratic societies. To do this the stories have to catch and hold student interest and enthusiasm. The idea of a well-dressed, middle-class woman strolling into an important art gallery and attacking one of its most valuable works of art with a meat cleaver grabs students' interest from the beginning. However, the springboards do not have to be quite so public or focused on key political movements (such as the struggle for women's rights). Often situations much closer to the lives of the children in class will serve very well. For example, we have launched interesting considerations of the meaning and limits of personal freedoms by using a story about children fined for not wearing bicycle helmets. In another case we have begun the study of the protection of privacy in democracies with a story of parents reading their daughter's personal diary.[41]

- They should be succinct. Again, the situations themselves are not the focus of the learning but rather the ideas and concepts inherent in them. The purpose of the situation is to begin student engagement in both inter- and intra-personal dialogue (more about these below) about these ideas, as well as to provide a context for this dialogue. The Russian teachers we work with often use a single painting as a springboard. One of the best examples is a work titled *The Old Believer* (Boyarynya Morozova), a nineteenth-century work depicting a female member of a banned sect being carted off to prison for her beliefs. Most Russian children immediately recognize the painting and know its subject, so the teachers use it to launch a study of freedom of religion, a contested idea in Russia both past and present.[42]

- They should be multidimensional. That is, they should allow for and promote the consideration of the ideas involved at a number of levels and/or from a number of perspectives. In regard to the latter, the story of Mary Richardson presented at the beginning of the chapter includes descriptions of her act as outrageous and heroic. This encourages students to consider a wide range of views about this and other acts of dissent. The painting *The Old Believer* includes a number of spectators, some of whom clearly sympathize with the woman being carried away while others are celebrating her detention. As we said earlier, most important ideas in the social world have a range of meanings and interpretations, and the situations used as springboards should open up consideration of as much of this range as possible.

- They should be deliberately ambiguous. The purpose of the situations is not to provide answers but to stimulate questions: therefore they must be open-ended and open to interpretation. In the literature about Problem-Based Learning (a particular form of situated learning) good problems are referred to as "ill structured," meaning that there is some question about what exactly the problem is and no clear direction about what the solution or solutions might be.[43] If the situations or problems are clearcut and unambiguous, consideration of them will be short and very limited.

- Finally, the springboards should be representative. That is, they should include within them features of the ideas or concepts that are common across a number of situations or contexts and not unique to the specific incident referred to. The story of Mary Richardson and the suf-

fragettes, for example, mirrors features of dissent in many other contexts. Protest begins in legal and relatively moderate ways—writing letters, demonstrating, making speeches—and is largely ignored; it escalates to more confrontational tactics—chaining protestors to public building and monuments, disrupting public events—and finally, in the face of intransigence from the government, moves to illegal and violent methods including the destruction of property. In the midst of this, there is a debate within the women's movement about the escalation and the movement splits between those who remain committed to legal means of protest and those, like Mary Richardson and Emmeline Pankhurst, who decide violence is the only way to move the cause forward, and is therefore necessary.

Many features of this evolution of dissent are common to other situations. The *Autobiography of Martin Luther King, Jr.*, for example, details the evolution of the civil rights movement in the United States, including the contentious debate between emerging Black Power advocates in the 1960s, who argued the oppressive nature of American society and the slow pace of reform justified violent means being employed to push for equal rights, and Dr. King, who was committed to non-violent action and, following his mentor Mahatma Gandhi, argued violence was never justified.[44] In considering the particular case of the suffragettes, students can investigate other dissenters and protest movements for the purpose of comparing and contrasting. The point is the situations or springboards should open up a wider world related to the central ideas, not narrow the focus to particular circumstances.

The situations serve as a reference point for testing ideas and a launching pad for exploring them in other contexts. Rather than the study of history or social studies being driven by narrative from which teachers and students might identify ideas to examine, we are arguing the first step is to decide on the ideas to be learned and then to identify the narratives that will drive their exploration. This would allow for the consideration of any of the important events or topics that are currently in the curriculum, but with a different focus. Instead of looking at the story of Louis Riel as part of a narrative about settlement of the West, for example, we might use the story as a launching pad for looking at ideas of Aboriginal peoples' rights, self-determination, loyalty, or regional accommodation. Students will come away from such a study knowing something about key personalities and events in Canadian history but also with more complex understanding of ideas that apply in a much wider range of contexts. In this way, we bring to bear in our field of social studies education, however it is conceived, the findings of cognitive science over the past decades. It is a drive to include both the ethos and instructional approaches of situated learning and anchored instruction.[45]

Fostering Dialogue

If the situations or springboards are designed to launch the study of important ideas, what comes next? Vygotsky argued that people learn through two kinds of activity, which he called interpsychological (among people) and intrapsychological (within ourselves).[46] In moving these ideas to teaching, we argue that teachers need to structure activities to promote interpersonal and intrapersonal dialogue about the concepts or ideas being studied. In other words, students should encounter a wide range of thinking about the ideas being studied and, in light of that, be led to deep reflection about what they think about these ideas.

Interpersonal dialogue will most often begin among the members of a class and between these students and their teacher. The activities we outlined above that were designed to get at students' prior understandings of the concept of dissent begin this interpersonal dialogue, as students come together to rank the particular examples of dissent and then present their rankings to the class. After presenting the Mary Richardson story, we ask students to consider her particular actions and decide whether they were effective and appropriate. A good springboard will generate much interpersonal dialogue and we would agree with others who have argued there is often much untapped knowledge among students

in any class that ought to be opened up and considered. Class discussion and debate, we believe, is a great way to begin the interpersonal dialogue about any idea. It is not, however, sufficient to complete the consideration of an idea. We share Hodgetts' view that classroom discussion uninformed by voices from beyond the classroom is often "democratic idle talk" or, as one of us has written elsewhere, "Debates in ignorance."[47]

A fundamental part of the teacher's job is to extend the interpersonal dialogue to include voices from across both time and space. In considering the question of whether or not the destruction of property is ever justified as an act of dissent in a democracy, students should hear from each other and their teacher, but they also need to consider what Mary Richardson had to say, how the police and authorities in London felt, and the arguments of the women's rights advocates who had decided not to join the suffragettes in their move to violence. Moving beyond that particular context, they might consider the ideas of other dissenters in other contexts. Martin Luther King, Jr. has already been mentioned but many others quickly come to mind, such as Mahatma Gandhi, Henry David Thoreau, and Nellie McClung. In addition to these historical figures, students might examine more contemporary examples of violent dissent such as the so-called Battle in Seattle in 1999, or the protests at the Summit of the Americas in Québec City in 2001. Chances are there will be examples much closer to home for most classes, as protests, strikes, and other kinds of dissent are relatively common in most Canadian communities.

Our point is this: interpersonal dialogue need not be face to face. It can take place as students encounter the ideas of others in books, articles, films, works of art, and in virtual environments. To be really informed and knowledgeable about ideas, students need to know not only what their peers think about them but what a wide range of knowledgeable others think and have thought in various places and times. Teachers need to connect students with the thinking of others and design activities to foster serious consideration of that thinking.

Judith Torney-Purta writes about one example of this.[48] She examined the process that a number of classes around the world went through as they engaged in a simulation of the United Nations dealing with an international crisis. Participating classes were assigned the role of one of the member states of the United Nations (not their own country) and provided with written background material about both the crisis and their country's policies in the area. Classes were expected to develop an initial position for their country and they then signed on to two kinds of online conferences to engage in the simulation. The first type of conferences were multi-lateral, that is all countries were on at once in real time. These ran like a meeting of the UN Security Council, with the various countries stating their positions and making arguments to support them. The second kind of conferences were bilateral, that is, when two countries, say Russia and Canada, would collaborate to try to work out a joint position or a compromise that might be presented in the general meetings.

Torney-Purta argues that a number of "discourse communities" were apparent in this exercise. There was the community in each class as students and teachers interacted with the written material and each other to try to work out their country's position, the multilateral community as many different voices weighed in from around the world, and the bilateral communities as individual classes interacted with each other. Students were engaged in interpersonal dialogue with peers from their own classes and peers from around the world, as well as with the historical, political, and sociological material provided as background information. According to Torney-Purta, they demonstrated clear gains in their understanding of the ideas and issues related to the simulation.

In addition to providing opportunities for wide-ranging interpersonal dialogue about ideas, teachers need to design activities that will cause students to think deeply about how they understand these ideas, particularly in light of the alternatives they have encountered in the interpersonal dialogue. The Russian teachers we have been working with over the past five years do this very well. In one small village school in rural Russia we saw grade 11 students wrestling with the concepts of equity and equality. The situation they chose to explore concerned women in the military, and the specific an-chor was the draft notice received by the teacher's son while young women of the same age remain exempt. The interpersonal dialogue included Internet discussions with the local military commander, consideration of the policies on women in the military from a number of other countries, and a survey of opinions from their village and another village more than 1,000 kilometres away. At the conclusion the teacher asked her students to draft their own policy regarding women in the Russian military, including consideration of whether or not they should serve at all and if so, what limits, if any, should be put on that service. This kind of activity encourages students to think about how they understand the issue in light of all the ideas they have encountered in the study. It fosters intrapersonal dialogue, a conversation within.

Dialogue is a key component in constructivist teaching, but not just any dialogue. Students need to engage in discussions of important ideas, come into contact with a range of thinking about those ideas (including that of their peers and important thinkers from history and the contemporary world), and be pushed to think about how they understand the ideas and whether or not they need to do some adjusting in order to incorporate changes in their thinking. The teacher's role is to stimulate dialogue with engaging and significant situations, connect students to a wide range of voices about the ideas in ways that are accessible to them, and design activities to promote serious introspection about the ideas.

Conclusion

In 1918 the president of Czechoslovakia, Professor Masaric, said, "Democracy is a discussion."[49] We could not agree more. Democratic ideas and the democracies that seek to put them into practice are not static; they are in a constant state of flux. We continue to try to work out how to live together. Our belief is that the role of social studies education is to introduce students to this discussion in an informed way. We cannot tell them the right way to think about ideas like justice, equity, due process, and human rights, though some would have us try, but we can help them to understand what people have thought about these ideas over time and in different places, and we can connect them to the current debates about these ideas in Canada and the world. This is hard work for the teacher and somewhat unsettling for students who might prefer firm and clear answers, but as the first president of the Czech Republic said, democracy is "the long tunnel at the end of the light."[50]

Endnotes

[1]   The *Guardian,* March 11, 1914, quoted in "The Consent of the Governed and the Right to Dissent: Civil Disobedience; The Suffragettes, *The Rokeby Venus*," http://www.unb.ca/democracy/Project/IdeasInDemocracy/TheConsentOf/CivilDisobedience/CivilDisobedience4.html.

[2]   Criminal Record Office of New Scotland Yard Memorandum, quoted in ibid.

[3]   *Votes for Women,* March 13, 1914, p. 491, quoted in ibid. Emmeline Pankhurst was the leader of a radical wing of the suffragette movement called The Women's Social and Political Union, which had as its principal aim obtaining the vote for women. Mrs. Pankhurst had been arrested and jailed the day before Mrs. Richardson damaged *The Rokeby Venus.*

[4]   Western Canadian Protocol for Collaboration in Basic Education, *The Common Curriculum Framework for Social Studies: Kindergarten to Grade 9* (Winnipeg: Manitoba Education, Training and Youth, 2002) 57, 69.

[5]   Mark Windschitl, "Framing Constructivism in Practice as the Negotiation of Dilemmas: An Analysis of the Conceptual, Pedagogical, Cultural, and Political Challenges Facing Teachers," *Review of Educational Research* 72, no. 2 (Summer 2002): 131–175.

[6]   Ibid., 141.

[7]   See, for example, The Youth Action Network, http://www.youthactionnetwork.org/ and Brown University's student-led organization, The Association for Children's Suffrage,http://www.brown.edu/Students/Association_for_Childrens_Suffrage/.

[8]   Department of Justice Canada, "Do Two Wrongs Make a Right? The Right to Vote for Inmates," http://canada.justice.gc.ca/en/justice2000/135mile.html (accessed October 28, 2003).

[9]   Ibid.

[10] Centre for Research and Information on Canada, *Voter Participation in Canada: Is Canadian Democracy in Crisis?* (Montreal: Author, October 2001).

[11] http://www.canadianalliance.ca/english/policy/index.asp#_Toc8204945 (accessed October 28, 2003).

[12] Guy Bourgeault et al., "Recognition of Cultural and Religious Diversity in the Educational Systems of Liberal Democracies," in *Citizenship in Transformation in Canada,* ed. Yvonne

Hébert (Toronto: University of Toronto Press, 2002), 81.

[13] Bishop William Hockin would often speak of this in sermons or talks.

[14] Windschitl, "Framing Constructivism in Practice," 135.

[15] Ibid., 137.

[16] Ibid., 136.

[17] Ibid., 140.

[18] Ibid., 138.

[19] Ibid., 145.

[20] In addition to Seixas' chapter in this book, see also, Peter N. Sterns, Peter Seixas, and Samuel Wineburg, eds., *Knowing, Teaching, and Learning History: National and International Perspectives* (New York: New York University Press, 2000); and Samuel Wineburg, *Historical Thinking and Other Unnatural Acts: Charting the Future of Teaching the Past* (Philadelphia: Temple University Press, 2001).

[21] A.B. Hodgetts, *What Culture? What Heritage? A Study of Civic Education in Canada* (Toronto: OISE Press, 1968), 41.

[22] Ibid., 51.

[23] Windschitl, "Framing Constructivism in Practice," 147.

[24] Ibid., 135

[25] Kevin Oliver, Educational Technologies at Virginia Tech, http://www.edtech.vt.edu/edtech/id/models/cog.html (accessed October 21, 2003).

[26] You can read more about these teaching and learning strategies at www.spiritofdemocracy.com.

[27] Windschitl, "Framing Constructivism in Practice," 148.

[28] R. Driver and J. Easley, "Pupils and Paradigms: A Review of Literature Related to Concept Development in Adolescent Science Students," *Studies in Science Education* 5 (1978): 61–84.

[29] Andrew Hughes and Alan Sears, "Macro and Micro Level Aspects of a Programme of Citizenship Education Research," *Canadian and International Education* 25, no. 2: (1996): 17–30.

[30] Stephen J. Gould, *Wonderful Life: The Burgess Shale and the Nature of History* (New York: WW. Norton, 1989).

[31] Windschitl, "Framing Constructivism in Practice," 162.

[32] Ibid., 151–152.

[33] Peter Seixas, "Mapping the Terrain of Historical Significance," *Social Education* 61, no. 1 (January 1997): 22–27.

[34] Manju Varma-Joshi, "Multicultural Children's Literature: Storying the Canadian Identity" (doctoral dissertation, University of Toronto, 2000).

[35] Hughes and Sears, "Macro and Micro Level Aspects," 17–30.

[36] There is a diverse literature in this field. See, for example, Sterns, Seixas, and Wineburg, *Knowing, Teaching, and Learning History*; and Wineburg, *Historical Thinking and Other Unnatural Acts.*

[37] Jere Brophy and Janet Alleman, "Primary-Grade Students' Knowledge and Thinking About the Economics of Meeting Families' Shelter Needs," *American Educational Research Journal* 39, no. 2 (Summer 2002): 426. See also, J. Brophy, J. Alleman, and C. O'Mahony, "Primary-Grade Students' Knowl-

edge and Thinking About Food Production and the Origins of Common Foods," *Theory and Research in Social Education* 31 (2003): 10–49.

38 Ibid., 461.

39 See, for example, Barbara Corbett, "Children's Understanding of the Concept of Dissent" (master's thesis, University of New Brunswick, 1997); Barbara Hillman, "Grade Eight Students' Understanding of the Concept of Dissent" (master's thesis, University of New Brunswick, 1997); Michael Kimberly Bourgeois, "Colouring Outside the Lines: Grade 12 Students' Prior Knowledge of the Concept of Dissent" (master's thesis, University of New Brunswick, 1998); Carla Peck, "Children's Understanding of Ethnic Diversity" (master's thesis, University of New Brunswick, 2003); and Andrew Hughes et al., "A Constructivist Approach to Studying and Teaching Democratic Citizenship" (paper presented at the Fourth International Citizenship Education Research Network forum, Halifax, Nova Scotia, June 1, 2003).

40 The Velasquez painting *The Rokeby Venus* is reproduced in "The Consent of the Governed and the Right to Dissent," http://www.unb.ca/democracy/Project/IdeasInDemocracy/TheConsentOf/CivilDisobedience/CivilDisobedience4.html.

41 You will find a number of springboards on our website, http://www.spiritofdemocracy.com.

42 The painting *The Old Believer* is on our website, http://www.unb.ca/democracy/English/Workshop/Freedom/Freedom.html, using the link to Boyarynya Morozova.

43 W.H. Gijselaers, "Connecting Problem-Based Practices with Educational Theory: Bringing Problem-Based Learning to Higher Education," *New Directions for Teaching and Learning* 68 (Winter 1996): 20. Many of the other articles in this volume also deal with the issue of ill-structured problems. See also Andrew S. Hughes, Alan M. Sears, and Gerald M. Clarke, "Adapting Problem-based Learning to Social Studies Teacher Education," *Theory and Research in Social Education* 26, no. 4 (1998): 531–548.

44 Carson Clayborne, ed., *The Autobiography of Martin Luther King, Jr.* (New York: Warner Books, 1998).

45 See, for example, J.S. Brown, A. Collins, and P. Duguid, "Situated Cognition and the Culture of Learning," *American Educator* 18, no. 1 (1989): 32–42; Jean Lave and Etienne Wenger, *Situated Learning: Legitimate Peripheral Participation* (New York: Cambridge University Press, 1991); J.D. Bransford et al., "Anchored Instruction: Why We Need It and How Technology Can Help," in *Cognition, Education, and Multimedia: Exploring Ideas in High Technology*, ed. Don Nix and Rand Spiro (Hillsdale, NJ: Lawrence Erlbaum, 1990), 115–141; Cognition and Technology Group at Vanderbilt, "Anchored Instruction and Its Relationship to Situated Cognition," *Educational Researcher* 19, no. 6 (1990); 2–10; and ———, "Anchored Instruction and Situated Cognition Revisited," *Educational Researcher* 33, no. 3, (1993): 52–70.

46 Joan Wink and LeAnn G. Putney, *A Vision of Vygotsky* (Boston: Allyn & Bacon, 2002), 91.

47 Hodgetts, *What Culture?*; Alan Sears, "Buying Back Your Soul: Restoring Ideals in Social Studies Teaching," *Social Studies and the Young Learner* 4, no. 3 (1992): 9–11.

48 Judith Torney-Purta, "Conceptual Change among Adolescents Using Computer Networks and Peer Collaboration in Studying International Political Issues," in *International Perspectives on the Design of Technology-Supported Learning Environments*, ed. Stella Vosniadou et al. (Mahwah, NJ: Lawrence Erlbaum, 1996).

49 Professor Masaric, President of Czechoslovakia, 1918, cited in Bulgaria-Belgium Friends Association et al., "Democracy is a Discussion," (Razgrad, March 14, 1997), http://www.flgr.bg/site/97democrac.htm (accessed November 7, 2003).

50 Vaclav Havel, cited in Jean Bethke Elshtain, "Patience Is a Virtue," *Women's Freedom Network Newsletter* 10, no. 4 (July/August 2003): 10, http://www.womensfreedom.org/articA42.htm (accessed February 5, 2004).

CHAPTER 19

Democratic Experiences for Early-Years Students

Ann Sherman

Introduction

Making decisions, being given choices, questioning routines, imagining that things can be done differently, and offering opinions are all things that can be associated with a democratic society and yet these very situations are rarely found in classrooms. How do children learn to question the status quo, how can they learn to make choices, how can they learn to share their opinions, to take a stand and make their voice heard, if they never have practice at doing any of these things? We have the opportunity as teachers to focus carefully on aspects of democratic community- and relationship-building through making choices, sharing opinions, and learning to listen to others. Together, these can help children learn to make decisions about what they value, what they accept, and what they want to change in a democratic society. If all members of democracies utilized these skills and attitudes effectively, societies might find themselves with a more democratic citizenry.

There has been a growing interest in the idea of teaching citizenship[1] in schools to children of younger ages, and while considerable agreement exists about the purposes of citizenship, little agreement appears to exist on what exactly citizenship means. In addition, the debate continues on what is appropriate citizenship with regards to the level of participation it entails. Sears suggests a range of possibilities exists between passive and active citizenship.[2] Westheimer sees three attributes of citizenry—responsibility, participation, and a social justice ori-entation—positioned on a continuum that we want to help students move along, from being more than only responsible or participatory to a position where they become democratic citizens who are oriented towards social justice.[3] We want children to see the need to move beyond giving handouts to the homeless (responsibility), past organizing a clothing drive for the homeless (participatory), to reach the point where they ask why homelessness exists (justice oriented). If, as Becker and Couto suggest,[4] democracy is not just a political system but also indeed a way of life, a way to help construct community, then as teachers we need to ask ourselves questions about the role of democracy in our classrooms. Not only do we need to ask what role the learning of democracy plays in the development of citizenship but also what role should the teaching of democracy play in the schooling of our children.

Teachers of young children can find many ways of ensuring opportunities exist for students to experience the types of activities that will help them develop the skills needed to experience a democratic society to its fullest. We need to provide the space for children to explore their own questions and intuitions while, at the same time, finding ways to guide and even, at times, disagree with them. Some of these opportunities include simple activities such as sharing circles, where important issues and ideas from home are shared and children learn to listen and to respect the speaker. Other opportunities include times for children to share important events from their lives, show-and-tell sessions, or sessions where "questions of the day" can be asked and everyone's questions are important and valued. In other situations debates can be planned, even at a young age, where decisions are needed. By allowing children to vote on class decisions, as well as to make individual decisions about what activities they choose, the skills of democracy can be encouraged. Classroom time can be scheduled where children have the chance to practise listening to a friend read a story in a paired reading activity. Real practice in the skill of communication, including listening, can bolster a child's ability to resolve conflict and support others, and in the process, become a more democratic citizen.

How can social studies help with this? In many elementary/primary classrooms the teaching of social studies is limited to only a few brief time blocks each week. But developing the skills and perspectives described here need not be limited to social studies time. Opportunities to learn and practise the attitudes and dispositions that may encourage a stronger understanding and commitment to relationships through opportunities to "live in community" with others occur throughout the school day. Living in a democratic community doesn't mean a place where everyone thinks and acts the same, nor is it a place of perfect harmony. By the phrase "living in community" I mean a group of people who are working through a process that includes a variety of opinions and perspectives, and a way of making decisions.

Making Decisions/Offering Choices

Opportunities for decision-making must be explicitly provided for young children if they are to learn how to make choices. For five-year-olds it isn't as important to offer a myriad of choices, but by letting them choose between two activities, students can start to learn to make decisions. Teachers can start with basic choices that they normally make for the class and let students make those decisions. For example, a teacher can offer two choices for the destination of a class walk. Or the teacher can tell the students that they can either do a painting after listening to a piece of music or write a short story.

In a primary/grade 1 classroom with forty-eight children, in which I co-taught, the students were given many opportunities to make decisions and state their opinions. Each morning included lengthy sessions of independent time when stations or centres were set up throughout the classroom. The children were guided in the selection of their initial choice each morning, but after completing their first station, they chose where to go next by selecting a tag, which they wore around their necks. Only a designated number of tags existed for each station, thus controlling the number of participants there at a time, but the children chose freely from the available tags according to their own interests. This act of choosing gave the children a sense of responsibility and ownership for their work. At the end of station time, during a sharing circle, children proudly displayed work, described activities to classmates, and encouraged other children to try stations they had enjoyed. This helped them gain confidence not only in speaking publicly, but also in their decision-making, as their classmates responded positively to their choice of activities. The sharing circle also provided a stage for children to learn to listen to the opinions of others, another key element of this kind of classroom community. At other times, the children were told that two activities needed to be accomplished during the afternoon and that they could be completed in any order. Allowing children to decide which activity they completed first provided a simple opportunity for making a decision.

Opportunities for Dialogue

In preparing students to participate as democratic citizens, providing opportunities for dialogue at a young age is important. In the classroom this can take several forms, including providing opportunities for students to interact with peers and encouraging them to share their opinions.

Interacting with others

The opportunity to interact with peers is critical in developing social competencies deemed valuable in a democratic society. The opportunity to interact is important if students are to learn to share their opinions and listen to the opinions of others. Direct interaction with other children is also a primary source of social knowledge for children of all ages. Talking is essential for intellectual development, but more than that, this skill also prepares young people to have a voice in society and to be able to question the status quo. To lose the experience of social discourse is a greater loss than can be imagined. Teacher-initiated talk and teacher-directed talk does not permit students to develop the confidence necessary to express their own opinions and ideas for fear they will not be accepted as worthy. Ideally, as Grumet describes:

> A curriculum designed for my child is a conversation that leaves space for her responses, that is transformed by her questions. It needn't replicate her language or mine, but it must be made accessible to our interpretation and translation.[5]

Giving voice to children

Giving voice to children "reveals the deeper meanings and perspectives of individuals and reflects learners' personal realities."[6] However, as Harris states, "the contemporary pressures upon teachers make it more difficult to find the space and time to plan and nurture student [voice] in school."[7] If teachers work to create a sense of democratic community in their classrooms, students can become full members of that community, sharing their voices and opinions.

In order to learn to think critically and to constructively criticize something, practice is needed in developing the ability to share opinions from a young age. Being able to discuss and criticize our ideas and the ideas of others is one way to encourage this development. Providing students with a safe environment for sharing their thoughts is another. This takes time and explicit planning, where teachers allot specific time at the end of activities for questions to be asked, or where safe, comfortable areas in the classroom are used for discussions and teachers do not

shut down the conversation. Teachers can provide space for questions by modelling questioning themselves. If they share with their students the questions they have about content and processes, they will help students find ways to question and problematize ideas and issues. To learn without such an environment is to place young children at a disadvantage with regard to their ability to think critically. Teachers who explicitly make time for students to share their work, their concerns, and their questions will help students think about other possibilities than the ones presented to them. This means ensuring an opportunity each day for talking time. Learning to question is a basic first step in learning to problematize. In order to make changes in a democratic society, citizens are required who can see where changes are needed through a process that includes both problematizing and problem-solving.

It is ironic that in school, a place where there is virtually no chance to be alone, children are most often discouraged from talking. In a study in the United Kingdom, fifty children, all five years of age, were interviewed as part of a research project on children's perspectives on schooling.[8] These children gave examples of not being allowed to discuss their work assignments with classmates seated directly beside them. To do so would lead to "getting in trouble." The alternative was to "sneak a little chat" and risk "Miss yelling at us if we talk because we can't learn by talking." Even though, in some cases, seating was arranged so that it appeared to encourage talking, no talking was allowed.

While no single lock-step program of cooperation can truly recreate real circumstances where interaction with others is required, some aspects of the philosophy behind cooperative classrooms can be beneficial, in particular in classrooms where talking has been viewed as something detrimental. Children interviewed after only four months in school were most adamant about the "no talking" rule. They were convinced that talking did not provide any benefits in the learning process, and the only talking valued was that of the teacher. To help children understand that their voices and opinions are important, the teacher must think about specific strategies to encourage discussion. These strategies may include group work, where the activity is structured so everyone's input is required, or an activity where the children are asked to interview someone at home. Where talking is encouraged, discourse becomes a valued commodity, promoting learning and creating new opportunities for both students and teachers to develop relationships, to develop stronger understandings of others, and to develop ways to communicate within a community setting. Only then will students "think of themselves as citizens who are willing and able and equipped to have an influence in public life."[9]

Community-building/ Building Relationships

Instead of focusing on skills and processes associated with relationships, schools focus primarily on ability.[10] We tend to reward children who succeed academically and who remain quiet. Unfortunately, this orientation fosters competition and differentiation, and a set of values that teachers may convey implicitly through their interaction with students, especially if they also fail to encourage caring interaction among students. If, as Spindler suggests, schools in general encourage only character types regarded as most desirable, leading to conformity for the sake of adjustment, then "individuality and creativity, or even more, originality, are not stressed or valued.[11] Even forty years after Spindler's research, this is evident in schools when student voices are stifled for the sake of a quiet classroom.

As a young child, feeling confident in sharing your opinion and in making strong decisions is also partially based on the trust and strength of relationships you have developed. Does relationship development bring about an understanding of democracy? Not necessarily, but the skills and understandings needed to develop strong and caring relationships are at the very least helpful in understanding and participating in a democratic society. If, as teachers, we want to encourage dialogue in a classroom community, we need to find ways to encourage the development of relationships based on caring and trust. Strong, supportive relationships between teachers and students and among classroom peers will help

students develop the confidence to share their opinions and make decisions. In supporting caring relationships, teachers may increase not only the students' social development but also their academic achievement.

Through an intentional focus on classroom community, teachers can make room for dialogue and decision-making in their classrooms. But the intention here is not to create a community where everyone is the same. As several authors have suggested, and Shields explains here:

> Rather than thinking of school as a community that finds its centre in the commonly held beliefs of its members, it is necessary to explore an antithetical concept—that of community of difference or otherness, in which the centre would develop through the negotiation of disparate norms, beliefs and values of its individual members. Communities of otherness or difference, then, would not be based on traditional or unchallenged assumptions about their members; rather they would emerge through careful listening to the cacophony of voices of those who, together, make up the school community.[12]

Such a community is best created when the relational nature of the community is acknowledged and incorporated into its structure, and when all participants are involved in discussion and decision-making. Using Clandinin and Connelly's[13] metaphor of landscape, marginalization can be eliminated if we think about a place in the landscape for all students, where the ontology or way of being of all participants is vital to the composition of the landscape. The current landscape often values ability and provides little opportunity for input into decisions. Teachers can solicit children's opinions about classroom rules, ask advice on how to proceed with an activity, and allow children to make suggestions about how to include everyone in the landscape.

"Service learning" is one approach to a practical pedagogy that can help to instill a desire to interact with others. Engaging students in participating in social causes—picking up litter and asking why it is important; organizing classroom recycling and talking about how we are all responsible both individu-ally and as a group—can build an understanding of community and increase students' sense of partici-pation in the community. By engaging them at an early age with social issues, students, even at five years of age, can begin to understand the need to interact with and include others in solving societal problems. In one school, students of all ages from kindergarten to grade 8 worked on a recycling project on Saturdays. Each class from K to 4 had a partner class in grades 5 to 8. With a grade 8 partner class, kindergarten students spent Saturday mornings pil-ing and collecting old newspapers as community members dropped them off. These students gained a sense of belonging to the whole school and the surrounding community, and they learned about cooperating with children of a different age. The kin-dergarten students also asked important questions about why their town did not have a recycling project prior to the school initiating one. This helped them better understand the consequences of decision-making, and the teacher talked explicitly about what happened when they did recycle, and what happened when they didn't.

The teachers in this project used a variety of models, including webs and role play, to help the children understand why the town did not have a recycling project. The children were also involved in evaluating how their project helped the environ-ment. Their involvement at many levels helped en-hance the feelings of community and deepened the students' understanding for the need to make in-formed decisions.[14] By including all students, incorporating open conversation and discussion, and valuing student voices, practices such as this service learning project facilitate learning both inside and outside the classroom.

Classroom structure and routines

Routines and structures play an important part in the daily lives of most institutions, including school. As we live our public lives, we encounter many ex-pectations about our behaviours and attitudes. Teach-ers use a variety of strategies, including rewards and stickers, to encourage students to comply with so-cial conventions and attitudes. Some of the behaviourist reinforcement of school/public expec-tations is intentional on the part of teachers, but much of it represents the underlying beliefs that adults have about what is socially acceptable. These include notions about following rules and routines, about using a public voice and solving solutions ver-bally, not physically. In an early childhood classroom, these are important and valuable things to learn. A large part of what teachers of young children do in-volves teaching routines. Generally, for the children, compliance with the routines ensures inclusion as a student in the teacher's school world. However, sometimes our expectations about rules and routines are understood by the children as so structured as to never be questioned. In some instances it appears to the children that absolutely no alternative routine could exist.

As part of the research study cited earlier, fifty children were interviewed in their fourth month of schooling about the routines in their classrooms.[15] Each child was able to describe the morning routine and the afternoon routine without deviation. When questioned about the order of morning activities such as completion of the daily register and the collection of milk money, the children were convinced that absolutely no deviation in the routine was required or even allowed. When alternatives were suggested, the children argued that they should not be consid-ered.

Part of the young child's dependence on the rou-tine of the classroom comes from a five- or six-year-old's need for security. However, the consistency that can provide this security is not one that says math-ematics must take place every Wednesday at 10:00 a.m., but a consistency that reassures the child that he or she is valued, a consistency in the way the teacher reacts, a consistency in what is expected in the classroom.

Within the structure of the classroom and the routines of the school, teachers must ensure the flex-ibility to enable the children to make decisions and share opinions. By ensuring large portions of unin-terrupted time exist in the classroom, the ability to offer choice is increased. Too often, schools sched-ule pull-out programs such as music and physical education in a way that is convenient for teachers, instead of providing large blocks of time for students to choose their own activities. We need to get away from the idea that every child must be doing the same thing at the same time and instead, think about what it is we want to accomplish over a large period of time, allowing children to work through a series of activities in their own time and in a sequence that makes sense for them.

Acknowledging the power/ sharing the power

Part of why children accept the routine of the classroom is because they defer to the power we hold as teachers and adults in their lives. Teachers can use this power both explicitly and implicitly. If we truly want to change the way relationships develop in our classrooms, the way students are valued in our classrooms, the way decisions are made in our classroom, we need to acknowledge this power and work to change the way it affects the classroom community. If democratic practices include a sharing of the power in society, then power must also be shared within the classroom.

The skills and attitudes that foster a democratic society cannot be learned if the instructional strategies in the classroom foster competition instead of collaboration, promote individualism instead of communitarianism, and provide little or no room for dialogue and shared decision-making. We also shouldn't wait to use strategies that promote choices and children's voices until such a time as we believe the children can fully understand how and why things like choice and voice are important. If we wait for that, it will be too late. We need to present children with a learning environment in the early years where strategies that encourage the development of decision-making and the sharing of opinions and the fostering of a democratic classroom occur on a daily basis across the curriculum.

Endnotes

1. Bernard Crick, "Advisory Group for Citizenship and the Teaching of Democracy in Schools (The Crick Report)," presented to the Secretary of State for Education and Employment, UK, September 22, 1998; Richard M. Battistoni, *Civic Engagement Across the Curriculum: A Resource Book for Service-learning Faculty in all Disciplines* (Providence, RI: Campus Compact, 2002); and Anne Colby, *Educating Citizens: Preparing America's Undergraduates for Lives of Moral and Civic Responsibility* (San Francisco: Jossey-Bass, 2003).

2. Alan Sears, "What Research Tells Us about Citizenship Education in English Canada," *Canadian Social Studies* 30, no. 3 (Spring 1996): 121–127.

3. Joel Westheimer, "Citizenship Education for a Democratic Society," *Teach Magazine* (March/April 2003): 17–19.

4. Theodore L. Becker and Richard A. Couto, eds., *Teaching Democracy by Being Democratic* (Westport, CT: Praeger, 1996).

5. Madeleine R. Grumet, *Bitter Milk: Women and Teaching* (Amherst: University of Massachusetts Press, 1988), 32.

6. Karin L. Dahl, "Challenges in Understanding the Learner's Perspective," *Theory into Practice*, 34, no. 2 (1995): 125.

7. Alma Harris, *School Improvement: What's in It for Schools?* (London: Routledge/Falmer, 2002), 62.

8. Ann Sherman, *Rules, Routines, and Regimentation: Young Children's Views of Schooling* (Nottingham, UK: Educational Heretics Press, 1996).

9. Crick, "The Crick Report," 7.

10. Martin L. Maehr and Carol Midgley, *Transforming School Cultures* (Boulder, CO: Westview Press, 1996).

11. George D. Spindler, *Education and Culture: Anthropological Approaches* (New York: Holt, Rinehart & Winston, 1963), 135.

12. C. Shields, "Learning from Students about Representation, Identity, and Community," *Educational Administration Quarterly* 35, no. 1 (1999): 107. Shields cites G. Furman, "Postmodernism and Community in Schools: Unraveling the Paradox," *Educational Administration Quarterly* 34, no. 3 (1998): 298–328; and C. Shields and P.A. Seltzer, "Complexities and Paradoxes of Community: Toward a More Useful Conceptualization of Community," *Educational Administration Quarterly* 33, no. 4 (1997): 413–439.

13. D. Jean Clandinin and F. Michael Connelly, *Teachers' Professional Knowledge Landscapes* (New York: Teachers College Press, 1995).

14. The author was vice-principal and part-time grade 5 teacher at this K–8 school during the time this recycling project was initiated.

15. Sherman, *Rules, Routines, and Regimentation*.

CHAPTER 20

Computer Technologies As Supportive Tools to Enhance Learning in Social Studies

Susan Gibson

Computers have become commonplace tools in most Canadian schools. Both this ready availability and the introduction of information and communication learning outcomes as part of the school curriculum have put increased pressure on teachers to become competent and confident users of computer technology. Alberta's Information and Communication Technology Program of Studies, for example, has three interrelated categories of general learning outcomes for students:

- those intended to develop a foundation of knowledge, skills, and attitudes, including understanding the nature and impact of technology

- those that address specific productivity processes such as composing, organizing, and manipulating information

- those that require the application of these processes through inquiry, decision-making, collaboration, and problem-solving[1]

Alberta teachers are mandated to implement these outcomes into their teaching of all core subjects beginning at the primary level. Teachers have primarily been using computers to develop students' technological skills and competencies, thus addressing the first two outcomes. The third outcome, using technology to support inquiry, decision-making, collaboration, and problem-solving, has been addressed less frequently. This chapter will focus on ideas for implementing this third outcome.

It's About More Than Simply "Using" Computers

According to the research literature, only a small proportion of social studies teachers are regularly integrating computer technologies in their teaching, and few of these could be regarded as promoting advanced learning using information and communication technologies.[2] According to Glenn Kleiman, "Many computers in schools, even up-to-date multimedia computers with high-speed Internet access, are not being used in ways that significantly enhance teaching and learning."[3] The main problem seems to be that teachers still tend to use computers as add-ons to the ways they have traditionally taught. As noted by Howard Gardner, "When the [computers] are plugged in, they are all too often simply used to 'deliver' the same old 'drill-and-kill' content."[4]

The key to best use is not the fact that computers *are* being used, but *how* they are being used. Maisie McAdoo contends:

The issue of equity now centers not on equality of equipment but on quality of use. The computers are there yes, but what is the real extent of access? How much computer training are teachers getting? And are schools able to raise not just students' level of technical proficiency but also their level of inquiry, as advanced use of technology demands?[5]

Computer use needs to go beyond low-level tasks that require students to demonstrate understanding of how to operate the various technologies with proficiency, to more challenging tasks that encourage more advanced learning using computers as "mindtools." When teaching is transformed through the use of computer technologies and when learning happens in ways that would be difficult or impossible without the use of these technologies, only then have we achieved success.

The Promise of Constructivism

According to Cameron White, the merging of technology and constructivism offers much hope for the future of education.[6] Sharon Adams and Mary Burns concur, saying "constructivism provides a valuable framework for using computers and other technologies in productive, interesting ways."[7]

Constructivism is a theory about how people learn. In connecting constructivist learning principles and pedagogy, Mark Windschitl identifies the following features that characterize teacher and student activity in a constructivist classroom: [8]

- Teachers elicit students' ideas and experiences in relation to key topics, then fashion learning situations that help students elaborate on or restructure their current knowledge.

- Students are given frequent opportunities to engage in complex, meaningful, problem-based activities.

- Teachers provide students with a variety of information resources as well as the tools (technological and conceptual) necessary to mediate learning.

- Students work collaboratively and are given support to engage in task-oriented dialogue with one another.

- Teachers make their own thinking processes explicit to learners and encourage students to do the same through dialogue, writing, drawings, or other representations.

- Students are routinely asked to apply knowledge in diverse and authentic contexts, to explain ideas, interpret texts, predict phenomena, and construct arguments based on evidence, rather than to focus exclusively on the acquisition of predetermined "right answers."

- Teachers encourage students' reflective and autonomous thinking in conjunction with the conditions listed above.

- Teachers employ a variety of assessment strategies to understand how students' ideas are evolving and to give feedback on the processes as well as the products of their thinking.

Chris Dede suggests:

By putting learning in the hands of the students, the 'constructivist' model turns on its head the old style of schooling in which a teacher stands in front of the room and lectures. . . . Classroom environments become places in which students take charge of their own learning.[9]

Cameron White calls for constructivist activities that promote inquiry, that begin with students' prior background knowledge and experience, and that engage learners in creatively applying the resultant new knowledge. These types of learner-centred activities, he argues, can "encourage students to develop problem solving and critical thinking skills, and to apply, analyze, synthesize, and evaluate knowledge, skills, and attitudes."[10]

The challenge for teachers then is to transfer these understandings of constructivist learning principles to the use of computers as teaching and learning tools. According to the research, the most effective uses of computer technologies in schools occur when computers are integrated into teaching and learning in ways that promote problem-solving, collaborative inquiry, creative and higher-level thinking, decision-making, and both the constructing of and the representing of knowledge for an audience.

Computer-Enhanced Constructivist Learning Environments

This section examines some of the ways that computer technology can be used to address the features of the constructivist classroom as identified by Windschitl and as supported by research on effective uses of computers as learning tools. These applications have been synthesized under the following headings:

- student engagement in problem-solving activities

- students revealing and reflecting on their prior and new knowledge through multiple representations

- students learning with a variety of information resources and tools

- students working collaboratively

Student engagement in problem-solving activities

One approach to using the Internet as a tool for teaching and learning in social studies is using WebQuests. WebQuests use problem-based learning to encourage students to apply critical and creative thinking, problem-solving skills, and content knowledge to real-world problems and issues.[11] A WebQuest is a specially designed website that engages students in a task or inquiry to solve a problem or to create something new.[12] Through a WebQuest students can actively explore issues, find answers, and reach moral and ethical decisions about contemporary world problems. Students can also engage in activities that help them look at historical events from a number of different perspectives. While engaging in inquiry through a WebQuest, students are constructing their own personal meaning about the problem under investigation. WebQuests can also enhance students' social skills, as many involve working in cooperative groups or role-playing. Posting the results of the WebQuest online adds to the collaborative nature of

the learning, as students then interact with others beyond the classroom walls.

Usually a WebQuest consists of an introduction, a task, a process, an evaluation tool (usually in the form of a rubric), and a conclusion. The introduction lays out the task or the problem to be investigated. Students are then assigned roles or provided with different perspectives on the issue or problem being investigated. Working either independently or in groups, they explore, analyze, and synthesize the information they access, and then transform it in some way to demonstrate their understanding of the problem. The goal is for students to use the information collected to construct an argument based on evidence. They then share their findings with the class. The teacher acts as facilitator, checking to see that students understand their roles and stay on task. Most of the resources used for the inquiry are other websites that have been vetted by the teacher and linked directly to the WebQuest. Many WebQuests allow direct access to experts, current news sites, and searchable databases.

A WebQuest can be chosen from a series of pre-designed WebQuest collections (see http://webquest.sdsu.edu/ or http://www.kn.pacbell.com/wired/bluewebn/) or the teacher can create one to address a specific topic of study. The latter allows for more active student involvement in deciding what problem to investigate and then designing an interesting and relevant learning experience. The WebQuest can easily be tailored for diverse learning needs in the classroom. Students can be encouraged to try developing their own WebQuests and sharing them with classmates. For a database of sample student-developed WebQuests, visit the ThinkQuest Library at http://www.thinkquest.org.

One example of a pre-designed WebQuest is "Does the Tiger Eat its Cubs: A WebQuest on Children & China," http://www.kn.pacbell.com/wired/China/childquest.html. The question that students investigate is, "What's the truth about how children are treated in orphanages in China?" Students are directed to research a number of perspectives. They are divided into three teams. One team reads international news reports; another reads responses from the Chinese people; the third examines the government of China's position as stated in China's One Child Policy. The students then come back together to discuss their findings, the challenge being to reach consensus on the issue. The culminating activity is to write a letter to the government of China expressing what they feel should be done about the situation. A series of other WebQuests about China can be found at http://www.kn.pacbell.com/wired/China/ChinaQuest.html. A WebQuest more appropriate for high school students, entitled "DNA for Dinner?" has students research genetically engineered crops and then develop legislation on this topic and present it to a governing body (see http://www.angelfire.com/ma4/peacew/webquest.htm#Introduction).

A WebQuest is just one structured approach to developing problem-solving skills using the world wide web. Other websites are available that can be used to develop and apply students' critical thinking and problem-solving skills. One such site, "Decisions, Decisions Online," http://ddonline.tomsnyder.com/issues/animaltesting/intro.cfm, engages users in investigating contemporary issues such as the death penalty, cloning, energy and the environment, TV violence, Napster, and animal testing. On the issue of animal testing, students are presented with this question: "Is it acceptable to use animals for human benefit, or should there be stronger laws to protect animals from harm?" Students role-play a decision-maker faced with a critical situation related to the problem, and they are directed to gather and review information, discuss options, and decide upon what action to take. Since this is an American site, Canadian teachers should pre-select the issues that are appropriate in a Canadian context. Finding informational websites with Canadian content on each issue would also be helpful.

Students revealing and reflecting on their prior and new knowledge through multiple representations

Constructivist learning theory argues that new knowledge should be integrated into existing structures in order to be meaningful and remembered.

An important beginning point for any new learning is a student's preconceptions about a topic or concept. By helping the student to uncover the ideas and beliefs about a particular topic that she or he is bringing to the learning situation, the teacher is better able to identify where the student's knowledge is inaccurate or incomplete.

One commonly used approach for eliciting students' prior knowledge about a topic is through visual organizers. David Jonassen argues that students show some of their best thinking when they try to represent something graphically.[13] There are now computer-based tools for organizing ideas in visual ways. See, for example, Inspiration, http://www.inspiration.com/, and the more child-friendly version for kindergarten to grade 5, Kidspiration. These tools can be used in the early stages of research to brainstorm ideas and check on students' understandings about a topic or concept. They can also be used to generate and organize ideas for a research project. A concept map can serve as a vehicle for organizing the information collected around key ideas. Concept maps can be reconstructed at any stage of the learning process, thus allowing for inclusion of new knowledge and deletion of inaccurate ideas. The tool allows the learner to convert complex and messy collections of information into meaningful displays.[14] The website Inspiration provides opportunities to create cause-and-effect diagrams that help students see dynamic relationships among events as well as the impact that multiple factors can have on outcomes. Older students can use a more challenging tool such as SmartIdeas™, http://www.smarttech.com/products/smartideas/index.asp.

Ongoing teacher assessment and feedback is a feature of constructivist classrooms. The teacher can use graphic organizers as assessment tools to better understand how students' ideas are evolving as a result of the learning experiences. As well, a teacher can gain access to and provide feedback on students' thinking processes.

Other tools that students can use to represent their learning are multimedia authoring programs such as Hyperstudio, Hypermedia, and PowerPoint, which allow them to create their own interactive multimedia presentations. With Hyperstudio and Hypermedia they can make use of graphics, video, animation, and sound to meet their differing learning needs. Using these tools, students are able to express their individuality and unique perspectives in their presentations.[15] Students can be highly motivated by using such product-oriented tools to design multimedia presentations.

Students learning with a variety of information resources and tools

A constructivist learning environment has a variety of informational resources and tools that students can use to mediate their learning. Computers can provide this variety of resources, particularly when it comes to supporting students' research in social studies. The technological tools and resources available include educational software, spreadsheets, databases, simulations, and educational games. Tools such as these provide options for learners, as information is presented in a variety of forms (graphs, pictures, text) and through a variety of modalities (auditory, visual). Individuals can further develop their unique strengths by being able to access information through their preferred modality and by having opportunities to represent their learning in a variety of ways. Tools such as the Internet also provide students with quicker and easier access to extensive and current information sources.

There is a fairly extensive collection of educational software available to support the teaching of social studies; however, much of the existing software mainly promotes information retrieval. According to Chris Dede, to prepare children to function in a technology-driven society, teachers must facilitate students' ability to master sophisticated, globally generated knowledge by learning to manage information rather than to memorize it.[16] The better software selections encourage students to organize and analyze the information presented, as well as providing opportunities for them to interact with the content through exploratory environments.

Database software can be an excellent tool for integrating information from a variety of sources and

for allowing manipulation and analysis of that information to better understand concepts. Databases can also be used to stimulate higher-level thinking as students are challenged to make predictions, do comparisons, observe trends, generate hypotheses, formulate generalizations, draw conclusions, create alternative solutions to problems, and decide what actions to take based on certain conditions. As well, databases can be effective for helping students to visualize complex historical relationships and to develop an awareness of the personal reality of history. Spreadsheets are another computer-based tool that can be used to store, organize, and analyze data for purposes of problem-solving and decision-making.

Educational games and simulation software are also readily available as sources of information. They can be powerful tools for making abstract content and complex ideas more accessible to learners.[17] As well, these representations and visualizations can help students negotiate concepts and abstractions.[18] As Chris Dede writes, "Utilizing computer modeling as a visualization [can be] a powerful bridge between experience and abstraction."[19] Participatory simulation software can also help students to develop empathy for the subject and to abandon contemporary assumptions and values in order to understand an event as it really was.[20] Providing students with such alternative ways to learn, including both verbal and non-verbal experiences, can be beneficial for students who have mild learning disorders.[21]

The SIM software series, including SimCity, SimTown, and The SIMS, encourages interactivity, critical and creative thinking, and application of learning. In SimCity, for example, the user takes on the role of a city planner and designs a city, providing infrastructure and services, and confronting problems and making decisions about various issues such as resource allocation and planning for disasters. Through this software series, the user is engaged in an imaginary environment that is realistic enough to provide meaningful issues and appropriate consequences, thus lending authenticity to the learning. Other software that has been designed specifically for the educational market and helps to promote higher-level thinking and decision-making skills is from the Tom Snyder series. Decisions Decisions 5.0 engages students in collaboratively and interactively investigating issues such as prejudice, violence in the media, lying and cheating, and saving the environment.

Students can also access the collections of a number of museums that have been put on the world wide web. Through these sites, they can engage in further authentic tasks and in the processes that historians use, such as analyzing primary documents.[22] Another recommended website that provides artifacts addressing Canadian history, culture, Aboriginal communities, and landscapes is http://collections.ic.gc.ca, Canada's Digital Collection. There is a component to this website that has students submit proposals to create their own web pages about some aspect of Canadian history. Students can be encouraged to take their learning one step further by constructing their own archives and then sharing their findings by publishing them on the web for review by a wider audience. Creating and posting their own archives adds authenticity and relevance to the learning and broadens the role of students by allowing them to become designers and publishers rather than simply users of web-based information.[23]

Virtual field trips are another particularly powerful resource because students can travel through both time and space to places that would otherwise be out of reach. Often these tours provide both images and text describing the particular site being toured. For example, when studying China, students can access interactive sites such as http://www.rims.k12.ca.us/china/, which features the Great Wall of China, the Emperor's Imperial Palace and other royal palaces, the terracotta warriors, Tiananmen Square, views of the cities and the countryside, and other geographical features of the country. These visuals give students important contextual information to help them personalize their study of a country from afar.

Students work collaboratively

A constructivist learning environment encourages collaborative work that engages students in dialogue.

Computer technologies can be helpful tools for developing such collaborative skills. Students are fascinated by the possibilities of electronic communication for contacting other students and adults all over the world to exchange ideas about topics of mutual interest. They view information gathered in this fashion as being more connected to "real" local, national, and global issues. In "Changing How and What Children Learn in School with Computer-Based Technologies," Jeremy Roschelle et al. write, "Using technology to promote collaborative activities can enhance the degree to which classrooms are socially active and productive and can encourage classroom conversations that expand students' understanding of the subject."[24]

Interactive web-based collaborative projects are an excellent way of extending the learning by engaging students in projects with other students and experts from around the world. In a report from Industry Canada on the success of their collaborative project-based GrassRoots program, some of the important features of these projects included placing students in a position of discovering the world and sharing the results of their experiences; encouraging content construction by students; involving students in new roles as active participants, creative interpreters of the world, and experienced collaborators; and providing for a greater range of learning by doing.[25]

Communication tools like email, listservs, bulletin boards, newsgroups, and chat groups build on students' desire to communicate and share their understandings. Online conversations through email can prompt reflection and help students to think about their ideas and how best to articulate those ideas so that they are clear to others. Such conversations also encourage self-checking for understanding and identification of inaccuracies in one's expressed ideas, which can lead to rethinking and reframing of prior ideas. In these ways, email and threaded discussions can "act as a conduit rather than an impediment to conversation."[26]

Online chat allows more than one student to "talk" at the same time. A web opportunity like e-pals allows students to interact with a real audience without the inhibiting factor of peer pressure.[27] Some researchers contend that gender bias pervades computer technologies and makes computers less friendly for girls; however, electronic participation has been found to counteract male dominance and be more gender equitable.[28] Providing opportunities for collaborative activity through the use of technology has been shown to actually heighten girls' interest in computing.[29] Online interaction has also been found to "free the child with special needs from fear of being stigmatized as well as enabling them to network with other children to share feelings about having a disability."[30]

There are numerous collaborative project opportunities available through the world wide web. One example, The Global Schoolhouse, http://www.gsn.org/, provides opportunities for students to engage with adventurers as they travel around the world. Through daily updates on the web and through conversational discussion boards, students can ask questions of the adventurers and keep in touch with the latest discoveries as the journeys unfold. There are also opportunities to plan an individualized online expedition and to find worldwide partners who may wish to partner up with other classes for an adventure.

Two other examples of websites offering online expeditions can be found at http://www.ctcexpeditions.org/ and http://www.quest-connect.org/. Both of these sites provide opportunities for students to be involved in explorations of different parts of the world and to accompany real people as they engage in those explorations. The real-life explorers post journals, research logs, and photos to authenticate the experiences for the students, and classes can send messages directly to them. Another website, The Electronic United Nations, http://www.simulations.com/, is designed to help classes utilize interactive learning by developing a "classroom country." This classroom country then "interacts" with other classroom countries around the world in a simulated United Nations. The process teaches students many life skills, and empowers both students and teachers. By using such collaborative activities, Chris Dede writes, "Students construct meaning through an exchange of perspectives on shared experiences."[31]

Another possibility, video conferencing, allows for interactive, face-to-face virtual discussions in real time between students and experts from around the world. For example, a connection between an Ontario high school and an Alberta high school with a third link to a provincial minister of the environment recently allowed students and the minister to discuss and debate the Kyoto Protocol.

As students gain first-hand knowledge of other cultures through online learning communities, there is potential for computer technologies to contribute to the development of effective citizens. Such increased exposure to first-hand information has the potential to overcome students' insular views of the world. David Staley refers to these online discussions as "a type of democratic performance."[32] Increased access through the Internet can spread democratic ideals internationally and help to stem the growth of potentially incendiary nationalism by giving students broader exposure to other cultures and providing them with opportunities to compare other cultures to their own.[33]

The Intercultural Email Classroom Connections website, www.iecc.org/, provides a service to help teachers link with partners in other countries and cultures for email classroom project exchanges. A site such as World Links for Development, www.worldbank.org/worldlinks/, sponsored by the World Bank, partners schools in developing countries with schools in developed nations. One project available through this website, entitled Our Human Environment, links several Canadian, South African, and Ugandan schools in online discussion groups and collaborative projects about natural habitats and questions of sustainable development in those countries. According to Wambui Githiora-Updike, "As secondary students in Kampala work online with students in Toronto, an international community of learners is being established—one that may extend beyond their school years. Certainly such sharing of ideas . . . represents a significant step in the building of a global community."[34]

Concerns arising from computer use

While computer technologies are now a reality in schools and there are ways that they can be used to support and enhance teaching and learning, there are also issues around their use that need to be considered by social studies educators. Many of the concerns with computers in schools arise around social and economic issues and particularly the influence that technological innovation is having on social change.[35]

The issue that seems to get the most attention in the educational literature and in the public debate about computers in schools is that of the digital divide—the "haves" and the "have nots." If the presence of technology in the hands of a knowledgeable and skilled teacher can have as many benefits as have been outlined in this chapter, then it goes without saying that the absence of technology in the classroom and school can be detrimental to those who do not have adequate access to computers. Ensuring equal access to all will continue to be a critical issue, especially as the cost for replacing aging computers continues to escalate.

Also related to access is the issue of training teachers to use these technologies. If new technologies are to have the impact on learning that has been argued for in this chapter, then teachers need professional development activities that expose them to these ways of thinking about technology integration. This, too, requires a substantial allocation of funding.

The following are among the social issues with technology use that have been raised in the research literature: loss of personal identity and the extinction of individual self and privacy; increased individual isolation; loss of face-to-face collaboration; loss of community; loss of caring; and the loss of master narratives.[36] In addition, the Internet is still a resource of privilege. According to Wambui Githiora-Updike, more than 80 percent of all websites are written in English, so non-English speakers automatically have diminished access to the benefits of the Internet. At least 60 percent of the Internet's host computers are in the United States. Although many strides have been made in accessing the Internet in the non-English-speaking world, it is clear that the English-speaking world will continue to dominate conversation in cyberspace, a possible deterrent to bringing together those of different "tongues." Solving that challenge will be a great educational task for the twenty-first century.[37]

Marc Belanger notes that since Canada is responsible for only a small portion of the English content on the Internet, we "must create content which reflects its particular Canadian personality if it is to maintain its cultural identity."[38] Belanger also cautions that there is a threat of "potential marginalization of groups such as women, persons with disabilities, seniors and aboriginal peoples"[39] in relation to their level of Internet use. All of these issues are important to consider as the technology invades our private lives more and more. Educators and students alike need to think critically about computer technology and make informed decisions about its appropriate use.

Conclusion

This chapter began with a challenge to all social studies teachers to think beyond the use of computer technologies for low-level tasks to ones that encourage more advanced learning with computers as supportive tools. Such advanced learning would include using computers to support and enhance opportunities to think critically and analytically, to engage students in inquiry centred around real-world problems, to encourage students to work collaboratively, and to create and share innovative products to demonstrate what has been learned. When technology tools such as databases, spreadsheets, multimedia, email, interactive software, and the Internet are used to complete authentic projects requiring students to use information to solve problems, there is greater potential to promote cognitive and social development as well as a positive attitude towards learning. These computer tools also have the power to stimulate the development of intellectual skills such as inquiry, reflection on learning, and learning how to learn. When such tools are used, the emphasis of the learning is more on student understanding than on "getting the right answers." Technology-enhanced learning experiences such as those discussed above have the greatest potential to enhance students' learning in social studies. Using computers in ways that support constructivist learning principles by actively engaging learners and offering them opportunities to take more control over their learning can make social studies more exciting and relevant for both students and teachers.

Endnotes

1   Alberta Learning, *Information and Communication Technology, Program of Studies* (Edmonton: Author, 2000), http://www.learning.gov.ab.ca/k_12/curriculum/bySubject/cts.

2   Mark Windschitl, "Framing Constructivism in Practice as the Negotiation of Dilemmas: An Analysis of the Conceptual, Pedagogical, Cultural, and Political Challenges Facing Teachers," *Review of Educational Research* 72, no. 2 (2002): 131–175.

3   Glenn Kleiman, "Myths and Realities about Technology in K–12 Schools," in *Digital Classroom: How Technology is Changing the Way We Teach and Learn*, ed. David T. Gordon, (Cambridge, MA: Harvard Education Letter, 2000), 8.

4   Howard Gardner, "Can Technology Exploit Our Many Ways of Knowing?" in *Digital Classroom*, 33.

5   Maisie McAdoo, "The Real Digital Divide: Quality Not Quantity," in *Digital Classroom*, 143–144.

6   Cameron White, "Preservice to the 'Real World': Transforming Social Studies through Technology," in *Technology and Teacher Education Annual* (Charlottesville, VA: Association for the Advancement of Computing in Education, 1997), 290–293.

7   Sharon Adams and Mary Burns, *Connecting Student Learning and Technology* (Austin, TX: Southwest Educational Development Laboratory, 1999), 4.

8   Windschitl, "Framing Constructivism in Practice," 137.

9   Chris Dede, "A New Century Demands New Ways of Learning," in *Digital Classroom*, 171–174.

10 White, "Preservice to the 'Real World'," 2.

11 Barbara B. Levin, *Energizing Teacher Education and Professional Development with Problem-based Learning* (Alexandria, VA: Association for Supervision and Curriculum Development, 2001).

12 Bernie Dodge, "Active Learning on the Web (K–12 Version)" (presentation, Faculty of La Jolla Country Day School, La Jolla, CA, August 20, 1996), http://edweb.sdsu.edu/people/bdodge/active/ActiveLearningk-12.html.

13 David Jonassen, ed., *Handbook of Research for Educational Communications and Technology: A Project of the Association for Educational Communications and Technology* (New York: Macmillan Library Reference, 1996).

14 Jamie McKenzie, "A Picture is Worth . . . A Thousand Words: Graphical Organizers as Thinking Technology", *FNO.org* 7, no. 2, (October 1997), http://optin.iserver.net/fromnow/oct97/picture.html.

15 Martha Boethel and Victoria Dimock, *Constructing Knowledge with Technology: A Review of the Literature* (Austin, TX: Southwest Educational Development Laboratory, 1999).

16 Chris Dede, ed., ASCD *1998 Yearbook on Learning With Technology* (Alexandria, VA: Association for Supervision and Curriculum Development, 1998).

17 John Schaeter and Cheryl Fagnano, "Does Computer Technology Improve Student Learning and Achievement? How, When, and Under What Conditions?" *Journal of Educational Computing Research* 20, no. 4 (1999): 329–343.

18 Shelley Goldman, Karen Cole, and Christina Syer, "The Technology/Content Dilemma" (paper, Secretary's Conference on Educational Technology 1999: Evaluating the Effectiveness of Technology, Washington, DC, July 12–13, 1999), 8.

19 Dede, "A New Century," 172.

20 David J. Staley, "Technology, Authentic Performance, and History Education," *International Journal of Social Education* 15, no. 1 (2000): 9.

21 Margie K. Shields and Richard E. Behrmann, "Children and Computer Technology: Analysis and Recommendations," *Future of Children* 10, no. 2 (Fall/Winter 2000), 4–30.

22 Randy Bass and Roy Rosenzweig, "Rewriting the History and Social Studies Classroom: Needs, Frameworks, Dangers, and Proposals," *Journal of Education* 181, no. 3 (1999): 41–61.

23 Staley, "Technology, Authentic Performance."

24 Jeremy M. Roschelle et al, "Changing How and What Children Learn in School with Computer-based Technologies," *Future of Children* 10, 80.

25 TeleLearning Network, *Canada's SchoolNet GrassRoots Program, A Study of Grassroots Projects: Online Project-based Collaborative Learning* (Ottawa: Industry Canada, SchoolNet, 2002), http://www.schoolnet.ca/alasource/e/resources/toolkit/tele/index.asp

26 G.A. Richards, "Why Use Computer Technology?" *English Journal* 90, no. 2 (November, 2000): 39.

27 Ibid., 38–41.

28 Eleanor Linn, "Gender Equity and Computer Technology," *Equity Coalition for Race, Gender, and National Origin* 5 (Fall 1999): 14–17.

29 Debra Butler, "Gender, Girls, and Computer Technology: What's the Status Now?" *Clearing House* 73, no. 4 (March/April, 2000): 225–229.

30 *Shields and Behrman*, "Children and Computer Technology," 13.

31 Dede, "A New Century," 172.

32 Staley, "Technology, Authentic Performance," 11.

33 Wambui Githiora-Updike, "The Global Schoolhouse," in *Digital Classroom*, 63.

34 Ibid.

35 Michael Bersen, "Rethinking Research and Pedagogy in the Social Studies: The Creation of Caring Connections Through Technology and Advocacy," *Theory and Research in Social Education* 28, no. 1 (2000): 121–131.

36 See Michael Bersen, John Lee, and Daniel Stuckart, "Promise and Practice of Computer Technologies in the Social Studies: A Critical Analysis," in *Critical Issues in Social Studies Research for the 21st Century,* ed. W.B. Stanley (Greenwich, CT: Information Age Publishing, 2001), 209–229; and Patrick Fitzsimons, "Changing Conceptions of Globalization: Changing Conceptions of Education," *Educational Theory* 50, no. 4 (2000): 505–520.

37 Githiora-Updike, "The Global Schoolhouse," 66.

38 Marc Belanger with TeleLearning Network, *The Social Impacts of Information and Communications Technologies* (Ottawa: Industry Canada, SchoolNet, September 13, 1999), 2.

39 Ibid., 1.

CHAPTER 21

Assessment and Evaluation in Social Studies Classrooms

A Question of Balance

John Myers

What Is the State of Assessment and Evaluation in Social Studies Today?

Since public education began in Canada 150 years ago, assessment has identified and ranked students using tests, essays, and quizzes. This limited role for assessment has broadened over the past twenty years for a number of reasons: First, the goals of education in general, and social studies in particular, have greatly expanded as we attempt to help our children acquire the knowledge, skills, attitudes, and behaviours required for living in the twenty-first century. As social studies educator Joseph Kirman argues, social studies is not about the accumulation of selected facts for later recall but should aim to:

> Produce a responsible person able to cope with change, capable of making reasonable decisions, who is an intelligent consumer and controller of science and technology, able to live with and appreciate human diversity, and support and defend human dignity. Such a person should be able to settle differences honorably, avoid the use of violence, be cognizant of, and active in, the stewardship of our planet, and have the skills necessary to maintain a functional economic system and democratic government.[1]

This expanded view of the purposes of social studies education is reflected across the curriculum and requires a much more sophisticated approach to assessment and evaluation.[2] Assessment reform has also been driven by increased knowledge about learning. After decades of viewing learning as a relatively passive accumulation of facts and discrete skills, we now recognize learning as a more active process in which learners construct knowledge and make connections among facts and concepts. Innovations in recent decades, such as curriculum integration, authentic assessment, and cooperative learning, reflect these current theories.[3]

A third factor driving assessment and evaluation reform comes from the widespread view that traditional ways of reporting student achievement—the evaluation side of things—are not telling us what we really need to know. It is not enough to want students to learn and to express our best intentions by setting course, unit, and lesson objectives. These objectives need to be achieved. We need results: clear evidence students have met the outcomes set for them. Many provincial ministries/departments of education are responding to this concern by trying to determine standards of achievement in various subject areas, including social studies, to help make grading more accurate.

Concurrent with these trends to broaden the scope of what and how to assess student progress has been a rise in large-scale, standardized assessments of various types including provincial, national, and international achievement tests. The term "standardized" refers to the fact that the results of such tests, if administered according to their instructions, can be interpreted the same way in different circumstances. The standardization occurs as a result of field-testing with thousands of students. They are administered system-wide or province-wide. The instructions to students, the test conditions, the timing, and scoring are the same in all places. They are generally norm-referenced and provide comparative data on students. They usually test for what the test authors determine to be basic skills and knowledge, and are considered to be objective; i.e., free of teacher bias in scoring. Commercial standardized tests are supposed to be content-free; that is, they are not designed to fit any particular district or provincial curriculum. In Canada, students are usually given standardized tests in language and math. Alberta is the only province that currently gives standardized tests in social studies at a number of grade levels. Provincial examinations in all subjects including social studies contain many if not most elements of standardized tests.[4]

Whatever benefits such tests have in determining student acquisition of basic facts and simple skills, they do not set a standard as to what students should be able to do. They do not define clear expectations, other than to get the highest score possible. They seldom assess complex thinking and behaviours. Even the advocates of standardized tests express concerns for their overuse. Most importantly for the purposes of this chapter, standardized tests are incapable of providing teachers with the day-to-day, moment-to-moment information they need for making instructional decisions. What follows will therefore focus on classroom-based forms of assessment and evaluation.

Even at the school and classroom levels there are competing trends in assessment and evaluation. This chapter tries to make sense of these as they influence the assessment and evaluation of student achievement in social studies. The key focus is to promote "assessment literacy"; i.e., the capacity to better match assessment methods and the information desired about student achievement, make sense of the student achievement data we collect, communicate assessment results effectively, use assessment to maximize student motivation and learning,

and identify current trends and issues in the field for further investigation and research so that we can be more proactive and better able to hold our own in debates about assessment, evaluation, standards, and accountability. As assessment expert Ruth Childs put it in the title of a recent address to a group of student teachers, "Critical Consumers Needed."[5]

What Is the Vocabulary of Assessment and Evaluation?

One of the confusing factors in the field of assessment is that professionals often use the same terms to mean different things. It might be helpful then to define some important terms and see how they relate to each other.[6]

The terms "assessment" and "evaluation" are often used interchangeably but they do not always mean the same thing. For many, assessment is the process of collecting data on student performance that is then used to evaluate (make judgements about) the attainment of certain expectations, objectives, or outcomes. Because we speak of judgements, evaluation is never neutral. It can only be objective in that assessments provide us with a quantity and quality of information sufficient to make judgements that are fair to the strengths and needs of all learners; precise in that students and others gain clear insights into how they are learning and what they can do to improve performance; and true in that our verdicts are valid, consistent, and accurate. It is important to remember that all assessments and evaluations are limited in that they do not tell us everything there is to know about the learning of particular individuals or groups.

Assessment and evaluation are continuous activities in the classroom and they can be both informal and formal. *Informal assessment* occurs when a teacher collects information to use for the purposes of shaping ongoing instruction. At the end of a segment of a lesson, for example, the teacher might orally ask a random sample of students around the room to respond to questions about what was just taught. The responses to these questions will give the teacher a sense of how well the class has learned the information, concept, or skill in question and whether they are ready to move on. Teachers might also carry out informal assessment of individual students by observing the way they are completing tasks assigned in class. This can tell them which students might need corrective feedback or more instruction in a particular area.

While informal assessment is a continuous and sometimes almost unconscious process, *formal assessment* is normally more overt and systematically planned. We are all familiar with typical manifestations of formal assessment: quizzes, tests, essays, and projects. But formal assessment may take a wide range of forms, including teacher observation of student performance. For example, a typical outcome for social studies is that students become more open-minded. One could imagine assessing progress towards that goal by having students write position papers on issues from various points of view, but observing students interacting in class with people expressing views different from theirs might also accomplish this. What makes this kind of observation different from an informal assessment is the structured nature of the data collection, perhaps using a checklist or taking notes, and sharing the information gathered with the students involved and perhaps others to provide *feedback*.

A key to effective assessment and evaluation is clarity about purpose. Broadly speaking in terms of purpose, there are two types of assessment: *formative* and *summative*. The purpose of formative assessment is to provide teacher and student with feedback that can direct future teaching and learning. For example, following some instruction on the skill of comparing and contrasting, the teacher might assign students the task of writing a short essay comparing and contrasting Napoleon's and Hitler's invasions of Russia. When the teacher examines the essays she finds that the majority of students tend to describe both invasions but do not actually develop comparisons and contrasts. This information tells her that there are areas of the skill that need further work. She can then develop a lesson showing students both the strengths and weaknesses of their work in terms of the skill, and provide further direction in devel-

oping the skill. Most of the assessment and evaluation we do will be formative, and the feedback loop that results (see Figure 1) is very important in the teaching and learning process.

Central to formative assessment is the provision of quality feedback. Feedback consists of information that tells us how we are doing and what we need to do next, in the light of our intentions and goals. Feedback is not the same as praise and blame, rather it is precise information about where someone is in relation to the goals they are trying to attain and what they might do in the future to make progress towards those goals.

A research synthesis by Marzano, Pickering, and Pollock noted the following principles of quality feedback:[7] First, feedback should be timely (the longer we wait the less effect it has on achievement). Feedback should be specific (criterion-referenced) and "corrective" in order to show what went well, what needs improvement, and how to improve (all three components needed for maximum achievement). Feedback can be verbal and written and can come from teachers, peers, or the student him/herself. It should ask students to interpret data and self-assess in the light of their goals and intentions, rather than ask them to react to our interpretation. Finally, feedback should allow students to make decisions as to the nature of the improvements and adjustments that need to be made. The great inventor Thomas Edison had his own way of describing the importance of feedback: "I've never made a mistake. I've only learned from experience."

Summative assessment provides an accounting of student progress at a particular point in time. It is normally a measurement that describes where the student stands in regard to some sort of standard such as curriculum outcomes. An end-of-unit test, for example, is designed to let students know how well they have accomplished the goals of the unit in terms of knowledge and skill acquisition. The most familiar summative assessment is the report card that communicates to students and their parents the degree to which students are meeting expectations with regard to the curriculum. Of course summative assessments can be used in a formative manner—a report card might help students focus on particular

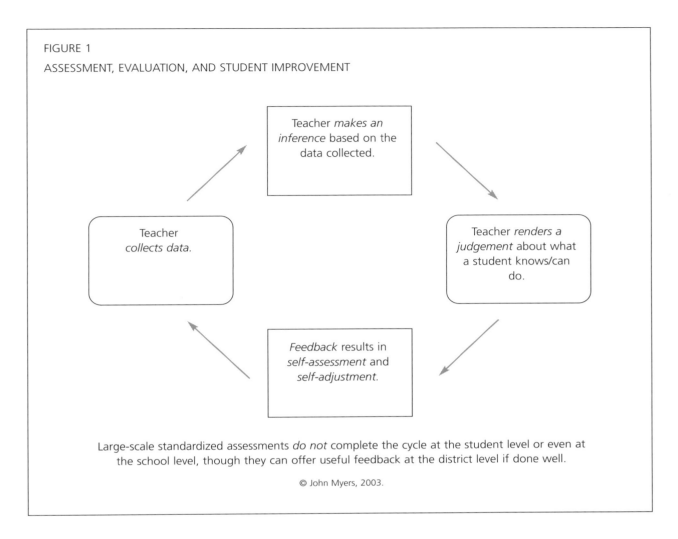

FIGURE 1

ASSESSMENT, EVALUATION, AND STUDENT IMPROVEMENT

Teacher *makes an inference* based on the data collected.

Teacher *renders a judgement* about what a student knows/can do.

Teacher *collects data.*

Feedback results in *self-assessment* and *self-adjustment.*

Large-scale standardized assessments *do not* complete the cycle at the student level or even at the school level, though they can offer useful feedback at the district level if done well.

© John Myers, 2003.

areas where they need extra work—but that is not their primary intent.

In order to overcome the limits and minimize the errors in our assessments and evaluations, the assessment tools we use must be valid and reliable. *Validity* and *reliability* are terms usually associated with standardized testing, but the underlying ideas are important to assessment and evaluation more generally.

Validity simply means that the data collected is truly related to the outcomes we intend to measure. For example, social studies curricula across Canada call for students to develop conceptual and procedural understanding related to the disciplines of social studies including history. The new curriculum for Alberta calls for students to develop "historical thinking" which, among other things, involves "the sequencing of events, the analysis of patterns and the placement of events in context."[8] Much assessment in history, however (including surveys and tests that have garnered wide media attention), focuses on collecting information on discrete facts such as names and dates. Sam Wineburg's research demonstrates that knowing a set of discrete facts is not the same as understanding the concepts of the discipline at a sophisticated level or the procedures used in an inquiry for making sense of contradictory accounts.[9] He found that high-achieving senior high students studying the American Revolution knew more facts measured in a test and could outscore some history professors whose specialties were elsewhere. Yet the professors were superior in analyzing primary sources depicting the period, since they had a much deeper understanding of the procedures for making valid historical claims about the past. Assessment instruments that only collect data on discrete historical facts, then, are not valid in assessing curriculum outcomes related to developing historical thinking.

Reliable assessment instruments are ones that will produce the same (or very similar) results in different situations. There are two components to be concerned about in producing reliable instruments. First, the activity itself should produce clear, consistent evidence of student achievement in the desired area. For example, ambiguous test questions that can be read and answered in many different ways are not particularly reliable because they might produce very different responses from students of similar ability in the same class. They cannot be relied upon to provide a relatively objective sense of student achievement. Second, the evidence should be interpreted the same way by independent observers. In the case of an essay, for example, reliability is demonstrated when qualified independent markers reach similar conclusions about the quality of the work. This kind of inter-rater reliability is achieved when both the assignment and the criteria for success are clearly understood. In standardized testing raters are trained in evaluating student work so that grading is consistent and fair. This is not possible in classroom situations but it is important that those involved—teachers, students, parents, and administrators—know the criteria for evaluation and can see they are being correctly and consistently applied.

It is important to remember that no single instrument, no matter how carefully constructed, can collect all the information needed for a comprehensive evaluation of student progress or be completely valid and reliable. The evaluation of student progress is a very complex process and good teachers build a wide repertoire of approaches to both collecting information and making sense of it.

What Are Some Particular Assessment and Evaluation Challenges for Social Studies Teachers?

Designing and implementing appropriate mechanisms for tracking student progress and providing feedback is a complex endeavour for all teachers, but social studies presents some unique challenges for assessment and evaluation. Social studies includes many ways of thinking and knowing: from the narrative of history and the mathematical and statistical reasoning of economics, to the visual and graphic components of geographic study and the deep understanding of differing perspectives and beliefs underlying the study of public issues and current affairs. Even within a single social studies discipline, the kinds of learnings to be assessed cover a wide range.[10]

Many key social studies outcomes such as critical thinking, social responsibility, and informed decision-making are hard to define compared to outcomes from other subjects. Furthermore, some of these complex goals such as the development of responsible citizenship, may not be evident until after students have left school and engaged in tasks such as informed voting, social action, and other forms of civic participation.

As a result of these varied and contested outcomes, the field of social studies has had great difficulty reaching consensus on its key concepts and purposes, including what constitutes sound assessment and evaluation. Because social studies is concerned with affairs in the real world, it has always been subject to pressures from that world (the political dimension noted earlier). This has certainly been true in the area of assessment. Tests or quizzes purporting to test student knowledge of history, geography, or civics are routinely published in the media, with subsequent blaming and hand-wringing about our wayward youth.[11] These challenges lead to our next question.

How Do I Plan for Sound Assessment and Evaluation?

Sound assessment begins with the learner in mind. This "backwards design" or "design down" process requires we: (1) determine what the learner needs to know and or do as a result of the learning;

(2) identify clear evidence of learning; and (3) design instruction so that students will have opportunities to learn and demonstrate their learnings.[12] Good teachers will keep the following questions in mind when planning for assessment.

1. What is to be assessed? As mentioned above, assessment instruments should be valid; that is, they should provide information about specific, clearly defined elements of students' knowledge or skills. In order to design appropriate methods of assessment, teachers must be very clear about exactly what it is they want information on.

2. What is the purpose of the assessment? The means of collecting information and reporting on it will vary depending on whether the purpose of the assessment is formative—to provide information for the student and teacher to use to monitor or improve progress—or summative—to provide end-point information for students, parents, and/or administrators.

3. What assessment tools will best provide the information we need? Tools will vary depending on what is to be assessed and the purpose of the assessment. For example, an essay might not be the best way to assess students' ability to work with scale and symbols on a map, but an exercise requiring them to plan the best route between two points might work well for this purpose.

4. What form will the data take? This is obviously related to the previous question but there may be some variety within particular assessment tools. A teacher might, as suggested above, ask students to compare and contrast Napoleon's and Hitler's invasions of Russia, allowing students to present their report in written, oral, or graphic form. In the case of students who have difficulty writing, the latter two forms might provide better information about their facility with the skill being evaluated.

5. Who will collect the data: teachers, students, or outside judges? Involving students in self- or peer-assessment can be a very effective teaching

and assessment technique. Asking students to use a checklist to rate their peers' performance in a debate by collecting data on several criteria (content, presentation, argument, etc) both directs the students to pay specific attention to these important criteria (teaching) and provides information on how well they understand them (assessment).

6. How often and when will the data be collected? As stated above, teachers assess students all the time. To paraphrase Thomas Jefferson, "The price of democracy is constant vigilance," and constant vigilance applies to assessment as well. Having said that, particular types of, and purposes for, assessment should guide our response to this question. Giving formal written tests to students every day will probably not prove effective, but research on skills teaching indicates that in the early stages of learning a skill, it is very important to provide timely and frequent corrective feedback.

7. What will be done with the data making up the assessment? As stated above, we assess for different purposes and, depending on the purpose, different things will be done with the data. If the assessment is formative the data needs to be provided to the students involved in an understandable way so they can use it to monitor and improve their progress. This is the feedback described above. We have all had the experience of getting back a test or an assignment on which we have not done well, but if we receive little or no feedback, we don't know where we went wrong. This is not particularly useful for understanding how we are doing so far and what we might do to improve. On the other hand, if the assessment is summative, information needs to be provided to the relevant people about student achievement. In the case of large-scale international assessments, for example, the information gathered is of little use to individual students who have probably moved on to the next grade or graduated before the results are even available. It is valuable, however, for curriculum planners, administrators, and teachers in

understanding the degree to which particular groups of students are meeting the objectives assessed.

Underpinning all these questions, of course, is the principle that our assessments must align with curriculum outcomes. Constraining our use of the full range of techniques and tools is our ability to manage, assess, and teach at the same time. So manageability is a factor in our assessment planning decisions. No one can do it all, even the most skillful of teachers! So we should strive to be fair by taking advantage of the many informal opportunities for assessment, such as simply watching our students while they work and giving them opportunities to reflect on their own learning. Such opportunities are built into sound lesson planning. With good instruction we are well on our way to making those first steps towards assessment literacy.

Is sound assessment easy? No, but nothing of value is. Even if we have useful answers for all of the above questions, they will not be perfect answers for all students on all occasions. We will now turn to an examination of some of the specific assessment and evaluation tools that might be helpful in teaching social studies.

What Specific Forms of Assessment and Evaluation Can Be Used in Social Studies?

As stated above, assessing and evaluating student progress is a complex endeavour. Good teachers will develop a range of tools for helping with this task. Some will be traditional forms with which we are all familiar and some will be newer forms such as performance or authentic assessment, which have been developed in response to recent knowledge about teaching and learning. Some options are outlined below but these represent only a small part of what is possible. It is important to remember that each of these tools has strengths and weaknesses and teachers need to be able to select appropriate ones to serve their particular assessment and evaluation purposes.

Selected response tests

Selected response tests, often called "objective paper and pencil tests" consist of multiple choice, true-false, matching, and fill-in-the-blank items. The phrase "selected response" is most accurate since it reflects the procedure of selecting correct responses from a range of possibilities. We use them because we perceive that they are objective, because we experienced these types of tests when we were students, and because the ease of marking makes evaluation more manageable.[13]

In true-false tests, data is quickly collected on a range of knowledge targets such as generalizations or propositions, with little demand on reading ability. Among their limitations are the strong possibility of guessing and the difficulty of designing items beyond the factual knowledge level.

Fill-in tests work for outcomes such as vocabulary understanding and, unlike other forms of selective response, do not promote guessing. On the other hand, poorly designed items and students' poor spelling can result in ambiguous answers that are difficult to score. With matching items, data is collected speedily with fewer demands on reading ability. Matching is particularly useful for assessing student recognition of how ideas are associated. In social studies examples of associations are countries and capitals; definitions and terms; or historical figures and their accomplishments/discoveries. Matching items are also prone to student guessing, and unless designed carefully, are susceptible to the use of irrelevant clues or obvious answers when more than one topic for the matching set is used.

Multiple-choice items, usually consisting of a complete statement of the problem or question (stem/lead); construction of plausible distracters (wrong answers); random placing of the key (correct answer), are the most versatile form of selective response, ranging in use from recall of basic information to interpretation, analogies, and other complex outcomes. Furthermore, guessing is discouraged and well-designed items of the type used in standardized tests are high in reliability. However, they take time and effort to design well.[14] Reading ability may influence some scores, thus threatening the validity of the assessment. Moreover, while some complex thinking can be assessed, prior knowledge possessed by students can easily turn multiple choice questions into recall items.

Selected response items have the advantage of being easy to administer and score and, if well constructed, are high in validity and reliability. Using selective response for assessment beyond routine knowledge or simple skills, however, is difficult. Furthermore, it is too easy to include irrelevant data in selective response items, allowing students to guess a correct answer without actually knowing anything.

Extended- or essay-response tests

Essays are items that require an extended or constructed written answer to a relatively open-ended question for which a variety of appropriate responses are possible. Along with short-answer questions, selective and essay responses constitute the traditional assessment options in social studies classes.

Essay responses can come in various forms such as writing a letter to the editor of the local newspaper about a current issue or writing a detailed analysis of a case similar to what a judge would write. Essay tests or assignments may be more valid than selected response items in that they are more likely to provide data on important outcomes such as the ability to identify an issue, organize relevant information into an argument, reveal cause-effect relationships, recognize human-environmental interactions, weigh evidence, and so on. The essay can range from a short paragraph to many pages.

Essays do, however, raise serious design and scoring issues. Without clear and precise scoring criteria, applied consistently by teachers, one person's "A" can be another person's "C." The unreliability of teacher scoring on essay items is one reason for the rise of standardized testing. This lack of reliability can be offset somewhat by the use of carefully developed examinations at the provincial level, as is the case in British Columbia and elsewhere. Committees of specialists, especially teachers, meet to design questions based on curriculum outcomes, to be assessed with clear criteria and reliable scoring systems. Where there are no carefully designed, administered, and scored provincial examinations,

social studies teachers can work together using the above process to reach consensus on scoring.

Language joins reliability as a scoring issue in essays. Social studies requires a high degree of literacy. Throughout Canadian classrooms, there are many students who struggle with basic literacy skills or for whom the language of instruction is not their first language. Thus, in designing, administering and scoring essay-type questions we should not penalize students unduly for difficulties in initial comprehension of questions or writing of answers, if the goal of the essay question is to reveal other abilities. We are increasingly aware of the need to support students' learning by providing supports or scaffolds. Scaffolding helps many learners write appropriate responses until they are able to respond more independently. The elements of the writing process in language arts classrooms, including the role of collaborative small group talk, can prepare students for doing higher-quality work than when left to sink or swim on their own.[15]

How can we modify an essay question to meet the diverse needs of our students? We can narrow or broaden the content focus by increasing or decreasing the factors or variables to consider. For example, an essay may challenge students to focus on a narrow historical period such as the 1920s. Other essays might have students look at a larger period such as the 1920s and 1930s. Still other essays could require students to examine (usually for purposes of comparison and contrast) the interactions among geographic and economic patterns in two regions of Canada or reduce the cognitive demands to an analysis of these interactions in one region.

We can also specify the cognitive demands. Some questions can provide additional support for learners by specifying what is required in an answer; for example, which events need to be examined or what factors need to be compared. Some questions offer a context that can serve as a thesis statement while other questions require students to develop their own thesis statements.[16] Vague instructions offer no support for students, as these instructions fail to define criteria for success.

Some questions personalize responses through role play to offer a more authentic context for writing; for example, students are asked about an event or an idea using a newspaper story format, including an appropriate headline. Other essays present a quotation or provocative proposition and ask students to make an argument based on evidence to support or refute the validity of the statement.

Finally we can direct students to respond in structured ways using action verbs connected to Bloom's Taxonomy of Cognitive Objectives (i.e., describe, explain, analyze, synthesize, and evaluate).[17] This works if students know the meaning of the verbs and see examples of their use in sample responses.

Document-based questions

As outlined above, Alberta and most other provinces have identified procedural understanding as a key goal for social studies education. In other words, students are supposed to be able to use the concepts and procedures of the disciplines involved in social studies such as history, geography, and economics. It is not enough to know what the causes of World War I are; students should also understand something of the way historians arrived at those causes, including what evidence they considered and how they made sense of that evidence. In teaching history in primary grades, curricula across the country recommend the use of primary sources: pictures, artifacts, maps, and written and oral accounts. We have been less successful in using these in assessment. In North America, document-based questions (DBQs) used to be considered appropriate only for senior high students in International Baccalaureate or Advanced Placement programs, though the British have been using "sources" for decades. Now we can use them to bring more authenticity to instruction and assessment. The Begbie Contest in British Columbia has used document-based questions since 1994 for high-school students.[18] Some jurisdictions have used them in elementary grades as well. These questions are not designed to test student's recall of information but rather their abilities to critically use sources as the basis for constructing historical accounts.

PERFORMANCE ASSESSMENT

Performance assessment is considered new although it is as old as assessment itself. Unlike selected response, the assessor does not count correct responses in order to render a judgement. Instead she or he collects data on the process or makes a judgement about the quality of the final product as students actually do something. In some jurisdictions performance tasks serve as end-of-unit assessments or culminating activities instead of the traditional quiz or project. Performance assessment tasks are not add-ons, fillers, or breaks for the teacher, but opportunities to combine instruction with assessment. There are many examples of social studies performance tasks, such as the following:[19]

- Three prominent international conflicts are drawn from newspapers. Students select one of the three, write a summary of the conflict, and discuss the influence of climate, resources, and location on the conflict. As well, the students sketch from memory a map of the region of the world showing national boundaries, capitals, and salient landforms. A legend and compass rose are included.

- Students identify, then compare and contrast, a diverse set of examples of societies organized under, or attempting to organize under, the democratic ideal, with examples drawn from three continents.

- Students analyze a transcribed excerpt of a discussion of a recurring public issue, distinguishing among factual, definitional, and ethical issues, and judging the quality of each participant's contribution.

- The federal deficit is about $500 billion. Students translate this number into a form the average reader of the local paper can understand.

According to Bower, Lobdell, and Swenson, culminating performance activities or projects:[20]

- are central to the unit and its big question

- are known to students in advance

- require students to think deeply about important issues

- ask students to create a meaningful product or performance

- demand students use different learning styles and intelligences

- make clear to students the standards by which their work will be judged

- foster the habit of self-assessment

- allow teachers to act as coaches

AUTHENTIC ASSESSMENT

Authentic assessments are a particular form of performance assessment where students are required to perform a real-life activity and an assessment is made based on that activity. Students in a grade 3 class studying their community, for example, might be asked to do an assessment of the area around their school (sidewalks, parks, public places) for wheelchair accessibility and prepare a report for a relevant civic body such as a committee of city council. The activity does not necessarily have to relate to contemporary situations. Currently, some Acadian people are asking that the Queen apologize for the expulsion of their ancestors from the Maritimes. Students might be asked to prepare a recommendation for the Crown on whether or not, considering the historical evidence, such an apology would be justified.

STRUCTURED OBSERVATION

Many performance and authentic assessments will include "hard" evidence of student progress such as written components, constructed models, and visual representations, but often much of the evidence of student progress will be gathered through watching them work. For example, many social studies outcomes are related to that important and hard-to-define term "thinking." However thinking is defined, conventional tests reveal only so much. One approach is to determine what thinking looks like when

we see it. Such "intelligent behaviours" are "habits of mind": a repertoire of mindful strategies we use when faced with problems or decisions. If we are going to provide useful feedback, either of a formative or summative nature, about something like thinking, we need to say more than, "John has shown great improvement in critical thinking." We need to be able to be more specific about what we mean and that kind of specificity can be obtained by structured observation: watching for, and collecting evidence on, particular behaviours. In the area of thinking, for example, we might watch for: [21]

- Perseverance: Do students give up or back up and use a different strategy if the first ones do not work?

- Decreased impulsiveness: Do students blurt out answers and make many corrections in their written responses or do they pause before answering, make sure they understand the learning task, and consider the responses of others in building arguments?

- Flexible thinking: Do students use the same approaches for different problems or do they use and weigh the merits of alternative strategies, consider the approaches of others, and deal with more than one classification system simultaneously?

- Metacognition: Are students unaware of how they learn or do they describe and reflect on the processes they used in learning?

- Careful review: Do students hand in uncorrected or unedited work as soon as it is done or do they take time to review and edit?

These observations would be structured not only in the sense that the teacher looks for evidence for precise criteria like these but also in the sense that some form of record is kept of the observations such as checklists or anecdotal notes.

For all of these assessment tools other than limited response items a difficulty is designing consistent and fair ways to make evaluations based on them. A common way to deal with this challenge is to design rubrics that describe clear criteria for making evaluative judgements. A rubric is an achievement scale: a set of scoring guidelines for evaluating student work. Rubrics answer questions such as: By what criteria should performance be judged? What should we look for when we judge performance tasks? What is quality? How can different levels of quality be described and distinguished from one another? The word "rubric" comes from the Latin word for "red." In the European Middle Ages it referred to the highlights of a legal decision as well as the directions for conducting religious services, found in the margins of liturgical books—both written in red.

When an activity requires a complex performance to assess complex outcomes scored at more than two levels, then a rubric is required. In one of our studies we asked grade 9 students from more than a dozen schools to write a personal letter at a specific point in historical time and place to a public figure in Canada. They were asked to write a letter in the first person and allowed to choose their role from either gender and from a range of occupations authentic to the time and place.

Before determining specific criteria, it is important for students to discuss what quality looks like. Fortunately, writing in role is a common activity in the Canadian history course in Ontario, so students could see and critique samples. Students also had access to real letters written during such periods as World War I and the Depression. If students have a role in determining criteria they are more likely to understand what is required and develop some sense of ownership and commitment to achieving the learning goal.

The teachers and student teachers scoring the hundreds of responses first did a scan of the letters to sort into three general categories: "good," "ok," and "poor." Then they discussed why letters were placed into each category. Veteran teachers' experience enabled them to better articulate and defend their reasons on the basis of some shared values about the nature of historic empathy and the role of evidence, two key concepts in historical understanding. From this task and discussion the following ru-

bric was built based on what students could actually demonstrate.

Student work should demonstrate:

1. Historical Argument: Could students present historically accurate and relevant arguments well supported with evidence?

2. Context: Could students display a strong sense of historical empathy reflecting a broad understanding of historical circumstance, events, and relationships?

3. Role: Could students articulate a personal point of view within a clearly identified historical role?

4. Organization: Could students offer a well-organized and coherent letter in paragraph form?

5. Persuasiveness: Could students use persuasive language appropriate for the historical audience?

A word on weighting criteria for grading purposes: the issues around converting performance levels to marks or grades are complex.[22] Teachers should consider which criteria are absolutely critical, without which the task cannot be accomplished. Which are very important, without which the quality of the product is seriously flawed? Which criteria may not be critical to the product though they may affect the quality?

Does this sound subjective? Yes, but remember that evaluation using a grade or rubric represents a judgement about what is valued. If we take the mystery out of these judgements, students are more likely to meet our standards.

Conclusion

The trends in assessment and evaluation in social studies, as in other parts of the curriculum, are in a state of flux. The issues are complex; easy solutions are impossible. Assessing student progress is one of the most difficult and public things teachers do. It takes time and hard work to develop the range of procedures and instruments necessary to adequately provide feedback to both teacher and students (formative assessment) and end-point information for students, parents, and others in the education system (summative assessment). Informed, reasoned discussion by researchers, practitioners, and policy-makers is a must. If this chapter offers us a direction for becoming more assessment literate, then it has done its job.

Endnotes

1   Joseph M. Kirman, *Elementary Social Studies* (Scarborough, ON: Prentice Hall, 1991), 11.

2   Overviews of this expanded role can be seen in Kieran Egan, "Testing What for What?" *Educational Leadership* 61, no. 3 (2003): 27–30; and Steve Alsop and Larry Bencze, "A Tale of Two Scientists: Professional Scientist/Citizen Scientist," *Orbit* 31, no. 3 (2000): 21–24.

3   Three collections of articles illustrating recent assessment reform can be found in *Orbit* 30, no. 4, (2000); *Canadian Social Studies* 34, no. 1 (1999); and Roland Case and Penney Clark, eds., *The Canadian Anthology of Social Studies: Issues and Strategies for Teachers* (Vancouver: Pacific Education Press, 1997).

4   Charles Ungerleider, *Failing Our Kids: How We Are Ruining Our Public Schools* (Toronto: McClelland & Stewart, 2003), 252–253 provides an overview (already out of date) of the changing provincial testing scene in Canada.

5   Ruth Childs, "The EQAO Tests and the OTQT: Critical Consumers Needed" (keynote address, OISE/UT Preservice Assessment and Evaluation conference, Toronto, February 11, 2004).

6   This section is an adaptation of two earlier publications by John Myers and Fiorella Finelli: *Canadian History: Patterns and Transformations, Teachers' Resource Guide* (Toronto: Irwin, 2003); and "Assessment and Evaluation", in *Civics Today: Teachers' Resource Guide*, ed. Jennifer Watt, et al. (Toronto: Irwin, 2000), 18–32.

7   Robert J. Marzano, Debra J. Pickering, and Jane E. Pollock, *Classroom Instruction that Works: Research-based Strategies for Increasing Student Achievement* (Alexandria, VA: Association for Supervision and Curriculum Development, 2001).

8   Alberta Learning, *Social Studies Kindergarten to Grade 12 Validation Draft* (Edmonton: Author, May 2003), 9.

9   Samuel S. Wineburg, "Historical Problem Solving: A Study of the Cognitive Processes Used for the Evaluation of Documentary and Pictorial Evidence," *Journal of Educational Psychology* 83, no. 1 (1991): 75–87.

10 See, for example, Canadian Council for Geographic Education, *Canadian National Standards for Geography: A Standards-based Guide to K–12 Geography* (Ottawa: Royal Canadian Geographic Society, 2001), for the range of learnings to be assessed in just one component of social studies.

11 Daniel Gardner, *Youth and History: Policy Paper and Survey Results* (Toronto: Dominion Institute, 1997) was the first of a series of results based on national quizzes of Canadian students' knowledge of Canadian history and citizenship.

12 Grant Wiggins and Jay McTighe, *Understanding by Design* (Alexandria, VA: Association for Supervision and Curriculum Development, 1998).

13 Richard J. Stiggins, *Student-involved Classroom Assessment*, 3rd ed. (Upper Saddle River, NJ: Merrill Prentice Hall, 2001).

14 John Myers et al., "Doin' the DBQ: A Project in Designing Useful Assessments" (in progress, Toronto, OISE/UT; first phase finished in 2003). This project, carried out with the assistance of fifty-eight student teachers, has demonstrated, among other things, both the importance and the challenge of designing useful multiple-choice questions.

15 The literature on the role of talk in small groups is vast. See, for example, the International Association for the Study of Cooperation in Education website, www.iasce.net, and its links.

16 See, for example, the essay questions in the Begbie Canadian History Contest, http://www.begbiecontestsociety.org/, which held its first contest in British Columbia in 1994 and is now a national contest.

17 R.J. Cornfield et al., *Making the Grade: Evaluating Student Progress* (Toronto: Prentice Hall, Canada, 1987).

18 The Begbie Canadian History Contest, http://www.begbiecontestsociety.org/.

19 Adapted from Walter C. Parker, *Renewing the Social Studies Curriculum* (Alexandria, VA: Association for Supervision and Curriculum Development, 1991).

20 Bert Bower, Jim Lobdell, and Lee Swenson, *History Alive! Engaging All Learners in the Diverse Classroom*, 2nd ed. (Palo Alto, CA: Teachers' Curriculum Institute, 1999).

21 Art L. Costa and Bena Kallick, *Habits of Mind: A Developmental Series* (Alexandria, VA: Association for Supervision and Curriculum Development, 2000).

22 See Ken O'Connor, "Grading—An Exercise in Professional Judgment," *Orbit* 30, no. 4 (2000): 40–42.

Notes about the Contributors

Kathy Bickmore is an associate professor at the Ontario Institute for Studies in Education, University of Toronto, a board member of the Association for Conflict Resolution, and on the Peace Education Commission of the International Peace Research Association. She teaches and conducts research regarding education for constructive conflict, conflict resolution, equity, and inclusive democracy in public-school contexts. Her work appears in books such as *Handbook of Conflict Management* and *How Children Understand War and Peace*, and journals such as *Conflict Resolution Quarterly, Theory and Research in Social Education, Curriculum Inquiry, Alberta Journal for Educational Research*, and *Theory into Practice*.

Wanda Cassidy has taught secondary social studies and law and has been director of a provincial program in law-related education. Currently she is an assistant professor of education and Director of the endowed Centre for Education, Law and Society at Simon Fraser University. She works extensively with teachers in various law-related education initiatives and researches and writes in the areas of LRE, social studies, citizenship education, the ethics of care and justice, and at-risk youth. Her new book (with Ruth Yates) is titled *Once Upon a Crime: Exploring Justice Through Storybook Mock Trials and Conflict Resolution Activities* (Emond Montgomery Publishers, 2004).

Mark Evans (http://home.oise.utoronto.ca/~mevans/markevans.html) is Director of the Secondary Teacher Education Program and Senior Lecturer in the Department of Curriculum, Teaching and Learning at the Ontario Institute for Studies in Education, University of Toronto. Mark has been involved in a variety of curriculum reform initiatives, teacher education projects, and research studies with teachers and schools locally, nationally, and internationally. Most recently, Mark's work has focused on pedagogical perspectives and practices related to political learning and citizenship education. Mark began his career with the Peel District Board of Education in Ontario where he served as a secondary school teacher, department chair, and district consultant.

Linda Farr Darling is an associate professor in the Department of Curriculum Studies at the University of British Columbia where she teaches courses in social studies, philosophy of education, and curriculum theory. Her research interests are in the areas of young children's moral understandings and the moral dimensions of teaching.

Susan Gibson is an associate professor in the Department of Elementary Education of the Faculty of Education at the University of Alberta. Her subject-area specialization is social studies education. Dr. Gibson's research interests include constructivist uses of technology to enrich students' learning in social studies, teacher professional development and technology integration, and the role of technology in teacher education.

Andrew Hughes is professor of education and university teaching professor at the University of New Brunswick. He has taught middle and high school and has worked with prospective social studies teachers for some thirty years. His current research is concerned with mapping children's understanding of the ideas of democracy. He is Director of the Spirit of Democracy Project, which is a Canadian-Russian collaboration designed to assist students in confronting the contested concepts that comprise the democratic ethic. See www.spiritofdemocracy.com.

Ian Hundey began teaching in 1968. For seventeen years he was a teacher and curriculum consultant in schools in Ontario and England. He taught at Moray House College of Education, Edinburgh, in the mid-1970s and at the Ontario Institute for Studies in Education, University of Toronto, from 1988–2001. He has also taught at Aga Khan University in Pakistan, at Lulea University in Sweden, and at the University of New Brunswick. In 2003 he was Manager of Education Outreach at the Library of Parliament. Now semi-retired, Ian is continuing his writing career, having already written or contributed to twenty social studies resources.

Wanda Hurren lives in Regina, Saskatchewan, and is an associate professor in the Faculty of Education at the University of Regina. She is chair of the social studies subject area and teaches a variety of courses in both social studies education and curriculum theory. Her research and teaching interests focus on the mingling aspects of space, identity, and curriculum. She is the author of *Line Dancing: An Atlas of Geography Curriculum and Poetic Possibilities*, and co-editor of *Curriculum Intertext: Place/Language/Pedagogy* (Peter Lang Publishers).

Stéphane Lévesque is an assistant professor of history education at the J.G. Althouse Faculty of Education, University of Western Ontario. His research focuses primarily on Canadian history (French and English relations), citizenship education, and students' historical understanding. He has published several chapters and articles in journals such as *Canadian Social Studies, Theory and Research in Social Education*, and *Encounters on Education/Encuentros Sobre Educacion/Rencontre sur l'Éducation*. Dr. Lévesque is co-editor of the Canadian and international journal *Historical Studies in Education/Revue d'histoire de l'éducation* and a board member of the Historica Foundation—Institute for Teaching Canadian History.

Lisa W. Loutzenheiser is an assistant professor of Curriculum Studies at the University of British Columbia. Her research interests include identity, pedagogy, bringing sexuality and race into teacher education and secondary classrooms, feminist, poststructural and/or critical race theories, and methodology.

John Myers is a curriculum instructor at the Ontario Institute for Studies in Education, University of Toronto. Among his research interests are the uses of assessment in social studies classrooms. He is completing a study in the use of performance assessment tasks in history classes due for publication in 2004. His writings in this area include a chapter on classroom assessment in *Trends and Issues in Canadian Social Studies*.

Jeff Orr is a social studies teacher educator, and Chair of the Department of Teacher Education at St. Francis Xavier University. Prior to this he taught elementary, middle, and secondary school in northern Saskatchewan. He has broad interests in social studies curriculum research related to citizenship, Aboriginal and multicultural education, and pedagogy. He has recently co-authored *Canada's History: Voices and Visions*, a required grade 11 textbook for Canadian history in Nova Scotia. He continues to engage in teaching, advocacy, and research alongside First Nations educators in areas related to Aboriginal pedagogy, curriculum, school reform, and life history.

Ken Osborne was educated at the universities of Oxford, Birmingham, and Manitoba. He taught history in Winnipeg high schools through the 1960s before joining the staff of the Faculty of Education at the University of Manitoba. He has written extensively on history and history education and is now a professor emeritus of education at the University of Manitoba.

Carla Peck is a PhD student in the Faculty of Education at the University of British Columbia. She is currently working in the Centre for the Study of Historical Consciousness. Her research interests include children's conceptions of ethnic diversity and students' uses of and understandings of the past.

Douglas Ramsay has been a social studies teacher, department head, and specialist for over twenty-five years. In 1996, he became the executive director of a non-profit citizenship education organization and has been extensively involved in the area of citizenship education, both in Canada and internationally. He has written a variety of social studies resource materials for the classroom and has been involved in a number of curriculum research projects, connecting social studies curriculum to different initiatives. He has continued to work with teachers, both through research activities and professional development initiatives, including the coordination of the 1999 Historica Teachers' Institute.

George Richardson is currently an associate professor of Social Studies Education at the University of Alberta. He has over twenty years' experience as a classroom teacher and has taught in northern Canadian schools and in Ukraine. His research interests include the role of education in national identity formation, citizenship education, multicultural education, international education, and action research.

Alan Sears is a professor in the Faculty of Education at the University of New Brunswick. He has been a social studies teacher for more than twenty-five years, working at all levels from primary to graduate school. In addition to co-editing *Trends and Issues in Canadian Social Studies*, he has published extensively in the area of citizenship education. He is currently principal investigator on an SSHRC-funded research project designed to map how middle-school students in Canada and Russia think about key ideas related to democratic citizenship.

Peter Seixas is a professor and the Canada Research Chair in Education at the University of British Columbia and Director of the Centre for the Study of Historical Consciousness (www.cshc.ubc.ca). He is editor of *Theorizing Historical Consciousness* (University of Toronto Press, forthcoming), and co-editor, with Peter Stearns and Sam Wineburg, of *Knowing, Teaching and Learning History: National and International Perspectives* (New York University Press, 2000). He contributed the chapter on

"Social Studies" for the *Handbook of Research on Teaching* (American Educational Research Association, 2001) and has published in journals such as the *Canadian Historical Review, Journal of Curriculum Studies,* and the *American Journal of Education.*

Ann Sherman has taught in public schools in Nova Scotia and Alberta and was vice-principal in a large elementary school in Fort McMurray, Alberta. She completed her initial teacher education at St. Francis Xavier University and went on to complete a graduate diploma in Educational Administration at the University of Alberta, an MEd at the University of New Brunswick, and a PhD at the University of Nottingham. She is now the director of the School of Education at St. Francis Xavier University, teaching both elementary education courses in the BEd program and educational administration courses in the MEd program. In addition, she is the Coordinator of the St. Francis Xavier Service Learning Program. Her main research interests lie in the areas of children's perspectives on schooling and women's roles in educational administration.

Patricia Shields has worked as a classroom teacher, educational consultant, and writer over the past twenty-four years. She has taught as a sessional instructor in the Department of Elementary Education at the University of Alberta and has worked as a consultant for Alberta Learning. She is a past-president of the Social Studies Council of the Alberta Teachers' Association. She has developed a number of social studies resources and been involved with a variety of research projects, focusing on social studies curriculum across Canada. She has continued to work with teachers through a variety of professional development initiatives, including coordination of the 1999 Historica Teachers' Institute.

Manju Varma-Joshi is an assistant professor in the Faculty of Education at the University of New Brunswick. Her research pursuits include the integration of children's literature and national identity, multicultural education in predominantly white locations, and issues of immigration and diversity in rural locations. Prior to working at the university level, her teaching experiences included English-as-a-second-language institutes, First Nations schools, and elementary education.

Ian Wright is a professor emeritus in the Faculty of Education at the University of British Columbia. He retired after a teaching career spanning four decades. He is the author of *Elementary Social Studies: A Practical Approach*, published by Prentice Hall, now in its sixth edition. His most recent book is *Is That Right? Critical Thinking and the Social World of the Young Learner* (Pippin, 2002).

Index

Page numbers in bold refer to tables, figures, and illustrations.